ULYSSES S. GRANT

ULYSSES S. GRANT

Soldier & President

★ ★ ★ ★

GEOFFREY PERRET

RANDOM HOUSE

NEW YORK

Library of Congress Cataloging-in-Publication Data
Perret, Geoffrey.
Ulysses S. Grant : soldier and president / by Geoffrey Perret.
p.   cm.
Includes bibliographical references and index.
ISBN 0-679-44766-0
1. Grant, Ulysses S. (Ulysses Simpson), 1822–1885.   2. Presidents—
United States—Biography.   3. Generals—United States—Biography.
4. United States. Army—Biography.   I. Title.
E672.P44   1997   973.8'2'092—dc21
[B]   97-9171

Random House website address: http://www.randomhouse.com/
Printed in the United States of America on acid-free paper
Book design by J. K. Lambert
2 4 6 8 9 7 5 3
First Edition

To Dr. John Sellers,
who has helped countless writers
on the Civil War

ACKNOWLEDGMENTS

My greatest debt is to Dr. John Y. Simon, who has acquired an unrivaled knowledge of Grant during the thirty-five years that he has edited Grant's papers. John's impeccable scholarship is surpassed only by a generosity of spirit such as I have rarely encountered and shall never forget.

I am grateful, too, for the expert help at the Library of Congress of Dr. John Sellers and Jeffrey M. Flannery. And at the Army Military History Institute in Carlisle, Pennsylvania, I was aided in my efforts once again by Dr. Richard Sommers, John Slonaker and David Keough. I would also like to thank John Grant Griffiths and Keith Poulter.

My researches into the Hamlin Garland Papers at the University of Southern California profited from the assistance of the head of Special Collections there, Dr. John Ahouse, at West Point Special Collections, Alan Aimone and Suzanne Christoff were, once again, models of helpfulness.

My thanks are extended, too, to the skilled staff members who smoothed my way at the Huntington Library in San Marino, California; the Bancroft Library at U.C. Berkeley; and the National Archives in Washington, D.C., and College Park, Maryland.

Like many others who write about the Civil War, I have never failed to be impressed by the knowledge and enthusiasm of the National Park Service rangers who preserve Civil War sites. To those who guided me around Fort Donelson, Shiloh, Vicksburg, Chattanooga, Petersburg, Richmond and Appomattox, I offer my appreciation and admiration.

Finally, I acknowledge for the fifth time the debt I owe my editor, Robert D. Loomis. His is always the unseen hand behind a thousand improvements. There is no such thing as a perfect book, but that never stops him from trying to make them so.

CONTENTS

LIST OF MAPS

ULYSSES S. GRANT

CHAPTER 1

──── ★ ★ ★ ★ ────

"I WON'T GO"

When Ulysses Grant came mewling and spluttering into the world on April 27, 1822, in the remote settlement of Point Pleasant, Ohio, the American West was broad and green—the color of hope, of spring, of youth. The line of permanent settlements ran from the Wisconsin dells down to New Orleans. The nation had few decent roads, and its highways were the big rivers—the Hudson and the Susquehanna, the Delaware, the Ohio and the mighty Mississippi. The spring thaw each year unleashed a swiftly gathering stream of flatboats onto the Ohio River, carrying settlers from the East to claim a piece of the western future.

Life on the frontier was vigorous, the pace of change rapid. The hand of government was light upon the land and its people. Nowhere on Earth were people so free to move around, to speak their minds, to make money, or just make a new start as they were in the West. But this frontier was no earthly paradise. The western lands were driven by impatience, their privations made tolerable to many only by the heavy consumption of corn licker and vinegary wines wrung from indifferent grapes, from gulping down coarse beers stinking of yeast and rough applejack that brought a few fleeting hours of oblivion, followed by a headache that was slow to clear. Frontier life was cruelly hard on women, who fought never-ending battles against dirt, poverty and disease, a struggle that made many look and feel old at forty—if they managed to survive that long. Families were large, but death reaped a terrifying harvest among infants and small children. To preserve a family's name and make some provision for old age, there was safety only in numbers.

The land they farmed, fished and hunted on had been wrested from the original inhabitants only since the Revolution. Many an early dwelling was a blockhouse, half buried in the ground and fortified against Indian attack. The War of 1812 had ended with the crushing defeat of Indian tribes from the Canadian border to the Gulf of Mexico. Their abandonment by the British broke forever the power of Native Americans to resist the white man's advance to the Mississippi.

Massacres were the stepping-stones on the advance over the Alleghenies and into the dark green forests that cloaked the reverse slopes with huge oaks, sycamores and black walnut trees. The West was haunted in its winning. By the standards of the long-settled East, with its Indian wars now behind it, the western frontier when Grant was born was peopled by savages of every description. The veneer of civilization that separated the white man from the red was so thin that when conflict erupted it took an act of faith, or denial, to believe it even existed.

The settlers were almost without exception simple people, boasting little education or refinement. When they fell ill, they treated themselves with "sheeps'-turd tea" or potions that included human urine. As with farmers and artisans everywhere, theirs was a society where the hand that shook yours was almost certain to be strong and horny, with fingernails broken and black. The familiar elements of daily existence—the tick-infested bearskin coat hanging from a nail behind the door, the powder horn grubby with frequent handling on the bench next to the long Kentucky rifle, the jar of bear grease that men rubbed into their long, lank hair in a doomed pursuit of elegance, the feeble tallow candles and the whale-oil lamps with rags floating in them for wicks that filled the tightly closed, poorly ventilated small log houses with a smell of smoked fish, the itchy, louse-harboring homespun garments—were the fulfillment of nothing. They simply made a rude existence possible.

The hardships and privation of frontier life were there to be transcended, not embraced, the first muddy rungs on the ascent to a better life. Ulysses Grant was fortunate in having a father, Jesse Root Grant, who had already left the lowest rungs behind by the time his first child was born and was rapidly scaling the middle section of the social and economic scale. By 1822 Jesse was well on his way to putting the harshness and squalor of the typical frontier existence behind him. Jesse was a frontier success story, one of the handful who had made it. He had not risen to prosperity from nothing, but from less than nothing—from being the abandoned child of a drunken wastrel of a father who had squandered a substantial inheritance on rotgut whiskey.

The Grants had been established in America early. Jesse's ancestors, Matthew and Priscilla Grant, landed in Plymouth, Massachusetts, one day in the summer of 1630 aboard the *John and Mary.* They were country people from Dorset, one of the most picturesque counties in southwest England. By the time of the Revolution, descendants of Matthew and Priscilla formed the core of a moderately prominent family in Connecticut. Jesse's father, Noah Grant, claimed to have fought more than six years for American independence, beginning as a minuteman standing on Lexington Green when the first shots were fired and ending the war as a captain in the Continental Army. But neither the Revolutionary War records of Connecticut nor those in the National Archives contain any confirmation of his claim.[1]

What is not in dispute is that Noah married during the Revolutionary War and his wife bore him two sons, but toward the end of the struggle, she died. What steadiness marriage and a settled family life might have provided was gone. Over the next five or six years he drank steadily, possibly heavily, and used up the inheritance that five generations of Grants had thriftily accumulated. His property and money gone, Noah did what countless Americans have done since—headed west to make a fresh start. He dumped his elder son, Solomon, on his parents-in-law and, taking his younger son, Peter, for companionship, lit out for western Pennsylvania. He wound up in a hamlet called Greensburg, a desolate spot twenty miles southeast of Pittsburgh, which was not yet a town, merely a remote frontier village of five hundred inhabitants.[2]

To many, Greensburg might seem a better place to escape from than to, but for Noah Grant it was a kind of boozy Nirvana deep in the forest. Greensburg was located in Westmoreland County, whose role in the frontier economy consisted largely of brewing cider, beer and whiskey and shipping them downriver to Ohio and Kentucky. Here was a place where a hard-drinking man could pass for a (wobbly) pillar of the community. Noah scraped together a living of sorts as a trader in animal skins and married a young widow of these parts, Rachel Kelly. She bore him seven children and stoically shared his poverty. Rachel's fourth child was Jesse Root Grant, born in January 1794, just as the frontier burst into flames.

Shortly before Noah Grant's marriage, the Federal government imposed an excise tax on liquor to pay off debts from the Revolutionary War. Tempers were inflamed across the West, and in the summer of 1794 local militiamen burned down the home of the tax collector for western Pennsylvania. The Whiskey Rebellion brought the power of the new national government down hard on the stupefied malcontents. George Washington led an army over the mountains to impose Federal authority on the hard-drinking, tax-evading inhabitants of the West. Thirteen thousand soldiers with money in their breeches and energy to burn descended on Westmoreland County and Pittsburgh.

Everything that was edible, drinkable or fornicatory brought a high price. Many of the Whiskey Rebellion soldiers never went back to their old homes, having discovered a new world where land was cheap and the soil fertile. Within five years the village of Pittsburgh had been transformed into a thriving industrial town and forges pounded heavy metal on the outer rim of the civilized world.[3]

It was time, Noah Grant decided, to move on. The man had a drifter's soul. No place could hold him long. He loaded his wife, his children, his two cows and his horse aboard a flatboat and floated down the Ohio during the 1799 emigration season, coming to a halt in Fawcettstown, Ohio.

Three years later Noah set off again, eventually settling in a village in south-central Ohio called Deerfield. Shortly after arriving there, Rachel bore her seventh child; less than two years later she died, at the age of thirty-eight. At this point, Noah abandoned all pretense of bearing up under the responsibilities of fatherhood, scattered his children like chaff, and decamped to the home of his son Peter, who had started a tannery in Maysville, Kentucky.

Jesse, just turned eleven, was left to make his own way in the world. For three years he struggled as an undersize, underage hired hand on local farms until, twenty miles from Deerfield, he went to work for George Tod, a judge on the Ohio Supreme Court. Before he met the Tods, Jesse had not attended school for a single day, yet he was beginning to itch with a desire for learning. Mrs. Tod taught him to read, made sure his wages were sufficient to buy some decent clothes, and paid for him to go to school for six months.

The Tods introduced him to a better life than any he had glimpsed or even dreamed of in Noah's wayward care. The Tod household possessed the epitome of culture to a rough-hewn western youth—silver spoons, not wooden dippers, and china bowls, not dull, gray hammered pewter, heavy in the hand and with a taste of tin and lead. Real china! Something deliberately made fragile and pleasant to the touch. What refinement. For the first time in his young life he had collided with the world beyond a rough frontier existence. Jesse yearned with all the intensity of an adolescent's white-hot spirit to acquire silver spoons and china bowls of his own. A man who raised a silver spoon to his lips and supped from a china bowl commanded respect.[4]

Jesse's strategy for rising in the world could not have been simpler or more charged with emotion. It consisted mainly of being as unlike his father as possible. He intended to marry at twenty-five—but only if he could afford to support a wife. He would accumulate enough wealth to retire at sixty, unlike his father, who had forced himself in old age on one of his sons and eked out his last years as a useless lump that soaked up money and whiskey. Jesse would be sober, hardworking, reliable, and successful in life, a burden on no one, least of all his children. And whatever children he had, they would be cherished and supported, not starved of affection and thrown away when the going got tough.

Literate by now but far from educated, Jesse knew only two lines of work—tilling the soil and the business of animal skins. Farming was unlikely to provide him with anything more than food on the table, but tanning was an enterprise that looked likely to prosper. As western towns grew—and they were growing rapidly now—the demand for leather was rising with them. People needed boots and aprons for themselves; harnesses, saddles and traces for their livestock. The creak of leather was as much the sound of westward expansion as the concussive popping of gunfire on the prairie.

Tanning was not a trade that had much appeal to able people. However bright its prospects, like most work involving dead animals, it put a man virtually at the bottom of the social ladder, because it depended on some of the dirtiest work around. The hides were treated in a lime solution before the hair or fur could be scraped laboriously from the outer side of skins that stank of dried blood. Rotting scraps of flesh had to be scraped from the inner side. The skins were then steeped in malodorous vats of sulfuric acid, to get rid of the lime, before being dumped into tubs filled with a kind of sludge made from ground oak bark. After several months of being "cured" in the bark, the hides were washed, scrubbed, and finally rubbed with tallow and fish oil until supple enough for use.

There was nothing remotely pleasant, glamorous or mentally stimulating in a tan yard. The smells—of decay, of blood, of the lime, of the acid vats, and of the oak-bark sludge—lingered on a man's skin and saturated his hair. But roses grow on dunghills and Jesse was the kind of hard-driving man who would swim an ocean of feculence if it promised to bring him out rich on the other side.[5]

At sixteen he left the Tods and returned to Deerfield, where he apprenticed himself to a tanner and scraped skins from dawn to nightfall. Two years later he went off to Maysville, Kentucky, to learn advanced tanning under his half-brother Peter Grant. Shortly after he went to work in Maysville, the War of 1812 ignited martial passions all along the western frontier. The West was the only region of the United States that was clamoring for war, and no place was more bellicose than Kentucky.[6]

Jesse's surrogate father, Judge Tod, went off to war as a colonel of militia, but young Jesse let militancy—against the Indians, against the British who armed them and invaded the United States—pass him by. He stayed close to the tannic acid vats of Maysville, scraping skins and dubbing strips of leather with tallow. His father, Noah, claimed to have spent six years in the Continental Army, and what did military life leave him with other than a fund of war stories and a weakness for whiskey? Eighteen-year-old Jesse Grant, five feet, ten inches tall, strong in body and clear in mind, was a fine specimen for carrying a musket, but here was one frontiersman immune to the militia-recruiting sergeant's eloquence. Jesse avoided military service as sedulously as any pacifist. Ulysses Grant could not have found a father more resolutely deaf to the bugle's scalp-tingling call.

After the war ended, slavery spread rapidly into Kentucky, and Jesse claimed he found that intolerable. "I would not own slaves," he said, "and I would not live where there were slaves." He moved back to Ohio and became a partner in a small tannery in a village romantically called Ravenna.[7]

In January 1819, the day he turned twenty-five, Jesse was ready for marriage. He was worth $1,500 and the tan yard was doing well. He could afford to take a wife and begin a family. Hardly had his bride-hunting begun before malaria put him, shivering and sweating, flat on his back for nearly a year. His savings seemed to evaporate with each morning's dew. When he was strong enough to work again, Jesse found employment at a new tannery that had opened in Point Pleasant. With his experience as his stake, he soon gained a partnership in the business.

As his health and fortunes revived, so did his determination to find a wife. Jesse's hide-buying journeys took him to a six-hundred-acre farm in western Pennsylvania owned by a family named Simpson. The household included a daughter named Hannah, who was not particularly pretty but was, like Jesse, unusually bright. She was a devout Methodist, remarkably quiet, invariably self-possessed, and with her twenty-third birthday not far off, she was at risk of becoming an "old maid."[8]

As a rule, frontier girls married young. Hannah was in danger of being left on the shelf when Jesse—no great looker himself, but obviously able and ambitious—came along. She may well have had her own plans for marriage, and the up-and-coming Jesse Grant could as well have suited her designs as Hannah Simpson suited his. At all events, in June 1821 they got married, following a brief engagement. During their honeymoon Jesse, more determined than ever to prove himself—and married now to a woman who had grown up in a family where book reading was taken for granted—attended classes in English grammar.

He had the zeal for learning characteristic of people who discover the world of books and ideas comparatively late in life. Jesse also had the lack of intellectual confidence that goes with self-education and tried to compensate by showing off to his neighbors and friends. He wrote vehemently outspoken political articles for local newspapers and penned yards of jokey doggerel on any subject that struck his fancy. This was as close as he ever got to poetry. His autodidact's need to be seen as a highly cultivated man made his humble origins as plain as if he had never sweated over past participles or pondered the correct usage of the gerund.[9]

Exactly ten months after becoming a husband, Jesse became a father. The Grants' first child, a son, was born in a small frame house covering barely three hundred square feet, divided into just two rooms. There was no porch, no verandah. In the front room, Hannah did the cooking at a large fireplace that provided warmth as well as hot food. The second, larger room, at the back, was taken up with a four-poster bed and some rough-hewn chests for the family's clothing. Cramped, cold in winter, stuffy in summer, it was nevertheless a cut above a log cabin.[10]

The child was named Hiram Ulysses Grant—Hiram because Hannah's father, John Simpson, thought it "a handsome name," Ulysses because Jesse had recently read a biography of the Greek hero Ulysses, the enterprising warrior who had brought the downfall of the Trojans by means of a wooden horse. Jesse invariably referred to his son as Ulysses, never as Hiram. No point in having a heroic name and not using it.

Jesse adored his infant son. "My Ulysses," he declared, "is a most beautiful child." With his russet hair, blue eyes and pink complexion, Ulysses Grant looked in childhood like a glowing miniature of his robust, energetic father.

★

There are vintage years for people as there are for wine, and for any young man with a spark of ambition to push him and the light of intelligence to guide him, 1822 was one of the best. Ulysses Grant was going to grow up able to participate, while in the full vigor of young manhood, in the great adventures shaping the destiny of the United States. Born in 1822, he was young enough to fight in two major wars yet old enough—if only barely—to be a credible candidate for the White House at the end of the second one. The great struggles ahead—over slavery, over expansion beyond the Mississippi, over Indian relations, over the survival of the Union—would test his character to the limit and provide him with a life's work.

For someone who would spend twenty-three years as a soldier, Ulysses Grant came usefully equipped with a remarkable imperviousness to the sound of gunfire. When he was less than two years old, a neighbor thought it would be interesting to frighten the child by firing a pistol close to him. Jesse challenged him to just go ahead and try it, confident his son would not so much as flinch. Simple amusements. The pistol was fired close to his head, but far from screaming out in terror or bursting into tears, the child was enthralled. Clamoring, "Fick it again! Fick it again!" the infant Ulysses reached out for the weapon with pink baby hands.[11]

It was at about this time that Jesse moved from Point Pleasant to Georgetown, twenty-five miles away. Although set in Brown County, a region whose principal crop was tobacco, Georgetown was surrounded by dense oak forests. There were vistas of tanbark from horizon to horizon. Wherever he looked, Jesse gazed on a wonder that lifted his spirits—money growing on trees.

Georgetown stood seven miles back from the Ohio River, near the center of Brown County. At the time the Grants arrived, Georgetown was a mere hamlet, inhabited by only a dozen or so families. Brown County, however, was developing rapidly. Home to one of the two important grape-growing areas of Ohio, it was reputedly the most bibulous region in the whole state. People as sober as Jesse Grant were unusual in these parts. At the very least, men were expected to celebrate national holidays by getting rip-roaring drunk. The man who didn't, said a contemporary chronicler, "could hardly maintain his standing in the community, or in the local churches."[12]

Jesse Grant built a new house, this time of brick. Owning a brick house so far out west made a man "an aristocrat" in the eyes of the vast majority of settlers, who still lived in dank dwellings crafted from logs and planks. To Hannah, the important thing was that they now had room for more children. When Ulysses was three, his mother gave birth to another son, this one named Samuel Simpson Grant. In time there would follow four more children—Clara, Virginia, Orvil and Mary.

Although the proud papa of six children, there was no mistaking Jesse's feelings. The firstborn remained his favorite child. Jesse never ceased to extol Ulysses as a prodigy. By implication, the other children of Point Pleasant were nothing much, little rustics his son would easily surpass. Jesse was not popular among his neighbors. They much preferred his silent wife. And not only silent: Hannah would walk out of a room rather than remain there and hear someone praise her son.[13]

As Jesse knew from his own haphazard upbringing, reading is the straightest road to knowledge. Sometime around his fifth birthday, Ulysses was enrolled in Georgetown's one-room school, a venture supported by the town's parents, who paid an annual subscription to keep it in business. The education on offer was rudimentary. The school's textbooks were basic readers and grammars. There were books on arithmetic, but not one on algebra or geometry. Instruction consisted of little more than rote learning, and everyone present, from children like

Ulysses Grant to brawny youths pushing twenty-one, learned the same things, at the same pace, while seated side by side on hard benches.

The subject he seemed to like best was mental arithmetic, and he shamed the older boys by calling out the answers before they had even digested the question. One of his teachers, Isaac Lynch, was impressed by how carefully Ulysses studied any book he got his hands on.[14]

Ulysses attended school only thirteen weeks a year, during the winter. The rest of the time his education was in the hands of his parents. It was Jesse, not the schoolteacher, who taught his eldest son to read. By the age of six, Ulysses could read unaided books written for adults—there was almost no literature for children in the early nineteenth century. He was by far the most intellectually able student the little school possessed. But to the other children of Georgetown, there was nothing unusual about him. If anything, they were inclined to misread his long silences as a sign that he was mentally slow.[15]

Ulysses Grant rarely hunted with the other boys, and he simply refused to kill anything when he did so. Throughout his life he would not even touch red meat if there was the least trace of bloodiness about it. He was different, too, in his choice of firearms. The other boys carried shotguns, but he became an expert with handguns and won a Fourth of July shooting competition as proof of his marksmanship.[16]

When he joined in games with other lads he was neither a leader nor a follower. Grant always seemed ready to belong to a group, yet remained slightly outside at the same time. He chose his friends from among boys who were about three years older than himself, but probably preferred the company of adults best of all.

While other boys his age expressed themselves by being competitive and aggressive, he went his own way, managing to avoid all but a few fights and rarely getting involved in disputes or rivalries. Ulysses Grant's taciturnity and composure reflected a temperament shaped more by his mother's example than his father's. He himself told people that his intelligence—"such as I possess"—was an inheritance from his mother.[17]

His withdrawn and watchful nature made him stand out in a place as small as this. At least one neighbor noticed there was something different about the Grant boy: When other lads of his age were playing in the street or whooping and splashing around in the creek, he was instead standing slightly apart, deep in thought.[18]

Behind the silence he had all the normal yearning for self-expression as other boys, but he had found a way to do so in a language that his friends did not understand—and horses did. Grant was born with what seems suspiciously like a gene for horse-handling. If such a thing actually exists within human DNA, Grant had it.

A traveling menagerie passed through Point Pleasant when Grant was about five years old. The show's promoter brought out a pony and asked if any child there wanted to ride it. The first boy who tried it ended up sprawled in the sawdust. Little Ulysses Grant, still in petticoats, begged to be hoisted aboard. When the pony tried to shake him off, almost instinctively he threw his arms forward, got a firm hold of the pony's mane, and held on tight until the pony calmed down and submitted to being ridden. He was lifted off chortling with delight at his adventure. A love of horses stayed with him the rest of his life.[19]

By the age of eight, he was earning money hauling wood with a horse and cart. At nine, he had saved enough to buy his own horse, a colt, owned by a farmer called Ralston. His father tried to negotiate on his behalf and offered $20, but Ralston rejected it.

Ulysses had his heart set on the colt, so his father told him to offer $20, because that was all the horse was worth. If Ralston rejected that price again, he should offer $22.50. And if even that wasn't enough, he should go up to $25.

When the boy arrived at Ralston's house, the first thing the farmer asked him was, "How much did your father tell you to pay?"

"Papa says I may offer you $20 for the colt, but if you won't take that, I am to offer $22.50. And if you won't take that, to give you $25."

Ralston told him that what with one thing and another, he couldn't accept a penny less than $25. Ulysses handed over the money without further ado and took the colt home.

The story soon spread around Georgetown, and the other boys made fun of him for being so simple, so stupid. What a fool! What a perfect idiot! Being a good horse trader was the mark of a western man. Blurting out your best right off! Only a simpleton would do something like that. One of Grant's nicknames was "Useless," and was it any wonder? The lash of small-town scorn cut deep. Even as Grant lay dying a painful death from cancer more than fifty years later, it still hurt.[20]

But now he had the colt, paid for with his own money, and a first horse is special, like a first love. Ulysses trained and rode his colt for four years, until the animal went blind. He caught his last glimpse of it some years later when he boarded a ferryboat. There was his former colt plodding sightless into nowhere—working the treadwheel that turned the boat's paddle.

There wasn't a horse in that part of southwestern Ohio that Ulysses Grant couldn't handle. Small for his age and clinging on for dear life, he broke some of the most unruly horses in the area for farmers who had despaired of ever subduing them. Sometimes he could be seen standing in the tan yard holding the reins of horses while his father negotiated business with their owners. Ulysses seemed content to stand there for hours, gazing into the large, lustrous brown eyes of horses. Not surprisingly, he grew up with hands much bigger and stronger than most young men his size and weight.[21]

At times he rode a spirited horse at breakneck speed through the town using nothing but a bridle. Even more spectacularly, he taught himself to ride standing on one foot on a sheepskin tied to a horse's back, and he galloped down Georgetown's main street that way as if it were the most natural thing in the world. "Horses seem to understand Ulysses," said his mother. It was the nearest she ever came to bragging about her son.[22]

Skill with horses brought the opportunity to travel. Equipped with a two-horse carriage, Ulysses provided a kind of frontier limousine service, taking people as far as Chillicothe, sixty miles away, and returning alone. That was quite a distance for a youngster barely in his teens. Like his grandfather Noah, who had died shortly before he was born, Ulysses Grant was driven by an intense curiosity to see the wider world. From childhood he was eager to discover what lay beyond Georgetown, and his horses took him there.

Adults seemed to take his abilities for granted. They climbed into the carriage he drove without hesitation, trusted him with their lives, and had him haul their property, deliver their mail, and fetch their wood. Before he was even in his teens he regularly took people to Cincinnati, fifty miles away, checked himself into a hotel when he got there, and scoured the growing burg the next morning for people seeking transportation down to Brown County.[23]

Children worked hard on the frontier. It took many hands, including small ones, to tame the wilderness. Grant was able from an early age to earn a living, and while the other boys chortled at his ineptitude as a horse trader, it may have been partly from jealousy that he, at the age of nine, had already earned enough money to buy and keep a horse of his own.

Grant found any kind of work that involved horses agreeable. As soon as he had enough strength to control a team, he went to work plowing his father's land. Jesse owned fifty acres on the edge of Georgetown. The farm put food on the table and money in the bank. Jesse's eldest son plowed, harvested, milked the cows and sawed the wood. Ulysses Grant found there was something agreeable about farming. It wasn't just the horses—a farm offered a lifetime of peaceful and productive work and allowed a man to stand on his own feet. Equally important, though, was the fact that every hour spent farming or handling horses was an hour he did not have to spend in the tan yard, a place he detested.

Grant survived the common illnesses of youth and the typical risks of a boyhood spent largely outdoors. He nearly drowned once, when he fell off a log into a swollen creek, but was pulled out of the water by one of his playmates. On another occasion, he saw one of his friends perish. The other youth was riding a horse behind him and trying to keep up with the fast-riding Ulysses when he lost control. The animal reared up, threw its rider, then fell on him. Grant himself narrowly escaped serious injury or death when, on a long drive far from home, an unbroken horse nearly pulled him and his carriage over a steep, high embankment.[24]

He remained calm in a crisis and never seemed to lack confidence. Once when he was transporting two young women in a buggy across a swollen river, white water came above the wheels. As he drove on, the water continued to rise, reaching the buggy's seats. The women cried out in alarm. Grant turned around. "Don't speak. I shall take you through safe." And he did.[25]

Unlike his father, Ulysses grew up with what children need and want most—total emotional security. His parents never scolded him or made him do anything he disliked. They simply loved him and made that as plain as they could. The boy grew up in an atmosphere of neatness, self-restraint and mutual devotion. Mrs. Grant was reputed to keep her home in immaculate order, and Jesse's home library, with its thirty-five books, was considered a marvel. But while Jesse was turning his home into a temple of hard work and ambition, Mrs. Grant was turning it into a shrine to silence. She was not a demonstrative person, and her grip on her emotions seemed unshakable. "I never saw my mother cry," Grant told a friend.

The Grant home banned alcohol, swearing, blasphemy, gambling, whippings and dancing. The only exception to the injunction against alcohol was a jug of blackberry cordial kept in the cellar. Infused with various herbs, it was claimed to prevent cholera. When Grant was eleven or twelve, he and several friends drank it all, unbeknownst to his parents, over several weeks. One of the survivors of this adventure later reported, "I don't know whether we took it right or not, but certain it is that we did not take the cholera."[26]

Grant was, in the combination of his abilities, probably the most remarkable youngster in and around Georgetown. He claimed not to be a book reader, but in all likelihood he was the best-read boy in town. It seems a safe bet that he read his way through his father's private library, the biggest collection of serious reading for miles around.

He had an avid curiosity but was easily bored. He was, that is, the stereotypical intellectually able child stuck in a backward school and surrounded by friends he had already left behind. They couldn't figure him out, simply because it did not occur to them—and it would probably be too painful for them to acknowledge—that he wasn't like them at all. Chances are that had there been intelligence tests available at the time, Grant would have scored close to the top of the scale, while they—with only two exceptions—were clustered somewhere around average. The exceptions were Daniel Ammen, who eventually became an admiral, and Absalom Markland, who was a major figure in the early history of the U.S. Postal Service. Grant had Markland assigned to his headquarters through the Civil War and Ammen dined at the White House regularly during Grant's presidency.

★

There is probably no greater complexity in the universe than the human personality, and every age cooks up some modish nonsense that pretends to explain it. Nineteenth-century man was bamboozled into slack-jawed credulity by a practice known as phrenology. This consisted of getting a pompous, self-important authority figure—"the phrenologist"—to run his money-itching fingers over the subject's head and feel the bumps. These, much like tea leaves or sheep's entrails, were claimed to reveal the inner man and, within that psychic space, the phrenologist could chart the ley lines of individual destiny.

Frontier bump-readers were like snake-oil salesmen, "wise women" and seventh sons—there was no escape from them. Inevitably, a wandering phrenologist showed up in Georgetown one day when Grant was twelve or thirteen to feel bumps and separate the gullible from their ready cash. Jesse was ripe for the plucking—the richest man in town, and by his own lights a shrewd one, but besotted with his eldest son and forever bragging that his Ulysses was going to be a great man. The phrenologist who hit Georgetown that day struck lucky.

When Ulysses Grant was presented to him, the phrenologist reached out his hands, fingered the little scalp, and declared, "It is no very common head! It is an extraordinary head!" Groping some more, he pronounced, "It would not be strange if we should see him President of the United States!" Jesse could not have been more delighted, and it seems safe to assume that the phrenologist, who probably found future Presidents among the sons of prosperous (and grateful) fathers all over the West, was suitably rewarded for his prophetic insight.[27]

In 1836, when Ulysses was fourteen, his father sent him to Maysville, Kentucky, for the winter. There, he attended a school run by a pair of male teachers, Richeson and Rand. Ulysses had extracted as much education from the small Georgetown school as it had to offer. To his disappointment, Richeson and Rand, who were reputed to provide a demanding curriculum, did not teach him anything he didn't already know. He grew bored all over again, chanting the same formulas that passed for education in Georgetown, including such half-baked gems as "A noun is the name of a thing."

The tedium was relieved when he enrolled in the local Philamathean Debating Society, where he expressed himself forcefully on the issues of the day—the annexation of Texas and the abolition of slavery—and on eternal questions with obvious answers, such as whether the written word is more important than the spoken.[28]

When spring came, he returned to Georgetown. Life continued much as before, but one day in the summer of 1838 his father found himself shorthanded in the tan yard. Ulysses pitched in and his father set him to work in the beam house. This was the shed where hides were stretched across beams and the hair was scraped from one side and the remnants of flesh from the other. It wasn't physically demanding work, but the stench, the dirt, the gilt-edged squalor were too much for his sensitive nature. At the end of the day, he told Jesse frankly, "Father, this tanning is not the kind of work I like. I'll work at it, though, if you wish me to, until I am twenty-one. But you may depend on it, I'll never work a day at it after that."

His father replied, "I want you to work at whatever you like and intend to follow. Now, what do you think you would like?"[29]

Ulysses had three possibilities in mind—farming, being a trader on the Mississippi River, or getting a college education. Jesse mulled it over. The fifty acres he possessed did not amount to much of a farm and the land Hannah had inherited was rented out. As for being a trader on the river, that obviously appealed to the boy's craving for travel, and there was money to be made there. It was a common sight along the Mississippi those days to see long flatboats go by carrying more than a thousand barrels of pork to feed the settlers moving into Texas. But however much money a trader might make, life on the river was bad for the morals. Hannah would never approve. Traders drank and gambled and consorted with disreputable women. That left education.

Ulysses Grant always claimed he had not done well in school, and he had had—still has—a reputation for intellectual mediocrity. Yet his father maintained that he was, in fact, a "studious" youth. If Grant truly found learning half as irksome as he always claimed and other people liked to believe, it was pretty remarkable that as a sixteen-year-old who had already shown he could make his way in life without any further education, he nevertheless nurtured a desire to go on to college. This was at a time when barely one person in a hundred did so. A college education automatically made someone a member of America's intellectual elite. It was a distinguished band he was seeking to join, but in his shy and shrewd way, he made it seem he blundered into higher education rather than admit he had gone looking for it.

Any expressed interest in more schooling was certain to win his parents' approval. That winter of 1838 Jesse sent his son to what both of them hoped would be a demanding and rewarding school, the Presbyterian Academy in Ripley, Ohio, ten miles from Georgetown. Disappointed again—"A noun is the name of a thing," etc. Ulysses seemed to have exhausted the wellsprings of knowledge in that part of the United States. In the meantime, though, Jesse had hit on a shrewd idea for getting the boy a college education. If he sent him to West Point, Ulysses would not only obtain it for nothing, but the government would pay him while he was there.

Thomas L. Hamer, the congressman whose district included Georgetown, already had a local young man at the military academy. In fact, it was the boy next door, Bartlett Bailey. The Grants and the Baileys lived side by side and their sons had been playmates together. But young Bart Bailey was failing the challenging West Point course and was due to be dismissed in February 1839. When Ulysses came home from Ripley to spend Christmas 1838 with his family, Jesse told him, "Ulysses, I believe you are going to receive the appointment."

"What appointment?"

"To West Point. I have applied for it."

"But I won't go!" He had asked for an education, but not one like this—not one wrapped in a gray uniform, punctuated by drum rolls, and enforced by military discipline and bellowed commands! He had a profound and lasting aversion to music, and the sound of military bands would forever be torture to his nerves. The last place on Earth he ever intended to go was West Point; the last career he had ever considered was a soldier's life.

Until now, Jesse had not demanded his favorite child do anything. Hannah was a devout Methodist, but the boy had never been baptized (unlike his siblings) or forced to go to church, possibly because of his strange, tormented physical reaction to the sound of music. Ulysses Grant had enjoyed the freest of boyhoods—had been allowed to go far from home unsupervised, to handle dangerous horses, and to spend his own money, even if he sometimes struck a bad bargain. This time, though, Jesse was adamant. West Point was for the boy's own good, after all. He had asked for an education. Well, he was going to get one. "I think you *will* go!" said Jesse.[30]

Ulysses had never seen his father behave like this, at least, not toward him. He did not know what to do, what to say. Bowing to a parental pressure he barely knew existed until then, he did not argue. If his father felt that strongly about it, there was nothing for it but to go there and do his best.

———— ★ ★ ★ ————

CHAPTER 2

"I, CADET U. S. GRANT"

West Point has been blessed by nature. It stands on a bluff overlooking a wide bend in the Hudson River eighty miles north of New York. Trophy Point, on the edge of the Plain, the forty-acre parade ground, offers one of the most magnificent views in the whole of the picturesque Hudson highlands. Its strategic position on the river had made West Point an important military objective to both the British and the patriots during the Revolutionary War. Afterward, it became the site of a school that taught artillery tactics and military engineering, and in 1802 President Thomas Jefferson created the United States Military Academy there.[1]

The Academy's superintendent would be the chief engineer of the Army, and its top graduates would be commissioned in the Corps of Engineers. But in creating the United States Military Academy, Jefferson was aiming to do something besides improve military engineering. Here was an opportunity to reform American higher education. There would be, for the first time, an institution of higher learning that taught modern languages, not dead ones, and a college that offered technology rather than theology. Ever since the establishment of Harvard in 1636, the main role of American colleges had been to produce lawyers and preachers. West Point was a different kind of college, and Ulysses Grant was going to get what was probably the best education the United States had to offer.

The military academy guarded its elite status zealously. The fact that Grant—or anyone else—had received a highly coveted congressional appointment was not enough to get him in. In reality, all Hamer could provide was an opportunity to take the West Point entrance exam. Every aspirant, including those who had the President's own imprimatur, was required to take it. And this entrance exam was no mere formality. Roughly one in four who took it failed and returned home without ever donning cadet gray.

At the end of May 1839, seventeen-year-old Ulysses Grant stepped off the steamer that had carried him up the Hudson and checked into Roe's Hotel. Here was a chance to try out his new name. He had never much cared for Hiram. Like his father, he preferred the ring of Ulysses. He signed the hotel register as U. H. Grant. He had not informed his parents he was planning to alter his name. He probably did not want to upset his mother.[2]

Grant was unaware that Hamer had inadvertently ruined his plan by signing the papers for his appointment the day before Hamer's term as a congressman came to an end. In his haste—too busy packing?—he had scrawled "Ulysses S. Grant" on the paperwork that went to the War Department. He knew Jesse always called the boy Ulysses, and Hannah's maiden name was Simpson, so there was elementary logic behind his mistake. It wasn't until Grant reached the adjutant's office at West Point that he discovered what Hamer had wrought.

He was, he informed the adjutant, Ulysses *Hiram* Grant, and attempted to register under that name. The adjutant replied that as the appointment was in the name of Ulysses S. Grant, that was who he was and that was who he was going to remain, at least as long as he wore the Army's uniform.[3]

Dressed in butternut jeans and a pair of stout clodhopper shoes obviously fashioned with mud holes rather than drawing rooms in mind, he looked just what he was—a country boy from out west.[4] His chances of passing the entrance exam looked poor. Even if he surmounted that hurdle, the odds were stacked against him. Two-thirds of all westerners who had gained entrance to West Point had, like poor Bart Bailey, failed to finish the course.[5]

Grant had no illusions about what he was up against. Passing through Cincinnati, he had bought a book on algebra. It was the first he had ever seen. As he studied the eternal question of what is the value of *x,* he found himself bewildered. It might as well have been a book of magic spells or an ancient text written in Sumerian.[6]

He joined nearly a hundred other candidates in a barracks on the edge of the Plain. For the next two weeks, they got their first taste of military discipline. They also got a physical examination. A board of three Army surgeons pounded their chests for signs of tuberculosis, examined their feet for bunions, counted their teeth and probed them for caries, twisted their arms and legs to make sure they were sound, felt once-broken bones to judge how well they had healed, felt their backs for slipped disks, and parted their hair for signs of lice. A medical orderly held up a dime at a distance of twenty-five feet, and the cadets were asked whether it was showing heads or tails. That was the sight test.[7]

They were weighed and measured. Grant, at five feet one, was only an inch taller than the minimum height requirement. Weighing only 117 pounds, he was one of the smallest youngsters there.

Two weeks after arriving, Grant and the others who had passed the physical took the dreaded entrance exam. To his surprise and delight, he was one of the seventy-three who passed it. If anything, it had been easier than he expected. Once the exam results had been posted, the successful appointees received uniforms and haircuts.

A barber known only as Joe removed their locks faster than they could believe was humanly possible. Joe was not only the fastest hair cutter they would ever meet, but he was equally renowned for his ability to get down virtually to the scalp without drawing blood. Almost bald and struggling to carry all their possessions, which were crammed into small boxes exactly two feet square, the newest cadets staggered out onto the Plain. There they would spend the summer months under canvas and play their allotted role in the ritual known as summer encampment.

They were still mere plebes, and upperclassmen were allowed to torment them at will before everyone moved into barracks in September. The hazing could, at times, be brutal. It produced fistfights, unabashed tears, broken spirits and swift departures for home. Nearly as bad for young Grant were the dancing lessons. The new cadets were obliged to learn how to negotiate a dance floor by practicing their terpsichore on one another. The effect on Grant, who already loathed music, was to make him allergic to dancing for life.

Although the faculty loved the stately rituals, few plebes ever looked back on "summer camp" with fondness, but they too could appreciate distractions such as dress parades, female visitors, and the presence of America's most important soldier, Major General Winfield Scott, the commanding general of the Army. Scott had not graduated from West Point, but he loved the place, defended it against all criticism, and liked to visit summer encampment.[8]

Scott had tremendous presence and a flair for the melodramatic. He stood six feet, five inches tall and was one of the great heroes of the War of 1812. Grant, along with the rest of the Corps of Cadets, looked on in awe as Scott made his way around West Point that summer, imperious with the officers, avuncular toward the cadets, and oozing charm in the direction of the younger and prettier women visitors. He was, Grant thought, "the finest specimen of manhood my eyes had ever beheld, and the most to be envied." And some faint stirring of ambition touched young Grant's soul—an odd feeling "that some day I should occupy his place . . . although I had then no intention of remaining in the Army."[9]

When summer encampment ended, the cadets moved into barracks. On September 14, 1839, he belatedly signed his enlistment papers: "I, Cadet U. S. Grant . . . do hereby engage, with the consent of my guardian, to serve in the Army of the United States for eight years, unless sooner discharged by the proper authority . . ."[10]

Life in barracks could hardly have been more spartan. Cadet rooms were small, dark and cold. Light came from whale-oil lamps. There was no heating in the barracks, apart from fires that were allowed in the small fireplaces only on the coldest winter nights. There was no running water in the rooms. Water had to be fetched from wells and carried up the iron staircases, which in winter months were treacherous with ice due to overflowing buckets. The food at West Point was so abysmal it was clearly part of the policy of testing the character of the cadets, and they were sternly forbidden to supplement it by buying their own fare. Smoking was not permitted—in the barracks or anywhere else. Alcohol was completely banned, even outside the limits of the Academy grounds.

There was one place where smoking and drinking were possible: a nearby tavern run by a gregarious Irishman named Benny Havens. Benny offered tobacco, alcohol, buckwheat flapjacks and a knowledge of West Point exam questions going back many years. His establishment blazed warmly, alluringly, like a beacon of sanity and civilization in a wilderness of privation and pomposity. But being caught at Benny's grog shop was almost certain to result in dismissal from the Academy. Not that the risk ever stopped cadets from chancing it.

Grant visited Benny Havens's tavern only once. He was talked into it by Rufus Ingalls, a fellow cadet in the Class of 1843, but three years older. As throughout his life in Georgetown, Grant preferred the company of people older than himself. He and Ingalls roomed together during Grant's first two years. Ingalls, a wellborn Yankee, would one day be quartermaster general of the Army of the Potomac and renowned for his logistical abilities. Grant may well have calculated that if they got caught at Benny Havens's tavern, it was the senior and sophisticated Ingalls who would have to take most of the punishment for dragging this innocent from out west into bad behavior and thus he would be spared from dismissal himself. Having sampled Benny's forbidden delights once, Grant's curiosity was satisfied and his reputation for being as daring as his fellows was assured.[11]

The West Point day began at five A.M. with an abrupt and jarring outburst of drumming. In the darkness, a small band of drummers began sadistically pounding away outside the barracks. It is hard to imagine a more trying start to the day for Grant, with his horror of music. Cadets went to class to the sound of drumming, to the dining hall to the sound of drumming, to bed to the sound of drumming. There was no respite from the rattle of drums, and Grant's inability to follow a drumbeat made him one of the worst marchers ever to parade across the Plain. Nonetheless, despite the discomfort, the slop that passed for food, the fearful specter of algebra, and all the damn drumming, he was determined to stick it out. He could not bear the disgrace of quitting—not so much from pride, strong as that was, but because of the embarrassment and pain it would cause his mother.[12]

His one hope of early release was a move in Congress to abolish the Academy. Grant followed the story in the press, but the Academy had too many powerful supporters in Congress for abolition ever to pass.[13]

And all the while, West Point was getting into his blood. "West Point," he rapturously informed his cousin R. McKistry Griffin four months after he enrolled, "is decidedly the most beautiful place I have ever seen. . . . From the window near by [*sic*] I can see the Hudson . . . its bosom studded with hundreds of snow white sails. . . . On the whole I would not go away on any account. The fact is if a man graduates here he is safe fer [*sic*] life. Let him go where he will. There is much to dislike but more to like. I mean to study hard and stay if possible. . . . Contrary to you and the rest of my friends I have not been the least *homesick* no!"[14]

★

The Corps of Cadets in Grant's day numbered around 240. It was a small and select group, and at the end of his four years, a cadet would know not only the members of his own class but many of those in the three classes preceding his own, and many from the three following it. The number of cadets destined for fame during Grant's time at West Point was probably unsurpassed— there was William Tecumseh Sherman, for example, who first saw Grant's name posted on a bulletin board as "U. S. Grant" and wondered what it stood for—"Uncle Sam," perhaps? Or maybe "United States"?[15] Like other cadets, Ulysses soon had a nickname. He became known as Sam, although a cadet who looked less like lanky Uncle Sam would have been hard to find in any class that ever passed through West Point.

The Academy introduced him to the future of the Army and, to a remarkable degree, to the future of the country. Grant knew both Thomas (later "Stonewall") Jackson and an intellectual prodigy named George B. McClellan, who had finished two years at the University of Pennsylvania before entering West Point. McClellan was considered such a rising star that the Academy waived its age requirements to allow him to enter at the age of sixteen years and seven months.[16]

Grant became friendly with a tall, lean southerner named James Longstreet and made the acquaintance of a distant cousin named Don Carlos Buell. He also met William S. Rosecrans and Simon Bolivar Buckner; George Thomas and George E. Pickett; Fitz-John Porter and Ambrose P. Hill; and a dozen more young men besides, who would someday rise to high command or political importance. Not one of his cadet acquaintances seems to have made much of an impression on him, yet the Class of 1842, the year that preceded Grant's, was considered by the West Point faculty to be the finest the Academy produced in the first half-century of its existence.[17]

Ironically, few cadets at the time, however promising, really wanted to pursue military careers. In that, Grant was much like the rest. Graduation from West Point was merely the direct road to a well-paid career, such as building railroads, or into something interesting and prestigious, such as becoming a professor. "A commission," wrote a contemporary observer, "is unquestionably a letter of introduction into the envied circles of polite society . . . prima facie evidence of the gentleman and the scholar."[18]

West Point not only conveyed social graces such as dancing; it provided opportunities for fresh-faced youths from western tan yards or southern farms to mingle on terms of complete equality with the sons and grandsons of Presidents and with the dandified offspring of rich families from New York, Boston, or Philadelphia. All got the same education and the same opportunities to shine, the same chances for failure—and an equal risk of being disciplined for not keeping their rooms neat and their appearance impeccable.

The bedrock of the curriculum was mathematics and its related branches—physics (known then as "philosophy") and engineering. Each course was weighted, and the combined weight of these three subjects was equal to all the others—from infantry tactics to drawing—combined. Ulysses Grant would have discovered early that as long as he did well in these three, there was little chance of his failing.

Because he was one of the smallest cadets, it was inevitable that his physical courage would be tested. One of his classmates, Jack Lindsay, a tall, solidly built youngster whose father was a colonel in the Army, pushed Grant out of his rightful spot as the cadets lined up to enter the mess hall. Grant calmly told Lindsay to be more careful in the future. The next time they formed up to enter the dining hall, Lindsay did it again. Grant pitched into him and knocked Lindsay flat on his back.

Back home, Grant had not gone in for fighting. As far as is known, he had only four fights in Georgetown—all against the same youth, who was both older and bigger than he was. Grant lost the first three, but learned something each time. He won the fourth so conclusively that it settled the series. And now, outside the mess hall, he jumped on the sprawling Lindsay. With his large, rock-hard fists—after more than a decade of horse-handling, they were probably as powerful as those of even the biggest cadet—he proceeded to give his tormentor a beating severe enough to act as a deterrent. Once word spread of how little Grant had thrashed tall Jack Lindsay to a pulp, he could look forward to being left alone by other bullies as well.[19]

Despite his small size, Grant participated, reluctantly, in the cadets' favorite sport, rugby. He was too light to play forward and get mixed up in rucks and mauls, but he proved a speedy and capable right-winger.[20]

West Point had no fraternities. What it had instead was the Napoleon Club. The top students and interested professors met about once a month in a room decorated with portraits and busts of their hero and discussed the emperor's battles and campaigns. The intellectual ethos of the Academy in the thirty years prior to the Civil War was set largely by a single, brilliant mind—that of Dennis Hart Mahan. Education at West Point was controlled by the academic board, and Mahan, the renowned professor of military engineering, dominated the academic board.[21]

It was Mahan's ideas, including his worship of Napoleon, that formed the intellectual core of West Point. The closer a cadet came to fulfilling Mahan's vision of the perfect soldier, the more highly he would be esteemed by his professors and the loftier his standing in the pure meritocracy that was the Corps of Cadets. The Napoleon Club was but an extension of Mahan's mental universe, and the handful of cadets who were allowed to enter on the evenings when it met stepped into the realm where legends came alive, warming the blood of a new generation with the glowing embers of heroic deeds. And just as it was certain that a prodigy like McClellan would be invited to join, it was equally predictable that Grant would not. He had no interest in military history, had no ambition to be one of the top students in his class, and preferred reading light fiction anyway.[22]

Cadets were not allowed to leave West Point until the end of their second year, at which time they got a sixty-day home leave. At the end of two years, Grant returned to Ohio. His family was now living in Bethel, ten miles from Georgetown.[23]

One day in May 1841 he stepped off the stagecoach that dropped him as near to Bethel as its route took it. He then hired a driver to take him the rest of the way in a carriage. He cut quite a dash in his cadet uniform—dazzling white pants, a dark blue jacket glittering with gold buttons, and a large, jaunty round cap of Morocco leather. To the driver's astonishment, however, when Grant got out of the carriage in Bethel and his family crowded around, there were no hugs, no tears of joy, no fervent kisses. Jesse and Hannah simply said, "How are you, son?" as if he had been gone for a few days. His brothers and sisters were the same—"How are you brother?" Ulysses was equally undemonstrative with them.[24]

The entire Grant family—Jesse apart—tended to shyness and emotional restraint. The personalities Ulysses and his mother presented to the world were cool and reserved. This made them seem odd to many who knew them. Even people who spent years close to Ulysses Grant were likely to wonder whether they knew him at all. Such intense emotional reserve was bound to seem unusual in the hurrying, dynamic open society of the New World, but Grant's close control over his emotions would have gone unremarked in the land that both his Grant and Simpson ancestors came from. In England, it would have merely passed for politeness. Ulysses, Jesse explained to people, was "like his mother. He rarely ever laughs, never sheds a tear or becomes excited . . . never says a profane word, or indulges in jokes."[25]

Grant and his mother were not without mutual devotion. Far from it. They simply knew that emotion runs deeper and endures longer for being channeled than it does if allowed to overflow in outbursts of passion, before trickling away into the sand. The restraint that made Ulysses Grant seem unemotional did not indicate the absence of feeling. On the contrary, it was the mute testimonial of feelings too deep for words and too precious to waste. However distant they may have appeared in the eyes of strangers, Grant and his mother were emotionally close.[26]

Having coolly welcomed her son home, Mrs. Grant stepped back and looked at him. He had not only grown a few inches, he no longer slouched the way he used to. "Ulysses, you have grown much straighter," she remarked.

"Yes," came the wry reply, "that was the first thing they taught me." It was also something he would soon forget. Grant was probably the slouchiest, most round-shouldered soldier ever to disappoint an Army uniform.[27]

Having survived the first two years, Grant could be completely confident of surviving the rest of the course, assuming he did not get dismissed for breaching the Academy's strict disciplinary code. The vast majority of cadets who were expelled were thrown out for one reason only—they were not good enough in math. Mathematics and its offspring provided the intellectual steam that drove the West Point curriculum. Grant had arrived badly prepared by the schools he had attended back in Ohio in this fundamental subject. He was also competing against classmates who were, on average, eighteen months older than him—and at a time in life when eighteen months is a lot. Worse still, some of his rivals had a year or so of college behind them before enrolling at West Point. Most had covered part of the West Point curriculum. But it was all new to him.

The competition Grant faced was formidable, yet he rapidly mastered algebra, geometry, trigonometry and calculus and never came close to failure. He had an aptitude for mathematics that was great enough to compensate for the poor foundation, the slow start and West Point's idiosyncratic system of instruction. Grant had discovered, once exposed to algebra and geometry, that math was easy. So easy, he modestly said, "as to come almost by intuition." But no one is born with a knowledge of pi. What it amounted to—but he would never say outright, for fear of seeming to boast—was that he taught himself the fundamentals of algebra and geometry, while all around him other young men with more preparation than he were being thrown out of the Academy for poor grades in math.[28]

Grant's roommate during those first two years at West Point, Rufus Ingalls, acknowledged that "in his studies, he was lazy and careless. Instead of studying a lesson, he would merely read it over once or twice. But he was so quick in his perceptions that he usually made a very fair recitation even with so little preparation. . . . In scientific subjects he was very bright and if he had labored hard he would have stood very high in them."[29]

Grant, however, saw no point in studying hard. West Point, he decided, was "the best school in the world." But the strange way that class standing was arrived at was simply perverse. A cadet could be a mathmatical wizard, but if he forgot to button his coat properly or did not manage to tie his shoelaces to the satisfaction of some martinet, the demerits he received would count for as much as his genius. Where, then, was the incentive to shine academically? It took a supreme effort of will to endure such nonsense—which he bridled at as "an injustice"—and it deprived Grant of one of the greatest pleasures a good education can offer: a sense of intellectual fulfillment.[30]

What he would have done had he been exposed to able teachers early on and sent to a college without drums, drill and demerits, nobody will ever know. But the charlatan who called himself a phrenologist was right about one thing: This was no ordinary head.

Secure in the knowledge that he had what it took to finish the course, Grant could devote himself entirely to the pleasures of leave—forget the drumming, the spartan discomforts and the discipline that reduced a cadet's life to a round of tedious routine. He enjoyed these two months at home "beyond any other period of my life."[31]

When Grant returned to West Point, he was appointed a sergeant in the Corps of Cadets. His academic standing placed him roughly in the middle of his class, he had committed no serious offenses, and his military bearing was, as his mother had noticed, dramatically improved, if from an admittedly low base. The next two years offered every prospect of being better than the two just past.

★

Paradoxically, although it was a military academy, West Point offered little military training. There was some basic instruction in infantry drill and artillery tactics, but it did not amount to much. Graduates learned how to command troops and fight their country's battles only after they left West Point. The principal military challenge the United States faced during Grant's time as a cadet was fighting Native Americans, but virtually nothing that was taught at West Point was of any use for Indian fighting.

The sole practical military skill that all West Pointers possessed was an ability to ride. Equestrian classes were introduced during Grant's second year, to determine suitable officers for the cavalry, and when it came to horsemanship, he was easily the number-one man in his class, if not in his generation of Army officers. Cadets spent several hours each week learning to ride with a saber in one hand, the reins in the other, to slash at the heads of straw dummies and take horses over hurdles.

Some cadets loathed riding practice, if only because of the horses, which were, by and large, a dreary bunch of nags. They were mainly the animals used to haul the post's artillery batteries around the Plain for gunnery practice. "Jounce, jounce, jounce," complained William Dutton, a cadet three classes behind Grant. "Some of the horses are the hardest I ever rode, [with] the hardest of all possible saddles . . . and *without any stirrups.*" But around and around the riding hall the cadets went, gingerly picking themselves up at times from the thick layer of tanbark that covered the area after being thrown by an unobliging horse.[32]

Something similar may have happened even to Grant. In May 1841 he was disciplined for kicking a horse. As everyone who has ever handled horses knows, they can be the most delightful animals, but they can also provoke almost anyone into a bad temper. For some reason, his self-control snapped that day and he applied his boot to horseflesh.[33]

Despite this, the long West Point riding hall provided Grant with some of his happiest hours at the Academy. Years later, after Grant had become famous, one of his old professors remembered him vividly: "He was a tiny-looking little fellow, with an independent air and a good deal of determination. It is a long time ago, but when I recall old scenes, I can still see Grant, with his overalls strapped down on his boots. . . . It seems but yesterday since I saw him going to the riding hall, with his spurs clanging on the ground, and his great cavalry sword dangling by his side."[34]

He seemed able to ride anything, including a large, difficult mount called York. Grant delighted in making this long-legged but balky beast outjump every horse on the post, but one of his friends warned him, "Sam, that horse will kill you someday."

Grant was unmoved. "Well, I can't die but once."[35]

His love of horses went back, as we know, to childhood. His interest in girls developed more slowly. During his sixty-day furlough in Bethel, however, he appears to have become infatuated. Exactly who she was isn't known for certain, although he told one of his earliest biographers, "My one thought at West Point was of her."[36]

Chances are her name was Mary King, and he wrote a poem to her before returning to West Point:

> *My country calls and I obey,*
> *And shortly I'll be on my way,*
> *Removed from home far in the West,*
> *Yet you with home and friends are blest.*
>
> *Kindly then remember me*
> *(I'll also often think of thee),*
> *Nor forget the Soldier story*
> *Gone to gain the field of glory.*[37]

There were few chances for a cadet to meet young women at West Point. Some cadets spent the entire four years there without having the chance even to speak to a young woman, but that hardly stopped them from dreaming. Grant, however, came back from Bethel thinking he was in love and hoping he would marry the girl once he had graduated.

Back at the Academy, he was elected president of the Dialectical Society, which combined an interest in literature with staged debates. Grant also helped form a completely different organization, called the TIO. Like the Apostles, there were only twelve members. The mystical-sounding name simply stood for "Twelve in One." Each member wore a ring with TIO engraved upon it, and the society's rules required that the ring be worn until marriage. It would then be presented to one's bride. Something went wrong, however. It seems that the young woman in question did not reciprocate Grant's feelings. His TIO ring would have to go to someone else.[38]

His entire last year at West Point was fairly traumatic. During his first two years, he got a slightly below average number of demerits. They were for the usual petty offenses common to most cadets—room not clean enough, lateness to drill. He was gigged, too, for the most predictable Grant offense of all—"unmilitary appearance generally." That was one failing he never even tried to overcome.

Such offenses were paid off by walking punishment tours. But in May 1842 he was confined to quarters for two weeks for "speaking to a superior officer in a disrespectful manner."[39] Grant maintained his grades during his third year, but his conduct slipped so much that when it ended, he lost his stripes and reverted to being just another private in the Corps of Cadets.

The top graduates in a class were usually commissioned in the Corps of Engineers. They could expect to spend their careers managing important construction projects. Those just below them would become topographical engineers, with responsibility for mapping and surveying and exploration. Below the engineers came ordnance officers, and below them came the artillery.

Grant, however, had no interest in the technical branches of military service. He was much more interested in the cavalry and being a horse soldier. A cadet did not have to graduate anywhere near the top of his class to get a commission in the Army's regiment of dragoons. If he graduated somewhere in the middle, he stood a good chance of becoming a cavalry officer, and if he demonstrated a high level of skill with horses, his chances would be excellent.

At the start of his fourth and final year as a cadet, Grant applied for a commission in the dragoons. For his second choice he put down infantry. But that was about all that would be open to him anyway if he did not get into the cavalry. Grant had every reason to think he was going to spend his time as an officer in the company of creatures he loved—horses.

Then came disaster. One day in March 1843 he lost his temper with a horse and struck it, probably with his saber. It amounted to a far more serious offense than kicking a horse. He was placed under arrest and confined to his room for two weeks as punishment.[40]

The only sanctions more severe were suspension for a year or outright dismissal. His former good conduct and—it seems reasonable to assume—genuine and obvious remorse at his behavior probably helped him avoid being suspended or dismissed. But he had, in a moment of anger, wrecked his chance of getting into the cavalry. No one, however skilled a rider, could be known as a man who maltreated horses and hope to be accepted among the dragoons, whose very lives depended on the animals they rode.

Grant tried to redeem himself at one of the great spectacles the Academy presented each year, the graduation ride. Scott would be present among the visiting dignitaries. Most of the faculty would be there, along with the entire Corps of Cadets. The riding master, Sergeant Herschberger of the dragoons, had the bar that was used for jumping raised to six feet, three inches, a height that seemed almost impossible. He then called out, "Cadet Grant!"

What followed was described by one of the visitors. "A clean-faced, slender, blue-eyed fellow, weighing about one hundred and twenty pounds, dashed from the ranks on a powerfully-built chestnut-sorrel horse and galloped down the opposite side of the hall. As he turned at the farther end and came into the stretch across which the bar was placed, the horse increased his pace, and, measuring his stride for the great leap before him, bounded into the air and cleared the bar, carrying his rider as if man and beast had been welded together. The spectators were breathless 'Very well done, sir!' growled old Herschberger . . . and the class was dismissed."[41]

No one had ever jumped so high at West Point. It is possible no one until then had jumped so high in the entire world. News of Grant's record-breaking jump on York spread his name among skilled riders in and out of the Army. It was even claimed that a plaque was put up in his honor at the Spanish Riding School in Vienna, but this hardly seems likely.[42]

The next day, Grant graduated twenty-first in his class, which numbered thirty-nine members. His roommate, Frederick Dent, of St. Louis, Missouri, narrowly escaped being the goat of the class and graduated thirty-third. While Grant's overall standing placed him in the middle of his class, his professors would have noticed that this was far from the whole story, or even the important part of the story. In mathematics, he stood tenth in his class; in philosophy (or physics), he stood fourteenth; and in engineering, he stood sixteenth. In other words, in the subjects that really counted, he was in the top third of the West Point class of 1843. And he got into the top third without even trying to excel. The professor of mathematics, Alfred Church, was so impressed with Grant's innate abilities that he wanted him to return to the Academy as an instructor as soon as possible.[43]

Grant had not given up hope of joining the dragoons, and his spectacular jump on York may have been an attempt to impress his superiors into giving him a second chance after his conviction for maltreating a horse. Before he departed West Point, he left an order at the post tailor's shop for a uniform but told the tailor not to start cutting cloth. Grant would let him know later what kind was needed—a glamorous cavalry officer's outfit or the more pedestrian ensemble of an infantry soldier— once his commission came through.[44]

He returned to Bethel, and shortly afterward came word from Washington: Grant had been commissioned a brevet second lieutenant in the 4th Infantry Regiment, stationed at Jefferson Barracks, Missouri. His commission was made out in the name Ulysses S. Grant. He finally accepted that his struggle to be known as Ulysses Hiram Grant had failed comprehensively. From this point on, he signed himself U. S. Grant and let it go at that.

For the rest of his life Grant would claim he did not much care whether he became a horse soldier or a footslogger. His assertions amount to nothing but a severe case of denial. The truth was, being rejected for service with the dragoons was a crushing disappointment. It was no consolation to reflect that he had brought it on himself. Several weeks after reporting for duty with the infantry, he could bear it no longer and wrote to the adjutant general of the Army: "Sir, I have the honor to apply for a transfer from the 4th Infantry to the Dragoons . . . which was my first choice on leaving the Military Academy." He pointed out that there were fewer brevet second lieutenants in the dragoon regiment than there were in the 4th Infantry. If anything, he suggested, the 4th Infantry had too many.

The adjutant general was unimpressed. In the small world of the military, Grant's West Point record was going to be crucial in deciding what kind of a commission he got, and that decision had not been taken lightly. The AG replied with the traditional dusty reply of the military bureaucrat: "Due regard for the interest of the service, will not justify the exchange you propose."[45]

An infantry officer he was and would remain, despite the fact that he had shown himself to be the finest rider in the Army. Grant had just learned an enduring lesson in the importance of keeping a viselike grip over his feelings.

Besides pretending he did not care whether or not he joined the cavalry, Grant also chose to pretend he had never liked West Point. This was merely another measure of his disappointment. In truth, he never ceased to love the place, even if his feelings about it were mixed. He told Army friends that he wanted to be buried there. He was also determined that at least one of his sons would follow him to the granite monastery on the Hudson, march across the Plain as he had done in cadet gray, and see that inspiring view for himself. Say what he might, Grant never got West Point out of his system.[46]

———— ★ ★ ★ ★ ————

CHAPTER 3

"BE SHURE AND WRITE"

In a dull provincial town where nearly everyone wore rough homespun of gray or brown, the sight of a few gold buttons, the yellow fire flashing from brand-new gold braid, a big black-and-gold West Point ring, and a pair of sky blue nankeen pants were certain to turn girls' heads and stir envy among other young men. Grant could hardly wait to get into his fancy new uniform and impress his country cousins. Each time he appeared on the street in uniform, people gathered around and he told them about West Point and the great men he'd seen, such as the general-in-chief, Winfield Scott, and the President, Martin Van Buren.[1]

Bethel was a small stage. He soon needed a new audience for his West Point stories. Grant got into his uniform one day and headed for Cincinnati, ten miles away, astride his best-looking horse. As he rode through the somber, unpaved streets, basking in what he took for silent approbation from passersby, a barefoot youth in a dirty shirt and ragged pants crossed his path. The boy took in the sight with a scornful glance, then hollered derisively, "Soldier! Will you work? No, siree—I'll sell my shirt first!"

It was the low comedy of any democratic society, but Grant, his overly sensitive nature bleeding from every pore, was devastated. He could not bear to be mocked. And being held up to ridicule in public was the ultimate humiliation. Most men would simply laugh off the childish nonsense of a guttersnipe, be momentarily irritated, and let it pass. Not Grant. He brooded on his embarrassment.

Returning to Bethel, he was mocked yet again, and by someone not much more august than a street urchin—a stable hand at the local tavern. The youth, Harrison Scott, who worked at the town's livery stable, was parading barefoot down Bethel's main street in blue pants with a white stripe sewn down the outside seam in a parody of that fancy-dan Grant boy back from West Point.

Instead of taking this dumb show for the small-minded, small-town jealousy it represented, Grant was wounded all over again. He reacted as if he had just been told he was inadequate by two people whose opinion mattered—say, Winfield Scott and Dennis Hart Mahan. Grant's youthful and harmless delight in being an Army officer was destroyed in an instant. A ragamuffin and a stable hand, both of whom were probably illiterate and unlikely to accomplish much, left a lasting mark. Between them, he said, they "gave me a distaste for military uniform that I never recovered from."[2]

At the end of September he reported to the 4th Infantry Regiment, stationed at the biggest military base west (if only just) of the Mississippi—Jefferson Barracks, Missouri. The barracks consisted of a collection of large stone buildings primly surrounded by white picket fences on a high bluff overlooking the west bank of the Mississippi, ten miles south of St. Louis. The buildings, arranged in an arc like the fingers of an open hand, were set among expansive lawns and sported large verandahs, where young officers sat in the shade for hours, booted feet insouciantly planted on the railing, gossiping, smoking, dreaming of women, promotions, and war and what they would do if any or all came their way.[3]

Although denied the dragoons, Grant got a desirable posting. The 4th Infantry was generally considered one of the elite units of the small U.S. Army, which numbered only seven thousand men.[4] And given the size of the Army, Grant could count on finding himself among friends virtually anywhere he was stationed. At Jefferson Barracks he would meet up again with a score of people he had known at West Point, including Frederick T. Dent, his roommate during his last two years at the Academy. He counted himself lucky, too, that Dent's family lived only five miles away and that officers from Jefferson Barracks were always welcome there.

It might have been a delightful household had it not been for the crabbed nature of the head of the family. Fred Dent's father, Frederick F. Dent, had left home at fourteen to work as a road builder. By the age of eighteen he was a surveyor but had had enough of roads. He used his savings to set up as a trader, which consisted mainly of swindling Indians out of furs. Within a few years he was worth $20,000—a huge fortune on the frontier, where cash was rare and barter was common.[5]

In 1813 Frederick F. Dent had returned to Maryland and married a strikingly pretty young Englishwoman, Ellen Bray Wrenshall. Two years later, when the War of 1812 ended and the Mississippi was at last securely in American hands from Canada to the Gulf, Dent put his wife, his possessions and his three slaves aboard several flatboats and headed for Missouri. Dent, it seems, had grown tired of being a merchant and aspired to be something grander. He bought 925 acres of land, which included a large house, on the banks of Gravois Creek, south of the fur-trading settlement of St. Louis.[6]

Dent called his new estate White Haven, in honor of the picturesque small port on the northwest coast of England with which he had an ancestral connection. Behind the large white farmhouse surrounded by spruce trees and locusts, Dent erected some miserable little shacks for his slaves, whose number eventually reached eighteen. He was, in truth, just another farmer, but in his fancy he saw himself as a more imposing figure—the highly cultivated owner of a quasi-southern plantation. Dent, who also imagined he was related to the British aristocracy and court, had no hesitation about granting himself a title. Without a single day of military service to his credit, he called himself Colonel.

A quarrelsome, bullying man, with vehemently expressed political opinions, Dent was quick to sue his neighbors over trifles and, in his grasping way, equally quick to seek a chance to make money. If anyone outside his overawed children actually liked Frederick F. Dent, there is no record of it. Grant, who eventually became his son-in-law, never said or wrote a word in his favor. The self-styled "colonel" was not a man he could ever like, or even respect. Dent, according to a local doctor, was "masterful in his ways, of persistent combativeness and . . . inclined to be vindictive." Not, that is, the kind of person the sensitive, introverted Grant would ever feel comfortable around.[7]

While his slaves tried to wring enough of a living from the farm's poor soil to cover his bills, Dent spent most days from Easter to Thanks-

giving on his front porch, seated in a rocking chair, reading the newspapers, smoking a long churchwarden pipe, and growing splenetic at the
rising chorus against slavery. In the winter he did the same thing
indoors, sitting close to the fire.[8]

One afternoon shortly before Christmas 1843 a young Army officer
mounted on a thoroughbred with a flowing mane and impressive tail
rode up to the house and dismounted at the gate. Several enslaved black
children and Dent's youngest daughter, eight-year-old Emma, rushed
up to him. "Does Mr. Dent live here, little girl?" Grant asked the awestruck Emma.[9]

The Dents had already heard of Brevet Second Lieutenant Ulysses S.
Grant from Fred. They made their son's onetime roommate warmly
welcome. During the next two months this lonely young man rode out
to White Haven once a week, seeking a chance to relax amid the comforts and distractions of a lively civilian home. Military routine in
peacetime in any barracks tends to be dull. And while Grant did not
have much in common with the colonel, it was really the company of
the females of the family that drew him there anyway.

The Dents had four sons and three daughters. There was little
Emma, her sixteen-year-old sister, Nellie, and the eldest, Julia, who was
spending the winter with a rich family in St. Louis. There was also the
short but remarkably good-looking Mrs. Dent, whose refinement stood
in stark contrast to the boorish ways of her husband. Ellen Wrenshall
Dent never ceased to yearn for the life she had known in the East. To
her, the frontier was a big step down.[10]

Grant was always happy to talk farming and horses with the self-
styled colonel, but whenever Dent brought the conversation around to
politics, there was an insurmountable barrier between them. Jesse Grant
had always loathed slavery and roundly criticized his southern relatives
who owned slaves as lazy good-for-nothings whose children would
grow up unable to black their own shoes.[11]

Southwestern Ohio was embroiled in the slave issue from the days of
Grant's childhood, and Ripley, where Grant had gone to school for a
time, was one of the principal stations on the Underground Railroad,
which helped bring slaves out of the South and into freedom. In the
1840s the question of slavery dominated political discourse. Grant had
views on the subject that were as strong as Dent's. He saw the use of
other human beings as property for the evil it was, but would not argue

the issue with Dent, or anyone else. Grant never argued anything with anyone. Outside the limits of a formal debate, he viewed all argument as a waste of time and a source not of enlightenment but of ill feeling. "He never had a personal controversy with man or boy in his life," marveled Jesse Root Grant, who gave every appearance of liking nothing better.[12]

In February 1844 Grant was finally introduced to the light of Dent's narrow, cantankerous existence, his eighteen-year-old daughter, Julia. Mrs. Dent had borne four sons before, to her husband's intense joy, she finally had a daughter. From that moment, Julia was her father's favorite. He delighted in her as in none of his other children and gave her a slave all her own, known as Black Julia. Slaves were not human beings, merely dark reflections of their owners' whims and fantasies. Julia happily accepted the gift, and to the day she died never thought there was anything wrong with slavery. When it came to black people, Daddy knew best, and Daddy thought slavery was actually good for them.

Even so, Julia preferred, as did other members of the Dent family, to avoid the word *slave.* In the Dent household they were usually called *servants,* as if they were free to come and go as they pleased, demand wages for their labor, strive to rise in the world and seek a better life for their children. The Dents probably treated their slaves better than some families did, but that was hardly the issue.

Shortly after returning home from her winter sojourn in St. Louis, Julia attended a dance at Jefferson Barracks. She often went to dances with her tall, handsome cousin, Lieutenant James "Pete" Longstreet, who had known Grant at West Point. Longstreet always claimed that it was he who had introduced them to one another.[13]

Julia was five feet tall, sturdily built and plump. She had thick, dark brown hair pulled into a chignon, small but strong hands and strabismus in her right eye. Photographed often throughout her lifetime, there are few pictures that show her looking straight at the camera. She was, to anyone who wanted to be critical, dumpy, cross-eyed and plain. But appearances aside, she was full of life, voluble, strong-willed and optimistic. Julia was the antithesis of Grant's mother, but in some ways a lot like old Jesse. Her warmth and sociability broke down his shyness and almost pathological hypersensitivity.

A young woman who could break through those barriers was just what he needed. Far from home once more, Grant almost certainly craved a woman's love, but having declared his feelings to one young woman and been rejected, he was not going to risk rejection again. Julia, though, looked like a fairly good bet. Although the shortage of young white women out West made all of them desirable to some degree, there would be less competition for Julia than there would be for many others. She was not particularly well educated, but neither was she stupid. She was quick-witted and had few illusions about her physical charms. Within a few weeks, possibly even less, Grant decided he was in love with Julia Dent and was going to marry her. "He became a daily visitor," Julia recalled.[14]

The fact that she was an exceptionally fine horsewoman surely counted heavily in her favor and they rode together often. Sometimes they walked up and down Gravois Creek, picking flowers, flirting shyly, talking about everything but what was really on their minds. Sitting on the banks of the Gravois, they read poetry to one another. On one occasion they came across an elderly slave who had cut his foot badly with an ax. Together, they saved the man from bleeding to death. While Grant improvised a dressing from the slave's tattered vest, Julia remarked, "I always had the impression that it was the mission of the soldier to make wounds, not bind them up."

He looked up at her with his steady blue-eyed gaze. "Perhaps it's both."[15]

When Julia's pet canary died, Grant made a tiny coffin for it and painted the casket yellow. Then he organized a funeral ceremony and got eight other officers to attend this solemn occasion. Julia thought it a moving farewell.[16]

Unlike her mother, who was fastidious to a fault, Julia loved the outdoor life, but that had not prevented her from acquiring the requisite social graces of a young woman of her time and class. She played the piano and could sing fairly well. She was an excellent dancer but, she was dismayed to discover, Grant never danced. He simply refused to take the dance floor after leaving West Point.

Grant tended to tarry so long at the Dents that he often returned to Jefferson Barracks after all the other officers in the 4th Infantry were already seated for dinner. The president of the officers' mess, Captain Robert C. Buchanan, was a martinet who had a stiff punishment for tardiness: Anyone arriving for dinner after the soup had been served had to buy the mess a bottle of wine. Decent wine was a luxury item on the frontier and Grant never had much patience with pettiness. He finally told Buchanan bluntly that he had paid enough. "I have been fined three bottles of wine within the last ten days," he declared, "and if I am to be fined again, I shall be obliged to repudiate."

Buchanan's response was, "Mr. Grant, young people should be seen and not heard."[17] This blunt—and dismissive—assertion of authority may be acceptable in dealing with children, but Grant can hardly have taken it lightly, as he approached his twenty-second birthday, to be rebuked like a child in front of his brother officers. What's more, Buchanan's failure to make out a good case for the punishment he imposed would hardly have persuaded Grant that he was dealing with a truly superior officer. The two men were destined to clash again, more seriously, some years later.[18]

Grant had never been a good timekeeper, and with Julia rather than mess regulations at the center of his thoughts, he could easily have sunk his entire salary into wine for the mess. But what was going to keep him apart from her wasn't Captain Buchanan—it was Texas. In 1844, as tempers became inflamed over slavery, the entire country seemed to be sliding into a red mist.

The Mexican government had opened Texas to settlement by Americans, but the Americans resented, and finally resisted, Mexican rule. In 1836 American settlers had fought the Mexicans for their right to remain in Texas and rule themselves, but Mexico still claimed the region between the Sabine and the Rio Grande as Mexican territory.

Slaveholders everywhere were clamoring for the annexation of Texas, because it was almost certain, they believed, to enter the Union as a slave state. This was so despite the fact that no more than 15 percent of Texas was suitable for slave labor. But with their backs increasingly to the wall as the North developed a modern economy and left the South far behind, slave owners were driven more by visions of impending poverty than by any realistic appraisal of macroeconomic developments. They looked to politics to shore up a system that was as doomed as an economy based on barter or the exchange of seashells.

Frederick F. Dent had no doubts about what to do—annex the land between the Sabine and the Rio Grande and bring it into the Union. Take it from Mexico by force if necessary, but one way or another, Texas must become part of the United States. Dent was a typical slaveholder of his time.

In April 1844 Grant obtained a three-week leave and was about to depart for Ohio. Sitting outside the Dent house with Julia one evening, he removed his West Point class ring. These were the very first college rings and had not yet been copied elsewhere. They were something special—the mark of a new elite. He had told Julia some weeks earlier that he intended to give his as an engagement ring to the woman he chose for his wife. As he timidly offered the ring to her now, Julia ducked the issue. "Oh no," she said. "Mama would never approve of my accepting a gift from a gentleman." It was as if he had just offered her a necklace or a silk dress. She didn't say anything about marriage. Neither did he.

Grant was obviously pained by her refusal to take the ring—"rather put out," as she described it. Baffled and hurt, he asked if she would miss him. He was almost desperate for a crumb of emotional nourishment, but Julia gave a noncommittal reply. The lieutenant was moving much too fast for her and heading in a direction she did not want to go.[19]

In his memoirs, he makes no mention of this incident, claiming instead that it was only when he had been separated from her for a week or so that he realized he was in love with Julia.[20] But she knew better. It was Julia who recorded what actually happened. She could hardly forget his attempt to arrive at an engagement by a flanking movement rather than by a frontal assault. It was typical, too, for Ulysses Grant first to try and declare his love for her indirectly, thus avoiding, if possible, the need to say outright that he was in love and wanted to marry her. Nothing mattered more to Grant than a woman's love, but like Cyrano de Bergerac—and untold more male millions—it was agony for him to declare his feelings to the woman he loved while in her presence, under her possibly rejecting gaze. So the ring stayed on his finger and a couple of days later he boarded the steamer that would take him upriver to Cincinnati.

The vessel had hardly vanished over the northern horizon before orders reached Jefferson Barracks deploying the 4th Infantry to Natchitoches, Louisiana. Tension over Texas was building up like a summer thunderstorm, and the Mexican government was threatening to provide the lightning—it was ready to fight, it declared, if the United States annexed Texas. Messages were sent to Grant, canceling his leave and ordering him to return to his regiment.

During the two weeks that he was gone he missed Julia intensely. It wasn't quite the same with her, but she found that she missed him, too—much more than she had expected. Julia's bedroom had just been refurbished and her father had bought her a brand-new bed with large wooden bedposts. She named one of these penile-looking objects Lieutenant Grant. And one night, when she fell asleep beneath it, what did she dream of but the charming lieutenant himself?[21]

The next day, Grant rode down the Gravois, like a maiden's dream come true, hurrying back to White Haven after reporting in at Jefferson Barracks. The spring thaw and heavy rains had swollen the normally placid creek into a raging torrent. As he rode into the creek, the force of the current swept Grant off his horse. He managed to hold on to the saddle, and the horse pulled him over to the opposite bank, half drowned and completely soaked. He arrived on the Dents' doorstep looking like an orphan of the storm.

The following morning he drove Julia to St. Louis so she could be a bridesmaid at a friend's wedding. Along the way, he halted the carriage by a bridge. Awkwardly, self-consciously, haltingly, Grant asked her to marry him. She replied brightly, "It would be charming to be engaged, but married? No! I would rather be engaged." As that was the best she would offer him, he stolidly accepted it. They were engaged. There was one more thing, though, said Julia—"Don't tell Papa!" He removed his class ring, and this time she accepted it.[22]

★

A paddle-wheel steamer carried Grant down the Mississippi, toward New Orleans. There, he boarded a smaller vessel that would take him to Natchitoches. The little steamer was seriously overcrowded. The intense heat and humidity of the Mississippi delta in early summer made the cramped conditions aboard almost intolerable. Many of the male passengers struck Grant as cutthroats—rough, aggressive men, quick with a knife, a gun, or a deck of cards. They turned the cramped vessel into a gambling den, open all hours. Much as he loved travel, this was one journey Grant couldn't wait to complete.

Arriving in Natchitoches, he found his regiment was encamped three miles away. There was a military base, Fort Jesup, twenty-five miles southwest of the town, but it was too small to accommodate an extra regiment of infantry. The 4th had pitched its tents on a high, well-drained ridge set among pinewoods. The ridge caught whatever breezes blew toward it from the nearby river. A spring provided wonderfully pure, refreshingly cold water. The men of the 4th were so delighted with this place they called it "Camp Salubrity."[23]

Despite "the hottest sun I think I ever felt," Grant made the three-mile uphill hike to camp rather than pay the exorbitant amount demanded by local drivers to carry him there.[24] He settled down in a tent with a floor covered with pine needles and waged a constant war with the abundant insect population that the pinewood bred. When it rained, his tent turned into a comically sodden sieve, although he did not find it funny.

Apart from cutting a military road through the woods, there was not much for the troops to do. Grant learned to play cards and proved to have no card-sharping talents whatever. He lost small sums nearly every time he sat down to play.[25]

His greatest pleasure was still horses. Grant bought a fine thoroughbred and rode it in local races. He soon became a favorite among the horse-crazy local plantation grandees, who were delighted to invite him to ride their spirited mounts, grace their homes and talk horseflesh.[26]

Grant spent much of his time daydreaming about Julia, but he was given a fright. Shortly after he reached Louisiana, an officer's wife arrived from Jefferson Barracks and told him he had a dangerous rival for Julia's affections. He could hardly believe it, but suppose it was true? Grant wrote Julia immediately, saying he did not believe a word of the tale. After all, if anything like that happened, Julia would have been the first to let him know . . . wouldn't she? The crisis soon passed. There was no rival. If there were any other serious suitors for Julia Dent's plump little hand, no record of them survives.[27]

Meanwhile, Grant had a lock of her hair to gaze upon and tried willing her from far away to write to him and seal her letters with his West Point ring, as she had promised she would. They had also promised each other, before he departed, that at sunset each day, no matter what they were doing, each would think of the other and of the love that bound them despite absence and distance.

Even though he wrote her regularly, Grant remained something of a mystery to Julia. It was typical of him to send his beloved a letter containing blank spaces—visible representations of his silences. The only way he could tell her how passionately he loved her was to let Julia provide the subtext. Only, she didn't. She stared at the blanks in disbelief and amazement. What could they possibly mean? she wrote him. It is almost possible to hear the sigh as Grant patiently explained that the blanks "were only intended to express an attachment which words would fail to express."[28] He signed his letters "Most Truly and Devotedly Your Lover" and fervently implored her, "be shure [sic] and write soon," but Julia sent few letters to Camp Salubrity.

Grant was gone for a year. In that time, he heard scarcely a word from her. Then, in May 1845, he got leave. Grant hurried back to Jefferson Barracks, mounted a dappled gray horse and rode over to White Haven. He arrived to find Dent outside the house saying farewell to various neighbors. The "Colonel" was about to set off for Maryland on business, and the pockets of his long black frock coat bulged with letters he had been asked to carry east and lists of things his family wanted him to buy them once he reached the civilized world, where there were real stores. Grant asked to be allowed to ride into St. Louis with Dent. There was something urgent he had to discuss.

Grant implored Dent to accept him as a future son-in-law. Impossible, Dent replied. "Now, if it were Nellie," he said, trying to offer an alternative, "I would make no objections. But my Julia is entirely unfitted for such a life." Oh, no! She would never be happy in the Army. Well, said Grant, I don't have to stay in the Army. He told Dent he could get a professorship and teach math at a civilian college in Ohio. He was willing to resign his commission if that was the price of Julia's hand.[29]

Dent wasn't interested. He advised Grant to stick to his profession. Army life wasn't good enough for Julia, Dent seemed to be saying, but it was good enough for Grant. In the end, Dent did not say no. He said he would leave it for Julia to decide, but it was clear what advice he intended to give her. The most he would concede was that the pair might correspond while Grant was away, and if they still wanted to get married in a year, maybe two, he would not try to stop them. As for Mrs. Dent, she simply refused to take the engagement seriously, and treated it as a mere infatuation, something her daughter and the nice lieutenant would eventually outgrow.[30]

When Dent returned from Maryland, he remonstrated with Julia. "You are too young and the boy is too poor! He hasn't anything to give you."

Julia responded, "I am poor, too, and haven't anything to give him."[31]

Dent remained convinced that Ulysses Grant's limited prospects meant he was not the kind of promising young man an ambitious father would consider suitable for his daughter, but the fact is that Grant was a far better catch than Julia. Jesse Grant was a successful businessman and died rich. Dent was a blowhard who lived far beyond his modest means. He was destined to die poor and in his final years depended on Grant for the food on his plate.

The real reasons Dent objected to Lieutenant Grant were neither his modest salary nor the rigors of Army life but his irritating northernness and his unshakable hostility to just about every political and social view that Dent loved to spout. Had Grant been a slaveholding young officer from Mississippi whose father owned a plantation as successful as Jesse's leather business, Dent would have thrown his arms around the slender lieutenant and called him "Son."

★

Conditions at Camp Salubrity had improved dramatically in a year. The officers moved into small wooden houses and a woman was hired to do their cooking. Grant and a fellow officer jointly hired a free black named Valere to be their servant. Grant pretended to be severe with Valere, teasing him by threatening dire punishments for minor infractions. Valere spoke English, French and Spanish—something likely to prove useful if, as the officers of the 4th Infantry expected, they were sent to the Mexican border.[32]

There was little doubt among them that war was coming. The government was creating "an Army of Observation" to be sent into Texas if annexation was voted by Congress. The army commander, Brevet Brigadier General Zachary Taylor, arrived at Fort Jesup to take charge of this burgeoning force.

Grant had been mightily impressed as a cadet by the magnificent sight of Winfield Scott, but Taylor provided a different education entirely in *le style militaire.* While Scott was nicknamed "Old Fuss and Feathers," Taylor was indifferent to appearances and allergic to fuss. He was as phlegmatic as a high-ranking officer could be and dressed like a farmhand, in baggy jeans and a palmetto hat. He had spent much of his life fighting—first against the British, then against the Seminole Indians. It was Taylor rather than Scott who was going to provide Grant with a role model of generalship that stripped everything to the essentials.

In January 1846 the Army of Observation was ordered to move to Corpus Christi, Texas. Congress was moving inexorably toward annexation and the Mexican government was moving just as steadily toward a declaration of war. Grant's mind, however, was less on these dramatic developments than on some other unfinished business. "After an engagement of sixteen or seventeen months," he wrote Julia, "ought we not to think of bringing that engagement to an end, in the way that all true and constant lovers should?"[33]

He was, he insisted, ready to leave the Army and go teach mathematics at Hillsboro, a small college in Ohio. Even his father, who had insisted on sending him to West Point, was now urging him to quit. Julia, however, wanted him to remain. She knew how entirely Army life suited him.

Grant could never express openly any desire to serve under fire, to see the elephant, to get himself shot at, or to lead men into battle, but his entire life demonstrated a character that was irresistibly drawn to danger and adventure. He was one of the first antiheroes of the Western world, emerging at a time when the romantic glow of figures such as Byron and Napoleon still filled educated young men's hearts with thrilling visions of the glorious deed conducted in a bravura—and preferably well-publicized—manner. Fame was ever the spur to nineteenth-century poets and soldiers.

Grant wanted the deed, but couldn't have cared less about the bravura manner. He was easily bored, and his taciturnity camouflaged a longing for a life that transcended the mundane. The Army—not teaching math—at this historic moment offered him exactly that. "Really," he told Julia, "I think there can be no happier [sic] place to live."[34]

The Army of Observation moved to the level white sands of Corpus Christi, at the junction of the Nueces River and the Gulf of Mexico. Row upon row of pyramid tents stretched along the shore as four thousand soldiers established their camp. The shoreline was choked with oyster beds, and it was difficult to get supply boats over them from the ships anchored offshore. On one occasion, while Grant was supervising troops who were wrestling boats across the oyster beds, he jumped into the water and joined the men in this difficult and dangerous task. Taylor noticed it and remarked, "I wish I had more officers like Grant."[35]

The officers of the Army of Observation drilled the men during the day on a huge expanse of open ground and amused themselves at night with gambling, drinking and amateur dramatics. Grant's preference, though, was what it had always been—to buy a horse. But what he bought was a wild stallion that no one else would even attempt to ride.

Grant paid twelve dollars for it, got onto its back, held on in seeming defiance of logic, common sense, and the laws of gravity, and then disappeared over the horizon as the horse streaked away with him. Man and mount returned three hours later, both covered with sweat, but the horse had his head down and the rider had his up.[36]

Horses were so cheap in those parts, thanks to the presence of huge herds of wild horses, that he soon owned three mounts. He entrusted their care to Valere, but one day the lad lost control of them when taking them to a watering hole and all three ran away, reducing the lieutenant to walking again.

Grant joined the theater troupe that some 4th Infantry officers had organized and was cast as Desdemona in a production of *Othello*. It was a natural piece of casting. Grant had an almost feminine prettiness at this stage of life. His rosy cheeks, clear skin and frank blue eyes prompted other officers in the 4th Infantry to call him "Beauty," and Julia's sister Emma thought he was "as pretty as a doll."[37]

Grant was also as demure and sensitive as a young woman. When he was nearly sixty, he claimed that no one had seen him naked since childhood. He had, thought James Longstreet, "a girlish modesty." In the rough male world of the military, Grant's prudishness was remarkable.[38]

Grant was not only slender but looked much shorter and smaller than he really was. Most accounts give his height as being five feet, eight inches, although one credits him with being five feet ten.[39] Even so, he is regularly described as "short," but this was an illusion. Grant stood approximately five feet, seven inches tall. The average height of soldiers in the Revolutionary War was five feet, four inches. By World War II, the average height of American soldiers had risen to five feet, eight inches. This strongly suggests that the average soldier of the Civil War era was roughly five feet, six inches tall.

Grant would have been of average height for his time, and possibly a little taller. But he slouched so severely that he appeared to be at least two inches shorter than his true height. Looking smaller only added to his almost feminine appearance. All in vain, though. The officer playing the Moor, Lieutenant Theodoric Porter, found he could not act with convincing passion when the object of his adoration was Lieutenant Grant. He sent to New Orleans for a professional actress to come and fan his ardor.[40]

Rejected in favor of a real woman, Grant grew a beard, ruling out future ingenue roles, and pined for Julia. She wrote as infrequently as before, but at their last parting she had given him a ring with her name engraved inside it. He spent hours looking at the ring and a lock of her hair, wondering why she didn't write him more often.[41]

In March 1846 the 4th Infantry was ordered to move a hundred miles south and deploy on the Rio Grande, opposite Matamoros. Shortly afterward, the Mexican government declared war on the United States.[42]

Although Mexico claimed it was waging "a defensive war," on April 25 a force of Mexican cavalry numbering sixteen hundred men ambushed sixty-three dragoons on the American side of the river, killing eleven, wounding more than a dozen more, and taking most of the survivors prisoner. Taylor sent a signal to Washington—"Hostilities may now be considered as commenced"—and called on the governors of Texas and Louisiana to provide him with eight regiments of volunteers. He wanted an army large enough to enable him, if it became necessary, to advance into Mexico.[43]

———— ★ ★ ★ ★ ————

CHAPTER 4

"THE FLAG

IS PARAMOUNT"

I f there is one thing that everyone who has ever written a life of Grant seems keen to tell us it is that he was opposed to the war with Mexico. But what could he do? "With a soldier the flag is paramount," he explained to a journalist more than thirty years later. "I know the struggle I had with my conscience during the Mexican War. I have never altogether forgiven myself for going into that. I had very strong opinions on the subject. I don't think there was ever a more wicked war than that waged by the United States upon Mexico. I thought so at the time, when I was a youngster, only I had not moral courage enough to resign . . . I considered my supreme duty was to my flag."[1]

For all the strength of Grant's feelings in late middle age, the fact is there is absolutely nothing that indicates he expressed so much as a hint of opposition to the war with Mexico in his letters or conversations at the time. He probably had doubts about the war—many Americans did—but there is nothing to show he was even half so opposed to it as he later claimed. Like many of us, what he did long after the event was to project the sentiments of maturity onto the fallible memory of the actions and emotions of a youthful self swiftly receding over the misty horizon of the past. By the time he got around to denouncing the war so vehemently, the romantic spirit that had once thrilled Ulysses Grant

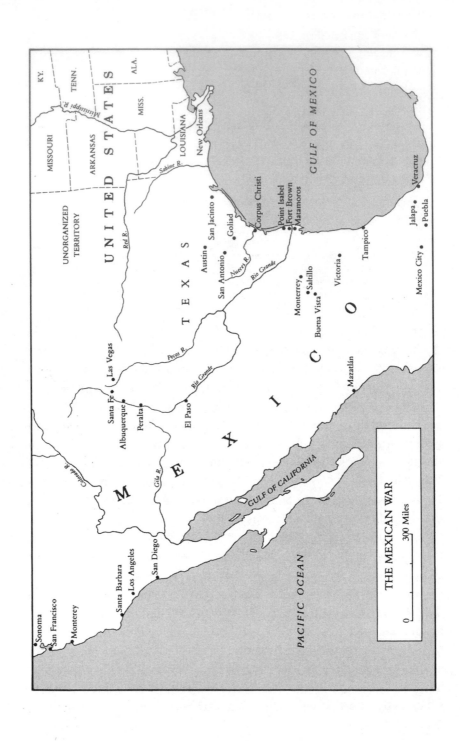

THE MEXICAN WAR

0   300 Miles

with its promise of escape from the dull rhythms of an ordinary existence had been sated or tamed. Life's greatest public drama—nations at war—did not look the same as he neared sixty as it had at twenty-four, when it bore the seductive face of adventure and the magnetic pull of a warehouse fire.

This fierce if retrospective opposition to the Mexican War owed much to Grant's acceptance following the Civil War of the abolitionist interpretation of American history. Abolitionists invariably portrayed the conflict with Mexico as the centerpiece of a plot to spread slavery by acquiring vast new territories for the creation of more slave states. "We were sent to provoke a fight," Grant asserted in his memoirs, "but it was essential that Mexico should commence it." To achieve this goal, Taylor's army was ordered to cross the Nueces River, said Grant, but "Texas had no claim beyond the Nueces River, and yet we pushed on to the Rio Grande." The Mexicans fell straight into the trap and, unwisely, struck the first blow.[2]

This was memory uncontaminated by history, but no Grant biographer has ever questioned it. When the Texans under Sam Houston had defeated the Mexicans at San Jacinto in 1836, they took prisoner the Mexican dictator Antonio López de Santa Anna. In return for peace and being set free, Santa Anna had not only conceded the independence of Texas but explicitly accepted the Texans' claims to all the land between the Sabine and the Rio Grande. Once he regained his freedom, Santa Anna repudiated the document he had signed. Ever since then, Mexico had continued to claim all of Texas up to the border of Louisiana. Mexican politicians regularly threatened war to reverse the defeat at San Jacinto, and Santa Anna had mounted two token invasions of Texas in 1842 in an attempt to give substance to Mexico's claims and propel himself back into power. Yet half a dozen countries not only recognized Texas as an independent state but took the Rio Grande as its boundary with Mexico.[3]

As for the "plot" to expand slavery by annexing Texas, the truth is simply that Americans kept moving west—as individuals and as families—and no government, American or Mexican, could stop them. What's more, few of those who moved into Texas owned slaves or grew anything that called for slave labor. Texas never became a slave economy, despite its later adherence to the Confederacy.[4]

In the months leading up to the outbreak of war, President James K. Polk took none of the steps that someone plotting to wage war would take, such as increasing the size of the Army and stockpiling military supplies. The perennially unstable Mexican government, on the other hand, was currently beating the war drum in an attempt to cement its hold on power and prevent the return of Santa Anna's dictatorship. Yet, like most Mexican governments, it groaned under the crushing weight of a mountain of foreign debt. Polk's solution to the problem of annexing Texas was to offer the Mexicans not cold steel but cold cash.[5]

Unfortunately, Mexico's leaders decided that the hostile terrain where the war would be fought was to their advantage, that there was not enough popular support in the United States for Polk to wage war for more than a few months and, crucially, that their own, much larger, army was certain to defeat the small American army led by Taylor. Victory beckoned, and the great prize Mexico reached for was the recovery of Texas.[6]

Grant's presentation of the war as an immoral act stemming from a slave drivers' conspiracy was based on complete ignorance of the documentary record, yet it served a valuable purpose. His melodramatic view of a wicked, stronger America outsmarting and then beating to a pulp a weak and innocent Mexico helped obscure something about his younger self that he found slightly embarrassing in later life. Like any intelligent person, Grant deplored war. Like any imaginative one, he empathized with those who suffered from its carnage, wastefulness and cruelty. But temperamentally he found it irresistible. There was something in war that tugged like a child's importuning hand on his dark blue sleeve. Just how urgent that pull was, he would soon find out.

On May 8, Taylor and some twenty-three hundred American soldiers clashed in the shadow of a patch of tall trees, called Palo Alto, with a force of nearly four thousand Mexicans. Santa Anna, who had overseen the creation of the Mexican Army, was an ardent Bonapartist and styled himself "the Napoleon of the West."[7]

What Santa Anna had created was a miniature version of the bedazzling Grande Armée. Grant, awestruck at the spectacle of the Mexican Army deploying to attack, was thrilled beyond words—at least, beyond any words of his own. What came to his mind in this feverish moment was Byron:

> *The Assyrian came down like the wolf on the fold,*
> *And his cohorts were gleaming in purple and gold;*
> *And the sheen of their spears was like stars on the sea . . .*[8]

The gorgeously arrayed Mexican columns were soon being raked by Taylor's artillery. While the enemy's guns were antiquated relics of Spanish rule, covered with ornate rococo inscriptions boasting in Latin that these iron mouths barked "the Final Word of Kings," Taylor possessed modern, quick-firing guns that were highly mobile and accurate. And while all the Mexicans could fire was solid shot, Taylor's batteries fired explosive shells. Grant marveled at the way these shells tore deep rents in the enemy's columns, gaping wounds that were swiftly filled in, as if the opposing army were a living organism that healed itself even as it advanced. He marveled, too, at the ineffectiveness of the fire from the smoothbore muskets on both sides of the battle line—"A man could fire at you all day without you finding it out."[9]

The Mexicans suffered nearly three hundred casualties from Taylor's artillery before deciding to withdraw. Taylor's loss came to five dead and forty-eight wounded.[10] The Americans continued their advance toward the Rio Grande. It had been a remarkable victory, but all Grant had to say in his memoirs about his feelings during this initial phase of the war was, "I felt sorry I had enlisted," an observation that was almost certainly untrue.[11]

Having failed to defeat Taylor's army by attacking it, the Mexican commanders now prepared a strong defensive position, taking advantage of the terrain at a spot called Resaca de la Palma. Here there was a four-foot-deep channel carved eons earlier by the Rio Grande. It provided an instant trench for the defenders, a trench that was obscured, moreover, by a tangle of trees. The approaches to the Mexican position were choked by dense chaparral and a wet necklace of swampy ponds. The narrow paths threading between the ponds funneled the advancing Americans straight toward enemy strong points.

This terrain, with its obscured fields of view and restricted fields of fire, ensured that Taylor's artillery would not play much of a role in the upcoming battle. The contest was going to be an infantry fight, man against man, bayonet against bayonet, and the Mexicans, having been reinforced, were confident that their two-to-one advantage in numbers would allow them to prevail.[12]

Grant's company commander was assigned to take charge of a party of skirmishers operating in front of the main body, leaving Grant to command his company in this action. He took the men forward through the chaparral until they ran into intense enemy fire, then he ordered the troops to lie down. When the fire slackened, he got them up on their feet again and tried to find another route into the enemy's lines. Spotting a gap between two ponds, Grant waved his sword, shouted "Charge!" and led a rush forward. A brief, confused melee followed—typical of a hundred similar episodes up and down the line. Grant captured a wounded Mexican colonel. To his chagrin, he soon discovered that the colonel was already an American prisoner.[13]

The aggressiveness and sound small-unit leadership of the American infantry snatched a victory at Resaca de la Palma despite the adverse odds. The battle ended in a total rout. Scores of Mexicans drowned in the Rio Grande in their efforts to flee. Grant wrote to Julia, describing his first two battles, and could not resist throwing in a flourish that Miles Gloriosus himself might have savored—"I am writing on the head of one of the captured drums," he began. Grant proceeded to describe the action in some detail, and confessed the worst moment of the fighting as far as he was concerned: "Although the balls were whizing [*sic*] thick and fast about me I did not feel a sensation of fear until nearly the close of the firing a [cannon]ball struck close by me killing one man instantly, it nocked [*sic*] Capt. Page's under jaw entirely off and broke the roof of his mouth, and nocked [*sic*] Lt. Wallen and one Sergeant down . . ."[14]

Taylor advanced into the city of Matamoros, rested his army there, and waited for the volunteer regiments he had demanded to be organized, while Polk continued his efforts to buy peace from the Mexican government. The troops delighted in the sensuous, languid ways of Mexico. Matamoros, the first Mexican city they saw, came as a revelation. The ways of Mexican women particularly shook their puritanical Anglo-Saxon souls and drove them half-crazy with lust. "They all wear shoes and stockings when they go to church, and when they squat on the floor they are very careful you shall not see even their feet, but they will bathe before us in the river and show themselves perfectly naked to the waist and sometimes lower. They just strip off and think no more of showing their titties than they do their faces, entirely bare," recorded one astonished Army lieutenant.[15]

Grant, however, was not distracted. Having already decided that love matters far more than sex, his mind was on other things, such as making sense of his first exposure to enemy fire. "You want to know what my experiences were on the field of battle?" he wrote an old friend. "I do not know that I felt any peculiar sensation. War seems much less horrible to those engaged in it than to those who read of the battles." And he informed Julia in the same vein: "Do not feel alarmed about me my Dear Julia for there is not half the horrors in war that you immagine [*sic*]."[16]

In mid-August Grant was made, to his dismay, regimental quartermaster of the 4th Infantry. This assignment brought a slight increase in pay, but he challenged what he regarded as an inexcusable attempt to remove him from the firing line. Grant appealed to Lieutenant Colonel John Garland, commander of the 4th Infantry Brigade. His regiment was assigned to Garland's brigade and Garland had the authority to overrule a regimental order. "I respectfully protest against being assigned to a duty which removes me from sharing in the dangers and honors of service with my company at the front . . ." It did no good, of course, but the rejection he received contained a compliment from Garland: "Lt. Grant was assigned to duty as Quartermaster and Commissary because of his observed ability, skill and persistence in the line of duty."

Grant scribbled angrily on the back of Garland's reply: "I should be permitted to resign the position of Quartermaster and Commissary . . . I *must* and *will* accompany my regiment in battle . . ." Even, he concluded, if it meant a court-martial.[17]

It was a hopeless protest. The position of regimental quartermaster was something new in the U.S. Army. Taylor himself was interested in seeing how it worked out, and believed that Grant, who approached every problem in a systematic manner, who since childhood had been something of an expert in transportation and was a superb manager of horses, was just the man for the job.[18]

Grant's new duties involved traveling over much of northern Mexico in search of supplies. He scoured Matamoros for a decent map and bought from a Mexican teamster a stolen map that may well have been the best example of cartography in the entire city. The completeness and accuracy of Grant's map, which had once belonged to a Mexican general, made it shine like a light in a cave. The American Army had marched into Mexico knowing little about its topography, the size of its towns, the layout, quality and gradients of the roads, the height of its hills, and the distance from here to there. Taylor's staff officers came to take a good look at Grant's map. So did a much-admired captain of engineers named Robert E. Lee.[19]

Taylor's army meanwhile was being reinforced by the arrival of some of the volunteers he had called for. Among them was Thomas L. Hamer, the former congressman from Ohio who had appointed Grant to the military academy. Hamer still had political ambitions and powerful political connections. Polk gave him command of a brigade of volunteers and a major's commission even though he knew almost nothing of military science beyond the evolutions of a militia company's drill. Grant undertook Hamer's education in strategy and tactics. It was assumed that once Hamer had learned something of the business, Polk would elevate him to a brigadier general's star.[20]

Grant and the greenhorn major occasionally rode into the countryside around Matamoros so Grant could use it as a classroom. Here, let us say, is your army, he told Hamer, conjuring up a compact but powerful force. To deploy it for battle on this ground, Grant would explain, you should arrange your infantry in this way, deploy your cavalry there and there, and put your artillery back here, where the ground is level and the fields of fire good. Now, an opposing army would deploy in another way, taking what advantage it could of this terrain, depending on whether it intended to attack or defend. Soon they had an imaginary battle going, with charges and retreats, their mutual fantasies of death and destruction inflaming dreams of military glory.

During one of these sessions, Hamer realized he had brought his force to the brink of defeat. Grant then suggested a way of maneuvering his troops to extricate them from impending disaster. It was even possible—just—to snatch a victory, he said, and explained how it could be done. Hamer gave the necessary orders and Grant, conceding defeat, bowed, drew his sword, and offered it in surrender. "Lieutenant Grant is too young to command," Hamer wrote a friend, "but his capacity for future military usefulness is undoubted."[21]

Polk's attempts to purchase a peace failed and in mid-September Taylor pushed his force deep into Mexico, advancing on the city of Monterrey, roughly two hundred miles west of Matamoros. The Mexican Army, too, had been replenished and reinforced. Taylor intended to strike it before it struck him. Attacking it in Monterrey, however, seemed close to madness. The city was a fortress built by nature and improved upon by man. Steep hills, a wide river and a strong fort guarded the approaches. There were more than seven thousand well-armed defenders already dug in, supported by forty artillery pieces.[22]

Taylor was nevertheless determined to wrest the town from them. The result was a three-day battle that brought heavy losses to both sides. On the first day Grant, listening to the sounds of fighting from three miles in the rear, could stand it no longer. Mounting his horse, he rode pell-mell for the roar of gunfire.

When Grant arrived, his brigade was about to charge a Mexican artillery position. He joined in the fighting, unable to resist. The brigade's attack was meant to be no more than a diversion to aid the Army's main effort, but Garland mishandled it, in Grant's opinion. The brigade made a frontal assault instead of approaching its objective by an indirect route and taking advantage of the available cover from enemy fire.

The brigade suffered unnecessarily high casualties, including the 4th Infantry's adjutant, who was killed. Grant was ordered to take his place, but to continue as regimental quartermaster.[23] Two days later the struggle raged on. American troops were still attacking the Mexicans, who had lost the fort and the two steep hills but were now barricaded in houses around the town's central plaza. This was street fighting, brutal and bloody.[24]

Close combat invariably consumes large amounts of ammunition, and by late afternoon the men of Grant's regiment were running short. They were in danger of being overrun if the enemy counterattacked. Garland turned to the officers around him and told them he would have to send word back to the division commander, Major General David Twiggs, demanding either more troops or more ammunition. "It's a dangerous job," said Garland, "and I don't like to order any man to do it. Who'll volunteer?"

"I will," responded Grant, and he played his ace: "I've got a horse!"

"There goes a man of fire," Garland later remarked.[25]

He rode through the streets of Monterrey like a trick rider in the circus, hands gripping his horse's mane, one foot hooked under the saddle, and his body on the side of the horse away from enemy fire. Dozens of Mexicans took potshots at him as he rode by, but not one managed to hit either him or the horse. Once out of the range of fire, Grant swung himself up and into the saddle and galloped the rest of the way. He got through to the division command post and delivered Garland's message.

Before anything could be done, however, Garland's brigade withdrew. Taylor's entire army was played out. But so were the Mexicans.

They asked for talks, and Taylor, bluffing them into believing that he was prepared to continue his attacks, got them to accept a truce. The Mexicans were allowed to leave with all their arms and equipment; the Americans would get the battered carcass of the town.[26]

Grant had now participated in three battles and discovered that being a quartermaster in war did not have to be the dull blanket-counting business it was in time of peace. One of his responsibilities was supervising the work of the ambulances and bringing out the wounded under fire. He had a free hand to rove the entire battlefield, and whichever place had the most wounded would likely be the spot where the fighting was hottest and the struggle won or lost. "He could see the whole line," his friend James Longstreet remarked, "and knew all that was going on by personal inspection."[27]

Not that they were aware of this back at White Haven. When "Colonel" Dent heard of Grant's QM assignment, he assured Julia that Ulysses was out of danger now. Grant, however, was keen to let her know differently. "Your Pa . . . pronounced me safe for Qr. Mrs. did not have to go into battle," Grant wrote her. "That is very true but on the 21st of September I voluntarily went along with the regiment and . . . continued through the fight."[28]

There was fighting even when there were no battles under way. Grant's foraging expeditions across northern Mexico in search of supplies brought clashes with Mexican soldiers, bandits and peasants. Any small party of Americans was in danger of being ambushed. On one occasion he came back and jubilantly reported to Garland, "I lost one man and had a horse wounded. We captured three of the enemy, three horses and a flag, and we had a handsome fight!"

The great fear among senior commanders was that the Mexicans might one day wake up. As long as they fought a war of pitched battles, the Americans stood a chance of winning it, but if Mexico resorted to guerrilla warfare, the Americans were likely to suffer the kind of military and political defeat that Napoleon had suffered in trying to subdue Spain. Bringing in supplies was crucial, but not at the cost of setting rural Mexico on fire and unleashing a thousand guerrilla bands. So Garland told Grant sternly, "That speaks well for your bravery, but remember we are in an enemy's country, that enemy alert and enterprising. Be careful to always temper bravery with prudence and caution."

As Grant strode back to his quarters with his good friend Lieutenant Calvin Benjamin, he vented his irritation. "Yes, caution I will observe, but when there's not more than two of *him* to *one* of me, we'll have a fight. That's what we are here for."[29]

In November, Hamer fell seriously ill with typhoid fever, which was reaching epidemic proportions in Taylor's army. Grant spent hours at Hamer's bedside, watching his friend rapidly grow weaker, but optimistically convinced himself that Hamer would pull through somehow. Instead, Hamer died as Grant, his pale blue eyes brimming with hot, salty tears, helplessly clutched his hand.

Grant wrote to Hamer's family: "He died as a soldier dies, without fear and without a murmur. His regret was that, if death must come, it should not come to him on the field of battle. . . . He was buried with the 'honors of war,' and with the flag of his beloved country around him. . . . Personally, his death is a loss to me which no words can express."[30]

No one's life truly ends with his death. The lives of the deceased are completed in the imaginations and spirits of those who love them. And Grant, stricken with grief at Hamer's demise, saw in his own mind the course that Hamer's life would probably have followed. Hamer had been re-elected to Congress three weeks before he died. Grant convinced himself that Hamer the war hero, not Franklin Pierce, would have been elected President in 1852.

This revelation opens a small window on Grant's undemonstrative nature, allowing a shaft of light to penetrate that seemingly phlegmatic personality. In his grief for his friend he immortalizes him in a romantic fantasy. But for himself he sees a different fate had Hamer lived, something ironic rather than glorious. Hamer, he believed, would have promoted him to the staff of the paymaster general of the Army. And there Grant would have remained until retirement, an obscure Army officer bent over payrolls and tally sheets. But, he concluded stoically, Hamer's sudden, unexpected death only shows "how little men control their own destiny."[31]

Grant was a typical example of the educated and introspective Victorian, with an electric strand of nervous tension running through his core beliefs. Like any enlightened man of his time, he had a strong faith in social progress and justice, but like many another doubter, he simply could not shake off a suspicion that any individual's life, for all its strivings and supposed achievements, is ultimately futile. He found it easy to believe in God but almost impossible to believe in religion, with its exalted claims of individual damnation or salvation.

Grant ran up his doubts like a banner in his *Personal Memoirs*. The very first sentence declares: "Man proposes and God disposes." A nagging feeling that human beings do not count for much was blood of his blood, bone of his bone, learned at his impassive mother's knee. What he had seen of war, with its fatal miscalculations, random destruction, and unnecessary deaths, could only underline in vermilion the fatalism that lay like an insoluble residue at the bottom of Ulysses Grant's soul. What he believed in was not the one but the many; not the individual but the whole.

Why, then, should anyone attempt to do anything? Because despite their impotence on a cosmic scale, human beings needed some kind of structure simply to be human and serve the purposes of the God who created them. To that extent, the flag *was* the paramount symbol in Grant's life, because it was patriotism—the claims society made on him—that made it possible to reconcile the inherent tensions in his fundamental beliefs. Patriotism filled a void that religion could not reach.

──── ★ ★ ★ ★ ────

CHAPTER 5

"THE LAST CHANCE
I SHALL EVER HAVE"

President James Polk was counting on a short war, but Zachary Taylor had failed to provide one. Worse, Taylor was developing political ambitions. As 1847 drew to a close, Polk turned to the Army's
senior general, Winfield Scott, and demanded that he go to Mexico and
"conquer a peace." Scott had insisted from the start of the war that the
best way to fight it was to land at Vera Cruz, some two hundred miles
east of Mexico City, advance on the Mexican capital, capture it and
compel the Mexican government to end the war. Here, then, was his
chance.

Scott's plan called for taking only twelve thousand men into the
heart of a country of twenty million people. His supply lines would be
long and tenuous, running for much of the way through Mexican territory, and the forces he would have to defeat were sure to outnumber him
by more than two to one. Yet, convinced of his own star, he probably
never lost a moment's sleep over the challenge ahead.

Taylor's army was stripped of its regulars to provide the backbone
for Scott's expeditionary force. Early in 1847, the 4th Infantry received
orders to ship out, but the epidemics that were sweeping Monterrey and
that killed Hamer had also brought Second Lieutenant Grant low. He
seemed too ill to travel.[1]

This was a wretched time for him. Not only had Hamer died virtually in his arms, not only was he ill himself, but the money entrusted to him to buy supplies was stolen from under his nose while he was sick. "On the night of 6th of Jan. 1847," he reported to the quartermaster general in Washington, "I had stolen from my Quarters in Monteray [*sic*] a chest containing all my Quarter Master funds besides several hundred dollars more. This money I am not at present able to replace and as it was not through negligence of mine that it was stolen it would be but justice that [the] Government should loose [*sic*] the amount and not me."[2]

When the regiment packed for the sea voyage to Vera Cruz, Grant insisted he was well enough to travel. But he was frustrated at the way the war was developing. There seemed no end in sight. Just before embarking for Vera Cruz, he poured out his irritation in a letter: "Don't you think Julia a soldiers life is insupportable in time of war? Just think in all this time there has been but three battles fought towards conquering a peace. If we have to fight I would like to see it done all at once then let us return."[3]

Such sentiments were not unique to Grant. They were those of the professional officer of a Western army. It is how Western countries have tried to manage war since the time of the ancient Greeks—fight one huge, decisive battle (preferably on a fine summer's day) and get the business over with. Somebody wins, somebody loses, but at least the issue has been settled and normal life can resume. Not, of course, that it usually turns out that way, but the decisive battle still haunts soldiers' dreams.[4]

Grant spent much of the voyage to Vera Cruz being seasick, but consoled himself with the thought that the landing was certain to bring a huge, and possibly conclusive, battle. If it turned out like that, he would finally be reunited with Julia, whom he had not seen for more than a year. However much Grant was drawn toward the sound of the guns, he longed to be with Julia, too.

On March 9, 1848, Scott's army landed on a long white beach four miles south of Vera Cruz. Grant, recovering from his illness, was still shaky as he waded ashore from one of the scores of surf boats ferrying the troops from the invasion fleet. What greeted him as he reached dry land wasn't Mexican opposition—there wasn't any—but blistering heat and stinging sand that lashed at his face and blew relentlessly into his eyes and mouth and up his nose.[5]

Scott threw a ring of steel around Vera Cruz. The town was defended by nine forts and forty-four hundred soldiers. As the most heavily guarded spot in the Western Hemisphere, Vera Cruz looked like a good place to avoid, but Scott absolutely had to take it for his plan to succeed. He set his artillery to work, pounding the town into submission. A shell was lobbed into the city every twenty seconds, day and night.

The enemy's guns barked back. When the 4th Infantry moved into trenches outside the town, it came under heavy bombardment from Mexican 24-pounders firing cast-iron round-shot, which threw up towering plumes of dirt and gouged huge craters. Grant came under artillery fire regularly but, like other officers, he soon grew used to it. There was little for infantry soldiers to do during the siege but keep their heads down and wait. A siege is the business not of the infantry but of engineers and artillery.

Grant was occupied anyway with his commissary and QM chores, but it wasn't enough. Whenever he had the chance, he went to join the engineers or the gun batteries. He studied the way an army conducted a siege—where the guns were placed, how trench systems were organized, how revetments, abatis and glacis were constructed under enemy fire, how even the strongest position could be reduced by bombardment. Grant rode along the siege line nearly every day, absorbing lessons in modern warfare.

One morning he rode up and joined Captain Robert E. Lee and several other officers, including Lieutenants George B. McClellan and P.G.T. Beauregard, as they prepared to observe the fire of a new artillery battery that had just been brought into the fight. While most of the party was satisfied with its vantage point, Grant and Beauregard went forward fifty yards to get a better look. They took cover in a small adobe building as an artillery duel between American and Mexican gunners rent the morning air with its screams.

The Mexicans, seeking to get the range of the new battery, sent a shell smashing into the roof of the adobe building. The shell penetrated the roof, buried itself in the floor and exploded. The entire structure was shattered, sending up a huge spume of devastation. All that remained was a mound of white adobe dust and splintered beams. At the bottom of the mound, gasping, choking on the dust, but otherwise unscathed, were the two American officers.[6]

After a three-week siege Vera Cruz surrendered to Scott. The defeated Mexican soldiers filed sullenly past the 4th Infantry that afternoon as they abandoned the town to the Americans. Over the next week, officers and men of the regiment were allowed to enter and see what modern artillery had wrought.[7]

Vera Cruz, one of the most picturesque fortress towns in the world, had been turned into a shambles of shattered, blood-smeared stones. Remnants of its former charm seemed like an indictment against the devastation visited on it. In a world where man creates little enough to compare with the beauty of nature, the destruction of even a small part of the beauty human beings can create wounds the human spirit. For anyone as sensitive as Grant, the broken body of Vera Cruz was a dismal sight. There was no sense of exultation at victory over the foe. Instead, there was a mood of depression. A fellow officer wrote home, "I cannot relate [the scene] to you . . . my heart sickens at the attempt. What a horrible thing is war!"[8]

Cutting loose from his base at Vera Cruz, Scott pushed his army inland, taking the road to Mexico City that Cortés's small band of conquistadors had cut in 1519. Some fifty miles from the coast, Santa Anna prepared to stop him. A Mexican army of fifteen thousand men was digging in along both sides of the road at a place in the mountains called Cerro Gordo.

Lee undertook one of the scouting feats of the century. Personally reconnoitering deep in the enemy's rear, he found a scratch of a trail that a goat might have shunned. Scott's artillerymen disassembled their 24-pounders, then dragged and carried the pieces up the trail and into the mountains. Several thousand American infantry crept along the trail behind them. The artillery was reassembled virtually under the enemy's nose. It was the greatest feat of its kind between Napoleon's achievement in getting artillery over the Great St. Bernard Pass in the winter of 1796 and the success of the Vietminh in smuggling artillery into the mountains overlooking Dien Bien Phu in 1954.

Grant was busy with his quartermastering as preparations for battle commenced. Whenever the 4th Infantry was in motion, he was the first man to arrive at the spot where fresh supplies were delivered. He operated not only ahead of the regiment but behind it, too, overseeing the slow-moving wagon train that brought up the rear and trying to get the regiment's balky mules to cooperate in the conquest of Mexico.

Grant spent much of his time in the saddle, and his days were long. Reveille was blown at four A.M. and forward movement nearly always began at five. The march usually halted in late afternoon but Grant, because he had to cover a greater distance than most officers in the course of a day, was not likely to return to his tent until after dark. The pressure was clearly getting to him. He had tried smoking at West Point, found it disgusting, and concluded he was averse to tobacco. Somewhere on the road between Vera Cruz and Mexico City, he found nicotine helped with the stress, and started smoking the cigars that would eventually kill him. He also took up drinking.[9]

As Scott's troops deployed to assault the Mexican positions at Cerro Gordo, Grant, who had been busy since before dawn with the supply train, spurred his horse up the mountain road to rejoin his regiment, but he was too late. The 4th Infantry was so far ahead he could not hope to reach it in time. Reining in his mount, he went to join a battery of 24-pounders commanded by Lieutenant George McClellan.

Grant took up a field glass, to help direct the battery's fire onto the Mexican defenses. The battlefield, with its dense forest, steep slopes, and the thin white scar of a road winding between the trees, was set out before him like a picture. Even if all he could do was act as a forward observer, Grant intended to take part. As Longstreet had noted, "You could not keep Grant out of a battle."[10]

The fight commenced, to the astonishment of the Mexicans, with an intense barrage of heavy artillery fire from their rear! Meanwhile, American infantry was charging up the road to strike them from in front. Grant was profoundly impressed to see the big guns in action. "It was war pyrotechnics of the most serious and brilliant character," he wrote a friend. But when he saw smoke rising from the Mexican lines in reply, it pained him to think that each innocent-looking white puff from the enemy's artillery spelled death and wounds to American soldiers. Even the scene of the infantry attack as it went in left him in a melancholy mood: "As our men finally swept over and into their works, my heart was sad at the fate that held me from sharing in that brave and brilliant assault."[11]

Panic seized the Mexican troops as American soldiers jumped into their positions, and they fled into the mountains. Grant and McClellan rushed forward to join in the final stages of the battle. Coming across a group of stragglers, they laid about them with the flats of their swords. Grant damned the stragglers as "cowards," then began barking commands: "About face . . . forward . . . on quick time, march!" But before he could get his impromptu platoon back up the mountainside, the fighting had more or less petered out.[12]

Scott halted his army and awaited reinforcements. Once he held their capital in his hands, the Mexican government would surely have to sue for peace. The city was defended, however, by more than thirty thousand soldiers. During comparatively quiet spells such as this, Grant relaxed by studying Spanish baroque architecture and taking an interest in Mexican flora and fauna. He became a bird-watcher and identified more than two hundred species.[13]

It was mid-August before Scott's army closed on Mexico City and began fighting a series of battles to break through its multilayered defenses. Lee performed another astounding feat of scouting, enabling Scott to strike the Mexican defenders at Contreras with complete, overwhelming surprise. The Mexicans were still asleep when American troops charged their camp at first light on August 20. The battle lasted less than fifteen minutes. Grant and the 4th Infantry barely had time to make contact with the enemy, who simply fled the field as rapidly as possible.[14]

This easy victory lulled Scott into making a second assault later that day against a hamlet called Churubusco. He threw his army at a sturdy thick-walled convent crammed with Mexican troops well supported by artillery. The bludgeoning frontal attacks at Churubusco nearly cost Scott the war. He came within a whisker of losing the battle. The Mexicans, however, fled during the final assault, when the Americans got into the convent through shell holes in the walls and the battle turned into a grim and sanguinary hand-to-hand struggle.

On September 8, Scott set the army in motion once more, with a collection of stone buildings called El Molino del Rey—the King's Mill—as its objective. Intelligence reports had reached Scott that the Mexicans had turned the mill into a gun foundry. The reports were wrong. El Molino del Rey was, instead, Mexico City's biggest grain-storage facility. Scott threw an entire division, commanded by William Jenkins Worth, at the mill without realizing that it was strongly defended. Worth's thirty-two-hundred-man force, which included Grant's regiment, ran straight into an entire Mexican division concealed in a ditch and supported by three artillery pieces deployed on the huge stone threshing floor in front of the mill.

The initial assault was thrown back with heavy losses. Grant and James M. Robertson, an artillery sergeant with whom he had become friendly in recent weeks, saw that the green crews of four American light-artillery pieces were failing to provide support where it was needed. They ran over to help the artillerymen place their pieces correctly and bring their fire against the Mexican guns. Taking advantage of the cover provided by a stone wall, they pushed the guns forward to less than two hundred yards from the Mexican defenders. At this distance even neophytes could knock out the Mexican battery on the threshing floor.[15]

Once American shells started exploding around them, the Mexican artillerists fled into the mill. Robertson drew his short sergeant's sword, and he and Grant, followed by a small party of American infantrymen, set off in pursuit. Near the huge wooden doors, Grant halted abruptly in his tracks. He saw his old friend and former roommate, Julia's brother, Fred Dent, slumped over, bleeding from a bullet wound in the thigh suffered in Worth's futile initial assault.[16]

Grant stooped to pick up Fred and carry him over to the wall, where he was more likely to attract medical attention than lying on the ground among hundreds of other dead and wounded men. As Grant straightened up with Fred in his arms, he saw a Mexican soldier rush into view and take aim at Garland's aide, Captain Hermann Thorn. "Look out, Thorn!" cried Grant. The Mexican hesitated for a moment as Thorn swiveled around to face him. In that instant Robertson ran the Mexican through with his sword, while Thorn, almost by reflex action, shot him in the head.[17]

After placing Fred Dent on the wall, Grant rushed into the mill with Robertson and Thorn. At about the same time another party of Americans was breaking into the mill through a door at the far end of the building. The fight for El Molino del Rey drew rapidly to a close, but American losses amounted to more than seven hundred dead and wounded. Hardly worth it for a grain store.

Five days after taking El Molino del Rey, Scott reached out to seize one of the key pieces in the defenses of Mexico City—the hill of Chapultepec. At its peak stood the Mexican military academy. The defenses were subjected to a heavy bombardment before the infantry made its assault. Scott's soldiers virtually raced each other up the hill in their eagerness to seize Chapultepec. Grant joined a pack howitzer battery early in the action, but abruptly left it to join in the final infantry assault.[18]

The Mexicans defended Chapultepec bravely but briefly. The battle was over in less than two hours. American losses were heavy once more—roughly eight hundred dead and wounded out of fewer than five thousand engaged. Mexico City was virtually an island surrounded by lakes. The city could only be reached by long, wide causeways, which led to a handful of imposing gates set in towering stone walls. Scott's plan was to make a feint from the south that would pin down the defenders and draw Santa Anna's reserves into the wrong position. Then he would make his real thrust, from the west, along the San Cosme causeway, using Worth's battle-hardened division as his battering ram.

When the time came for them to make their assault, Worth's troops were halted a hundred yards or so in front of the *garita,* the gateway where the causeway met the city walls. The Mexicans had erected a barricade across the road and posted riflemen on the roofs of houses overlooking the barricade.[19]

The causeway was wider than the barricade, and ten feet above it was a stone aqueduct that carried water into the city. Using the cover of a low wall and ducking among the stone pillars that supported the aqueduct, Grant, Sergeant Robertson and half a dozen men managed to slip around the barricade unnoticed by the combatants, who were furiously shooting at one another from either side. Grant's small group pressed on and, to their surprise, were able to slip through the *garita,* which the Mexicans had inexplicably left unmanned.[20]

Grant noticed a small church nearby and, taking Robertson with him, banged on the door. In halting Spanish, Grant persuaded the priest who greeted them through a small peephole in the heavy door to open up. Otherwise, he said, his troops would have to break it down and the church would be damaged, to the benefit of no one. The priest agreed and unbolted the door.

Once inside, Grant and Robertson rushed up to the roof of its bell tower to continue their reconnaissance. The small roof of the belfry proved to be flat. If they could get a mountain howitzer up here, they decided, they could fire directly onto the defenders at the barricade and clear the riflemen from the rooftops of the houses around it.[21]

They managed to sneak back out of the city and find a mountain howitzer. Disassembling this small but powerful gun, they hand-carried it back in pieces, sneaking back to the church this time by sloshing through ditches filled with water that came up to Grant's chest. Grant and Robertson each carried a wheel. Once the gun was reassembled atop the bell tower, Grant watched the first couple of rounds fired strike their target, then left Robertson in charge of the gun while he went back down to join the street fighting near the barricade.

Worth saw the gun burst into action and sent one of his aides, Lieutenant John Pemberton, the future defender of Vicksburg, to find the officer responsible. Grant reported to Worth a short time later. "This is mighty fine work, sir," said the general. "Every shot tells. I'll send you another gun."

"Thank you, General," said Grant, saluting. He did not tell Worth there was not enough room on the roof for a second piece of artillery. Junior officers do not, if they are sensible, contradict generals.[22]

While Grant's howitzer was doing its work from behind and above, an enterprising artillery officer named Henry Hunt managed to get a howitzer onto the causeway directly facing the barricade and started blowing holes in it. By dusk the barricade had been captured, and as night descended, word reached Grant that his closest friend in Mexico, Lieutenant Calvin Benjamin, had been fatally wounded.

He found Benjamin close to death, lying on a cot out in the street and guarded by several soldiers. Grant knelt down, took one of Benjamin's hands and kissed it in farewell. Minutes later, Benjamin died. Grant took a canteen, moistened a handkerchief and, in an act full of symbolism and emotion, wiped the grime of battle from the dead man's face. This moment and the death of Hamer were his two worst experiences of the war.[23]

Grant departed to join the infantrymen who were busily burrowing their way into the city. They made their way from house to house by attacking the walls with pickaxes, bursting inside, rushing up to the roofs and killing any Mexican soldiers still there. Scott's troops were well into the city by first light the next day, when word reached Scott that Santa Anna had fled and the city wanted to surrender. At noon Scott and his retinue rode into the central plaza of Mexico City to the sound of American bands and the sight of American flags and the roar of ordinary Mexicans rejoicing that their city had been spared the kind of devastation visited on Vera Cruz. There were no more battles, only minor skirmishes while peace was negotiated.

★

Grant had had a remarkable war. He had excelled as both a military manager and a fighting soldier. For him there were two wars in one and he had distinguished himself in both. Nevertheless, when the shooting ceased and the smoke cleared away, Grant received a crushing blow.

Once Mexico City surrendered, Scott's headquarters was able at last to get around to making awards for gallantry. The U.S. Army at this time had no decorations in its gift. What it had instead was brevet promotions, which were more honorary than real. The brevet system was untidy and confusing. A brevet rank carried no extra pay, yet an officer could be ordered to duty in his brevet rank. When Zachary Taylor took command of the Army of Observation, he was still only a permanent colonel, but he commanded that army as a brevet brigadier general.

Grant's valor at El Molino del Rey, he was informed, was going to be recognized with a brevet promotion to first lieutenant, but his initial reaction was to try to turn it down. For one thing, he had recently been made a permanent first lieutenant on the basis of seniority within his regiment. But the main reason he felt like rejecting this brevet was disgust. Among the officers recommended for brevet promotions for their actions at El Molino del Rey was one who, to Grant's critical eye, had shown a streak of cowardly behavior. A brevet for such a man was nothing but favoritism or stupidity. "If he is entitled to a brevet," Grant commented scornfully to a fellow officer, "then I am not." In the end, the craving for distinction proved too strong. Grant accepted his brevet promotion.[24]

He had also been recommended, he was informed, for promotion to a brevet captaincy for "gallant conduct at Chapultepec." Grant was happy to accept this. But for his even more brilliant feat—getting that howitzer into the bell tower—he got nothing.

"Didn't you see me go first into that work [the San Cosme *garita*] the other day?" he asked Henry Hunt, whose splendid performance at the barricade had just been rewarded with a brevet promotion.

"Why, no," said Hunt, "though I don't doubt you were in first."

"Well, I *was* in first," Grant responded bitterly. "Colonel Garland has not recommended me. The war is nearly done, so there goes the last chance I shall ever have of military distinction!"[25]

He felt once again the sting of injustice, made more odious still by the blind workings of stupidity. The Army simply seemed incapable of according him the recognition that his talents deserved. At West Point Grant had been denied the chance to distinguish himself intellectually, even though he was probably as bright as any cadet in his class. Excel as he might in math or physics, he was sure to collect more than enough demerits to lower his class standing. William Tecumseh Sherman, for example, would have graduated third in the Class of 1840 on the basis of his grades but had fallen to sixth place because of demerits.[26]

No system could have been more unfair to Grant, who possessed as much military bearing as a sack of potatoes. He was usually neat and clean, but he could not fuss over the thousand tiny details that West Point considered essential to a cadet's education, as if his life depended on them. It simply was not in his temperament or upbringing to treat intrinsically petty concerns as if they were important. West Point had made him an officer but missed his quality. And now, despite having proven himself in battle, the Army had done it again.

Grant deserved a third brevet, but Garland was seriously wounded just before Mexico City surrendered. When he recovered, he recommended Grant for a third brevet, but his letter was misfiled in the War Department.[27]

Fewer than a dozen officers won three brevets in Mexico. These triple-award winners left Mexico regarded as officers with brilliant military careers ahead of them. They included Lee, Don Carlos Buell, Joseph Hooker, and an artillery officer who was widely considered the most quarrelsome man in the Army, Braxton Bragg.[28] Had Grant been awarded a third brevet for his actions at the San Cosme *garita,* he might have confidently anticipated rising, however slowly, to colonel. This latest disappointment only served to justify his fatalism. Individuals had no control over their destiny. Man proposes . . . foolishly.

★

Grant's mental universe was peopled with heroic figures. For all his conviction that man proposes but God disposes, the world made no sense to him without heroes bestriding it. In the tiny pantheon that he allowed, the foremost soldier was not Napoleon or Julius Caesar or Washington or Scott. It was Zachary Taylor.

"Old Rough and Ready" Taylor had advanced into Mexico at the head of a small army, seized the military initiative and taken the fight to the enemy. Taylor's unmilitary appearance—long, grimy duster, straw hat, scuffed boots—was matched by a casual manner that made strangers to his headquarters assume he was somebody's servant rather than everybody's commander. It was claimed that a newly arrived lieutenant noticed this scruffy, gray-haired old man with a weather-beaten face walking around the camp and offered him a quarter to polish his sword. Taylor, so the story goes, took the sword, polished it till it gleamed and collected his two bits. Next day the lieutenant buckled on his shining sword, went to pay his respects to the army commander and nearly fainted when he was ushered into the general's tent.[29]

In Taylor there was all the proof Grant needed that appearances have nothing to do with military ability. He was deeply impressed, too, by Taylor's calm assumption of responsibility for the lives of thousands of men. Grant found moral courage to be rarer and more ennobling than physical bravery. But the lesson that really stuck was Taylor's way of handling an army in combat. Taylor, claimed Grant, "could put his meaning so plainly there was no mistaking it. He knew what he wanted to say in the fewest well-chosen words . . ." In the midst of confusion, excitement, the sudden death of close friends, false information and the blundering of subordinates, there was one clear guide an officer could turn to—the general's commands. That was a standard worth adopting as one's own.[30]

Scott was the antithesis of Taylor. "Old Fuss and Feathers" lived and breathed ceremony, military bearing and ritual. Grant did not care for the way Scott bore himself or for the way he referred to himself in the third person (a trait later adopted, incidentally, by Douglas MacArthur). Even so, Grant readily acknowledged that Scott had waged one of the most impressive campaigns in the annals of war. Outnumbered by as much as four to one, Scott had advanced more than two hundred miles into the enemy's heartland and captured his strongly defended capital. His troops had won every battle, met every challenge and tried to conduct the war with as much humanity as their mission allowed. It was a campaign worthy of comparison with Napoleon at his best.

That did not prevent Grant, after he had acquired experience directing the operations of armies, from casting a critical retrospective gaze over the Mexican War. It would have been better, he decided, had Scott not driven straight for Mexico City, thereby making it easier for the enemy to prepare defenses to stop him on the hills and causeways south and west of the city. Scott, he believed, ought to have swung around to the east, broken contact with the Mexican Army, then struck quickly at the capital from the north. But this was all twenty-twenty hindsight, as Grant conceded, and he concluded, "Scott's successes are an answer to all criticisms."[31]

On one thing Grant and Scott were in complete accord: Victory had been possible in Mexico only because of the superb quality of Scott's regular soldiers and the excellence of the officer corps, especially the West Point graduates. Without these professionals, Scott was convinced, an army four times the size of the force he led could never have conquered Mexico.[32]

The performance of the regulars in Mexico was of a different order of magnitude than that of the volunteers, whose military effectiveness was almost ruined by the dysentery that volunteer officers allowed to rage within their camps. Ten volunteers expired in their own excrement for each one who perished in battle.[33]

Appropriately for one of the Army's elite units, the 4th Infantry emerged with ten battle honors—Palo Alto, Resaca de la Palma, Monterrey, Vera Cruz, Cerro Gordo, Contreras, Churubusco, El Molino del Rey, Chapultepec and Mexico City. No regiment in the Army had participated in more battles than the 4th Infantry, nor had any soldier in Mexico taken part in more fighting than Grant. The 4th had paid heavily for its battle honors. No regiment had suffered more casualties, and only five of the regiment's officers when the war began saw it to a finish without being killed or wounded. Grant emerged without a scratch.

With the fighting ended, he was free to enjoy the country for a while. His attitude toward the land and its people had undergone a profound change in the course of the war. When Grant first encountered Mexico and the Mexicans, he was indifferent to the country and contemptuous of the people. He was struck by the fact that the overwhelming majority of Mexicans were Indians or *mestizos*—people of mixed blood, that is. He had assumed Mexicans would be like Americans—largely descended from white Europeans. Finding they were far more Indian than European at first excited only his scorn. They were, he told Julia, not just Indians but "of the sort that lost Ohio."[34]

This seems a gnomic remark until we remember that Grant's boyhood was spent on the frontier at a time when clashes between Indians and settlers were still commonplace. They ended with the Indians of western Ohio being virtually wiped out. In the meantime, and by way of justification for the white man's actions, Grant would have heard countless stories about the treachery of the Indians, their shiftlessness, their filthiness, their diseases, their lewdness and their cruelty, and of the unspeakable things they did to their captives, especially white women. He would have been raised to believe there was nothing quite so vile, so evil or so cowardly as an Indian. Especially the sort that lost Ohio.

In northern Mexico, he came face to face for the first time in his life with large numbers of Indians and dark-skinned *mestizos*. His initial reaction was affronted disgust. And when he went to Vera Cruz with Scott, he found the people of central Mexico were no different from those in the north—"the mass of the people are the same degraded looking beings."[35]

As he studied the Mexican Army, however, Grant saw that it was a microcosm of Mexican society, and that the elements that made Mexico weak were the same elements that made it possible for the Americans, who were invariably outnumbered and outgunned, to defeat them. A small Spanish-descended elite provided the officer corps and the Indians provided the conscripts who filled the ranks. The social gulf between the two was enormous, and officers treated their soldiers like serfs or worse, like beasts fit only to be driven to the slaughter. These Indian and *mestizo* conscripts may have been dressed like men of the Grande Armée, but they did not fight like them. "The better class are very proud and tyranize [*sic*] over the lower and much more numerous class as much as a hard master does over his negroes . . . ," Grant wrote Julia.[36]

Increasingly he found his sympathies were with the ordinary Mexicans, while their masters were worthy only of his contempt. Grant discovered what a beautiful country Mexico was and how agreeable were its more prosperous towns, their streets and plazas made delightful by Spanish baroque architecture and languid ways. And yet, "I pity poor Mexico. With a soil and climate scarsely [*sic*] equaled in the world she has more poor and starving subjects who are willing and able to work than any country in the world. The rich keep down the poor with a hardness of heart that is incredible."[37]

Grant's idea that once the fighting ended the Army would be withdrawn and he could be speedily reunited with Julia was cruelly disabused. Peace negotiations dragged on through the winter of 1847 and into the spring of 1848. Grant and the other officers grew restless and some were tempted to resign their commissions. But Scott informed them that even this would do no good. They would not be permitted to leave the country, no matter what. The American army occupying Mexico City was a gun held to Mexico's head. Scott had no intention of seeing it emptied of bullets.

It was May 1848 before a treaty was signed and Scott could lead his victorious army back to Vera Cruz. Along the road disaster struck Grant.

Before the regiment began its march to the coast, Grant received a thousand dollars in quartermaster funds. He arranged to keep the money in a locked trunk owned by one of the regiment's senior officers, Captain John H. Gore. "On the night of the 16th of June 1848," Grant reported, "the trunk containing these funds was Stolen from the tent of Capt. Gore whilst he and Lieut De Russy 4th Infantry were both sleeping in the tent . . ."[38]

A board of inquiry investigated the theft and concluded "that no blame can attach to Lt. U. S. Grant." But this did not exempt him from a legal obligation to repay the money. The government had been prepared to overlook the earlier loss of three hundred dollars. This time, however, Grant was expected to make good the theft. The missing thousand dollars would dog him for years to come. This baleful reminder of the Mexican War was curse enough, but it seemed a harbinger, too, of a running theme in Grant's life thereafter—that he and large sums of money would never keep company for long.

──── ★ ★ ★ ★ ────

CHAPTER 6

"I WAS NO CLERK"

D uring his two years in Mexico the sturdy, bronzed fighter had a recurring dream. It came to him in the subtropical night with the vividness, the urgency, the tantalizing hyperreality of any deeply rooted fantasy, and like most dreams that fill a young man's slumbers, if it was about anything, it was about sex. Night after night Grant saw himself being married to Julia. She was finally his and his alone. And once married . . . well, he did not have to spell out for her what happened in marriage. Julia was no sheltered urbanite, removed from earthy realities. Like him, she had spent many hours around horses and other farm animals. Both of them could easily picture what came next. Grant told her about the wedding in his dreams, eager to know whether her dreams matched his.[1]

Although he wrote her every time there was a chance to send a letter out of Mexico, Julia was never more than a sometime correspondent. Still, that did not prevent her from complaining peevishly that he did not write *her* often enough. While Grant was growing into manhood during their long separation, was learning to handle life-and-death responsibilities, and was required to prove himself in his chosen profession, Julia remained much as when he last saw her—an adolescent. She was the product of a particular time, place and social milieu, none of which encouraged her to grow up.[2]

During the three years they were apart, Grant not only dreamed regularly of marriage and sexual fulfillment with the woman he loved, but in his waking hours his thoughts often turned to her—what was she doing at this minute? was she all right? He got into the habit of removing the ring she had given him and studying the name engraved inside it—JULIA. Every letter he sent her, he kissed before mailing. Every letter he received from her, he kissed before opening. He wrote to Julia begging her for a daguerreotype—this precursor of photography was all the rage those days—but no example made its way to him from chez Dent. He wore a beard throughout the Mexican War and one day tore some russet hairs two inches long from his chin. He enclosed them in a letter to his beloved. They survive to this day, glued by some conscientious archivist to a sheet of paper—curly and almost unfaded by the passage of nearly 150 years.[3]

Moved to respond with something symbolically similar, Julia sent him some rose petals she had pressed. Grant eagerly ripped open the envelope, unfolded the letter containing the petals, and a stiff desert breeze blew them away before he realized what they were![4]

Despite the coolness of Julia's parents toward him and their obvious wish that a long separation would see this supposed "engagement" lose its charm and interest, Grant remained convinced that once he was reunited with Julia, marriage would inevitably follow. For Julia herself had, in a moment of high emotion, given him exactly the promise he craved almost at the start of the Mexican War. The day after news reached St. Louis that the first battle had been fought, at Palo Alto, she had written to Grant in a fervor that mingled love of country with love of Ulysses, pledging that if he chose to remain in the Army, she would gladly share his tent; and if the fortunes of war brought him captivity at the hands of the Mexican enemy, she would just as gladly share his prison cell. How she wished, she said, that they had married before he left for the war.[5]

Their long separation was made tolerable to Grant by the new experiences it brought. Always eager to see the world and what it contained, he had a chance to travel throughout Mexico—a chance, too, to discover his mettle under the challenge of close combat. But once the fighting finally ended, even travel began to pall and he fell into long periods of depression. "I have the *Blues* all the time," he wrote Julia.[6]

She, on the other hand, was enjoying herself immensely. No blue period for her. Julia did not spend those three years pining for the lieutenant. Much of her time was passed at parties and dances and visiting her friends. Her father had rented a small house in St. Louis for his daughters while they attended school in the city each winter. He may well have been hoping, too, that the more time Julia spent there, the better her chances of meeting someone more suitable than her damned Yankee admirer. "I am sure no country lasses ever had three gayer or more delight-ful winters there than we did," is how Julia described these unchaperoned days in St. Louis. She and her sister Nell had young men for company most evenings, and their noisy revels irritated the neighbors. They also held open house on Sunday afternoons. None of the gallants who came calling took much interest in Julia, however. All they seemed interested in was pursuing pretty Nell.[7]

One reason Grant felt so depressed was he feared that he was about to lose his fiancée. "I believe you are carrying on a flirtation with someone, as you threaten of doing," he wrote in the spring of 1848. In a bluff man-of-the-world kind of way, he pretended he did not mind if that helped Julia pass the time while he was gone. But Grant was so fiercely monogamous in his own behavior, this assertion of broad-mindedness was hardly convincing.[8]

Meanwhile "Colonel" Dent's pretense of prosperity was falling apart. Julia's explanation for her father's sudden poverty was partly defensive, partly denial, and wholly absurd. He had ruined himself, she claimed, by being "most kind and indulgent" toward his slaves. Why, he pampered them by buying barrels of fish simply because they liked herring. Such extravagance.[9]

That he paid his slaves nothing for their labor, would never permit them to be educated, and denied them all hope of a normal family life did not register with Julia. Slavery, lacking any moral foundation, was based entirely on violence and could be maintained only by terror. Yet the part of conscience that in any truly refined person was certain to recognize the fundamental immorality of slavery had, in her case, been cauterized in childhood.

Down the years Dent had sat on his porch in a black frock coat and starched, ruffled shirt looking balefully out over his dull stretch of northern Missouri landscape, with dogs and newspapers scattered at his feet, fulminating against his neighbors, cursing them, issuing writs. And when the law did not suffice, there were always other means. His son Louis had hunted down one of their neighbors, an abolitionist named

Sigerson, with a shotgun, but Sigerson managed to turn the tables on Louis Dent and beat him senseless with a cudgel.[10]

The view the Dents had of themselves as well-bred gentlefolk was elastic enough to include attempted murder. But like all bullies, the "Colonel" finally overreached himself. He lost an important lawsuit, a setback that cost him much of what remained of his fortune. Julia informed Grant that as her prospects had changed dramatically, she considered him free to end their engagement. Grant would not hear of it. The engagement was still on.[11]

In early July 1848, the 4th Infantry Regiment arrived back in the United States and made camp at Pascagoula, Mississippi. Grant promptly applied for, and received, a two-month leave to go to St. Louis and make his wedding arrangements.[12] He arrived suddenly at the Dent farm at the end of July, riding a handsome gray horse and accompanied by a Mexican servant boy named Gregorio, with whom he conversed in Spanish.

The Dents greeted the warrior warmly. Here was the gallant officer who had saved Fred's life, as they saw it, during the battle at El Molino del Rey. They were struck, too, by how much older Grant seemed than the youth of three years earlier. He had gone to war as a pale young man prone to chest infections and suffering indifferent health, only to return as a robust figure deeply tanned by long exposure to sun and wind. He urged Julia to set an early date for their wedding. All he needed was sufficient time to travel to Kentucky, see his family, and, if they chose to attend, bring his parents back for the ceremony. The date he and Julia agreed on was August 22.[13]

While Grant's parents were delighted to see their son home safe from the war, they declined the invitation to his wedding. Their absence suggests that Jesse, and possibly Hannah, were still not reconciled to their son's choice. It may not have been Julia they objected to so much as her father. The rich, energetic Yankee tanner never ceased to despise the indolent, impoverished southern slave driver—a sentiment the choleric "Colonel" was going to repay in full.

The Dents' reduced circumstances were reflected in the spartan wedding arrangements for their eldest daughter. Instead of at the spacious farmhouse out near Gravois Creek, the ceremony would be held in the small, rented house in St. Louis. Had the wedding been performed at the farm, the guest list would be expected to include just about the entire haute bourgeoisie of St. Louis. As it was, the list must of necessity be limited to a handful. There was no room for an orchestra, only a solitary fiddler, and instead of a grand wedding feast there was merely a small table holding refreshments at the back of the house.[14]

Grant's groomsmen were three brother officers: James Longstreet, Cadmus Marcelus Wilcox and Bernard Pratte III. One day they would surrender to him at Appomattox Court House. What mattered, though, was now. And now he was married. Now his dream could come true.

★

Following the Mexican War, the U.S. Army was reduced to a force of eight thousand men, barely 15 percent bigger than its prewar size. Victory had virtually doubled the size of the United States, however. Army units were stretched so thinly across the country they were almost invisible. The 750 men of Grant's regiment were about to be scattered among posts stretching from Green Bay, Wisconsin, to Plattsburgh, New York.[15]

Following the wedding, Grant took his new bride to meet his family, who made her feel as welcome as their plain, undemonstrative lifestyle allowed, yet there was an undercurrent of tension, and always would be. "They considered me unpardonably extravagant," said Julia, "and I considered them inexcuseably the other way."[16]

Before reporting for duty in Detroit, Grant secured a two-month extension to his leave so Julia could return to St. Louis and say farewell to her family. It had not really dawned on Julia until now that her old life was over, that as Mrs. Grant she would not be Daddy's little girl any longer. "Parting with papa! I could not, could not, think of it without bursting into a flood of tears and weeping and sobbing as if my heart would break." Grant was able to cope with almost anything, but having a weeping woman on his hands turned him into just another helpless male. He couldn't think of what to do . . . but the "Colonel" could. "Grant," he said, "I can arrange it all for you. Join your regiment and leave Julia with us. You can get a leave of absence once or twice a year and run down here and spend a week or two with us. I always knew she could not live in the Army."

Grant put his arm around her. "Would you like this, Julia?" he asked, probably incredulous. "Would you like to remain with your father and let me go alone?"

Julia had enough sense to realize that, in effect, she was being asked if she wanted to destroy her marriage before it had really begun. Her father was more than willing to help her do so. "No, no," she said, to Grant's immense relief.

"Then dry your tears and do not weep again. It makes me unhappy."[17]

It was November before they set off for Detroit, the new headquarters of the 4th Infantry. When Grant arrived, he was astonished to receive fresh orders. As regimental quartermaster, his post was at HQ. But winter was at hand and the officer who had been acting quartermaster during Grant's four-month leave, Lieutenant Henry D. Wallen, had no intention of giving up the comforts of Detroit for a cold, remote duty station out in the boondocks. Wallen went to work on the regimental commander, Colonel William Whistler. The aged colonel had not shared the dangers and discomforts of the Mexican War with his regiment but had remained in the United States while the bullets flew. He and Wallen were cut from the same piece of well-preserved cloth. Not surprisingly, then, Wallen was able to talk Whistler into keeping him in Detroit and banishing Grant to the wilderness. Grant was told not to tarry but to keep moving. He was being sent to Sackets Harbor, New York.

Pleasant enough in the summer, Sackets Harbor is one of the coldest places in the entire eastern United States in the winter. Grant was stunned, but he had no choice. He and Julia set off for Sackets Harbor, at their own expense, when the first snows of winter were in the air. Over the next few months, while Wallen was snugly settled in a warm house in Detroit, Grant and Julia found themselves shivering in dreary stone barracks overlooking the eastern shore of Lake Ontario. Grant protested furiously to the War Department and the question of where a regimental QM belonged went all the way to the commanding general, Winfield Scott, who ruled emphatically in Grant's favor. But victory, when it came, was pretty academic: With the rivers and lakes now turned to ice, Grant would have to wait until spring 1849 before he could travel back to Detroit.[18]

As might have been expected, Julia turned out to be a hopeless cook and a worse housekeeper. Grant was never bothered by that. What *was* worrying was the way she could make money disappear even in places where there was nothing much to buy. Julia, by her own admission, came close to bankrupting her husband during the early years of their marriage.

When the thaw came, they returned to Detroit. All they could afford to rent was a tiny wooden house in one of the poorer parts of the city, which had grown to a population of twenty-one thousand and boasted more than six hundred brick dwellings. Grant raffled off his gray thoroughbred mare, but he could not imagine life without a horse to communicate with and through. He soon bought a small, fleet-footed mare that he raced for cash prizes. But he had to part with Gregorio, who was hired away for better pay than Grant could afford.[19]

As Grant soon discovered, being a quartermaster and commissary in a thriving American town demanded little of him. There was no real foraging to be done; there were no exciting rides through the enemy's country to unearth hidden stores of grain, no "grand fights," no flags to be captured and carried back in triumph. He craved for a company of soldiers to command in addition to his paperwork. Drilling the men, trying to keep them out of trouble, taking an interest in their welfare, trying to turn them into the best company in the regiment, maybe the best in the department, would have occupied his time and engaged his emotions. But for now all Grant had before him day after day was bureaucratic routine, and routine invariably brought out the fatalism, pessimism and ennui that lay just under the skin.

Reports went unwritten, bills were paid late, letters piled up, crying like orphans for answers. "I was no clerk, nor had I any capacity to become one," he admitted in his *Personal Memoirs*. It was one of those confessions that looks a lot like bragging in disguise. "The only place I ever found in my life to put a paper so as to find it again was either in a side coat-pocket or the hands of a clerk more careful than myself."[20]

Yet there was another side to it. His QM job brought out an important trait, important because it would set Grant apart from nearly all other major field commanders during the Civil War—his belief in using what the system provided and not demanding more and more resources from his superiors. It was a trait he shared with his hero, Zachary Taylor. But the quartermaster clerk working for him in Detroit, the felicitously named Friend Palmer, was baffled and irritated. That wasn't how things were done in the Army as Palmer—and probably most other soldiers—knew it. What you did was ask for twice as much as you expected to get, knowing that some fool higher up the chain of command was likely to cut any request you made by half, possibly more. "Why in the world have they put that lieutenant in as quartermaster

and commissary?" an exasperated Palmer asked the headquarters sergeant one day. "Is it because he knows less than any other officer in the
regiment?"

The sergeant came to Grant's defense. "The Captain," he said, refer-
ring to Grant by his brevet rank, "is not much good when you come to
papers, accounts, returns and all that sort of thing. But when you get to
the soldier part of it—drill, the manual of arms, fighting—he can handle this regiment as well, if not better, than any other officer in it." One
day Palmer, after he had risen to become a general himself, decided the
sergeant was right—Grant *was* the most capable officer in the 4th
Infantry, even if he had a strange approach to obtaining supplies.[21]

In the fall of 1849, Julia became pregnant. As soon as her pregnancy
was confirmed, she returned to St. Louis, leaving Grant to brave the
winter without her. Julia maintained that she left only at the urging of
her doctor, but this hardly seems likely. Women had babies in Detroit
every week and medical conditions there were much the same as in St.
Louis. The difference, one suspects, was that winters were milder in
Missouri than in Michigan. Besides which Julia probably, and understandably, wanted to have the child in familiar surroundings, with the
presence of her mother and sisters to sustain her. Childbirth was still a
dangerous ordeal wherever a woman happened to be. Grant could only
stand aside and wait out the winter. In May 1850, Julia gave birth to a
son and named him Frederick Dent Grant, in honor of her father.
Whether her husband was even consulted is open to doubt, and the fact
that not one Grant letter survives from the eight months they were apart
suggests that he was far from reconciled to Julia's decision to return to
Papa.[22]

After the birth of his son, Grant got a prolonged leave to be with his
wife and newborn child and brought them back to Detroit in October.
That winter, Julia and other officers' wives diverted themselves by organizing a fancy dress ball with a Turkish theme. While an excited Julia
dressed up as a tambourine girl at the sultan's court, Grant dressed up
as a brevet captain in the 4th Infantry Regiment—no silly costume
for him.

At about this time Grant slipped on the ice outside the home of one
of Detroit's up-and-coming businessmen, Zachariah Chandler. An indignant Grant sued Chandler for neglecting "to keep his Side walk free
and clear from Snow and Ice . . ."[23] The case was put before a jury,

which found Chandler guilty but showed what it really thought by imposing a derisory fine amounting to all of six cents.

It was not only the jurymen who mocked Grant. Chandler handled his own defense and openly derided Grant during the trial. "If you soldiers would keep sober," he fumed, "perhaps you would not fall on people's pavements and hurt your legs!" Was Grant drinking in those days? Almost certainly—which may explain the pointedly minuscule fine.[24]

By the inexplicable workings of fate, twenty years after this courtroom confrontation, Chandler, who had gone on to become a United States senator, was appointed secretary of the Interior in Grant's cabinet. In middle age they simply laughed away the encounter that had first brought them together.[25]

The Army, under severe pressure from Congress to save money, decided to move the headquarters of the 4th Infantry from Detroit to Sackets Harbor. Julia had no intention of spending another winter in that frigid spot. She returned to St. Louis, leaving Grant to make the move without her.

Once more, he wrote to her regularly. Once more, she wrote to him when she felt like it, which was rarely. His wife's apparent unconcern infuriated Grant. He was almost pathetically eager for news of his son—"the little dog," as Grant affectionately called him. What were the child's first words? Was he active and adventurous? Was his health good? "After a lapse of more than one month," Grant protested to Julia, "I at length received a letter from you yesterday. I do not see that you had any excuse whatever for not writing before. . . . Do not neglect to write for so long a time again." It did no good, of course.[26]

Grant amused himself that summer of 1851 by traveling to Canada. He visited Quebec and Montreal, before heading south and making his first return visit to his alma mater. He arrived at West Point during summer encampment. He was too shy—and too averse to music—to attend any of the parties and dances alone, but West Point still cast its spell. "Next summer," he promised Julia, "if we are still at Sacket's [sic] Harbor I will get a leave for a week and bring you here. It is one of the most beautiful places to spend a few days you ever saw."[27]

That fall, Julia reluctantly came to join him at his new station. She spent only part of the winter with him, but when she set off for St. Louis she was pregnant again. Left on his own once more, Grant was depressed. What had he to look forward to but snow, boredom, more snow, numbing cold, more boredom and still more snow? Many a soldier got through the long, bitter winter by taking refuge in an alcoholic haze. But heavy drinking was dangerous. For ordinary soldiers, habitual drunkenness brought loss of all pay and allowances, a shaved head, branding on the hip with the letters HD and a dishonorable discharge. For an officer, there was no branding and no head-shaving, but he risked being compelled to resign his commission in disgrace.[28]

As winter closed in on Sackets Harbor, Grant prepared to do battle with the temptations of drink. A moderate drinker up to now, but sensing how easily loneliness can push a man from moderation into addiction, Grant sought help. He enrolled at the Rising Sun Division, Lodge No. 210, of the Sons of Temperance. Meetings were held weekly at the Presbyterian church. Grant not only attended regularly but took an active part in lodge activities. He dressed in the red, white and blue regalia of the movement, marched in temperance parades and talked the wonders of temperance to other sinners. On a wall in his quarters Julia had proudly hung his membership certificate before departing for St. Louis. As the certificate proclaimed, Grant was pledged not to "make, buy, sell, or use, as a beverage, any Spiritous or Malt Liquors, Wine, or Cider."[29] The Sons were sworn not only to stay off the booze but to give up smoking and swearing, too. The main thing, though, was the bottle. "I have become convinced," Grant declared, "that there is no safety from ruin by liquor except by abstaining from it altogether."[30]

The Sons of Temperance was one of the most important efforts at self-improvement in America at mid-century. Among the half-million men who signed the pledge were P. T. Barnum, Abraham Lincoln and Rutherford B. Hayes. Grant joined the Sons at the peak of the movement. But like most promises of redemption, it demanded more than frail humanity can deliver. At least half the Sons eventually fell off the wagon. The failure of this evangelistic movement would nonetheless prove to be a major step along the road to Prohibition. For Grant, despite the parades; the red, white and blue sash; the white apron of purity; the certificate on the wall; and the fervently sworn pledge, joining the Sons turned out not to be a lifelong commitment after all. It was just a prop to help get him through another godawful winter at Sackets Harbor.[31]

With the melted snows came news that the regiment was moving to California. Grant got a brief leave and headed for Bethel, where Julia had gone to show off young Fred to Jesse and Hannah and to have her second child. There was a cholera scare in St. Louis, otherwise she would almost certainly have waited out her pregnancy at White Haven.

Julia offered to go with Grant to California, but he adamantly refused to expose his pregnant wife and young son to the rigors of the journey. Travel between the East Coast and the Pacific Coast involved either a long and hazardous voyage around Cape Horn or sailing to Panama, crossing the isthmus on muleback, then embarking on another ship, usually to San Francisco. While the sea voyage was often uncomfortable, crossing the isthmus meant a hazardous trek through the jungle. Disease was rife, serious accidents common, and little white crosses marked the narrow, muddy mule paths—besides which, the California Gold Rush had sent the price of nearly everything on the West Coast far beyond the reach of a mere lieutenant's pay. "You know how loath I am to leave you," he told Julia, "but crossing Panama is an undertaking for one in robust health. And then, my salary is so small, how could you and my little boy have even the common necessaries of life out there?"[32]

The regiment moved to Governors Island, in New York Harbor, to await the ships that would carry it to Panama. Weeks passed. In July 1852, Grant took advantage of the prolonged delay to slip away to Washington for a few days. He was curious to see the city, for one thing. But more than that, he wanted the Army to write off the thousand dollars of quartermaster funds that were stolen from him just before he left Mexico. Although the government was not pressing for restitution, this crushing debt—which exceeded his annual salary—weighed on him. Attempts by sympathetic congressmen to have it waived had achieved nothing. He wanted to get the issue resolved before he left for California.

Grant was disappointed by the appearance of the nation's capital— just a dull southern small town with far fewer majestic buildings than he had seen in Mexico. The city was also in a somber mood. The day Grant arrived saw the funeral of the great Whig politician Henry Clay, and the District of Columbia was in official mourning.

As he strolled the almost deserted streets, there was little to enchant Grant's eye, and the monument begun by his hero, Zachary Taylor, was still nothing but an ugly marble stump south of the White House. After Taylor's election to the presidency in 1848, he pushed Congress into raising a large Egyptian-style obelisk to Washington's memory. Taylor died in 1851, only days after the dedication ceremony, and Congress soon lost interest. When Grant saw the Washington Monument, it was barely seventy-five feet high. Work stopped for twenty years—until Grant became President.[33]

He soon discovered that the House Military Affairs Committee would not meet for another week. Grant returned disconsolately to New York, visiting some of his mother's relations in Philadelphia along the way. It was nearly midnight on July 4 when he got back to Governors Island.

The regiment would board ship in the morning, he was told, and sail on the afternoon tide. Grant was flabbergasted. After catching a few hours' sleep, he barely had enough time to make sure everything and everyone was safely aboard ship and dash off a short letter to Julia: "We sail directly for the Isthmus!"[34]

CHAPTER 7

---- ★ ★ ★ ★ ----

"HOW FORSAKEN I FEEL HERE!"

His name, destined to become part of the nation's geography, sang on the tongue. If you could measure a man by his moniker, the euphoniously named Benjamin Louis Eulalie de Bonneville would have been a titan. Instead, he was merely an officer who demonstrated that mediocrity was not an obstacle either to fame—as an explorer—or to a successful career in the Army. Almost comically vain, the French-born Lieutenant Colonel Bonneville advertised his singularity by shunning military headgear. He wore a large white beaver hat instead. Here I am, it announced, and I am not the short, stout, balding, testy and unprepossesing person you probably take me for but a man of some consequence. I am Bonneville, the explorer who traveled up the Columbia River all the way to Hudson Bay.

That he got so hopelessly lost he could not find Fort Vancouver, which he was heading for, and that his touted exploration was in truth mainly a search for a commercial opportunity that would make him rich (he didn't find that, either) was not dwelled on by the man who made him famous, the writer Washington Irving. Bonneville, moreover, liked to suggest that he was the illegitimate son of the Marquis de Lafayette, spicing an innate dullness with a whiff of sexual scandal and a dusting—a *saupoudrage*—of revolutionary glory.[1]

Shortly after the 4th Infantry learned that it was to move to the Pacific Coast, Bonneville took over from Colonel Whistler. In the nineteenth-century Army, an officer could be assigned to a regiment yet see hardly a day's service with it. He could even, like Whistler, decide he was too old for the rigors of Mexico, too infirm for the hazards of life on the West Coast, and stay safely at home, collect his pay, and see someone else handle the regiment in his stead. And that was how Bonneville got command of the 4th Infantry—he would command it in fact while Whistler, thousands of miles away, practiced the zen of leadership and continued collecting his pay. There was no retirement pension, so officers had a powerful incentive to cling grimly to the payroll and die in harness.

The person principally responsible for the nuts-and-bolts business of ensuring the regiment had all its equipment ready for its long journey to the Pacific Coast was Grant. For some reason, Bonneville took an instant dislike to Grant, and one of his first actions was to look for a new quartermaster.[2] Given Bonneville's querulous nature and insufferable airs, it was inevitable that Grant would dislike him in return. For months to come Grant kept wishing—in vain—that Whistler would change his mind and decide to rejoin the regiment. As for being ousted as quartermaster, nothing could have pleased him more.

Unfortunately for Grant, his brother officers protested vehemently to Bonneville that while Grant might not be a typical QM, he got things done without making a great show of getting things done. Bonneville backed down. "Everything devolvs [*sic*] upon me," Grant stoically informed Julia, explaining why he had so little time to see her before he left, unlike other officers, most of whom were given at least a month's leave before departing.[3]

The War Department had waited until the last minute to book passage for the troops. It seemed somnambulently unaware that the California Gold Rush was creating a kind of panic for places aboard every vessel that was Panama-bound. When it did finally make a move, the department acted as if there was nothing more urgent in the world than getting the 4th out to the West Coast ASAP and booked passage for the regiment aboard a brand-new steamer, the *Ohio*. The government pressured the steamship line into taking the regiment even though every berth on the *Ohio* had already been sold. But the War Department was trying to make up for lost time. There were problems with miners, Mexicans and Indians out west. Troops must be sent without delay.

As 650 soldiers of the 4th Infantry, accompanied by sixty Army wives and twenty children, trooped aboard the *Ohio,* it was left to Grant to try and find places for them to bed down in the holds and the corridors, and on deck. He counted more than 1,100 crammed aboard a vessel designed to carry 350. Everyone was in for an uncomfortable voyage. Not only was the ship dangerously overcrowded, but the weather was so hot that even night brought no relief. The rats-in-a-cage conditions and high temperatures produced endless friction between soldiers and civilians.

The excitable Bonneville was of no help when it came to resolving these petty squabbles. It was left to Grant to keep people calm. He also had to smooth agitated feathers that the self-important colonel had unnecessarily ruffled. Grant was lucky that from the outset he found someone willing to help him—the captain of the *Ohio,* J. Finley Schenck, a former commander in the Navy.

Schenck, like everyone else, had first to get past Grant's shyness and his preference for silent communication to find the real man. What he discovered came as a pleasant surprise—a first-rate mind and a powerful will. And far from being taciturn from want of anything to say, Grant turned out to have clear and interesting ideas on just about every subject Schenck raised. Between them, Grant and Schenck managed to keep the tensions simmering aboard the *Ohio* under control.[4]

Almost the moment he put his foot on the overcrowded steamer's deck, Grant fell off the wagon. Schenck noticed how conscientious Grant was, how little sleep he seemed to need, and how he lived on his nerves, sustained by tobacco and alcohol. "He never went to bed before three in the morning," remarked Schenck, "but he would walk up down the deck smoking a cigar . . . had an excellent taste for good liquors. I had given him the liberty of the sideboard in my cabin and urged him frequently never to be backward in using it as though it were his own, and he never was. Every night, after I had turned in, I would hear him once or twice, sometimes more, open the door quietly and walk softly over the floor, so as not to disturb me; then I would hear the clink of a glass and a gurgle, and he would walk softly back."[5]

After eight days at sea, the *Ohio* arrived at what is now the port of Colón. Its passengers disembarked to begin the transit of the Isthmus of Panama. In a straight line, it was a mere thirty-five miles, but the route was so tortuous that the actual distance covered was nearly twice that figure. And in the opinion of the surgeon of the 4th Infantry, Major Charles S. Tripler, crossing the isthmus was going to be a descent into a green, wet hell. For one thing, summer is the rainy season in Central America. For another, a cholera epidemic had broken out in Panama shortly before the *Ohio* left New York. Tripler tried to convince the War Department that it would be "murder" to send the regiment into a cholera zone. The surgeon general of the Army brushed his protests aside. The epidemic, he said, would be "quickly over." As guesses go, this one deserves a prize. The onset of cholera in Panama was the prelude to one of the greatest cholera epidemics in the history of the Western world. In 1853 it would spread across North and South America, killing more than a hundred thousand people.[6]

The journey into the interior of Panama was made in dugout canoes poled along the Chagres River by strapping, virtually naked Indians. The next part of the journey consisted of a short ride on a railroad train. Along the way, however, it became clear that the cholera epidemic was raging—there were dead and dying construction workers pathetically clustered in squalid huts all along the track. The epidemic would kill nearly half these men.[7]

At Cruces, a village barely ten miles from the coast, Bonneville dropped off the slowest-moving and most vulnerable element—the sixty women and twenty children—plus one infantry company to serve as a guard, the regimental band, all the regimental baggage, and nearly a dozen people who were already ill. Brevet Captain Grant was ordered to shepherd this motley, and increasingly sickly, group across. Bonneville and the remaining seven companies of infantry continued along the river a few miles to Gorgona. Disembarking there, they moved rapidly through torrential rains and across a landscape that seemed nearly as liquid as the ocean.

Meanwhile, Grant's party was plunged into a slow-motion nightmare, beginning with the mules. When travelers from the *Ohio* discovered that most of the available mules had already been hired by the Army, they simply offered to pay more than twice as much and rode away on beasts that were rightfully Grant's. He found himself forced to pay far more than he had been authorized simply to get hold of the few mules still available. Even then, he obtained fewer than half the number he needed. The women and children had to walk much of the way. The sick were carried in hammocks.[8]

As his party pressed doggedly on, the cholera epidemic began killing its members. A strong young soldier could seem in perfect health on a Monday, fall ill on Tuesday, and be buried in a shallow grave alongside the treacherously muddy mule path on Wednesday. The first signs were diarrhea and vomiting. Then came agonizing cramps in the legs and abdomen, followed by a thirst so intense it was torture. The skin turned blue, and the voice was reduced to a hoarse whisper—the "vox choler- ica." Death followed soon after. It was a horrible way to die and unnerv- ing to anyone who witnessed it.

Almost every mile between the Atlantic and the Pacific, Grant had to bury someone in the mud. There was nothing solid enough to dig into and make a real grave. While the jungle sometimes burst into life with cheerful tropical birdsong, the sound arising from the trail was a dirge of sobbing by the recently bereaved.

Grant himself avoided cholera by never touching water and drinking only wine. He urged others to do the same and the soldiers tended to heed his advice, but the women and children were likely to ignore it— the sight of what looked like attractive springs gushing pure, cool water was too tempting. But the springs were polluted by cholera sufferers who had tried to wash away the traces of diarrhea from their clothes and their bodies. And it was not only the water that spread the disease. So did the flies, which transported it from the feces of the dead to the food of the living.[9]

From his experience bringing in the wounded from battlefields, Grant knew how to handle a burial quickly but with dignity, help Major Tripler tend the sick, and practice the sanitary measures needed to keep other diseases, such as malaria, in check. He also managed to keep panic and demoralization at bay, despite the ceaseless anguish and ter- ror. But with the inevitable confusion and absence of normal security, most of the regimental baggage was lost or stolen. Guarding the 4th's silver dinner service was less compelling that trying to keep people alive.[10]

On July 26, Grant and his survivors stumbled down to the Pacific shore. Of those who had set off from Cruces with him two weeks ear- lier, one in three had perished. Relieved though they were to reach the Pacific, Grant and Tripler were horrified to discover that Bonneville had already loaded the entire main body, including dozens of people who were showing signs of cholera, aboard a steamer—the aptly named

Golden Gate—that had been hired to carry the regiment to San Francisco. It could only be a matter of time before the disease spread throughout the entire ship.[11]

Grant and Tripler turned a beached vessel into a makeshift hospital for the sick. The cholera victims were to remain there until they died or recovered. Grant spent most of his time aboard the hospital ship. According to one officer, Grant "took a personal interest in each sick man. [He was] a man of iron, so far as endurance went, seldom sleeping, and then only two or three hours at a time. . . . He was like a ministering angel to us all."[12]

Only those who appeared to be in perfect health were allowed to reboard the *Golden Gate,* but there was no way of knowing for sure, as Grant soon discovered. He was playing euchre one evening aboard the steamer with one of his closest friends, Brevet Major John Gore, when Gore suddenly put his cards down. "My God!" said Gore, his face turning white. "I've got cholera!"

Grant refused even to consider the possibility. "You have only eaten something that disagrees with you." Tripler was summoned at once, but Gore was dead before morning.[13]

The sole redeeming feature of the whole ghastly business was that Julia and little Fred were spared it. Grant had no doubt that had they attempted to cross the isthmus both would have perished, as would the child Julia was carrying, which was due any day now. He could not bring himself to write to her about the ordeal he had just witnessed, been part of, and survived, until it was far behind him.

He took up his pen as the *Golden Gate* steamed past Acapulco: "My dearest, you never could have crossed the Isthmus at this season. . . . The horrors . . . are beyond description. . . . I will say however that there is a great accountability some where for the loss which we have sustained . . ." He did not give her a detailed description of anything that had occurred. It was still too fresh, too painful.[14]

Crossing Panama was the kind of traumatic experience that remains with someone for life. In his later years Grant was always willing to talk about the Civil War in the company of friends, but the subject he kept coming back to over and over again, without any prompting at all, was what he had gone through in Panama. It was as if he felt a huge burden of guilt that he had not been able to keep all of his stricken party alive crossing the isthmus.[15]

The more Grant reflected on it, the more convinced he became that no one—and certainly not women or children—should ever have to undergo such a dangerous and primitive journey. When he became President, the first message Grant sent to Congress called for the United States to build a canal across Panama and carve "a Path Between the Seas."[16]

★

In 1842 a young Army lieutenant named John C. Frémont blazed a trail west, looking for a safe and easy route to Oregon. That was the publicly stated reason, but there was also a half-hidden agenda: to arouse American interest in the Pacific Northwest and to make the British, who claimed most of what is now Oregon and Washington States, think of leaving.

This venture made Frémont the most famous lieutenant in the Army. Dashing, dapper, handsome, married to the daughter of one of the most powerful men in the Senate, Thomas Hart Benton of Missouri, here was someone the nation readily adopted as everyone's son when he returned after marking out the Oregon Trail.

In 1843 Frémont set off again. He went back to Oregon and then headed south, into California. His poetic descriptions of the richness of the soil, the healthiness of the climate, and the overwhelming magnificence of the scenery aroused every emotion from avarice to mystical reverie. His report, read eagerly around campfires or in the yellow glow of whale-oil lamps or by the flickering light of candles, was California's first—and probably most important—publicity coup. People warmed themselves that winter thinking about the magical place Frémont described. Here was the beginning of the American West of romance and legend, the West of the lemonade springs and the Big Rock Candy Mountain. And then, in 1849, after California had been wrested from Mexico, came something guaranteed to drive people half-crazy with desire—gold. Why, there were nuggets as big as acorns. No, there were nuggets as big as a man's fist. Call that big? Well, latest report says nuggets as big as a man's head![17]

So when Ulysses Grant stepped off the *Golden Gate* in August 1852 to see what San Francisco had to offer, he was not completely surprised to find himself walking into something wilder, more colorful and more thrilling than anything short of war. The city offered everything from stupefying wealth to desperate poverty, but mostly what it generated was excitement. The entire population of fifty thousand was living on its nerves. The only occupation known to man or woman was to get rich—by any means possible—and the city was growing so rapidly that for Grant it was like seeing an entire civilization shoot up before his eyes. What elsewhere had taken a decade was here crammed into a month; the progress of a century could be reproduced in a year. Nothing seemed normal or ordinary. Grant, with his low tolerance for the mundane or routine, felt at home from the first. This was "a different country from any thing that a person in the states could imagine in their wildes [*sic*] dreams," he excitedly informed Julia. "There is no reason why an active energetic person should not make a fortune evry [*sic*] year." Even so, he wondered, was it all a mirage, an electrifying vision of riches, not riches itself? Maybe it was a shade too good to be true.[18]

Grant spent a couple of months at Benicia, fifteen miles northeast of San Francisco, recovering from Panama. He was emaciated, ashen and plagued by a wide variety of minor ailments. As strength returned, however, he self-prescribed his favorite tonic—travel. Grant made several trips through the East Bay area. He also visited the foothills of the Sierra Nevada to visit two of Julia's brothers, John and Louis Dent, who had come west to seek their fortunes. John had gone into the mining business, while Louis ran a small rope ferry on the Stanislaus River.[19]

"The climate is unequaled," Grant marveled. And, "The whole country from Benicia to the southern limits of the state . . . abounds with luxuriant growth."[20] Compared to the dull landscapes and of the prairies of Ohio and Missouri, California seemed a gift the gods gave to those with enough fire in their soul to appreciate it. The outwardly prosaic Grant, a man who was careful to reveal only oblique glimpses of his hinterland, was as much a romantic as anything else. There was in him a heightened sensitivity that invariably responded to a cerulean sky, the fragrance of flowers, the hypnotic attraction of birds going about their business, the delicious tension of traveling along a river, wondering what was around the next bend, and the soul-cleansing high of jumping a spirited horse over logs in a clearing in the woods on a sunlit day. After only a month, he declared himself, "a Calafornian [*sic*] . . . wanting but one thing"—his family to come and join him.[21]

Grant continued to consider himself a "Calafornian" at heart long after he returned to the East. Drunk or sober, confronting bankruptcy or victory, he regularly promised himself he would go back one day, for good. Nearly everyone has a fantasy of escape. California, as he saw it in the heady days of the Gold Rush, was Grant's.[22]

★

Once he had regained his health and strength, he boarded a steamer that would take him to Fort Vancouver, eight miles north of Portland, Oregon. As the ship plowed northward, he fell into a reverie about his wife—"I dreamed that I got home and found you and Fred and a beautiful little girl, all asleep. Is my dream true . . . ?"[23] It wasn't. While he was crossing the isthmus, Julia had given birth to another son. In accordance with Grant's wishes, this time the boy was named after him.

From the moment he reached his new post, and probably long before then, Grant was looking for ways to make some money. His Army pay plus allowances for a servant, a horse and the high cost of living on the Pacific Coast amounted to fifteen hundred dollars a year.[24] That was not only sufficient for him but, provided he lived simply, he could send enough money to his wife to maintain her and the children. What he could not do was have them join him. His wife could never have managed without a servant of her own, and there was no question of her bringing along the four slaves her father had given her.

However much Julia fancied that her "servants" were outrageously pampered at White Haven, the fact was that the minute any able-bodied slave reached free territory, he or she was likely to take a walk. So Grant would have to be able to pay for a servant—a real one—for Julia and meet the high cost of supporting a family of four in boom-time California. To do that, he had to try making some money. His first venture was to bankroll a merchant he had known at Sackets Harbor, Elijah Camp, in setting up a general store at Fort Vancouver. The store did so well that Camp soon insisted on buying out Grant's share in the business, and Grant agreed. In the space of one month he had made fifteen hundred dollars—equal to an entire year's income. But "I was very foolish in taking it," Grant soon decided, "because my share of the profits would not have been less than three thousand per year."[25] He also planned to grow potatoes for sale in San Francisco, where the current price was eight dollars a bushel. The local Hudson's Bay Company representative, a man named Ogden, agreed to let Grant plant his crop on land he owned in exchange for fixing up the fences around Ogden's farm. By late fall Grant felt his financial prospects were good enough to ask Julia to come out and join him that winter. To his bitter disappointment, she never showed up.[26]

Julia was proving, as ever, to be one of the world's least satisfying correspondents. Months could pass without her putting pen to paper. To Grant, a happy marriage should be a love affair, and his devotion to his wife was the main subject of his letters. All the same, it seems likely that there was something more to Julia's prolonged silences than indifference. She had an infuriating habit, when she did bother to write, of producing a page or so, then stopping abruptly on one excuse or another—someone had just arrived, someone was about to leave, etc. It infuriated Grant that when he did get a letter, often after a silence of two or three months, it ended suddenly just as it started to get interesting. Yet it is not too difficult to see in Julia's fitful approach to outgoing mail a form of protest at her husband's prolonged absence, a protest she had no other way of making.

Grant was also disturbed on reaching Fort Vancouver to discover that the post quartermaster, Brevet Captain Thomas Lee Brent, demanded that the regimental quartermaster, Brevet Captain Grant, should be under his authority, because his brevet antedated Grant's. Here was one instance where Bonneville and Grant were in perfect accord: It was Brent who should be under Grant. The issue was not resolved until May 1853, when Brent was transferred elsewhere. Grant took over as post QM while remaining QM of his regiment.[27]

As post quartermaster, he was entitled to what was the finest house in the territory, a splendid two-story structure that had been constructed in New England, shipped to the West Coast and reassembled at a picturesque spot on the banks of the Columbia River. His most important task was fitting out surveying parties, and while he was gathering the supplies they needed, the surveyors stayed in his spacious house. Grant was a highly sociable man and was always delighted to have company, even if he had little to say. But get him on a subject that interested him, and he could be eloquent and compelling. What he liked to talk about most was the Mexican War. "How clear-headed Sam Grant is in describing a battle!" remarked another officer. "He seems to have the whole thing in his head!"[28]

Getting the surveying parties outfitted, however, was irksome. The surveyors made endless—sometimes impossible—demands and did not appreciate how difficult it was to get adequate supplies all the way out to such a remote spot on the frontier. One of these parties was led by someone he had known in Mexico, Brevet Captain George B. McClellan. Grant made the mistake of getting drunk while McClellan was his guest, thereby forfeiting his respect forever. Surveying this vast, largely unexplored territory was a dangerous business and no one wants to trust his life to a drunk. The claim of many of Grant's admirers that he never let his drinking get in the way of his duties is wrong.[29]

On the other hand, stories that his life in the Northwest revolved around the bottle are exaggerated. The trouble with Grant was not that he was a hopeless drunk but that, like F. Scott Fitzgerald, he was so lightly built and highly strung that he could not handle the stuff. Robert McFeely, an officer who served with him at Fort Vancouver, noticed that "one glass would show on him and two or three would make him stupid."[30]

By and large, assignment to Fort Vancouver was tolerable. There was congenial company there among both the officers and the NCOs. Grant met up with his West Point roommate Rufus Ingalls, and they spent many hours playing cards or on long horseback rides through the dense forest. As at most frontier posts, the people who liked Fort Vancouver best were usually those who loved hunting and fishing, but Grant never found any pleasure in killing other creatures for sport and left the wildlife alone. He was excited, though, by a trip to Mount Hood, sixty miles from Fort Vancouver.[31]

Grant also enjoyed working the land. It was hard work repairing the storm-battered fences around Ogden's farm and putting in a large crop of potatoes. But any task that involved horses always satisfied Grant's deep need for mutual trust and admiration. It thrilled him, as it had done in youth, to break virgin land with a shiny plow, and it gave him an almost childish delight to discover he could still handle a team and score the face of the Earth with a pattern of straight furrows. Day after day he toiled in the fields, dressed in a canvas coat, canvas pants, stout boots and a straw hat, puffing contentedly on a cigar.[32]

When harvesttime came, it looked as if half the people of northern California had decided to get rich by growing vegetables for San Francisco. The city was awash with fresh produce. The price of potatoes crashed from eight dollars a bushel in the summer of 1852 to twenty-five cents in the spring of 1853. Grant made nothing from his crop. An attempt to provide the city with logs also came to grief. So did a venture into pig farming. He even went into partnership with several other officers to lease a hotel in San Francisco and turn it into a private club. The venture prospered until the manager disappeared with the profits.[33]

Grant's failed business ventures were dismaying, but they were as nothing compared to the guilt and loneliness caused by separation from his wife and children. By the spring of 1853 it was clear that Julia had no intention of coming to California. Not only was she refusing to come to California, she would not even take the children to visit their grandparents in Ohio, and "Colonel" Dent was evidently boasting that the two boys would grow up at White Haven as little Dents.[34]

Grant found himself in an impossible situation. He desperately wanted his family to join him yet was terrified of what would probably happen if they tried. Seventeen of the twenty children aboard the *Ohio* had perished in Panama. The three who reached California died soon after. What chance, then, for Fred and Ulysses, Jr.? So while he yearned for his family to come west, Grant really did not want them to attempt it.[35]

The answer to his dilemma was obvious—if they could not come to him, he would have to go to them. In the fall of 1853 he learned he had been promoted to captain in the regular Army. In the meantime he was trying to get a transfer to the Quartermaster's Department in Washington. It was imperative, he claimed, that he return to the East Coast to resolve the issue of his thousand-dollar debt to the government. The War Department disagreed and told him he would remain out west.[36]

Frustrated and despondent, Grant wrote Julia several times to say he was going to be reunited with his family even if he had to resign his commission. One day he burst into tears while reading a letter from Julia and told the NCO's wife he employed to cook for him, "Mrs. Sheffield, I have the dearest little wife in the world. I want to resign from the Army and live with my family!"[37]

Hope, however, is always the last thing to die. As long as Grant was at Fort Vancouver, he felt there was a chance of working things out. But in January 1854 he reported to a much smaller, much less pleasant post, Fort Humboldt, on the coast of northern California, to take command of Company F. A winter on Humboldt Bay would test any man's spirits. For Grant, who was already miserable, it was a ghastly prospect. It might have been different had there been at least one old friend there, but there were only four other officers assigned to the post. Three were strangers, and the fourth, the post's commander, was Grant's old adversary, Brevet Lieutenant Colonel Robert C. Buchanan.[38]

While Buchanan was a competent soldier and had won two brevets in Mexico, he was considered one of the most disagreeable men in the Army. "Elated at his own importance," according to one of his adjutants, Buchanan seemed to delight in making people afraid of him. He kept boredom at bay by sadistically wounding the feelings of junior officers and watching them squirm, knowing they were unable to retaliate. And boredom was a constant menace in wet, foggy, cold and isolated Fort Humboldt.[39]

When Grant reported to his new post he was sick with the flu, in agony from a rotten tooth, prone to migraine headaches, and suffering acutely from rheumatism in his legs. Almost overwhelmed by despair, he wrote Julia, "How forsaken I feel here!"[40]

The only distraction available in this wet, gloomy place was at Ryan's store, in the village of Eureka, three miles down the road. Ryan offered a warm stove to sit next to, a fresh audience for Grant's war stories, and a barrel of whiskey with a long-handled dipper in easy reach— basic comforts for a lonely man feeling under the weather and without much to do apart from avoiding a superior he detested.[41]

Somewhere between Ryan's store and Buchanan's desk, Grant reached a decision. He *was* going to resign, after all. But he would do so on his terms—he would leave not as a permanent lieutenant but as a permanent captain. Although Grant had been promoted back in the fall of 1853, the promotion would not take effect until his commission was signed, and it would be months before President Franklin Pierce got around to signing his. Grant would have to wait a while longer.

On April 11, 1854, his commission finally arrived at Fort Humboldt. He was now a permanent captain, one of only five among the thirty-nine members of his West Point class. Grant had shown that far from being mediocre officer material, he was in fact one of the most able young men in the Army. If he chose to remain, he would almost certainly rise higher. But if he chose to quit, then the fault must be with the system, not with the man. He had not failed the Army. It was the Army that had failed him.[42]

Grant penned a brief note to the adjutant general, saying he accepted his commission as a captain. Then he dipped his pen into the ink again and wrote a second letter—"I very respectfully tender my resignation of my commission as an officer of the Army . . ."[43]

★ ★ ★ ★

CHAPTER 8

"I WAS HAPPY"

Man proposes. On January 23, 1854, Jesse Grant turned sixty. From his home in Covington, Kentucky, he could survey his domain, content to see that what he had proposed for himself when young had pretty much come to pass. His still large and powerful frame was slightly at odds these days with the little wire-rimmed spectacles—an old lady's glasses, a pair, in fact, almost identical to those Hannah wore—perched on his nose. But even as old age began to put a gentle curve in his broad back he remained a model of self-education, ambition and willpower. Jesse had made it. A thousand may have failed for every frontier youth who succeeded, but what of that? The stink of the beam room was far in the past. The malodorous frontier tan yard had grown into a leather business that covered much of the Midwest. With a net worth of a hundred thousand dollars, he was the 1850s equivalent of a 1990s multimillionaire, and still the money was piling up. Jesse had vowed to quit when he reached sixty, and he could do it. He had all the money he would ever need, and his six children could each look forward to a substantial inheritance. His daughter Mary had married, and Virginia still lived at home. His son Simpson ran the leather store in Galena, Illinois, and Ulysses was one of the youngest captains in the Army. He would probably end up as a colonel in command of a regiment if he hung on long enough.

Then, in early June, Jesse learned that Ulysses had resigned his commission. He was appalled. The waste of it! The stupidity of it! Jesse
appealed directly to the secretary of war, Jefferson Davis, to reject his
son's resignation. It was only prolonged separation from his family that
had forced his son to act so rashly, Jesse informed Davis. He begged
him to grant Ulysses a six-month furlough so he could come home and
see his wife and children. Many officers had enjoyed such furloughs,
but not Ulysses. Besides, "I think after spending so much time to qual-
ify himself in the Army, & spending so many years in the servis [*sic*], he
will be poorly qualifyed [*sic*] for the pursuits of privet [*sic*] life . . ."
Davis coolly replied that the resignation, having been accepted, could
not be reconsidered.[1]

Meanwhile, Captain Grant was recovering from his various illnesses
and putting his regimental quartermaster accounts in order. That done,
he left Fort Humboldt and made his way to San Francisco, intending to
reclaim the $1,750 he had on deposit with a former Army officer, now a
banker, Captain Thomas H. Stevens. What he got from Stevens was not
hard cash but dishonest excuses. It wasn't until 1863, when Grant was a
man to be reckoned with, that Stevens, under strong pressure from Julia,
finally coughed up.[2]

Fortunately, Grant had $250 in accumulated Army pay and
allowances to collect, but he spent some of that in San Francisco while
waiting for a ship to carry him to Panama. He was disappointed with the
way the city had changed. In just two years it had become "staid and
orderly." It was no longer the rip-roaring, wide-open, colorful place he
remembered fondly but a place that was safe for women and children . . . if not for innocent investors.[3]

While crossing Panama, Grant gave forty dollars to an old soldier
who was sick and broke, and bailed out a couple of other travelers who
were down on their luck. By the time he arrived in New York, on June
25, Grant was virtually penniless, but he expected that would soon be
put right.[4]

Back at Fort Vancouver, when he had formed a partnership with
Elijah Camp to build a general store, the business had flourished. But
this was just about the only business Grant ever put money into that
turned into a profitable venture. Camp had later pressured and cajoled
Grant into selling him his half-share in the business for $1,500. Grant
accepted $700 in cash and Camp's note for the remaining $800.

Shortly after buying Grant out, Camp saw the business go up in smoke. The store sold mining supplies, including gunpowder, and one day an almighty explosion reduced the store and its contents to matchsticks and dust.[5]

A bitterly disappointed Camp left California soon after and returned to Sackets Harbor to start anew. When Grant reached New York he still held Camp's note for $800 and (unwisely) sent a message to Camp to let him know he was coming to Sackets Harbor.

Grant made the long trek across New York State. When he reached Sackets Harbor, he learned that Camp was doing even better back east than he had ever done out west. Business was booming and he had recently bought a brand-new yacht . . . which he was sailing somewhere on Lake Ontario when Grant arrived.[6]

Unable even to see Camp, except perhaps on the distant horizon, Grant headed back to New York City and checked into a hotel. He sent messages to his parents and his wife that he had returned from the Pacific Coast. With virtually all his money gone he was in serious straits.

An old Army friend assigned to Governors Island, Captain Simon Bolivar Buckner, had to vouch for his bill at the Astor House Hotel, reassuring the anxious manager that he would be paid, eventually. Jesse sent him some money and Grant traveled to Covington. His return was more a new humiliation stoically borne than a new venture boldly begun.[7]

His father was reported to have said bitterly, "West Point spoiled one of my boys for business," forgetting whose idea it had been for his eldest son to go there in the first place. Hannah, on the other hand, was far from upset. "I was sorry Ulysses ever had anything to do with this Army business," she told her cousin.[8]

From Bethel, Grant made his way back to the Dent farm. One afternoon near the end of August, he drove up to White Haven in a rented buggy. Two small boys were playing on the front porch—four-year-old Fred and the son Grant had never seen, two-year-old Ulysses, Jr. The children weren't used to seeing strange men with long beards driving up to the front gate like that, jumping down from a buggy and coming straight toward them, and they shrieked in alarm, until a female slave rushed out from the kitchen, and saw the cause of the commotion. "For the Lord's sake, here is Marss Grant!"[9]

★

The year 1854 produced a bumper crop of resignations from the Army. Promotion was glacially slow and pay was poor. Many of the most promising officers quit to start again as bankers and engineers, lawyers and businessmen. Braxton Bragg, who had won three brevets in Mexico, left for a plantation in Mississippi. Henry Halleck, considered one of the smartest men in the Army, departed abruptly, seduced by the appeal of California, where he set up as a mining expert and lawyer. George McClellan, the former child prodigy, left to become president of a railroad. William S. Rosecrans departed for a career as a civil engineer. All told, more than a dozen officers who would soon be back in uniform, whether of blue or gray, and rise to a general's stars left at about the same time Grant did. But nobody started from a lower base than he.[10]

Jesse offered him a place in the Grant store in Galena, Illinois, but Ulysses turned it down. He preferred to try farming instead. Julia owned nearly a hundred acres, given to her as a wedding present. This tract of land offered nothing but a grinding struggle. Most of it was too hilly for arable farming, making it more suitable for grazing sheep and cattle than growing prairie wheat, which currently brought a high price in the fast-growing cities of the East. Much of the land that was level enough to be harvested was still covered with trees, so it would have to be cleared. Not a single building stood on Julia's property. Not a dollar had been spent on improvements. Everything would have to be done from scratch. Grant was nevertheless excited. "When I resigned from the Army and went to a farm, I was happy" was how he remembered it.[11]

In the late fall of 1854 he and Julia moved into the house her brother Louis had built, a large and ugly farmhouse called Wish-ton-Wish (the local Indian word for "whippoorwill"). Living under any Dent roof had no appeal for Grant. To Julia's bewilderment, as soon as spring 1855 rolled around he started building a house on her hundred acres. He wanted a home he could call his own, something simple and robust, an expression of his spirit, not Louis Dent's. For the next eighteen months he put every hour he could spare into building a house with his own hands, from cutting down the trees to provide the wood to putting in the windows and chimney. He gently mocked the pretensions of the Dents, who gave their homes fancy names. Grant called his place Hardscrabble.[12]

Jesse put up most of the money Grant needed to stock his farm and build a house on it. There was no doubt that Grant loved farming. The land was poor, however, and the farm was never going to provide much beyond food for his own table and enough money to get by on. While he waited for his crops to grow, he relied on cutting down his trees and selling firewood in St. Louis and pit props to local miners. At times, he also rented out his horses for cash.

However much Grant may have enjoyed working the land and steering a team of horses from behind a plow, the life he had chosen was likely to put him into an early grave. His present contentment was caused not only by having his family with him but because he had work to do, in abundance. Grant had a hunger for work that the peacetime Army had rarely satisfied; like his appetite for liquor, it proved greater than his slender physique could stand.

Work kept depression at bay and provided a sense of accomplishment. As for any man, work gave Grant a chance both to lose himself, if he chose, and to find himself, if he chose. At this stage of his life, he probably preferred the losing to the finding. But wherever he was, he had to have work to do—hard work, serious work, and plenty of it—to keep boredom and restlessness away.

He threw himself into it now as if trying to make amends for countless idle hours out west. Building up a farm provided labor enough for any man; trying to build a house at the same time was too much. Grant aged rapidly and was often stiff-jointed and in agony from rheumatism. Malaria, which he had picked up in Nicaragua during his return from the West Coast, periodically forced him to remain in bed shaking, sweating and exhausted. And his old chest problems returned, reviving the old fear that he would die of tuberculosis, or "consumption."

What work had to be done, he did mainly by himself. If he had to resort to having black people work alongside him, he preferred hiring freemen to those enslaved. And to the disgust of neighboring farmers, he paid his freemen more than the current rate for black farmhands.[13]

Although Julia owned four slaves—two male, two female—Grant made it clear to his wife and her family that he was "opposed to slavery as an institution." And he told his wife's slaves that it was his ambition to give all of them their freedom "as soon as I am able." Grant never doubted that there was, ultimately, only one race—the human race. When a neighbor questioned the potential loyalty of one of the Dents' slaves, Grant responded, "I don't know why a black skin may not cover a true heart as well as a white one."[14]

Far from exploiting blacks, said a neighbor, Grant was "tyrannized over by the Negroes given to his wife." At times, Julia tried to get him to punish them for some offense, real or imagined. "Aren't you going to whip [them] for doing that?" she wanted to know. Grant would reply, "No—I guess not," and smile at her, which was as good a way as any of indicating the subject was closed. On one occasion when he saw a neighbor whipping a slave, he intervened and put an immediate stop to this barbarity.[15]

The evidence is only circumstantial, but Grant appears to have bought a slave from his father-in-law in order to set the man free. It was certainly in keeping with his goal of eventually freeing all of Julia's slaves. This venture appears to have begun in October 1858, when Ulysses sounded out Jesse about sending a slave to him to learn to be a farrier—"He is a very smart, active boy, capable of making anything."[16]

Nothing came of this, but six months later, Grant signed a certificate of manumission, freeing a slave known as William Jones. A male slave in good health was worth about fifteen hundred dollars, and Grant was financially hard-pressed. Setting William Jones free under these circumstances bordered on the melodramatic. It was an unspoken declaration of how he felt about slavery, especially when it involved an intelligent and capable person.[17]

Even though he had left the Army, Grant was bound to it emotionally. When he went into St. Louis with a cartload of wood for sale, there was always a good chance he might see old Army friends in the street. Sometimes he took his load over to Jefferson Barracks, where he was sure to catch up on the gossip and be able to reminisce about the great adventure, Mexico. His friends, in their gold braid and youthful vitality, could see him dwindling from year to year, like a light that was fading. The old blue Army overcoat got shabbier and turned to a sludgy gray, the muddy pantaloons tucked into the tops of the cracked boots got more threadbare, the old slouch hat pulled down on Grant's small head became increasingly disreputable.

One day in September 1857 he encountered Sherman walking down the street. Sherman had left the Army in 1853, gone to San Francisco, prospered briefly, then failed miserably as a banker. "I'm a dead cock in the pit," said Sherman glumly. He did not have to ask how Grant was doing. It was pretty obvious. Anyway, Sherman was feeling too sorry for himself to worry about Grant's problems. He blamed his fate on West Point and the Army—"not good schools for farmers and bankers," he said bitterly. Grant could have replied that no one ever believed they were, but he didn't.[18]

On these visits to St. Louis, Grant was likely to look in at the Planters House, a hotel favored by Army officers. He sat in the lobby smoking a clay pipe. When a group of officers invited him to join them in the bar for a drink, he told them, "I will go in and look at you, but I never drink anything." This was an exaggeration. Grant still drank occasionally, but these days decent alcohol, like good cigars, was a luxury he could not often afford.[19]

On a rainy day when Longstreet was at the Planters House, he found several officers willing to play poker, but they said the game would be better if they had at least one more hand. Longstreet went to the front of the hotel to see if he could rustle up another player and found Grant there, obviously eager for company. Longstreet took Grant inside. The deck was shuffled, cards were dealt. And Grant sat there, the living embodiment of just how far a man could fall when he threw away a promising career in the Army. It was a subject that nagged at the back of everyone's mind, but no one even hinted at it. They talked about everything and anything except what Grant was doing these days.[20]

Besides, Grant much preferred talking about war. There was not only Mexico to recall. In 1859, when France went to war with Austria, Grant bought some maps, read the newspapers assiduously, traced the campaign as it unfolded, and offered a critique to anyone who would listen. This was Grant the armchair strategist, living in his imagination battles between armies he had never seen, fighting over issues he knew almost nothing about. War, which he always claimed to dislike, fascinated Grant like no other subject in the world.[21]

After nearly two years of effort, Hardscrabble was finished. Grant insisted on moving his family into it. The house was a two-story structure with three bedrooms and a certain roughhewn charm. Julia had been against his building it and disliked it long before it was finished. To her, it was little better than a shack compared to Wish-ton-Wish. She lived at Hardscrabble only three months, until her mother died. Julia was then able to convince Grant they had to move into White Haven to help look after her grieving father.[22]

Living with "Colonel" Dent made Grant squirm. He loathed the old man, and Dent made no bones about his contempt for his son-in-law the failure, the Yankee fool who had thrown away a promising Army career, unlike Fred Dent, who was sticking it out and doing well in the military. Thought he could be a farmer and failed at that, too. It gave Dent a malicious satisfaction to tell Julia that her husband had made a mess of his life.[23]

Then, in October 1857, the economy crashed. One of the worst depressions in American history closed thousands of banks, wiped out tens of thousands of businesses, and put millions of people out of work. St. Louis had been booming, but almost overnight its economy fell apart as the price of prairie wheat went into free fall. Grant's precarious venture into farming was close to collapse, and now he was trying to save not only his own farm but Dent's, too.

Even the small sums of cash from selling firewood at four dollars a cord dried up. Grant was broke, and just before Christmas 1857 he pawned his gold watch for twenty-two dollars, probably to buy presents for his three children (a daughter had joined the family) and Julia, who was pregnant again.[24]

Two months after Christmas, in February 1858, Julia gave birth to her fourth and last child, a son named Jesse Root Grant. Ulysses, meanwhile, was begging his father to help save the farm, but the old tanner had already sunk two thousand dollars into this doomed enterprise. Besides, the economic crisis was creating problems for his leather business. Jesse was more reluctant than ever to put hard-earned Grant money into worthless Dent land. He urged his son to walk away from the wreckage and bring Julia and the children to Kentucky. Grant was willing, but Julia would not even consider it. The whole Grant family, she was convinced, despised her, with the possible exception of Hannah.[25]

Grant persevered with the farm until his health broke down under the strain. In the summer of 1858 he rented it out. He lacked the strength to work it and the money to hire others to work it in his stead. Grant sold off his farming implements and the horses. Desperate for an income, he formed a partnership with a local property tycoon, Harry Boggs, who was one of Julia's cousins. Grant became a rent collector.[26]

A less likely person to put the pressure on debtors to turn out their pockets would be hard to imagine. Anyone with a hard-luck story was sure to get a break. Similarly, when Grant assumed responsibility for finding tenants for empty properties, he was inclined to take them on trust. One of the tenants he found for Boggs proved to be a prostitute, and for her, home was also her workplace.[27]

Grant was a tenderhearted and sentimental man, an inevitable reflection of his fundamentally romantic nature. Few things gave him more pleasure than to sit in a flower garden grasping the beauty of the blooms with his eyes while his nose absorbed their bouquet.[28]

People did not have to come to him and ask for help. Grant had a social reformer's conscience. There was, for example, a day laborer whose mule was seized to satisfy a court judgment. The man was poor and had sometimes worked for Grant. When the mule was put up for auction, Grant bought it for fifty dollars and gave it back to the original owner. But the writ called for a "change of possession," so the mule was seized again. This time, however, no one would bid against Grant at the auction and he bought the mule for five dollars. He gave it back to the man once again—and it was seized for the third time! No "change of possession" had taken place. Grant bought it, this time for one dollar, but advised the owner to take it to another county and trade it for another mule. But if even this did not work, said Grant, "I am going to have that old mule even if I have to buy it once a week all summer!"[29]

Not surprisingly, Grant's venture into debt-collecting was as hopeless as his efforts at farming. But Grant, the offspring of ancient Puritan root-stock, remained convinced that tenacity brought better answers to life's challenges than mere intelligence, cunning or riches. He believed that a man's life was shaped by his character, not that character was a malleable medium that took its shape from a man's life. Unlike "Colonel" Dent, a Jeeter Lester type who spiraled on down when the going got rough, Grant never quit trying. As his quixotic venture into debt-collecting drew to its swift and inevitable close, he thought he saw the way ahead. He would turn his West Point training and military experience to advantage and become superintendent of roads for St. Louis County.

The West Point curriculum provided the best engineering education in the United States, and Grant's time out west had taught him more than a little about surveying. Thirty-five of the most prominent men in St. Louis put their names to a testimonial recommending him for the job, which paid sixteen hundred dollars a year.[30]

Nevertheless, Grant feared his qualifications were irrelevant, along with the thirty-five signatures. "I am not over sanguine about getting the apointment [*sic*]," he informed his father.[31] This was a political sinecure, and in 1859 there was only one political question—slavery.

Grant was against slavery. No one who knew him well doubted that. Of the five people who would vote on the appointment, three were not only vehemently antislavery, they were looking ahead to the possible breakup of the Union. And what they noticed was not Grant's training in engineering or his experiences out west but the fact that he was living in the home of "Colonel" Dent, a man whose splenetic proslavery views marked him out as a potential rebel. What's more, Grant's wife owned four slaves. One way or another, Grant had chosen to live in the bosom of the slavocracy.[32]

According to Grant, the appointment went to a German immigrant. This imagined slight still rankled more than twenty years later, when Grant wrote in his *Personal Memoirs,* "My opponent had the advantage of birth over me [he was a citizen by adoption] and carried off the prize." Frustrated, terrified of poverty and deeply hurt, Grant reacted by joining the Know-Nothings, a nativist political faction that was anti-immigrant and anti-Catholic. He was a Know-Nothing for only one week, the time it took him to cool down, but this was hardly Grant's finest hour. In fact, the engineer's post actually went to someone called Edward Gray, as native-born as himself.[33]

Meanwhile, he had swapped Hardscrabble for a small house in one of the poorer parts of St. Louis plus a note for three thousand dollars. The family that signed the note soon fell behind in their payments and Grant had to sue them to get his property back, a process that took eight years.[34]

In the winter of 1859 he was, for a month or so, a customs officer. But he had hardly managed to get back onto the Federal payroll before he was unceremoniously dumped when the incumbent collector died and a new man was appointed. In early 1860 his situation was about as desperate as it could be. Julia, who had resisted every attempt by Jesse to get his eldest son to leave the domain of the Dents, finally relented. She suggested he go and ask his father to help him. Grant was reluctant. "I do not see that I can very well. It will cost something, and we have nothing to spare."[35]

Grant really had no choice. In March 1860 he made the three-day journey to Covington, Kentucky. Not surprisingly, he arrived with one of his migraine headaches. Before long, however, he and his father had reached an agreement. Ulysses would join Simpson and the youngest son, Orvil, in the Galena leather store.[36]

Jesse was almost certainly glad to see the prodigal son come home at last. For one thing, it meant that he and Hannah would see a lot more of the grandchildren. For another, Simpson was seriously ill, dying slowly of tuberculosis. As for Orvil, a young man of twenty-four, he was simply not to be trusted. Orvil was the black sheep of the Grants and would one day help disgrace his brother's presidency.[37]

Back in 1854, when Jesse retired, everything was going according to plan. By 1860, though, the economy was still mired in depression and the leather empire that he had built up from nothing faced an uncertain future. God disposes.

CHAPTER 9

"THE SOUTH WILL FIGHT"

One April day in 1860, Grant came down the gangway of the steamboat *Itasca* to embark on a new career. The two-hundred-foot bluff of Galena rose before him like a gigantic green tabula rasa inviting a fresh beginning. The town looked as lively and promising as most trading centers along the Mississippi. The truth, though, was that Galena had blown its chances. This bustling home to fourteen thousand people, with dozens of well-established businesses huddled at the bottom of the bluff, their roots deep in the river, had kissed tomorrow goodbye. It was Grant, an unremarkable-looking bearded man in a black slouch hat and carrying a couple of kitchen chairs in each hand, to whom the future belonged, and not the busy town.[1]

Galena had thrived by shipping out huge quantities of the lead ore mined from the hills of northwestern Illinois. For twenty-five years it had profited handsomely from its excellent location on the broad river. Then, in the mid-1850s, the Illinois Central Railroad sought to make the town a major railhead. Galena's business elite complacently said no, the town would cling to what it knew—trading up and down the river. The Panic of 1857 ended Galena's prosperity virtually overnight. Once gone, it never came back.[2]

Grant rented an attractive two-story, seven-room house on fashionable Cemetery Hill, with a graveyard behind and magnificent views of the river and the town from the front porch. Julia was going to have to try managing it with hired help. Her father had used the servant question to try talking her out of leaving White Haven. "You know you cannot do without servants," he warned her brusquely, and it was true. Julia could not bake as much as a biscuit, let alone manage an entire house on her own. Yet she dared not take her four slaves to Galena. Illinois was a free state. It would not be long before her slaves started demanding proper wages and humane treatment or else. Out of the question. They would have to remain with Papa at White Haven, where uppity niggers got whipped.[3]

Julia resigned herself to dependence on a servant girl hired in Galena. One servant—that was all Ulysses, on his salary of eight hundred dollars a year from the leather store, could afford. To Julia's surprise, seeing her command shrink from four to one did not ruin her life. She marveled at how efficiently the house got cleaned, the laundry got done, the meals were cooked. One person who worked willingly accomplished as much as four who did not, but Julia failed to make that connection.[4]

Since Jesse Grant's retirement, Simpson Grant had done most of the traveling to buy hides and supervise the outposts of the empire—the Grant stores in La Crosse and Prairie du Chien, Wisconsin, and Cedar Rapids, Iowa. These days, though, Simpson was dying. Tuberculosis was killing him painfully and slowly. It would be Ulysses who did most of the traveling from now on, keeping an eye on the other stores, buying up hides, shipping them to the Grant tanneries in Kentucky, and seeing them come to Galena, finally, as treated leather, ready to be turned into belts and saddles, boots and bridles.

Grant's other major responsibility was collecting money owed the business, but he was as inept at dunning debtors as he had ever been. His father grumbled that what he recovered barely covered the cost of hiring a horse and buggy to go put the bite on the deadbeats.[5]

When he was not traveling, Ulysses Grant helped Orvil in the store, keeping track of the inventory and balancing the books. It was a life that promised nothing but dullness, security and routine, and all in sufficient abundance to smother the old craving for adventure. The work might have been more tolerable had he not found himself, for all intents and purposes, taking orders from Orvil, who was thirteen years his junior.[6]

And there were the customers—wanting to look at a bridle, wanting to haggle over shoes. That was clerk's work, and Grant had not changed. Now as before, "I was not a clerk." So he did not bother to learn the price of things. His mind was not made for cluttering with such trivia. Whenever Grant had to serve a customer, he guessed at the price and charged either too much or too little, indifferent to the error either way.[7]

He was also having to manage without one of the great sources of joy in his life—a handsome, spirited horse. Living in a nice house, paying for a servant, providing new clothes for the children and trying to pay off old debts left nothing for horseflesh. Grant, we may be sure, missed the company of horses, but there was nothing he could do about that.

All the while, he worried over his debts as if they were a kind of curse or a secret grief. Grant had left the Army owing money to various people and departed Missouri owing even more. It would be a long time before he got out of debt, and he was too rigidly bound by puritanical notions of duty and honor to live as a debtor without sacrificing some peace of mind to Mammon. But he was finally making progress. Near the end of 1860 he wrote a friend, "In my new employment I have become pretty conversant and am much pleased with it. I hope to be a partner soon, and am sanguine that a competency at least can be made out of the business."[8]

Grant passed almost unnoticed among the citizens of Galena during his first year in their town. Few knew anything much about him. At noon each day he went home for lunch, climbing the wooden steps that led from the business district to the top of the bluff two hundred feet above. The Grants did not visit other families, and other families did not visit them.[9]

Little Jesse sometimes waited on the porch for his father to appear, greeting him with a shrill challenge—"Mister, do you want to fight?" Grant's answer was usually, "I am a man of peace, Jess, but I will not be hectored by a person of your size." Falling to his knees, he let Jesse pummel him for a while with his tiny fists, before grabbing the boy. Then, laughing and rolling over while hugging his son, Grant would shout, "I give up! I give up!"[10]

Occasionally Grant played cards with the few people he knew in this part of the world, which gave him the chance to reminisce about Mexico, but the only time the Grants went anywhere *en famille* was on a Sunday morning, when they attended the Methodist church at the bottom of the wooden steps. Julia probably attended out of habit. Besides, it was a chance to leave the house for a while. Grant's motive was less the worship than the hope of a interesting sermon. Theology bored him rigid, but a passionate speaker with a vigorous line in damnation was free entertainment.[11]

Most evenings, while Julia sat by the fire with her needlework, Grant slumped in a nearby chair, smoking his clay pipe and reading. He was unusually well read, yet it was part of his mystique never to appear bookish. Grant had acquired the reading habit at West Point and it remained with him for life. Much of his time in California had been spent reading. So too had passed many hours on his failed farm. And now, during the long, cold nights of a winter in northern Illinois, he read assiduously. Besides, books provided more than intellectual stimulation. They offered a welcome if brief escape from the depressing contents of newspapers.[12]

★

The hour of the failures was at hand. The life of a great nation is both peace and war. Every man therefore gets his chance. For Grant, peace had brought only setbacks. He had excelled only in war. So, too, had another Mexican War veteran, Colonel Robert E. Lee. After nearly thirty years in the Army, he still did not have command of a regiment, let alone a star. Lee felt he had failed in his chosen career, for he sprang from generals. Sherman was another who had failed. The "dead cock in the pit" had recently become superintendent of a new and fairly unpromising military college down in Louisiana, for want of anything better to do. Disaster, however, was about to snatch yesterday's warriors from provincial obscurity.

Grant took comparatively little interest in politics but in November 1856 he happened to be riding past a polling station in St. Louis during the presidential election, which was being contested by Democrat James Buchanan of Pennsylvania and John Frémont, the "Pathfinder" and former Army officer who had surveyed Oregon and California. Frémont was representing the new Republican party and Grant couldn't stand Frémont. Too much a show-off, too shallow a man. He dismounted and tied his horse to a tree. Partly out of duty, but mainly for the sheer pleasure of it, he cast a vote against Frémont.[13]

Grant had hopes, all the same, that Buchanan would somehow find a compromise that would settle the slavery issue once and for all. Two

days before he was inaugurated, Buchanan made a thrilling announce-
ment: The Supreme Court was about to hand down a ruling that would
do just that. In the 1830s, a St. Louis farmer named Peter Blow had
owned a slave called Dred Scott and sold him to an Army surgeon
named John Emerson. During his time with Emerson, Dred Scott lived
in Minnesota and Illinois, both of which were free states. In 1847, Scott
filed a suit for damages. By virtue of having lived on free soil, he hoped
to establish that he was no longer a slave. By this time, Emerson was
dead, and as the case dragged from year to year, Dred Scott came, by a
complicated series of events, into the ownership of Taylor Blow, the son
of Peter Blow.

The legal decision, when it came, was a stunner. The seven Democratic judges, led by Chief Justice Roger Taney, declared that while
Dred Scott was a citizen of Missouri and might be considered free by a
Missouri court, he was not an American citizen, on account of being a
black man, and therefore had no rights under the Constitution that any
white person was obliged to respect. The two Republican judges vehemently, but impotently, disagreed.

The Dred Scott decision, like all irrational behavior, created alarm.
Its implication that slavery was a national institution created anger
throughout the North. By upholding the Constitution's view that black
people were not even human beings, it was simply nauseating to public
opinion in states such as Massachusetts and New York, where free
blacks were already considered citizens under state law, with equal
rights.[14]

Passions unleashed by this ludicrous judgment were still running
high when one of the most fervent of the abolitionist fanatics, John
Brown, struck back. In October 1859, Brown and a handful of like-
minded terrorists raided the Federal arsenal at Harpers Ferry, Virginia.
His aim, to the extent that someone so confused was able to formulate
one, was to create some kind of antislavery stronghold in the Appalachi-
ans and foment a black Spartacist uprising. The raid was, predictably,
botched—the first person shot dead by Brown's followers was a free
black man—and doomed to failure anyway. A company of Marines
commanded by Robert E. Lee soon recaptured Harpers Ferry and
Brown was taken prisoner and hanged a few weeks later.[15]

Grant did not simply follow these tumultuous events in the newspapers. He knew Taylor Blow, the man who owned Dred Scott. Back in St.

Louis, Taylor's brother Henry had been one of the local worthies who tried to get Grant appointed superintendent of county roads. Owen Brown, the father of John Brown, had been Jesse Grant's partner when he had set up his first tannery in Ohio. And although Ulysses Grant chose to avoid making an issue of it, understandably putting the happiness of his marriage ahead of all other concerns, he could never be happy that his wife owned slaves.[16]

The excruciating division over slavery that tormented America sorely troubled Grant despite all his efforts to avoid confronting it directly. His psyche became an arena where the tensions, passions and fears that slavery created did not simply converge but came to him with familiar faces and names. Several times a friend found Grant alone in his office at the back of the store, clutching a fresh newspaper, lost in despair. "It made my blood run cold to hear friends of mine, Southern men . . . discuss dissolution of the Union as though it were a tariff bill," said Grant some years later. "I could not endure it. . . . I wanted to leave the country if disunion was accomplished."[17]

Grant was unable to vote in the crucial presidential election of 1860. He had not lived in Illinois long enough to meet the residence requirements. Had he been able to vote, he would have cast his ballot for Stephen A. Douglas, the pint-sized, barrel-chested Democratic orator who had defeated the Republican candidate, Abraham Lincoln, in the Illinois senatorial election of 1858. Douglas, the "Little Giant," faced Lincoln again in 1860 for the biggest prize of all.

While Grant strongly favored Douglas (a point he carefully obscured in his memoirs), the fact was the "Little Giant" had no more idea of how to defuse the slavery time bomb than Buchanan. Cleverer than Buchanan, Douglas employed his superior intellect to construct a position that was nothing but evasion, ambiguity and legalistic hair-splitting. It was a position calculated to get him elected. He would tackle slavery—maybe—after that.

Lincoln, on the other hand, grasped the nettle. There was only one issue in this election and that issue was a clear moral choice. If black people were human beings, then slavery was wrong. Not even the equivocating Douglas could bring himself to say black people weren't human. All Douglas offered was more delay, but for someone like Grant, who had no illusions about the alternative, there seemed to be hope in delay and none in war.[18]

The streets of northern towns already echoed to the heavy rhythmic cadences of marching men. Radical Republicans organized marching clubs called Wide Awakes. Democrats organized themselves as the Douglas Guards, and the Galena chapter invited Grant to join it and take responsibility for training. He turned them down cold. "Having held a commission as captain in the Army of the United States, I do not think it becoming for me now to serve a citizen body, though semi-military, as its orderly sergeant." In other words, I was a regular soldier and an officer and I won't waste my time on a bunch of amateurs who want to play at being soldiers. Even so, curiosity got the better of him a couple of times and he stopped by to see how they were doing.[19]

On Election Day, November 8, 1860, Galena narrowly voted for Douglas—by only twenty-nine votes of more than fifteen hundred cast. The nation, however, made Lincoln the first President with only a plurality in the popular vote. That night, with returns clacking over the telegraph wires, the Wide Awakes dragged a pair of cannon up the bluffs, lit bonfires, blew martial blasts on brass trumpets, set off fireworks and rocked the town with explosions from the cannon. Down at the Grant store Orvil, a radical Republican like his father, handed out oysters and beer. But while Orvil was jubilant, Grant's mood was grim. "The South will fight," he told the Grant company's lawyer, John A. Rawlins.[20]

★

The unthinkable had become thinkable. The South, unable to manage either transition to a postslavery economy or irrevocable economic decline, was now talking only to itself as it sought to defend the indefensible, slavery, and deny the undeniable, union. It had become a paradigm of the closed society. And like closed societies everywhere, it was driven by extreme emotions into paranoid delusions and reckless action. There was such anger with the world beyond its narrow perspective that the South seemed at times almost to welcome its own destruction, like a suicide leaping with a shout into the raging sea.

A month after Lincoln's election, South Carolina passed the Ordinance of Secession. By February 1861 six states had declared their secession from the Union, and delegates from all six, meeting in Montgomery, Alabama, created the Confederate States of America and elected Jefferson Davis their President. An excited prosecessionist acquaintance of Grant's burst into the store to tell Grant what had happened. Grant was appalled. "Davis and the whole gang of them ought to be hung!"[21]

Two months later, on April 15, Fort Sumter, guarding the harbor of Charleston, South Carolina, was bombarded into submission by Confederate artillery. News of the fort's surrender ignited the passions that northerners had, until now, managed to control. Galena, like a thousand other northern towns, erupted with patriotic fervor.

A town meeting was called for the evening of April 16. The Galena courthouse was packed with agitated men—politics was man's work—excited, fearful, angry, desperate for leadership. The mayor, Robert Brand, was a Democrat and tried to temporize. What the South had done was wrong, he acknowledged, but brother shouldn't fight brother Surely some compromise could be worked out even now.

The mayor's advice was rejected by Galena's congressman, a Republican named Elihu B. Washburne, who proposed several militant resolutions. But it was John A. Rawlins who demolished Brand's equivocation. In an impassioned forty-five-minute speech, Rawlins reviewed the events leading up to the crisis. "I have been a Democrat all my life," he concluded. "But this is no longer a question of politics. It is simply Union or disunion, country or no country. I have favored every honorable compromise, but the day for compromise is past. Only one course is left for us. We will stand by the flag of our country and appeal to the god of battles to vindicate our flag!" The word *battles* brought a satisfying, bellicose roar that rocked the stone courthouse.[22]

Grant was sitting somewhere near the back of the room. As he listened to Rawlins's speech, it seemed to crystallize and focus his own emotions. Whatever lingering doubts remained in his mind were dispelled by Rawlins's eloquence. Until now, he had not been much impressed by Rawlins, a young man of twenty-nine who had clawed his way up from a wretched, impoverished upbringing to become the most successful trial lawyer in Galena. Grant tended to dislike lawyers anyway. Rawlins had an unhealthy pallor (and was destined to die of tuberculosis before he reached forty), a bushy dark beard, glittering black eyes, a blunt and abrasive way of talking to people, an obvious lack of social graces, and an equally evident inferiority complex. That night, however, he reached deep into himself and pulled out the inspirational climax this momentous occasion demanded. Grant made a mental note on Rawlins.[23]

Lincoln responded to the attack on Fort Sumter by calling for 75,000 men to serve for the traditional militia term, three months. The regular Army, numbering only 17,000 officers and men, was far too small and too widely scattered to bring the Confederacy to its knees. A mere 75,000 volunteers were not going to do that either, but Lincoln knew what he was doing. The first task was to protect Washington, which involved occupying Maryland and northeastern Virginia.

The quota for Illinois was six volunteer regiments. Galena's patriots promptly organized a meeting to recruit a company, and Congressman Washburne shrewdly manipulated the situation so that Grant, the one man in town who had any real military experience, ended up presiding over the meeting. Washburne evidently hoped this would lead to Grant taking command of the company, but Grant declined. He had greater ambitions than being a captain again—a captain of regulars was at least the equal of a colonel in the militia. So he turned down the captaincy, but would help recruit the men and drill them.[24]

In the meantime, he wrote a letter to his father-in-law, essentially to rub the "Colonel's" nose in some unpalatable truths. "The North is responding to the President's call in such a manner that the rebels may truly quaik [*sic*]. I tell you, there is no mistaking the feeling of the people. The Government can call into the field not only 75000 troops but ten or twenty times 75000 if it should be necessary and find the means of maintaining them too. . . . No impartial man can conceal from himself the fact that in all these troubles the South have been the aggressors and the Administration has stood purely on the defensive. . . . In all this, I can but see the doom of Slavery."[25]

To his father he wrote to explain why the store would have to manage without him: "We are now in the midst of trying times when evry [*sic*] one must be for or against his country. . . . Having been educated for such an emergency, at the expense of the Government, I feel that it has upon me superior claims, such claims as no ordinary motives of self-interest can surmount."[26]

There were enough volunteers to man not one company but two. Grant drilled them on the expansive lawn of the Washburne mansion, with pine laths substituting for muskets. He also designed a uniform for them to wear. On April 25, the first company of Galena volunteers marched proudly through town, in brand-new uniforms of dark blue frock coats and light gray trousers, to catch the train to Springfield, where volunteer companies were being assembled into regiments.

Galena was drowning in flags and bunting. Its people were almost mad with patriotic fervor at the sight of their sons and husbands going to war. This was war as sport, as adventure, as righteousness, its immanent tears and heartbreak as distant and unimaginable as the stars. When the column of 150 men, their faces beatifically wreathed in delirious grins, approached the "dee-po," Grant appeared as if from nowhere. Still a civilian, still slouching toward his destiny, he fell in at the rear, carrying a well-traveled carpetbag.[27]

————— ★ ★ ★ ★ —————

CHAPTER 10

"I CAN'T WAIT
ANY LONGER"

Lincoln, his gaunt, gloomy face looking out from the White House onto streets echoing to the tramp of marching men and the rattle of artillery caissons, had saved the nation's capital with his call for 75,000 short-term militia. The response had been phenomenal. It showed the North was ready to fight. It showed something else, too—that if the President wanted a large and powerful army to prosecute the war, all he had to do was ask.

On May 3 he called for 42,000 volunteers who would serve for three years. The recruiting stations were swamped all over again. Lincoln showed how big he really expected the war to be not in the modest number he had asked for but in the huge number he accepted—230,000 men. These three-year volunteers became the bedrock of the Union Army.

The commanding general, Winfield Scott, meanwhile made a serious mistake. Some members of his staff thought he ought to break up the regular Army and distribute its officers and sergeants—its experience, that is—among the huge volunteer force the President was creating. It would have been possible to assign two regular officers to every volunteer regiment raised in 1861 and put a regular sergeant in every company to advise on training, discipline and hygiene.[1]

Old Fuss and Feathers was too attached to the regular Army to consider breaking it up. He advised Lincoln to enlarge it, but tried to prevent regular officers leaving to take command of volunteer units. Only those with strong political connections managed to get away during the twelve months following Fort Sumter. Most regulars remained where they were when the war began—out west, fighting the Indians. It was the Confederacy that demonstrated the benefits of having experienced officers and sergeants distributed among amateur regiments and divisions. The Union Army consisted almost entirely of inexperienced officers leading totally ignorant troops. With a leavening of regulars, the Union Army could have become an effective fighting force in a year. Without an infusion of experience, it could not hope to reach that goal in less than two.

While Lincoln was trying to create an army, Grant was in Springfield wondering if he would ever get into the war. He carried a short letter from Washburne to Governor Richard Yates recommending him for a colonelcy. While he waited for Yates to act—and by this time the governor probably had dozens of applications for regimental command to consider—Grant made himself useful in the office of the state adjutant general. For five weeks he performed menial clerical tasks, compiling an inventory of the state's armories and advising how to handle Army paperwork. It was a chore, but at two dollars a day it easily covered his modest expenses.[2]

When Yates began awarding colonel's eagles to others and seemed to take no notice of him, Grant felt slighted and convinced himself his failure was the result of his rectitude, the payoff from his refusal to plunge into the sordid scramble for advantage that he saw swirling around him. He informed his father that he was "perfectly sickened at the political wire pulling for commissions" and that this accounted for his lack of success.[3]

The greatest obstacle to Grant's hopes was not his high-mindedness but the fact that Yates had been told he was "a deadbeat" Army officer who had been forced to leave active service under a cloud. Yates had no objection to employing him on mundane tasks, but a colonelcy was out of the question.

The adverse reports on Grant may have been poured into the gubernatorial ear by Captain John Pope, who had served in Mexico with Grant. Pope, still on active duty with the regular Army, was mustering in the six Illinois regiments that were called to serve for thirty days. Mustering in consisted mainly of compiling an accurate roll of the men in each regiment and swearing them in to military service. As Yates's military adviser, Pope was in a powerful position to decide who got what, and for now Grant got nothing.[4]

While the six regiments were being mustered in, an election was held for a brigade commander. Pope expected to be elected brigadier general. Instead, another officer was chosen and Pope departed Springfield in a mighty huff. Yet there was still mustering in to be done. Yates asked Grant to go to Mattoon, where the Seventh Congressional District Regiment was being assembled, and muster it in.

The regimental commander, Colonel Simon S. Goode, was a former city clerk from Decatur who, a few years earlier, had taken part in an attempt to seize Nicaragua. Goode shoved three revolvers and a bowie knife into his belt, draped himself in an impressive cloak, spouted Napoleonic aphorisms and claimed he never slept. Even his amateur soldiers did not take long to figure out that Goode was just another bullshit artist. When Grant showed up, he proceeded in his prosaic and conscientious way to show the regiment how a professional soldier operated. The contrast between Grant's grasp of reality and Goode's feverish embrace of fantasy made a lasting impression on some of the regiment's officers.[5]

His mustering in chore done, Grant went to St. Louis, to visit "Colonel" Dent, see some old Army friends and, he hoped, get command of a regiment from Missouri. His efforts to secure a colonelcy failed. His Army friends were glad to see him but unable to help. He also had to endure a lecture from his father-in-law on the glorious opportunities available to him in the Confederate Army. The old man's arguments were wasted not only on Grant but on young Fred Dent, too. Like Grant, Fred was sticking with the Union. As for Grant, he returned to Springfield, broke and depressed.

Once more he hung around the state capitol like a mendicant—too dignified to beg outright, but pathetic in the way he flaunted his availability. An acquaintance who saw him there looking forlorn asked him what he was doing these days. "Nothing," said Grant glumly. "Waiting."[6]

The amateurs having failed him, he turned to the professionals. On May 24 he wrote to the adjutant general in Washington, begging for command of one of the new infantry regiments being raised in the regular Army. "I would say that in view of my present age, and length of service, I feel myself competent to command a Regiment," wrote Grant. In the haste and confusion of the most rapid mobilization in American history, his plea was, not surprisingly, misfiled. But even had it been carefully weighed, the chance of his getting one of the new regiments was close to zero. They would go to officers who had *not* resigned their commissions during the dull, testing years of peace.[7]

Grant went to see his parents in Covington, Kentucky, and took advantage of the proximity of Cincinnati, on the other side of the river, to go visit the headquarters of an acquaintance from Mexico and California, George McClellan, who was presently overseeing the creation of militia regiments on behalf of the governor of Ohio. McClellan was away from his headquarters, but after the war he stoutly claimed that had he been aware of the visit, he would have readily given Grant a command. In the dazzling glare of Grant's triumph over Lee, he could hardly have said anything else without appearing a complete idiot. It seems unlikely, though, that McClellan would have offered Grant anything except his regrets back in 1861.[8]

The situation was beginning to look desperate. Grant was convinced the war would be over in six months. It was mental torture to contemplate a war for the salvation of the United States without any role for himself. Throwing all scruples aside, Grant reached for the only political wire within his grasp and pulled hard. He was already acquainted with the governor of Ohio, William Dennison, and had served in Mexico with a member of the Ohio legislature, a former Army officer named Chilton White.

Before leaving Cincinnati, Grant went to see White, reminisced about Mexico, and told him plaintively, "I've tried to re-enter the service, in vain." Ohio was currently raising regiments of three-year volunteers and needed colonels to command them. White promised him, "I'll see what can be done."[9]

While Grant was in Ohio, Simon Goode's Seventh District Regiment was falling apart. The men went into Mattoon every night and got riproaring drunk. They raided local henhouses, mutinied over the bread they were given, and when Goode tried to punish the offenders, they burned down the guardhouse. As their thirty-day enlistments drew to a close, the men were being encouraged to volunteer all over again, this time for three years. They refused to do so and would not serve any longer under Goode. Half the twelve hundred men Grant had mustered in had already gone home.

Yates needed someone to take command of this problematic regiment. By now, it was far too unruly for an amateur soldier to handle. Besides, the regiment's officers had a preferred candidate—that quiet, efficient Captain Grant, who had mustered them in. On June 15, a reluctant Governor Yates sent a telegram to Grant, offering him command of the Seventh District Regiment.[10]

Grant immediately wired his acceptance to Springfield. Later that day a second telegram arrived, this time from William Dennison, offering him command of the 12th Ohio Volunteer Infantry. Too late. Illinois had won the race.[11]

Grant had his colonelcy at last, and the way he remembered it, he got *his*—unlike some people—entirely on merit. In truth, though, what happened was that Grant had found it impossible to wait for a colonel's bird to alight on his shoulders. The only thing he would not do was put himself up for election by the men, which is how most militia colonels got their commands. Other than that, he had tried everything he could think of, including political wire-pulling, contacting old Army friends, trying to cultivate the goodwill of Governor Yates, trying to see McClellan, and writing directly to the War Department. He had refused to put his trust in providence. And his efforts finally paid off.[12]

The search for a regiment revealed something about the kind of commander Grant was likely to be. He was not a man to wait on events. Once his objective was fixed, he became restless and energetic. If one approach failed, he was quick to try something else. Yet when he came to write his memoirs, how easy—how human, too—to forget how desperately he had sought a colonelcy back in the dusty days of obscurity.[13]

★

Farm boys—the unpolished gems of the infantry. Raw-boned, fresh-faced, used to getting up early, accustomed to being cold and wet, inured to hard physical labor, strong in limb, and no strangers to blood, mud and sudden death. Down the ages farm boys have been the preferred raw material for infantry commanders to turn into soldiers. Grant's regiment was made up mainly of farm boys, dressed in their old work clothes, still waiting to receive uniforms from the Army, and full of promise.[14]

He himself did not have a uniform or that other essential for a colonel, a horse. He returned to Galena and a former business partner of his father's endorsed a note for five hundred dollars. That allowed Grant to get himself measured for a uniform and buy a fine horse, saddle and spurs.[15]

The six hundred men of the Seventh District Regiment who had agreed to sign on for three years were presently encamped at Camp Yates, on the outskirts of Springfield, sheltered in a collection of miserable huts. During the first couple of weeks that Grant commanded the regiment they probed the limits, much as schoolchildren test out a new teacher. The first and most obvious thing they disliked was his down-at-the-heels appearance, and some muttered loud enough for him to hear, "What a colonel!" and "Damn, such a colonel!" One soldier came up behind him and slapped him on the back hard enough to dislodge Grant's hat. Some of the officers even seemed to mock him, showing up at a dress parade in their shirtsleeves. He terminated the parade, calmly told the officers they were out of uniform, and dismissed the men.

Grant handled every infraction coolly, guided by a firm idea of what was needed. He intended to turn his farm boys into soldiers—real soldiers, as good as regulars. If he could make them want the same thing, they would arrive there eventually. But if they thought for a minute that he might accept something less, they would not even come close.

When morning roll call took place an hour late, he told the officer in charge, "Captain, this is no time for calling the roll. Order your men to their quarters." The troops found they had nothing to eat that day. The morning report had not been completed, because the roll had not been called. And without a morning report, rations could not be distributed. The men spent the next twenty-four hours feeling hungry. There was no angry scene, no threat, no harsh words, just a memorable low-key demonstration of what happened when sand was thrown into the gears of the military machine. It was the last time roll call was late.[16]

When Grant took command on June 16, there were eighty club-wielding soldiers assigned to guard the camp, mainly to keep the men in at night. Yet the guardhouse was full, day after day. And not even the guards could be trusted. They took off one night, along with the men they were supposed to be guarding, to sample the local nightlife. Grant pointed out the possible consequences—in time of peace, a fine and thirty days at hard labor, but "in time of war the punishment of this is death." He recognized that the soldiers involved did not realize how serious an offense they had just committed, but "it will not be excused again in this Regt."[17]

Grant systematically but calmly punished the drunks, the absentees, the tardy and the recalcitrant, telling his soldiers just what he was doing and why he was doing it. Yet even as he presented himself as a picture of reasonableness, he was making greater demands than Goode had ever dreamed of, but he made even this palatable by creating a more varied routine.

Goode had tried to keep the men occupied by drilling them for up to six hours a day. Grant's regime called for three one-hour drill sessions a day. The rest of the time the men improved and cleaned their quarters, learned how to look after their equipment, kept the camp sanitary and fired their muskets, loaded with blanks, in volleys.

To develop the regiment properly, Grant first had to train the officers so they in turn could train the men. He taught them the ways of the regular Army and in the evenings they sat in their tents bent over books that tried to explain the mysteries of command and infantry maneuvers. Grant recognized that he, too, needed to study. Warfare had moved on since Mexico. He pored over William Hardee's *Tactics* and wrote away for a copy of the report that McClellan had written as an observer in the Crimean War of 1853.[18]

Unlike most Civil War officers, Grant did not believe in charismatic leadership. Until then, outstanding commanders had generally been those who could rally men on the field of battle, inspire them with visions of glory and lead them in heroic deeds. The other possibility was to rely on the harshest kind of military discipline, making men more afraid of their officers than of the enemy.

Anyway, Grant was too shy for charismatic leadership, and an army of American militia would never accept the brutal discipline of European armies. Inadvertently, he became the forerunner of the modern school-trained infantry officer, whose leadership depends far less on the variable elements of his own personality than upon systematic training, good communications with the troops and moderate discipline. He also had the born leader's understanding that nearly everyone yearns for a chance to succeed. If Grant could offer them that, his farm boys would follow him anywhere, with or without the aid of personal charisma or draconian punishment.

The Seventh District Regiment, including its commander, was sworn into Federal service as the 21st Illinois Volunteer Infantry on June 28. Two congressmen, John A. McClernand and John A. Logan, traveled to Springfield for the swearing-in ceremony. "The regiment is a little unruly," said Logan to Grant. "Do you think you can manage them?"

"I think I can," Grant replied equably, and stepped forward to review the troops. The entire regiment then paraded past him and formed up in long lines. Dressed in a disreputable old hat with a feather stuck in it and a threadbare blue overcoat, a sash around his waist, a sword hanging from his belt, and a beard that was long and slightly unkempt, he looked like a figure out of a comic opera. Yet when he clutched the regimental muster roll in his right hand as if it had some totemic power and significance and demanded in a loud, firm voice, "Are you willing to be mustered into the service for three years?" what the troops heard was the voice of command.

They enthusiastically shouted back, "Yes!"

"Then hold out your hands," said Grant, and swore them in as three-year men.[19]

Once Grant finished, McClernand and Logan roused the 21st with impassioned patriotic orations for two hours. Grant listened impassively, probably bored rigid. Finally, Logan concluded his oration. "Allow me to present to you your new commander—Colonel U. S. Grant!"

The regiment started chanting, "Grant! Grant!" Some men bellowed, "Grant—a speech!" in the mistaken impression that he, like other colonels, was really a politician at heart.[20]

It was important to let them know once and for all that he was not a political colonel, not a speechmaker, not a rally-to-me-and-I-will-lead-you-onward commander, but a professional soldier, neither more nor less. Grant stepped forward and waited for the chanting and excitement to die down. When everyone was perfectly still, perfectly silent, he said clearly and firmly, "Men . . . go to your quarters!" What could they do but obey?[21]

★

The regiment was under orders to deploy to Quincy, Illinois, on the east bank of the Mississippi. Grant chose not to move by rail, but marched his men across central Illinois, covering a hundred miles in a week. It would not have been arduous but for the intense heat of mid-summer. A long march provided a good opportunity for instilling discipline. When some men took advantage of passing through a small town to fill their canteens with whiskey, Grant personally sniffed at every canteen and emptied into the ground the contents of those that reeked of booze. The offenders were then tethered by lengths of rope to the baggage wagons and spent the rest of the day at the end of the column, eating the dust of the regiment and enduring the taunts and jeers of the crowds who gathered at towns along the way to watch the 21st Illinois pass by.[22]

The main point of the march was pride rather than punishment. A trek such as this gives soldiers both a feeling of accomplishment and a sense of solidarity as men encourage one another to keep going despite the blisters, the heat, the weight of the packs, the arms aching from the dead weight of muskets.

By the time the march ended, Grant felt proud of them. He told Julia, "I don't believe there is now a more orderly set of troops now in the volunteer service. I have been very strict with them and the men seem to like it. They appreciate that is all for their own benefit." He expressed his thanks to the men for the way they had conducted themselves, telling them they compared favorably with "veteran troops in point of Soldierly bearing, general good order, and cheerfull execution of commands." It was plainly exaggerated to put men who had only two months of military experience on a par with professional soldiers, but Grant's pride in his regiment was such that he was in no mood to be objective.[23]

The 21st crossed into northeastern Missouri, where Confederate guerrillas were attacking railroads and bridges. The regiment was at Palmyra when Grant was ordered to advance on a band of twelve hundred rebels led by Brigadier General Thomas A. Harris and destroy them. Harris was reported to have set up camp twenty-five miles away, along a creek bottom near Florida, Missouri. Grant set off at once with his regiment, not at all convinced that Harris was anywhere near Florida.

As he approached the enemy's position, however, Grant began to feel a new kind of dread. It wasn't physical fear. That had troubled him only once in Mexico and he soon threw it off. This was a different kind of fear—the fear of failure, paid for in other men's lives. Suppose he did it all wrong and his regiment was beaten? routed? disgraced? This was the fear of the commander, the man with a greater responsibility than physical courage. And it grew heavier, more crushing, as the hill that screened the creek bottom from view loomed in front of him. "My heart kept getting higher and higher until it felt to me as though it was in my throat. I would have given anything right then to be back in Illinois . . ." But there was no turning back now. Grant led his men onward, up the slope, until he could see the valley on the other side. The creek bottom bore all the signs of a recent encampment—burned-out fires, wagon ruts, hoofprints, holes made by tent pegs, scattered detritus and impromptu latrines. But no Harris, no guerrillas. Not a guard was posted, not a warning shot fired. "It occurred to me at once that Harris had been as much afraid of me as I of him. . . . From that event to the close of the war, I never experienced trepidation upon confronting an enemy, though I always felt more or less anxiety."[24]

From the point of view of a commander with a green regiment, these weeks in Missouri, with their almost palpable sense of danger, were nearly ideal for training. Like most border states, Missouri was not completely convinced which way it should go. Grant was slightly bemused to find that many of its people wanted to support the Confederacy yet expressed little real desire to depart from the Union. There were slaveholders who were strongly opposed to secession, just as there were people who had never owned a slave who were clamoring for it.

The 21st did not find itself plunged into a struggle to survive, but the threats it faced were serious enough to concentrate the soldiers' minds. When guard was mounted at night, it was no longer to keep the adventurous away from whiskey and women but an act of self-preservation. When men cleaned their muskets, they knew their lives might depend on it.

★

One day, Grant was sitting in his tent when the regimental chaplain, John Crane, came looking for him, carrying a copy of the *Daily Missouri Democrat*. "Colonel, I have some news here that will interest you." According to the newspaper, the War Department had just announced the creation of thirty-four new brigadiers. One of them was Ulysses S. Grant. His date of rank was given as May 17, making him eighteenth in seniority among these new generals. "Well, sir," said Grant, "I had no suspicion of it. That's some of Washburne's work."[25]

On August 7 Grant received orders to deploy his regiment to Jefferson Barracks. Like every superior infantry commander down the ages, Grant believed in the critical importance of rapid action. Here, then, was a chance to impress this lesson on the troops. By evening, he had the entire regiment and its equipment loaded aboard a train for St. Louis. He expected to have enough time in the city to find some books on strategy and tactics and to be fitted for a general's uniform, but before he had the chance to find a tailor or a bookseller, he received fresh orders. He was to proceed to Ironton, seventy miles south of the city, and take command of all Federal forces in southeastern Missouri.

Ironton was both an important railhead and the center of an area rich in mineral resources vital to the Union's war industries. It was reportedly threatened by eight thousand Confederates. Grant reached Ironton with his regiment that afternoon, having moved his command 110 miles in twenty-four hours.[26]

Grant received reports of five thousand rebels massing somewhere in the low hills near Ironton under William Hardee, the author of that same *Tactics* that he was reading, preparing to mount an attack. He refused to be alarmed. Grant needed cavalry to patrol the railroad and provide him with reconnaissance, and he had to find artillery to help him defend critical points. Yet Grant remained confident that even if all he had was the four regiments of green troops that comprised his brigade, he could hold Ironton. Hardee's men were no more experienced and no better equipped than his own.

He set up his command post on the estate of a local luminary, John W. Emerson, whom he had known in St. Louis before the war. Emerson went to see him one day and found Grant sitting at a table beneath an ancient oak tree studying a map. This map, Grant grumbled, is virtually useless. What I need is one that provides a detailed picture of the whole of southeastern Missouri.

Emerson found him a decent map and was gratified to see how Grant studied it for hours, making marks on it with a red pencil. What he was looking at was not the hills or the railroads but the rivers—the Mississippi, the Cumberland, the Tennessee—all flowing south, each a highway leading deep into the Confederacy. The first thing, though, was to drive the enemy out of southeastern Missouri.[27]

When word came that far from preparing to attack, the rebels were withdrawing, Grant immediately decided to chase after them. He dashed off a letter to Julia first. "No doubt you will be quite astonished, after what the papers have said about the precarious position of my brigade . . . to learn that tomorrow I move South."[28]

He had not gone far, though, before Brigadier General Benjamin M. Prentiss showed up at his headquarters. Prentiss had just been assigned to take command in southeastern Missouri by Major General John C. Frémont, the commander of the Western Department. Grant had never had a high regard for Frémont, and Frémont had just demonstrated an ignorance of Army regulations that would shame a second lieutenant. Paragraph 5 clearly stated that between officers of equal rank in the militia, seniority belonged to whichever one had held senior rank in the regular Army. Both Prentiss and Grant were militia brigadiers, but Grant had been a permanent captain in the regulars, while Prentiss had been only a permanent lieutenant. Grant had been ousted in what amounted to an illegal act.[29]

After arguing the issue with Prentiss, who proved so thrilled to get a major command he could not be made to see sense, Grant sent a protest to the War Department and reported to Frémont's chaotic headquarters in St. Louis for further orders, dressed in shabby civilian clothes. His colonel's uniform had been finished just as word came through of his promotion to brigadier general and he had never worn it. He was still waiting for a general's outfit, complete with sword and sash, to be finished. In the meantime, he looked like a careworn civilian puffing on an old clay pipe and seeking employment in some menial capacity around headquarters. He had a long wait before Frémont found time to see him.

The headquarters was a theatrical spectacle, unlike any headquarters Grant would ever tolerate. Aides dripping gold braid dashed in and out of doors and up and down the stairs in a state of excitement. There were contractors bawling and jostling in the corridors and banging on doors, determined to sell the Union Army everything from hardtack to harnesses at inflated prices. Amid all this bustle and noise Mrs. Frémont acted as the Pathfinder's secretary, while a white-haired former slave, known only as "Uncle Ralph" and liberated by Frémont's mother thirty years earlier, served as doorkeeper to the great man.[30]

Frémont was intensely patriotic, energetic, outspoken, aggressive and impulsive. He had a high regard for his own abilities, which were considerable, but what was lacking was ballast. It could be only a matter of time before he toppled over.

Frémont was surprised to see Grant and was unconvinced when Grant told him that he ranked Prentiss. The only new assignment he could think of was to send Grant to Jefferson City, another spot presently threatened by Confederate guerrillas, and take charge of its defense. Grant was disgusted. This was not a job for a brigadier general. He requested leave to return to Galena but was turned down. Reluctantly but obediently, he headed for central Missouri, removed, he feared, from the action.[31]

★

The general-in-chief, Winfield Scott, saw it all from the first, from the day Fort Sumter surrendered. The Union would have to raise, train and equip a huge army. While it did so, a much strengthened Navy would begin a progressively tighter blockade on Confederate ports on the Atlantic and Gulf coasts. A powerful force of steam-driven gunboats would have to be constructed to dominate the great rivers. Once the Army was ready to take the war to the enemy, it would use the water-ways—especially the Mississippi—to drive deep into the South and cut the Confederacy in two.

It would then proceed to crush the life out of the rebellious states, like an anaconda remorselessly and steadily killing its prey. Scott's strategy would take three years to carry out—and in its realism, its thoroughness and its heroic scale, it left no scope for even the most brilliant Confederate commander to triumph and no prospect of a stalemate for southern politicians to negotiate into an acceptable peace.[32]

It was a masterly vision. No one else—not even that strange, tormented genius Abraham Lincoln—shared it. Yet whoever carried it out, it would not be Old Fuss and Feathers. He was too stout these days even to mount his horse. But more than that, he was simply too old, too infirm, in too much pain from a bullet wound of the Mexican War to command an army at war anymore. All he could do was imagine the terrible future and wait for a commander to emerge with the vision and the will to put an anaconda strategy into effect.

No one seeing Grant in Missouri could have imagined he might be the man; Grant himself could not have imagined it. But he was only in Jefferson City a week before the War Department informed Frémont that Grant really *was* senior to Prentiss and therefore should never have been ousted from his command. To rectify this blunder, Frémont brought Grant back and increased his responsibilities. Grant was to head immediately for Cairo, the southernmost town in Illinois. Strategically placed where the Ohio River flows into the Mississippi, Cairo was one of the most important sites in the West and under constant threat from rebel forces. Frémont had reinforced it several times, but never ceased to worry about it.

Grant's new command embraced southeastern Missouri, southern Illinois and adjacent areas of Kentucky, which at present claimed to be neutral in the war between North and South. Good Union men were convinced it was a policy aimed mainly at keeping the Union out while doing nothing to discourage Confederate troops from moving in.

Grant set up his headquarters in a former bank building overlooking the river and had his office on the second floor. An Army paymaster who visited the headquarters often said he "always found it a place of business, and free from all the pomp and circumstance of war." The staff in the rooms below went about their duties quietly and calmly, "while General Grant, sitting at one of the windows overlooking the flotilla of gunboats in the river, and the Kentucky shore beyond, was always absorbed in meditation, probably blocking out in his mind the grand movements of the campaign."[33]

When Grant took command in Cairo, his first assignment was implementing an elaborate plan that Frémont had devised to trap a notorious Confederate guerrilla leader, M. Jeff Thompson. "If Jeff Thompson moves ten miles, we haven't the least chance," said Grant, seeming to find Frémont's plan almost funny in its unrealistic optimism. Given the fact that mounted guerrillas moved ten miles most days, he did not expect the plan to work, and it didn't.[34]

What Grant really had his mind on wasn't Thompson but events in Kentucky. Frémont had sent a small force to capture the steamboat landing at Belmont, Missouri, across from Columbus, Kentucky, whose high bluffs dominated the Mississippi. The force at Belmont was incapable of doing anything much beyond giving the Confederates something to worry about. Meanwhile, Frémont had another small force "demonstrating" across the Ohio River from Paducah, Kentucky. All this shadow-boxing was too much for the Confederate commander, Major General Leonidas Polk, a West Point graduate who had abandoned a promising military career to become an Episcopalian priest. Polk had risen to become bishop of Louisiana, but hardly had he grown accustomed to the purple vestments before the Civil War began and he changed uniform.

Inevitably dubbed "the Fighting Bishop," Polk assumed command of Confederate forces in the West. He soon became irritated at Frémont's ceaseless shadow-boxing and, encouraged by Gideon Pillow, a Tennessean who had commanded a division of volunteers in the Mexican War, Polk seized the strategic heights at Columbus on September 3, effectively nullifying Frémont's seizure of Belmont, across the river.

Polk's action was a political blunder. Until now Kentucky had been able to proclaim its neutrality. The Confederate seizure of Columbus was seen by many Kentuckians as an invasion, and made it politically possible for Union forces to move into the state as putative liberators, assuming there was a Union commander ready and willing to act.

On September 5, while the news from Columbus was still sizzling, a Union officer who had gone behind enemy lines, Captain Charles de Arnaud, arrived at Grant's headquarters bruised and battered. Arnaud claimed he and another Union spy had been captured by the Confederates. His companion had been shot dead, while he was roughed up before making a daring escape. And now, he said, nearly four thousand Confederates were moving toward Paducah, roughly forty-five miles northeast of Cairo. Paducah was crucial to any Union strategy based on the inland waterways of the upper South. The town dominated the area where the Tennessee and Cumberland rivers flowed out and south from the Ohio.

Grant believed him. In any case, he was simply incapable of sitting where he was and watching the Confederates snap up Paducah like a lost wallet. He immediately dispatched a telegram to Frémont: "I am getting ready to go to Paducah. Will start at 6½ o'clock."[35]

Grant expected Frémont to send a message back granting authority to move on Paducah. Six-thirty came and six-thirty went, without a word from St. Louis. Grant grew restive as the hours ticked by. Finally, at ten P.M. he told his aides, "Come on. I can wait no longer. I will go if it costs me my commission!"[36]

He had already put fifteen hundred men and four artillery pieces aboard three steamers. Guarded by two wooden gunboats, the steamers set off downriver in the darkness at ten-thirty. Grant landed his troops on the Paducah waterfront at half past eight the next morning and seized the town. He claimed he had gotten there with less than twelve hours to spare, although in fact Polk had never planned to seize the town. Simply grabbing Columbus was hardly worth invading Kentucky, but Polk lacked the strategic sense to try scooping up two key towns in a single daring movement.

Secessionist flags were hastily pulled down by Union troops, and Grant issued a proclamation. "I have come among you, not as an enemy but as your friend and fellow-citizen, not to injure or annoy you, but to defend and enforce the rights of all loyal citizens. . . . I am here to defend you. . . . I have nothing to do with opinions. I shall deal only with armed rebellion. . . . The strong arm of the Government is here to protect its friends, and to punish only its enemies . . ."[37]

Grant left most of the force that had captured Paducah in the town and installed Brigadier General C. F. Smith with orders to hold it. His relationship with Smith was slightly uncomfortable for both of them, because Smith had not only been commandant of cadets during Grant's four years at West Point, but had also been his instructor in infantry tactics. After the Civil War Grant liked to boast, in a lighthearted way, that he had been "last in infantry tactics." This wasn't strictly true, but it conveyed enough of the truth to make him uneasy when he met up with Smith in 1861.

Back in Cairo, Grant found a telegram from Frémont giving him carefully hedged permission to take Paducah, but only "if you feel strong enough." This message had been delayed twelve hours en route because it had been translated into Hungarian before being transmitted, for security reasons, and then had to be translated back into English before being delivered. Grant was unaware of this and considered the telegram from St. Louis little more than a posterity paper, designed to make Frémont look good if the mission was a success but to cover his backside with armor plate if it went badly.

Grant's boldness had paid off, and Frémont tried to make it seem as though grabbing Paducah had been his own idea. Indeed, long after the war ended, Frémont shamelessly tried to claim that every victory Grant had won in the West could be traced back to some idea that he had put into Grant's mind during the early months of the war.[38]

The contempt he already felt for Frémont was only deepened by the Paducah experience. Grant knew that while he had acted boldly to seize a strategic position, Frémont had lacked the moral courage to back him promptly and completely. And Grant had no doubt that he had pulled off a major coup. For all his innate modesty, he craved praise. He found the admiration of strangers slightly embarrassing and cringed at the thought of ever being considered vain, yet he yearned to be admired within his family. What boasting he did, he did mainly to them—usually to Julia, but sometimes to Jesse. So now he could not resist telling his wife, "I suppose you have seen from the papers that I have quite an extensive and important command. It is the third most important in the country. . . . You have seen my move upon Paducah, Ky! It was of much greater importance than is probably generally known."[39]

By October, Grant's growing command numbered thirteen thousand men. The critical point was western Kentucky, where Confederate forces continued to threaten communications along the line of the Mississippi. As ever, his innate restlessness nagged at him. Grant was never any good at waiting patiently. More than that, though, he had absorbed the strategic outlook of Napoleon and the most important lesson Mexico had to teach: Only the offensive is decisive in war. The Mexicans had fought mostly on the defensive and lost, while Scott, always outnumbered, had taken the war to the enemy and won. That was war as Grant understood it, the only kind of war he was willing to fight.

———— ★ ★ ★ ★ ————

CHAPTER 11

"WE WILL CUT
OUR WAY OUT"

For weeks following his coup de main at Paducah, Grant fretted, sifted reports from spies, monitored the buildup of his troops, who were skirmishing regularly with rebel pickets, and studied the maps with which he covered the walls of his headquarters, like a man seeking a chance to strike. Yet his force was too thinly spread out to allow him to mount an attack anywhere. Impotence only amplified the inner call to action and made frustration worse.

Then, on November 1, Grant received instructions from Frémont that he was to "make demonstrations" on both sides of the Mississippi and to keep his columns in constant motion, but not to attack the enemy. Frémont was currently commanding in the field, hoping to destroy Sterling Price's army, which was operating in southeast Missouri. The Pathfinder had spent a month searching for Price and still hadn't found him.

What worried him now was a report that Confederate forces under Leonidas Polk, "the Fighting Bishop" from Louisiana, were about to cross over from Columbus, Kentucky, to Belmont, Missouri, the steamboat landing some fifty miles south of Cairo. Frémont did not want to find himself caught with Price in front of him and Polk in his rear.

He need not have worried so much. Polk was not about to sneak up on him. Tall, thin and balding, Leonidas Polk prayed and fretted and hauled in artillery from across the upper South until he turned Columbus into the Gibraltar of the Mississippi. By November, the bishop-general had crammed 140 artillery pieces onto the bluffs towering 150 feet above the river. His arsenal included a ten-inch Columbiad, firing a 128-pound shot, that his troops called Lady Polk. Yet even as he turned Columbus into an impregnable fortress, Polk worried endlessly that the Federals might somehow find a chink in the shield he was raising against the sword point of southern Illinois, already thrusting, or so it seemed, into the heart of the South. Having been too aggressive for the Confederacy's good when he seized Columbus, and thereby being blamed for "invading Kentucky," he spent his energies now on God and defenses.[1]

As for Frémont, his days as Grant's superior were coming to a close. He had incurred Lincoln's wrath, for reasons that will become clear later. Shortly after Frémont's November 1 order reached Grant, Frémont was relieved of his command.[2]

Meanwhile, in compliance with Frémont's instructions, Grant had set virtually his entire command of twenty thousand men in motion, organizing seven columns. Most of his troops were devoted to chasing guerrilla bands, in keeping with Frémont's wishes. He ordered Brigadier General C. F. Smith at Paducah to send a column toward Columbus. That would provide a demonstration on the eastern side of the river and have the effect of pinning down Polk's troops in their fortress. The other demonstration, the one on the western side of the Mississippi, he would take charge of himself. Explaining to one of his brigade commanders, John A. McClernand, that they were about to make "a reconnaissance in force," he put three thousand men aboard five steamers and headed for Belmont the evening of November 6.[3]

Nine miles south of Cairo, Grant halted for the night. He had the steamboats drop anchor on the Kentucky side of the river, barely ten miles above Columbus. No attempt was made to maintain silence or a blackout aboard either the transports or the two wooden-hulled gunboats that stood guard over them, the *Tyler* and the *Lexington,* and a large guard was noisily posted onshore. Grant intended his fleet to be not only noticed but misunderstood. He wanted Polk to think Columbus was about to be caught in a two-pronged attack, by Grant from the river and by Smith overland.

The steamers were horribly overcrowded. Grant and his staff dozed fitfully in chairs aboard the *Belle Memphis* that night for want of space to lie down. The troops sprawled on deck or excitedly crowded the rails and stared into the darkness. The sight of the Kentucky shore, black against black in the chilly fall night, had them telling one another with all the confidence of ignorance, "We're going to Columbus!" War was still an adventure to them. All volunteers, their enthusiasm had not yet been tempered by carnage and tears.[4]

Around two in the morning, a message arrived informing Grant that Confederate troops were crossing the river from Columbus with the intention of threatening two of the columns he had sent in pursuit of guerrillas. This news convinced him, he later informed the War Department, that he had to attack Belmont. Doubts have been raised as to whether such a message ever existed, because it has never been corroborated. Grant, however, was not a man to invent a story out of whole cloth. It may have been an oral account from a spy or a scout, or simply a rumor. But that hardly seems to matter, seeing that he told his military secretary, Adam Badeau, he would have attacked Belmont anyway.[5]

Grant's prize-winning biographer, William McFeely, believes that in turning a demonstration into an attack, Grant was insubordinate. This ignores the fact that in the nineteenth century field commanders had considerable leeway to interpret their orders—much more so than in these days of instant and secure communications. As Frémont's orders to Grant made clear, the primary objective Frémont sought was to secure his rear from an enemy threat. If a demonstration would achieve that, nothing more was needed. If Grant decided that a demonstration would fail, however, it was for him to provide a better solution. He could, of course, have balked, pulled out, returned to Cairo, and left Frémont to his fate. Some other officers would have done exactly that. Not Grant.

Having decided that a demonstration would not suffice to achieve Frémont's objective Grant was not only free to act on that conclusion, but it was his responsibility to do so. It was that ability to read the situation—nearly always on the basis of incomplete or misleading information—and to seize the initiative and act aggressively that would eventually take him to supreme command in the Army, while scores of other generals, less enterprising, closer to the McFeely ideal of subordination, failed.[6]

At dawn, the steamers cut their lines and followed the two gunboats south. Around eight o'clock the transports pulled away from mid-channel and headed for the Missouri shore, aiming for a point three miles from Belmont, where the wide river made a large bend to the east.

The gunboats steamed beyond, bringing them in sight of Columbus. The big guns on the bluffs opened up, the gunboats briefly and ineffectually engaged some of the enemy batteries, steamed around in a circle, then pulled back upriver. They did this three times that morning, hoping to bluff Polk into holding his troops in Columbus instead of moving men across the river to Belmont.[7]

While the gunboats were barking defiance at Columbus like a pair of Pekingese yapping at an angry Doberman pinscher, Grant was disembarking his troops. Three hundred men were formed into a reserve and left in a hollow near the landing. The rest, including a small cavalry detachment and two artillery pieces, set off on a southeasterly course, toward Belmont and the Confederates' camp. Mounted on a fine bay horse and erect in an expensive saddle with his name on it, Grant had a good view of the terrain ahead as it unfolded this fine autumn morning.

The troops advanced first through fields filled with well-ripened corn and, being farm boys, admired it. Beyond the cornfields, they came in sight of a dense woodland. Grant ordered each of his five regiments to send two companies forward as skirmishers to develop the enemy position. "They had gone but a little way when they were fired upon," Grant informed his father, "and the *Ball* may be said to have fairly commenced." As he rode forward, the firing grew intense and his horse was shot. Grant dismounted safely and took the horse of his aide, William Hillyer, but with bullets flying all around there was no time to rescue the expensive saddle or his silver mess kit, engraved U.S.G.[8]

Polk had entrusted Belmont to Brigadier General Gideon J. Pillow, whose conduct in command of a division of volunteers in Mexico had made him a laughingstock among regular officers. Pillow had been given a division not because he had any military experience but because his good friend James K. Polk happened to be President.

There was a fund of Pillow stories from the Mexican War, including the one about how he had ordered entrenchments to be dug at Camargo, but demonstrated his ignorance of the situation by putting them *behind* his troops. At Chapultepec, he had been bruised in the foot by a spent ball, which he described in an official report as "being at the very Cannon's mouth, where I was cut down." Grant despised him. "I do not say he would shoot himself," Grant wrote to his father. "Ah, no! . . . I think, however, he might report himself wounded on receipt of a very slight scratch . . ."[9]

Pillow was holding Belmont with approximately two thousand men, although when Polk heard that Grant was coming south, he immediately started ferrying reinforcements over to Belmont. In the opening stages of the battle, each commander put around twenty-five hundred men into the fight. Grant's great advantage was not in numbers but in surprise. The Union troops advanced into the woods and fought their way from tree to tree. A Confederate counterattack was defeated and Pillow's men began to fall back toward the river.

The Confederate camp, named Camp Johnston in honor of Albert Sidney Johnston, the commander of Confederate forces in the West, was screened by an abatis, several hundred yards long and created from recently felled trees, which was lightly manned. The onrushing Federals scrambled over the thousand sharp points of the abatis and jumped in among the defenders. A brief hand-to-hand struggle sent routed Confederates fleeing over the top of the riverbank. Around two P.M. the shooting and screaming stopped abruptly as Grant's men found themselves in undisputed possession of the enemy camp. From here, it was possible to see people moving about in Columbus, on the opposite shore.

Pillow's demoralized troops were out of sight, down by the river, or skulking in the dense timber. His command was on the brink of annihilation. All it would take to round them up was to continue the pursuit. Instead, Grant, his two brigade commanders and his five regimental commanders sat on their horses, talked among themselves, and surveyed the chaotic scene before them while the troops threw a victory party and looted Camp Johnston in a frenzied search for booty. The band of the 22nd Illinois appeared as if from nowhere and pounded out "Yankee Doodle," "The Stars and Stripes" and other tunes bound to annoy the Confederates in Columbus. A captured flag, with the Stars and Bars on one side and the golden harp of Erin on the reverse, was mockingly paraded, before being draped across an artillery caisson. The eternal politician in John McClernand, commanding one of Grant's two brigades, was roused to deliver an impromptu oration on the glory of the Union and the treachery of secession.[10]

For thirty minutes, Grant lost control of his troops. Here was the volunteer spirit in action—the fight was won, the job was done, time to celebrate. Regular troops under regular officers would have continued the pursuit until ordered to stop. Grant, however, had to assert himself through brigade commanders and regimental commanders who were amateur soldiers, and one of them, McClernand, was too powerful politically to risk antagonizing. McClernand had been Lincoln's neighbor in Springfield and had been a congressman before securing a general's commission. There were practical limits to Grant's command authority when it came to handling volunteers. He stayed well within them, at Belmont as back in Cairo.

The "volunteer spirit" affected not only the troops but their company officers as well. Having been elected by the men they led, they were always more likely to join the revelry than to try curbing it. And as Grant saw to his disgust, that was exactly what they did at Belmont. To restore control over the troops, he must first re-establish control over the officers, and he did not know how to do it. Grant had to wait until this stupidity had run its course.

The absurd scene over at Belmont may well have seemed to Polk to be close to divine intervention. Even while the battle raged he was pushing thousands of men aboard steamboats and sending them across. Cannily, he had two of them steam north. An alert lieutenant rode up to Grant and pointed to where their smokestacks, poking above the treeline, were making a black line that moved steadily toward where his own steamboats lay. A medical officer, John Brinton, rode up to Grant at the same time and made the same point.[11]

Grant was incredulous. At first he refused to believe they were Confederate steamboats. But they had to be. And if they *were* disgorging troops to the north of his present position, he was in danger of being cut off from his own steamers. His cavorting regiments were courting their complete destruction.

Grant turned to an aide and commanded, "Fire the tents!" A good blaze would soon put a stop to the looting of Camp Johnston. Union officers set fire to the tents, to the grief of souvenir-hunting Federals.[12] Until now, the Confederate gunners at Columbus had restrained from opening fire on Camp Johnston for fear of killing their own men. The eruption of fires was a signal that there were only Federals there now. Polk's biggest guns opened up on Camp Johnston. Most of the huge projectiles flew harmlessly overhead as excited, poorly trained gunners set about their work, but when Lady Polk was fired, she was right on target. Her 128-pound round, nearly a foot in diameter, screamed down at the camp's dismal little parade ground—freezing Union soldiers in their tracks—ricocheted back into the air, and tore a frenzied, splintering path through the trees.[13]

Companies were hurriedly re-formed into line as Confederate reinforcements fresh off their steamboats came crashing through the woods. They launched a vigorous counterattack, and panic seized the Federal volunteers. A frightened aide, his face white with terror, rode up to Grant. "Why, General, we are surrounded!"

Grant calmly replied, "Then we will cut our way out."[14]

It was now for him to manage what is generally considered the most difficult feat of arms for an infantry force—the fighting withdrawal. Facing the stark prospect of disaster, Grant's volunteers sobered up, formed a ragged line, and began to pull back toward the landing, three miles to the northwest, where the Union steamboats were still waiting.

This was the point where the reserve ought to have entered the picture. The function of a reserve is to reinforce success if all goes well and help stave off disaster if it doesn't. Grant, however, had completely mishandled his reserve. It was left too far in the rear to be of much use. Nor had he left clear instructions on what it should do, although his intention was evidently to have it cover a retreat if his main force found itself fighting its way back to the landing—the very situation he now faced. But when the reserve force commander heard the Confederate counterattack erupt less than a mile away, he rushed his men back to the landing and put them aboard the *Belle Memphis,* out of harm's way, instead of marching to the sound of the guns. When Grant rode back to the hollow where he had posted his reserve to order it to advance and cover the withdrawal, he was bewildered. Where had it gone? The reserve was no help in his retreat.[15]

Nor had he handled his cavalry properly. The squadron of horse soldiers that Grant took to Belmont ought to have been scouting the flanks of the Federal line, monitoring Confederate movements. News that the enemy was building up a threat on the left flank should have come from Grant's cavalry and not from a doctor.

Once the initial shock of the Confederate charge had been absorbed without shattering Grant's line, the risk passed of the retreat turning into a rout. Aided by effective fire from the two Union artillery pieces, Grant's men withdrew steadily through the cornfields until they reached the steamboats. The entire force boarded in good order.

Grant was the last Federal soldier to quit the field. He rode through the high corn toward the landing, passing a company of Confederates barely fifty yards away. Polk, who had come over to see the battle first-hand, noticed him and said to his men, "There is a Yankee. You may try your marksmanship on him if you wish." No one bothered to take a pot-shot at Grant's receding back.[16]

When he reached the riverbank, every steamboat but one was making for mid-channel. Grant shouted to a group of soldiers standing alongside the vessel, "Get aboard the boat—they are coming," and called to the ship's captain, "Chop your lines and back out." Once the lines were cut, the vessel instantly began drifting away. A plank was hurriedly pushed out from the lower deck to the riverbank. Grant, the nonpareil horseman still, got Hillyer's mount, which he may never have ridden before, to set-tle down on its haunches, slide down the muddy bank, then tread care-fully across the bending, swaying plank and onto the deck.[17]

Grant headed for the captain's cabin and lay down for a few minutes, collecting his thoughts on this hectic day. Then he stood up. Just as he did so, a Confederate musket ball crashed through the cabin wall and ripped into the head of the sofa where he had been resting a moment before. Three times in one day he had brushed against death, and he was as lucky in this war as he had been in Mexico. Nothing seemed able to touch him. Grant possessed the military gift Napoleon considered the most important any general can have—good luck.

He had lost nearly one hundred killed and three hundred wounded. Around fifty Union soldiers were missing in action. Confederate losses were slightly higher. The Federals had burned a collection of Confeder-ate tents, spiked several cannon, and seized a barnload of souvenirs. On the other hand, they had left behind nearly a thousand muskets, a wind-fall for their poorly armed foes.[18]

Grant informed the War Department that he had advanced on Bel-mont "to make a reconnaissance toward Columbus," to protect the two columns he had on the move in southeastern Missouri, and to prevent Polk from reinforcing Sterling Price. Meanwhile he sent a report back to headquarters in St. Louis claiming, "The victory was complete." Nei-ther report so much as hinted that his troops had stopped for a looting break in the middle of the engagement.[19]

It may be hard to believe Grant was serious when he penned this report, yet he almost certainly was. In truth, though, he had not discovered anything from his "reconnaissance" that he did not already know about the strength of the defenses at Columbus or the fact that Belmont was untenable so long as the enemy posted artillery on the bluffs opposite. The two columns he was trying to protect were moving away from Belmont, not toward it. They were never threatened by Polk's troops in Kentucky even though when the sun went down on November 6, there was nothing in the world to stop Polk from moving men from Columbus over to Missouri to reinforce Sterling Price. Grant's attack, however, had demonstrated how vulnerable Belmont was to a raid from the north. That strongly discouraged Polk from sending any force west.

Grant sent a revised report on Belmont to the War Department in June 1865, after the Civil War ended, still seeking to justify his actions but his mistakes and those of his amateur soldiers were never acknowledged.[20]

Even in his memoirs Grant sought to portray the inconclusive engagement at Belmont as a kind of victory, for victory justifies every action, excuses every mistake. The truth was, neither side had much to boast about. Even so, something *had* been gained. Grant insisted that Belmont was good for morale. If he had not taken his troops into a fight, they would have lost confidence in him and themselves—the subtext of which is that Belmont instilled discipline, self-confidence and experience in his green soldiers, which would pay dividends in future, more important fights.[21]

Belmont was not only a school for the troops but a classroom for their commander. Until November 1861 Grant had never commanded more than a dozen men in a battle. At Belmont he commanded three thousand men, committed major errors in tactics and troop handling, yet redeemed himself by waging a fighting retreat and emerged with a down payment on the renown that he secretly craved. Little wonder, then, that he considered it worthwhile.

———— ★ ★ ★ ★ ————

CHAPTER 12

"THIS IS NOT WAR"

From Alexander the Great to the Civil War, generals fought their campaigns without the aid of professional staff officers. The modern staff officer, doctrine at his fingertips and standard operating procedures deep in his brain, is a post–Civil War creation. A general created a "household" around himself, often including a son (if he had one) or a nephew or two, and was likely to drag in a few of his or his wife's relations, the whole rounded out with a handful of able officers who served as his aides and secretaries. More likely than not, he spent from dawn until close to midnight dictating orders, letters and messages before falling into bed exhausted. It was a cumbersome method of command and the rapid expansion in the size of armies and the breadth of battlefields in the second half of the nineteenth century made it ludicrously inefficent.

Grant, like other Civil War generals, was left to fight the war with what was still really a household, even if he called it "my staff." Like most households, his was an untidy collection of people of varying abilities, clashing temperaments and petty resentments. First among equals on Grant's staff was John A. Rawlins. A thin man of average height and stooped like Grant himself, Rawlins was emotionally intense, highly intelligent and remarkably handsome. He was blessed with high cheekbones and a pair of large and lustrous black eyes that seemed to burn in his deathly pale face like embers, hot without smoke or flame. Those eyes beneath an untidy shock of raven hair conveyed a sense of some barely contained elemental force tormenting Rawlins and driving him on.

Rawlins was that American perennial, the poor boy made famous. His father was a shiftless, ne'er-do-well farmer who managed to eke out an existence as a charcoal burner when not too busy being indolent. Rawlins had only a few years of formal schooling. Beyond that, he was self-educated, and even though he had managed to become Galena's most successful lawyer by the age of thirty, he never shook off the intellectual uncertainty of the autodidact or the wavering self esteem of any man ashamed of his roots. Here, then, was one of those able people who drive themselves to remarkable achievements only to discover that the higher they rise, the stronger—not weaker—grows their sense of inferiority, for as they ascend they meet others not only much better educated than themselves, but possessing an abundance of confidence and families worth bragging about.[1]

He had won Grant's admiration with his rousing speech the night after the firing on Fort Sumter—"We will stand by the flag of our country and appeal to the god of battles!" When Grant received his general's commission, one of the first things he did was offer a place on his staff to Rawlins, even though Rawlins had not a day's military experience to his name. Grant was going to draw on that keen intelligence and turn all that smoldering intensity to the service of the Union cause. Rawlins's wife, however, was dying and it was September before he could join Grant's headquarters.

So Rawlins came to Grant at Cairo that fall of 1861 eager to serve but openly awestruck at the way professional soldiers talked confidently about the arcane and bloody mysteries of war and ill at ease around officers with polished manners and a college education. Rawlins added to his unhappiness by a tendency to burst into a stream of "goddamns" and "son of a bitches" whenever he became agitated. Given his highly strung nature, that happened a lot. Grant, who rarely said anything stronger than "doggone it," found Rawlins's swearing amusing and laughingly told people that it was why he kept Rawlins around. It was not a joke that Rawlins, who took himself all too seriously, would ever find amusing.[2]

Rawlins went along to Belmont and was awestruck. He reported back to his mother, with pride in his courage and surprise at himself, "I never thought of running [even though] I was in the midst of danger and within reach of the rebel fire more than once in the day."[3]

Grant's principal aide was William Hillyer, an amiable lawyer who had befriended Grant back during the ghastly last year in St. Louis, when Grant tried being a rent collector. Hillyer and his wife were good friends of Julia's, and having Mrs. Hillyer near would assure agreeable company for Mrs. Grant. Unfortunately, Hillyer and Rawlins never got on well. For one thing, Hillyer was an outgoing, fun-loving man, while Rawlins was a dour, duty-haunted individual. For another, each was fiercely jealous of his relationship with Grant. Rawlins would succeed in forcing Hillyer out long before the war ended.[4]

In Cairo, Grant and Rawlins worked side by side at a round table placed behind the counter at Safford's Bank, drafting orders, letters and dispatches, Grant puffing contentedly on a pendulous meerschaum, Rawlins wreathed in the general's smoke, both scribbling away diligently.[5]

Rawlins, Hillyer and the other amateurs on the staff were there for Grant to shape to his own ends. There were few people he could actually turn to for advice on military problems. The most important of these few was Major Joseph D. Webster, who understood two areas in which Grant sorely needed an expert—military engineering and artillery tactics. Webster was also an exceptionally able administrator. Grant paid tribute to Webster in his revised report on the battle of Belmont: "[he] accompanied me on the field, and displayed soldierly qualities of a high order."[6]

In the long tradition of generals' households, Grant wanted to keep Fred, his eldest son, with him at headquarters. The lad had accompanied his father to Springfield when Grant got command of the 21st Illinois. He sent the boy back to Galena, however, when the regiment set off for Missouri. "We may have some fighting to do," he explained in a letter to Julia, "and he is too young to have the exposure of camp life." Julia replied sternly, "Do not send him home. Alexander was not older when he accompanied Philip." It did no good. Fred was already riding the train to Galena when Julia's letter reached Grant.[7]

Following Belmont, he felt Cairo was safe enough for him to send for his wife and family. Julia arrived and let him know, as wives will, how much she disliked the long, unkempt beard he had grown. Grant promptly trimmed it and improved his appearance generally. He delighted in the paterfamilias role, and having his children around was one of the great joys of his life.

Shortly before Christmas 1861, Fred was allowed to visit some old family friends of the Dents in Caseyville, Kentucky, midway between Cairo and Paducah. But when the boy tarried, Julia worried. She told Grant that Confederate guerrillas might learn that their boy was within reach, kidnap Fred and hold him hostage against the release of prominent Confederates in Union hands, such as Mason and Slidell. Fred was abruptly summoned from Caseyville to rejoin his parents.[8]

Apart from this exaggerated and totally false alarm, Julia was thrilled to be in Cairo. She loved the parades and reviews, the color and bustle of an army headquarters at war. In fact, being a general's wife was delightful—altogether different from being married to a struggling lieutenant in some remote, freezing outpost in peacetime, when promotion was glacially slow, money short and comforts lacking. Julia was finally reconciled to her husband's choice of career.[9]

★

Like every war President, Lincoln had to sell the conflict to the people. The best way to do that was to present it as a war to save the Union, not as a struggle to end slavery. Had Lincoln presented the war as a fight to free the slaves, the volunteers he needed would have stayed away in the millions. Offer them the flag to defend, however, and young men would swamp recruiting stations across the North.

Only when the Union was secure would Lincoln be free to turn the war into a fight against slavery. The best way to help enslaved blacks was, paradoxically, to fight a war that was not about slavery—at least, not in the early years. In its later stages, however, the war would increasingly turn into a moral crusade. It had to, if only to justify the ghastly bloodbath it had become.

John Frémont's boiling anger against slavery, however, made him deaf, dumb and blind to the political realities. At the end of August 1861 he issued an emancipation proclamation, declaring that slaves owned by secessionists in his Western Department were hereby set free. He began issuing instruments of manumission to runaway slaves.[10]

Lincoln was horrified. He wrote to Frémont and told him that what he was doing was likely to "alarm our Southern friends, and turn them against us—perhaps ruin our rather fair prospect for Kentucky." As if to confirm Lincoln's fears, he heard shortly after writing this letter that an entire company of Kentucky volunteers had thrown down their arms and disbanded when they heard of Frémont's proclamation. "I think to lose Kentucky is nearly the same as to lose the whole game," he told Congressman Orville H. Browning. "Kentucky gone, we can not hold Missouri, nor, as I think, Maryland. These all against us, and the job on our hands is too large . . ."[11]

Frémont had not even bothered to discuss the matter first with the President's political representative in St. Louis, Colonel Francis Blair, Jr. Once Frémont realized how seriously he had antagonized the President, he compounded his error by sending his wife to Washington to explain his actions rather than explaining them himself.[12]

Grant, on the other hand, had seen the situation the way Lincoln did from the day Fort Sumter was attacked: If the North won the war, slavery would inevitably fall. He shared his fear of what might happen if abolitionism was allowed to undermine the war effort. "My inclination is to whip the rebellion into submission, preserving all constitutional rights," he told his father. "If it cannot be whipped any other way than through a war on slavery, let it come to that legitimately. . . . But that portion of the press that advocates the beginning of such a war now, are as great enemies to their country as if they were open and avowed secessionists." Already Grant and Lincoln, who had never met, shared an identical outlook on how the war must be fought.[13]

Frémont was fired while chasing Sterling Price across southern Missouri. Grant only learned of the change in command when he returned to Cairo following Belmont. Frémont's deputy, Major General David Hunter, held the command briefly, only to hand it over to Major General Henry W. Halleck, author of *Elements of Military Art and Science.* A man of much learning and not a day's combat experience, Halleck was tall and solidly built. He was also graying and somber. His bulging, almost exophthalmic eyes made him appear to be looking right through people and some found it unnerving, but ordinary soldiers thought he looked weird and made fun of his imposing forehead. They called him "Old Brains." Although an acknowledged authority on military history, he had much of the crabbed outlook of the born civil servant, to whom there is no solution without a problem. Halleck was fussy, idiosyncratic—a fountain that spurted theories of war, but a dry creek in action. He could no more be bold than Grant could be patient.

One of the first things Halleck did on reaching St. Louis was issue an order that runaway slaves would not be allowed to seek refuge with the Union Army. It was as good as declaring that Frémontism was dead. This was welcome news to Grant, who had been pursuing exactly this policy since his days commanding the 21st Illinois. When slaves sought sanctuary within his lines, he had turned them away. As he explained to the regimental chaplain, whose sympathies were understandably with the runaways, the role of the soldier was not to protect the slaves but to defeat the rebels.[14]

Halleck was also facing another challenge—cleaning out the stable. George B. McClellan, the "Little Napoleon" who had succeeded Winfield Scott as general-in-chief, had warned him melodramatically that in St. Louis he was going to confront "a system of reckless expenditure and fraud perhaps unheard of before in the history of the world."[15]

It wasn't half as awesome as that, but what Halleck found was bad enough: a headquarters redolent with the ripe odor of palm grease and vibrating to the agitation of snouts deep in the trough. He got most of the crooked contractors out of his corridors and off his stairs, tore up some of the crooked contracts, cut down on the large number of people who were doing too little to justify their pay, and organized the headquarters along military lines, to the grief of those who had grown to like the Ruritanian court Frémont had created—lively with braid and good-looking women, but short on direction and purpose.[16]

While trying to follow McClellan's demand that he "reduce chaos to order," Halleck was also pacing the big office on the second floor, abstractedly scratching at his elbows and casting his capacious mind over the strategic problems his command faced along the waterways of the Mississippi River valley.

His first and most pressing task, he believed, was to secure Missouri. That meant destroying Sterling Price's army. Halleck launched a relentless pursuit of Price with a force that was ably led by Samuel Curtis and which possessed a cutting edge that Frémont had failed to develop—a strong cavalry arm.

While trying to concentrate on securing Missouri, Halleck was under strong pressure from the President to take the offensive against the Confederates in Kentucky. Lincoln was similarly pressing the commander of the Army of the Ohio, Don Carlos Buell, to advance into Tennessee. The place to break into the South, the President strenuously and repeatedly insisted, was east Tennessee, which was strongly pro-

Union. What awaited the Union Army there was, in effect, a second army willing to rise up and aid the invaders.

Halleck was appalled. Any plan that had him driving into Kentucky while Buell attacked Tennessee, he maintained, would fail. All military history showed that a movement which set advancing forces heading in directions that steadily drew them apart led to defeat ninety-nine times out of a hundred.[17] The only strategy that would work was one that saw the forces in motion converging, the strength of each augmenting the power of the other until the whole movement became irresistible. Halleck was right, but Lincoln was President. It was only a matter of time before Halleck would have to yield.

Buell resisted the President's plan as strongly as Halleck. The two generals, Lincoln was discovering, were like wheelbarrows—hard to push, easy to upset. Even so, he was not going to allow Union armies to sit out the winter, musing on future glories, staying warm, and drawing up plans for spring campaigns. It was no use Halleck complaining, "I am in the condition of a carpenter who is required to build a bridge with a dull ax, a broken saw, and rotten timber." The pressure had to be maintained on the tautly stretched forces of the Confederacy.[18]

The Confederate commander in the West, Albert Sidney Johnston, was holding a 150-mile front from Belmont, Missouri, to Bowling Green, in central Kentucky. Strategically, Johnston appeared to be in a strong defensive position. There were only three broad highways south—the Mississippi, Tennessee and Cumberland Rivers—and he had all three covered. Columbus blocked movement down the Mississippi, while two new forts—Henry and Donelson—guarded the Tennessee and the Cumberland. Tactically, however, Johnston lacked the men and the firepower to hold a front as broad as this against a determined, well-armed opponent capable of striking simultaneously from the rivers and overland. The two forts were hastily erected and badly sited. Far from being strong points, they were weak ones.

Grant was itching to attack them, but there seemed little chance of that. Halleck had no faith in Grant, whom he barely knew. He was not only "Old Brains" but Old Army and had heard the rumors—about Grant's drunkenness, his scruffiness, his taciturnity, his unceremonious departure from the prewar Army under a cloud distilled from barrel whiskey, followed by failures in civilian life. And then there was Belmont. To a military thinker like Halleck, Belmont was an example of how not to make war. It could only have convinced him that Grant should not be trusted with a field command.

Lincoln was pushing harder than ever for action in Kentucky and Tennessee, and Halleck, who felt as desperately short of troops as Johnston, grudgingly agreed to comply, but he had no intention of taking chances. On January 6 Grant was ordered to advance into Kentucky, make a demonstration in the direction of Mayfield, and drop hints that he was heading for Dover, Tennessee, a small town just south of Fort Donelson. But, "by all means avoid a serious engagement," Halleck demanded.[19]

Meanwhile, Brigadier General C. F. Smith, still holding Paducah, would also make a demonstration in the direction of Mayfield. If possible, Grant and Smith were to give Polk the impression that they would advance beyond Mayfield, converge on Camp Beauregard, which stood roughly midway between Mayfield and Dover, and attack it.

The real point of all this shadow-boxing was to discourage Polk from sending troops to reinforce Bowling Green, because if Buell did move through the Cumberland Gap toward east Tennessee, the rebel position at Bowling Green would be right on his flank. The weaker that position, the better; the stronger, the worse.

Grant was disappointed at being told to demonstrate once again. "I wonder if General Halleck would object to another 'skirmish' like Belmont," he mused scornfully. When a staff officer talked about the benefits of maneuvering against the enemy's rear to force him out of frontline positions like Columbus, Grant retorted, "Better attack and capture the entire force where they are. Why allow them to withdraw and follow and fight them in the interior of Mississippi or Alabama under greater disadvantages?"[20]

He was forced to delay his movement from Cairo because of dense fog, but on January 10 he set two columns in motion toward Mayfield. The weather was abysmal—nothing but biting winds, snow showers and sleet. Much of the countryside seemed virtually abandoned. Grant and a small mounted party rode nearly all the way to Mayfield without being challenged. For the footsloggers, however, it was an appalling, if typical, infantry experience. Short of shoes and blankets, they suffered keenly. After three days of misery the two columns were turned around and hurried back to the shelter of winter quarters. Dreary huts and tents had never seemed so appealing.[21]

Grant's demonstration accomplished nothing except to bewilder Confederate commanders. They could not understand what the point was. It never occurred to Polk to reinforce Bowling Green from Columbus. As for Grant, although he claimed in his memoirs that he had prevented Polk from reinforcing Bowling Green, he felt frustrated at not having an objective to attack. He had no illusions about the futility of his demonstration. "This sloshing about in the mud, rain, sleet and snow for a week without striking the enemy, only exposing the men to great hardships and suffering, is not war," he complained to his staff. So much movement, so little action. If only he had been allowed to attack Camp Beauregard, "this would have been a demonstration with an object and a reward."[22]

Grant returned to Cairo deeply depressed. He was all too aware that Halleck despised him, and probably suspected that moves were afoot in St. Louis to get him out of his command. Rawlins told a friend that if he had to endure the scorn that Halleck reserved for Grant, he would resign his commission.[23]

While Grant's advance was fruitless, C. F. Smith's foray brought an intelligence windfall. Traveling down the Tennessee River aboard the gunboat *Lexington,* he discovered the truth about Fort Henry: It was almost defenseless. He sent Grant a sketch of the position, with a note that read, "I think two iron clad gun-boats would make short work of Fort Henry."[24]

On January 24, Grant went to St. Louis to try to convince Halleck that he should let him try to capture Fort Henry. His pretext for visiting Halleck was that he was coming to report on what he had learned during his advance toward Mayfield.

Halleck greeted him disdainfully. Grant, abashed in Halleck's intimidating bug-eyed presence, unfolded a map and started talking in a faltering way about taking Forts Henry and Donelson. Halleck interrupted Grant before he had gone very far. "Is there anything concerned with the good of your command you wish to discuss?" Grant tried to draw his attention to the map again, but Halleck brushed it aside. "All of this, General Grant, relates to the business of the general commanding the department. When he wishes to consult you on this subject, he will notify you."[25]

Halleck did not need Grant to advise him to attack Fort Henry. He had already arrived at that conclusion some weeks before. What he was doing was biding his time until mortar boats had been built, to pound the forts with plunging, high-angle fire. This meeting seems to have prompted Halleck finally to take steps to find a replacement for Grant, because that same day he wrote to McClellan urging him to get Ethan Allen Hitchcock, one of the most widely respected figures in the Old Army, to return to active duty as a major general of volunteers. Hitchcock could serve as Halleck's field commander, leaving Grant to shuffle papers at rear-area headquarters.[26]

"I returned to Cairo very much crestfallen," recalled Grant many years later.[27] Even so, it was only a few days before he bounced back. He was nothing if not tenacious, a quality he considered as important in life as intelligence. Grant got the commander of the growing naval force that would support the Army's advance, Flag Officer Andrew H. Foote, to send a telegram to Halleck saying he and Grant believed that with just four gunboats they could seize Fort Henry. Grant meanwhile sent a telegram of his own to Halleck: "With permission I will take Fort Henry on the Tennessee and hold and establish a large camp there."[28]

Halleck responded with a message telling Grant to be ready to move, but still he withheld permission. He had not yet had a reply from McClellan about the possible return to active duty of Ethan Allen Hitchcock.[29]

Grant's reaction was to fire off an exasperated telegram. Unless both Henry and Donelson were attacked without delay, he asserted, "the defenses on both the Tennessee and Cumberland rivers will be materially strengthened." Besides, an order to advance would raise troop morale. Grant concluded, in a tone close to insolence, "The advantages of this move are as perceptable [*sic*] to the Gen. Comd.g Dept. as to myself . . ."[30]

Halleck might have sent a stiff rebuke had he not received some startling intelligence that same day from McClellan. P.G.T. Beauregard, the victor at Bull Run, was reported moving to Kentucky with fifteen regiments to bolster Albert Sidney Johnston's front.[31]

Halleck had to make a preemptive strike whether his mortar boats were ready or not, whether he had heard from Hitchcock or not, whether he trusted Grant or not. Within twenty-four hours a message was on its way to Cairo: "You will immediately prepare to send forward to Fort Henry, on the Tennessee river, all your available forces. . . . Fort Henry should be taken & held at all hazards. . . . You will move with the least delay possible . . ."[32]

When the message arrived, Rawlins joyfully pounded the bank walls with his fists. Other officers threw their hats in the air, shouted with delight, and kicked their hats around like footballs. Grant laughed. Look, he told them when they caught their breath, we had better not make so much noise or Polk will hear us all the way down in Columbus and know something is up.[33]

For months Grant had fretted that he was likely to lose his command. He had fathomed its imminent possibilities as a likely arena for fame from the moment he reached Cairo. Ever since, he had expected others to see what he saw and lived in dread of being summarily relieved so that some other general, with powerful political connections or a famous name—someone like Hitchcock—would take his place. He had boasted to members of his family about the importance of his command but agonized over the prospect of losing it.[34]

Here, though, was his chance at last. This would be no inconclusive skirmish like Belmont; even less a sterile demonstration in sleet and mud. Fort Henry was a real objective, a prize to be torn from the clutches of the hated Confederacy.

—— ★ ★ ★ ★ ——

CHAPTER 13

"Unconditional
and Immediate
Surrender"

It took only a few days to assemble an army at Paducah for the advance on Fort Henry. Grant was taking twenty-three regiments, totaling nearly seventeen thousand men, supported by ironclad gunboats and a large flotilla of steamers to carry his troops. He wired Halleck on February 3: "Will be off up the Tennessee at six (6) o'clock."[1]

The steamboats could not carry the entire army south in a single lift. They took McClernand's division in the first phase, and halfway to Fort Henry a small cavalry force was dropped off to reconnoiter the enemy's positions. Five miles north of Fort Henry the steamers disembarked McClernand and the 1st Division. McClernand's troops were going to make the direct attack on the fort, while two other divisions seized the high ground around it.

Next day Grant decided to take a good look at the defenses of Fort Henry for himself and boarded one of the ironclads, the gunboat *Essex*. There was a broad stream, known as Panther Creek, only two and a half miles north of the fort. Grant wanted to see whether he could land McClernand's troops closer to their objective, sparing the men from having to cross the stream under enemy fire.

The *Essex* moved south until it was slightly below Panther Creek. A 24-pound shell whistled past and crashed into the riverbank nearby.

This was a ranging shot. The next one screamed toward the *Essex,* smashed through the officers' cabins on the stern deck—fortunately missing Grant and the gunboat commander, William D. Porter—before going out at the stern and splashing into the brown waters of the Tennessee. The gunboat promptly withdrew.[2]

McClernand's men were re-embarked and landed just north of Panther Creek. They would have to advance on foot from there. Despite this minor setback Grant had, he informed Julia, "a confidant feeling of success." And so, in his own way, had the naval commander, Flag Officer Andrew H. Foote, who taunted Grant and his staff, "I shall take it [Fort Henry] before you get there with your forces."[3]

As dusk gathered along the river, creating mists and fogs, a torpedo—or mine—that had been fished out of the Tennessee a few hours before was carried up to the fantail of the gunboat *Cincinnati.* A naval armorer began to disarm the mine for the edification of a handful of curious brass, including Grant, Foote, McClernand and C. F. Smith. The black ugly-looking object began fizzing loudly.

While the enlisted men remained rooted to the spot, the officers made a dash for the ladder leading to the deck above, Grant in the lead. When they reached the deck safely, Foote teasingly asked Grant, "General, why this haste?"

Oh, for no particular reason, said Grant, making fun of Foote's gibe, "except that the Navy may not get ahead of us!" Meanwhile the mine on the deck below fizzled out. A dud.[4]

Late at night on February 5 Grant wrote out orders for the next day. McClernand was to set his division in motion at eleven A.M., the time that the gunboat flotilla would begin steaming toward the fort. McClernand's troops were to cut the roads near Fort Henry, preventing reinforcements from getting in, the defenders from getting out.[5]

Foote was unhappy. He objected that Grant was not allowing enough time for the troops to slog their way through the muddy countryside and still to be certain of launching a ground assault that coincided with the naval attack. Grant ignored Foote's protest. Field Orders Number 1 remained as written.[6]

In the morning, four ironclads set off shortly before eleven and by twelve-thirty were in line abreast, ready to duel with the gunners of low-lying Fort Henry. Heavy rains had raised the Tennessee almost to record levels. The raging river was already swamping the fort, making it untenable. If the gunboats did not force the defenders out, the water soon would. There is an old naval adage that one gun ashore is equal to three guns afloat, but on this occasion the advantage was clearly on the side of naval gunnery. The battle began at a distance of little less than a mile.

Foote was an aggressive old salt. He pushed his gunboats forward until they had closed to three hundred yards. His gunners found themselves firing point-blank into the tormented earthen heaps that had passed for a fort only an hour or so earlier. Confederate gun crews were remorselessly driven from their pieces by intense and accurate fire. To fight on was to die. A little before two P.M. the Fort Henry commander, Brigadier General Lloyd Tilghman, hoisted a white flag. The fort would surrender to the Navy.[7]

McClernand's troops were still floundering in the mud more than a mile away. The 1st Division had not even cut the roads leading east from Fort Henry. This failure allowed some 2,500 of its 2,600 defenders to escape under McClernand's splendid Roman nose. McClernand looked like a conqueror but wasn't.

Having played no role in the battle, McClernand's command found itself little more than the tardy mud-spattered witness to Fort Henry's surrender. Foote had made good his boast, while Grant's badly conceived order showed he still had much to learn about combined arms operations.

Not that arriving second dampened the spirits of his volunteers. When they reached Fort Henry around three P.M., it was the Camp Johnston experience all over again. They looted the tents, wrote jubilant letters of triumph on captured stationery, fired the enemy's muskets, smoked the enemy's pipes, and threw an impromptu victory party in celebration of their lucky, victorious selves. There was no sense of chagrin at having been beaten to the objective by Foote's sailors. "We had enough of fighting ere the war was over," wrote one of them, "and after [Belmont] we never begrudged other forces the honor of gaining victory without our help."[8]

Most of the ninety-two Confederates who were captured were wounded men. Those who got away departed in good order, carrying most of their arms and equipment right past the slackly led and unenterprising 1st Division. Vain, boastful and almost comically ambitious, McClernand demonstrated no talent for military command and little grasp of military realities. He seemed oblivious to the importance of the mission spelled out in Grant's orders. The Confederates who paraded across McClernand's front would fight another day, at nearby Fort Donelson.

Grant tried to cover up this failure in his official report on the battle by asserting that because McClernand's troops were asleep at eleven P.M. the previous night, when he had written out Field Orders Number 1, "I did not deem it practicable to set an earlier hour than 11 O'clock to-day to commence the investment."

The feebleness of this excuse reflects something Grant never discussed and rarely hinted at—his lack of confidence in his volunteer troops and their officers. The history of war is hardly short of examples of commanders being told in the middle of the night that they would advance on the enemy at dawn. Scott had done it in Mexico. Grant tried to confuse the issue by claiming, "The garrison I think must have commenced their retreat last night or early this morning," which he would have known was simply untrue from conversations with the fort's captured officers, as well as from McClernand.[9]

Believing that Fort Donelson, only twelve miles to the east, was a mere outpost, lightly manned and now ripe for the taking, Grant penned a telegram to Halleck that was a trumpet blast: "Fort Henry is ours. . . . I shall take and destroy Fort Donaldson [*sic*] on the eighth and return to Fort Henry."[10]

★

Victory worried Halleck. Fort Henry captured was another place to defend. And suppose the Confederates launched a strong counterattack? What if Polk even launched an attack on Cairo from Columbus? An army in the flush of victory is always likely to be overextended and vulnerable on its flanks or in the rear. And there was no doubt about it— Cairo was virtually undefended. Grant had stripped the place of men and munitions when he set off for Fort Henry. He paid almost no attention to the crucial need to secure flanks and rear areas during any major advance. It is a need that is all too easy to forget about in the giddy days of a successful offensive.

Grant had run huge risks, probably never gave them more than a moment's thought, and won, while the vaunted Albert Sidney Johnston was proving to be indecisive. If Fort Henry was Grant's opportunity to strike, Cairo was his. One strong thrust at Cairo and chances are that Grant would have been forced to scramble back from Fort Henry. At the least he would have abandoned all thought of pressing on to Fort Donelson. The Confederates could have gotten Grant off their backs forever.

Such recklessness only reinforced Halleck's conviction that Grant was a bad investment, bound to go bust one day. Grant was completely unaware of the machinations in St. Louis, but following the fall of Fort Henry, Halleck was almost desperate to get rid of him, although he still hadn't heard anything from Ethan Allen Hitchcock. Not even Halleck would deny that the advance had been a splendid, albeit hair-raising, success. Union forces had cracked the center of the Columbus to Bowling Green front, but by all accounts it was the Navy that had won down at Fort Henry, not Grant.

Halleck sent him a message: "Hold on to Fort Henry at all hazards. Picks and shovels are sent and large reinforcements will be sent immediately." Along with entrenching equipment, Halleck also dispatched his own chief of staff, Brigadier General George W. Cullum, to Fort Henry. On arriving there, Cullum told Grant he had come "to facilitate your very important operations," but Grant wouldn't have been fooled for a moment. He surely saw Cullum for what he was—Halleck's spy.[11]

Four days after Fort Henry fell, Hitchcock reluctantly returned to active duty. There was no chance of getting Hitchcock out west before Grant moved on Fort Donelson, but the first part of Halleck's plan was working. At least the old warhorse was now back in harness. Halleck promptly urged McClellan to have Hitchcock assigned to the Western Department.[12]

★

The morning of February 12 Grant informed Halleck: "We start this morning for Fort Donaldson [sic] in heavy force."[13] Then he rode out from Fort Henry at the head of fifteen thousand troops, chatting animatedly with his staff, excited as only movement and the thrilling phenomenology of war could excite him. Suddenly the spirited stallion ridden by surgeon John H. Brinton broke into a fast walk. "Doctor," called Grant. "I believe I command this army and I think I'll go first." The staff burst out laughing while a chagrined Brinton reined in his horse and fell in behind Grant.[14]

It was a magnificent day—blue skies, balmy temperatures—a heady taste of spring in the middle of winter. Grant's innocent volunteers threw their overcoats and blankets aside, and their volunteer officers, no wiser than they, made no attempt to stop them.

When Grant first told Halleck he intended to seize Fort Donelson, his confidence bordered on complacency. He seemed to imagine it would be no harder to take than Fort Henry, and if he could, he would have gladly seized it without the help of the self-satisfied sailors. "The Army is rather chop fallen," a gloating Flag Officer Foote had informed his wife after Fort Henry fell and Grant came to proffer congratulations through gritted teeth.[15]

By the time Grant set off for Fort Donelson, carrying no more baggage than a toothbrush in a waistcoat pocket, he had revised his earlier opinion. He now believed there might be as many as ten thousand Confederates at Fort Donelson. Bad guess. There were more like twenty thousand. Albert Sidney Johnston had allowed two of the officers there—Brigadier Generals Gideon Pillow and Bushrod Johnson—to talk him into making a do-or-die stand.

For one thing, defeating Grant on the Cumberland would redeem the loss of Fort Henry. For another, the position was strategically placed, surmounting a 120-foot bluff overlooking a bend in the river. It was, in effect, the rampart that blocked a Union advance on Nashville, seventy miles to the southeast, which was one of the most important railheads in all of North America.

The defenses at Donelson consisted of the fort itself and several defensive layers. There were entrenchments, an impressive abatis and thousands of rifle pits. The outer defenses snaked out to embrace the village of Dover, less than a mile away. As Grant's leading units approached defensive positions three miles west of the fort, brisk firefights erupted. A Confederate cavalry force under the intrepid Nathan Bedford Forrest—probably the finest cavalry commander of the war—harried Grant's overly confident troops.

The moment was ideal for a spoiling attack against Grant's army as it picked its way along two narrow roads winding through heavily wooded and hilly terrain. Yet apart from this sporadic skirmishing, no attempt was made to block its advance. Confederate commanders in the West seemed too embroiled in heated arguments over strategy to pay attention to tactics.

That night Grant and his staff bedded down at the widow Crisp's small log farmhouse, four miles from the fort. The general was snug in a double feather bed set up in the kitchen, which also boasted a large fireplace. For Grant, who was suffering from a severe and lingering cold, it could hardly have seemed more welcoming.[16]

However, his soldiers, out in the open, were incredulous at the fickleness of Tennessee weather. When the sun went down on a springlike day, it was followed by a bitter, mid-winter night that fell like a hammer blow, stunning Grant's young volunteers. They suffered for want of the heavy brown blankets and warm blue overcoats they had so gleefully thrown away only that morning. Their only comfort was provided by the pigs.

The woods between Henry and Donelson were dotted with farms, and most seemed to have at least one large pig herd roaming the February woods gorging on acorns. Throughout the fight for Fort Donelson, the evening air was spiced with the aroma of roasted pork rising from huge bonfires in the Federals' camp.[17]

Grant's plan for taking Fort Donelson was a reprise of his plan at Fort Henry. He would place a cordon around it to prevent reinforcements from coming in and block its defenders from getting out. The gunboats would wreck the fort's artillery. An infantry assault would crush the demoralized survivors.

Fort Donelson was commanded by John Floyd, who had served as secretary of war under Lincoln's predecessor, President James Buchanan. His principal subordinates were Gideon Pillow; Grant's old friend Simon Bolivar Buckner, a fellow cadet at the Academy; and Bushrod Johnson. Buckner had helped Grant out when he was in New York in 1854, desperately short of money. Floyd had never been a professional soldier; nor had Pillow, who, like Floyd, had been made a general more for his political connections than any military ability. Nevertheless, the sole professional, Buckner, carried less weight than either of the two politicians.

As scouts reported in and prisoners were interrogated, it became obvious to Grant as he sat at Mrs. Crisp's kitchen table the morning of February 13 that Fort Donelson was much more strongly held than he had imagined. He sent a message to Halleck saying he needed reinforcements, and gave his two division commanders—John McClernand and C. F. Smith—firm instructions. They could probe the enemy's position, but they were not to bring on a battle.

As Smith's troops deployed on the Union left and McClernand's advanced toward high ground on the right, they got involved in heavy fighting that had no purpose at all. For a couple of hours Grant's army was at risk of being drawn into what is known as "a soldier's battle"— one where men fight simply because they are fighting. There is no objective to be seized, no victory to be won.

While volleys of musketry erupted and cannon roared back at cannon, Grant—almost gray from head to foot after galloping down muddy roads—was boarding Foote's flagship, the *St. Louis*. Over the next hour or so he insisted that Foote had to send his gunboats against the fort. Halleck had already demanded as much in a message to the Navy Department and here was Grant applying the pressure in person. The normally aggressive Foote was reluctant to attack. The fighting at Fort Henry had left him in need of replacements for his injured sailors, and his ironclads were still suffering serious battle damage.[18]

Foote had four mortar barges ready to be launched, and he begged Grant to wait a little longer so he could get them into action. Grant refused to wait. Every hour's delay only worked to the defenders' advantage. In the end, rather than risk being blamed for any failure to take Fort Donelson, Foote had little choice but to do as Grant and Halleck demanded. A confident Grant left the flagship in a jaunty mood. Swinging himself up onto his horse, he couldn't resist telling a knot of curious bystanders that with the help of the gunboats he could take Fort Donelson and capture every one of its defenders. Then he galloped away like a man heading for a party.[19]

The next day, February 14, Foote's gunboat flotilla—four ironclads in the lead, followed by two timberclads—steamed toward Fort Donelson. Foote repeated the tactics that had paid off at Fort Henry: he had his flotilla get in close. It was a mistake. Fort Donelson's artillery consisted largely of medium-calibers. The heavy ordnance aboard the ironclads had every gun in Fort Donelson but one outranged. They could have given the defenses a leisurely pounding. Instead, as the gunboats pressed steadily on, the effectiveness of Fort Donelson's artillery increased with every yard they advanced. Two of the ironclads were knocked out of action. They drifted away down the Cumberland, their steering shot away.[20]

Defeating the gunboats ought to have provided whatever encouragement the defenders of Fort Donelson needed to mount a strong counterattack. Foote's failure was a serious rebuff, an opportunity to be exploited. But, no—Floyd and Pillow were as inert as ever.

Grant's position was far from brilliant at this point. Even after receiving reinforcements, he had only twenty thousand men at Fort Donelson, while another five thousand guarded the two roads over which his supplies traveled. Each side had a roughly equal number of troops to put into battle. Yet it is an axiom of war that the attacker nearly always needs an advantage of at least three to one to be sure of defeating a well-entrenched enemy. Had Grant made a frontal assault on Fort Donelson, he would have run up a casualty list longer than his blue-clad arm and might still not have won a victory, as he was well aware.

The alternative, a prolonged siege, was not without its own risks. The fort might eventually fall, but not before Halleck had found a way of getting Grant out and someone Halleck knew and respected, such as Hitchcock, in. Grant did not discover until after the war that Halleck had been trying hard to replace him. The reason for his burning impatience now was not the knife threatening his back but something even more compelling: A siege was simply not in Grant's nature. The very thought made him squirm. War was movement, battles, the clash of arms, the decisive result. He wrote gloomily to Julia late that night, "The taking of Donelson bids fair to be a long job."[21]

Grant was lucky once again, luckier than most generals can ever hope to be. But he had his own way of generating luck: Press the enemy hard, press him often, and he is almost sure to make a major mistake. With a Federal army now camped at his door and Foote's gunboats still in the river at his back, the volatile Pillow grew panicky. Having earlier insisted the fort absolutely had to be held, he now began arguing it would have to be abandoned. He wanted the defenders to launch a surprise attack early the next morning, punch a hole in the Union lines, and make a break for it, but not before coming back and collecting all their supplies and artillery. It hardly takes a West Point graduate to spot the crucial flaw in this plan.

After an early breakfast in the widow Crisp's kitchen the morning of February 15, Grant dictated some messages, including one to Halleck: "Appearances now indicate we will have a protracted siege."[22] Then he rode off to see Foote, who had suffered a leg injury during the previous day's engagement and was in no condition to travel. It was a bitterly cold morning and sleet blew across across the battlefield. Grant and Foote had a brief, inconclusive discussion aboard the *St. Louis,* anchored out in the Cumberland.

The gunboats were too damaged to mount another attack, said Foote. He would not be able to do much before the mortar boats were available. Grant returned to the landing in a somber frame of mind when his aide, William Hillyer, galloped up ashen-faced. A ferocious battle had erupted, Hillyer panted. The rebels were making an all-out assault and McClernand's division was in full retreat. Grant galloped back to the farmhouse.[23]

That dawn intense artillery fire had poured down on McClernand's 1st Division, on the right of Grant's line. For the next few hours the Confederates attacked repeatedly, driving McClernand's troops back, never giving them time to consolidate in a new position. C. F. Smith and the 2nd Division were too far to the left to offer support, but help was at hand.

Only the previous day Grant had organized the fresh regiments Halleck had sent him into a provisional division and entrusted it to Brigadier General Lewis Wallace, a man destined to be far less famous for anything he did in the Civil War than for his best-selling novel *Ben-Hur.* Wallace's bright-green division was hurriedly wedged into the center of the Union line. When the pressure on McClernand's division became overwhelming, Wallace moved one of his three brigades to the right. McClernand's survivors retreated through it, taking shelter behind.

The Confederates had succeeded in punching a hole in the encircling Union line. A road south was wide open. Floyd and Pillow could now make a fighting retreat toward Nashville. There was nothing to stop them getting most of their army out by nightfall.

Grant galloped up to his headquarters at the farmhouse, and his staff quickly briefed him. He scribbled a note to Foote, urging him to have his gunboats open fire. Grant's note said he needed to raise the morale of his troops and depress that of the foe. "If all the Gun Boats that can, will immediately make their appearance to the enemy, it may secure us a Victory. Otherwise all may be defeated. . . . I must order a charge to save appearances. I do not expect the Gun Boats to go into action but to make their appearance and throw shells at long range." Shortly afterward the Navy obliged.[24]

Riding on to inspect the situation, Grant arrived on the battlefield at the left of the line. C. F. Smith's 2nd Division was well posted on the frozen ground and intact. As Grant rode through Wallace's division, everything at first seemed under control. But at the right-center of the line there was confusion, and when he reached the right wing he found a mood close to panic. Men were milling around complaining they were out of ammunition, yet there were hundreds of ammunition boxes piled up nearby.

Volunteer officers sometimes had to be led by the hand, even in the middle of battle, and problems of ammunition supply in close combat persisted throughout the war. Grant pointed to the nearby ammo crates and said bluntly to the troops within earshot, "Fill your cartridge boxes quick and get into line. The enemy is trying to escape and must not be permitted to do so."[25]

Wallace and McClernand were conferring when Grant galloped up, holding a sheaf of what looked like telegrams in his left hand. McClernand grumbled, "This army wants a head"—an implied rebuke for Grant's absence during the crisis.[26]

Grant ignored that, blandly responding, "It seems so." He told Wallace and McClernand to pull their men back onto higher ground, dig in and hold until reinforcements arrived. McClernand replied that it was too late for that—the enemy had a clear road out.

Grant's face flushed and he crushed the papers in his left hand. Then, willing a calmness he clearly did not feel, he said in a matter-of-fact way, "Gentlemen, the position on the right must be retaken."[27]

Shortly after this, the pressure slackened abruptly. Instead of making a fighting withdrawal, the Confederates were returning to their own lines to collect supplies and artillery. This was war à la Pillow, and a weird godsend it was to the Federals. Grant turned to Colonel Webster. "Some of our men are pretty demoralized, but the enemy must be more so. He has attempted to force his way out, but has fallen back. The one who attacks first now will be victorious, and the enemy will have to be in a hurry if he gets ahead of me."[28]

It was obvious to Grant that if the Confederates had put nearly all their weight into an attack against his right, they must be wide open to a powerful counterstroke over on the left. Grant cantered up to C. F. Smith's command post. He found Smith, the awe-inspiring West Point commandant of his cadet years, sitting under a tree. "General Smith," said Grant. "All has failed on the right. You must take Fort Donelson."

Smith, a tall, handsome and slender sixty-year-old, got to his feet, pulled himself erect, brushed his flowing white mustache, and responded, "I will do it."

When Smith's division charged it found the Confederate position as lightly manned as Grant had foreseen, but a huge abatis blocked any direct assault on the fort. Smith rode among his men, holding his cap aloft on the point of his sword, shouting, "Damn you, gentlemen. I see skulkers! I'll have none here. . . . You volunteered to be killed for the love of your country, and now you can be. . . . I'm only a [professional] soldier and I don't want to be killed, but *you* came to be killed . . ."[29] His men scrambled over the abatis and fell on the defenders behind it. Many a Confederate fled rather than fight. Night and a light snowfall descended on a Confederate army that was hunkering down and on thousands of Smith's men, who were now inside the last line of Donelson's defenses.

Grant and Webster rode over the battlefield at dusk. Icy temperatures were freezing the dead into grotesque attitudes that only accentuated the violence that had killed them. The wounded, suffering from pain, thirst and terror of dying, groaned, sobbed and called out for help. Grant felt suddenly depressed. "Let's get away from this dreadful place," he said to Webster. "I suppose this work is part of the devil that is in us all."

Riding away, words came to him, a few lines of poetry. Grant had remembered a poem of Byron's during his first battle in Mexico. Now a poem by Robert Burns flashed through his mind. To any sensitive soul, there is steel in great verse and the downcast Grant recited to himself Burns's "Man Is Made to Mourn," like a secular prayer.

> *Man's inhumanity to man*
> *Makes countless thousands mourn . . .*[30]

In the middle of the night, a Confederate officer approached Smith's lines with a message from General Buckner. The defenders, he said, were asking for an armistice. When Smith was informed, he burst out hotly, "I make no terms with rebels with arms in their hands—my terms are immediate and unconditional surrender!" Smith took the letter the Confederate officer was carrying and rode off with it to the widow Crisp's house. He handed the letter to Grant while Grant, roused from sleep, was still struggling to get dressed. *"There's* something for you to read, General," Smith announced.

"What answer should I send to this, General?" asked Grant when he had finished it.

"No terms to the damned rebels!" Grant, amused, laughed quietly and sat down at the kitchen table to write a reply to Buckner:

> Yours of this date proposing Armistice and appointment of Commissioners to settle terms of Capitulation is just received. No terms except unconditional and immediate surrender can be accepted. I propose to move immediately upon your works.
>
> Your obt. svt.
U.S. Grant
Brig. Gen.[31]

When he finished writing, he read the letter aloud. Smith harrumphed. No ornate courtesies for him. A soldier didn't waste his time on folderol. "It's the same thing in smoother words," Smith said bluntly, then stalked out of the room, carrying Grant's letter.[32]

During the night, Floyd and Pillow made their escape by boat, leaving Buckner to endure the obloquy of surrender alone. Buckner considered Grant's terms unduly harsh, but he had no choice. And when the two men came face-to-face later that day, they chatted and joked, plainly delighted at meeting up again. Grant, eager to repay an old kindness, drew Buckner aside and told him that now that he was a prisoner, he might find himself in need of money. If so, Grant's purse was available.[33]

Capturing an entire army is a rare and spectacular moment in any general's career. Washington had done it at Yorktown. Scott had done it at Vera Cruz. Surgeon John Brinton was looking forward to seeing the enemy regiments paraded in front of the victors while Union bands played patriotic airs and Buckner formally handed over his sword. Like victory, capitulation too had its rituals. Brinton asked Grant just when the surrender ceremony would be held.

"There will be nothing of the kind," Grant replied. "The surrender is now a fact. We have the fort, the men, the guns. Why should we go through vain forms and mortify and injure the spirit of brave men, who after all are our own countrymen and brothers?" It was, thought Brinton, a strange note to end on. But Grant's idea would prove to be the modern one, and the truly novel always seems strange at first.[34]

That night Grant wrote to Julia and couldn't resist boasting, "After the greatest victory of the season . . . some 12 or 15 thousand prisoners have fallen into our possession. . . . This is the largest capture I believe ever made on the continent."[35]

He could be forgiven if he believed that now, finally, his hold on command was secure. But he would have been wrong. Halleck still intended to shelve him, maybe even dump him. Grant's next battle would be a fight to save his career.

★ ★ ★ ★

CHAPTER 14

"It Begins to
Look Like Home"

B y January 1862 Lincoln was running out of patience. Did his generals have *any* intention of driving into the rebellious South and
crushing the Confederacy? There were five hundred thousand Union
soldiers drawing pay and rations, yet nowhere could he find a sense of
urgency to close with the foe. He did not realize how long it was going
to take to turn the Union Army into a truly effective force, but his impatience was the country's impatience and a factor that commanders like
McClellan and Halleck ignored at their peril.

On January 27 Lincoln issued President's War Order Number 1,
demanding a "general movement" of all Union forces on February 22,
Washington's birthday.[1] With Lincoln's deadline only days away,
Grant's triumph at Fort Donelson gave the President a boost that he and
the Union needed almost desperately. Since Fort Sumter, there had been
ten galling months of defeats, retreats, setbacks, frustrations. Here at
last was a beacon as bright as a gas flare, a coruscating promise that the
North could and would defeat the Confederacy, for all its famous martial virtues. Bells were pealed, hats were thrown, steamboat whistles
tooted, champagne was gulped, cannon boomed, flags were waved,
toasts were offered, throats bellowed sore, bunting draped feverishly,
diaries were enlivened, backs pounded, hands shaken, cigars puffed

with deep satisfaction, couples coupled, newspapers snatched, diners addressed, juvenile recruits scratched x's on enlistment papers and lied about their age as bands blared, oraters orated, paraders paraded, maps were pored over, and in large houses strategy was explained by Papa while he solemnly deployed forks, spoons and cruets across the breakfast table to demonstrate the movements of armies.

Everybody within reach of it rushed to grab a slice of the glory. Halleck, McClellan, McClernand, even Frémont, each claimed that it was he who had really brought the fall of Fort Donelson. Grant was at most the tool they had so brilliantly, so farsightedly, so boldly and so cleverly used. The man himself was nothing much.

Halleck's response to Fort Donelson was to credit success not to Grant but to C. F. Smith, who, he reported, "when the battle was against us turned the tide . . ."[2] And instead of exploiting the victory, Halleck chose to pour his energies into politicking for the creation of a "Department of the West," with himself in command. He had tried persuading Buell to agree to come under his control while Grant was at Fort Donelson, by promising to get Grant transferred out of the department. He evidently thought—probably with good reason—that Buell despised Grant as much as he did.[3]

The opinion that really mattered, though, was Lincoln's. Hours after the news flashed into the telegraph office at the War Department that Buckner had surrendered, he signed the papers nominating Grant for promotion to major general. There would be other promotions in days to come, but Grant would be senior to everyone in the West but Halleck.

Grant's message to Buckner was savored as a marvel of prose at its pithiest. The line about "unconditional and immediate surrender" sent otherwise sober men into raptures. What's in a name? As much as a delirious country can cram into it. Grant's initials instantly came to stand for "Unconditional Surrender." A newspaper report that he liked the occasional cigar brought a flood of coronas, cheroots and cigarillos to his door. Boxes of cigars piled up at his headquarters like ammunition, and in the end proved just as fatal.

Halleck, living in a world that to a large extent consisted of Halleck talking to himself, was meanwhile throwing away much of what Grant had gained. The Confederacy had been poleaxed, like a boxer hit hard and flush on the point of the jaw. Albert Sidney Johnston's entire front had just collapsed. The Confederacy hurriedly abandoned both Columbus and Bowling Green, leaving behind mountains of matériel the South could ill afford to lose. A new front would have to be created more than one hundred miles to the rear. Virtually the whole of Kentucky and Tennessee were written off by the Confederacy.

The time was ripe for another heavy blow, but Halleck held Grant back. "Had any license or discretion been given to Grant," wrote a sympathetic visitor to whom Grant poured out his anger and dismay, "he would have occupied Alabama and Mississippi two weeks ago and scattered any forces the enemy had up there."[4]

Following the capture of Fort Donelson, Halleck explained his grand design to Assistant Secretary of War Thomas A. Scott. His plan was to have Major General David Hunter, presently still chasing Sterling Price into Arkansas, command the westernmost areas of the department, and have Hitchcock take over in Missouri and Tennessee while Buell retained command in Kentucky and Ohio. There was no mention of a role for Grant.

The best he could have hoped for, if Halleck got his way, was some minor post in the rear, where he would oversee the paperwork while Hunter, Hitchcock and Buell, all cautious men in the Halleck mold, commanded the field armies and advanced slowly, entrenching every step of the way to New Orleans, digging rather than fighting the road to victory. Of course, what Halleck conjured up before Scott's wondering eyes was an exciting vision—earthshaking victories won at little cost and achieved in no time at all. If only Washington had the wisdom to give him all that he asked for.

While there was need for a better command arrangement in the West, Halleck's proposal was based less on a dispassionate appraisal of the military situation than on two personal projects—winning a greater role for himself and a smaller one for Grant. In the end, Halleck got most of what he wanted, and Buell was placed under his command. Even so, the prolonged negotiations with the War Department over reorganization helped give Johnston the time he needed to create a new defensive line. Nor, in the end, did Halleck get the services of Ethan Allen Hitchcock. Grumbling and unhappy as he struggled back into uniform, the old warrior refused to take a field command. He was assigned to the War Department instead.[5]

Grant was appalled and amazed at the inertia that fell like a wet blanket over his army. He did not know what was taking place at Halleck's headquarters, how the wires sizzled between St. Louis and Washington with schemes to push him into a backwater. All he knew was that the day after Fort Donelson surrendered, his command was designated "the Department of West Tennessee." Halleck put Sherman, who was something of a protégé, into Grant's old headquarters at Cairo.

Grant's every instinct was to drive on at once, capture Nashville, and smash Johnston's army while it was still withdrawing, still in shock. He wrote to Halleck three days after Buckner capitulated: "I can have Nashville on Saturday week." Halleck refused to let him advance on the city. Nashville, he was informed, was in Buell's command, not his.[6]

He champed at the bit for a week, growing increasingly frustrated, and finally took action. A division of troops from Buell's Army of the Ohio had been sent to reinforce Grant during the Fort Donelson campaign. They arrived too late for that, so he had to send them back. Grant ordered the division's commander to report to Buell . . . in Nashville. At this point Buell was making halting progress toward the city. Grant had hit on a way of speeding its capture. It was a clever and ingenious move but not one that Halleck or Buell was likely to appreciate. The city fell without a fight on February 26.[7]

Even so, Buell was outraged and complained bitterly to Halleck. Like Halleck, Buell could not move without thinking he heard Albert Sidney Johnston sneaking up behind him. His reaction to the news that Nashville had fallen was to demand reinforcements, immediately and in large numbers. Grant, fearing nothing from Johnston, went to take a look at the city. This provoked even more bleating from Buell.

His protests fell on receptive ears. Halleck was so determined by now to get rid of Grant that he had few scruples about how he did it. "It is hard to censure a successful general," he informed McClellan, "but I think he richly deserves it. I can get no returns, no reports, no information of any kind from him. Satisfied with his victory, he sits down and enjoys it without any regard to the future. I am tired out with his neglect and inefficiency. C. F. Smith is almost the only officer equal to the emergency."[8]

Under normal circumstances, Halleck would have been justified in complaining that Grant was slow to report the strength of his command to St. Louis, but Halleck never sent any specific request for this information or told Grant it was needed urgently. Besides, it was difficult to obtain information from his widely scattered forces, many of which were presently in motion. Furthermore, Halleck was well aware that the telegraph line to Fort Henry was not completed until a week after the fall of Fort Donelson. He had also been informed more than once that flooding and other problems made the line unreliable even after it was completed. On top of which, Grant claimed, a rebel sympathizer in the Fort Henry telegraph office was stopping many of his messages from getting through to St. Louis.[9]

Be that as it may, any assertion that Halleck got no information from Grant was absurd. There are more than a dozen letters and telegrams in the National Archives and the Library of Congress sent from Grant to Halleck and to Halleck's chief of staff in the two weeks following the capture of Fort Donelson. It is likely there were others that have not survived.

In the extant correspondence, Grant offers ideas on how to exploit the success at Fort Donelson. Far from sitting down and savoring his victory, he is champing at the bit, eager to get on with the war. His great fear is not that Albert Sidney Johnston might attack him but that, having been elevated to two stars, he could find himself stuck behind a desk when what he wanted most was to get back into the saddle. "If a command inferior to my rank is given me," he wrote Julia, "it shall make no difference to my zeal."[10]

Halleck complained to the War Department that Grant had left his command without authority when he visited Nashville. He did not mention that Grant had specifically informed him in advance: "I will go to Nashville . . . should there be no orders to prevent it." Halleck was trying to build a case for Grant's removal, and anything would do.[11]

He even suggested to McClellan that the problem might have been due to Grant's getting drunk. "If so, it will account for his neglect of my oft-repeated orders." There was not a shred of evidence for this, but in his eagerness to rid himself of Grant, what was truth when rumor might do?[12]

McClellan gave Halleck the carte blanche he was looking for: "Do not hesitate to arrest him at once if the good of the service requires it and place C. F. Smith in command. You are at liberty to regard this as a positive order . . ."[13] As nutty ideas go, this one was a pecan pie.

Arresting Grant on any charge short of provable treason only three weeks after the capture of Fort Donelson would have provoked a command crisis that gave comfort to no one apart from Albert Sidney Johnston, Robert E. Lee, Jefferson Davis and six million other Confederates. The northern press—especially in Illinois and Ohio, both of which were bursting with pride over Grant—would have screamed that the war effort was being damaged. So too would powerful members of Congress who admired Grant, such as Elihu B. Washburne, who had a lot of influence with Lincoln.

The President and the secretary of war, Edwin Stanton, would inevitably have been drawn into the fray had Grant been arrested. The War Department would be virtually paralyzed until the situation was resolved, which could take weeks, possibly months. McClellan had no more sense of the seamless web between war and politics than Halleck. But as good soldiers should, they considered themselves far above politics, and confident of McClellan's backing, Halleck proceeded to put the next part of his plan into operation.

Grant was preparing to advance into southwestern Tennessee when he received a blunt telegram from Old Brains: "You will place Major General C. F. Smith in command of the expedition and remain yourself at Fort Henry. Why do you not obey my orders to report strength and positions of your command?"[14]

Grant was hurt and bewildered. This was the first indication he had that Halleck was trying to dump him. What really hurt, though, was that Smith had just been given his combat units and would lead them south. He showed the telegram to a friend, tears filling his eyes. "I don't know what they mean to do with me. What command have I now?" He later claimed he was "in disgrace and practically under arrest." This was a gross exaggeration, but the fact that he remembered it that way indicates the depth of his anguish and a bitterness that never lost its cutting edge.[15]

Washburne's brother Colonel Cadwallader C. Washburn (they spelled their names differently) happened to be at Fort Henry when Halleck's message arrived. The excuses Halleck used to strip Grant of most of his troops were so frivolous, the colonel informed his congressman brother, that they had to be false, as indeed they were.[16]

Halleck piled on the humiliation with a follow-up telegram. "Your neglect of repeated orders to report the strength of your command has created great dissatisfaction and seriously interfered with military plans."[17]

Grant was incensed. The claim that he had so neglected his duties as to delay the prosecution of the war was as unjust as it was false. "If my course is not satisfactory," he cabled Halleck angrily, "remove me at once. . . . I respectfully ask to be relieved from further duty in the department."[18]

Halleck longed to be rid of Grant and probably saw Grant's threat as bringing him closer to his goal. He responded by sending a lying message designed to deflect Grant's attention and muddy the waters. He told Grant that the root of any trouble between them was McClellan. Here was the bureaucratic infighter, demonstrating all the pusillanimity that back-stabbing inevitably breeds.[19]

Grant replied by sending Halleck a breakdown on the number and disposition of his forces. He also sent a stiff rebuke: "You had a better chance of knowing my strength whilst surrounding Fort Donelson than I had." After all, every soldier he commanded was sent to him by Halleck.[20]

Then, on March 13, Grant received an anonymous letter forwarded in the first instance to Halleck by Judge David Davis, a friend of Lincoln's. The letter asserted that Grant's troops had looted Confederate supplies captured at Fort Donelson. Halleck attached a note to the letter before sending it on to Grant: "The want of order and discipline and the numerous irregularities in your command . . . are matters of general notoriety. . . . Unless these things are immediately corrected I am directed to relieve you of your command."

Fizzing with fury, Grant wrote an angry response. He drew Halleck's attention to the orders he had published the day after Donelson fell to prevent looting. He had followed this up with other orders and stiff punishments. Grant saw the issue for what it was—a breakdown of discipline, and nowhere is discipline more important than in combat units in the front line. Even so, at Fort Donelson, as elsewhere throughout the war, Union soldiers were resourceful and enthusiastic pillagers. The nub of the problem was not that Grant was slack but that many volunteer officers were as ready as their troops to steal anything within reach.

His anger by this time boiling over, Grant concluded by shoving his ace right down Halleck's throat: "There is such a disposition to find fault with me that I again ask to be relieved from further duty *until I can be placed right in the estimation of those in higher authority* [italics added]." This could mean only one thing—Grant was going to appeal to the War Department, possibly to Lincoln, and demand a court of inquiry.

Less than forty-eight hours before Grant sent this message, word had reached St. Louis that Lincoln, his patience with McClellan exhausted, had fired him as general-in-chief. When Halleck received Grant's angry telegram, he found himself holding a bomb, and it was about to

explode. Halleck had been priming McClellan to back him in any showdown with Grant. With McClellan in severe presidential disfavor, he
was too weak and shaken a reed to rely on now. Halleck's great interest
had instantly changed from getting rid of Grant to making sure Grant
did not explode and wipe both of them out. He was suddenly desperate
to avoid any inquiry that might bring into the light of day the shabby
way he had tried to get Grant sidelined.

And the whole underhanded scheme was threatening to get completely out of hand. Halleck had just received a telegram from the War
Department asking whether it was true that Grant had "left his command without leave," failed to provide strength returns, or acted "not in
accordance with military subordination, or propriety." McClellan had
evidently been playing his part in Halleck's scheme. But with McClellan out and Grant demanding a court of inquiry, Halleck may have had
visions of himself vanishing down a black hole. The documentary
record he had been trying to build up to justify Grant's ouster suddenly
looked sick. If anything, it was virtually all on Grant's side, not his.
That record has damaged Halleck's reputation to this day.[21]

The first thing he had to do was to get Grant to drop all thought of
demanding an inquiry. He sent him a telegram immediately. "You cannot be relieved from your command. . . . Instead of relieving you, I wish
you as soon as your new army is in the field, to assume the immediate
command and lead it on to new victories."[22]

Grant was too elated to waste time trying to figure out what was
going on between St. Louis and Washington. He would not learn the
truth until after the war. His mind and emotions switched instantly to
the tens of thousands of Union troops already advancing into southwestern Tennessee for a move against Corinth, Mississippi. Back in the
saddle again.

Before leaving Fort Henry for the last time, he dropped a line to
Julia; "What you may look for is hard to say, possibly a big fight. I have
already been in so many it begins to look like home to me."[23]

CHAPTER 15

"Lick 'Em Tomorrow"

He was the man who had the North worried. Albert Sidney Johnston was built like John Wayne—six feet, one inch, 210 pounds, with a confidence-inspiring barrel chest and a jaw that looked like it could be used for breaking rocks. His square-cut, ruggedly handsome features were accentuated by a vigorous black mustache and a penetrating blue-eyed gaze. He was brave and he was charismatic. After graduating from West Point in 1826, Johnston served in the first cavalry regiment the U.S. Army raised, fought in the war for Texan independence, compiled an impressive combat record in Mexico, and achieved national fame leading a punitive expedition against the Mormons in 1857.

When Fort Sumter was attacked, he was commanding the Western Department. Lincoln tried to win his services by offering him promotion to major general, but Johnston chose to throw in his lot instead with his close friend Jefferson Davis and serve the Confederacy. That first year, northern generals held him in greater respect than all other rebel army commanders.[1]

Not even the loss of Forts Henry and Donelson shook the South's faith in its hero. It looked to him now to work a minor miracle and, with some help from Halleck, he obliged. Johnston got seven weeks after Fort Donelson fell to pull together a new army. By April he had more

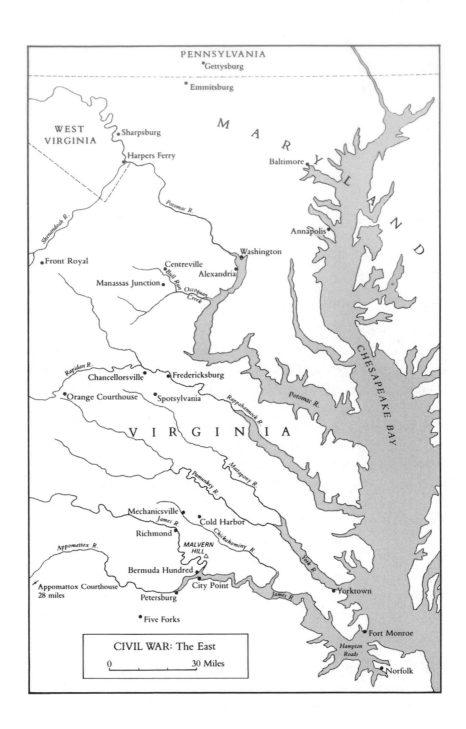

PENNSYLVANIA
• Gettysburg

• Emmitsburg

MARYLAND

WEST
VIRGINIA

• Sharpsburg

• Harpers Ferry

Baltimore •

Potomac R.

Shenandoah R.

Annapolis •

• Front Royal

Centreville •
Alexandria •

Washington •

Manassas Junction •

Bull Run

Occoquan Creek

CHESAPEAKE BAY

Rapidan R.

Chancellorsville •

• Fredericksburg

• Orange Courthouse

• Spotsylvania

Rappahannock R.

Potomac R.

V I R G I N I A

Mattapony R.

Pumunkey R.

Mechanicsville •
Richmond •

James R.

• Cold Harbor

Chickahominy R.

Appomattox R.

MALVERN
HILL △

Bermuda Hundred •

York R.

Appomattox Courthouse
28 miles

City Point •

Petersburg •

James R.

Yorktown •

• Five Forks

Fort Monroe •

CIVIL WAR: The East

0   30 Miles

Hampton Roads

• Norfolk

than forty thousand men concentrated at Corinth, where two major railroads met close to the Tennessee-Mississippi border. Johnston's plan was to establish a defensive position there and make it strong enough to halt Grant's advance and save the lower South.

Grant meanwhile was overseeing the buildup of the Army of the Tennessee, which numbered roughly forty thousand men, organized in six divisions. Grant concentrated his force twenty miles northeast of Corinth, at Pittsburg Landing. The landing, on the west bank of the Tennessee River, had once been busy with steamboats loading cotton. In recent years it had fallen into disuse as the railroads penetrated western Tennessee.

Sherman, commanding one of Grant's six divisions, had recommended it as a good place to establish a military base. Grant went one better. He moved virtually his entire army into Pittsburg Landing. As new units arrived, they went down there and reported to Sherman, who told them where to pitch camp. The exception was Lew Wallace's division, which was placed at Crump's Landing, roughly five miles to the north.

Grant himself chose to move into a brick mansion, owned by a strong Union man named Cherry, nine miles from Pittsburg Landing, in the village of Savannah, on the eastern side of the river. Here he brought his staff, here commanders reported to him, and here he awaited the arrival of Buell and the Army of the Ohio, numbering twenty thousand men, moving down from Nashville. Once the two armies combined, Grant would advance on Corinth.

When Johnston heard that Buell was about to reinforce Grant, he scrapped his plan to fight a defensive battle. His best—probably only—hope now was to defeat Grant before Buell arrived.

Halleck ordered Grant not to bring on a major battle. He was to dig in and await the arrival of Buell. But Colonel James McPherson, Grant's able engineer officer, advised against entrenching. The best position for entrenchments was on the higher ground at the rear of the position, not on the low-lying and wooded forward areas in the direction of Corinth. Besides, the landing enjoyed good natural defenses. A creek secured the right flank, another creek ran across much of the front, and the left flank was based on the Tennessee River. After heavy spring rains, the creeks were almost small rivers.

C. F. Smith, who was lying—in fact, dying—in an upstairs bedroom at the Cherry mansion, was also against digging in. Smith had scraped his right leg against a seat while getting out of a rowboat on the Tennessee, suffering a painful shin injury. It was simply assumed he would recover. Instead, the leg became infected and gangrene set in.[2]

When Grant asked what he thought about entrenching the army, Smith said bluntly that it was bad for morale. "The men have come here to fight and if we begin to spade, it will make them think we fear the enemy." Grant paid close attention to whatever Smith said. Halleck was not alone in thinking Smith was the best general in the department. "I was rather inclined to this opinion myself at that time," said Grant.[3]

With both McPherson and Smith opposed to entrenching, Grant felt free to do what he probably wanted to do anyway, and that was concentrate on training his army. Although it contained veterans from Donelson, most of it was as green as spring buds. The men needed to drill, to acquire the habit of instant obedience to commands, and to develop confidence in themselves and their officers, more than they needed holes in the ground.

Grant rode a steamboat each morning from Savannah to Pittsburg Landing, and returned in the evening to the Cherry mansion, much like a modern commuter. He took over a small log house on a hill overlooking Pittsburg Landing and made that his forward headquarters.

At dusk on April 4 Grant was out inspecting Sherman's outposts, where Federal soldiers had skirmished with rebel cavalry that afternoon. Rain was falling in torrents and Grant's horse lost its footing, stumbled, rolled over, and crushed his left leg. Had the ground been dry and hard, he might have lost it. Even if he kept the leg, he could have been left lame for life. The mud saved him. Grant struggled to his feet with a badly bruised leg and an excruciatingly painful ankle but no shattered bones.[4]

He and Sherman were agreed: These clashes between Federal pickets and rebel patrols were not the prelude to a battle. After Donelson, Grant's confidence was sky-high. He had seen through the myth of Albert Sidney Johnston. The man might look magnificent, but something had happened: The hero had shown weakness and uncertainty, maybe even a lack of moral courage, in the way he handled Fort Donelson. He had not made a stand when he should have made a stand, had chosen not to fight when his chances were at least as good as Grant's. In any event, something about Fort Donelson convinced Grant he would beat Johnston no matter what. It made no difference whether Johnston attacked him or he attacked Johnston.

He wrote to Julia and told her the biggest battle of the war was going to be fought soon, and he had no doubt that he would win it. "Knowing however that a terrible sacrifice of life must take place, I feel concerned for my army and their friends at home."[5]

As he contemplated the battle to come, he grew almost cocky. Grant estimated the enemy had him outnumbered by roughly two to one, yet informed Halleck, "I have scarcely the faintest idea of an attack [a general one] being made upon us." And when an old childhood friend, Colonel Jacob Ammen, arrived at the Cherry mansion on Saturday, April 5, leading one of Buell's brigades, Grant told him, "There will be no fight at Pittsburg Landing. We will have to go to Corinth, where the rebels are fortified [because if] they come to attack us, I can whip them."[6]

★

Johnston's troops might as well have been advancing through a tunnel for all they could see of the battlefield ahead of them and for all the maneuver room they enjoyed. Some forty-one thousand men had to advance along two narrow, muddy roads that wound through dense timber, and when they emerged they were to deploy immediately into a line of battle. The trees would mask their movement, but their being limited to two meager roads made it impossible for them to get into action quickly in large numbers. What was more, the creeks that covered the flanks of the Union position were going to confine the Confederates to attacks from one direction only, the southwest. There was no chance of making a feint, and little hope of taking the Federals by surprise.[7]

When night fell on April 5 and the advance was about to begin, Johnston's second in command, Pierre Gustave Toutont Beauregard, was suddenly gripped by anxiety. There was no doubting Beauregard's courage or skill. He had won the first battle of the war, at Bull Run, for the Confederacy. But surely, he now argued, skirmishing with Union pickets over the past few days must have alerted the enemy that an attack is coming? Johnston brushed all doubts aside. "I would fight them if they were a million."[8]

Grant was having breakfast at seven o'clock on Sunday morning, April 6. He had no plans for going anywhere today. Buell was expected to reach Savannah sometime that afternoon and Grant was going to be on hand to greet him. Then, as he raised his coffee to his lips, he heard it. At first, the noise resembled the growling of distant thunder, booming somewhere upriver. Colonel Joseph D. Webster, his chief of staff, said, "General, that is the noise of cannon."

"It very much sounds like it," Grant replied.

"Where is it? Crump's Landing or Pittsburg?"

"That's what I am trying to determine," said Grant. "I think it is Pittsburg." He put the cup down. "Gentlemen, the ball is in motion. Let's be off."[9]

Grant scribbled a brief note to Buell—"Heavy firing is heard . . . an attack has been made on our most advanced positions. . . . This necessitates my joining the forces up the river instead of meeting you to-day as contemplated." Another note went to Brigadier General William Nelson, commanding the leading division in Buell's army. Nelson was approaching Savannah, but Grant ordered him to change the line of his march and go south, so his men would reach the river at a point opposite Pittsburg Landing. From there, they could be ferried straight across to the battlefield. Hobbling on crutches and still suffering intensely from his damaged ankle, Grant boarded the steamboat *Tigress* and headed for the battle he had been so convinced was not going to happen.[10]

At Crump's Landing, roughly halfway to Pittsburg, the *Tigress* pulled up alongside Lew Wallace's command boat. While boatmen held the two vessels together, Grant and Wallace conferred briefly. Grant told Wallace to hold his division in readiness to move at a moment's notice. Wallace replied that his men were already prepared. As they were talking, a young journalist, twenty-four-year-old Whitelaw Reid, threw a few effects into a small carpetbag, clambered over the rail of Wallace's boat, then over the rail of the *Tigress*.

Reid had spent the past two days in bed aboard Wallace's boat, suffering from diarrhea. The Federals had been drinking water from contaminated springs the past few weeks and Reid was only one among thousands of sufferers. Wallace had allowed him to stay on his boat while he recovered. Reid was tall, wore his hair long in the back like a southerner, and affected the Napoleon III approach to facial hair—a prominent mustache and pointed tuft of beard poking out from the chin. His articles in the *Cincinnati Gazette* appeared under the pen name Agate, which meant either ruby or marble or small type to most people but probably had some more portentous meaning to Reid.[11]

Grant's steamer pulled away from Crump's Landing and continued its passage, heading for the noise of battle—not any battle, but by far the biggest of the war, the biggest ever fought in the New World up to that bloody Sunday.

The crash of musketry, the fearsome boom of artillery, the screams and shouts reached a crescendo as the steamer pulled in to Pittsburg Landing at around nine A.M. Grant disembarked only to find the 16th Iowa at the riverbank. The regiment had pulled out of the battle line to go in search of its ammunition, which was still piled up alongside the landing.

The first action Grant took in the battle was to order his staff to get an ammunition train organized. He then formed the 16th Iowa and its sister regiment, the 15th Iowa, which had arrived only the previous night, into a reserve. They would protect the landing and could, if necessary, shoot stragglers heading for the rear.[12]

Webster lifted Grant onto a horse. Grant tried to make himself easily identifiable to his troops by wearing a sword and a buff sash. The cigar that seemed welded to his molars was also a good clue. But there were still men who had no idea who he was. The colonel of the 15th Iowa, for instance, simply stared blankly at him when he gave the man orders. Grant had to tell him, "I am General Grant." Later that morning, when Grant crossed the line of sight of an soldier sending a semaphore message, a signal corps lieutenant bellowed at him, "Get out of the way there! Ain't you got no sense?"[13]

The critical point as Grant rode onto the field was over on the right, where Sherman's division was posted. There, the Union line was being forced back. Grant sent a written order to Lew Wallace—he was to move down from Crump's Landing and come in on Sherman's right.

When the Confederates attacked, they had found an army that was just stirring, still yawning and stretching and scratching itself awake, getting dressed and heating water for coffee. They also found the 53rd Ohio out on a limb and awaiting destruction. Two weeks earlier Grant had ordered that regiments be posted virtually shoulder to shoulder. The 53rd's colonel had ignored that and moved his men four hundred yards out in front so they could take advantage of a sweet-tasting spring. The first thing the charging Confederates hit was the 53rd Ohio.

The men struggled to form a line. They managed to fire a couple of volleys before their colonel panicked. "Fall back and save yourselves!" he screamed, then took off and spent most of the day hiding behind a log far in the rear.[14] By the time Grant reached Sherman, around ten A.M., the 53rd Ohio had virtually ceased to exist. With this huge rent in his front, Sherman had to pull the rest of his division back toward the Tennessee River.

Grant's five division commanders were, reading from right to left, Sherman, McClernand, W.H.L. Wallace (no relation to Lew), Benjamin Prentiss and, nearest to the river, Stephen A. Hurlbut. As the oncoming Confederates struck into the gap left by the 53rd Ohio, they collided with McClernand. His troops stood their ground, ably supported by some of W.H.L. Wallace's regiments.

Johnston's plan was to pin the Union line down on his left—that is, where Sherman, McClernand and Prentiss were deployed—then break through near the river, the area defended by W.H.L. Wallace and Hurlbut. Not that he was aware of any weakness on the Union side or had a clear idea of the topography near the river. He could not have chosen a worse place to try breaking through, because to do so his men would have to cross a swamp, and behind the swamp was a ravine with steep sixty-foot slopes. Johnston's plan would not work this side of a miracle. The best place, really the only place, where the Confederates could break through was over on the Union right. That was why Grant had assumed that if the enemy did attack him, the blow would fall there.

As the attack developed on the Union right and center, the pressure built up on Prentiss's division. It became the pivot of the entire Federal position. So long as Prentiss held fast, the rebels could not do much more than push Sherman, McClernand, Wallace and Hurlbut back. Grant rode up and told Prentiss he had to hold on "at all hazards" and ordered a Missouri regiment to reinforce Prentiss.[15]

This was the same Prentiss who had refused to obey Grant's orders earlier in the war, in the mistaken belief that he outranked Grant. He was no better now than he had been then. By ten A.M. Prentiss's division had been virtually routed. Whitelaw Reid, who had followed Grant from division to division, chose to stay with Prentiss, and before noon he, Prentiss, and at least half of Prentiss's division had fled to the riverbank. Grant's army, he believed, was on the brink of destruction.

Hurlbut, who was not under much pressure yet, extended his line until his troops covered much of the gap. Meanwhile, the sole regiment of Prentiss's division that stood its ground was fighting stubbornly and effectively. The position it occupied became known as the Hornet's Nest and for six hours it withstood repeated Confederate attacks.

Grant sent an urgent message to Buell: "If you can get upon the field, leaving your baggage on the east bank of the river, it will be a move to our advantage and may possibly save the day for us. The rebel force is estimated at over 100,000 men . . ."[16]

What he was counting on even more than Buell was for Lew Wallace to appear over on the right at about noon. Something strange had happened to his order, however. It had been lost. Wallace admitted receiving it, but never gave a clear, precise account of what it actually said. His adjutant admitted having taken possession of Grant's order, but claimed he had stuffed it under his belt buckle, and the next time he reached for it, the order had vanished.

Even so, there was a well-known rule for what to do in case of doubt—march to the sound of the guns. Wallace did not do that. He marched instead to the sound of his own drummer. Wallace argued for years afterward that had he done as Grant wanted he would have found himself out on his own, confronting half the rebel army, because Sherman's troops had fallen back toward the river. A competent commander, however, would have sent scouts forward to inspect the roads leading south and staff officers to confer with Sherman and coordinate the linking up of the two divisions.[17]

Wallace had been speaker of the Indiana state legislature and came from an important political family. He also had military experience, having commanded a company of volunteers during the Mexican War. After Mexico he pursed his military interests through involvement in the Indiana militia. He had raised a regiment shortly after Fort Sumter and seen action in West Virginia early in the war. For all his keen interest in military service, however, Wallace lacked the temperament for combat command. What he possessed was the base metal—a romantic attachment to military glory. He was a talented young man, with a brilliant imagination and an artistic temperament. Wallace had a novelist's mind, not a soldier's. And now his vivid imagination detected an opportunity for fame.

Instead of advancing straight toward Sherman as Grant directed, he would swing far to the west, pass around Sherman and enter the battle poised to make an attack of his own. With any luck he might fall on the unsuspecting Johnston's open left flank and save the day. It might have worked, too, under someone who knew the local road net or could at least read a map. Trouble was, Wallace got hopelessly lost. He spent the entire day leading his seven thousand desperately needed men up one country lane, then down another, like Marshal Soult at Waterloo.[18]

Grant sent an aide, William R. Rowley, in a frantic search for Wallace, but it did no good. Once Wallace got lost, he stayed lost. Grant sent another aide, William Hillyer, to hurry up Nelson's division. That did no good either.

Nelson was one of Lincoln's most quixotic appointments. Standing six foot five, weighing three hundred pounds, he was a huge, bearded and cantankerous sailor. Joining the Navy at fourteen, he decided twenty-three years later—when the Civil War began—that he preferred ground combat to naval warfare. Lincoln considered him some kind of a catch, because he promptly awarded Nelson a brigadier general's commission. Without ever showing the ability to handle as much as a platoon effectively, he nonetheless commanded a division.

There *were* Union generals who were worse than Nelson, but they were few in number. He was destined only four months later to come close to losing half of Kentucky. On this April day he played a crucial role in the way the battle developed by completely fluffing his part in it. Ordered to move to Pittsburg Landing at about seven-thirty, he did not move an inch for the next six hours. Difficult, irascible and bizarre, Nelson really took orders from no one.

To most of those involved, a battle is little more than terror and confusion. Grant was one of those few who could look into the dust and smoke and see the underlying pattern. He possessed an ability to read a battle as other men can read a book, without ever losing track of the plot and with a swift grasp of what the likely conclusion would be. His saying that he felt at home on the battlefield was no empty boast. Grant's orders and actions that April morning were those of a man who saw a priceless possibility in front of him and not the disaster that other men thought they were looking at.

Pittsburg Landing was not the South's great lost opportunity but the North's. By noon, Grant's actions had a clear pattern: He was trying to deploy his army to bring off one of the greatest battles of annihilation in the history of war. If Wallace advanced as ordered on the right and Nelson advanced as ordered on the left, the Army of the Tennessee would be poised to launch a double envelopment, much as Hannibal had done at Cannae. Around mid-afternoon most of the initial energy from Johnston's assault would be expended. The rebels would be tired, overextended and vulnerable. The appearance of two fresh divisions at full strength and poised to turn the enemy's flanks at that moment might well have brought the destruction of Johnston's army.

The war in the West could have been won in a day had it not depended on a fictioneer advancing on one flank and a strange sailor on the other. They moved slowly, haltingly, like men lost in the fog, unable to comprehend simple orders or to grasp a simple idea. Trying to get them to act decisively was like trying to push a couple of pieces of string.

Wallace's idiosyncratic wandering and "Bull" Nelson's bovine inertia cost so much time they not only deprived Grant of his Cannae but ruined even the hope of seizing the initiative. All he could do was fight the kind of battle he liked least, a defensive one. And he would have to do it with what he already had on the field—five infantry divisions, around twelve hundred cavalry, a hundred cannon, and himself.[19]

Throughout the day he rode from place to place as the Union line was bent back, talking to regimental and brigade commanders, sometimes positioning regiments himself. He rounded up stragglers and led them back into the battle. Cantering from one hot spot to another, Grant plainly thrilled to the din and the danger. Reid was not the only journalist there. At least half a dozen were covering the battle for northern newspapers. Irving Carson of the *Chicago Tribune* was decapitated by a cannonball while standing only six feet from Grant, taking notes.[20]

A terrified staff officer came up to him and said bluntly, "General, we must leave this place. It isn't necessary to stay here. If we do, we shall all be dead in five minutes." Grant considered the density of the bullets ripping past them, the frequency with which men nearby were falling down dead or wounded, weighed the volume and accuracy of the artillery fire exploding around them, and concluded calmly, "I guess that's so," then rode away, his relieved staff close behind.[21]

As the afternoon wore on, Grant became increasingly convinced that the Confederates had shot their bolt. They had made two crucial errors, and never showed any sign of correcting either one. First, instead of concentrating their force at any point, they were fighting an entirely linear battle, yet the terrain was too broken up for a line of any length to be maintained. Nor had Johnston created a reserve to exploit a breakthrough if one occurred.

The result was that roughly 34,000 Confederates (that is, 41,000, minus the sick, the dead, the wounded and the skulking) broken up into small formations were fighting dozens of fierce, uncoordinated fire-fights to push back a ragged line of 25,000 Federals (40,000, minus the sick, the dead, the wounded, the skulking and Lew Wallace's division). At no point had Johnston massed a force strong enough to break Grant's line or crush a flank, and with an advantage of only four to three, it would have taken a tactical genius to do so with so little room to maneuver. Apart from shattering the hapless 53rd Ohio, the rebels made heavy weather of their battle.

They forced two-thirds of the Union line back through forty-five degrees. Instead of flowing around Prentiss's position at the Hornet's Nest, isolating it, and moving behind it to threaten Grant's rear—which was their best bet—they kept pounding away as if hammering a horseshoe on an anvil. They mounted eleven frontal assaults on Prentiss's steadily shrinking salient. That was their second blunder.

There was no tactical advantage to possession of the Hornet's Nest. It just happened to be where Prentiss, who had no combat experience, chose to make his stand—or, rather, from where one of his regiments refused to budge. He returned to it in the early afternoon with a handful of reinforcements, but most of his troops remained where they were, down by the river, being interviewed by Whitelaw Reid.

The men in the Hornet's Nest could not resist indefinitely, but the longer Confederate troops expended their strength on this one not particularly vital spot, the more time there was for Nelson to arrive, for Lew Wallace to appear, and for Colonel Webster to form an artillery reserve—consisting of the biggest guns in the army—above the ravine that secured the Union position near the river.

Grant seems to have understood the value of an artillery reserve under central control before most Union Army commanders. Webster spent much of the afternoon rounding up the army's big guns and posting them on the bluffs overlooking Pittsburg Landing, at the far left of the Union line. This was the ground that Hurlbut was withdrawing toward. Hurlbut established a line that provided a clear field of fire to the south and west. In front of him was the ravine, turned by recent rains and an inflow from the river into something that resembled a swamp, and just to reach the ravine the enemy would have to cross open ground easily swept by both musket and artillery fire.[22]

While Webster was still forming the artillery reserve, Albert Sidney Johnston was out in the field encouraging the regiments attacking the Hornet's Nest. "Men, they are stubborn," he boomed. "We must use the bayonet!" At two o'clock, while he was watching his troops make yet another charge, a Union musket ball struck him in the left leg, severing the femoral artery. His boot started filling with blood. An aide noticed Johnston turning into a waxwork. "General, are you hurt?"

"Yes, and I fear seriously," Johnston stoically replied. He was lifted off his horse and by two-thirty he had bled to death. A simple tourniquet could have saved him, and there was one inside his coat, but no one thought to look for one or fashion one from his clothing. Beauregard took command, but news of Johnston's death was kept from the men until after the battle.[23]

Buell finally arrived and was appalled at the sight that greeted him when he met Grant aboard a small steamboat moored in the Tennessee. In the lee of the riverbank, barely fifty yards away, he could see at least five thousand Union soldiers—maybe as many as ten thousand—huddled or milling around. They seemed leaderless and panic-stricken. To Buell, it was obvious that Grant's army stood on the brink of defeat.[24]

It isn't surprising that Buell jumped to that conclusion. Others who saw it—Whitelaw Reid, volunteer officers, Confederate prisoners—thought the same. They, like Buell, had far less experience of combat than Grant, and Grant wasn't alarmed. While there *were* thousands of troops taking cover rather than fighting, there were also many who were wounded, along with men who had carried wounded comrades to the rear and still others who were neither wounded nor stretcher bearers but simply sick. Dysentery, influenza and other illnesses were rife in the Army of the Tennessee. Better than 20 percent of Grant's command was on sick report in the week leading up to the battle. "What preparations have been made for retreating?" asked Buell.

"I haven't despaired of whipping them yet," Grant replied.[25]

He didn't waste time discussing the troops huddled on the riverbank. Instead, he showed Buell the scabbard of his sword, where a musket ball had made a large dent, trying to impress on him that he had been in the thick of the fight and knew the situation firsthand. All he needed now was for Buell to get his army into the battle as quickly as possible, but Buell was no longer the man he had once been. In Mexico, he was dashing and bold. In this war, the weight of an army command made him ponderous.[26]

It was close to five P.M. when the twenty-two hundred men in the Hornet's Nest realized they were completely surrounded. Their flanks were caving in and concentrated artillery fire was pouring in. There was nothing for it but to surrender. A white flag went up. Prentiss, who later wrote the report on this action, covered up the fact that most of his division—himself included—had fled during the first few hours of fighting. As a result, he emerged from the battle as a Union hero, but Grant knew better. Prentiss's career as a combat commander was over.

Having taken the Hornet's Nest after a six-hour struggle, the Confederates turned it into a tourist site. They lost interest in fighting and went over to collect souvenirs, gloat in the faces of the damned Yankees, and marvel at what they had wrought. A lull fell over the battlefield.

News of Prentiss's surrender sent a shiver of alarm through Grant's officers. One asked him if it portended a rebel victory. "Oh, no," he answered like a man who has it all figured out. "They can't break our lines tonight. It is too late. Tomorrow we shall attack them with fresh troops and drive them, of course." He was exactly right, but he may have been the only man there who could see it.[27]

Rawlins, so proud of his steady nerves at Belmont, grew apprehensive. "Do you think they are pressing us, General?" he asked nervously.

"They have been pressing us all day, John," replied Grant coolly, "but I think we will stop them here."[28]

When the Union artillery reserve—fifty-two guns in all—opened up shortly after Prentiss surrendered, the effect of the bombardment was breathtaking. From that opening salvo it should have been obvious to Confederate commanders that they could no longer mass their troops for a breakthrough close to the river. Any large, compact formation would be blown to shreds before it ever reached the Union line.

By this time steamboats were crossing the Tennessee, bringing Nelson's division into the battle. They disembarked with regimental bands pounding out patriotic airs, flags streaming in the breeze, and the swagger of men who feel they are coming to the rescue of their comrades. The flags, the band music, the swagger brought ecstatic cheering from exhausted Federals who had been fighting all day long.

The light was fading and evening was nigh by the time Nelson's division was deployed. It saw hardly any fighting that day. Shooting had become sporadic as Lew Wallace finally arrived, taking up a position in Sherman's rear. He entered the battlefield roughly three miles from where he had started that morning, but had marched his men at least fifteen miles to reach it, resting from time to time.

Throughout the night, the two ironclads in the river—the *Tyler* and the *Lexington*—fired eight-inch shells into the Confederate position, to keep the enemy from getting much rest. Rain fell. Grant and Buell went to see Sherman. "Well, Grant, we've had the devil's own day, haven't we?" said Sherman.

"Yes." Grant puffed on his cigar. Sherman had not yet figured out the meaning of Sunday. He knew only what had happened in his part of the battle. Grant had seen it all. He knew the enemy was going to be driven from the field as surely as he knew the sun would rise. "Lick 'em tomorrow, though."[29]

After the brief conference with Buell and Sherman, he tried to rest under a large oak tree at the rear of the artillery reserve. Army quartermaster troops put down hay to keep him out of the mud, but the hay was soon wet and the ground was muddy and cold and his ankle was giving him hell. He had to leave his boots and his spurs on in case he needed to ride off at a moment's notice, but the pain from his swollen ankle, which had bounced against the side of his horse for much of the day, was torture.[30]

His forward headquarters, in the log house, had been taken over and turned into a hospital. Maybe it would be better up there. Around midnight, he hobbled up to it. Stretchers with wounded men groaning in agony were scattered all around. Inside, blood-covered surgeons were bent over in the light of kerosene lamps, performing the most common surgical procedure on the nineteenth-century battlefield— sawing off shattered arms and legs. "The sight was more unendurable than encountering the enemy's fire and I returned to my tree in the rain."[31]

★

As Beauregard studied the reports flowing in from his four corps commanders, his earlier doubts and fears fell away. The loss of Johnston was a cruel blow, but the results of the battle were a triumph that would make the dead man's name live forever. Beauregard sat down in Sherman's captured tent and dictated a telegram to Jefferson Davis: "After a severe battle of ten hours, thanks be to the Almighty, we gained a complete victory, driving the enemy from every position."[32]

All he had to do now, Beauregard believed, was reach out and grasp the trophy his soldiers had won. The exhaustion of the troops and the onset of night alone had prevented the victorious Confederates from completing their triumph, but a little rest and a new day would take care of that. Grant's Army of the Tennessee would be driven into the river, and most of those who survived would become Confederate prisoners.

While Beauregard tried to get some sleep, virtually the entire Army of the Ohio was crossing the Tennessee. With seventeen thousand men from Buell's command now at Pittsburg Landing, plus Wallace's fresh division ready to join the fight, Grant would be stronger on the second day than he had been on the first. Up to forty-five thousand Union troops would advance against Beauregard's twenty-five thousand. At first light, he sent orders to his division commanders: "Advance and recapture our original camps."[33]

At dawn, as Beauregard's troops formed up to renew the fight, the Union advance began. Grant's line was still ragged and bent back almost parallel to the river. Units were jumbled and officers galloped up and down the line trying to stitch regiments back together. Movement was slowed, too, by the tiredness of the men. Many of Buell's soldiers had marched all night just to get there.

The Confederates were already in line and, well supported by their artillery, put up stiff resistance for several hours. The sheer weight of Union numbers nonetheless pushed them steadily back. By afternoon, every foot of ground the Federals had lost had been recaptured. Grant, sensing the end was nigh, rounded up two regiments, personally placed them in position, and shouted "Charge!"[34]

Beauregard, his dreams of glory shattered, his doubts of victory justified at last, had no choice. If his troops stood and fought it out, his entire army would be destroyed by nightfall. At two-thirty he gave the order to withdraw. The exhausted Union troops did not pursue them. Just to see butternut backs retreating into the woods and down the roads toward Corinth seemed victory enough. Men slumped to the ground, bone-tired, cold, hungry and wet to the skin. It was raining again.

Grant's losses came to thirteen thousand killed, wounded and missing; the Confederates had lost close to twelve thousand.[35] In the woods from which the Confederates had launched their initial attack, they had to march past a small log church that served local Methodists. The building was fairly crude and, set among dense timber, it was a dark and airless place. It took its name from a small town in a faraway land that itself was a famous theater of war down the ages, Palestine. Its congregation called it Shiloh Methodist Church. Across the North, the battle took its name from the log church. It seemed appropriate somehow—both biblical and bloody.

★ ★ ★ ★

CHAPTER 16

"Notoriety Has No Charms"

Three journalists came to Rawlins demanding passes. They had to get back to Cairo, they said, so they could let the country know what had happened here. A large steamboat was being loaded for Cairo with hundreds of the more seriously wounded and they could squeeze themselves in somewhere. Rawlins wrote out passes for the reporters, including Whitelaw Reid, and they hurried back to the landing and scrambled aboard Tuesday evening, barely twenty-four hours after the fighting ended.

Reid spent that night bent over wounded men, whispering gently, trying not to brush against their bloody bandages, stepping carefully to avoid their mangled limbs. The groans and screams of the wounded, inescapable in the cramped, dark spaces of the boat churning its way northward, fell on him, as they did on the other able-bodied men aboard, like an oppressive cloak. When Reid disembarked at Cairo the next afternoon, Franc Wilkie of the *New York Times* saw him make his way down the gangplank looking like a man in a trance. Wilkie tried to talk to him, but Reid stared back, hollow-eyed. His expression, thought Wilkie, was that of a man who had just escaped "some imminent and frightful danger."[1]

Reid caught a train to Cincinnati, but by the time he got there, other newspapers were already telling the story. Where was his copy, the anxious *Gazette* editor wanted to know. He was still working on it, said Reid. All he had written so far was the lead. He showed it to him:

Fresh from the field of the great battle, with its pounding and roaring of artillery, its keener-voiced rattle of musketry sounding in my ears; with all its visions of horror still seeming to seer my eye-balls, while scenes of panic-stricken rout and brilliant charges, and obstinate defences, and succor, and intoxicating success are burned alike confusedly and indelibly upon my brain, I essay to write what I know of the battle of Pittsburg Landing.

By the time he had finished writing the piece, it was one of the most vivid battle descriptions of the war. The smell of gunpowder seemed to rise from the page. Heroism could not have been more heroic; cowardice could hardly have been more abject. Reid's best passages cut like a magical scalpel that exposed a great human mystery—the internal dynamics of battle—to mortal view.

Shiloh, as he described it, was a bloody folly, the bitter fruit of complacency, a terrifying brush with fate that took the North to the brink of total defeat thanks to poor generalship. Only a near miracle—the sudden arrival of Buell's Army of the Ohio like the deus ex machina in a Victorian melodrama—had saved the Union. The day began with Federal soldiers being shot in their beds as fearsome Confederates in butternut came crashing out of the woods at first light, taking Grant's hapless troops completely by surprise. Thousands of Union soldiers had fled in terror toward the river and huddled there like frightened sheep the rest of the day.

A fresh Federal line was hastily cobbled together, only to collapse in mid-morning when Prentiss's division meekly surrendered to the enemy. Lew Wallace was nearby with an entire division, ready to march, but this bold paladin was not sent for until close to noon and, thanks to command blunders, did not reach the battlefield until dusk. Grant exercised little control over events. He was present but absent at the same time. According to Reid's account, Grant did virtually nothing that day.

It was in his treatment of Grant that Reid offered the most damning critique on this battle, and revealed how little he had actually seen. For the truth was, Grant had been all over the battlefield, deploying reinforcements to threatened sections of the line, rounding up stragglers, galloping from division to division, organizing ammunition trains, ordering the creation of an artillery reserve, and trying to put together one of the greatest battles of annihilation in history. Despite intense physical pain, he was resourceful, energetic, imaginative and daring. No one would ever imagine that from Reid's story.[2]

When the British military scholar Major General J.F.C. Fuller wrote his study of Grant's generalship, he pieced together Grant's activities that day. The result was a detailed list based on documentary evidence. Fuller's list covers two pages, and even then it is incomplete. Had Reid truly covered the battlefield as he suggested he did, he would have encountered Grant again and again. He might also have shared the fate of the three other journalists who tried to follow the fighting at close hand and were seriously wounded, to say nothing of the one who was killed.

Sherman dismissed Reid's piece as the work of someone who had spent virtually the whole first day at Shiloh down by the riverbank, talking to the wounded and the stragglers. Reid certainly hadn't seen Sherman, because he described Sherman as being wounded by "a musket ball through the hand." In fact, he had received only a slight wound when his right hand was struck by buckshot. The real proof of Sherman's peril that day was the fact that he had two horses shot out from under him, but Reid didn't know that.[3]

Reid's account was reprinted in newspapers across the North, cutting across an open wound and adding immeasurably to the nation's shock at the enormous loss of life. And the fact that many a soldier at Shiloh saw the battle much as Reid did—through a narrow, distorting lens of sheer terror—only convinced him that he had gotten it right. In truth, he and they were but strangers plunged at musket point into an uncharted, ghastly land where death was sovereign.[4]

★

The rumors and whispers had followed him around for years, ever since he quit the Army in 1854. He drank, people said, and seemed to drink not for conviviality but just to get drunk. Sometimes, of course, they were right. At other times, though, they were probably wrong. About once a month he got a migraine headache and had to lie down, even if it was the middle of the day. Or he might be sitting at his desk, unable to work, clutching his head.

Before Shiloh, the newspapers had kept the stories and rumors largely to themselves. But Reid's piece on Shiloh changed all that.

Somebody had to be blamed, some explanation offered, and Grant's weakness for liquor was too tempting to resist. Reid hadn't written anything about Grant's drinking, but he had brought Grant's reputation low enough that it was now safe for other people to do it. Grant's rivals and enemies suddenly felt free—maybe even licensed by patriotic duty—to pin the mistakes at Shiloh—and by implication the huge butcher's bill—on Grant's weakness for liquor.

Even today, people who could not find Shiloh on a map or tell you Grant's rank in the Civil War know one thing about him—that he drank. Grant the President is barely recalled, but Grant the alcoholic has a kind of perverse glory that never fades. He has become the most famous drunk in American history, despite a long line of distinguished public figures over the past hundred years who, on an average hooch day, could make Grant on his worst day seem positively sober.

The rumors had nipped at his spurred heels for months. He had barely settled in at his Cairo headquarters the previous fall before an acquaintance from Galena, Benjamin Campbell, felt obliged to write to Congressman Elihu B. Washburne: "I am sorry to hear on good authority, that Gnl. Grant is drinking very hard . . ." At about the same time, one of the proprietors of the *Chicago Tribune* informed the secretary of war, Simon Cameron: "Evidence entirely satisfactory to myself and Associate Editors of the Tribune has become so convincing that Gen. U. S. Grant commanding at Cairo is an inebriate that I deem it my duty to draw your attention to this matter."[5]

Washburne wrote to John Rawlins, who had appointed himself keeper of Grant's conscience—at least as far as the whiskey went. Rawlins responded forthrightly. Any claim that Grant was drinking heavily was "utterly untrue and could only have originated in malice. When I came to Cairo, Gen. Grant was as he is today, a strong total abstinence man, and I have been informed by those who know him well that this has been his habit for the last five or six years."

It was an odd version of total abstinence. As Rawlins himself acknowledged, various important well-wishers had visited Cairo several weeks after the battle of Belmont and Grant had taken a few drinks with them. He did so, said Rawlins, only to avoid giving offense.[6]

Rawlins did not yet realize—he would soon learn better—that what had seemed so innocuous, if anything a laudable attempt at courtesy, was in truth a significant moment: The total-abstinence man, the one-time Son of Temperance, had let down his guard after fighting his first battle as a commander and promptly fallen off the wagon. He may well have told Rawlins he took a few drinks with his visitors to avoid hurting their feelings, but that was not the true reason. It was simply a convenient excuse.

By returning to his old habits even for a single occasion, Grant was writing off those five or six years of sobriety. This did not mean he went to bed drunk every night for the rest of the war or even that he went on a bender after every battle. He was the binge-drinking type of alcoholic, one who can go for weeks, months, even years, without a drink, but once he starts, is as likely to drink a bottle as a glass. The best medicine he had to ward off the bottle wasn't the prickly, self-righteous Rawlins but Julia. The presence of booze nearly always indicated the absence of Mrs. Grant.

A couple of months before Shiloh, the matter of Grant's drinking was presented dramatically to Cameron's successor as secretary of war, Edwin McMasters Stanton, by an angry, incarcerated sailor named William J. Kountz. During the winter Grant had asked Halleck for a quartermaster to oversee the growing fleet of steamers that moved his men and supplies. Halleck commissioned Kountz, who was an experienced Mississippi riverboat master, and sent him to Grant.[7]

Kountz turned out to be a splenetic, incompetent and dishonest character who alienated many of the people Grant needed to run his fleet efficiently. When reprimands to Kountz failed to achieve anything, Grant had him arrested, no doubt hoping Kountz would resign his commission, go away and never be heard from again. He had misjudged the man. Kountz angrily retaliated by filing charges against Grant, accusing him of being "beastly drunk" while parleying with Confederate officers over a prisoner exchange after Belmont and of regularly being "so much intoxicated as to be unfitted for any business, thereby setting an evil example to the officers and soldiers under his command."

Kountz, still in confinement, brooded on the injustice of Army ways for a week or so, then came up with a longer list of charges, even more colorful than the first. This second list included drunkenness, of course, but now he had Grant "drinking with traitors" and "vomiting all over the floor of the cook's cabin aboard a steamboat." He was also accused of being so inebriated at a Cairo hotel that he lost his sword and his uniform; of playing cards and paying off his losses with Army secret service funds; of "getting so drunk he had to go up stairs on all fours"; and of spending the night with "a Harlot" in room number 5 at the same hotel where he'd lost the sword and the uniform.[8]

Julia had warned her husband to keep on eye on Kountz, but Grant wasn't worried. "He can do me no harm," Grant informed her. "He is known as a venimous [*sic*] man [and] is without friends or influence."[9]

He was right. Still, it probably brightened the normally gray day of the anonymous and probably overworked War Department clerk who had to transcribe all the sensational nonsense in Kountz's second list of charges. Nothing came of it. Government departments regularly receive obviously fictitious reports from embittered subordinates seeking revenge on a superior who, they claim, has wronged them.

Kountz was eventually released from arrest, mainly so he could be stripped of his silver bars and thrown out of the service. It was a phenomenal misjudgment at Halleck's headquarters, all the same, to give someone so obviously unbalanced a captain's commission.[10]

While Grant knew he had little to fear from Kountz, he was nevertheless worried about the political and newspaper criticism that was certain to follow Shiloh. He informed Julia what she should expect—"I will come in again for heaps of abuse from persons who were not here."[11] And he did. One of Washburne's old college friends wrote him from Boston only days after the battle: "The public seems disposed to give Grant full credit for ability and bravery but seems to think it 'a pity he drinks.' " An angry citizen wrote the congressman to demand rhetorically, "Must our army be sacrificed by the neglect and inefficiency of such drunken leaders?" A third claimed "the loss of life was terrific and seems wholly caused by bad management in the field, or no management at all. . . . Somebody has much to answer for . . ." And yet another informed him that a reporter for the *New York Herald* was telling everyone that "Grant was drunk in Sunday's battle." This is only a small sample. Grant was damned in newspapers and congressional mailbags across the North.[12]

It was not only journalists who circled like sharks tasting blood. McClernand, eager to supplant Grant and get command of his army, spread stories that Grant had been so drunk he had nearly lost the battle.[13]

The troops, too, were outraged at what they considered his appalling generalship. It was a time-honored volunteer tradition for amateur soldiers to take out their frustration at their own lack of success and want of military skills by roundly damning their commanders. Grant was cursed from tent to tent across Pittsburg Landing as a drunk, an incompetent and a butcher. The volunteers' howls of rage reached all the way back to their state capitols, and politicians such as David Tod, the governor of Ohio, demanded Grant's dismissal.[14]

In fact, there is absolutely no evidence that Grant had been drinking immediately prior to or during the battle. There is also a good witness to his sobriety. Colonel Jacob Ammen, commanding the brigade of Buell's troops that reached Savannah the day before the battle, informed his diary the evening of April 8, "I am satisfied Gen. Grant was not under the influence of liquor."[15]

The drumbeat of press criticism meanwhile grew so depressing that Grant more or less gave up reading the newspapers for a time. At least, that's what he told Julia. But she had not stopped reading the newspapers, and he had to reassure her that what they said against him was simply untrue. "Most or all that you have seen has been written by persons who were not here and thos [*sic*] few items collected from persons nominally present, eye witnesses, was from those who disgraced themselves and now want to draw off public attention."[16]

Grant was distressed, too, by the death of C. F. Smith. He had come to admire and love the old soldier and personally wrote Smith's widow to inform her of her husband's death. "It was my fortune to have gone through West Point with the Gen. and to have served with him in all his battles in Mexico, And in this rebellion. . . . Where an entire nation condoles with you in your bereavement no one can do so with more heartfelt grief than myself."[17]

Meanwhile he told his father, as he'd told Julia, not to pay too much attention to newspaper accounts of Shiloh. Grant was particularly stung by claims that he had been surprised. "If the enemy had sent us word when and where they would attack us, we could not have been better prepared," he told his father.[18]

Protestations aside, the fact remains that the Confederates had surprised him by launching an all-out attack when the most he had expected was a reconnaissance in force. The complacency Grant had felt about the outcome of the big battle he was preparing to fight had spread all the way down. The 53rd Ohio, for example, was out on its own four hundred yards ahead of the rest of the Army of the Tennessee, almost inviting attack. Sherman scoffed at the regiment's commander, Colonel Jesse

Appler, for reporting a strong buildup of Confederates immediately to his front. What Sherman should have done was order the 53rd to pull back and get into line with the rest of the division.

Not one division commander was vigorously patrolling his front, nor was there a strong line of pickets well in advance of the main encampment. Pittsburg Landing was a good place to assemble an army, but so close to the enemy that the outer perimeter had to be strongly patrolled. That was not only the proper military action; it was simple common sense. Grant reacted fiercely to the charge that he had been taken by surprise not because it was false but because it was true.

Jesse, as eager as any other father to see his son vindicated, made Grant's letter available to the press. This only stirred the cauldron again, providing his detractors with yet another opportunity. Grant angrily told his father not to make his letters public in the future. He was so angry, in fact, that for the only time in the war he took on his press critics openly. He wrote to a Cincinnati newspaper, continuing to insist that his army had not been taken by surprise.[19]

Grant also had one of his aides, William Rowley, write a long and detailed account of Shiloh to Washburne, assuring him that press accounts of the battle were wrong. The reporter on the *New York Herald* who was going around telling people Grant had been drunk was known to be "an infamous liar," and any assertion that the general had been drinking was "an unmitigated slander."[20]

Washburne loyally defended Grant on the floor of Congress and as the press furor simmered down, Grant wrote to thank him for his support, but conceded it had been a difficult time. "To say that I have not been distressed by these attacks upon me would be false, for I have a father, mother, wife & children who read them and are distressed by them. Then too all subject to my orders read these charges and it is calculated to weaken their confidence in me. . . . Notoriety has no charms for me and could I render the same services . . . without being known in the matter, it would be infinately preferrable [*sic*] to me." Of every wish he ever had, this was the last one that would ever be granted.[21]

Lincoln was so concerned by the reports of Grant's drinking that he had Stanton write to Halleck: "The President desires to know . . . whether any neglect or misconduct of General Grant or any other officer contributed to the sad casualties that befell our forces . . ." There was also a story spread by Alexander K. McClure, an important Republican politician from Pennsylvania, that he had spent two hours one April evening telling Lincoln why Grant had to go. Public sentiment demanded it, said McClure. Firing Grant was the only way the President could regain the confidence of people. Lincoln's long, gloomy face grew even longer, even gloomier, and he sank into a melancholy silence for what seemed to McClure like an eternity. "I can't spare this man," Lincoln said at last, with a depth of feeling that took McClure by surprise. *"He fights."*[22]

★

Halleck arrived at Pittsburg Landing from St. Louis three days after the battle to take personal charge. So far as he was concerned, Grant had performed badly, while his protégé Sherman had saved the day. Sherman, who Grant himself singled out for praise in his report on the battle, was swiftly promoted to major general of volunteers.

Although Halleck publicly praised Grant's army for its combat performance, he privately disparaged it as being unruly, disorganized and wide open to another attack. Given the shattered state of the retreating Confederates, this was nonsense, but he doubtless believed it. Halleck's mind was probably made up about the wretched condition of Grant's army before he even left St. Louis. Halleck took the field convinced he had been called upon to save this army from itself. He even managed to persuade himself that he was welcomed as a savior by its officers.[23]

One of his earliest actions was to organize a board to examine combat performance during the battle. The first day the board met, Sherman had Colonel Appler thrown out of the service. Sherman couldn't wait to get rid of him, and not all the bleating the governor of Ohio could emit was going to save this inept and cowardly officer.

Halleck had not given up hope of shelving Grant, but he would have to be subtler about it than he'd been in the past. Shortly after reaching Pittsburg Landing, he reorganized his forces into four components. Grant's Army of the Tennessee was reinforced by troops from Buell's army, designated the "right wing" and entrusted to George Thomas. Buell's Army of the Ohio became Halleck's "center." Major General John Pope was assigned to command the "left wing." Pope had recently taken New Madrid and Island Number 10 in a swift, clever and almost bloodless campaign that gave the Union control of the Mississippi as far south as Memphis and made the city vulnerable to a direct attack.

Completing his reorganization, Halleck put McClernand in command of the army's reserve. All told, Halleck had a field force of fifteen divisions, numbering close to 120,000 men, while another 30,000 protected his flanks and rear.[24]

Where did this reorganization leave Grant? Out in the cold. He was informed that he would be second in command, under Halleck. But Halleck did not work through Grant. He communicated directly with Thomas and Buell and Pope. It was about as galling as it gets. Grant was by turns incensed and depressed. He put up with this humiliating situation for ten days, then his patience snapped.

He wrote to Halleck, telling him that since the reorganization, "relieving me from immediate command of any portion of the *Army in the Field* I have felt my position anomylous [*sic*] and determined to have it corrected, in some way. . . . I felt that censure was implied. . . . I deem it due to myself to ask either full restoration to duty, according to my rank, or to [be] relieved entirely from further duty."

As before, Halleck brazened it out by lying unashamedly. "For the last three months I have done everything in my power to ward off the attacks made upon you," he replied. "If you believe me your friend, you will not require explanation; if not, explanation on my part would be of little avail."[25]

This convinced Grant that Halleck was not trying to demote him, but it did absolutely nothing to make him one bit happier with his position. He had virtually nothing to do. The little work that was required at his headquarters now was routine administrative stuff, and Rawlins could take care of that.

Meanwhile, Halleck was moving toward Corinth, one of the most important rail centers in the Confederacy. Two railroads passed through this small down-at-the-heels town, making a spidery cross on the map. The Mobile and Ohio Railroad went through on a north-south axis, while the Memphis and Charleston Railroad crossed it going east and west. And yet a third railroad, the Mississippi Central, threaded its own steel rails across the map a few miles from Corinth.

After Shiloh, Beauregard had pulled his badly mauled army back toward the town, to await reinforcements and to resupply his men. Grant had not mounted a pursuit, believing his troops were too exhausted after a two-day fight to make any rapid advance. Besides which, the roads were too muddy for him to move his artillery.[26]

All the same, he had more than a thousand fresh cavalry available to him; the horse soldiers had never really gotten into the fight. They could at least have harried the retreating foe. Grant's failure to do even this much has been justly criticized. It certainly came as a relief to Beauregard, whose force was demoralized and short of supplies. Even after receiving reinforcements at Corinth, he remained extremely vulnerable. He had an army of only fifty thousand men to face the oncoming Union juggernaut.

Halleck advanced on Corinth spade first. His troops moved less than a mile a day. They spent more time digging than marching. Their burrowing, molelike advance threw up line after relentless line of trenches across the northern Mississippi landscape—all neat, all regular, all cautious, all useless, given Halleck's crushing superiority in manpower and firepower.

Grant could only look on in dismay. "Corinth could have been captured in a two days' campaign commenced promptly on the arrival of reinforcements after the battle of Shiloh," he claimed in his memoirs, and he was almost certainly right.[27]

In the middle of May, Sherman's division hit a weak spot in Beauregard's outer defenses. Grant hurried over to Halleck's command post and explained that if Pope's corps followed up with a dawn attack, it could probably smash straight through and take Corinth while the rest of the army kept the Confederates pinned down. Halleck brushed it aside as if Grant's proposal was too stupid to be worth discussing. Grant departed, insulted by Halleck's reaction and profoundly depressed at a missed opportunity.[28]

While the slow-motion advance continued, that ripe source of interesting and unreliable information, army rumor, brought tales that Major General David Hunter, presently commanding Federal forces in the Carolinas, was about to get a new assignment. Grant had Rowley write to Washburne. If the story about Hunter was true, Rowley told the congressman, "I am certain that Gen. Grant would like *extremely* well to be assigned to the command that he now holds." Just to make sure, yet another aide, Clark Lagow, also wrote to Washburne, urging that Hunter's post be given to Grant, but claimed unconvincingly that Grant "knows nothing of my writing this." Grant's attempts to get a transfer to the East came to nothing. He was stuck with Halleck and Halleck's ponderous attempt to win the war by a maximum of maneuver and a minimum of combat.[29]

Corinth looked formidable to Halleck, a fortress bristling with guns and held, he convinced himself, by at least a hundred thousand Confederates. But hardly had he gotten his huge army digging industriously within the shadow of the town before Beauregard began to pull out. At first light on the morning of May 30, explosions were heard coming from Corinth and plumes of thick black smoke rose into the sky.

The Confederates were certainly on the move. They had begun their retreat the previous evening, and by dawn on the thirtieth they were gone, leaving behind an army of straw-filled dummies in threadbare uniforms, smiles mockingly painted on their vacant faces. While Grant quickly concluded the explosions and the movement of troops during the night meant the enemy was abandoning Corinth, Pope drew a different conclusion—that the enemy was being reinforced in order to attack him. Halleck agreed with Pope.

Around mid-morning, however, Pope's patrols pushed cautiously into the town and found it deserted save for a handful of civilians. They laughed at the straw-filled dummies and unmasked the formidable artillery that had worried Halleck. It consisted of "Quaker guns"—large logs of appropriate calibers painted black.

Grant was appalled. While it was important to take Corinth, "the victory was barren in every other particular [because] it was nearly bloodless." Halleck considered war to be a matter of capturing strategic points on the map, while to Grant it was as obvious as anything could be that wars were won by destroying the enemy's forces. Even the troops, he was convinced, shared his strategic vision, not Halleck's. "They could not see how the mere occupation of places was to close the war while large and effective rebel armies existed."[30]

To Grant's rage and disgust, Halleck made no attempt to catch and destroy the retreating enemy, although he had a cavalry force of more than five thousand well-mounted men ready to ride, the roads were good, the weather dry and the army eager to press on. Instead, Halleck had John Pope's divisions follow Beauregard south toward Tupelo, mainly to make sure he was not coming back. His way of campaigning harkened back a hundred years, to the pre-Napoleonic era of limited wars, when fortresses dominated much of Europe and campaigns were waged to seize strategic points. Everyone understood the rules of the game until the Corsican upstart came along, moved between and around the fortresses, and killed his opponents' armies. Grant waged war much like Napoleon.

Halleck moved into Corinth only to sit on it. If his troops thought the damned digging was over, they were in for an earthy surprise. He got them entrenching again, even though there were miles of entrenchments all around, yawning brown mouths ready to swallow them up, every last one. Beauregard had bluffed him by creating such huge earthworks that it would have taken a hundred thousand men to man them, and his bluff had worked flawlessly. And now, what the enemy had dug well, Halleck set about digging better.[31]

The clink of thousands of busy spades, the *thunk! thunk!* of axes biting into logs, the percussive pounding of hammer against rock from dawn till dark, was simply unbearable to Grant. He couldn't take any more of it. A few days after Corinth fell, Sherman was talking to Halleck when Halleck casually remarked that Grant was going to St. Louis on leave. Sherman rode over to Grant's command post and entered Grant's tent.

He found Grant standing at a crude table, chests crammed with his effects piled in the corners, diligently tying up bundles of official papers with red tape. "Is it true you are going away?"

"Yes," said Grant, looking up. "You know that I am in the way here. I have stood it as long as I can." Sherman wanted to know just where he was going. "St. Louis," Grant replied.

"Have you any business there?"

"Not a bit."

From this, Sherman got the idea that Grant was leaving for good, when in fact he was merely looking forward to spending a month at home with Julia and the children, away from Halleck, away from entrenching. Sherman urged him not to leave. The newspapers said I was crazy, he told Grant, and that got me so depressed I was ready to quit. But I didn't, and Shiloh brought me back: "It gave me new life. I am now in high feather." Well, he went on, if Grant stayed right here, when things changed—as they were bound to do—he too would bounce back. But if he left, when the situation changed, he would be completely out of the picture, his career finished.[32]

Grant, in his shy way, offered no reply to this, made no effort to set Sherman straight. In all probability, he would have been touched by this profession of loyalty, the more powerful for being totally unexpected and obviously sincere. When deeply moved, Grant invariably preferred silence to speech. He allowed Sherman to ride away with a wrong idea about his intentions. No wonder Sherman later decided he had never understood Grant. He also concluded Grant did not understand himself, but he was wrong about that. Anyway, Grant mulled over what Sherman had said and canceled his plans to go home on leave. After all, Sherman was close to Halleck—closer, probably, than anyone else in the Army. Maybe some big change was afoot. Better to stay with the troops and see what developed.[33]

Shortly after this, Grant sent Sherman a note to let him know he had changed his mind and would not be going to St. Louis after all. Sherman was delighted, thinking he had just saved Grant from a terrible mistake. He wrote back: "I have just received your note, and am rejoiced at your conclusion to remain. For yourself, you could not be quiet at home a week, when armies are moving, and rest would not relieve your mind of the gnawing sensation that injustice has been done to you."[34]

Following the fall of Corinth, Halleck had little idea of what to do next. He thought maybe he ought to make a move against Vicksburg, but on reflection decided that was really an objective the Navy could take. As he pondered strategic choices, Halleck decided to abolish the system he had created. It was simply too unwieldy, even for him. Grant, Buell, Thomas, Pope and McClernand resumed their former commands and Grant seized the opportunity this gave him to establish a headquarters of his own once again, but not here.

He would get away from Halleck, away from Corinth, away from the ever-growing entrenchments. He moved himself and his staff to Memphis. The city had been captured recently and was presently under the command of Lew Wallace. Grant arrived there on June 23, glad to have his old command once again.

While he was settling in, the war in the East was going badly. Under intense pressure from Lincoln, George McClellan had taken the Army of the Potomac down to the Yorktown Peninsula by water and advanced on Richmond, only to be stopped cold by Joe Johnston and, after Johnston was wounded, by Robert E. Lee. The Army of the Potomac suffered such a rebuff that it seemed, for a short time, to be in danger of being destroyed. A shock wave rippled through the North, spreading alarm and apprehension.

Since removing McClellan as general-in-chief in March, Lincoln had filled the role himself. Here, though, was a crisis that revealed his limitations. He could not run the country and coordinate the operations of the armies at the same time. Halleck was ordered to Washington to become general-in-chief.

The obvious person to assume command of the Western Department was Grant. It is equally obvious in retrospect that Grant was the last person Halleck would choose. For a time, Halleck toyed with the idea of giving the command to a quartermaster, Colonel Robert Allen. According to Allen, Halleck came to his tent one night and told him, "I could give you command of this army."

Allen was incredulous. "I have not rank."

"That," responded Halleck, "can easily be obtained." Allen had the sense to refuse to go along with this oddball scheme and it came to nothing.

If his story is true, it casts doubt on at least half of Halleck's nickname, Old Brains. Making Allen a major general and putting him in command could only have worked if all the other major generals in the department who outranked him—Grant, Buell, Pope, Thomas, Sherman, et al. were sent elsewhere or at least agreed to serve under the most junior major general in the Army. Given Allen's complete lack of combat experience, that was so unlikely it was simply ridiculous. All they had to do to block such a foolish move was ask to be relieved of their commands or transferred elsewhere.

A blizzard of resignations and transfer demands from the most experienced and successful of Union generals of the war thus far would have rocked the White House and the War Department to their foundations and demoralized the Union Army. Halleck was at times a bizarre, almost otherworldly figure. Whatever his understanding of theories of war, his grasp of human psychology was close to zero.[35]

In the end, he chose to break up the department rather than let Grant have it. It was an almost spiteful thing to do, but Grant knew nothing of this. On July 1 he received a telegram from Halleck ordering him to report to Corinth immediately and to plan on moving his headquarters there.

Before leaving Memphis, Grant managed to do something he had been longing to do for three months: He got Lew Wallace out of the Army. He sent Wallace back to Indiana on leave, where Wallace became involved in recruiting new regiments. Then, when Wallace grew bored with recruiting and let it be known he was ready to return, Grant informed the War Department there was no assignment in his command that Wallace might fill. This was the payback for Wallace's hopeless combat performance. Getting rid of Lew Wallace was Grant's farewell to the battle of Shiloh.[36]

———— ★ ★ ★ ————

CHAPTER 17

"ONE MORE FIGHT"

When the war began, Grant believed that one big battle—with the Federals triumphant, of course—would bring the Southrons to their senses and return them swiftly, if chastened, to the Union fold. Well, he had whipped the Secesh handsomely at Fort Donelson and bagged an entire army, but they hadn't quit. He still thought one more big battle would do the trick, but Shiloh turned out to be more of a hard-fought draw than a victory.

Then Halleck arrived and Grant, who was slightly in awe of Halleck's intellectual reputation and his comprehensive knowledge of military history and theory, expected all that brilliance was going to pay off with the destruction of Beauregard's army. Once that happened, the war in the Mississippi valley would be as good as over. Halleck would be able to take his huge army anywhere he wanted—down to the Gulf, pocketing Vicksburg along the way; or maybe he would move toward Chattanooga and free eastern Tennessee, which was sure to please Lincoln. A week after Shiloh, Grant confidently informed Julia: "One more fight, then easy sailing to the close of the war."[1]

Halleck's failure to annihilate Beauregard's army at Corinth put paid to those optimistic ideas. This war was not going to be settled by one more huge battle. It had taken a long time for Grant to realize that—

more than a year, in fact, with as many downs as ups, a disappointment or a setback to balance every advance—but the way it would be from now on was blindingly obvious. Much effort and bloodshed had gone into subduing the South, battles had been won, land had been conquered, yet the outlook could hardly seem worse. The suffering thus far was as nothing compared to what was certain to follow.

That realization came to Grant when he set up shop in Memphis. There hadn't been many civilians left in Corinth when that town fell, but Memphis was still a thriving, bustling southern city. And far from being reconciled to its occupation by Federal soldiers, the citizens were as outspokenly pro-Confederate as ever. If they were anything to go by—and they probably were—this was going to be a long and truly terrible war. In their mocking glances, their defiant utterances, their infuriating self-righteousness and unbending hostility to the Union and what he never doubted was the best government on the face of the Earth, the whole future of the war could be read plainly. He could now see what this struggle had come to.[2]

The one heartening part of moving to Memphis was that Grant was finally able to send for Julia and the children to join him. They arrived just in time for the booming Fourth of July celebration that Grant's soldiers had organized. The Union artillery, firing salvo after jubilant salvo, reminded the sullen inhabitants just who controlled their destiny these days.[3]

Ten days later Grant returned to Corinth. There, he promptly took over the spacious and gracious house of a local worthy by the name of Francis E. Whitfield. Although Mr. Whitfield later insisted he was "an original Union man," he had in fact come to this allegiance a little too late to hold on to his home. Before becoming an original Union man he had been an original contractor to the Confederate Army, but in those days he probably could not have imagined that he would ever, this side of a nightmare, find a Union army camped outside his house. His claims of loyalty were sincere only insofar as they expressed a genuine desire to get the Federal government to compensate him for the fact that Grant commandeered his home. As for where his true allegiance lay, his daughter never had any doubts. Papa, she boasted proudly, "was one of the hottest Rebels around here."[4]

So Grant moved into Mr. Whitfield's house. It was charmingly framed by large grounds planted with fragrant mimosas and magnolias, plantains and vines. In return, Mr. Whitfield got accommodation in the Federal prison at Alton, Illinois. For some reason, however, Grant completely forgot all this. When he came to write his memoirs, he blandly claimed, "I do not recollect having arrested and confined a citizen (not a soldier) during the entire rebellion."[5]

With a decent place to house them, Grant sent for Julia and the children to come down from Memphis. They arrived by train one night, and as they rocked along in an Army ambulance toward Mr. Whitfield's house, Grant escorted them on horseback, reaching out from time to time to give Julia's plump little hand an affectionate squeeze. Thousands of men gathered around campfires were singing "John Brown's body lies a molderin' in his grave . . ." as the ambulance and rider passed by. It was a thrilling, theatrical scene, an operatic moment charged with all the heightened emotions of a people's war.

Nothing cheered Grant more than having his children around him. He took a delight in them that was touchingly obvious and just as obviously limitless. Old Jesse, however, didn't think an army camp, with its rough ways and coarse language, was a suitable place for his grandchildren, and Jesse never kept his opinions to himself. Grant wrote back promptly to let him know he was wrong (again). "They are not running around camp among all sorts of people, but we are keeping house in the property of a truly loyal secessionist who has been furnished free board and lodging at Alton, Illinois; here the children see nothing but the greatest propriety."[6]

His father felt Ulysses had been slighted by not getting command of the Western Department, but Grant assured him, "I do not want to command a department because I believe I can do better service in the field." The only thing that bothered him was the thought of someone junior in rank being placed over him. Other than that, he was content to remain a combat commander, with a mission to take the war to the enemy.

Meanwhile, Lincoln was pushing for a campaign to free eastern Tennessee. He pictured the region as the domain of sturdy Union-loving mountaineers who were being killed or otherwise persecuted by Confederate fanatics. That was one good reason for capturing Chattanooga, but there was also another. This small unprepossessing town of five thousand dominated rail and water communications far into Alabama and Georgia. If the Federals could get hold of Chattanooga, they could drive deep into the South and possibly take Atlanta. Shortly after capturing Corinth, Halleck had ordered Don Carlos Buell and the Army of the Ohio to advance across northern Alabama and seize it.

Chattanooga was presently defended by some fifteen thousand Confederates under an 1845 West Point graduate and veteran of the Mexican War, Edmund Kirby Smith. He was not strong enough on his own to stop Buell's advance, but following the evacuation of Corinth, Beauregard was fired for not making a fight for the town. He was replaced by Braxton Bragg, and Bragg had taken his new command east, to Chattanooga.[7]

The arrival of Bragg with thirty-five thousand men changed everything. Chattanooga was no longer under threat of a siege. Smith and Bragg had enough manpower between them to hold the city and at the same time seize the strategic initiative in eastern Tennessee. They decided to move north, slip around Buell, and liberate Kentucky. This move would force Buell to retreat and would go a long way toward wiping out all that Grant and Halleck had so far achieved in the West.[8]

During his first month back in Corinth, Grant seemed content to consolidate what he held. His command numbered nearly eighty thousand men. It was the largest force he had handled so far, but it was dispersed widely across western Tennessee and northern Mississippi. Then, on August 10, Buell informed Grant that a large Confederate force was about to move north from Chattanooga. Grant sent two divisions to reinforce Buell and held two more in readiness.[9]

Four days later Kirby Smith set off from Knoxville at the head of twelve thousand battle-hardened Confederate veterans. With the enemy on the move, Grant sent Julia and the children back to St. Louis. Several days later, he wrote her, "From present indications you only left here in time. Lively operations are now threatened . . ."[10]

Kirby Smith made straight for central Kentucky. Buell had entrusted the defense of this area to William Nelson, the huge, bearded sailor who had failed Grant so miserably at Shiloh. Nelson's report on Shiloh (which Grant dismissed as "a tissue of unsupported romance from beginning to end"[11]) had made it appear that both he and his troops had performed gloriously. Lincoln seems to have agreed; he rewarded Nelson with a promotion to major general. Here, then, was another chance to show what kind of soldier he was.

His division consisted of seven thousand Indiana volunteers, recently mustered into service. They had virtually no training and had just received their rifled muskets. It was an axiom among professional soldiers that green troops could be counted on to do one of two things—"fight like hell or run like hell." Shiloh was a perfect demonstration of this adage in action. For every man who fled, three, maybe four or five had stood their ground, under intense pressure, choosing to risk death or mutilating wounds rather than yield. Nelson's recruits were no greener than those that Sherman and Prentiss had led in stubborn defensive fighting that memorable first day at Shiloh.

The commander of the Department of the Ohio, Major General Horatio Wright, urged Nelson to pull his division back to the north side of the Kentucky River. If his troops destroyed the few bridges and dug in on the bluffs that towered over the river, they stood an excellent chance of stopping Smith's advance cold. Smith himself was well aware that a contested river crossing would cost him more casualties than he could afford with a force this size. He had decided almost from the moment he entered Kentucky to fall back rather than attempt one, and if his small army withdrew, Bragg's own plans for invading the Bluegrass State would collapse.[12]

Kirby Smith was rescued by Nelson. As at Shiloh, this huge sailor, renowned throughout Buell's army for his inability to assemble a sentence without a solid substructure of bellowed profanities to prop it up, went his own heedless way once more. He decided to have his seven thousand men fight *south* of the river, out in the open, against Smith's superior numbers. He also decided, with the enemy racing up the roads toward him, that this would be a good time to make a tour of inspection of outposts in the rear.

Nelson did not bother to inform either of his brigade commanders where he was going or how he could be reached. A mounted messenger tracked him down at two-thirty on the morning of August 30 in the small town of Lexington, fifteen miles from where his division was camped. Appropriately enough, given their prospects, his troops had settled down next to a cemetery. The message said the enemy was close enough to attack.

The battle began in mid-morning, but Nelson did not arrive until a couple of hours later, just as the last shots were fired, one of which plowed into his thigh. His troops scattered in every direction. Nearly a thousand were killed or wounded. The Confederates rounded up some four thousand others. The rest seem to have scampered on home. Nelson's division had ceased to exist. So, shortly afterward, did "Bull" Nelson.

He managed to elude capture and survived his leg wound and, incredibly, was entrusted with another division. His undoing was not his ineptitude but an almost childish altercation with one of his former brigade commanders, an angry young man with the improbable name of Jefferson Davis. Their personal hostilities ended with Davis shooting Nelson dead in a hotel corridor.[13]

Following Kirby Smith's victory over Nelson's men, panic gripped Louisville and Cincinnati. Martial law was declared throughout Kentucky just as Bragg made his own northward advance from Chattanooga. Bragg's move posed Buell with a clear choice. He could either fight a battle somewhere east of Nashville to stop Bragg's advance or he could fall back toward Louisville, Kentucky, and give priority to protecting his line of communications. Buell being Buell, he withdrew nearly one hundred miles, ceding most of central Tennessee and nearly half of Kentucky without a fight.

★

When Grant returned to Corinth from Memphis, he kept his troops busy defending the railroads that snaked across the wooded and swampy landscape. It was mid-summer and the rivers were low. His army was dependent on the shining rails as never before. He lacked cavalry, though, and Confederate guerrilla bands kept attacking bridges, tracks and rolling stock. Union soldiers had so much track to replace and so many bridges to rebuild that Grant's army seemed almost as much a construction outfit as a fighting force. The War Department encouraged him to use freed or runaway slaves—"contrabands"—as laborers so his army would remain ready for battle, but able-bodied black men proved hard to find in any great numbers, which came as something of a surprise in what had until recently been slave territory

Grant's combat strength was undermined even more by his having to send three of his eight divisions to help Buell. Nonetheless he was itching to destroy the two small Confederate armies left in Mississippi. One, numbering twenty-five thousand men, was at Vicksburg, under the command of Earl Van Dorn, a small, blond West Point graduate who was probably too aggressive for his own good, or his men's. The other Confederate force consisted of fifteen thousand troops under Sterling

Price, the rebel commander who had caused so much trouble for the unlucky and unlamented John Frémont back in Missouri.

Price's troops had moved into Iuka, a small town on the railroad some twenty miles southeast of Corinth, where Price intended to wait until he heard from Van Dorn about bringing their two forces together. Grant, however, did not know that. He believed Price was planning to move to Tennessee to support Bragg's advance, and Halleck was urging him to do anything he could to prevent it. Almost as soon as Grant learned that Price was in Iuka he set in motion an operation to pin Price down and destroy him.

Two of Grant's divisions were entrusted to the very able Major General Edward Ord. The other two were commanded by Brigadier General William S. Rosecrans, an officer immensely popular with his troops but less so with his staff. A devout Roman Catholic, he had a bishop for a brother, a son in the priesthood, and a daughter in a nunnery. The genial, talkative Rosey kept his aides up late at night debating theology. He had graduated near the top of his West Point class and played a prominent role in the first Union victory of the war, the battle of Rich Mountain, West Virginia, in July 1861. Much was expected of him thereafter.[14]

Grant proposed to have Ord and Rosecrans link up, then advance toward Iuka jointly. When they reached it, Ord would strike the town from the north and Rosecrans from the south, thereby trapping Price and his army. Rosecrans rejected this idea. Having briefly occupied Iuka a few weeks earlier, he claimed to know the terrain and the few poor roads that ran through it. It would be far better, he argued, to have the two forces move separately and come together on the battlefield. Grant accepted that Rosecrans knew the area as well as he claimed and okayed Rosey's proposal.[15]

Ord would be able to field eight thousand men; Rosecrans would have nine thousand. The Union force closing on Price would enjoy no great superiority in numbers, but its tactical advantage was considerable. There were only two roads leading south from Iuka and if Rosecrans held both of them, Price would be trapped. His army could then be pushed out of the town, driven east to the Tennessee River, and there forced to surrender or die.

On September 18 Ord's troops, accompanied by Grant, moved by train to Burnsville, some six miles west of Iuka. Shortly after midnight a courier arrived at Grant's command post with a message from Rosecrans, who was still twenty miles southwest of the town. His column had set off on the wrong road, he reported. Not a good start for someone who claimed to know this area well. The attack would have to be postponed from the morning of the nineteenth until sometime in the afternoon. Grant was disappointed, but remained confident the plan would succeed.

While he waited, he sent a message to Price under a flag of truce demanding his immediate surrender. Stunning news had just clicked over the telegraph wires into Burnsville from Washington: a huge battle had been fought in Maryland, at Antietam Creek, two days earlier— General McClellan had destroyed Lee's Army of Northern Virginia! "I think this decides the war finally," he gleefully informed Ord.

Grant was hoping Price would reach the same conclusion. Instead, Price robustly informed him that he did not believe the news from the East. Besides, even if it were true, it would only make him and his men fight all the harder.[16] Everything now depended on Rosecrans.

Around noon on the nineteenth, two of Grant's aides, Clark Lagow and T. Lyle Dickey, found Rosecrans seven miles south of Iuka. He told them he was waiting to hear the sound of Ord's attack. They told him that maybe Grant was expecting him to attack first. Rosecrans brushed that idea aside and proceeded to advance cautiously toward the town. There was an obvious failure of communication here, because while Ord expected Rosecrans to strike first, Rosecrans assumed it was Ord who would open the battle. Grant had, in fact, sent Rosecrans a message telling him to attack first, but he did not receive it until late in the afternoon.[17]

By this time Rosecrans had made his own matchless contribution to the impending battle. The roads in front of him formed an inverted V, with Iuka at the apex, where they met. Rosecrans did not even consider putting a division on each of these converging roads and advancing on the town along them. Instead, he decided that if he split his force, the parts would be too widely separated to come readily to each other's support if either came under attack. Besides, it was a widely accepted axiom that a commander did not divide his army when close to the enemy.

Even so, Rosecrans had just made the wrong decision. The entire plan depended on both roads being denied to Price. Otherwise there was no point in trying to implement it. What's more, Rosecrans had nearly eight hundred cavalry available to him. With a little light artillery, the cavalry could have moved up one road and blocked it a few miles south of the town while the entire infantry force and the rest of the artillery attacked along the other.

The fundamental flaw in Rosecrans was that the man had appalling judgment: cautious when he ought to be bold, reckless when he ought to be cautious. And always, always too slow and poorly organized. There were risks in spreading his force out; that is undeniable. But although Grant was certain Price had only fifteen thousand men in Iuka, Rosecrans managed to convince himself there were really as many as thirty thousand Confederate troops. His hesitant progress toward Iuka was that of a man heeding his fears rather than his commander.[18]

As Rosecrans reached a point roughly two miles south of the town, the Confederates discovered Ord's regiments deployed only about one mile to the north of it. Even though Price had sent a defiant message to Grant, he had in fact already decided to evacuate Iuka. Finding the Federals so close was all the incentive needed to signal an immediate withdrawal. As they moved south, the rebels ran smack into Rosecrans's leading division. The Union troops had barely enough time to get out of column and into line to meet the Confederate attack. One of the fiercest engagements of the entire war erupted just south of Iuka, but Grant and Ord didn't hear a thing.

Why Union generals lacked the sense to get off their horses, stretch out, put an ear to the ground, and try to pick up the vibration of artillery fire when they knew a battle was pending is a mystery. It was well known among soldiers that during some of Napoleon's battles, such as Jena-Auerstadt, atmospheric conditions made it possible for the noise of fighting to be carried away by the wind so it could not be heard even a couple of miles away. This phenomenon, known as "acoustic shadow," had happened at Fort Donelson, so it should not have caught anyone by surprise. Yet Grant and Ord and their staffs and their aides waited passively all that afternoon, expecting to hear the sound of Rosecrans's attack at any moment. Rosecrans meanwhile had the fight of his life on his hands, at one point bellowing in despair, "Where in the name of God is Grant?"

The Confederates charged four times, but were stopped—only just—every time. In the space of two hours, nearly one-fourth of the men who blocked the rebels were killed or wounded. Night fell and with the onset of darkness the firing sputtered down into a tense, sullen silence. An infuriated Rosecrans wrote angrily to Grant. "You must attack in the morning and *in force . . .*" Even as he wrote, however, Price's troops were discovering the open road. By dawn they were fleeing Iuka along the route that Rosecrans had failed to block.[19]

Grant advanced into Iuka around nine A.M. behind marching regiments, fluttering flags, and the braying of military bands. He rode up to Rosecrans's command post and discovered that even though Rosecrans was well aware that Price's army was now fleeing south and had at hand an entire division that had not been involved in the battle—to say nothing of his well-rested cavalry—he had done nothing to pursue the retreating Confederates. Grant ordered him to organize a pursuit at once, but it was too late to catch them.[20]

At first Grant believed a victory of sorts had been won—at least Price had been stopped from going to join Bragg. In his official reports on the battle, he praised Rosecrans, yet the more Grant learned of what had actually happened, the more he found fault with Old Rosey. By the time he came to write his memoirs, he was scathing about the failed operation at Iuka.[21]

Following Iuka, Grant moved his headquarters to Jackson, Tennessee, nearly sixty miles north of Corinth. There he took over a rambling structure that had evidently begun as a log cabin but was later greatly enlarged by having a frame house as an addition. From Jackson he was able to run his widely scattered command while remaining poised to come to the aid of Buell if necessary.

He had installed Rosecrans in command at Corinth. Neither of them seriously expected that Rosecrans would soon have to fight for the town. Van Dorn, however, had not altered his plans because of the battle at Iuka. There was a Confederate spy in Corinth, and according to her, its defenses were not as formidable as they appeared. Van Dorn and Price joined forces on September 28, and as soon as Grant learned of it, he guessed that Corinth would be attacked. He sent a warning to Rosecrans, but Rosey at first refused to take it seriously.[22]

Rosecrans was convinced Corinth's defenses were so strong no enemy would dare attack them. He had fifteen thousand soldiers holding the entrenchments, with another eight thousand deployed in nearby outposts who could be pulled in very rapidly. Van Dorn's attack force itself amounted to no more than twenty-three thousand men. He would enjoy no superiority in numbers or firepower. His best hope was to trust his spy's reports and try to catch Rosecrans by surprise by striking at Corinth not from the south but from the northwest. Twenty-four hours before the attack, however, Rosecrans finally realized Grant was right and bolstered his defenses.

On the morning of October 3, Van Dorn's troops launched their assault and swiftly broke through the first of the three lines of entrenchments girdling the town. These were the trenches that Beauregard had dug. By midday they had penetrated the second line, the trenches ordered by Halleck. Late in the afternoon they pierced the third and final line, one that Rosecrans had played a major part in creating. Some Confederates managed to force their way into the town, but half a mile from the center were driven back by a Union counterattack.[23]

The Confederates counted the day a success, but they had paid dearly for it, if that's what it was. Van Dorn's faulty tactics had spread them out in a wide arc, exposing most of his assaulting force to galling Union artillery fire. He had also failed to create a reserve strong enough to exploit his breakthrough.[24]

Next day, the Confederates tried to renew their attack, but Rosecrans's artillery was too devastating and his men were too well dug in. Around noon the rebel assault fizzled out. Butternut dead were piled in heaps in front of Union positions. The very air seem to boil with hot lead. It was hopeless. By three P.M. a general retreat was in motion. The Confederates had suffered up to five thousand casualties. Federal losses came to roughly twenty-five hundred.[25]

Rosecrans had shown tremendous personal courage during the fight, riding from one hot spot to another, exhorting, inspiring, directing the Union defenses. He was always at his best in the middle of a fight, never in setting one up or in handling the aftermath. When the battle for Corinth abruptly stopped, he gave orders for his troops to rest. They would launch their pursuit of the enemy in the morning.

So far, thought Rosecrans, so good. Grant saw it differently. Like Napoleon, he was forever seeking battles of annihilation, but not because he was "Butcher" Grant. On the contrary. From what he had seen in Mexico, Grant knew that the biggest killer in war was not battle but disease. Paradoxically, a short, bloody, intensely fought war was more humane than one that dragged on from year to year, steadily filling the cemeteries with the victims of typhus and cholera, pneumonia and malaria. Far more soldiers in the Civil War would be killed by bacteria and viral diseases than perished in combat. The war Grant wanted would be horrifyingly bloody, but over in a couple of months. Preferably, it would be settled by just one more fight.

For now, what Rosecrans had to do was to cut off the Confederates' line of retreat, then destroy Van Dorn's army. Grant had dispatched one of his most trusted subordinates, Brigadier General James McPherson, to Corinth once it became certain an attack was imminent. McPherson arrived during the afternoon of October 4 with four fresh regiments of infantry. Grant had also ordered a division of troops to move to a point south of Corinth, with Ord in command. Once more Rosecrans had a sizable cavalry force available. With Ord's division, McPherson's four regiments, and nearly a thousand cavalry, the pursuit should and could have begun the evening of October 4. The fact that it was growing dark was neither here nor there. It was Gneisenau's night pursuit at the end of the battle of Waterloo that destroyed Napoleon's Grande Armée.

In other words, Rosecrans had all he needed to trap Van Dorn's battered and demoralized army in the countryside around Corinth and crush it. To Grant's indignation, the Confederates were not cut off, nor were they pursued vigorously. From the time the Confederate retreat began to the time Rosecrans's pursuit got moving, some fifteen hours passed—long enough for Van Dorn to elude him.

Rosecrans was not only slow to get started, but most of his troops took the wrong road. During the night of the fourth, he issued orders to McPherson to be "prepared to march," thereby immobilizing McPherson, whose regiments were already poised to set off at once in pursuit. Rosecrans also overloaded his men with extra supplies. They might as well have been dragging lead weights on their feet across the hot, dusty landscape.[26]

Ord cut the road ten miles south of Corinth and kept Van Dorn occupied for three hours in a battle for a bridge that spanned a narrow stream with steep banks. He assumed that McPherson, Rosecrans's cavalry and at least some of Rosecrans's infantry would by this time be attacking the enemy's rear, when in fact they were still looking for the right road. Van Dorn could not smash through Ord's line, despite an advantage in numbers of at least four to one. He broke off the engagement, marching away in search of another road and another bridge.

Rosecrans followed Van Dorn across central Mississippi, toward the small town of Ripley, while Grant grew increasingly apprehensive. There were reports that Van Dorn had been strongly reinforced by nine thousand Confederate veterans, paroled enemy soldiers who had broken their oath not to take up arms again. Besides, Van Dorn fell back toward Holly Springs and was far enough ahead of Rosecrans to have time to entrench his men on favorable ground before he got there. Grant could easily picture the volatile, unsteady Rosecrans losing his entire army in a reckless, doomed assault on Holly Springs. He ordered Rosecrans to halt the pursuit and return to Corinth.

Instead of doing as ordered, Rosecrans telegraphed a nettled reply: "I most deeply dissent from your views . . ." Grant felt obliged to refer the issue to Halleck, who came down on the side of Rosecrans. "Why order a return of our troops?" asked the general-in-chief. "Why not reenforce Rosecrans and pursue the enemy . . . supporting your army on the country?" Grant wired back, "An army cannot subsist on the country except in forage"—i.e., there was food enough for horses but not for men. He was wrong about that, but it would be six months before he discovered just how abundant foodstuffs were in what, to someone who has grown up in the Midwest, even now looks like a poor region for agriculture. Rosecrans was ordered to pull back to Corinth.[27]

During the failed pursuit of Van Dorn, Julia joined Grant in Jackson. Hardly had she settled in before Rawlins, then McPherson, told her something had to be done about Rosecrans. "We want to reach the general's ear through you," said McPherson. "In justice to General Grant— in fact, in justice to ourselves—General Rosecrans ought to be relieved."

Before the war was over, Julia would become accustomed to acting as a kind of unofficial, unpaid staff officer, one who could get the general's attention whenever she wished and on any issue that interested her. When she told him what Rawlins and McPherson had said, Grant responded, "Rosecrans's action was all wrong." Even so, he considered Rosey to be "a brave and loyal soldier." Besides, he was also a trained professional, "and of this kind, we have none to spare at present."[28]

Not surprisingly, then, when Grant wrote his official report on the battle of Corinth and its aftermath, he covered up Rosey's failure, as he had done after Iuka. The truth was he was disgusted by Rosecrans's generalship, both in the way he had fought to save the town and in the way he handled the pursuit. But there were a number of good reasons for keeping his feelings out of the official record.

Grant enjoyed a reputation for personal honesty that was extraordinary. Even so, that does not mean his reports should be taken literally.

Official documents, then as now, serve many uses. Whatever truth they contain, compromises, half-truths and hidden agendas clog the subtext. An important official report submitted by Grant—or any other army commander—was both an account of what had happened and a step toward what he wanted to happen.

That was not something Grant created; it was the system he had to deal with. His mastery of Army paperwork and bureaucracy was unmatched by any other soldier of the Civil War. Grant had a powerful literary gift, and he used it to make this huge, cumbersome military machine serve his purposes. Everything he wrote as a commander was crafted with his own ends in mind. History was not best served by his methods, but Grant didn't worry much about that.

Anyway, he knew that whatever he wrote would serve not only his purposes. It would be used by others to serve theirs. Although official reports could not be made public without the War Department's approval, portions were often leaked to journalists and politicians. If he indicated there was anything wrong within his command, he would be inviting them—and Halleck—to take an uncomfortably close interest in it. Besides, Rosecrans had strong supporters in Congress and a mentor in Halleck. It would be foolish to alienate Rosey's powerful friends if it could be avoided. Grant's contempt for Rosecrans *was* eventually made public, but it had to wait for an angry blast twenty years later in the memoirs.[29]

Even as Grant wrote his uncritical official report, Rosecrans was intriguing against him, going over his head to Halleck. He informed the general-in-chief that there were two problems. First, Grant's staff ("mousing politicians") had turned the general against him. Second, "he lacks administrative ability." All in all, the situation had become so bad, "I should be relieved from duty here . . ."[30]

This was brazen back-stabbing for any subordinate, but given Halleck's own disdain for Grant, Rosecrans wasn't going to be rebuked for it. If anything, he would get Halleck's sympathy. The irony of all this intrigue was that it worked to Grant's advantage.

While Rosecrans had been tangling with Van Dorn, Buell had at last stopped Bragg and defeated him at the battle of Perryville. Bragg retreated, but Buell's pursuit was so inept that Lincoln finally lost all patience with him. Buell was ousted and the Army of the Cumberland was created to secure eastern Tennessee. It would need a commander, and it did not take Halleck long to think of a suitable candidate.

On October 23 an Army messenger carried a telegram from Halleck into Grant's office, a room at the end of the long, low, south-facing piazza of the unusual log cabin–cum–balloon-frame house. Shortly afterward Grant stepped onto the piazza holding the telegram and smiling. "There is good news, good news," he told his staff. The message he held ordered Rosecrans to report to department headquarters in Cincinnati. "My greatest trouble has been solved," said Grant.[31]

It was a confident, even jubilant, beginning to the movement he had been pondering the past couple of weeks in that office at the end of the piazza—a campaign to capture Vicksburg.

CHAPTER 18

— ★ ★ ★ ★ —

"UNMANAGEABLE AND INCOMPETANT"

John McClernand was not much taller than Grant but was certain he towered over him. "I am the man to command this army, not Grant," he told his regimental commanders. The whole character was there in the look of him—in the spade chin and dagger beard, the vulpine, swarthy face, the black eyes glittering like jet, the bombastic pouter pigeon chest thrust out and up like a challenge to the world. Here was an embodiment of force and ambition, ego and will. It was a disgrace, McClernand raged, that a man of his abilities had to serve under a drunkard.[1]

The only reason such injustice was permitted in a democratic country was the vicious West Point clique that protected people like Grant. Academy graduates were strutting, pampered popinjays who assumed that professional soldiers knew just about everything in war and the patriotic volunteer knew just about nothing. Yet the only reason Grant had been made a general was not a talent for soldiering but the fact that he had a powerful congressman, Elihu B. Washburne, pulling strings for him all over Washington. Without Washburne's backing, Grant was nothing.[2]

Why, McClernand's own battlefield record showed what an overrated mediocrity Grant was. At Belmont, at Fort Donelson, and again at

Shiloh, Grant had brought his army to the brink of failure—probably even disaster—and every time he had been saved by McClernand's division, that rock on which Grant's reputation stood. But would Grant or any of the other professionals give him half the credit he deserved? They'd see him in hell first.

Be that as it may, the time was coming when the whole country would know the military qualities of John McClernand. He had in mind a project that would alter the whole course of the war. He was going to raise an army of his own, a Mississippi River Expedition. Instead of having to take orders from Halleck and Grant, he would be independent of them, reporting only to the President. With Lincoln's backing he would go on to achieve something that Halleck and Grant and the other professionals had failed to do—open the Father of Waters all the way to the Gulf.

At the end of September 1862 McClernand traveled to Washington to tell his former Springfield neighbor Abraham Lincoln how the Confederate stranglehold on the great river was choking the economic life of the Midwest. McClernand, as he probably expected, found he was pushing on an open door. Lincoln had lived and worked along the great river himself.

The President knew as well as McClernand how important it was to the economies of half a dozen midwestern states. He knew, too, that from a strategic point of view, the war in the West could not be won without first securing the river. He and Stanton talked over the Mississippi River Expedition idea with Halleck, but Halleck opposed it. The general idea was good; no argument there. What he didn't like about the plan was entrusting an independent command to McClernand. On the other hand, Rear Admiral David Porter, commanding naval forces on the Mississippi, supported it. His view of West Pointers was much like McClernand's. Porter thought he would get better cooperation from an amateur than from a professional, news that would have amazed Grant had he known of Porter's real attitude.[3]

In October Lincoln finally gave it the go-ahead—up to a point. He and Edwin Stanton, the secretary of war, were both skillful lawyers, and while they would never admit this to McClernand, they were virtually auxiliary members of that West Point clique. If the trouble with the professionals was that they tended to be too cautious—because they knew too much about all the things that could go wrong—the trouble with volunteers was that they were likely to be reckless—because they could not even begin to imagine half of the dangers they courted. A little bravado might be good if you had to pitch a regiment into a battle, but the Union could not risk throwing away an entire army on a volunteer's untutored impulse. So Lincoln and Stanton drafted a document that was so craftily worded it might fool someone as wrapped up in himself as McClernand into thinking he was getting what he wanted, without actually committing them to anything much.

At the very least, McClernand might raise tens of thousands of fresh soldiers. Even if he didn't capture Vicksburg and drive on to New Orleans, he would light a fire under Grant and Halleck. On October 21 McClernand was ordered to go to Illinois, Indiana and Iowa to recruit new regiments. These troops were to assemble at Cairo and Memphis "to the end that, when a sufficient force not required by the operations of General Grant's command shall be raised, an expedition may be organized, under General McClernand's command, against Vicksburg, and to clear the Mississippi River. . . . The forces so organized will remain subject to the designation of the general-in-chief, and be employed according to such exigencies as the service, in his judgement, may require."[4]

What these turgidly worded provisos meant in plain English was that Halleck and Grant would really control whatever force McClernand managed to raise. McClernand, however, was so intoxicated by the thought that he was getting an independent command that he didn't read the details too closely. He believed only what he wanted to believe. With this secret order in his pocket, he headed straight for the Midwest on a recruiting drive. In his nostrils, we may guess, was the giddying incense of victory, glory and, one day, the White House.

The War Department did not inform Grant about these moves. What he learned, he gleaned from Army rumor and the northern press. A week after McClernand got what he thought was the order to create an independent command for himself, Grant decided to move his headquarters from Memphis to La Grange, Tennessee, virtually on the border with Mississippi, as a preliminary to an advance on Vicksburg.[5]

He led his army forward in the approved nineteenth-century style—out in front of the troops, riding Jack, the powerful yellow stallion he had bought with borrowed money when he got his commission as a colonel. When he set off for La Grange the morning of November 4,

Grant rode ahead of his staff, with regiment after regiment marching behind them, while to the rear of the tramping infantry and stretching almost to the horizon, or so it seemed, came the army wagon train rocking and swaying to the crack of whips and the shouted "Goddamn!" of teamsters.

Cavalry rode around on the flanks and couriers dashed up and down the line of march carrying messages to and from the general, heedless of anything or anyone in their path. On this day, a courier allowed his horse to tread on Jack's heels and Grant, turning angrily in his saddle, rebuked him sharply, a rare occasion when Grant allowed his anger to show in front of strangers.

Most of the time when Grant led the army forward, he rode alone, deep in thought, but occasionally a staff officer kept him company. On this ride he allowed a journalist who had just been attached to the Army, Sylvanus Cadwallader of the *Chicago Times,* to accompany him for a while. Cadwallader's predecessor, Warren P. Isham, was currently in the Federal penitentiary at Alton, Illinois. Isham had filed entirely false stories whose only purpose seemed to be to provide aid and comfort to the enemy, by spreading alarm in Washington and demoralizing Union soldiers in the field.[6]

Grant was curious to see what kind of man had been sent to him this time. He talked to Cadwallader about horses, farming and the difficulties of raising hogs, but told him nothing more than he already knew about why headquarters was being moved to La Grange.[7]

His plan was to advance following the line of the Mississippi Central Railroad. Some thirty miles south of La Grange was Holly Springs, presently occupied by Van Dorn's troops. Grant ordered Sherman, presently commanding in Memphis, to send three divisions down. Once reinforced, Grant would move on Holly Springs, after which he would push on to Grenada. That would take him almost into central Mississippi, in position to threaten Vicksburg.[8]

As it turned out, he did not have to fight for Holly Springs. Earl Van Dorn's failed attempt to seize Corinth by frontal assault had led to suspension from his command and a court of inquiry. His troops were demoralized, hungry and suffering from the unseasonable winter weather that swept across northern Mississippi that fall. They abandoned Holly Springs to the oncoming Union cavalry, which entered the town on November 13. The Confederates fell back toward Grenada.

Van Dorn's successor as commander of the Department of Mississippi and Louisiana was Lieutenant General John Pemberton, whom
Grant had known as a promising young staff officer in Mexico. Pemberton was not a southerner but a Pennsylvanian. His adherence to the
Confederacy was inspired by devotion to his wife, who was not only
southern by birth but a staunch Confederate by conviction. At about the
time Grant was making plans to advance on Grenada, Pemberton was
setting up a field headquarters there and conferring with his staff on
ways to halt Grant's advance.[9]

As the Federals pressed southward, the leading elements of Grant's
force clashed periodically with Confederates, but the retreating enemy
seemed incapable of offering strong resistance. "How far south would
you like us to go?" Grant asked Halleck by wire on December 4. The
enemy was not the great obstacle, he explained. It was his tenuous supply situation that was slowing his advance. Much of his army was still
tied down guarding and repairing track, tunnels and bridges.[10]

Next day at Coffeeville, only eighteen miles north of Grenada, the
three regiments leading the army's advance were ambushed and driven
back two miles. It was a minor shock, and something of a warning.
Grant, with the threat of McClernand constantly at the back of his mind,
had stretched his army too thin and pushed it too hard. He informed
Halleck that he had now moved about as far as he could go.[11]

By this time Grant's supply line consisted of a single, vulnerable
steel thread—the railroad tracks stretching back deep into central Tennessee. He had to pause and consolidate, building up a supply depot at
Holly Springs to support any further advance. With active operations
winding down, he moved to Oxford, which was halfway between Holly
Springs and Coffeeville. It looked like he was going to be staying here
for some time, so he sent for Julia to come and join him.

Waiting was one thing Grant was never good at. It was galling to sit
still, accumulate supplies and repair railroad tracks. Every day that
passed without putting the enemy under pressure only allowed the
rebels to strengthen their defenses and prolong the war. And every day
he was immobilized gave McClernand an opportunity, too.

He poured out his downcast and fretful mood in a letter he wrote his
sister on December 15. "For a consciencious [*sic*] person, and I profess
myself to be one, this is a most slavish life. I may be envied by ambitious persons, but I in turn envy every person who can transact his daily

business and retire to a quiet home without a feeling of responsibility for the morrow . . . there are an immence [*sic*] number of lives staked upon my judgement and acts. I am extended now like a Peninsula into an enemies [*sic*] country with a large Army depending for their daily bread upon keeping open a line of rail-road runing [*sic*] one hundred & ninety miles . . . through territory occupied by a people terribly embittered and hostile to us. With all this I suffer the mortification of seeing myself attacked right and left by people at home professing patriotism and love of country who never heard the whistle of a hostile bullet. I pity them and a nation dependent on such for its existence. . . . With all my other trials I have to contend against is added that of speculators whose patriotism is measured by dollars and cents. Country has no value with them compared to money . . ."[12]

He was exasperated at the flood of cotton speculators and rapacious businessmen, the petty swindlers and brazen con artists who seemed to follow the Union Army south like garbage pulled into the powerful wake of a passing ship. There was a clamor in the North for cotton. The Treasury Department was attempting, ineffectually, to control the trade by issuing certificates to trade in cotton to reputable northern merchants.

To Grant, though, all these cotton buyers were thieves, and he had nothing but contempt for the Treasury's deluded idea that it could somehow keep them under control. The trade was so hedged about with government restrictions that it was impossible to make a profit from it honestly, yet many people were rapidly getting rich. The cotton traders were also getting their goods onto the railroads, but Grant's army was so dependent on the railroads that any civilian use of them undermined his fighting power. No wonder, then, he was delighted when he heard that Cadwallader had gotten into an argument with a cotton trader and beaten the man up. Rawlins even congratulated him. Cadwallader was on his way to becoming a favorite of Grant and his staff.[13]

The conquered areas of the South were rich with easy pickings, and one of those who showed up in Memphis that fall to grab a piece was Jesse Root Grant. Age had not withered the old man's acquisitive instincts. When Grant heard his father was on his way to Memphis, he had sent for Colonel T. Lyle Dickey, his chief of cavalry, and told him, "Some of the money sharks and cotton speculators here have gained an unwarrantable influence over the old man, and he is really coming down here to use his influence over me to gain favor for them."[14]

Then he explained his plan: Dickey would offer to share his tent with Jesse and would accompany Jesse wherever he went. Grant would visit his father every day, but never alone. If Jesse came to see him, Dickey had to make sure he was present, too. It worked. Jesse stayed for ten days and tried several times to see his son alone, but it was impossible. There were always other people around—the kind of people who were ignorant of business and how deals were done, the kind of people who might misunderstand and go blabbing it around that something funny was going on. Jesse went back to Covington glad to have seen his famous son, but frustrated all the same.

Grant had not been in Oxford long when he heard that his father was coming to see him again, bringing a Jewish business partner. At the same time, Grant was receiving reports that the worst—that is, the most successful—cotton speculators in his department were Jews. Not only were they buying cotton; they were doing so with gold. That only made the offense worse, because the Confederacy, with its worthless paper money, was desperate for gold to pay for its imports, including weapons. With the pressure on him to do something about the illegal cotton trade growing intense, Grant wrote out a pass for his father to travel through the Union lines but refused to issue one for his father's partner. Angered, one can guess, at Jesse's persistence and cupidity, and determined to show Washington that he was cracking down on the speculators, on December 17 he wrote out General Orders Number 11. It began, "The Jews, as a class, violating every regulation of trade . . . are hereby expelled from the Department."[15]

Grant was known, and not only to those who admired him, for his common sense. An order like this was obviously the sign of someone at the end of his tether, for once not thinking clearly; a fundamentally decent man for once not even trying to be fair. He later admitted, somewhat ruefully, "The order was made and sent out without any reflection . . ." He was looking for a scapegoat on which to vent his pent-up anger and frustration. Not for the first time in history, Jews fit the bill.[16]

Before this, Grant had made critical remarks about Jews, but those amounted to no more than passing irritation and the casual anti-Semitism that has been a commonplace in American life up to the present day. General Orders Number 11, however, gave that casual anti-Semitism a new and ugly twist. Besides being manifestly unjust, it was an insult to every honest and patriotic Jew who served the Union cause and so completely unenforceable it was ludicrous. Did Grant seriously mean to expel Jewish soldiers serving in his regiments? What about Jewish sutlers, who provided the troops with minor luxuries? And was he barring Jewish contractors, who provided crucial supplies to his army?

When Lincoln learned of the order expelling the Jews from Grant's department, he was appalled. Two weeks after it was issued, Halleck ordered Grant to revoke it. He did so promptly, with a sense of relief. He had no right, he readily admitted, to act in a sweeping way against an entire religious sect, and when he learned that he had been criticized severely in Congress, his response was that he deserved it.[17]

In the meantime, Julia was making her way toward him from Jackson, Tennessee, having stopped off for a week in Holly Springs while waiting for Grant's troops to improve the road down to Oxford. On December 18 she set off to join him, just in time to avoid being caught in one of the most daring Confederate moves of the war.

Following the court of inquiry into his attack on Corinth, Van Dorn was exonerated and given a new command, one more suited to his limited abilities. Pemberton entrusted him with thirty-five hundred well-mounted cavalry, to strike deep into Grant's rear and force the Federal army to halt its advance; maybe it could even be forced to pull back. As Van Dorn moved north, his cavalrymen were spotted by eight hundred Union horse soldiers commanded by Colonel T. Lyle Dickey, leading a mission to cut the Mobile and Ohio Railroad, running through eastern Mississippi. Dickey feared being drawn into a fight. Given the odds against him, he could count on being thrashed. Van Dorn, however, ignored the Union horse soldiers, whose presence his riders had easily spotted, and rode on.

Dickey had just blundered—twice. He had dispatched two messengers to Grant, with news that a large Confederate cavalry force was moving north. One of Dickey's couriers got lost. His instructions to the other were so unclear that the man remained in camp and never set off at all. Second, he began "demonstrating"—that is, he pretended to be about to attack part of Van Dorn's force. But his demonstration was treated with disdain. The Confederates declined to be drawn into a fight.[18]

At this point Dickey should have attacked. Just delaying the enemy by a day—even half a day—would have been worth heavy losses if it kept this large rebel cavalry force out of the poorly protected Union rear long enough for Grant to shore up its defenses. Dickey, however, seemed incapable in this, the critical moment of his life, of thinking clearly. He did not pause to wonder why the Confederates continued moving north after they noticed the Union cavalry.

It was late in the afternoon of December 19 when Dickey galloped up to Grant's Oxford headquarters and began reporting on his mission, thinking he had just snatched his men from the very jaws of death. Grant ignored all that. What he wanted to know was how many riders were with Van Dorn. Which direction were they headed? What was the condition of the road they were following? Then he walked quickly over to the telegraph office, several hundred yards away, and began writing telegrams.[19]

Cables were dispatched to officers in small towns across northern Mississippi, warning them that Van Dorn was heading in their direction. What had Grant worried most was Holly Springs. The railroad depot there had been turned in recent weeks into a huge supply base, overflowing with bullets and hardtack, rice and sowbelly, tents and blankets, rifled muskets and corn. Holly Springs was not only a magnet for an enemy raid, but it had just become one of the most vulnerable places in Grant's far-flung command—vulnerable because the colonel in command there was a fool by the name of Robert C. Murphy of the 8th Wisconsin. Murphy had been holding Iuka back in September, and when Sterling Price approached the town, Murphy had hastily abandoned it, without firing a single shot to discourage the rebels or destroying or removing the large supply of military stores that had been collected there. Murphy had done as much as, if not more than, Price's quartermaster, when it came to re-equipping his ragged army.

It was an abysmal performance, but Grant was not going to get embroiled in the dismissal of a mediocre volunteer colonel unless he was sure he could get rid of him with a minimum of fuss. Murphy had done badly, but not badly enough. Grant settled for putting him in charge at Holly Springs, never expecting it to come under attack. Grant ordered a cavalry force to head for Holly Springs immediately and notified Murphy that help was on the way.[20]

Julia reached Oxford that afternoon and was disappointed to find Grant wasn't waiting to greet her at the depot. When she arrived at his headquarters with little Jess at dusk, he came out from his office to embrace her. "I only have time to kiss you," he said apologetically.

"And, Jess, you little rascal, are you glad to see me?" Then he hurried back inside. Explanations could wait for later.[21]

Van Dorn's cavalry rode into the outskirts of Holly Springs that night. Every rebel raider carried a bottle of turpentine and a box of matches. Murphy learned (from one of his own officers) they were approaching the town at almost the same time the news reached Grant, yet Murphy did virtually nothing to put his own men on the alert. Nor did he summon help from other Federal units deployed in and around Holly Springs. Murphy more or less closed his eyes and hoped it would all soon be over.[22]

The Confederates easily evaded the few pickets he had posted. They charged into the town at dawn on the morning of December 20, catching most of Murphy's troops still asleep. While a handful put up a fight, Murphy abjectly surrendered his entire command. Van Horn's raiders looted the town and the depot, then put what remained to the torch. The mountain of supplies Grant had counted on to support his advance to Grenada and beyond smoldered for days.[23]

He was incensed. There were roughly two thousand Union soldiers in Holly Springs and plenty of cotton bales and brick walls to place them behind. "With all the cotton, public stores and substantial buildings about the [Holly Springs] depot it would have been perfectly practicable to have made in a few hours defenses sufficient to resist with a small garrison all the cavalry brought against them until the reenforcements [*sic*] which the commanding officer was notified were marching to his relief could have reached him," he reported to Halleck. This time Murphy was dismissed from the service.[24]

That was the only satisfaction Grant had from this entire sorry affair. The thick pall of smoke curling skyward from the Holly Springs depot marked the defeat of his hopes of advancing on Vicksburg that winter. On December 23 he pulled out of Oxford, withdrew to Holly Springs, and reduced his men's rations by 25 percent. This retreat hurt like a public humiliation. Everything now depended on Sherman, who was about to try taking Vicksburg by storm.

★

McClernand had raised more than twenty-five thousand men for his Mississippi River Expedition, but when the War Department made no sign of getting them into action under his command, he became restive.

In mid-December he sent a peremptory telegram to Halleck, demanding implementation of the "order of the Secretary of War of the 21st of October giving me command of the Mississippi expedition." He also fired off a message to Lincoln. The War Department, he complained, had ignored the President's order. "I believe I am been superseded."[25]

Grant was dreading the eventual—and inevitable—return of McClernand. He was afraid, too, that Lew Wallace, who had strong political connections, might get back into the war. "I am sorry to say it but I would regard it as particularly unfortunate," he informed Halleck, "to have either McClernand or Wallace sent to me. The latter I could manage if he had less rank, but the former is unmanageable and incompetant [*sic*]."[26]

Four days after he sent this message, the War Department informed him that his army was to be organized into four corps, one of which would be commanded by McClernand, and McClernand was to lead the advance on Vicksburg while remaining under Grant's command. This was the President's wish, Halleck told him. There was no getting out of it.

Grant's disappointment was more than matched by McClernand's. Stanton had just informed McClernand of the brutal truth—he was not going to get an independent command and would serve under Grant once again. But what was even worse was that when he arrived in Memphis to assume command of the troops gathered there, he learned that Sherman had already taken them on a mission to capture Vicksburg.[27]

Sherman had set off on December 20 with twenty thousand soldiers, many of them recruited that fall by McClernand. At Helena, Arkansas, another twelve thousand men joined the expedition. Sherman's seventy overcrowded steamers then proceeded down the Mississippi, guarded by eight Union gunboats. Grant and Sherman had put this operation together in a hurry and launched it without proper planning in an attempt to grab Vicksburg ahead of McClernand. The only element operating in its favor was the fact that the attackers would have the defenders outnumbered by nearly two and a half to one. Other than that, they hadn't a chance.[28]

As far as Sherman knew, however, Grant was still advancing into central Mississippi, a move which would force Pemberton to weaken the defenses of Vicksburg by sending part of his force to block Grant somewhere near Grenada. Instead, though, Van Dorn's raid on Holly Springs had made Grant pull back. Pemberton had indeed sent thousands of men to Grenada as anticipated, but with Grant's retreat he wasted no time bringing them back to Vicksburg to repel Sherman's attack.

On December 27 Sherman launched his four divisions against the northern defenses of the town. The weather was close to freezing and rain fell in torrents. His men had to cross a bayou to reach the enemy line, a line that was well entrenched on high ground overlooking the swamps that the Federals were floundering around in. Sherman's assault carried his men across the bayou, but that only left them more exposed than ever to enemy fire. Worse, in a way, was the fact that the approaches to the enemy's line were so hard to reach that only a small portion of his force could get into action at any time, which completely nullified their advantage in numbers.

The attack was renewed the next day and Union regiments were cut to ribbons. Sherman had incurred nearly two thousand casualties; Confederate losses amounted to no more than two hundred. It was hopeless. Sherman pulled his men out and reported to Grant, "I assume all responsibility and attach fault to no one."[29]

On January 2, 1863, McClernand arrived to claim his due. By then, Sherman and Porter had thought of a face-saver. They would attack the Confederate base at Arkansas Post, on the Arkansas River. They could reach it in a day and had enough firepower and manpower to overwhelm the defenders. McClernand was unable to resist insulting Sherman. He had, he announced, a way of reinvigorating the troops, "demoralized by the late defeat"—*he* was going to attack Arkansas Post.

When Grant learned that McClernand was going to attack Arkansas Post he was disgusted. "It will lead to the loss of men without a result," he reflected angrily. While there might be something to be said for it as a morale boost, it would do so only at the cost of weakening the force to be used against Vicksburg, which was the reason for the existence of McClernand's "army" in the first place. Grant may never have realized that Sherman and Porter, both of whom he respected, had planned to attack Arkansas Post even before McClernand arrived.[30]

Sherman was infuriated, as was Porter, by McClernand's contemptuous attitude, but there wasn't much they could do about it. McClernand took command of the four divisions and grandiloquently named this modest force "The Army of the Mississippi," with Sherman as one of his corps commanders.[31]

Grant sent a short telegram to Halleck, protesting, "Genl. McClernand has gone off on a wild goose chase . . ." But it was too late to cancel it. The attack went ahead. Porter's gunboats shattered the Confederate defenses. Sherman's infantry assault followed and Arkansas Post fell on January 12, 1863, with the surrender of five thousand Confederates.

Although Grant had not been able to stop this unnecessary attack on Arkansas Post, it was not without positive results. His brief, angry cable to Halleck brought a swift, liberating reply. "You are hereby authorized to relieve Genl McClernand from command of the Expedition against Vicksburg, giving it to the next in rank, or taking it yourself." A message like this could not have been sent without Lincoln's authority. It was like being let out of jail.[32]

A rejoicing Grant got Rawlins to draft a letter to McClernand—"You are hereby relieved of Command of the Expedition against Vicksburg." Before it could be sent, though, he had another thought: *". . . taking it yourself."* That was all he needed. Removing McClernand would stir up an unnecessary political storm. Why do that when he could go down there and assume command in the field? Besides, that was always his preference. It was the best way, maybe the only way, to take Vicksburg.[33]

─── ★ ★ ★ ★ ───

CHAPTER 19

"Fortifications

Almost Impregnible"

The Union's hastily improvised military machine had gotten into gear slowly and although the Army of the Potomac, operating in the main theater of war, had shown flashes of brilliance, these seemed only to be shafts of golden light that emphasized a generally grim picture of battles lost and campaigns botched. Even so, the repulse of Lee's thrust into Pennsylvania, at Antietam, combined with Grant's advance into northern Mississippi, put an end to southern hopes of foreign intervention and made plain the South's inability to mount a truly successful invasion of the North. The strategic initiative was now firmly in northern hands and was going to stay there, despite the inevitable setbacks and disappointments that are as much a part of human life as of the vicissitudes of war.

Since Fort Sumter, Father Abraham had justified the war as a fight for the Union. In the summer of 1862, the artist in this strange, melancholy genius sensed a shift deep among the roots of the struggle, deeper still in a society fighting for its life—a fluctuation in the current of emotion that makes war possible at all. While others not granted with his powers of divination for seeing beneath the surface of life would take a long time coming to the same judgment, he knew; he absolutely knew. It was time to move on, to change the moral foundations of the conflict.

Lincoln began turning the struggle for the Union's existence into a moral crusade for its soul. In October, after Lee's invasion of the North was repulsed at Antietam, Lincoln issued a preliminary emancipation proclamation that anticipated freeing slaves in the seceding states by government decree. On December 1 he followed up with a long and impassioned message to Congress, calling for a constitutional amendment to abolish slavery throughout the U.S., declared himself in favor of "colonization" of freed blacks, by which he meant sending them to Liberia, and said he was going to issue a proclamation that freed slaves owned by people in rebellion against the Union.[1]

In Washington, and in state capitals north and south, there was scoffing. It was all a bluff, veteran solons knowingly told one another. Lincoln was engaging in a little war propaganda. It was obvious there couldn't be any blanket liberation of the slaves, for how could the country cope, in the middle of a bitterly fought war, with millions of freed but destitute and homeless blacks?

Lincoln's new line alienated many Union soldiers. Then and forever, they preferred to see the conflict as a war to save the Union, not a mission to liberate the slaves. While a small, vocal and highly educated northern minority had long agitated for abolition, northerners as a rule tended to see all those involved in slavery—from the indolent master in his white pillared mansion to the swaggering overseer, bullwhip in hand and penis in black women, to the toiling, wretched slaves themselves— as disgusting and immoral creatures, an embarrassment, every one of them, to American life. Slavery might be worth fighting against, but that did not make the slaves worth fighting for.

There were, inevitably, protests from the ranks against Lincoln's new emphasis on emancipation, and within Grant's command at least one regiment, the 109th Illinois, more or less revolted. When Van Dorn raided Holly Springs, the regiment was guarding bridges south of the town. The 109th was not under attack, yet some of its officers encouraged their men to desert or be taken prisoner. One captain even suggested a plan to help the Confederate raiders. In January 1863 eight officers were punished for disloyalty and the regiment was broken up. Most of its soldiers, chastened and cowed, were absorbed by another Illinois regiment.[2]

Grant was presently struggling to prevent the large and growing force of "contrabands" within his command from bogging down the advance of the army. Thousands were already laboring on bridges, roads, entrenchments and other projects of military importance. Thousands more were hired directly by the troops, out of their own pockets. But this was no charity in blue. "All the Negroes here were slaves before we came," Sylvanus Cadwallader noticed. "They call themselves free now but have only changed masters. Our soldiers make them chop wood, wash, cook and do the camp work instead of doing it themselves."[3]

There was more than enough work to keep the able-bodied occupied. If anything, there was a shortage of black labor. When masters quit their plantations, they took all the healthy young adults they could round up, leaving behind the old, the children, the sick and the infirm. For many a contraband that late fall of 1862, freedom looked likely to consist of a fatal disease or death by starvation.

At first, Grant had thought maybe he could send his contrabands north, where they would provide servants for white families in big cities, such as Cincinnati and Chicago. It seemed a good idea, until word got back to Ohio and Illinois that thousands of recently liberated blacks were heading in their direction. Horrified—maybe even terrified—the putative employers of this mass of dispossessed humanity bellowed "No!" loud enough for Lincoln to hear it. Grant was told to keep his contrabands down south.[4]

He established a refugee camp in Grand Junction, Tennessee, guarded by a regiment of soldiers. He also managed to talk a reluctant chaplain named John Eaton into taking responsibility for the welfare of the contrabands throughout his department.[5]

There was a cotton crop waiting to be picked and there were all those northern traders panting to get their hands on it. Grant and Eaton soon had tens of thousands of blacks, women and children along with the men, out in the fields, bent over, and bringing in the cotton harvest. They were paid for their labor, for the first time in their lives, but what probably mattered more was the provision of rations, medical care, shelter and protection from former masters and Confederate marauders, whose barbarity to runaway slaves defies description.[6]

As the army advanced deep into Mississippi, Arkansas and Louisiana in early 1863, the tide of blacks fleeing toward the soldiers was turning into a human flood. Grant could not take responsibility for their welfare and prosecute the Vicksburg campaign at the same time.

For a while he had to forbid any more blacks from seeking shelter behind the army's line. Even so, he wryly remarked, "About the only loyalty in this region is possessed by the mules and contrabands."[7]

★

On January 16, Grant went down the Mississippi to see Logan and Sherman and Rear Admiral David Dixon Porter and to look for ways of attacking Vicksburg from the north or west. Then he reported back to Halleck. There were now four military departments in the West, all of them involved in the Vicksburg campaign to some degree, his own department most of all. The best thing to do, he told Halleck, was to merge them. It also made sense to put both banks of the river under a single commander, at least until Vicksburg was captured. And there was the question of what to do about McClernand. "I found there was not sufficient confidance [sic] felt in General McClernand as a commander, either by the Army or Navy, to insure him success." Which brought him to the nub of the matter: "It is my intention to command in person."[8]

Grant was making it appear that he had decided to take personal command only after making an inspection when, in fact, he had made that decision before he left Memphis. This way, though, the documentary record would look better. Instances such as this demonstrate that Grant was far from being the simple, guileless figure of legend. He could be trusting to a fault; that's true. Yet he could also be wily if he chose to be.

Needless to say, when McClernand realized he was really no more than one of the four corps commanders in Grant's army, he protested vehemently to Lincoln. "One thing is certain: two Generals cannot command this army." He demanded that Lincoln resolve the issue, but from Washington came only an eloquent, crushing silence.[9]

Halleck gave Grant command of all four western departments and authority to take as much of the western side of the Mississippi as he needed to tackle Vicksburg. Grant established his headquarters at Milliken's Bend, Louisiana, roughly twenty miles northwest of his goal. Although he was confident of eventual success, Grant described Vicksburg to his cousin Silas Hudson as "very strongly garrisoned [with] fortifications almost impregnible [sic]."[10]

At present, he had seventy thousand men in his command, of whom twenty thousand were deployed only ten miles north of the town. Even so, they were cut off from it by the river. It looped around, made a huge U-shaped bend, and was festooned with swamps and bayous, like stinking, wet jewels attached to the mile-wide silver thread. To attack the town they must first find a way to cross the river, push past its defenses, and position themselves on the high, dry ground to the northeast.

Meanwhile, the rest of Grant's force—some fifty thousand men on the Louisiana side of the river—was also looking for a way of getting across the Mississippi and seizing high ground on the eastern shore before it, too, could make an assault on Vicksburg. As if there wasn't enough water to contend with in the swollen river, the bayous, and the swamps, the rain descended across the sodden landscape day after day in those winter months, turning the few roads to mud and making Grant's troops regularly move their camps to escape drowning.

By the end of February he had launched three projects—one involved digging a canal; the other two called for advancing along tributaries of the Mississippi—to get his army onto dry ground on the eastern side of the great river. Lincoln read the telegrams, looked at the maps, drew on his own memory of the river, and for the life of him failed to see how any of Grant's projects could work. If the Confederates were able to block the Mississippi, which was a mile wide, they would have little trouble preventing Grant from moving toward Vicksburg along a canal or rivers that in some places were almost as narrow as the steamboats trying to navigate them. And everyone in the civilized world seemed to know exactly what Grant was attempting. People as far away as the sidewalk cafés of Paris and Rome were reading about the three projects.[11]

Yet despite the rain and mud, as troops and contrabands toiled through the winter, Grant's hopes were rising as steadily as the swamps and bayous. When Halleck informed him on March 1, "There is a vacant Major-Generalcy in the Regular Army, and I am authorized to say that it will be given to the General in the field who first wins an important & decisive victory," Grant confidently responded, "I will have Vicksburg this month or fail in the attempt."[12]

He did not capture Vicksburg—did not even make the attempt. All three projects for getting over to the eastern side of the Mississippi failed miserably. When the rains stopped and the sun came out and spring arrived, Grant was still marooned far from his goal.

As he wrestled with the rain, the mud and the river there were moments when he thought back ruefully to his withdrawal from Oxford following Van Dorn's raid on Holly Springs and regretted it. Grant blamed himself for his current dilemmas. If he had held his ground, lived on short rations, waited out the winter, and rebuilt his base, he would now be poised to continue his advance following the line of the Mississippi Central Railroad. There would have been rivers to cross and swamps in his path, but nothing compared to the mile-wide Mississippi. Grant had discovered what many another commander has learned down the centuries: It usually costs more to regain ground given up than it does to hold onto that same ground, even under ferocious pressure.[13]

Chaplain John Eaton, his "General Superintendent of Contrabands," was moved by his tired, careworn face, which had resolved into a cobweb of lines cut deep by work and worry. Grant even dressed like a down-on-his-luck farmer again—battered slouch hat, old brown linen duster considerably the worse for wear, and blue pants threadbare in the crotch and seat from long hours in the saddle.[14]

He had plenty to worry about, because his failed attempts to get onto the eastern shore of the Mississippi seemed to have lowered his standing with both the War Department and the President. Brigadier General Lorenzo Thomas, the adjutant general, arrived unannounced in Memphis. He was there on a sensitive assignment—the creation of black regiments. Grant welcomed the idea and supported it strongly. But Army rumor also had it that Thomas had come on a secret mission from the President: to take a good look at Grant's operations, and if he didn't like what he saw, to relieve Grant immediately. Julia was told by a friend fresh from the East that Thomas had the power to "make and unmake men" and that she should not be surprised if her husband was dismissed from his command.[15]

Thomas probably was asked to take a good look and report back, but it seems unlikely that he had any power to relieve Grant. In any event, even before he departed, another emissary arrived from Washington, Assistant Secretary of War Charles A. Dana. Rumor had it—and this time rumor was right—that Lincoln wanted to know if Grant was a drunkard, and Dana was there to settle the issue once and for all. Before the war Dana had made a name for himself as a journalist of progressive views. He was highly educated, highly sophisticated and well connected. He arrived in Grant's department claiming he was there to look into the efficiency and probity of Army paymasters, but no one believed for a minute that this was anything more than a smokescreen.[16]

Rubbing the smoke from their eyes, some of Grant's staff wanted to keep him at arm's length, or at least away from the general, for as long as possible. Rawlins, however, had a better understanding of what was required. Dana would know at once if he was being snubbed. Any action like that would alienate him, and it was going to suggest there was something to hide. Better to make this distinguished visitor feel welcome and give him as much time with the general as the war permitted. "I expect to see that a tent is always pitched alongside General Grant's for Mr. Dana's use as long as he remains at headquarters," said Rawlins. He would also have a place reserved for him in the general's mess, be assigned a horse and have the services of a couple of orderlies. In effect, he was being made to feel almost like an auxiliary member of Grant's staff. And long before the campaign ended, that was exactly how Dana behaved. He would make light of the tales about Grant's drinking, preferring instead to praise him unreservedly for his loyalty, courage and skill.[17]

When Dana arrived, though, he took a quick look around and concluded this campaign was as good as dead. Yet another Union Army failure. Not surprisingly for someone coming from Washington, he assumed Grant was much like McClellan and, given so many setbacks, would skedaddle on back to Memphis, demanding reinforcements and making excuses. He was wrong.

Even soldiers who had once admired Grant, such as Elihu Washburne's brother Brigadier General Cadwallader Washburn, had by this time written him off. "This campaign is badly managed," Cadwallader wrote to Elihu. "I fear a calamity before Vicksburg . . . all Grant's schemes have failed." He blamed the failures not so much on the general as on Grant's "drunken staff." This does not seem like much of an exculpation, seeing that Grant had personally chosen every member of that staff, and nearly always it was someone he already knew and trusted. Cadwallader Washburn concluded on a forlorn note—Grant was probably about to do something reckless and doomed, such as attempt another frontal assault.[18]

He, too, was wrong. Grant *was* briefly tempted to try storming the Vicksburg defenses as Sherman had done, but sometime in the last week of March he abandoned that idea. He did not, however, inform the congressman's brigadier brother. He used Cadwallader as a conduit to Elihu and nothing more.[19]

As Grant gnawed at the problem now, it came down to a simple, even obvious, proposition. It was a great gamble, but he had to risk it. He could hazard sending his slow-moving wooden steamers, piled high with rations and ammunition, south along the Mississippi, past the guns on the bluffs stretching fifteen miles, from Vicksburg down to Warrenton. He would then march his troops down the Louisiana shore to a point somewhere below Vicksburg and then ferry them across the river, using the steamers and barges that had run the gauntlet of fire.

Sherman, whom he admired and trusted, argued vehemently against Grant's idea. It could never work, Sherman insisted. The steamers and barges would be sunk and their cargoes of hardtack and ammunition end up at the bottom of the river. He offered instead a plan of his own— a plan that called for going back to Memphis, capturing Grenada, and starting all over again. His proposal was made complex by various diversions and secondary operations.[20]

Grant read it but probably did not give it five minutes' thought. Sherman's plan was not only complicated but relied on the railroads to move the men and their supplies. Grant had no intention of doing that again. His own idea was simple and daring, and it would turn the Mississippi, the source of most of his woes, into his highway. Their distinctly different approaches to the Vicksburg conundrum offer a good illustration of how unlike they were in temperament and mental processes—Sherman, the self-regarding intellectual getting lost in his own cleverness; Grant, his powerful mind cutting through the inessentials to seize hold firmly of the core of the problem, devising a solution that any intelligent officer would readily grasp.[21]

The question now was, Could the steamboats and barges needed to carry his troops across the Mississippi get past the immense firepower deployed from Vicksburg to Warrenton? Porter was willing, if anything eager, to give it a try. The admiral was a daring, supremely confident fighter, who seemed to love battles and arguments.

Twelve-year-old Frederick Dent Grant had come to join his father at the end of March. The sight of his son riding with boyish delight for hours on a lively pony cheered up Grant enormously during these worrying days. Shortly afterward he sent for Julia and his youngest son, Jess, to come down from Memphis. It was at stressful times like these that Grant, like many another man, yearned for his wife and children most. No matter how close he was to his staff, they were not his real family and chances are he never showed any of them more than a small piece of himself. Now, after six months of frustration and failure, although his health was good, his spirits were low. If the end was to be either crushing defeat or a great triumph, they had only one place to be, and that was with him.

Julia arrived in time to witness the Navy's most significant challenge yet to Pemberton's gun crews. Grant, his staff, his wife and eldest son boarded a steamer at Milliken's Bend the evening of April 16 and by midnight were in mid-stream several miles north of Vicksburg. Seven ironclad gunboats closed in to engage the enemy's batteries. A huge rebel flare arched into the sky, exposing the Union fleet to Vicksburg, its defenders and its people. Porter's gunners opened up. As shells screamed upward in graceful parabolic arcs, trailing scarlet tails of fire, and thunderous explosions sent thrilling shock waves across the stygian waters, three steamboats, towing ten barges, made an agonizing procession past the enemy's fortress and nearly fifty big guns.[22]

One steamboat was lost, but that was mainly because the crew panicked and abandoned their vessel when it took a direct hit in the engine room. The other two steamers survived with nothing but minor damage and most of the barges got through. That was enough for Grant to order McClernand to be ready to move his corps thirty miles south and prepare to cross the Mississippi.[23]

★

Colonel T. Lyle Dickey, Grant's cavalry commander, a man much liked by both the general and the staff, was gone. He had not performed brilliantly during the Holly Springs fiasco. If Dickey had acted more aggressively, or at least done a better job of getting a message to the general, Holly Springs might not have gone up in smoke. Dickey had done his best, but it wasn't good enough. He seems to have realized that. Certainly Grant did.

Although Dickey had risen rapidly to a colonel's eagles, his chances of becoming a general following Holly Springs were virtually nil. While Grant still liked Dickey personally, he had lost faith in him as a commander. Dickey evidently noticed the change, because only five weeks after the raid, he told Grant he wanted to return to civilian life, offering a variety of reasons, not one of which was convincing. They were merely camouflage for a swift departure.[24]

Grant made no effort to talk him out of quitting; nor did Dickey get a letter of thanks and personal regret, although Grant wrote a fulsome tribute to another colonel who quit at about the same time, George H. Pride, an engineer officer who had managed his military railroads.[25]

His new cavalry commander was a former music teacher from Illinois, Colonel Benjamin H. Grierson, a man who rode with a Jew's harp in his pocket. The tall, slender and handsome Grierson was an unlikely cavalry hero. He had been kicked in the head by a horse as a child, bore the resulting scar on his face and avoided horses for years after. Yet when the war came, he joined a cavalry troop and proved to be a daring and resourceful horse soldier. Even before he tried pushing transports past the Vicksburg batteries, Grant was planning a diversionary raid that would weaken the defenses of Vicksburg and confuse Pemberton when McClernand's 13th Corps crossed the river.

Grierson was to ride deep into Mississippi and near the state capital, Jackson, cut the railroads that funneled troops and military supplies from the East to Vicksburg. The operation was so hair-raisingly dangerous that Grant wanted it to be carried out entirely by volunteers, but that proved unnecessary. There was no shortage. The morning of April 17, Grierson rode out of La Grange, Tennessee, at the head of seventeen hundred cavalry and a battery of six light artillery pieces. The Federals were about to repay their debt to Earl Van Dorn.[26]

The night of April 22 a second flotilla, consisting of six steamers and twelve barges, braved the Confederate batteries. Only one steamer, Grant's old headquarters boat, the *Tigress,* was sunk, but the entire crew survived and roughly half the barges got through with their cargoes intact. There would now be enough shipping, rations and ammunition to make a river crossing and put his army on the Mississippi's eastern bank.[27]

McClernand's corps, followed by McPherson's, was already moving down the Louisiana side of the Mississippi to a landing called Hard Times, roughly thirty miles below Vicksburg. The troops marched day and night to Hard Times down muddy roads and were regularly drenched by heavy spring showers, but their morale was good. Being on the move lifted their spirits, much as it helped lift Grant's. He ordered Sherman to make a demonstration north of Vicksburg, to make it appear that another frontal assault was coming. Grant's aim was pin down Pemberton's army while a landing was attempted somewhere near

Grand Gulf, roughly thirty-five miles south of Vicksburg, where he intended to establish a base.

Grand Gulf itself was too well defended, he discovered, to attempt a landing there. He had to settle for a point seven miles farther south, at a hamlet called Bruinsburg. The morning of April 30, seven ironclad gunboats closed in and dueled with the Grand Gulf batteries. Once the Confederate gunners were fully engaged, barges and steamers began ferrying fifteen thousand men across. Next day, the troops advanced inland for about five miles before colliding with a Confederate force of five thousand men outside Port Gibson. Grant, accompanied by young Fred, arrived shortly after the battle opened. It was fought, he reported to Halleck, "over the most broken country I ever saw . . . a series of irregular ridges divided by deep and impassable ravines, grown up with heavy timber, undergrowth and cane."[28]

The battle lasted from dawn until dusk, but eventually the Confederates were forced back into Port Gibson by Grant's veteran troops, their fighting spirit rapidly rising to the excitement of battle after months of inactivity. When night fell, the outnumbered and outfought Confederates abandoned Port Gibson. The next morning, Grant rode into the deserted town.

He was immensely relieved at being, finally, on the eastern side of the river—immensely proud, too, of his army, ceaselessly extolling its virtues to his wife, to Washington, to visitors, to the press and to itself. Many of the men he led were by this time combat veterans, men who had fought at Donelson and Shiloh, Iuka and Corinth. He considered them every bit as good as regulars. For their part, Grant's troops felt a boundless confidence in themselves and in their commander. They had come to appreciate his quiet, undemonstrative presence, the lack of show around him and his staff, which was itself singular and striking. Grant felt completely at home with his men, and they with him. His relationship with his troops was close but unusual. During a battle, Grant rode from regiment to regiment in the thick of the fight instead of trying to direct his army from a tent safe in the rear. The troops called him "the Old Man," as if they knew him, yet chances are most would not know him if they met him.

Despite that, they sensed he was one of them. "He could stand any hardship they could stand," mused one officer, "and do their thinking beside. They went with him like men to a game; no despondency, all alert and eager, glad to know inaction had ended and vigorous work had begun."[29] It was the Zachary Taylor style of military leadership, free of gold braid, red tape and silver-trimmed saddles. Yet because it was a genuine expression of Grant's personality, free from affectation or calculation, he had made it his own.

His strategy for taking Vicksburg was off to a splendid start. Grierson had led his men to the outskirts of Jackson, cutting telegraph wires across the northern and central part of the state, tearing up railroad tracks, spreading panic, wrecking isolated Confederate outposts. But there was distraction as well as destruction. During the ride Grierson, the most uninvited guest in southern homes, played plantation pianos from one end of Mississippi to the other.

Pemberton was bewildered as reports flowed in daily of Union cavalry appearing in remote villages and towns. Warnings reached him several times that the Federals were about to land near Port Gibson, but he ignored them. At the time of the landing virtually all Pemberton's cavalry was away in hopeless pursuit of Grierson. This famous exploit ended a few days later, when Grierson led his saddle-weary troopers and worn-out mounts into Baton Rouge, after riding six hundred miles through enemy territory, leaving behind a broken telegraph network, its wire guts spilled across fields and roads.[30]

With Port Gibson secure, Grant and a small cavalry escort went to scout Grand Gulf, nearly ten miles away. According to contrabands he talked with along the road, the enemy had fled. Grant rode in and took Grand Gulf himself.[31]

As far as he was aware, his plan was unfolding perfectly. Once McPherson had his entire corps on this side of the river, Grant could send McClernand's command, consisting of four divisions, down to Port Hudson to reinforce Nathaniel Banks. That would provide enough strength to seize the town. Once Port Hudson fell, Banks and John McClernand would come up to join the rest of Grant's army in a massive assault on Vicksburg. Meanwhile he would turn Grand Gulf into a huge forward-supply base.

Grant had barely had a chance to take a look around Grand Gulf, however, when a messenger arrived, bearing a letter from Banks. The letter was three weeks old, and informed him that Banks had decided to take most of his troops off on an expedition up the Red River, leaving a small force besieging Port Hudson. He did not expect to return to Port Hudson before May 10.

Grant found himself deep in enemy territory, at the end of a long and shaky supply line, just as his plan to take Vicksburg with the combined force of Banks's army plus his own fell apart. It was obvious that he could not afford to stay where he was while the strategic initiative passed to the enemy. He must either withdraw or advance. The one thing he couldn't do was wait. "Every days [*sic*] delay is worth two thousand men to the enemy," he wrote to an aide charged with speeding the flow of supplies.[32]

This was the moment Grant showed his military genius. Almost any other Union Army commander would have pulled back to Louisiana, dug in, sent a stream of messages to the War Department complaining bitterly about Banks, and clamored for more men, more artillery, more supplies, before returning to the fray. Instead, he decided to take Vicksburg on his own, knowing that Halleck was certain to disapprove of anything so daring.[33]

Holding Grand Gulf shortened his supply line slightly, but his position was still precarious. He had more and more mouths to feed as regiments steadily disembarked from the steamers and barges that ferried them across from Louisiana. Grant's men could march and fight on short rations, but without bullets, grape shot and canister this entire venture was doomed. He told his men they would have to live off the country, and gave orders that the supply line be devoted almost entirely to hauling ammunition.

Having cut himself free from his base, Grant was gambling that he could feed his men off what the country provided, and what it provided turned out to be protein. Mountains of it. His men stuffed themselves on beef, pork, mutton and chicken until they were nearly desperate for hardtack. Never had they expected to eat steak and find themselves yearning for bread, but they did. This part of Mississippi had hardly been touched by the war. There was an abundance of food, even if all that meat soon grew monotonous. It was one of the war's little ironies that the deeper Grant advanced into Mississippi, the easier the supply of food became.

Having made his decision, Grant moved north, heading for the Big Black River and the railroad bridge that crossed it fifteen miles east of Vicksburg. There were two rebel forces for him to deal with. One was Pemberton's army of thirty-five thousand men at Vicksburg. The other, much smaller force, consisted of the six-thousand-man garrison defending Jackson.

Even before he learned that Grant had cut free from his base and was going to try taking Vicksburg without help from Banks, Lincoln feared that this new campaign was going to end in yet another defeat, another humiliating retreat. It was too unorthodox, too risky. Meanwhile Dana was reporting to Stanton that the inept and erratic McClernand was the weak link in Grant's command. Stanton sent a message to Dana that said, in effect, Grant could fire McClernand if that became necessary: "General Grant has full and absolute authority to enforce his own commands, and to remove any person. . . . He has the full confidence of the Government, is expected to enforce his authority, and will be firmly and heartily supported, but he will be responsible for any failure. . . . You may communicate this to him."[34]

Up until now, Grant had allowed McClernand to head the army's advance, but that was a sop to Lincoln and Stanton. Besides, he had expected that by this time McClernand would be down at Port Hudson, operating under Banks—one amateur yoked to another. As a commander, the man was simply hopeless. Grant's orders to McClernand were filled with detailed instructions on how he should deploy his men, the roads he ought to follow, where to place his artillery, and so on. Grant's orders to his other corps commanders—McPherson and Sherman—were different in tone and considerably shorter.

Grant had not moved far before learning that Lieutenant General Joe Johnston, the commander of all Confederate forces in the West, was heading for Jackson. He respected Johnston's abilities. It was too risky to leave Johnston undisturbed in Jackson, able to pose a threat to his rear. Grant shifted most of his army in the direction of Jackson, to take it before Johnston became strong enough, to hold the town.[35]

Grant placed McPherson's corps in the lead, with Sherman close behind, leaving McClernand out to the west, as far from Joe Johnston as he could position him. On May 12, McPherson's troops fought a meeting engagement with the Confederates near Raymond, fifteen miles southwest of the state capital. Once Grant was satisfied that McPherson had engaged Johnston's main body, he poured men into the fight and crashed through the heavily outnumbered Confederates to seize the town around midday on May 14. The Stars and Stripes was raised above the state capitol building, while Grant moved into one of the offices and triumphantly wrote orders that began, "Head Quarters, Dept of the Tenn. Jackson, Miss."

When darkness fell he would sleep in the room where Joe Johnston had slept the night before, but before he could do so, an order from Johnston was handed to him. Johnston had written to Pemberton the previous day, urging him to come out from behind the defenses of Vicksburg, threaten the rear of Grant's army near Clinton, some fifteen miles west of Jackson, and link up with the troops defending Jackson. Three couriers were entrusted with carrying this message to Pemberton—but one turned out to be a Union spy. His copy was handed not to Pemberton but to McPherson, who forwarded it to Grant.[36]

Had Johnston sent this message a couple of days earlier and Pemberton acted on it quickly, it might have caused Grant serious problems. McClernand's corps was deployed near Clinton, while Sherman and McPherson were attacking Jackson. Had Pemberton, with up to twenty-five thousand men ready to move out, struck the inept, unready and heavily outnumbered McClernand before Sherman and McPherson could come to his rescue, it might have been possible to halt Grant's advance. But by the afternoon of May 14 the time for a successful Confederate counterstroke had come and gone.

With timely warning of the enemy's intentions, Grant rapidly concentrated his forces and deployed them so that what Pemberton, unwisely making his sortie from Vicksburg, found himself up against was not Grant's exposed rear but a compact, well-deployed three-corps front, its men exulting over the capture of Jackson and poised to attack. As for Johnston, once forced to retreat, he had departed in a northeasterly direction with five thousand men, giving up all hope of combining his force with Pemberton's.

Grant's men drove west, following the railroad line toward the Big Black River. Pemberton found himself out on a limb, uncertain whether to turn back or fight a battle. Halfway between Vicksburg and Jackson, there is a low ridge grandiloquently called Champion Hill, and here at first light on May 16 Confederate skirmishers collided with the leading elements of McClernand's command. Not having any confidence in McClernand, Grant sent a blunt message—"Don't bring on a general engagement till we are entirely prepared." He wanted to get McPherson into position first.[37]

This cautionary message was to have consequences. One reason McClernand was totally unsuited for combat command was his inability to move and think at the same time. As the battle developed, McClernand dithered, moving tentatively throughout the action. Once McPherson had gotten his corps up to Champion Hill, it was obvious that McClernand should then push his four divisions straight into the enemy. Obvious, that is, to any experienced professional soldier reading Grant's orders, but McClernand was a professional politician; there was no dash in him, only cunning and calculation. During the battle Grant rode from regiment to regiment, giving orders and encouragement, managing his army from the saddle. He spent most of his time riding around McClernand's 13th Corps, trying to get McClernand to move more quickly; trying, too, to make sure that Pemberton did not take advantage of McClernand's incompetence. He sent messages to McClernand to hurry up, but these made no difference. McClernand was well to the rear, with only a hazy idea of what was happening in the front line.[38]

During that afternoon Grant's 30,000 men ultimately prevailed over Pemberton's 22,000 Confederates in what became a head-to-head, toe-to-toe battering contest. Each side lost roughly 400 men killed and 1,800 wounded, but Pemberton also lost eleven artillery pieces, and more than 2,000 of his men were taken prisoner. He had no choice but to pull out.[39]

The close of the battle left Grant angry and disappointed. McClernand's slowness had allowed the rebel army to escape. It was a mistake he never forgot or forgave, but for the moment there seemed little he could do about it.[40]

The retreating Confederates streamed back to their bridgehead at the Big Black River. At dawn next day Sherman attacked it, bringing irresistible pressure to bear. With five thousand of his men still waiting to cross, Pemberton had to blow the bridge spanning the river, buying just enough time to get the rest of the Champion Hill survivors into the entrenchments fanned out in a wide semicircle around Vicksburg.

Believing the defenders were completely demoralized by the failure of Joe Johnston to help them, by their defeat at Champion Hill, and by the dramatic collapse of their bridgehead over the Big Black, Grant threw his army at Vicksburg's defenders on May 19. Pemberton threw it back. From inside their entrenchments, the Confederates enjoyed excellent fields of fire. Every approach had been turned into a huge killing ground. The battle allowed Grant's divisions to tighten their grip on Vicksburg, but whether that was worth the sacrifice just made is arguable. They were closing in anyway.

As evening fell Grant went to visit Sherman at the Big Black, where engineer troops had built a pontoon bridge to replace the structure blown up by the retreating Confederates three days earlier. The two generals, sitting on a log by a pitch-pine fire that sputtered and hissed, pensively watched a column of troops coming toward them across the pontoon bridge, which danced lightly under the tramp of marching feet. It was a scene of field-soldiering that put both of them in a cheerful mood. Grant seemed undismayed by that day's failure to take Vicksburg by storm.[41]

He had good reason to feel happy. Grant had bet everything, and now knew he had won. Cutting loose from its base, Grant's army had marched north in the knowledge that it would not be secure again until it made contact with the great river. His men had marched two hundred miles in eighteen days, fought and won five battles along the way, and from where they were now deployed, they could see the sunlight flashing gold and silver on the waters of the Mississippi. It would not take long to re-establish contact with it north of Vicksburg, opening the way for a flood of reinforcements, rations and ammunition.

Buoyed up by this heartening prospect, Grant still intended to crush the enemy. He was leading a force that was as eager as he to finish this campaign. Like his men, he would much rather fight than spend a sweltering, enervating Mississippi summer in a long, dreary siege. After taking three days to prepare another assault, Grant attacked again, on May 22. By this time, he had thirty-five thousand men available, against Pemberton's thirty thousand.

Early in the fighting, a shell exploding near Grant covered him with a thick coating of yellow dirt. Other than that, he escaped without a scratch. A short time later, as he stood conferring with Sherman, a small youth, a drummer boy named Orion P. Howe, ran up to them, bleeding profusely from a wound in his leg, gasped that his regiment was out of ammunition, turned to return to the battle, but came back to tell them more precisely what was needed—"caliber 56!"—then collapsed at their feet. As he watched the pathetic broken body of young Howe taken to the rear on a stretcher, Grant's eyes filled with tears. The lad was not much older than Fred, who was just coming up to thirteen.[42]

Grant's eldest son was still with him. Dressed in his father's ceremonial sword and general's sash and mounted on a huge horse of advanced years purchased somewhere along the road from Port Gibson, young Fred had already seen more battles than most soldiers and had picked up a slight leg wound at Champion Hill. Grant did not inform Julia of that.[43]

The Union attack on May 22 ran out of steam around noon. The Federals had suffered close to two thousand casualties and had nothing to show for it. McClernand, however, reported that he had captured two forts and demanded reinforcements. Sending fresh units to him, Grant ordered Sherman and McPherson to renew their attacks, to prevent the enemy from wiping out McClernand's gains, although as he galloped around the field he could not see any sign that McClernand had made the progress he reported. In fact, McClernand had captured nothing. His report was false. Late that afternoon the assault was broken off. The toll of dead and wounded stood at thirty-six hundred men. Grant blamed half his casualties on McClernand's lying message. Without it, he would have ended the operation much sooner.[44]

It had become almost imperative by now to get rid of McClernand. Dana was regularly communicating with Stanton, and after this battle told the secretary of war bluntly, "McClernand has not the qualities for a good commander, even of a regiment." Grant was more than ready to wash his hands of his insubordinate subordinate, but decided to wait until Vicksburg fell. Then, with victory strengthening his hand, he would tell McClernand to request a leave of absence. Once gone, McClernand would never be allowed back.[45]

McClernand, however, saved him the trouble, by issuing an order that ostensibly congratulated his troops but was really a political pamphlet on the military triumphs of Major General John C. McClernand. In it he modestly described himself as "born a Warrior."[46]

When Sherman read this farrago of self-glorification in a Memphis newspaper, he was disgusted—and probably overjoyed. McClernand had just provided all the hemp needed for a public hanging. He sent the newspaper to Grant, reminding him that War Department regulations banned the publication of official letters, orders and reports and that the name of any officer guilty of violating this regulation was to be "laid before the President of the United States for dismissal." Grant relieved McClernand almost immediately, ordering him to go back to Illinois.[47]

Meanwhile, Grant was stuck with a siege. He kept the pressure on by pushing his men ever closer to the enemy's lines, by having his artillery fire into the town at regular intervals, and by having engineers tunnel under Vicksburg's defenses and explode huge mines, causing large sections of entrenchments to collapse.

Missing his wife and frustrated by the wearisome business of besieging, Grant fell off the wagon. On June 6 Rawlins wrote him a long, indignant and rebuking letter: "I find you where the wine bottle has just been emptied, in company with those who drink and urge you to do likewise . . . you pledged me the sincerity of your honor last March that you would drink no more . . ."

There is a hint of jealousy about this letter, with its suggestion that Grant preferred the company of officers who drank to that of Rawlins, the self-righteous teetotaler. More telling, however, is that it betrays Rawlins's deepest flaw—he was a man incapable of loyalty.

There can hardly be a more serious failing, for without loyalty there is neither love nor, on love's outer shore, true friendship. This and other letters from Rawlins to Grant on the subject of drinking are slightly hysterical. They are sulfurous with fury at being unable to get Grant to stop. Rawlins's fervent protestations that he is taking Grant sternly to task entirely out friendship for him and devotion to the Union cause ring hollow. A true friend would not have written any of this down but would have talked to him frankly, alone and without hysteria. Instead, Rawlins not only produced this and similar letters, but he preserved them for posterity. A true friend would not write to other people, to regale them with detailed descriptions of Grant's drinking and spread the news around, but Rawlins did. Within Rawlins's own secret vice was enfolded another—the desire to wound. The only way he could hurt Grant was by attacking his reputation. Rawlins went at it with cunning and determination, both during his own short lifetime and from beyond the grave. Grant drunk was a bigger and better man than Rawlins sober.

The entire staff, as well as most of Grant's division and corps commanders, was well aware of his drinking problem. McClernand tried to make capital out of it and one or two other officers expressed their disgust at Grant's weakness, but to the rest, it did not matter. A few were alcoholics themselves, but the main reason it was tolerated was that when Grant got drunk, it was invariably during quiet periods. His drinking was not allowed to jeopardize operations. It was a release, but a controlled one, like the ignition of a gas flare above a high-pressure oil well.[48]

The only obstacle between him and the bottle was Julia, and for a time he hoped he might be able to have Julia come and join him. She could stay aboard a steamer out in the river, he mused, and he would go visit her. But then he realized that was impossible. The roads were too crowded with supply wagons and newly arriving troops. His tent was six miles from the nearest steamboat landing. It would take hours he could not spare to go visit a steamer and return to his headquarters each day. Deeply disappointed, he told Julia she would have to wait until the campaign was over.[49]

Vicksburg was being starved into submission. In the closing days of this campaign, Pemberton's situation was the mirror image of what Grant's had been at its beginning—plenty of ammo, not enough to eat. The situation had become so desperate that his army was killing its mules and eating them. Pemberton's only hope was being rescued by Joe Johnston, who had assembled an army of thirty thousand men between Grenada and Jackson. Sherman's corps, however, was poised to block Johnston's approach. Whenever Johnston maneuvered for position, Sherman matched him step for step.

On June 28 rebel deserters told one of Grant's division commanders there were only six days' rations left in the town. A deserter picked up by the Navy said the same thing. All Pemberton was waiting for now, they said, was July 4. He was going to fire a salute to the Confederacy on Independence Day, then surrender. Grant believed them, writing to Julia the next day, "Saturday or Sunday next [July 4 or 5] I set for the fall of Vicksburg. You can come down then and bring the children with you."[50]

If Pemberton did not quit by then, Grant was going to end the siege his own way. Grant's strength had risen to more than seventy-five thousand men. He had amassed 220 artillery pieces, plus dozens of mortars. Porter's gunboats could bring their powerful ordnance to bear. As for ammunition, the days of shortage were over. He had a mountain of shot and shell ready to fire. The Army would make an all-out assault on July 6.

The morning of July 3 Pemberton sent a message to Grant, asking for an armistice and the appointment of three commissioners from each side, who would negotiate the terms of a capitulation. "I make this proposition to save the further effusion of blood."

Grant sent back much the same reply he had given Buckner more than a year earlier: "The useless effusion of blood you propose stopping can be ended at any time you choose, by an unconditional surrender of the city . . ." There was no need for peace commissioners; there was nothing to negotiate about.[51]

Pemberton somehow convinced himself that what Grant really wanted was a personal meeting, and Grant agreed to one, thinking Pemberton intended to surrender to him. So a meeting was arranged for that afternoon. In the shade of a magnificent oak tree, they reminisced briefly about Mexico. It was Pemberton who had brought Grant General Worth's compliments at getting a howitzer onto the roof of the San Cosme church. But when Grant realized that Pemberton was trying to dicker, not surrender, he told him bluntly, "All the terms I have are stated in my letter of this morning."

Pemberton bristled. "Then the conference may as well terminate and hostilities begin."

"Very well," responded Grant easily. "My army was never in better condition to prosecute a siege."

"You'll bury a good many more men before you get into Vicksburg," Pemberton blustered.[52]

The two men parted, but although nothing had been settled, Grant was not seeking to take the garrison captive. Pemberton's troops, once disarmed, would be paroled, much as the Fort Donelson garrison had been paroled. While Union and rebel officers worked out the details, Grant wrote to Porter, telling him what would happen if Pemberton did not quit: "I shall fire a national salute into the city at daylight." In other words, he was going to bombard Vicksburg as no town had ever been bombarded.[53]

Pemberton continued trying to negotiate better terms during the night, but Grant brought the issue to a head with an ultimatum: If the town did not surrender by nine A.M. on July 4, he would consider his demands rejected and launch his attack.

The besieging Union troops were having breakfast the next morning when a messenger arrived at Grant's tent. The general was at a table, writing. Fred was sitting on his army cot, nursing his leg wound. Grant opened the note the messenger handed to him, read it, sighed deeply, and looked up at his son. "Vicksburg has surrendered."[54]

CHAPTER 20

———— ★ ★ ★ ★ ————

"THE SPECTICLE

WAS GRAND"

Shortly after Vicksburg fell, Grant received a letter from Lincoln. It was a tribute any general would treasure. Lincoln wrote, "I do not remember that you and I ever met personally. I write this now as a grateful acknowledgement for the almost inestimable service you have done the country. . . . When you first reached the vicinity of Vicksburg . . . I never had any faith, except a general hope, that the Yazoo Pass expedition and the like [i.e., the three failed attempts to find a way to get across the Mississippi close to the town] could succeed—When you got below, and took Port Gibson, Grand Gulf, and vicinity, I thought you should go down the river and join Gen. Banks; and when you turned Northward East of the Big Black river, I feared it was a mistake—I now wish to make the personal acknowledgement that you were right, and I was wrong."[1]

An equally generous accolade came from Halleck. The general-in-chief was moved to pay what was, for him, the ultimate in compliments. Formerly convinced that Grant was a mediocre commander at best, Halleck told him he considered the Vicksburg campaign comparable to one of the most impressive victories by history's greatest soldier—Napoleon's capture of Ulm in 1805.[2]

Grant was rewarded, too, with promotion to major general in the regular Army, dating from July 4. Halleck had dangled this prospect before him like a two-star carrot back when the campaign began. This promotion assured Grant of retaining his rank after the war. At the age of forty-three he could expect a comfortable living for the rest of his life. A major general's salary was six thousand dollars a year, approximately ten times the earnings of the average man. Since returning to duty, Grant had saved diligently, almost strenuously. Having paid off his debts, he was now buying up most of what property Julia's feckless father and ne'er-do-well brother Louis still owned. From a financial point of view, he was ahead of where old Jesse Grant had been at a comparable age.

Even in the moment of triumph, though, with the praises of Lincoln and Halleck still fresh, Grant couldn't help worrying about McClernand. That saturnine figure cast a long, tenebrous shadow. Lincoln was, after all, a politician, not a soldier, and having been elected and gone to war with the backing of barely 40 percent of the voters, the President would never take his eye off the narrow political base that had put him into the White House and allowed him to prosecute a war that was turning into a vast bloodbath. Without knowing the details, Grant could be certain that even now McClernand was at work trying to get himself reinstated—trying, too, to undermine whatever confidence Lincoln had in Grant during the period of euphoria that followed Vicksburg's surrender.

Grant's official report on the campaign, from the moment he had assumed command in the field until Pemberton quit, left out nothing of importance, and provided interesting sidelights on various individuals who had distinguished themselves, from an obscure sergeant to William T. Sherman. He entrusted the report to Rawlins, who carried it to Washington, ostensibly to present it to the President and the War Department. Rawlins's real mission was to find out whether firing McClernand had done any permanent damage. The answer was, it hadn't. McClernand still had political pull. He got back command of his old corps, but not until January 1864, and by then Grant had gone east.[3]

When Vicksburg surrendered, more than thirty thousand Confederates were paroled. They were marched to a parole camp near Meridian, Mississippi, to await a possible future exchange against Federal parolees in Confederate hands. Nearly a thousand of the men surrendered at Vicksburg refused to sign parole pledges and were shipped to prison camps in the North. The 171 cannon that were captured, along with tens of thousands of small arms, were distributed among Grant's army and used to equip the new black regiments that were being formed.

Sherman had looked forward to seeing the fall of Vicksburg, but when the moment came, he was more than twenty miles away, keeping Joe Johnston at bay. With the siege lifted, Grant reinforced Sherman heavily, enabling Sherman to advance on Jackson. Fearing that Sherman was about to get behind him and trap him in Jackson, Johnston abandoned the Mississippi state capital for a second time, withdrawing to the east. Sherman pursued him for a week before grinding to a halt, his men exhausted by the stunning heat and panting for water.

Only five days after Vicksburg's surrender, Port Hudson capitulated to Nathaniel Banks. The Mississippi was now entirely under Union control. The Confederacy had been split in two.

In the sapping heat of that mid-summer, Grant was seeking a way to maintain the momentum, to keep the enemy under pressure. As he studied the maps, he looked long and hard at Alabama. The correct strategy, he was convinced, would be to push east and south once the weather improved. A landing at Mobile, combined with an overland thrust from eastern Mississippi, would make Chattanooga untenable to the enemy, virtually destroy the Confederacy's position on the Gulf, and allow Grant to mount a campaign against Atlanta.

He was now venturing beyond the role of a department commander and trying to devise national strategy, which was the business of the President and the War Department. It really was not his concern unless he was asked for his opinion, and he hadn't been. In the end, however, Grant could not resist presenting his idea to Halleck. But having given his views on Mobile, he felt obliged to throw in a disclaimer. "I have not studied this matter," Grant said, which obviously wasn't true, "because it is out of my Department."[4]

Halleck was also looking at the maps and was inclined to agree with Grant, but the President and the secretary of state, William Seward, were preoccupied by the recent French intervention in Mexico. Napoleon III had taken advantage of political turmoil in Mexico and the American descent into civil war to impose a European monarchy on the impoverished and strife-torn peasants who made up the vast bulk of the Mexican population. Lincoln and Seward believed that to curb French expansion into Central America, the United States had to place an army on Texas soil.[5]

They were wrong about that. As long as the United States was torn by civil war, the presence of Federal troops in Texas would not discourage foreign intervention in Mexico. The one sure way to do that was to achieve a speedy end to the conflict. Then a victorious United States, possessing a strong Navy and a large, lavishly equipped, powerful Army of veteran troops, would be able by threats alone to force the withdrawal of the opportunistic French. Nevertheless, Banks was pushed into Texas and Grant was ordered to reinforce him.

The momentum of Grant's Vicksburg triumph was thereby discarded, by people who had little idea of the value of momentum in war. Intangible and impossible to quantify, it is a great prize, invariably bought at the cost of much blood, but justified if properly exploited to speed an end to the fighting. Grant fretted at the way the enemy was once again being given a breathing space, but there was nothing he could do.[6]

For several weeks he had another cause for anxiety: It looked like he might be ordered east, to assume command of the Army of the Potomac. Lincoln was close to despair. This mighty force, on which so much depended, had still not been fought to the limits of its abilities. True, under George Meade the Army of the Potomac had defeated Lee's Army of Northern Virginia in a monumental three-day struggle at Gettysburg just as Vicksburg prepared to surrender. Yet Meade allowed the battered, nearly shattered Confederates to withdraw at their own pace, taking virtually all their artillery and supply trains with them. "There is bad faith somewhere!" Lincoln lamented to Gideon Welles, his secretary of the Navy. "What does it mean, Mr. Welles? Great God!"[7]

For Grant—who had turned the Army of the Tennessee from a collection of small-town mechanics and boisterous farm boys into a force of proud, confident, veteran soldiers who would attack anything he wanted to attack with an eagerness that was almost frightening, who would live in holes in the ground, march day and night, sleep in the mud and fight on empty stomachs without complaint or skulking, whose courage defied description but not appreciation—to move to any other army would be a step down, not up. Assistant Secretary of War Charles Dana, however, was able to convince Halleck and Stanton—and through them the President—to leave Grant where he was.[8]

On September 2 Grant arrived in New Orleans to confer with Banks on how he could aid the advance into Texas. Three days later Banks held a review of his army on the outskirts of the city and loaned Grant a horse to ride. It was a powerful, spirited beast that took two men just to hold it while Grant got into the saddle. This was exactly the kind of horse he enjoyed riding. When he put this lively mount into a gallop on the ride back into the city following the review, no one else could keep up. It was a thrilling mount, a challenge to his riding skills, right up until the moment the horse went down as if it had been shot in the head.

Grant's recollection was that his mount had been startled by a railroad train coming around a bend and blowing its whistle at a point where the tracks ran close to the road he was galloping along. The horse shied, lost its footing and fell on him. The adjutant general of the Army, Lorenzo Thomas, was there and in his diary that night added one important detail: a horse pulling a carriage as Grant passed by had been frightened by the train and reared up. Grant's horse was struck by the carriage, which "threw him over with great violence. The General who is a splendid rider maintained his seat in the saddle, and the horse fell upon him." A doctor who attended the injured Grant also recorded in *his* diary that the general's horse had been hit by a carriage.[9]

Inevitably, however, the word soon went around that it was all his own stupid fault, that he'd been drunk again. Banks had no doubt that's what had happened. One of Banks's corps commanders, William B. Franklin, said much the same thing.[10]

Although Bruce Catton, Grant's most acclaimed biographer, went to considerable pains to challenge them, there is nothing implausible about the assertions that Grant had been drinking. Both Banks and Franklin were eyewitnesses. This was exactly the kind of occasion when he could drink without it affecting operational decisions. Moreover, Grant was such a superb horseman it probably never occurred to him not to drink and ride.

All of these stories could be true. Grant might well have been drinking, a train almost certainly did come around a bend, startling not one horse but two—the mount Grant was riding and the horse pulling the carriage. Two frightened beasts were enough to produce a collision. The fact that Grant had no memory of the carriage isn't unusual. People involved in impact accidents often have only a partial recollection of what happened in the seconds before the world went black.

Drunk or sober, Grant was knocked out. Carried away on a stretcher, he regained consciousness in the Saint Charles Hotel as several doctors, bent over and feeling his body for broken bones, swam into view. Besides a badly crushed left leg, he had also suffered three cracked ribs. He was in excruciating pain and remained bedridden for the next week. Returning to Vicksburg on crutches, he informed Halleck two weeks after the accident, "My injuries are severe [but] my recovery is simply a matter of time . . ." Any expectations he might have had when he wrote this of a prolonged, restful recuperation came to nothing.[11]

★

In the fall of 1862, William S. Rosecrans was given command of the Army of the Cumberland with clear orders to do what Don Carlos Buell had failed to manage—drive Braxton Bragg's Confederates back to Chattanooga. Rosecrans caught up with Bragg at Murfreesboro, Tennessee, at Christmas, but although he had a four-to-three advantage in manpower and a substantially bigger advantage in firepower, he hesitated to attack. Bragg had a far more combative spirit and attacked him, on New Year's Eve. The two armies slugged it out for two days. Each suffered twelve thousand combat casualties, which hurt Bragg, with his smaller army, more than it hurt Rosecrans. The Confederates retreated and Rosecrans did nothing to hinder their going.

Halleck tried to inspire him by sending him the same message he had sent Grant—the first Union general to win a major victory would be promoted to major general in the regulars. Where Grant had responded enthusiastically, Rosecrans sent Halleck an affronted reply: "I feel degraded to see such an auctioneering of honor."[12]

While Grant was straining every nerve and launching one scheme after another to close on Vicksburg, Rosecrans was moving across middle Tennessee at a pace that made Halleck's slow-motion advance on Corinth after Shiloh look like a race. Lincoln grew impatient and in early June Halleck bluntly told Rosecrans that if he didn't use his army more effectively, some of his troops would be sent to help Grant take Vicksburg.

Rosecrans bombarded the War Department with reasons for not moving more quickly—his logistical situation was poor; he was waiting for the corn to ripen so he could feed his men; if Bragg was bottled up in Chattanooga, it would be harder to defeat him than in the open field; besides, Bragg might block the Army of the Cumberland with a small part of his force and send the rest to Mississippi, where they could be used to break the Vicksburg siege.[13]

All of Rosecrans's objections were plausible, but Grant would never have allowed them to halt an advance. He would have moved rapidly on Chattanooga, living off the country as he did so, besieged the place, waited for the corn to ripen once he got there, and worked on improving his road and rail links while starving the enemy into defeat. Such a strategy would never have found living room in Old Rosey's large, handsome head. It wasn't a question of intelligence. Rosecrans was a smart man. What was lacking was imagination and the spirit that drives events along.

With both Halleck and Lincoln bearing down hard on him, Rosecrans finally got going at the end of June. He maneuvered Bragg out of middle Tennessee in little more than a week, which said something about Rosecrans's skill but was equally eloquent on the subject of Bragg's weak position. The Confederate commander did not dare risk a fight. His army was too poorly equipped and too small for another pitched battle. He fell back steadily, and pulled out of Chattanooga to avoid a siege. Rosecrans moved triumphantly into the city, convinced of his military genius.

Chattanooga was one of the most important railheads in North America. Rosecrans did not reflect on the fact that it is one of the rarest events in the history of war for a strategic position as crucial as this to be given up without a fight. He was slow to comprehend that Bragg's withdrawal was merely the prelude to a counterattack.[14]

Bragg was being heavily reinforced by the arrival of James Longstreet's entire corps of veteran troops from the Army of Northern Virginia. He also got the benefit of a declaration by the Confederate government that thousands of men who had been paroled at Vicksburg had been exchanged for northern parolees and were therefore free to return to active duty. Halleck indignantly protested that there had been no such exchange, but at least one rebel division that had surrendered to Grant appeared two months later in Bragg's army.

Fearing he might be bottled up in Chattanooga, Rosecrans pushed his men out of the town and fifteen miles to the southeast, to deploy along Chickamauga Creek. On September 22 Bragg attacked and brought Rosecrans's army to the brink of destruction. The demoralized survivors fled back to Chattanooga.

From his sickbed, Grant dispatched two divisions to reinforce Rosecrans, but the situation continued to deteriorate as the Confederates closed remorselessly on the town from three sides. They had Chattanooga virtually besieged, and food supplies were running low. Early in October, Grant was ordered to report to Cairo. Accompanied by his wife, his youngest son, Jess, and his staff, he reached the town on October 16, after a five-day journey by steamboat.[15]

Next day he received a cable from Halleck, telling him to depart immediately for the Galt House in Louisville, Kentucky, where he would be met by "an officer of War Department." Grant was to take his staff with him "for immediate operations in the field."[16] With wife, son and staff in tow, he set off for Louisville by train, by way of Indianapolis.

Grant's train was about to pull out of the Indianapolis depot just as the special train bearing the "officer of War Department" arrived. A messenger scrambled across the tracks and ran up to Grant's train, shouting to the locomotive engineer to stay right where he was. The secretary of war, Edwin Stanton, wanted to see General Grant.[17]

The weather was miserable and Stanton, who was a martyr to asthma, on this bone-chilling damp day had his face buried much of the time in a handkerchief in a hopeless effort to stanch the outflow from a heavy cold. He also made a fool of himself when he boarded Grant's railroad car by advancing on a member of Grant's staff, Dr. Edward D. Kittoe, and shaking his hand vigorously while declaring that he would recognize General Grant anywhere, he looked so much like his photographs.[18]

Once this misunderstanding had been put right and proper introductions effected, Stanton dismissed his special train. He would ride to Louisville with Grant instead. Along the way, with Stanton coughing and wheezing and Grant stiff and in pain from his ribs and his leg, they talked about the crisis in Chattanooga. Stanton said he wanted Grant to assume command of a much bigger department, embracing the Army of the Ohio, the Army of the Tennessee, and the Army of the Cumberland. His new command would be called the Division of the Mississippi. This would give Grant nearly the whole western theater of war. He was free to relieve Rosecrans from command of the Army of the Cumberland, Stanton told him. But if he did so, the War Department had already decided that Rosecrans's successor would be George H. Thomas.[19]

Grant decided to remove Rosecrans, whom he disliked personally and deplored professionally, but he would have to be careful how he did it. Rosecrans had influential friends on Capitol Hill and strong backing in the northern press. Besides which, Grant can hardly have been pleased at not being allowed to make his own decision on who should get command of the Army of the Cumberland. As the most successful Union general of the war so far, Grant had gone far beyond the point where it was acceptable for the War Department to choose his principal subordinates for him. Yet Stanton and Halleck had not even had the courtesy to consult him before making this decision.

Thomas was a brave and competent officer who had performed superbly at Chickamauga, but he was not Grant's kind of commander. Given a free choice, Grant would have given the Army of the Cumberland to Sherman, because Chattanooga was now the critical point. Instead, he gave Sherman the Army of the Tennessee and resigned himself to doing the best he could with Thomas. Forcing Thomas on Grant was not only an insult to Grant, but it did Thomas no favors, either.[20]

When the train reached Louisville, Stanton checked into a hotel to rest and Julia and Grant visited various Dent relations and family friends. These were people who had treated her and Ulysses with disdain in years gone by, pitying her for marrying such a failure, despising him for dragging her into poverty. Grant was now one of the most famous men in the country, a successful general whose name was already being bruited about as a potential President. How sweet it was to lord it over these provincial mediocrities as Grant, still on crutches, hobbled through their parlors saying little, letting Julia do the talking, but basking in their newfound admiration for his talents. Julia and little Jess would remain in Louisville with Julia's aunt and uncle. Chattanooga was the front line.[21]

Grant was out riding when Stanton received a telegram from Dana, who was at Rosecrans's headquarters. According to Dana, Rosecrans was preparing to retreat. It wasn't true, but Dana had come to despise Rosecrans so heartily that he probably did not care whether it was true or not. What mattered was getting him out.[22]

When Grant returned from his ride, he was summoned to see Stanton at once. Still suffering from his heavy cold, Stanton was confined to his bedroom. Pacing the floor in his dressing gown, he agitatedly passed on the false story that Rosecrans was preparing to abandon Chattanooga. Grant immediately sent a telegram to Rosecrans telling him he was relieved. A second message, to Thomas, informed him he was now commander of the Army of the Cumberland: "Hold Chattanooga at all hazards. I will be there as soon as possible." To which Thomas sent the perfect reply—"I will hold the town till we starve."[23]

★

Vicksburg was such a phenomenal victory that from now on, Grant aroused expectations in people, the way the famous invariably do. Time and again, though, he disappointed them.

When people rub up against greatness they are likely to expect a certain *frisson* in return—a chill down the spine, perhaps, or a pleasant tingling sensation across the scalp, a surge of unexpected emotion. Something, anyway, that will confirm they have indeed enjoyed the special thrill of coming into direct personal and physical contact with one of that handful of people whose names and deeds will resound down the ages.

Grant did not offer anything like that. If anything, he seemed almost to go out of his way to avoid it. Many who met him were left feeling slightly puzzled. Some felt more or less cheated. He did not look like a great general, did not talk like a great general, did not dress like a great general, and did not even appear to consider himself a great general. Maybe he wasn't so great after all. Lucky, perhaps, but if so, he was no greater than the clerk who inherits a fortune or the panhandler who stumbles across gold in the mountains.

When Grant's train reached Stevenson, Alabama, on October 21, 1863, he dismounted slowly and painfully, then stood on the platform for a while, leaning on his crutches. Soldiers and civilians gathered there gawked at him in disbelief and wonder. Being stared at so intensely was still fairly new, but it would soon become part of his everyday life. Grant was waiting for Rosecrans's train to arrive from Chattanooga. Old Rosey was going to fill him in on the situation he would find there. As Grant leaned on his crutches, one of the Union soldiers standing nearby noted, "An army slouch hat with bronze cord around it, quite a long military coat, unbuttoned, no sword or belt, and there was nothing to indicate his rank. . . . When the boys called for a speech, he bowed and said nothing."[24]

The meeting with Rosecrans did not take long and did nothing except confirm Grant's conviction that Rosecrans had no idea how to manage an army in combat. The line ended at Bridgeport, Alabama, because the rebels had torn up long stretches of track, and much of what remained intact was within range of their guns.

The birthplace. Not exactly a log cabin, but only a cut above. *(Library of Congress)*

A romantic and idealized engraving done when Grant was stationed at Jefferson Barracks. It makes him appear older than he was and gives him much more regular features than he ever possessed.

(Library of Congress)

Grant and Alexander Hayes were West Point classmates, but it was in Mexico that they became good friends. This steel engraving is based on a daguerreotype made shortly before the war. Possibly the worst experience Grant endured the first day of the battle of the Wilderness was hearing that Hayes, who commanded a brigade in the Army of the Potomac, had just been killed.
(Library of Congress)

Hardscrabble, the house that Grant spent two years building with his own hands. This project nearly ruined his health, and the family lived there only three months.
(Library of Congress)

There were no dramatic photographs of Grant leading troops, so someone—probably one of Matthew Brady's assistants—created this photomontage. Although it lacks authenticity, this picture nonetheless conveys something of the reality of life around Grant's field headquarters.

(Library of Congress)

Grant shortly after he became a major general. The strain of trying to hold on to his command against the machinations of Henry Halleck is evident.
(Library of Congress)

Grant was considered the best equestrian in the Army, and possibly in the country. He is seen here with his famous "war horse," Cincinnati.
(Library of Congress)

This photograph of Grant on Lookout Mountain was taken a few days after he defeated Braxton Bragg in the epic fight for Chattanooga. It is still possible to stand where Grant stood, but it takes strong nerves and a head for heights—at his feet there is a sheer drop of approximately one hundred feet. *(Library of Congress)*

Grant a week or two after Lincoln presented him with his commission as a lieutenant general. He looks boyishly young and brims with confidence; he seems eager for the campaign ahead, the chance to defeat Robert E. Lee. *(National Archives)*

A difficult moment in the war. The Army of Northern Virginia has frustrated Grant in the race for Spotsylvania. The pews of a village church have been dragged outside for a staff meeting on the Army of the Potomac's next move, to the North Anna River. Surrounded by generals, Grant writes fresh orders. *(Library of Congress)*

This picture was taken in the summer of 1864, after the failure to seize Petersburg and possibly shortly after the botched operation at the Crater. One half of Grant's face presents a military commander's look of resolution and is fixed firmly on the future, but the other half reflects a sensitive man's dismay at the terrible human cost of war. *(National Archives)*

This is the famous painting done at City Point by Peter Ole Hansen Balling, showing Grant leading twenty-five other Union generals on the road to victory. Not great art, but as a depiction of a restless, irresistible force guided by one man's will, it is powerful propaganda.

(Library of Congress)

Julia left a large, comfortable house to live with Grant in this crude shack at City Point in the winter of 1864. She stands in the doorway while Jesse, Grant's youngest son, strikes an appropriately casual pose. *(Library of Congress)*

Grant's New York admirers bought him this large house on I Street, in one of Washington's most fashionable neighborhoods. He later sold it to his close friend and brother in arms, William Tecumseh Sherman. *(National Archives)*

Between the Civil War and the presidency, Grant continued to command the armies of the United States and was elevated to an unprecedented fourth star. This photograph, taken shortly before he became President, records the transition back into civilian life. *(National Archives)*

Julia, Nellie and Jesse pose with Julia's father, the cantankerous and self-styled "Colonel" Frederick Dent, shortly after Grant became President. Julia's father remained an unreconstructed southern Democrat and died in the White House an unrepentant believer in slavery and secession. *(Library of Congress)*

Grant's second inauguration. He can be made out, if only just, reading his inaugural address, in which he proclaimed that re-election was all the vindication he needed to answer his numerous critics. *(National Archives)*

Grant bought a house by the sea at Lo[ng] Branch, New Jersey, where he could esca[pe] from the pressures and irritations of the pre[si]dency. Julia stands behind him, and next [to] Julia stands the Grants' daughter, Nellie, w[ho] married at eighteen and moved abroad. To [the] right are young Jesse and the Grants' eld[er] son, Frederick Dent Grant, recently gradua[ted] from West Point. The three black servants a[re] probably in the picture as a way of indicati[ng] that they were part of the fam[ily]

(National Archiv[es)

The Treasury was planning a new gold coin and intended to show Grant in profile. Julia persuaded him to shave off his beard, probably thinking that it would make him look more imposing for the ages. Instead, he looked like a tired government clerk in his Sunday best. The coin was never struck, and Grant grew another beard.

(National Archives)

The country Grant enjoyed most during his two-and-a-half-year journey around the world was Egypt. He and Julia were photographed at the great temple at Karnak. The young man in the center is their eldest son, Fred, who made part of the journey with them. *(Library of Congress)*

Grant as Wall Street operator, looking more presidential than he ever did during his eight years in the White House. Shortly after this photograph was taken, the firm of Grant and Ward went bust. *(Library of Congress)*

One of the last pictures ever taken of Grant, who was probably the most photographed man of his time. As he writes his memoirs in pencil, his extraordinary powers of intellectual concentration not only help him to produce an American classic but distract him from the agonizing pain of the cancer that would kill him ten days after this photograph was taken. *(Library of Congress)*

From here the only way to reach Chattanooga was by taking a sixty-mile ride on horseback over a treacherous, winding mountain road that snaked into the town from the north. This road was now Chattanooga's only supply route, and with heavy rains already lashing the mountains, it took heroic efforts just to push a handful of supply wagons down it each day. Once winter arrived and cut the road with mudslides, it would be virtually impossible to get anything through. The troops in the town were already on half-rations, and unless something happened soon, they could be starved into surrender.

At dawn on October 22 Rawlins lifted Grant onto a horse and tied his crutches to the saddle. With his staff following behind, Grant set off in the rain from Bridgeport. Along the road he passed the stiff and stinking carcasses of thousands of mules and horses that had been killed in recent fighting or simply died of starvation. With the men so hungry, there was nothing left to feed the animals.

As he drew near to Chattanooga Grant stopped at the headquarters of Major General Oliver Otis Howard, a young, one-armed officer who had performed ineptly at Chancellorsville and splendidly at Gettysburg. Howard commanded the XI Corps in the Army of the Cumberland. It seemed to him that Grant was remarkably small, when in fact he was of average height and build. "Rather thin in the flesh and very pale in complexion," Howard reflected, "and noticeably self-contained and retiring."[25]

Similarly, a regular Army lieutenant colonel who met Grant a few days later was slightly shocked to discover that the general "wore his uniform more like a civilian than a graduate of West Point. . . . He walked with his head down and without the slightest suggestion of a military step."[26]

Thirty-six hours after leaving Bridgeport Grant reached Chattanooga, but as he rode into the town his horse went down. The road surface had the consistency of porridge, which spared his injured leg further damage.[27]

He reached Thomas's headquarters soaked to the skin, sat down near the fire and lit a cigar. Thomas seemed too interested in describing the current situation to notice that Grant was sitting in a puddle of water. An officer on Grant's staff grew irritated and said bluntly, "General, can't you get General Grant some dry clothing?"

"Why, bless me, yes, of course," replied Thomas, and gave the necessary orders to a black servant.[28]

Thomas then resumed his conversation with Grant. The pile of dry clothes that was placed at Grant's feet remained there, ignored, as Grant shook hands with Thomas's staff officers and listened, absorbed, as each man gave his own account of the problems the army faced. Then Thomas's chief engineer, Brigadier General William F. "Baldy" Smith, stepped forward. Smith claimed he knew how to open a secure and adequate supply line. Grant and Baldy (nickname due to premature hair loss) were West Point classmates but had not met since graduation, and Grant was thrilled by what Smith had to say.

Smith claimed he had worked out a solution to the puzzle created by the terrain and the enemy. It called for seizing two lightly guarded Confederate positions close to the winding Tennessee, crossing the river in three places, building a pontoon bridge, and getting two damaged steamboats patched up and brought back into service as ferries. If the plan worked, Grant would be able to re-establish the railroad link with Bridgeport. A "cracker line" consisting of steamboats and railroads would soon have the troops back on full rations.[29]

Smith was one of the most controversial figures in the Army. He was a lot like Rosecrans—high intelligence yoked to appalling judgment. His service with the Army of the Potomac had brought him a corps command, but he was so difficult that Congress would not give him a second star. Having done enough to prove that Congress was right to deny him promotion to major general, he was sent to the West. Besides being a pain in the posterior, Smith was also a raging egomaniac lusting for glory. Grant did not know that yet. He listened, fascinated, to Smith's plan, unaware that it wasn't, in truth, Smith's idea at all.

It had in fact been pieced together by various people, including Rosecrans, himself an accomplished engineer officer, and the very able George Thomas. What Smith claimed was his plan would have been implemented even if Rosecrans had not been fired—even if Smith had dropped dead the day before Grant arrived.

Afterward, however, Smith made a cause out of trying to get national recognition for himself as the man who saved Chattanooga. He created such a fuss that in 1900 the secretary of war felt obliged to order an official inquiry. To Smith's well-deserved mortification, the board found no evidence that he had originated this plan. "On the contrary," it concluded, "there is abundant evidence in the *Official Records* to show that the plan was devised and prepared by General Rosecrans."[30]

Next day Grant, Thomas and Smith made a horseback ride around Chattanooga. Grant was convinced the plan Smith described was feasible. That evening, back at Thomas's headquarters, Grant spent several hours at a small table in an upstairs room writing out orders that would implement the cracker-line plan, bring reinforcements into the town and allow him to take the offensive. He could see it all now—what the enemy was doing, what the terrain was doing, and what he needed to do to break the stranglehold placed by man and nature on this rain-swept, depressing place. In complete silence and without hesitation, page after page flowed from his pen. As each was finished, he pushed it off the small table, allowing it to fall to the floor. When he had finished he picked up the papers, arranged them neatly in a small stack, handed them to an officer to distribute to the designated recipients, and hobbled off to bed.[31]

At that small table, writing silently for hours, the mechanism of Grant's military genius was put into motion. It is the invariable signature of supreme accomplishment that it is the instrument—the pen or the paintbrush, the piano or the military machine—that appears to do the work rather than the individual who holds that instrument in his hands. Grant's ability to achieve great results without fuss or ostentation or by doing anything to attract attention to himself was not, as most officers around him supposed, a sign that he was, after all, not so very different from themselves. It was proof, in fact, of complete mastery of an instrument as complex and demanding as any that humanity has ever devised and he achieved it in what is probably the most competitive profession on Earth.

★

Chattanooga was a railhead because it sat on one of the few flat stretches of land in this part of the country. The Tennessee River makes a series of dramatic loops close to the town. A few miles to the west it sweeps north, then south, only to turn north again, and the town that Grant came to had taken shape within yet another, smaller, loop in the river. The winding Tennessee hemmed in Chattanooga so effectively it might as well have been several rivers rather than one.

To the south of the town rose the impressive heights of Lookout Mountain, which on a clear day provide spectacular views for more than twenty miles in every direction. East of Chattanooga ran the long purple spine of Missionary Ridge. What with the river hugging it on the west and the north and with so much high ground to the east and south, this modest town, which in peacetime had a population of five thousand people, was easy to besiege. All that Bragg had needed to do when Rosecrans had hunkered down in Chattanooga was grab Lookout, Missionary Ridge, and a few places along the river and the place was virtually cut off.

The night of October 26 the two attacks Smith had described to Grant were launched, and Smith led one of them. The advancing Federals were aided by fog and river mists and caught the Confederates completely by surprise. The positions needed to operate the ferries and build the pontoon bridge fell quickly into Union hands. With the Confederates driven away from the railroad line to Bridgeport, it was possible to replace the broken stretches of track. The evening of October 28 a cheerful Grant sent a cable to Halleck: "I think the question of supplies must now be regarded as settled . . . preparations may commence for offensive operations."[32]

He ordered Sherman to bring a large part of the Army of the Tennessee to Chattanooga, and the War Department sent him the XII Corps, under Joe Hooker, who had for a time commanded the Army of the Potomac. Grant expected he would soon have a force considerably bigger than Bragg's.

While awaiting Sherman and Hooker, he put the Army of the Cumberland on full rations. Morale soared. Yet hardly had his cracker line gone into operation before Grant—and the War Department—began receiving reports that Bragg had sent Longstreet's corps to attack Knoxville, ninety-five miles northeast of Chattanooga.

When Grant assumed command of the Department of the Mississippi, the Army of the Ohio, commanded by Major General Ambrose E. Burnside, was holding Knoxville. Burnside was another failed commander of the Army of the Potomac sent out west. Lincoln had long being urging that Federal troops be sent into eastern Tennessee to protect its hardy, Union-loving mountaineers. Burnside, with twenty-five thousand men, had seized Knoxville in the summer of 1863, but with Longstreet now moving toward the town, Lincoln was growing alarmed.

Baldy Smith recommended that Grant make a feint against Confederate positions at the northern end of Missionary Ridge. That might be enough to make Bragg call Longstreet back. Grant seized on this idea, but turned it into an order to Thomas to mount an attack. Thomas was appalled. Grant's inherent aggressiveness, his instinct to respond to a challenge by attacking the enemy, was a world away from the mental processes of either Thomas or, he was later going to discover, Baldy Smith.[33]

Thomas came to him and said, "If I attempt to carry out the order I have received my army will be terribly beaten." The Army of the Cumberland had virtually no transportation. Thousands of horses and mules had perished—as Grant had seen for himself—and those that survived were too weak to pull artillery. Grant's reply was that if Thomas took the horses owned by officers (and it seems a reasonable guess that there were at least a couple of hundred of these) to supplement the small number of draft animals that were in adequate health, he would find he had enough muscle power to move the cannon needed to support his attack.

Besides, Hooker's XII Corps had arrived only recently on the outskirts of Chattanooga, with three divisions of fresh troops and hundreds of horses in good condition. Thomas, who was never much good at improvising, ignored what Grant had to say about the availability of horses and still insisted the attack be called off.[34]

Smith agreed with Thomas. He said he had made a reconnaissance of the enemy position, and an attack would have to wait until Sherman arrived with reinforcements. Short of relieving Thomas and putting someone else in his place, Grant had little choice but to call off the attack. Nevertheless, he remained convinced for the rest of his life that Thomas was wrong. He did not yet realize that in advising him as he did, Baldy Smith was revealing both a talent for misreading enemy defenses and a fear of taking risks.[35]

Other Union commanders would have tried to save Chattanooga by nibbling away at Bragg's forces throughout the winter. Not Grant. He intended to bring Bragg to battle and crush him. He later tried to justify his strategy by claiming he was attempting to rescue Burnside, but this was an exaggeration, to say the least. The cautiousness Longstreet had shown at Gettysburg was still in full working order. He did not attempt to besiege Knoxville closely or try taking it by storm.

Whatever confidence Grant ever had in George Thomas had taken a blow. Grant did the best he could with what he had, and expected other officers, whatever their rank, do the same. There was no more certain way for anyone to lose his respect than to balk at an assignment. So it isn't surprising that even as Thomas prepared his troops for Grant's all-out attack, Grant was venting his frustration with Thomas in a telegram to Halleck: "I have never felt such restlessness before as I have at the fixed and immovable condition of the Army of the Cumberland."[36]

Even so, the future looked bright. Sherman had reached Bridgeport on November 15, and his army was less than a week behind. Grant trusted and liked Sherman above almost all other generals. On November 20 Bragg sent Grant a message, advising him to get all the civilians out of Chattanooga within forty-eight hours. Grant had invited Julia's cousin William W. Smith to come and see what a battle looked like and had Smith sharing his room. When Bragg's message arrived, Grant was amused. He was going to let Bragg have his answer, he laughingly told Smith, once Sherman's troops were in position. On the eve of battle, Grant invariably seemed the most carefree and confident man in his entire command.[37]

★

Union troop strength in and around Chattanooga had risen to roughly seventy-five thousand men, while Bragg had only forty-three thousand. The Confederates, however, held a lot of high ground—Lookout Mountain to the south and five-mile-long Missionary Ridge to the east. Most of Bragg's troops were posted on the ridge. Because the railroads Bragg relied on ran through the hills at its northern end, Grant made taking the northern end of the ridge the principal objective in the impending attack and entrusted this mission to Sherman.

The battle would open with "Fighting Joe" Hooker's XII Corps advancing to seize Lookout Mountain. From there, they would advance on the southern end of the ridge. Thomas's Army of the Cumberland would tackle the central portion of the ridge, but were expected only to mount a reconnaissance in force. That would uncover the heart of the Confederate position and place Thomas in a position to assist Sherman, as he thrust down the ridge from the north.

Rain delayed the operation for two days, during which Thomas beefed up his reconnaissance until it amounted to a three-division assault, with two more divisions in reserve. The morning of November 23 he pushed his five divisions into Chattanooga valley. It made quite a show—row upon row of bayonets glinted wickedly in the morning sun as the troops advanced beneath streaming battle flags and regimental bands blared martial music and cannon roared like gigantic cheering throats. It all looked so perfect, so splendidly done, that the Confederates deployed on Missionary Ridge leaned on their rifled muskets like happy interlopers at someone else's party. They thought the Yankees were holding a grand review, and very grand it was, too, until three of the bluecoat divisions set off at a rapid pace, marched straight across the valley floor, and swept toward the picket line in front of Missionary Ridge and started scaling the barricades of logs and stone that Confederate hands had raised in recent weeks. The lightly held line of pickets was quickly overrun.

Sherman, meanwhile, was moving against Missionary Ridge from a position several miles north of Chattanooga. He was advancing toward a hill that was penetrated by a railroad tunnel. First, Sherman's men had to build a pontoon bridge to cross the Tennessee River, which inevitably slowed him down, and not being familiar with the terrain, he advanced cautiously. In late afternoon he reached what he thought was Tunnel Hill and stopped for the night. In fact, Tunnel Hill was a mile away, across a valley that would expose his men to heavy fire from the hill's defenders. Worse, though, was a deep ravine that ran across the base of Tunnel Hill. Sherman's axis of advance was probably the worst possible way of attacking Tunnel Hill, but Baldy Smith, whose responsibility it was to have scouted this battlefield and studied the terrain, had provided him with a map that did not indicate this formidable natural moat even existed.[38]

Grant was thereby misinformed by Sherman that he had reached Tunnel Hill, and concluded that the plan was working perfectly. All his subsequent actions were colored by a completely false belief that the northern end of Missionary Ridge was in Union hands.

When night fell, Bragg moved a division from Lookout Mountain over to Missionary Ridge. That allowed him to send one of his best divisions from Missionary Ridge over to Tunnel Hill. These moves inevitably weakened the defenses of Lookout Mountain, which eased the task Hooker's XII Corps faced on the morning of November 24.[39]

Hooker's soldiers advanced through the kind of morning mists common in late fall where rivers run at the base of high ground. Throughout the day, as the troops moved up the steep slope of Lookout Mountain, the drifting mists created dramatic chiaroscuro effects, sometimes hiding the long blue lines of panting men, sometimes revealing them in the dazzling fall sunlight to staff officers and journalists watching from below. Grant rode partway up the mountain to follow the battle, and once it became clear that the Confederates were being driven from the defenses, he dismounted and, taking a sheet of paper and a pencil from his cousin-in-law William Smith, got down on one knee and wrote out an order to Hooker telling him to cut off the enemy's retreat.[40]

The fact that he felt he had to tell a corps commander something as basic as this suggests that he didn't have much faith in Hooker. Even so, the spectacularly theatrical assault on Lookout Mountain was instantly immortalized by journalists and soldiers alike as "the battle above the clouds." Grant scoffed at any such description as "one of the romances of the war. There was no such battle. . . . It is all poetry."[41]

He never gave the soldiers who took Lookout Mountain the praise they deserved, mainly because he disdained commanders like Hooker and Burnside, major generals who had failed in the East yet were considered good enough for important commands in the West. Grant was convinced, anyway, that western soldiers were better than their eastern counterparts. That belief made it impossible for him to do justice to what was a splendid feat of arms.

During the night the Confederates abandoned Lookout Mountain. The morning dawned clear but bitingly cold. Grant, his staff and Julia's cousin assembled, along with Thomas and other general officers, and rode forward in their overcoats. Grant's plan for November 25 called for Hooker's troops to move eastward from Lookout and cross the Chattanooga valley. They would then attack Confederate defenses at the southern end of Missionary Ridge, while Sherman tackled the defenses at the northern end from the vantage point of Tunnel Hill. Meanwhile Thomas would be poised to threaten, and if possible attack, the center, once pressure from the north and south forced Bragg to thin out the central portion of his line. Nothing, though, went according to plan.

First of all, Hooker's troops were counting on capturing a bridge to get them across Chattanooga Creek, which runs through Chattanooga valley. When they reached it, they discovered the Confederates had destroyed the bridge. They spent four hours building a new one. It was late afternoon before the XII Corps was in position to attack the southern defenses of Missionary Ridge.

Far worse, though, was Sherman's predicament. He moved toward Tunnel Hill, only to discover the ravine. He was blocked, and as his frustration mounted, he became convinced that columns of Confederates were being sent to attack his flanks. This really *was* poetry. What he faced was a single division, handled skillfully, making the most of what nature had to offer a robust defense.[42]

Around midday Sherman sent a message to Grant telling him he was facing a strong rebel force. Grant sent back an order that read, "Attack again." Sherman could hardly believe it. Had Grant lost his mind? He sent an officer to find out whether this order was to be taken literally. It was. As this news sank in, Sherman started clamoring for help. "Where is Thomas?" he signaled Grant frantically.[43]

Thomas was about to move on Missionary Ridge. His advance two days earlier had carried his men forward by about a mile. They now held two small hills, the higher of which was known as Orchard Knob, more or less in the center of what had been the enemy's picket line. A couple of hundred yards farther back, where the ridge began to rise above the valley floor, ran a long line of enemy rifle pits.

Grant and his staff, Thomas and his staff, and an important visitor from the War Department, the very capable quartermaster general of the Army, Montgomery C. Meigs, plus various corps commanders, were clustered on Orchard Knob, message pads and binoculars in hand, looking out over a parapet of logs toward the enemy's position. An artillery battery at the base of the hill fired over their heads toward the Confederate lines. As the generals peered over the log parapet, Thomas remarked to Grant it was a good thing the Confederates did not realize how much Union brass was assembled on this one small spot well within range of their artillery.

Beneath his invariably calm exterior, Grant relished moments of danger like this. He loved to ride powerful, difficult horses, the kind of horses that could kill or cripple any but the most skillful rider. Unlike other men, who will themselves to bravery in the presence of mortal danger or take refuge in fatalism, his confidence seemed to expand the more closely he courted a sudden and violent death. He never flinched, never showed alarm, never gave the least indication of fear. The unusual physical constitution that made him capable of losing control of his legs after only one or two drinks seemed also to make him totally impervious to physical danger.

Even so, as Sherman's increasingly anxious messages flowed in, it was obvious something had to be done to relieve the pressure. The center of Missionary Ridge still might prove invulnerable to a frontal assault. But if Sherman's messages were accurate, Bragg must surely have pulled some of his troops from the center and shifted them north. In fact, there were twenty thousand rebels in the center of Bragg's line, the same number there had been for the past few weeks. Grant did not know that, and decided to attack it.

He told Thomas to have his troops throw out two skirmish lines and seize the rifle pits at the base of Missionary Ridge, roughly three hundred yards in front of Orchard Knob. Once the rifle pits had been captured, there would be a pause, so that the troops, who would be strung out in a two lines each nearly two miles long, could be organized into columns. Only column formations, narrow but deep, had the weight to punch holes in fixed defenses. Once the columns were formed they would advance to attack the breastworks higher up the ridge.[44]

After telling Thomas what he wanted, Grant waited awhile, then in his usual unemotional, understated way, he said to Thomas, "Hadn't you better order out your troops?" Thomas continued studying the situation through his binoculars. Grant was prepared to wait a little longer, but Rawlins threw a tantrum.

Rawlins, whose addiction to profanity and overwrought lectures on the evils of drink betrayed a hysterical temperament, was coming unglued as the news flowed in that Hooker was building a bridge and Sherman was unable to advance. Only a week earlier he had written yet another denunciation of Grant's drinking, this one inspired by the fact that Grant's mother had sent her son a bottle of homemade wine, which hardly seems like an invitation to get plastered.[45]

And now, as the plan for the battle began to fall apart, Rawlins's nerves cracked. Shaking his fist angrily in Grant's face, he burst out, "If I was general of this army, by God, I would see that my orders were carried out!"

For a member of his staff to behave like this in front of Meigs, who was sure to carry the story back to the War Department, almost defies belief. Grant flushed with embarrassment and said mildly to Thomas, "General, the time has come for you to move out, sir."[46]

At three-thirty in the afternoon the six cannon posted at the base of Orchard Knob fired in rapid succession, giving the signal to advance.

Thomas's men stepped out briskly once more, flags flying, bugles blaring shrilly, drums beating thunderously. They swept over the line of rifle pits, only to make a terrifying discovery. Where they stood now, they were completely exposed to the massed fire of dozens of rebel artillery pieces deployed high above them. There was no fold in the ground to provide cover, and the rifle pits they had captured offered shelter for only a few hundred men. The ridge loomed like a rocky wall. If they stayed where they were, they could count on being killed or wounded. If they advanced, though, there was ground higher up that would screen them from the enemy's main line of breastworks. All they had to do was live long enough to reach it.[47]

A handful of men led by a sergeant here, a cluster somewhere else, rallied by a lieutenant or a captain, and that was all it took to start tugging the ragged blue lines forward. As the aggressive and resourceful spirits pressed on, shouting, cursing, inspiring, the momentum they generated was enough to set the whole twenty-three thousand men Thomas had put into the fight scrambling up the numerous paths and roads leading from the valley up the slope of Missionary Ridge.[48]

Grant watched them moving up with increasing alarm. He turned to Thomas. Who had ordered the troops to climb the ridge? Why hadn't they paused as he had ordered? Thomas said he had not done it, and Grant muttered that if this turned out badly, someone (and he surely meant George H. Thomas, "the Rock of Chickamauga") was going to pay.[49]

Fortune favors the brave. The Confederates had entrenched not on the military crest—the piece of ground that provided the best field of fire—but on the topographical crest, higher up. As Grant, Meigs and the others watched in appalled fascination, they saw three red silk regimental flags bobbing up Missionary Ridge like wine-stained corks carried along on a dark blue tide.[50]

Behind and around the banners flowed Union soldiers, moving almost on their knees toward the heart of Bragg's defenses. Remaining in plain sight of the officers on Orchard Knob, they disappeared from Confederate view for a while, only to reappear a short while later virtually on top of the rebel trenches. But now six regimental flags were visible as Thomas's men, panting hard from the climb, surged over them shooting, stabbing, slashing, exhilarated and eager, ready to strike down any butternut soldier who stood in their way.

Just then a Mississippi regiment began pulling out of the line, under orders to redeploy. This sudden movement, combined with the unexpected charge of Thomas's troops, was enough to send startled rebels fleeing down the reverse slope. The entire Confederate position along Missionary Ridge unraveled. It did not do so according to plan, although no one would ever guess that from either Grant's or Sherman's memoirs. It was a triumph against the odds, won by veteran soldiers.

Grant rode up the ridge with Julia's cousin, William Smith, jubilant and excited. "You were lucky to be here!" said Grant. "In half a dozen lifetimes you couldn't expect to see so much of a battle with comparatively so little danger."[51]

In the space of a month Grant had broken what amounted to a siege; restored the health and morale of a beaten and starving army; driven a well-entrenched enemy from mountain ridges and river lines; and successfully attacked with an advantage of only three to two. He had won even though his plan had failed. Grant deserved to win all the same. He had wrested the initiative from Bragg, brought on a battle and pressured him into making serious mistakes.

It is something of a truism that military plans begin to go wrong the moment battle is joined. But within any realistic plan there is almost a secret design, a plan that *will* work if commanders and the soldiers they lead have the wit and the audacity to grasp it. Veteran troops under sound leadership could improvise a victory even when Grant and his staff got the details wrong.

Not that Grant considered the battle in that light. Instead, what remained strongest in his memory was the heart-stopping theatricality of the scene. From his vantage point on Orchard Knob he could see almost the entire battle line, from Chattanooga Creek, where Hooker's men finally crossed, to Tunnel Hill, nearly ten miles to the north. "I am sorry you could not be here," Grant wrote to his champion in Congress, Elihu B. Washburne. "The specticle [sic] was grand beyond anything that has been, or is likely to be, on this Continent."[52]

CHAPTER 21

———— ★ ★ ★ ★ ————

"GET ALL THE SUNSHINE I CAN"

There had been only one lieutenant general in the history of the Republic, and that was George Washington. True, Winfield Scott had held three-star rank, but that was by brevet, meaning it was temporary and without any increase in pay. Following Grant's stunning success at Chattanooga his congressional mentor, Elihu B. Washburne, introduced a bill to revive the grade of lieutenant general so that Grant could be raised to three stars.

Grant himself was of two minds about this move. He wrote to Washburne, urging him to "recollect that I have been highly honored already by the government and do not ask, or feel that I deserve, any thing more in the shape of honors or promotion."[1] Grant had no objection to a promotion and the extra pay it was likely to bring. What had him worried was the possibility that three stars meant being chained to Halleck's desk in the War Department. As Halleck himself had found, his job was as much a political appointment as a military one. Besides running the Army, his energies went into fending off politicians seeking favors from the War Department, dealing with the irascible and self-righteous Stanton, and implementing the President's policy of rewarding political allies with major commands.[2]

Washburne nevertheless pushed his bill with an enthusiasm that indicated he hadn't grasped the point, so Grant got Rawlins to follow up with a letter that left the congressman in no doubt: "I can only say that if the confering [*sic*] of the distinguished honor on him would mean taking him out of the field, or with a view to the superceding of General Halleck, he would not desire it, for he feels that if he can be of service to the Government in any place it is in Command of the Army in the field, and that is where he would remain if made a Lieut. General." All of which amounted to saying that Grant would gladly take the three stars, provided he retained the drama and Halleck held on to the desk.[3]

While Washburne's bill was making its way through Congress, Grant was trying, and failing, to cash in on victory at Chattanooga. There had been virtually no pursuit of Bragg's defeated army. The only divisions in position to mount a pursuit were the four that stormed Missionary Ridge, and only one division commander—Phil Sheridan—showed the alertness and aggressiveness to pursue the enemy. The other three had sat down on Missionary Ridge and neither their corps commander nor George Thomas, their army commander, was inclined to make them move out. The aftermath of Chattanooga was that Grant's admiration for Sheridan went through the roof, while his already shaky faith in Thomas took another knock.[4]

The biggest obstacle to Grant's efforts to maintain the pressure on the enemy, however, was not Thomas but the aid he was forced to give to Ambrose Burnside and the IX Corps troops defending Knoxville against "Pete" Longstreet, a groomsman at Grant's wedding. During the climactic hours on Missionary Ridge on November 25, Grant had received a telegram from Lincoln that read, "Remember Burnside."

Grant had no confidence at all in Burnside. Shortly before the battle of Chattanooga he had sent James H. Wilson of his staff to Knoxville to see how Burnside was doing. Wilson found Burnside preparing to abandon the town. He told Burnside emphatically that Grant would not countenance a withdrawal. Burnside reluctantly remained where he was, afraid that Longstreet might attack him.[5]

On November 29, four days after the battle of Chattanooga, Longstreet finally launched a halfhearted attack against Burnside's lines. It achieved little beyond confirming that Burnside's men were well entrenched. Longstreet then pulled away and went up into the mountains fifty miles northeast of Knoxville and settled down for the winter, posing a threat to eastern Tennessee that kept Burnside rooted to the spot like a rabbit caught in headlights.

Grant sent strong reinforcements to Knoxville, in accordance with Lincoln's wishes, but it angered him when he thought of what might have been. With Bragg's army in full retreat, Grant could have driven from Chattanooga in any direction he wanted—to Mobile, perhaps, or on to Atlanta, and the Confederates would not have been able to stop him—if it hadn't been for the need to support the timorous, unenterprising Burnside.[6]

Grant was also ordered to send more troops to aid Nathaniel Banks's advance toward Texas, as the secretary of state, William Seward, demanded. The new year found Grant in no position to mount a winter campaign. So he turned his thoughts to the spring and came back once again to an operation against Mobile. He proposed to lay siege to the town with part of his force, but use the rest to clear the rebels from central Alabama. That done, he would be in position to move into Georgia and launch an Atlanta campaign.[7]

When this idea failed yet again to draw a positive response from Washington, Rawlins, Wilson and a young engineer officer, Cyrus B. Comstock, presented him with a memo that called for landing an invasion force of sixty thousand men near Norfolk, Virginia. From there, the Federals could advance on Raleigh, North Carolina, blockade Wilmington—currently the only Atlantic Coast port open to Confederate blockade runners—and threaten the railroads on which Richmond depended. Grant sent this proposal to Halleck, but with a major disclaimer: "You will be better able to judge of the practicability of it than I can."

On paper, the plan had its merits. In reality, however, it was likely to fail, because although it would almost certainly lead to the capture of Wilmington, Grant could find himself blocked a long way from Richmond. There were too many rivers, too many swamps and too few roads on the way north. He could easily find himself drawn into a siege for Raleigh, which would be pointless but might become unavoidable. Faced with that, it would be better to re-embark his army and send it back to Washington. If this operation failed it would shake the government to its roots, for it would be a replay of McClellan's failed Peninsula campaign of 1862.

Grant, however, did not want to discourage his staff or strain his relationship with them. It would be better if the plan was turned down by Halleck rather than by Grant. Halleck obliged. Once in the War Department, this plan swiftly arrived at its appropriate destination—the wastebasket.[8]

Grant, meanwhile, had moved to Nashville for the winter. Julia came to join him for a while and took to visiting the hospitals, which were filled with wounded men. When she started to tell him about it one evening, he cut her short. "Now, my dear, I don't want to hear anything about that. I don't want you to come to me with any of these tales of the hospitals. . . . I have all I can bear up under outside my home, and when I come to you I want to see you and the children and talk about other matters. I want to get all the sunshine I can." Shortly after this, the weather in Nashville turned Siberian. Julia went back to St. Louis and, to Grant's deep disappointment, had to remain there because of a painful affliction to her eyes.[9]

Washburne's bill finally came to a vote in the House on February 4. Given Grant's fame and the acclaim he enjoyed these days from a formerly hypercritical press, there was a surprising amount of political resistance. The opposition was led by James A. Garfield, until recently Rosecrans's chief of staff. Following Grant's removal of Rosecrans from command of the Army of the Cumberland, Garfield had resumed his congressional career. His resistance to Grant's promotion, aided by yet another whispering campaign that Grant was a hopeless drunk, failed. The bill passed by 96 votes to 41 in the House and by a 31-to-6 margin in the Senate.[10]

Grant's feelings at getting a third star were mixed. His pay would double, to twelve thousand dollars a year, which put him among the most highly paid people in the country. Nor would he be forced to take Halleck's place and try running the war from the War Department. Even so, a dream had died. Most people have a fantasy of escape and for him, as for countless others since, that dream was spelled C-A-L-I-F-O-R-N-I-A. The hope that Grant had clung to throughout the hardships and poverty of his life after he left the Army, the vision that helped sustain him during the long hours of unremitting toil and psychological strain of wartime command, was finally laid to rest. With such exalted rank, there would be only one place for him in the postwar Army, and that was in Washington. As a major general, he might hope to get command of the Pacific Division, but with three stars on his shoulder straps? Not a chance.[11]

★

For more than two years John Rawlins had, by his own lights, served Grant faithfully and well. He had sought to stand as a bulwark between the general and the bottle. If he had not always succeeded, he had always tried. And while serving on Grant's staff, Rawlins, an intelligent man even if he was uncouth, insecure and poorly educated, had learned something about army management and battlefield tactics. Not only had he been surrounded by professional officers, happy to advance his grasp of the military art, but he had been provided by fate with a chance to study at first hand the operations of one of the greatest soldiers of the age.

Yet from Grant's point of view Rawlins was little more than a glorified clerk— hardworking, conscientious to a fault and, Grant mistakenly believed, completely loyal. Everybody who ever suggested a military move to Grant convinced himself that he was the real mastermind behind the victories. Not even Julia could resist giving him advice on strategy. Halleck, Frémont and McClernand all lodged claims, but only Rawlins has been written about as Grant's chief military adviser, which is simply absurd. If Grant was prepared to reject the advice of Sherman, for whose military talents he had the highest respect, he was hardly likely to be guided by an amateur. All the same, enlisted men joked, "If you hit Rawlins on the head, you'll knock old Grant's brains out." This, though, simply shows how hard it was to believe that someone who looked and acted so ordinary could be a great general. And as soldiers often discover, there is a certain comfort to be had from mocking the general.[12]

More serious was the assertion by both staff member James H. Wilson and Sylvanus Cadwallader, the journalist who became a quasi-member of the staff, that Rawlins was "at least one half of Grant."[13] Now, this is an interesting claim, because if it were so, there would be at least some documentary evidence to support it. There is none. On the other hand, there is a mountain of evidence in the documentary record, corroborated by eyewitness testimony, against it.

For example, the chief enlisted clerk at Grant's headquarters, Sergeant Harrison Strong, strenuously maintained that Rawlins's duties were confined to administrative tasks. Grant did not turn to him for military advice. Other eyewitnesses to the headquarters scene, such as Horace Porter and Sherman, agree with Strong. Claims to the contrary come entirely from Wilson and Cadwallader.[14]

There is no doubt whatever that Grant wrote nearly all his own orders and his own reports and that where Rawlins's hand and mind can be detected, they are invariably operating as extensions of Grant's.

While Rawlins's efforts to express himself often resulted in the kind of turgid, convoluted prose that invariably reflects a mind that is muddy, Grant's *Personal Memoirs* is generally considered a masterpiece of nineteenth-century literature.

At times Rawlins and other officers proposed ideas on what should be done, but this is normal between a general and his staff. They are not there to provide him with friendship. The people he commands are there as tools to be used. This can be an uncomfortable thought to anyone who suffers, as Rawlins did, from problems of low self-esteem. Nor is it at all surprising that at times some members of commanders' staffs start flattering themselves that the general regards them as close friends. And there are exceptions, of course, such as John J. Pershing and George C. Marshall, between whom there were strong bonds of affection, but chances are that the commander regards his staff as just that— his staff, not his family and not his equals.

Grant made his true feelings about Rawlins almost brutally clear in his memoirs, when he dismissed Rawlins's contribution to the war in a perfunctory, impersonal paragraph. This debunking of Rawlins outraged Cadwallader and Wilson alike. Their anger was so intense at what they saw as Grant's ingratitude—"Such a man deserves to be scourged from the face of the Earth!" raged Cadwallader—as to raise the question of just what was it about Rawlins that inspired such posthumous devotion. Why all this fuss over an amateur military bureaucrat? Why the determination to immortalize him, and why the absurd overestimation of his abilities?[15]

The feelings Wilson and Cadwallader express about Rawlins are so intense as to suggest that this brooding, passionate man, the strange luster of his eye and the startling pallor of his skin intensified by the tuberculosis that doomed him to an early grave, exerted a powerful homoerotic attraction over both of them. In his finely chiseled cheeks, pouting mouth and intense gaze he bore a resemblance to James Dean and River Phoenix, beautiful young men doomed, like Rawlins, to an early grave.

There can be little doubt that Wilson was susceptible to the physical appeal of young men. Shortly before the war began, he was engaged in what was almost certainly a homosexual affair with Adam Badeau, who at that time was blatantly effeminate, a quasi-bohemian character attempting to make a name for himself as a writer.[16]

It appears from their correspondence that Wilson seduced Badeau in 1860. Three years later he got Badeau assigned to Grant's staff during the Vicksburg campaign so that they could be reunited, only to lose interest after Badeau was wounded in the foot at Port Hudson and became a whining, demanding cripple. Badeau's early letters to Wilson are *billets doux,* with allusions to physical intimacy. The letters from 1864–65, however, are cries of pain from a jilted lover.[17]

Rawlins's hold over Wilson—and over Cadwallader, too—has no basis in either logic or empirical evidence. It roots must therefore be sought in the realm of emotion. But if homoerotic attraction is the explanation, it is certain it went no further than that. Rawlins may not even have been aware of the passions he aroused. For Wilson, though, devotion to Rawlins sparked what became over time a withering hatred of Grant. When, in 1896, Hamlin Garland went to interview Wilson for his biography of Grant, what he got took him aback. "For two hours," Garland recorded, "he battered me with one of the most adroit and copious assault's upon General Grant's fame I have met."

Wilson sneered at any suggestion that Grant was either a strategist or a tactician. He claimed the credit for Grant's victories either for himself or for his friend. "Rawlins furnished all the motive power and the sagacity," said Wilson. As for Grant, he was nothing, just "a timid man. Not an aggressive fighting man at all." Given the obvious absurdity—not to say dishonesty—of assertions such as this, it is impossible to take anything that Wilson says about Grant at face value.[18]

Cadwallader meanwhile produced a memoir titled *Four Years with Grant,* which was a considerable exaggeration. He actually spent only two years covering Grant's headquarters during the war, and during that time weeks could pass without him exchanging a word with Grant. Cadwallader nevertheless felt he played a vital role, and when he compiled a list of those who had served on Grant's staff, he added at the bottom of the list "+ Sylvanus Cadwallader." He also awarded himself the courtesy title of "General." The heroic figure in Cadwallader's memoir isn't Grant, though, but Rawlins. Neither his nor Wilson's biography of Rawlins is remotely reliable, but hagiography isn't about fact, anyway; it is about love.[19]

As Rawlins contemplated Grant's three impending stars, he was less inclined to congratulate the general than to feel sorry for himself. The staff was bound to be much bigger now, and his influence—which he mistakenly believed was far greater than it truly was—could only diminish as able young West Pointers, with distinguished combat records, took up their places around the throne. "Oh, greatness!" Rawlins moaned histrionically and self-pityingly. "How dost thou lift up in themselves those whom thou favor . . . to go with them is ascending heights too far beyond the level of my plebeian birth; beyond the reach of any influence I can exert for my country's good." He sensed, that is, that while Grant had tolerated his sanctimonious lectures and letters on the evils of drink up until now, those days were probably over. Grant had become untouchable. But without his role as self-appointed conscience and busybody, what was Rawlins but another paper shuffler?[20]

And the fact is, Rawlins was right to be worried. Grant increasingly made it plain that he'd had enough of Rawlins's inability to control his language and his feelings. The immaturity that had prompted him to rebuke Grant in front of the quartermaster general of the Army had not been left behind on Orchard Knob. Rawlins was capable of acting the same way in front of the President or the secretary of war. Bad behavior might be excused or ignored out west, but in Washington, high command blended inextricably with high politics and, on the outer fringes, with high society.

Grant was not going to dump Rawlins. That might raise questions as well as eyebrows. Besides, Grant believed in loyalty down as well as loyalty up, and as far as Grant knew, Rawlins had been loyal, if in his own strange way. Moreover, there were army commanders who had brigadier generals as their chiefs of staff, and Grant did not intend his staff to suffer by comparison with those of two-star commanders. So Grant got Rawlins promoted to brigadier general, beating down objections from the House Military Affairs Committee that as a staff officer without combat experience Rawlins really should not have a star. "If his confirmation is dependent on his commanding troops, he shall command troops at once," Grant informed the committee chairman.[21]

It soon became clear, though, that Rawlins's promotion was not a mark of absolute confidence. Grant increasingly distanced himself from Rawlins. In the closing stages of the war, there was a widening gulf between them, something that pained Rawlins and his admirers.[22]

★

The story has been told dozens of times, of how Grant appeared at the front desk of the Willard Hotel on a rainy Tuesday afternoon, March 8,

1864, and the clerk, who had seen generals come and generals go, was studiously unimpressed, telling him that maybe he could let him have a small room at the top of the hotel. And Grant, in his shy, modest way, said that would be just fine, and the clerk half turned the register so Grant, who was standing there with his fourteen-year-old son, Fred, and two staff officers—John Rawlins and Cyrus B. Comstock—signed in as "U.S. Grant and son, Galena, Ill.," and the clerk's jaw dropped open like the trap on a gallows. But the man knew his business and he shifted from patronizing indifference to fawning obsequiousness in the blink of an eye, the way good hotel clerks know how to do all over the world, and said maybe the general would like Parlor 6. That was where Lincoln had stayed in the week before his inauguration.

Meanwhile, the lobby seems to have been filled with people who were staring at Grant, among them the novelist Richard Henry Dana, author of *Two Years Before the Mast.* "He had no gait, no station, no manner," Dana informed his wife. "Rough light brown whiskers, a blue eye and a rather scrubby look . . . the look of a man who did, or once did, take a little too much to drink . . . a slightly seedy look, as if he was out of office on half pay, and nothing to do but hang around the entry of Willard's, cigar in mouth."[23]

While those around him were losing their heads, he gazed at the throng with his usual mixture of shyness and almost inhuman self-possession. Fame left him what he had always been, Hannah Grant's son. She had taught him to treat this world as a place of meaningless noise, futile busyness and vain ambition. There was something of the Shaker temperament in Hannah Grant, and her eldest son showed the effects throughout his life.

The conduct of Washingtonians, who considered themselves a fairly sophisticated bunch, turning to Grant faces lambent with exaggerated curiosity and barely controlled excitement, only showed that Mother was right. They revealed something else, too—the desire for a savior, the one man who would solve the country's problems and thereby solve theirs. Yet, as Richard Henry Dana saw, Grant's attitude was as plain as could be—"an entire indifference to the world about him."[24]

Grant had no intention of playing the role the people who clustered around him yearned for him to fulfill. He shared with Washington far more than three stars. Both Grant and Washington were so honest, so sincere and so devoted to the simple virtues of public service and private morality that they were above trying to please any crowd. They did not know how to begin, had no intention of finding out. Privately, Grant deplored "this show business."[25]

What mattered was a man's character, not his fame, and certainly not praise. Grant's view of his true worth was much like that of a figure from our own time. "I am not a leader," says Nelson Mandela. "I am a servant."

When Grant descended for dinner at the Willard he barely had time to sit down before a nearby diner began pounding the table with his knife. "I have the honor to inform you that General Grant is present in the room with us!" Whereupon people sprang to their feet and started chanting, "Grant! Grant! Grant!"

He rose, bowed and sat down again. This, however, wasn't enough to appease the crowd, who mobbed his table, baying for his attention. They ignored the fact that he was clearly annoyed at being imposed on like this, insisted on shaking his hand, and made it impossible for him to eat. After forty-five minutes, he gave up and returned to his room, unfed.[26]

Later that evening Grant was escorted to the White House by former secretary of war Simon Cameron. As they entered the Blue Room they found it crowded with people drawn there by the promise of finally seeing the famous general from out west. Lincoln was there, too, towering above women in crinolines and men in dark suits. Hearing the commotion near the entrance, he strode over and introduced himself. "It is General Grant, is it not?" To which Grant monosyllabically replied, "Yes."

After a halting exchange of pleasantries, Grant was then escorted by Secretary of State William Seward to the East Room, to meet Mrs. Lincoln. An even bigger crowd was assembled here, and ignoring his pleas to be "let alone," Grant was lifted up and required to stand on a crimson sofa so everyone could see him. For an hour people pressed forward, eager to shake his hand and exchange a few words.[27]

It was nearly midnight before Grant and Lincoln were able to retreat upstairs and talk. Lincoln almost invariably tried to put people at ease by telling them jokes and he began by telling Grant about a monkey general called Jocko, of whom great things were expected in the Monkey War. Jocko said he was eager to fight but wasn't sure his tail was long enough for a commander of his rank. Monkey surgeons removed the tails from other monkeys and spliced them to Jocko's appendage. Jocko, however, demanded more tails, more splicing, to boost his confidence. He wound up with a tail so long and heavy it had to be draped over his shoulder and wrapped around his chest. It finally broke his back. So far, said Lincoln, he'd had a lot of generals like Jocko—always demanding, never fighting.

There was something important that Lincoln did not want Grant to misunderstand, though. The President had never wanted to get involved in fighting the war. He had done so only from necessity. "I don't give many military orders," said Lincoln. "Some of those I do give, I know are wrong. Sometimes I think all of them are wrong."[28]

Turning to the ceremony the next day, at which he would present Grant with his commission as lieutenant general, Lincoln handed Grant a copy of the remarks he intended to make. He wanted the general to respond with a short speech of his own, and there were a couple of points he wanted Grant to include. "First, to say something which shall prevent or obviate any jealousy of you from any of the other generals in the service, and second, something from you which shall put you on as good terms as possible with the Army of the Potomac."[29]

Grant returned to the Willard, and before he turned in, he tore a scrap of paper from a notebook and picked up a pencil. He wrote out a few lines and shoved the paper into a coat pocket. Next day, in the presence of the entire cabinet, young Fred Grant, John Rawlins and Cyrus Comstock, Lincoln presented Grant with his three-star commission and read out a statement reminding him of the great honor and responsibility it conferred. Now it was Grant's turn.

He fished from an inside pocket the scrap of paper on which he had scribbled four anodyne sentences just before going to bed. These he proceeded to mumble so anticlimactically that even his mother could not have said he was showing off, appearing vain or seeking applause.

"Mr. President: I accept this commission with gratitude for the high honor conferred. With the aid of the noble armies that have fought on so many fields for our common country, it will be my earnest endeavor not to disappoint your expectations. I feel the full weight of the responsibilities now devolving on me and know that if they are met it will be due to those armies, and above all to the favor of that Providence which leads both nations and men."

His remarks were even shorter than Lincoln's. But the message he was really seeking to convey was not in what Grant actually said. It was in what he did not say. He came from the kind of people whose folk wisdom on new beginnings was "Begin as you mean to go on."[30]

There was not a word, not even a hint, of the two points Lincoln had stressed about the feelings of other generals or winning over the Army of the Potomac. And Lincoln, who came from the same plain-living, up-by-the-bootstraps frontier stock as Grant, would have understood. What Grant, by silence and indirection, was telling the President was that he was his own man, wrote his own speeches, made his own decisions and would handle the Army his own way.

Shortly after this, Lincoln was asked by a member of the White House staff just what kind of soldier this new fellow was. Unlike other commanders, Lincoln told him, Grant did not make impossible demands on the government, then use its inability to satisfy them as an excuse for inaction. Instead, he looked for chances to fight. "Grant is the first general I have had!" said Lincoln, admiration mingling with relief. "He's a general!"[31]

CHAPTER 22

★ ★ ★ ★

"If It Takes Me All Summer"

Ever since its creation at the end of the Revolutionary War, the United States Army had been organized as a constabulary, based on garrisons, outposts and military departments. When military action was needed, units from the widely scattered posts were brought together to fight a battle or campaign. Once the military challenge had passed, the troops were dispersed across the country once more. The huge Union Army was organized along the same lines. The constabulary system had survived the War of 1812, the Mexican War, numerous clashes with the Indians and, until now, the Civil War. Halleck never did anything to alter it, because he couldn't see anything wrong with it.

Grant, however, had no time for antiques. He moved into a small brick house next to the railroad depot in Culpeper, Virginia, and began to demolish the constabulary method of making war. He was only the second truly strategic thinker the United States military produced, the first being Winfield Scott. Grant always protested that he was not a Napoleonic general. After all, he pointed out, a war in the United States could not be fought as if this were Europe. The Old World was densely populated. Its most prosperous regions were covered with good roads and historic towns. The United States, despite its riches and large population, was still mostly wilderness.

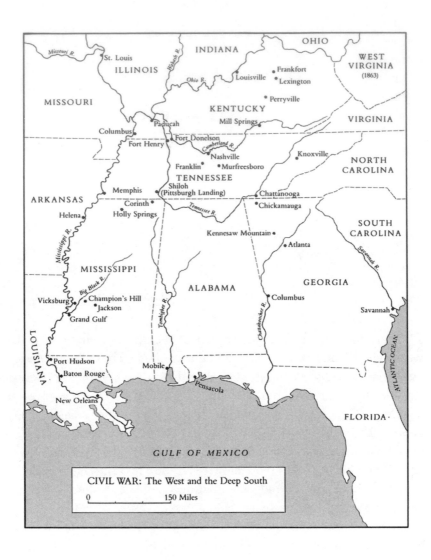

MISSOURI R.

St. Louis
ILLINOIS
INDIANA
OHIO
WEST
VIRGINIA
(1863)

Wabash R.

Frankfort
Louisville • Lexington
Ohio R.

• Perryville
KENTUCKY

VIRGINIA

Paducah
Columbus
Fort Donelson
Fort Henry
Mill Springs

Cumberland R.
Nashville
Knoxville
NORTH
CAROLINA

Franklin • Murfreesboro
TENNESSEE
Shiloh
(Pittsburgh Landing)
Chattanooga

Memphis
Chickamauga

ARKANSAS
Corinth
Holly Springs
Tennessee R.

Helena

SOUTH
CAROLINA

Kennesaw Mountain •

MISSISSIPPI
• Atlanta

Savannah R.

Big Black R.

GEORGIA

Vicksburg • Champion's Hill
• Jackson
ALABAMA
Columbus

Grand Gulf

Tombigbee R.

Chattahoochee R.

Savannah

LOUISIANA

Port Hudson
Baton Rouge

Mobile

ATLANTIC OCEAN

New Orleans
Pensacola

FLORIDA ·

GULF OF MEXICO

CIVIL WAR: The West and the Deep South

0   150 Miles

Even so, Grant had a Napoleonic grasp of war. His constant goal was the destruction of the enemy's armies. Halleck and others preferred to pursue victory by capturing strategic places. When Grant threatened a strategic point, however, it was always as part of a larger design, usually to make the enemy come out and fight. Napoleon had revolutionized eighteenth-century warfare by maneuvering between the huge fortresses of western Europe, and he made his enemies fight in the open field, which allowed him to annihilate their armies. This was widely denounced as turning war into massacre, and Grant, who fought similar campaigns, was tarred with the same brush, for the same reason.

It seems almost inevitable, then, that when he became general-in-chief, he immediately set about turning the Union Army into something that bore a passing resemblance to Napoleon's Grande Armée. Out went the constabulary principle. In its place he created a large, mobile army prepared for a war of maneuver. It was free to move in any direction, for any distance, living off the land (i.e., the enemy) where possible, and prepared to fight all year round. Its organizing principle was not fixed territories but powerful, converging columns, designed to apply pressure on the Confederacy from various directions, in season and out, the movements of each column coordinated with the advance of the rest.[1]

There would be five powerful columns, all advancing at the same time, all putting pressure on the beleaguered Confederacy, pinning its forces down while driving deep into its territory. Sherman instantly recognized the new design for the intellectual breakthrough it was. "That we are now all to act in a Common Plan, converging on a Common Center looks like Enlightened War," he wrote approvingly to Grant.[2]

The largest of these five forces consisted of the Army of the Potomac and the quasi-independent IX Corps, under Ambrose E. Burnside, which was more or less attached to it. The IX Corps's odd status reflected the fact that Burnside had once commanded the Army of the Potomac, failed miserably and been sent west to command the Army of the Ohio. His performance in defending Knoxville was mediocre. Recalled to the East to command the IX Corps, he posed a problem. Burnside was senior on the list of major generals to the current commander of the Army of the Potomac, George G. Meade.

It *was* possible for a senior commander to serve under a junior, but only if the senior agreed to do so. Grant, coming new to the Army of the Potomac and unsure how it would react to him, played it safe and did not press the issue. Burnside was allowed to continue with his corps as a separate command, and answered directly to Grant, not to Meade. It was a bizarre, and ultimately unworkable, arrangement. For now, though, the Army of the Potomac and IX Corps combined provided Grant with 120,000 men to take the war to Robert E. Lee and the 65,000-man Army of Northern Virginia.[3]

As the Army of the Potomac advanced and attacked Lee, the 33,000-man Army of the James, operating from Fortress Monroe, was going to land somewhere south of Richmond. Its commander, Major General Benjamin Butler, was a War Democrat whom Lincoln had seen fit to reward with two stars despite the fact that Butler had no talents as a combat commander. Once Butler's army landed, it would pose a threat to the Confederate capital that Lee would not be able to ignore, at a time when Lee was expected to have his hands full fighting off the Army of the Potomac.

During previous advances by the Army of the Potomac, Lee had been able to regain the initiative by sending a force north, usually by using the Shenandoah Valley to outflank the advancing Federals. The alarm Lee's ripostes created in Washington would be hard to exaggerate. To prevent Lee from using the Shenandoah Valley again, Grant was going to have yet another political major general, Franz Sigel, lead a force of nearly 25,000 men through the valley to Lynchburg. Having seen McClernand in action, Grant may have thought he had witnessed the nadir of military incompetence. Sigel was going to surprise him.

Grant installed Sherman in command of the Division of the Mississippi. Sherman would advance on Atlanta with an army of a hundred thousand men. His principal mission was not to take the city but to destroy the 65,000-man Confederate army assembled in Georgia under Joe Johnston. Meanwhile Nathaniel Banks, yet another political general, was ordered to wind up his futile campaign along the Red River and redirect his army toward Mobile.

This plan was hardly in motion, though, before it suffered a setback. On April 8 Banks allowed himself to be ambushed near Shreveport, Louisiana. His army was trounced and forced into a long, humiliating retreat back to New Orleans.[4]

Grant wanted to relieve him, only to be informed by Halleck that the President was opposed to that idea. Banks had too many supporters in Congress and the President did not want to alienate them. Although

Lincoln liked to think he was giving unstinting support—and Grant liked to pretend that was what he got—the President fell short of giving Grant what he really wanted.[5]

Sigel, Butler and Banks made Grant's task incomparably harder than it needed to be. They may, in fact, have prolonged the war. Grant was a realist, however, and promptly dropped the matter. It was only after there was such an outcry in the press against Banks's incompetence that he became enough of a political liability for Grant to be allowed to fire him.

Grant intended to command the five-hundred-thousand-plus troops deployed throughout the United States from the field. Thanks to advanced technology, Grant informed his father, "in these days of telegraph & steam I can command whilst traveling and visiting about." It really did not matter where he put his desk. He expected, in that early spring of 1864, to move around the country, shifting from army to army, as the need arose. That, however, was not how it turned out.[6]

Halleck claimed, "General Grant is my personal friend. I heartily rejoice at his promotion [and] if the government has no command for me, I am ready for the shelf," but he was merely putting a brave face on being elbowed aside as general-in-chief. He still had less than complete confidence in Grant, still did not understand Grant's way of making war.[7]

He had his uses, though. Grant created a new position, chief of staff of the Army, and shoved Halleck into it. His responsibilities did not resemble those of a chief of staff anywhere else, whether in the United States or the world. Nor did they even approximate those of a twentieth-century chief of staff of the Army. In his new post, Halleck found his primary role was to forward men and supplies for Grant to use. He also proved a useful conduit for back-channel communications between Lincoln and Grant. Halleck commanded nothing, nor did Grant turn to him for strategic advice. These days, Grant and Grant alone made the strategy. He did not even tell Lincoln what he had in mind, and the President said he preferred it that way. All that interested him was results.[8]

Officers in the Army of the Potomac expected Grant to give many of the most important assignments to people he already knew. Grant surprised them by offering combat assignments to only a few highly trusted subordinates from out west, such as Phil Sheridan, James H. Wilson and Baldy Smith. The existing corps and division commanders in the Army of the Potomac were left to continue with their commands. Meade, assuming that his presence would be an embarrassment to Grant, graciously offered his resignation at their first meeting. Grant just as graciously declined to accept it.[9]

Although when he first came east he had briefly considered putting Baldy Smith in command of the Army of the Potomac, Grant had decided not to go through with it even before he met Meade. There could have been no worse start for him with this army, which was immensely proud despite its failures, than to indicate the least lack of confidence in its fighting ability. Instead, Grant made improving its morale his first order of business. He was generous in his praise of officers and men alike and made few changes.[10]

One thing he did alter, though, was its cavalry operations. He put all its cavalry together for the first time. The result was a force of 12,500 horse soldiers, commanded by Sheridan. The natural mission of this newly created Cavalry Corps, in Sheridan's view and probably in Grant's as well, was to bring the rebel cavalry to battle and crush it. Until now the Army of the Potomac's cavalry arm had been wasted. What fighting it did was mainly against Confederate infantry. It was an even greater waste to use it to provide escorts for generals, carry messages, and ride picket duty to protect the infantry's camps, something Sheridan was determined to end.[11]

Grant intended to travel with the Army of the Potomac in its new campaign against Lee, giving general strategic direction and coordinating operations between it and the IX Corps but leaving the day-to-day running of the army to Meade. It was a strange, illogical arrangement rooted entirely in Grant's determination not to remain in Washington; his kid-glove handling of Burnside; and his decision not to relieve Meade. There was going to be a lot of improvising in an arrangement like this. But if Grant wasn't good at improvisation, he wasn't good at anything.

★

Lee's army was deployed along the south side of the Rapidan River, two corps strung out on a roughly east-west axis, with a third in reserve to the rear. The first question Grant had to decide was whether to try to get around Lee's right flank or his left. From a purely tactical point of view, the best line of attack was to go around the left flank. That would provide Grant with terrain suited to his cavalry and artillery and offer the chance of closing rapidly on Richmond. But being in open country, it would be hard to protect his immense wagon trains and if he tried to rely on the railroad, his army could easily get bogged down in guarding and rebuilding it rather than fighting the enemy.

The alternative, to go around the right flank, meant fighting in rough, densely wooded terrain, where there were no good roads and his cavalry and artillery would be useless. Yet he would be much closer to the point where Butler would land the Army of the James, his supply line would be shorter, it would be easier to protect his wagon trains, and he would be almost certain to pin Lee down.[12]

In the end, it was a question of how much confidence he really had in the Army of the Potomac—how good were its officers? how strong was its fighting spirit? This army had launched six offensives in its three-year history, and all six had been repulsed. The most recent advance had been in November 1863, when Meade crossed the Rapidan northeast of Richmond. He had soon been forced to halt, when he ran up against Confederate entrenchments along a stream called Mine Run. Once Meade halted, Lee had made a counterattack that ended with the Federals retreating back across the Rapidan.

There was also the Burnside question. From what he had seen of Burnside's defense of Knoxville, Grant had no confidence in Burnside at all. He was brave and patriotic and had some military ability, but his judgment was poor and it got even worse under pressure. He ordered Burnside's IX Corps to guard the trains—a huge force in itself, numbering 3,500 wagons, nearly 20,000 animals, and thousands of men. Grant's instructions to Burnside on how to do his job were so detailed they were comparable to the kind of orders he had formerly issued to McClernand.[13]

With Sherman, McPherson and a force of 120,000 western troops, Grant later told a friend, he would have turned Lee's left flank and risked everything on smashing Lee's army in the open field. With the Army of the Potomac, he had little real choice. He simply did not trust its senior officers enough. Grant ordered Meade to cross the Rapidan by way of three fords to the east of Lee's right flank.[14]

Just south of the fords there were only two halfway decent east-west roads. The one nearest the fords was the Orange Turnpike. The other, the Orange Plank Road, ran more or less parallel to the turnpike but was distant from it by a couple of miles most of the way before the two roads converged at Orange Court House, a crossroads within Lee's lines. Grant's plan was to have the army cross the Rapidan, get onto the Orange Turnpike and the Orange Plank Road, and turn west. He expected to push his troops quickly through the one hundred square miles of dense second-growth timber, known as the Wilderness, and have them emerge poised to strike Lee's right flank.

There was a major flaw in this plan: Grant did not have the army go far enough south before turning west to pin Lee. If anything went wrong, Grant could easily find himself fighting a battle in densely timbered terrain that was ideal for the Confederates, who would know it well, and sheer hell for Union troops, who had been comprehensively thrashed here once before, at Chancellorsville, in April 1863, when Stonewall Jackson had crashed through the woods, fallen on an exposed flank, and brought the Army of the Potomac to the brink of destruction.

Grant's plan now committed that same army to making a shallow envelopment when a deeper envelopment was not only feasible but preferable. He could have ordered the Cavalry Corps to ride south and seize the vital crossroads at Spotsylvania Court House, twelve miles south of the Rapidan. From there, he would have better roads from which to attack Lee, would be in a better position to link up with Butler's Army of the James, and would have the Wilderness well behind him. The cavalry force was strong enough to keep the Confederates at bay while the infantry marched down to Spotsylvania and the immense army trains, protected by Burnside's IX Corps, rocked and jolted their way through the Wilderness.

It is probable that Grant would have considered this possibility, or something much like it. But he handled the superbly equipped, magnificent looking Army of the Potomac with care. It was almost as if he felt he was teaching a spoiled, bad-tempered rich kid to walk.

★

The Army of the Potomac's wagon trains began moving out around midday on May 3, creating huge dust clouds that Confederate lookouts on Clark Mountain, twenty miles away, were certain to see.[15]

By nightfall nearly the entire army was in motion, heading for the Rapidan. At midnight Sheridan's cavalry seized the fords, and the leading infantry units were not far behind. With the three fords securely in his hands, Grant wired Halleck at 1:15 A.M. on May 4: "The crossing of the Rapidan effected. Forty eight hours now will demonstrate whether the enemy intends to give battle this side of Richmond." After talking for a while with some of his staff, he turned in for a few hours' sleep.[16]

He may not have been one for show, but whenever he set an army in motion Grant seemed to feel it was part of his duty to make a gesture. So, after breakfast on May 4, he mounted his magnificent bay, Cincinnati, and rode out at the head of his staff wearing his best frock coat, six large and glittering silver stars, a blue waistcoat, a pair of yellow cotton gloves, and a black felt hat with a golden cord; a blue-and-gold silk sash snaked around his waist and a sword jingled cheerfully at his side. After crossing the Rapidan, Grant stopped for lunch and from the porch of an abandoned farmhouse watched contentedly as regiment after regiment swung past in high spirits.[17]

After lunch, as Grant sat smoking and chatting with his staff, a reporter approached and asked how long it would take him to capture Richmond. Grant replied calmly, "I will agree to be there in about four days." The reporter's amazement was matched by the looks on the faces of Rawlins and the rest. Having gotten them nicely wound up, Grant said almost as an aside, "That is, if General Lee becomes party to the arrangement. But if he objects, the trip will undoubtedly be prolonged." That set them all laughing uproariously, at him and at themselves.[18]

Mid-afternoon saw virtually the entire army come to a gentle halt. There was a danger that if the slow-moving, heavily laden wagons fell too far behind the infantry, a gap would open up that the Confederates could plunge into, smashing and plundering the trains and forcing the entire army to retreat. The early halt was to allow the trains time to catch up with the infantry before night fell. It wasn't ideal, but there didn't seem to be much risk to advancing in this halting way. No one, least of all Meade or Grant, expected a quick, strong Confederate response.

When Meade had crossed the Rapidan back in November and been snagged on the entrenchments along Mine Run, it had taken Lee thirty hours to get there in force and launch his counterattack. The positions where the Army of the Potomac halted the afternoon of May 4 were close to Mine Run. On past performance, then, there seemed little chance of any Confederate riposte before the morning of May 6, by which time Meade's army would be virtually out of the Wilderness.[19]

Unfortunately, Lee was moving faster this time. Confederate troops were already moving east along the Orange Turnpike in force. That afternoon Grant received a report telling him of this development. He sent a message to Burnside, whose IX Corps was guarding the trains, telling him to move south quickly and march through the night.[20]

The army renewed its advance at first light on May 5. There was no change of plan, but during the night two Confederate divisions had moved down the Orange Turnpike and Lee was already shifting eastward Longstreet's corps, which had redeployed to Virginia from Tennessee a few weeks earlier, but he was not looking for a general engagement. At least, not yet. When he counterattacked, Lee intended to do so in strength. He did not want to feed his army piecemeal into a major fight, although that is exactly what happened.[21]

Around seven A.M. there were volleys of musketry on the turnpike as Confederate skirmishers collided with the advancing Federals. Grant had promoted James H. Wilson, the engineer officer who was devoted to Rawlins, to brigadier general and given him what he wanted most— command of a cavalry division. Wilson's division was leading the army's advance. It was expected to fulfill the traditional cavalry missions of screening its own army's advance from enemy scouts while pressing forward and uncovering enemy positions. Wilson did a masterly job of failing to do either.

Grant received a report at breakfast from Meade—"The enemy have appeared in force . . ." It was the infantry, not the cavalry, that had made first contact with the enemy. Meade went on to say that he had directed the commander of the V Corps, Gouverneur K. Warren, "to attack them at once with his whole force."[22]

Grant saw a chance here to seize the upper hand and promptly endorsed Meade's action. "If any opportunity presents itself for pitching into a part of Lee's Army," he informed Meade, "do so without giving [him] time for disposition."[23]

Warren's troops, however, were strung out along the road. It would take time to redeploy them so they could make an attack—time during which the Confederates got even more men down the turnpike. One of the great defects of the Army of the Potomac, as Grant was about to discover, was that only two of its four corps commanders, Winfield Scott Hancock and John Sedgwick, were capable of handling a corps command. Already well aware of Burnside's limitations, Grant was about to learn something about Warren, one of the heroes of Gettysburg.

Warren had graduated high in his West Point class of 1850 and been commissioned in the elite Corps of Topographical Engineers, the select band of Army officers who explored and surveyed much of the trans-Mississippi West. It was Warren, with his trained topo engineer's eye, who had spotted that Little Round Top was the key to the Union position at Gettysburg early in the fight and gotten an infantry brigade plus a battery of artillery up there just in time to prevent the Confederates from capturing it.[24]

This feat had brought him a corps, yet Warren had neither experience of handling infantry in close combat nor the habit of instantaneous obedience to orders from a superior. He was an intellectual and liked to think things over first, and maybe talk about them for a while. The hours passed while Grant fumed and smoked and Warren got his corps rearranged.

A Sheridan or a McPherson would have organized a reconnaissance in force to uncover the enemy's position and ascertain his strength while preparing to make their attack. This would not only give them a chance to seize the initiative but was likely to delay, if not halt, the enemy's forward movement. In the event, it was early afternoon before Warren was in position to make the attack ordered at breakfast. Even then, it wasn't Warren's troops who led the way but a division from John Sedgwick's VI Corps, which was coming up close behind Warren's.

The division commander, Brigadier Charles H. Griffin, was outraged when he discovered that Warren's tardiness had left his men with exposed flanks to left and right. He rode off to look for Meade and found him in a clearing in the woods talking to Grant, who was sitting on a tree stump, drawing heavily on a cigar. Griffin rode up to them, angry and voluble, damning Warren and demanding to know what Meade intended to do. Griffin's outburst only triggered off Rawlins, who began bawling to the skies that such intemperate language from a subordinate to a superior amounted to mutiny.

Grant turned to Meade, asking mildly, "Who is this General Gregg? You ought to arrest him." ·

"His name's Griffin, not Gregg," said Meade. "And that's only his way of talking."[25]

While Warren was trying to get his corps into action on the Orange Turnpike, fierce firefights were breaking out two miles farther south, along the Orange Plank Road. Wilson had bungled his mission again. He was still supposed to be leading the advance and probing for Confederates, but it was the infantry of Winfield Scott Hancock's II Corps who stumbled across Confederate divisions under A. P. Hill cutting the Orange Plank Road. Hancock instantly threw his corps into a ferocious attack.

Visibility in these woods was already limited and now, as gunfire erupted, dozens of little fires were started by sparks shooting from the barrels of rifled muskets. As smoke drifted between the trees, soldiers from both sides soon found themselves fighting in what amounted to a fog, groping blindly for each other's lines and becoming increasingly unsure of their own position. Being shot was bad enough; being burned to death was even worse.[26]

As fires began breaking out, thousands of Hancock's troops panicked and fled to the rear. Grant and Meade were standing side by side on a small rise, and as the men raced past them it looked as if Hancock's entire corps was about to fall apart. Grant said nothing, did not look the least bit worried. Here was a test not for him but for Meade, for Hancock, for the men themselves. Meade began running up and down, barking orders at his staff officers, his agitation all too evident. The orders he gave were coherent, but his body language was a dance of hysteria.[27]

Hancock's division, brigade and regimental commanders rallied their men. The line steadied. The crisis passed, but one of Grant's oldest friends, Alexander Hayes, a tall, distinguished-looking officer, was commanding one of Hancock's brigades. When his men began running away, Hayes rode to the front line and just as he got them back under control, a Confederate sharpshooter shot him dead. The news reached Grant shortly afterward. Now his composure cracked. He slumped to the ground, his back against a tree for support. He spoke haltingly, close to tears, to his aide Horace Porter. "Hayes and I were cadets together for three years," he said, an agonized pause slotted between every word. "We served for a time in the same regiment in the Mexican War. He was a noble man and a gallant officer. I am not surprised that he met his death at the head of his troops. It was just like him."[28]

Hancock's men began fighting stubbornly. Their blows grew stronger and by nightfall Hill's divisions were exhausted, their line was broken and ammunition was running low. The Army of the Potomac was close to smashing through in corps strength and rolling up the entire rebel line just as darkness fell and the sound of gunfire gradually died away.

Grant did not realize how close he had come to success. What he did know, from prisoner interrogations and intercepted messages, was that Lee was preparing to attack with all his available strength the next day. Grant's every instinct was to strike first. His best, maybe only, hope was to hit Lee hard while the Confederates were still maneuvering for position.

The Army of the Potomac launched its attack at five o'clock on the morning of May 6. The Federal line, reading from north to south, consisted of Sedgwick's VI Corps, Warren's V Corps, Burnside's IX Corps, just coming into the fight, and Hancock's II Corps. The line they formed faced west, more or less. The focal point of the renewed attack was Hancock's corps, which sought to snatch the victory that had only just eluded it the previous evening. Hancock piled into Hill, only to discover that Hill had been reinforced by the arrival of his third division during the night. And not far behind was Longstreet, with an entire corps of fresh Confederates.[29]

Longstreet got into the fight around mid-morning, just as the momentum of Hancock's renewed attack began to fade. He struck Hancock such a blow that he nearly crushed the II Corps's left flank. In the course of this action, however, Longstreet was seriously wounded and Hill, already in poor health, was too ill to think straight. By mid-afternoon the Confederate pressure eased and Hancock was able to consolidate his position.

There was little Grant could do at a time like this. In previous battles, his command style was urgent and direct. To Grant, a life fully lived was motion or emotion. His habit in battle was to swing himself into the saddle without a word, then ride off at top speed to where the fighting was hottest, leaving his staff to follow as best they could. He ignored roads. He improvised shortcuts, splashing through streams, darting among trees at a gallop, or riding across open ground in plain view of thousands of the enemy, like pure energy unleashed, an added measure, his physical presence, thrown into the scales of battle. Grant could stay in the saddle for eighteen hours a day, gathering up the threads of other men's actions and weaving them into a design all his own, exhausting his staff, not even pausing to eat.[30]

In the Wilderness, he had to bow to another command style. His place was in the stratosphere, a realm that was nearly all thought and little movement, days of talking, not galloping. He could no longer canter across the battlefield to watch the troops fight, have a hurried word with division commanders, organize ammunition trains, and improvise tactical moves. Whatever he did now he had to do it through Meade and operate through the headquarters of the Army of the Potomac.

So he sat and whittled furiously, smoked one cigar after another, tore threads from his fancy yellow gloves and tried to make sense of the sounds of fighting and the fragmentary reports brought to Meade by hard-riding couriers. Brigadier General Marsena Patrick, provost marshal of the Army of the Potomac and a cantankerous figure of Victorian rectitude, grumbled to his diary, "I do not see that Grant does anything but sit quietly about, whittle, smoke and let Genl. Rawlins talk Big."[31]

Lee, meanwhile, was not handling his side of the battle well. Late in the afternoon, Confederate divisions counterattacked Sedgwick's VI Corps, near the Orange Turnpike. Attacking the Union left several hours after the attack on the Union right had failed did not make much sense. The two attacks ought to have been made at the same time. For now, though, the battle rolled on.

Even so, the rebel onslaught took Sedgwick's troops by surprise. More than five hundred were taken prisoner, including two brigade commanders. A flustered officer from Sedgwick's staff came riding up to Meade's headquarters at dusk. General Sedgwick had been killed, he panted, and the VI Corps routed. Grant looked at him for a moment, removed the cigar from his mouth, and uttered a crushing reply: "I don't believe it."[32]

Meade shifted troops from Warren's corps to support Sedgwick, but a steady stream of officers continued arriving with bad news. One of them didn't seem to think Grant was taking the situation seriously enough and started telling him that the army was in the throes of a major crisis. "I know Lee's methods well by past experience," the officer said. "He will throw his whole army between us and the Rapidan, and cut us off completely from our communications."

Grant's patience snapped. "I am heartily tired of hearing about what *Lee* is going to do. Some of you always seem to think he is suddenly going to turn a double somersault and land in our rear and on both our flanks at the same time. Go back to your command and try to think what we are going to do ourselves, instead of what *Lee* is going to do!"[33]

By nightfall, the position along all four corps fronts had stabilized. Two days of fighting had cost the Union some fifteen thousand casualties. Confederate losses are likely to have been between eight and nine thousand men.[34]

Grant knew by now that he had failed to get past Lee's right flank, failed to seize the two east-west roads, and failed to avoid being drawn into a major battle in the Wilderness. He could not defeat Lee in these woods any more than Lee could eject him from them. He would have to find another place—a better place—to fight the Army of Northern Virginia.

According to Wilson, the tremendous strain of this hectic day was more than Grant could handle. His nerves shattered, Grant went into his tent, threw himself on his cot and broke down. Not that Wilson was there. He claimed he got this story from Rawlins. Wilson, however, almost surely invented this incident as part of his larger design to belittle Grant, and Grant biographer Bruce Catton wasn't sure what to make of it, so he buried it in his footnotes when he wrote his account of the battle of the Wilderness. Someone who *was* there, however, was Horace Porter. He went into the tent shortly after Grant and found him not sobbing but napping.[35]

It had been a terrible day, no doubt about that—nothing but one crisis after another. The fingers of the yellow gloves had been reduced to grubby and pathetic shreds. He had smoked twenty cigars, more than he had ever consumed in a single day before, and whittled God only knew how many small sticks to the size of matches. Yet to nearly everyone who saw him, he seemed unmoved by the flow of reports bringing news of disaster. "Grant smokes and whittles all the time and is the coolest man I ever saw," was how one officer described him in his diary that night.[36]

When Grant emerged from his tent following his nap, a fledgling reporter from the *New York Tribune,* Henry Wing, approached him. Wing said he would be leaving in the morning to take dispatches to Washington for his newspaper on how the recent fighting had gone. Did Grant have anything he would like to add?

"Well, yes," said Grant emphatically. "You may tell the people that things are going swimmingly down here."

Wing was incredulous, but took out his notebook and wrote down what Grant had said, expressed his thanks, and turned away, hardly able to credit his ears. Suddenly he realized Grant was walking behind him.

Once they were out of earshot of the officers clustered near Grant's tent, Grant put a hand on Wing's shoulder. "You expect to get through to Washington?" When Wing said that was exactly what he had in mind, Grant said quietly, so only Wing could hear, "Well, if you see the President, tell him from me that whatever happens, there will be no turning back." Grant shook Wing's hand and went back to his tent.[37]

The question he faced that night was not whether he would move on but where he would move to, and the few roads traversing this lightly populated area virtually dictated the answer. Early the next morning, Grant wrote a note to Meade: "Make all preparations during the day for a night march to take position at Spotsylvania C. H."[38]

★

May 7 turned out to be foggy and rainy, and the bulk of the army did not set off until evening. One of the problems Meade faced was that there was only one route south which would take large numbers of men, and that was the Brock Road. He would have to put virtually his entire army on it.

As the troops broke camp and marched onto the road, many— possibly most—expected they would be ordered to move by the right flank, which would mean they were heading north; that this was yet another failed offensive; that Lee had whipped Grant. Once they reached the Brock Road, however, Grant, seated on Cincinnati, was off to one side, watching them, and as their officers barked out the commands to move by the left flank, which would take them south, they realized this wasn't like the other offensives at all. This campaign had barely begun.

Their spirits soared and they cheered Grant, wave after wave of them, while he, chewing on a cigar, simply bowed, then turned to his staff officers and told them to go tell the regimental commanders to put a stop to this demonstration—it might alert the enemy that something important was happening. The statue of Grant that guards the Capitol, with water seeming to drip from his battered felt hat, commemorates this moment, that wet, cold night when the Army of the Potomac accepted Grant as its own.[39]

Meanwhile, Meade had done an appalling job of organizing the move to Spotsylvania. Lee's troops had to cross the Po River if they were going to head off the Union advance. Sheridan should have been ordered to send a cavalry force immediately to block, or destroy, the bridge across the Po. Instead, Meade ordered one cavalry division to head for Spotsylvania while another guarded the army's right flank. The bridge crossing the Po was left for Lee to use as he pleased.[40]

Sheridan assigned James H. Wilson's 3rd Cavalry Division to lead the army south, but Wilson's riders only managed to get tangled up with the infantry. For several hours the Brock Road was blocked by a congealed mass of footsloggers and horse soldiers screaming abuse at each other, neither willing to give way. An angry Meade sent an order to Sheridan, telling him to get the cavalry out of the way and let the infantry through, but the order never reached Sheridan. Precious hours were lost before traffic began moving smoothly down the Brock Road.

The Confederates were doing much better. For one thing, they had the advantage of operating on interior lines and in country they knew well. The Federals did not even have adequate maps. For another, there was a fire in the woods that night, which worked to the rebels' advantage.[41]

When Longstreet was wounded, his corps was given to Major General R. H. Anderson. Shortly after Grant ordered Meade to head for Spotsylvania, Lee told Anderson to do the same thing. Both sides set off at roughly the same time. The Federals took a few hours' rest around midnight, which was hardly the wisest way to begin a race. There was a general lack of urgency anyway to the Union advance. Once in motion, some Federal infantry units were shuffling along at a rate of half a mile an hour. Anderson planned to rest his men at some point along the line of march, but the woods he was passing through were smoldering, so he simply kept moving throughout the night of May 7 and reached Spotsylvania shortly after dawn on May 8.[42]

The leading Confederate regiments arrived just in time to beat off the advance of Wilson's cavalry. During the afternoon, the Union infantry arrived and hurriedly launched an attack, but as more Federals were arriving on one side of the line, so were more rebels appearing on the other.

Around the middle of the day Sheridan rode up to Meade's headquarters and got a tongue-lashing. Meade was a highly capable officer in his ability to manage a large military force. He was not a great combat commander, however, and was a choleric figure at the best of times. These were far from that. His nickname was "the Old Snapping Turtle," and his staff lived in dread of his explosive temper. When he took umbrage at a misleading account of the Army of the Potomac in a New York newspaper, he arrested the reporter who had written it and drummed him out of camp with a sign around his neck reading LIBELER OF THE PRESS. This was the kind of move guaranteed to put Meade in bad with journalists, who produce the first rough draft of what eventually becomes History. Meade's reputation has suffered ever since.[43]

And now, with reports coming in that the Confederates had won the race to Spotsylvania, he damned Sheridan up one side and down the other. Sheridan, whose aggressive streak was about as wide as the Mississippi and as deep as the Marianas trench, hit back. Once aroused—and it didn't take much—he was as emotionally volatile as Meade, and it mattered nothing to Sheridan that Meade outranked him by a long way. He blamed Meade for everything that had gone wrong, by hampering the cavalry's advance.

Sheridan concluded angrily, "I could whip Jeb Stuart"—Lee's renowned cavalry commander—"if you would only let me. But since you insist on giving the cavalry directions without even consulting or notifying me, you can command the Cavalry Corps yourself. I will not give it another order." He was quitting. Then he stormed out.[44]

Meade went and told Grant about it, probably expecting Grant to get Sheridan back under control and maybe even throw in a reprimand for blatant insubordination. Grant did not seem much interested in this contretemps between his two prima donnas. He seemed almost bored, until Meade repeated Sheridan's boast about defeating Stuart. "Did he really say that?" asked Grant. "Well, he usually knows what he's talking about. Let him go ahead and do it."[45]

By nightfall Sheridan was leading ten thousand riders on a circuitous route that took him to the outer suburbs of Richmond. A comparative handful of cavalry—roughly two thousand men—remained with the army. Sheridan not only made good on his boast of defeating the Confederate cavalry, but Stuart was killed. Even so, nothing that Sheridan accomplished on this ride deep into enemy territory and back was of any use to Grant as he sought to capture Spotsylvania and its crucial crossroads.

It isn't likely that Grant expected any major results from cutting Sheridan loose. It was obvious that Meade and Sheridan could not get along. Letting Sheridan try to make good on his boast was the quick fix to something that if left to fester was going to turn quickly into a showdown where one of them would have to be fired, and Grant did not intend to lose the services of either.

Next day, the Army of the Potomac advanced through woods that seemed to be crawling with Confederate snipers. One of those they shot dead was John Sedgwick, commander of the VI Corps and one of the most popular men in the entire army. With his round, red face, stocky frame, unassuming manner, and frayed straw hat, Sedgwick could easily have passed for a farmer rather than a career soldier with a West

Point background and a love of infantry fighting. "The loss of General Sedgwick," said Grant to his staff, "is as bad as losing an entire division of infantry."[46]

While Grant was making preparations for a major attack, the Confederates were digging in furiously, creating a line of entrenchments six miles long to the north and east of Spotsylvania, complete with abatis and artillery. Although the country here was more open than in the Wilderness, frontal assaults on entrenched positions almost anywhere were virtually guaranteed to take a heavy toll.

Even so, there were two weak points in Lee's hastily established position. When the Army of the Potomac made its attack on May 10, a Union infantry brigade on the extreme right of the line outflanked the Confederate left and established a bridgehead in Lee's rear. Grant, however, was not informed of this and the brigade, lacking support, was forced to withdraw later in the day by furious Confederate counterattacks.[47]

Meanwhile, around six P.M. a promising young colonel named Emory Upton organized twelve Union regiments to attack the other weak point in the Confederate line, a salient called the Mule Shoe, that stuck out incongruously from the left-center of Lee's defenses. The salient was cracked open by Upton's attack and more than a thousand Confederate prisoners were taken. Lee's entire line was in danger of breaking wide open, but Upton was forced to withdraw when night fell, for want of support on either flank. Grant took advantage of the powers recently given him by Congress to promote officers in the field and made Upton a brigadier general.[48]

The tragedy in all this was that the Army of the Potomac still had tremendous fighting spirit. That spirit was being wasted, thought Andrew A. Humphreys, Meade's highly competent chief of staff, because of the cumbersome command arrangement that gave it, in effect, two heads. Grant claimed he did not tell Meade how to run his army, but that was at best a half-truth. It would be more accurate to say that Grant tried not to tell Meade how to run his army and often failed. All of which was complicated by the anomalous status of Burnside and the IX Corps.[49]

There was no sense of there being clear, firm direction from the top. Instead, there was a built-in hesitation, like a heart that has an unpleasant habit of skipping a beat. The result was seen in attacks launched too late to capitalize on success; in the abundance of debate; in the dearth of initiative. Grant's staff told him plainly that the only solution was to get rid of Meade. Grant would not consider it. Instead, he kept Meade but increasingly took control of Meade's army.[50]

No attacks were launched on May 11. Grant wrote to Stanton, bringing him up-to-date on the fighting of the past six days. Sitting on a tree stump, puffing so fiercely on a cigar that his head seemed almost to vanish in a cloud of smoke, he also wrote a letter to Halleck. "I am now sending back to Belle Plaines all my wagons for a fresh supply of provisions, and Ammunition, and propose to fight it out on this line if it takes me all summer." There was something wrong there. It sounded too personal somehow, too much like boasting. Grant drew a neat straight line through "me."[51]

Next day, May 12, he attacked Lee's lines again, concentrating on the Mule Shoe. While Union soldiers battled their way into the salient, Lee was digging a line of entrenchments across its base. The Federals got the salient, but the enemy got a shorter, more easily defended position.

Having failed to crack Lee's center, Grant decided to try turning his right. He was delayed five days by torrential rains, but on May 18 he attacked again. The assaulting troops soon discovered that Lee's position was not only well entrenched but strongly supported by twenty pieces of artillery. The attack, launched at dawn, was called off in midmorning. Grant finally gave up on Spotsylvania.[52]

Late at night on May 20 the Army of the Potomac pulled out but, still moving south, finally headed for a linkup with Ben Butler's Army of the James.

──── ★ ★ ★ ★ ────

CHAPTER 23

"WILLING TO RUN THE RISK OF DEFEAT"

The essential Grant lived between the cigar and the ears. At this stage of his life, in the spring of 1864, he was thinking tenaciously. It wasn't enough simply to hold on and try to grind down Bobby Lee. Allowing Lee to pull back into the trenches around Richmond and to turn the campaign into a protracted siege might only add to war weariness in the North and weaken Lincoln's chances of re-election in November. Like a virtuoso musician, Grant was doing several things at once: He was trying to keep Lee out of those trenches, turn Lee's right flank, and place himself between Lee's army and Richmond—all the while keeping Lee pinned down so that even if the turning movement failed, Lee would not be able to pull most of his army out, head north, and threaten Washington, forcing Grant to withdraw hastily and defend the capital.

Every time Lee succeeded in preventing Grant from getting between his army and Richmond, it became less likely that Grant would ever be able to crush him in a head-on clash of arms. And by fighting on the defensive and mounting little more than raids and counterattacks, Lee had also come close to wiping out Grant's numerical advantage. Besides, the apparent two-to-one margin of manpower superiority that Grant possessed was something of an illusion. So much of his army was engaged in guarding his lines of communication, occupying conquered territory, and handling his supplies that up front, where the fighting took place, he barely outnumbered the Confederates.

Grant's biggest advantages were not greater manpower or matériel but superior firepower and greater mobility. It was for him to turn these into the instruments of victory. That was what he was thinking about as he whittled and smoked or seemed to stare vacantly into space while slumped in a folding chair next to his tent.

The thirty-five hundred wagons, the fleet of steamers and gunboats, the tens of thousands of modern repeating arms, and the thousands of well-mounted cavalry under his command were what, in a later day, would be known as force multipliers. That is, if used properly, they could make up for the fact that Grant did not have the three-to-one advantage in frontline manpower needed to crash through the defenses of a well-entrenched foe. Superiority in firepower and mobility might make his infantry as effective as if they really did have greatly superior numbers. He possessed advantages that would allow him to strike at Lee's flanks, rear and logistics. That was how he would ultimately prevail over someone as capable as Lee, who not only had fixed defenses to retreat into, but also had the benefit of interior lines, knowledge of the ground, and a local population eager to aid the Confederacy and harass the invaders.

Between receiving his commission as lieutenant general and mid-June 1864, Grant figured out how to do it. In those three months he evolved the future of the United States Army, even though that was not what he was attempting to do. Nonetheless, that is the untold story at the heart of his Virginia campaign, the story that makes sense of what otherwise looks like a sequence of horrifyingly bloody battles, heartbreaking disappointments, desperate improvisation, high-command failures and ultimate success.

It began with Grant's strategic vision before he crossed the Rapidan, of five converging columns putting pressure on the Confederacy. Sherman's army would move across Georgia, Franz Sigel's army would advance into the Shenandoah, Nathaniel Banks's army was under orders to head for Mobile, the newly created Army of the James under Ben Butler was going to land somewhere south of Richmond, while the Army of the Potomac crossed the Rapidan and descended on the rebel capital from the north.

Grant's strategy of converging columns did not require all five of them to succeed. The design was sound enough that it would work even if some columns failed. After the war, converging columns were used—on a much smaller scale—to crush the Sioux. They were employed again in the Philippine Insurrection, in World Wars I and II, and in Korea.

Grant did not invent the idea of converging columns, or pincer movements as they are sometimes called. What he did was to reinvent them to suit American needs and capabilities. In doing so, he intended to give the two most important elements in the U.S. Army's way of making war—maximum firepower, maximum mobility—the central role that they deserved. He did this at a time when soldiers on both sides entrenched rapidly, skillfully and almost enthusiastically. In the spring of 1864 the Civil War seemed poised to descend into a struggle of sieges and trenches, of spades rather than rifles. Grant, however, never really stopped moving. It wasn't in him to do so.

The strategy of converging columns merged with what is sometimes known as grand tactics—the tactics, that is, not of a division or a corps but of an army or an army group. At this level, Grant relied on the wide envelopment, a movement in which one part of a commander's force moves forward to pin the enemy in place while the rest of his force maneuvers to attack a flank or get into the rear. He had attempted to envelope Lee's right in the Wilderness and failed. He tried again at Spotsylvania and failed again. Before the war ended, however, his approach to grand tactics would eventually triumph.

The intellectual pattern that Grant wove into the fabric of the American military tradition wasn't Napoleonic, even though it contains Napoleonic elements. It wasn't Clausewitzian, although it embraces Clausewitz's premise that only the offensive is decisive in war. It was, more than anything else, an expression of a singularly restless spirit, a spirit that since childhood had sought movement, drama, adventure. The result in maturity was a commander fighting battle after battle in a relentlessly aggressive campaign, forever wreathed in cigar smoke, puffing deeply on optimism and opportunism, trying and failing, trying and succeeding, and—consciously or not—sending a message.

A generation after the Civil War ended, the Army took possession of that message. It did so not only by studying the headache-inducing old maps and reading the one hundred thousand pages of documents embalmed in the *Official Records,* but also by taking over many of the battlefields and using them as outdoor classrooms. That is why Shiloh, Donelson, Petersburg, and others survive to this day instead of being buried under housing developments called Grant Condo Towers or Rebel Retreat. Grant's clear, easily grasped strategy and tactics are still there, embedded in his battlefields as eternally as the rocks that trip up the unwary tourist on a hot summer's day.

When the Command and General Staff School was created at Fort Leavenworth following World War I, its students—all of them potential corps and army commanders—learned only one grand tactic: the wide envelopment. What's more, it is with us still. The wide envelopment was the army-level tactic used with devastating effect by American ground troops in the Gulf War of 1991. Two strongly supported Allied divisions advanced to apply pressure on Kuwait, thus pinning the Iraqis in place, while Allied armor and infantry divisions swung wide around Kuwait, advancing through the desert to strike the Iraqi Army in the rear.

The small-unit version of the wide envelopment is known as the holding attack. It became the only tactic taught at the Infantry School after George C. Marshall took control there in the late 1920s. What both the Infantry School and the Command and General Staff School sought was a realization of Grant's vision, which called for a systematic approach—from strategy, at the highest level, to tactics, at the lowest level—so coherent and so simple that even an army of half-trained amateurs could soon learn to fight effectively. Like all truly imaginative and creative people, Grant was both a man of his time and at least one generation ahead of it.

This simple but powerful strategy, these simple but effective tactics, the whole geared to an army rich in firepower and mobility, are the context of Grant's Virginia campaign. But they offer something else, too—a window on an unusual mind. As windows go, this one is admittedly obscured by clouds of black powder smoke; obscured, too, by the enduring powers of folk memory, nagging us into a distracting acknowledgment of terrible scenes in which young men, most of them decent and idealistic, did appalling things to one another and suffered for it with wounds and deaths worse than anything inflicted on our most appalling criminals. Up close, though, that window shows something of Grant at his best, Grant as man thinking.

★

Ben Butler and Baldy Smith were the most wildly mismatched prima donnas of the Civil War, a Dickensian odd couple, too busy trying to get rid of each other to have much left over for fighting the enemy. At forty-six, Butler looked like a weary walrus, with a large and sad-looking mustache and beady, crossed eyes that were almost lost within fleshy, heavily creased pouches. Bald on top, he compensated by wearing his hair long at the back. It fell in oily curls over his collar.

A man not much above medium height, Butler wedged his two-hundred-pound bulk into a uniform that seemed several sizes too small. He thereby gained all the sartorial grace of a man wearing a straitjacket while making it perfectly plain that he was seriously overweight. Butler's eccentricities included wearing white denim slippers instead of boots, and he thought nothing of putting cavalry spurs on the slippers. Well read and highly intelligent, he relaxed with midnight horseback rides, reciting poetry to the moon and stars.

After failing to get into West Point, the young Butler had attended an obscure Baptist college in Maine. On graduation he took up the practice of law, but the soldiering itch was still there and he got a commission in the Massachusetts militia and swiftly rose to the rank of colonel. His law practice, combined with successful investments, made Butler one of the richest men in New England. He married a well-known actress and lived in a mansion. All the same, he enthusiastically defended the interests of the mill workers of the Merrimack valley against their often rapacious employers. Butler's standing among ordinary people in his district provided him with an unassailable political base when he ran for Congress, but when he ran for governor, the mill owners got their revenge.[1]

Days after Fort Sumter was fired on, Butler raised a regiment and moved it to Washington ahead of all other volunteer units vying for that honor. Lincoln was so thrilled, and relieved, that he made Butler the first major general of volunteers in the Union Army. His seniority thereafter made it impossible to overlook Butler, not that Lincoln ever tried. As a pro-black, antislavery War Democrat, Butler was the kind of opposition politician whose support was crucial in allowing Lincoln, with only 40 percent of the electorate behind him, to prosecute the war.

Butler had been sent to handle the occupation of New Orleans following its capture in April 1862. His order that southern women who showed disrespect to Federal soldiers be treated by the law as common prostitutes outraged southern opinion. For many years thereafter, southerners of both sexes lowered themselves onto chamber pots lovingly hand-painted with the hated cross-eyed features of "Beast" Butler.[2]

Itching for a combat role, "Old Cockeye" was recalled from New Orleans and given command of the Department of Virginia and North Carolina. It was Grant's task to try and make use of him in the upcoming campaign. On April 1 Grant went to see Butler at his headquarters in Fortress Monroe and spent two days talking to the only man in uniform who looked more unmilitary than himself. Afterward, Grant dropped heavy hints that he was favorably impressed, but it would have been a mistake to do anything else.[3]

What he really thought can be inferred from what happened next: Grant sent him Baldy Smith. The significance of this is that Grant had recently had Smith promoted to major general and called him "one of our best generals." He even thought of replacing Meade with Smith in command of the Army of the Potomac.[4]

Convinced, then, that Smith was a superb combat commander, whatever his personality defects, Grant had sent him to Butler. What he did not foresee was that the volatile elements in Butler would become combustible when brought into contact with the neurotic and erratic Smith.

Grant still believed that Smith had masterminded the plan for breaking the siege of Chattanooga. He may have been impressed, too, by the fact that Smith had graduated near the top of his West Point class and been commissioned an engineer. Although still in his mid-thirties, Smith already looked middle-aged, thanks to the spreading bald spot on the back of his head and the fact that in a search for gravitas he had chosen to emulate the waxed mustache and small pointed beard of Napoleon III. To anyone with a grain of sense it was obvious that Napoleon III, the comic-opera emperor of France and nephew of Napoleon Bonaparte, was a hollow man. It was hardly a secret by 1864 that Napoleon III was a charlatan and a fool. In his misguided yearning to look important, Smith had chosen to ape a strutting buffoon.[5]

As if sending Smith to Butler were not enough, Grant also sent him another West Pointer, Brigadier General Quincy Gillmore. Smith and Gillmore commanded the two infantry corps that comprised the Army of the James's combat elements. The idea was that the two professionals would fight the battles, leaving Butler to handle the headquarters paperwork. He was, by all accounts, a brilliant administrator. The trouble with Grant's plan was that Butler would not take a backseat, Smith would not fight, and Gillmore was barely capable of handling a regiment, still less a corps.

Grant ordered Butler to put the Army of the James into motion on May 4, the same day that the Army of the Potomac crossed the Rapidan. The principal point Grant made in these instructions was that the Army of the Potomac and the Army of the James would act in concert. When Meade and the Army of the Potomac advanced into the Wilderness, Butler and the Army of the James were to proceed up the James River. Exactly how the operations of the two armies would develop was impossible to say at this point, but what was being set up here was a wide envelopment in the making—one army would pin Lee down while the other maneuvered against him, probably by advancing on Richmond. It hardly mattered which army did the pinning and which the maneuvering as long as they operated in concert.

"Take City Point," Grant wrote to Butler. "Fortify, or rather intrench [*sic*], at once. . . . From City Point directions cannot be given at this time for further movements [but] Richmond is to be your objective point . . . the minor details of your advance are left entirely to your direction." Shortly after this Grant sent a supplementary instruction, telling Butler to "secure a footing as far up the south side of the river as you can."[6]

At first light on May 5 a huge fleet of steamers set out from Fortress Monroe behind five ironclad gunboats. When Butler reached City Point at three P.M., he allowed a black regiment the honor of going ashore first, followed by the rest of his army. He ignored Grant's orders to move as far up the James as possible *and* take City Point. As it went ashore the thirty-thousand-man-strong Army of the James found itself facing nothing beyond a few curious and surprised Confederates, who soon took to their heels.

Instead of placing his army on the south side of the James, Butler chose to put most of it on the north side, within a loop called Bermuda Hundred. This piece of land had one military merit: its base was only five miles wide, which would make it easy to defend. Butler's army spent six days digging five miles of trenches on the north side of the river, while also entrenching furiously around City Point.[7]

He pushed a raiding party west to tear up a stretch of nearby railroad line but, beyond that, seemed oblivious to the fact that he was conducting an offensive operation, and with a timid figure like Smith at his elbow, he wasn't likely to be reminded. Nor was Gillmore any better. When Butler ordered Gillmore to make a demonstration to keep any potential rebel force in the vicinity distracted, Gillmore, convinced there was no point in making a demonstration, simply ignored him. Butler promptly retaliated by urging Congress to reject Gillmore's impending promotion to major general.[8]

Had Butler done as Grant ordered and advanced past City Point he would have made a startling discovery: Grant was pressing Lee so hard that the crucial railhead city of Petersburg was virtually undefended. There was no more important railroad junction in the entire Confederacy. Every line but one that provided Richmond with food and Lee with reinforcements ran through Petersburg.

Butler, however, was too busy digging to bother with a reconnaissance in force. He proudly reported to Stanton (completely bypassing Grant): "We have landed here, intrenched [sic] ourselves . . . and got a position which, with proper supplies, we can hold against the whole of Lee's army." Butler was proving to be as timid and cautious as Buell or Rosecrans.[9] This, of course, made a mockery of the fact that Grant had told him in half a dozen ways that his role was an offensive one. Even allowing for the fact that he had been told to entrench, two days would have sufficed for his purposes.

Nevertheless, Lee was taking alarm at the threat the thirty-thousand-man Army of the James posed to his rear. He faced a stark choice: He could either push most of the twenty thousand Confederate troops currently south of the James into Petersburg, or he could bring them up to Drewry's Bluff, the high ground between Richmond and Bermuda Hundred, to block any northward movement by Butler. He lacked the manpower to do both. Lee gambled and brought fifteen thousand men north to hold Drewry's Bluff. Petersburg remained wide open to attack.

In the next act in this comedy of blunders, Butler recalled that he had been told by Grant that Richmond was "your main objective point" and got Smith and Gillmore moving north. He still had not probed the miles of almost empty trenches to the west, around Petersburg. Under the inert leadership of Smith and Gillmore, the troops moved as if in a trance. It was three miles from Bermuda Hundred to Drewry's Bluff, yet it took three days to get there. Even allowing for the fact that the weather was stormy and the roads ankle-deep in mud, this was inexcusably slow.

The Federals brushed the Confederate pickets aside and got onto the bluff. Smith, whose corps was posted on the right, cleverly rounded up telegraph wire. He may have been overrated, but he wasn't a complete fool. Stringing the wire between tree stumps, he protected his left flank against a possible Confederate attack. This was probably the first-ever military use of wire to strengthen a defensive position.[10]

The morning of May 16 dawned foggy. Unable to see more than thirty feet in front of him, Smith took fright that his artillery might be captured and ordered it sent to the rear. It got there just as the fog thinned out and the Confederates charged Smith's position. Hundreds of Confederates piled up in a heap when they hit the wire, got tangled in it and accidentally bayoneted one another as they fell. Nonetheless, Smith was alarmed at the pressure developing on his left, fearing it might be overrun now that he lacked artillery support. Instead of calling the artillery back, he ordered a withdrawal.[11]

The entire Federal position collapsed as Smith's units pulled out. Butler had little option but to order a return to the shelter of Bermuda Hundred. The troops covered the distance this time in three hours, not three days. They were followed by jubilant Confederates, commanded by P.G.T. Beauregard. They proceeded to dig their own line of entrenchments facing the five miles of fresh Union earthworks. Butler's army was, as Grant cuttingly observed, "shut off from further operations directly against Richmond as if it had been in a bottle strongly corked."[12]

★

The Army of the Potomac pulled out from Spotsylvania on May 20, heading south for a linkup at some point with the Army of the James. Following the Drewry's Bluff fiasco, Grant knew there was something wrong with the Army of the James, but he wasn't sure just who was to blame. If it was Butler, there was little he could do about getting rid of him. Or was it Smith, who, he told Halleck, "is obstinate and likely to condemn whatever is not suggested by himself"?[13]

Meanwhile Grant, Meade and the Army of the Potomac were moving south. Along the way, Grant finally put a stop to the nonsensical arrangement that had the IX Corps under Burnside acting independently and simply folded it into the Army of the Potomac. He may have expected some kind of protest from Burnside, in which case Burnside would have to go—a development that would not cause Grant any grief. Burnside, however, not only did not protest. He said he applauded the move and patriotically declared his willingness to waive his seniority at any time for the good of the cause.[14]

As he moved on from Spotsylvania, Grant tried to lure Lee into fighting a pitched battle. He had Hancock's II Corps lag behind, to encourage Lee into mounting an attack on it. Grant was betting that he would be able to rush back and join the fight before Hancock's force was destroyed.[15]

Lee made exactly the same calculation, and instead of aiming at the rear of the long blue columns snaking over the open, gently undulating landscape of east-central Virginia, he urged his commanders to get in front of it before Grant could deploy along the North Anna River. If Grant reached the river first, he might be able even now to get around Lee's right flank, something he had been trying to do since crossing the Rapidan.

The Confederates, having a shorter distance to travel, again won the race. When the Army of the Potomac reached the North Anna, Grant found thousands of butternuts already there. Both sides sparred for a couple of days before he pulled out yet again. His confidence was so great, however, that he had the army cross the river right in front of the Confederates. For a time, part of Meade's command was north of the river and the rest south of it, yet Lee did not dare mount a general attack against either portion. His strategy by this time consisted of talking offensive moves while fighting ever more defensively. Grant, like Napoleon and every great general in history, knew one thing if he knew nothing else—an army that fights entirely on the defensive is doomed. Lee would have known that too. On May 26, when Grant resumed his southward advance, he sent a long report to Halleck. He concluded confidently, almost triumphantly, "I may be mistaken, but I feel our success over Lee's army is already insured."[16]

He had not given up hopes yet of getting between Lee and Richmond. Nor had Grant any intention of allowing twenty thousand men to remain bottled up in Bermuda Hundred. He ordered Smith to bring his corps north, using the vast steamer fleet at Grant's disposal. On May 30 Smith disembarked at Grant's new base, White House, on the Pamunkey River, with sixteen thousand men. White House was twenty-five miles due east of Richmond. Grant was now nearly as close to the Confederate capital as Lee.

Sheridan's cavalry led the advance toward Richmond and on May 31 was attacked by five thousand Confederates near a crossroads enigmatically named Cold Harbor. No one really knew what the name meant, but there was something memorable and strange in a name like that, and what happened during the next few days would make it historic, too.

Meade ordered Sheridan to hold on. The cavalry dismounted and, with their repeating rifles and the support of horse artillery, they kept the Confederates at bay long enough for infantry to come to their support. By the afternoon of June 1 Meade had nearly half his army in action at Cold Harbor with the rest hurrying toward it. When night fell, both sides were digging in.[17]

Meade was convinced that once he got the rest of his troops to Cold Harbor and was reinforced by Smith's sixteen thousand men, he would be able to break the Confederate lines. A breakthrough here would open a road straight to Richmond, barely twenty miles away. Grant might yet get between Lee and the city. He ordered an all-out attack for the morning of June 2.

The weather the past week had been stifling, even at night. Many of the troops who had been force-marched to Cold Harbor were exhausted. Smith's men had been particularly unlucky. The orders they received had set them marching in the wrong direction. By the time they had countermarched and been put on the right road, they were worn-out. Grant postponed the attack until four P.M. to give the troops some rest, but they were so weary even this didn't seem enough. He postponed the assault again, this time until dawn on June 3.[18]

The twenty-four-hour delay enabled Lee to get his army into position, with his left flank secured by a river and his right by a creek six miles away. Throughout June 2 the Confederates entrenched energetically, digging down about four feet in the scrub-pine woods, then fashioning log parapets from hurriedly felled trees along the top of the trenches. Lee's army numbered sixty thousand men, of whom roughly half could be put into frontline positions. This meant he would have at least three rifles to defend every yard.

Meade, meanwhile, prepared the Army of the Potomac for the attack. Or rather, he failed to prepare it. Grant ordered that every corps commander have a reconnaissance made of the portion of the enemy line in front of him. Not one of them did so. When the Union divisions advanced, their commanders would have little idea of what they were moving toward. Many soldiers, however, had a grim premonition. They sewed labels on their coats, giving instructions on where to send their bodies.[19]

Grant chose to let Meade handle this battle, something Meade later boasted about to his wife. Unfortunately, it was at times like this that Meade showed his limitations as a combat commander. He had not formulated a general plan but allowed each corps commander to make his own. Only strong columns well supported by artillery had any chance of breaking through if the enemy proved to be well dug in. But there were no assault columns. The attack would be made almost entirely by men advancing in line—the simplest formation but the one with the least chance of success. Nor was a strong reserve force established to exploit a breakthrough should one occur. These were matters for an army commander to attend to, and Meade simply failed to do his job. If Grant wanted a plan, Meade grumbled to an astonished Baldy Smith, let Grant provide one.[20]

The attack was launched at dawn. Union regiments advancing behind huge battle flags had barely picked up the cadence of the tunes pumped out by their bands before a louder music ripped from the Confederate trenches. Tens of thousands of tongues of flame, each like a deadly finger marking someone for death, pointed straight at the oncoming dark blue line and a shroud of acrid smoke reached out to embrace it. Those in the first wave fell in heaps, sending ripples through the ranks behind. Confederate rifles and artillery picked away relentlessly at the growing piles of fallen men, shaking and rocking them as if stirring bundles of rags with long, invisible sticks. Thousands fell dead or crippled in the first half-hour.

Meade, who had decided to command in person, was perplexed. For a brief moment, one Union division managed to penetrate the Confederate line, but there was no force on hand to support it. And elsewhere the attack had been halted in its tracks. He sent a message to Grant. "I should be very glad of your views as to the continuance of these efforts, if unsuccessful." Meade seems to have been trying to cover himself, shrinking from the responsibility of either ordering a new attack or calling off the present one. But in all probability he really did not know what to do.[21]

There was an inability to think clearly or act resolutely under pressure that made it impossible for Meade to be a truly successful combat commander. He had never handled a company or a regiment, and his understanding of infantry fighting and leadership was no better than that of most engineers. Grant's reply—"The moment it becomes certain that an assault cannot succeed, suspend the offensive, but when one does succeed push it vigorously . . ."—was the kind of advice that could be found in any textbook on tactics. The fact that in the middle of a major battle Grant had to try to educate Meade on something every infantry captain in the regular Army knew as well as his name almost defies belief. Shortly after scribbling this note, Grant set off from his place in the rear to go steady Meade.[22]

On receiving Grant's message, Meade had ordered that the attack be relaunched, but this time Smith refused to send his corps forward. Elsewhere many a Union soldier, seeing how hopeless it was, simply hugged the ground, not moving, not fighting, simply waiting for somebody to call this grisly farce to its inevitable halt. Grant, riding from one corps commander to another, didn't take long to see how futile it was. He wrote out a brief message to Meade, telling him to call the attack off and dig in.[23]

Grant returned to his tent, dismounted, and sat on a stone marker beside the road, head down, features drawn. Julia's cousin William W. Smith had been sharing the tent with him the past few days and came up to Grant. "What is the situation?" asked Smith.

"Bad," sighed Grant. "Very bad." Then he wrote out a brief report to Halleck. He made the Cold Harbor battle seem almost trivial: "Our loss was not severe . . ." Halleck would never have guessed that some seven thousand Union soldiers had been killed or wounded, as against only fifteen hundred Confederates.[24]

Cold Harbor haunted Grant. "I regret this assault more than any I have ever ordered," he told his staff that night. And when he came to write his memoirs, it returned to haunt him once more: "I have always regretted that the last assault at Cold Harbor was ever made," he wrote apologetically.[25]

The first assault was a different matter. When it was launched, he believed—and had reason to believe—there was a reasonable chance of success. Grant had not known that Meade had failed to make a proper plan or that the corps commanders had failed to reconnoiter the Confederate position. Had he been informed of these failures, Grant might well have canceled the assault. But he did not wring his hands over that. What he did not forgive himself for was failing to order Meade to desist the moment he received Meade's message, for it was obvious in retrospect what the message really meant—that the attack was in trouble and Meade hadn't a clue about what to do next.

After Cold Harbor, he was an easy target for those who called him "Butcher Grant." Lee was more reckless with men's lives, yet got away with it. The list of costly, doomed frontal assaults in Lee's career is remarkably long, but he was not known as "Butcher Lee." Pickett's hopeless charge at Gettysburg, for example, was a pointless, bloodily repulsed attack twice as costly as Grant's failure at Cold Harbor.[26]

The criticism bothered Grant for the rest of his life. "They call me a butcher," he said to an old friend one day after the war. "But do you know, I sometimes could hardly bring myself to give an order for battle. When I contemplated the death and misery that were sure to follow, I stood appalled."[27]

There were hundreds of wounded men between the lines when the battle ended. Grant proposed to Lee that each side should allow the other to come out and collect its wounded. There was a traditional, bureacratic and time-consuming ritual called "the flag of truce" for bringing in wounded men. It was exactly the kind of military antique Grant ordinarily had no time for, but if he thought Lee, whom he respected, was as progressive as himself, he had misjudged his man. Lee bridled at Grant's suggestion. Cold Harbor or no Cold Harbor, Lee by this time probably realized he was going to end up on the losing side and sought consolation in winning a debating point. Had their positions been reversed, and Lee asked Grant to waive formalities to speed up aid for the wounded, Grant would almost certainly have obliged him.

With Lee refusing to budge, however, Grant was forced to do it Lee's way and organize a flag of truce. In the meantime, the hundreds of helpless men between the lines, already suffering from their wounds, had to endure 100-degree temperatures and torturing thirst. When stretcher parties were finally allowed to go forward, there were only two men left alive. The rest had perished to gratify Lee's flag-of-truce obsession.[28]

★

The Army of the Potomac had neither turned Lee's right flank nor brought the Army of Northern Virginia out into the open and crushed it in a battle of annihilation. The only part of Grant's design to work so far was keeping Lee gripped so tightly that he lost the strategic initiative and could not move north to threaten Washington. Butler's Army of the James had also failed. It had not advanced on Richmond, nor had it moved into Petersburg.

From the beginning of the campaign, however, Grant intended to have the Army of the James move against Lee's supply lines running south of Richmond. The two questions that hadn't been decided were just how Meade's command and Butler's would coordinate their operations, and exactly how close to Richmond Butler would move to cut the railroads.

Following Butler's withdrawal from Drewry's Bluff and Meade's blundering assault at Cold Harbor, Grant decided to form a junction of the two armies by putting both of them south of the James and to cut the railroad lines by seizing Petersburg. Richmond and Lee depended completely on the railroad links with the rest of the South. Grant hoped as strongly as he had ever hoped for anything that once there were Union troops athwart his railroad lines, Lee would choose to fight a climactic battle rather than retreating into his trenches and pointlessly dragging out the war. A winter siege would exact a terrible toll in deaths from disease. On June 9, with these prospects teeming in his mind, Grant wrote to his congressional patron, Elihu B. Washburne. "All the fight except defensive and behind breast works is taken out of Lee's army. Unless my next move brings on a battle the balance of the campaign will settle down to a siege."[29]

First, however, he would have to disengage. Not easy, seeing that Union and rebel trenches were only forty to fifty yards apart in some places. Even so, on the night of June 12 the Army of the Potomac crept away from Cold Harbor. By dawn next day it was moving south in one of the most daring strategic moves in American history. When Lee's patrols reported the empty trenches, Lee was mystified. Had Grant and Meade given up and retreated to Washington? Or had they gone south, to lure him into a hasty move in pursuit, which might allow them to double back and get into his rear?[30]

While Lee wrestled with these questions the Army of the Potomac was hurrying south, crossing the Chickahominy River, eight miles from Cold Harbor. Once across, Meade's soldiers pushed onward another twenty-five miles, until they reached the wide, unfordable James River. At its narrowest, ten miles east of City Point, the James was seven hundred yards wide and eighty feet deep. It had a tidal range of four feet, and no one knew whether a twenty-one-hundred-foot pontoon bridge could ride out that kind of buckling rise and fall. No army had ever built a pontoon bridge more than a thousand feet long.

There was another danger—the Confederate flotilla at Richmond. This force included three ironclads with long-range, heavy-caliber guns. They could shell the steamers that carried the infantry across and send fireships downstream to wreck the pontoon bridge on which the rest of the army—its cavalry, its artillery, its thousands of supply wagons, and close to four thousand beef cattle—crossed the James. For two days and one night the Army of the Potomac would be wide open to a devastating attack during the most difficult operation in ground warfare, an opposed river crossing.

Nor could Grant count on the Union Navy tipping the scales. Although Union sailors dominated the eastern seaboard, they did not control the James River much beyond the tidal estuary, because their most powerful vessels, the heavy, slow and low freeboard monitors, had trouble navigating the sharp bends and treacherous currents.[31]

A few days earlier Lee had a hunch about what Grant might do and remarked to Jubal Early, commander of his II Corps, "We must destroy this army of Grant's before he gets to the James River. If he gets there it will become a siege, and then it will be a mere question of time."[32] Lee now had the chance of a lifetime, if he had the nerve to act on that hunch. The destruction of the Army of the Potomac at this stage of the war, when recruits were few and the deeply unpopular draft was about to go into force, would have been profound. It would probably have brought Lincoln's defeat that fall and assured the survival, in some form, of the Confederacy.

All Lee had to do was penetrate the thin cavalry screen deployed between the Chickahominy and the James to confirm Meade's movement south, wait until roughly two-thirds of the Army of the Potomac was across the James, summon the Confederate Navy to wreck the bridge and the ferries with long-range gunfire and fireships, then attack the surprised, and almost certainly demoralized, Federals stranded without hope of rescue on the northern shore of the river.

The Union force that had reached the southern bank would then find itself trapped around City Point, with much of its artillery and cavalry now at the bottom of the James. Its evacuation by sea would be almost inevitable and virtually certain to unleash a political crisis that would threaten to overwhelm the government. Grant's shift to the James gave the South the chance to redeem every failure, every defeat and every setback since the death of Albert Sidney Johnston at Shiloh two years before.

The chance of the move to the James ending in failure was high. No one in the history of war had ever moved a force of 115,000 men up to fifty miles in three days, crossed two rivers deep in enemy territory, and built a pontoon bridge more than two thousand feet long virtually under the guns of a hostile naval force. Grant, however, had a gambler's soul. He was willing to risk everything on a single throw. His cousin-in-law William Smith wasn't surprised. "He loved to gamble. He loved risks— chances—he liked to bet. He was not puritanical in that," said Smith.[33]

There was more to it, though, than the thrill of defying the odds. Risk played an important part in the way Grant thought about war. In a discussion one evening that summer about the abilities of Don Carlos Buell, the general extolled by Grant's critics as the man who saved him at Shiloh, Grant expressed his own admiration for Buell. When it came to tactics, he said, Buell was easily his superior. The trouble with Buell was his reluctance to fight unless he was sure of the result. "No man ought to win a victory," Grant concluded, "who is not willing to run the risk of defeat."[34]

He was betting now that Lee would not take the kind of risk with Richmond that he was prepared to take with Meade's army and the outcome of the war. Lee's obsession with defending Richmond had tied his hands and dulled his edge. Although Lee had repeatedly succeeded in preventing Grant from enveloping his right flank, the old daring was gone. "Lee's great blunder," Grant remarked later, "was in holding Richmond."[35]

While Meade's troops marched south, engineers were building the pontoon bridge and dozens of steamboats came upriver to act as ferries. The morning of June 15 dawned a brilliant blue, revealing the finished bridge, the 101 crude boats that held it afloat rocking gently on the moving waters, the steamers waiting to serve as ferries blowing short blasts on their whistles, while Grant stood atop the riverbank on the north side of the James, hands clasped behind his back, as the head of a blue column twenty-five miles long marched past him, bands playing, banners snapping in the breeze off the river, the sun making the points of bayonets glitter like gold and silver, and the dull boom of cannon somewhere on the northern horizon drifted lazily down, announcing that Warren's corps, at the other end of the column, was fighting a rear-guard action. Lee had regained contact, but was following rather than pursuing Meade.[36]

While this drama was being played out, so was another. Grant had already sent Smith's corps back to Butler by boat from White House and urged Butler to advance on Petersburg. In effect, he was setting up yet another wide envelopment—while Lee's army was being kept busy by Meade's, Butler was free to swing Smith's corps around from White House against Lee's extreme right flank, at Petersburg. Grant empha-sized in his instructions to Butler that he had to make a major attack. There was no point in launching a small-scale effort that achieved nothing except to stimulate the Confederates into strengthening Peters-burg's defenses. The force that hit Petersburg had to be strong enough to hold it if, as Grant was certain, it proved vulnerable to attack.[37]

Smith's corps got reinforcements that made good its losses at Cold Harbor, plus extra cavalry and artillery, bringing its numbers to eighteen thousand men. When he set off toward Petersburg the morning of June 15, Hancock's corps, twenty-eight thousand strong, was being ferried across the James. Grant intended to have Hancock keep on marching once he had his men across and to join Smith in the assault. With forty-seven thousand men advancing on Petersburg, its fate appeared sealed.[38]

Beauregard had only ten thousand men to contain Butler's force at Bermuda Hundred *and* to man the earthworks of Petersburg. Beaure-gard had put nearly all his infantry into the trenches at the base of Bermuda Hundred. That left only two thousand infantry and forty artillery pieces to defend the approaches to Petersburg.[39]

When June 15 dawned, Smith wasted two hours of daylight before setting off to cover the five miles from City Point to the trench line that ran east of Petersburg. He moved at a one-mile-per-hour crawl. It was noon before he got there, although there was no impediment barring his way. When he came up to the outer line of defenses, he rightly decided a reconnaissance was needed before launching his attack and wrongly decided to make it himself. Smith was, he later claimed, suffering from dysentery and nearly fainted several times. But what else could he do? He was the only engineer officer available, so he had to do it himself.[40]

After three years of war there were dozens, probably scores, of vet-eran officers and sergeants in a force the size of Smith's who could reconnoiter an enemy line. In Mexico, scouting and reconnoitering were engineer missions, but Petersburg wasn't Mexico. War had moved on. Smith, who could come up with a forward-looking innovation such as the defensive use of wire, could also entertain outdated notions of just who did what. Nor had he any unusual talent for this kind of work. He was, after all, the engineer officer who had failed to spot the mile-long ravine in front of Tunnel Hill just before the battle of Chattanooga, a ravine that Sherman's army stumbled into and never managed to cross.

By the time Smith finished reconnoitering at Petersburg it was the middle of the afternoon, and he was shaken by what he had seen— half a dozen strong artillery positions. What he did not notice was the long, empty entrenchments between them in which hardly a butternut stirred.[41]

After some difficulty getting his artillery into position, Smith shook his corps into a heavy skirmish line, to minimize casualties from Confederate artillery fire, and pushed it cautiously forward at seven P.M. Once the infantry got within rifle range of the artillery positions, Confederate gunners fled to the rear rather than be shot dead at their pieces. Petersburg was now as helpless as a kitten. Smith's soldiers walked into the entrenchments as the sun went down, taking more than two miles of earthworks.[42]

Meanwhile Smith, Meade and Butler all sent messages to Hancock, urging him to hurry. Smith's informed him that he was preparing to make a night attack. Hancock rode up to Smith at nine P.M. At that moment this became, in effect, a Hancock operation, because Hancock was senior to Smith.[43]

Hancock was generally considered the best corps commander in the Army of the Potomac, a potential successor to Meade. He had performed stoutly at Gettysburg, where he had been seriously wounded, and became something of a national hero. His wound still had not healed completely and, like his men, he was tired after marching twenty miles to reach Petersburg. By the time he got there, Smith was having second thoughts about a night attack. He greeted Hancock, then started telling him that maybe a night attack wasn't such a good idea after all. Smith said he had heard trains rumbling into the city from the north . . . looked like Lee was pouring in reinforcements . . . we've done well so far . . . why risk it all on something as hard to control as a night action? Hancock let himself be persuaded.[44]

All Smith and Hancock had to do was push until they hit something solid and the whole city, with the rail lines that ran through it, would be in the care of the Union Army by morning. A Sheridan or a Sherman would have done it. Not, though, a Smith or a Hancock.

Grant did not know how near the lip was the cup that slipped. Not yet, anyway. The morning of June 16 he jubilantly told Meade, "Smith has taken a line of works stronger than we have seen in this campaign!" thinking Smith had vindicated his trust.[45]

Grant ordered an assault to cash in on Smith's success, but by the time it was launched it was the evening of June 16. Beauregard was thus given nearly twenty-four hours to shift troops from Bermuda Hundred down to Petersburg and hold it, while Lee shifted troops down to hold the trenches at the base of Bermuda Hundred.[46]

All Grant got from Smith's bungled attack was part of the trenches along the eastern approaches to Petersburg. The three railroad lines entered the city over to the southwest. There would be no climactic battle for them after all. There would, instead, be a siege, with Grant steadily extending his siege line westward to attack the railroads one by one.

Grant's wartime successes were often written off by his critics as little more than luck, and there was no doubt about it—when Grant was on the spot, he could be amazingly lucky. When he wasn't around, though, luck seemed to desert the Union and go over to the enemy. In Smith, Hancock and Butler, as in Rosecrans and McClernand, the only kind of luck that came Grant's way was bad luck, in doses strong enough to make anyone choke. The failure of Smith and Hancock to launch a night attack on June 15 brought another ten months of war. That thought angered Grant to the day he died.[47]

CHAPTER 24

★ ★ ★ ★

"GEN. LEE SURRENDERED"

Under a broiling sun thousands of men, black and white, were heaving earth, pushing wagons, pulling on ropes, cursing, splitting logs, pounding rocks, and from time to time the crushed bodies of the unlucky or reckless bobbed away on crude stretchers to an obscure fate, while the work went on with hardly a pause, the dead and crippled little more now than soft debris. This swarming scene of muscular toil was only the latest panel in an endless tableau of monumental construction—the erection of the pyramids, the construction of the Great Wall of China, the building of the medieval cathedrals of Europe—acted out this time on an American shore to the eternal rhythms of manual labor, the sea smell of sweat, the groans of effort, the unspoken satisfaction men take in making anything on the heroic scale, and in the foreground, always the busy, fussing masterminds—the engineers—heads bent in conference. Grant was besieging.

The line of freshly dug earth snaking around half of Petersburg grew and grew. Grant's siege strategy was simple—keep extending the line of works at both ends, avoid frontal assaults and get across the five railroad lines that were Richmond's logistical arteries. Four of them ran through Petersburg. By the middle of July he possessed the two lines east and southeast of the city.

The three remaining in Confederate hands were the Weldon Railroad, which ran from Petersburg down to Wilmington, North Carolina, the last Atlantic Coast port open to rebel blockade runners; the Southside Railroad, running southwest of Petersburg toward Lynchburg, Virginia; and the Richmond–Danville railroad, which ran southeast from Richmond and intersected the Southside Railroad fifteen miles west of Petersburg. If Grant could cut these three lines, Lee would have to abandon his trenches, come out and fight.

While the Army of the Potomac was sweatily carving out trenches, abatis, redans, glacis, revetments and forts, Grant was hoping to get rid of Meade, by making him chief of staff, sending Halleck to California, and giving the Army of the Potomac to Hancock. Lincoln, however, had not really forgiven Meade for failing to pursue Lee after Gettysburg. So Meade stayed where he was, under Grant's immediate direction, and Grant was stuck with Old Brains as chief of staff for the rest of the war.[1]

One general Grant managed to part with was Baldy Smith. He still did not know what had gone wrong during the assault on Petersburg, but on July 19 he relieved Smith from his command. He fired Smith because he couldn't fire Butler. It was all too obvious that Smith and Butler would never get along, wouldn't even try. One of them had to go, so Smith found himself given indefinite leave in New York. A week or so later Grant finally learned just how horrendously Smith had blundered on June 15. After that he made sure Smith never got back into the war.

Smith sought revenge by writing to Senator Solomon Foot of Vermont and telling Foot that Grant was a drunkard and claiming Butler had used this knowledge to blackmail Grant into getting rid of Smith, all of which was absurd. By this time there was hardly a literate person in the United States who hadn't read that Grant periodically fell off the wagon, if not off his horse.[2]

Even as the siege works progressed, Grant was looking for a way to break through and swallow Petersburg whole instead of nibbling it to death. When he asked Meade and his corps commanders for ideas, all came up barren except for Burnside. The IX Corps included several hundred miners from western Pennsylvania and they were convinced they could tunnel under the Confederate trenches and blow a huge hole in them with a mine. Burnside told them to start digging.

Grant had exploded two big mines under Confederate trenches at Vicksburg, but they probably did not speed the fall of the town by a day. That wasn't enough to prejudice him against this proposal, though. It was Meade who threw cold water on Burnside's idea and gloomily said it wouldn't work. For want of anything better, however, the miners were told to continue digging. They burrowed 250 yards to reach the Confederate lines.[3]

The officer in charge of the operation, Edward Ferrero, commanded a division of black troops and trained them to lead the assault once the mine exploded. Ferrero, an Italian immigrant, had begun his military career as the first dancing master at West Point. Over the years he absorbed enough military knowledge that when the war came he was given a captain's commission in the Union Army. The Petersburg mine appealed to his imagination, and where trained engineers doubted, Ferrero believed.

He argued that the mine would have to contain at least six tons of gunpowder to be sure of success. Ferrero intended to push forward, widen the breach the mine created, and secure the ground immediately on the other side of the crater. With a mile-wide gap in the Confederate entrenchments held by Ferrero's men, the other three divisions in Burnside's corps could push straight through and seize Petersburg.

Three days before the explosion, Meade sent for Burnside and told him to change the plan. No black troops. Ferrero's division had no combat experience, for one thing, and if this crazy scheme somehow backfired, the Army would be blamed for treating black soldiers as if they were expendable. What Meade did not say but almost certainly felt was that black soldiers lacked the ability to lead a major assault.

Burnside argued strongly against any last-minute changes. Meade ended the discussion by saying the only thing to do was put the issue to Grant and let him decide. That was agreeable to Burnside, but he made a terrible mistake: he didn't insist on going with Meade to see Grant. Meade saw Grant alone and didn't tell him about Ferrero's plan. He simply offered him his own plan, which involved four tons of powder instead of six, and called for sending forward a brigade at a time. There was no mention of substituting a smaller explosion or of removing the division that had prepared for the assault from its leading role. Grant okayed Meade's plan, assuming it was the result of careful thought. After all, if Meade couldn't handle something like this, he hardly deserved command of an army.[4]

Grant sent Hancock's corps back across the James to create a huge diversion north of Petersburg and pull Confederate units away from the area of the mine. Burnside, meanwhile, had to find another division to make the assault. His three white-division commanders argued that it was ridiculous to change the plan so close to the operation. Their men wouldn't have time to prepare. No one volunteered. In the end, Burnside wrote each division commander's name (excluding Ferrero's) on a slip of paper, dropped the three slips into his hat and had them draw. The name that came out was Ledlie.

Unfortunately, James H. Ledlie was both an alcoholic and a coward. When his division formed up to make the assault in the early hours of July 30, Ledlie was in a bombproof shelter getting drunk. His division would go into the attack leaderless. So, for that matter, would the other divisions. In a kind of silent protest, the other division commanders also stayed behind rather than participate in what they considered a doomed operation, thanks to Meade's meddling.[5]

At 4:30 A.M. on July 30 Grant was leaning against a tree, watch in hand, peering intently into the darkness. At 4:45 the rocks beneath his feet skittered across the ground, the branches overhead waved to the graying sky, trench walls buckled, cracking the planks that held them fast, and tongues of orange flame shot upward through a rising cone of dirt as if the Earth's molten heart were erupting. An enormous pit opened beneath a mushroom cloud of smoke, and rocks flew upward into the dawn. A three-hundred-yard stretch of Confederate trenches containing artillery, teams of horses, and several hundred men disappeared. Where they had stood moments before there was now a crater up to thirty feet deep marked by strands of smoke shifting lazily in the morning breeze.[6]

Ledlie's troops rushed toward the crater without training or leadership, forethought or ladders. Their advance was as sensible as hurling thousands of men at a door. They got in each other's way, trampled one another underfoot, and became a barrier to the divisions that followed them into this pullulating pit. For half an hour there was not a single Confederate barring exit from the crater, yet no Union soldier reached the rim on the Confederate side.[7]

Then, butternut units came hurrying up. Infantry deployed along the crater's crest, artillery unlimbered close behind, and an hour after the explosion, shot and shell and musket balls were raining down on the seething blue mass churning impotently below. Grant, mounting his horse, rode forward to get a closer look, dismounted and elbowed his way closer still. Elements of four divisions were tangled hopelessly within point-blank range of Confederate fire. "The entire opportunity has been lost," he said to his aide, Horace Porter. "These troops must be immediately withdrawn."[8]

It took several more hours to get them all out. By the time the survivors returned to their lines, nearly five thousand Union soldiers had been killed, wounded or captured, among them several hundred blacks. The Confederates treated their white captives as prisoners of war. The blacks were murdered in cold blood, without protest from Lee or any attempt to prevent a repetition. Lee considered himself a fundamentally decent man, but he drew the line at blacks. Grant repeatedly demanded that black soldiers in Confederate hands be treated as prisoners of war; Lee invariably refused.[9]

Grant reported to Halleck that the crater fiasco was "the saddest affair I have witnessed in this war . . ." and told Meade bluntly, "So fair an opportunity will probably never occur again . . . the crest beyond the mine could have been carried. This would have given us Petersburg . . ." It was too bitter to contemplate. Grant lay in his iron camp bed for an entire day, too depressed to rise.[10]

★

Shortly after Grant and Lincoln met in March 1864, Grant explained in broad terms just how he intended to fight the war. There was, for example, Franz Sigel, who would take a small army into the Shenandoah Valley. Sigel wasn't expected to do much beyond keeping Lee from using the valley as a highway to come north and threaten Washington while the Army of the Potomac was advancing on Richmond. What Grant was describing was yet another wide envelopment—one force holding the enemy in place while the other maneuvered. "Oh, yes! I see that," exclaimed Lincoln. "As we say out west, if a man can't skin he must hold a leg while someone else does." Grant was so delighted with Lincoln's skinning analogy he later used it himself.[11]

Sigel was a German army officer who had immigrated to the U.S. some years before the war. He had become an influential figure among German-Americans and when the war began Lincoln had made him a general, both to get the benefit of his military know-how and to attract German immigrants into the Union Army. Sigel was not a commander Grant chose but one imposed from above.

Short and muscular, with beady eyes and a flowing black mustache, Sigel looked like a stage villain straight out of a Victorian melodrama. His spoken English consisted of guttural barks that were incomprehensible to most of his soldiers and did nothing to inspire confidence in their commander.

Advancing into the Shenandoah Valley in early May, he moved his twenty-thousand-man army hesitantly toward the most important town in the central Shenandoah, Staunton. Before he reached it, he was blocked by a Confederate force of fifteen thousand men, near New Market. On May 15, he prepared to attack the enemy despite the fact that rain was falling steadily and rain nearly always works to the advantage of the defender. Sigel formed a line of battle that was shorter than the one he was preparing to attack. This meant that when the two lines collided, his troops would be outflanked to both left and right. By midafternoon Sigel's army was in full retreat up the valley.[12]

Grant replaced Sigel with Major General David Hunter, who had performed moderately well early in the war. Hunter managed to put Sigel's scattered force back together, steadied it, and advanced through the valley in early June heading for Lynchburg, at the southern end of the Shenandoah. Lynchburg, roughly a hundred miles west of Richmond, was one of the biggest towns in Virginia. The Southside Railroad, connecting Lynchburg with Petersburg, was essential to Richmond's survival.

Lee rushed troops west to defend Lynchburg, and Hunter moved so cautiously that by the time he got there he found twenty thousand Confederates, including three veteran divisions under Jubal Early, holding the town. Hunter pulled back, followed by Early, then bizarrely withdrew into West Virginia, thereby leaving the valley wide open for Early, who sped north through the door Hunter had left unguarded. Early got as far as Pennsylvania, where he razed Chambersburg before pulling back into Maryland. The shrieks of alarm coming from the War Department as Early turned toward Washington irritated Grant. "Boldness is all that is needed [to drive] the enemy out of Maryland," he sternly informed Charles A. Dana, the assistant secretary of war.[13]

Grant had virtually stripped the capital of troops. It was defended now mainly by militia and dozens of outlying forts. Something close to panic gripped the District of Columbia. The kind of support Grant could expect to receive from the War Department in this crisis was exemplified by Dana, who liked then and later to pose as one of Grant's defenders. Yet whatever loyalty he possessed collapsed under pressure as news flowed in that Early was heading for Washington.

In a long and overheated letter to Rawlins, Dana raged at Grant. He derided Grant's decision to strip the Washington garrison as "poltroonery and stupidity . . . its probable consequences are likely to be the defeat of Mr. Lincoln and the election of Gen. McClellan to the Presidency . . ." For good measure, he damned the principal military commanders—presumably including Grant—as "mental dwarfs and moral cowards." He added a postscript to his letter: Rawlins should feel free to show it to James Harrison Wilson. Among them—Dana, Rawlins and Wilson—there wasn't enough understanding of Grant or commitment to him to make a single genuine friend.[14]

Nor could Grant expect much help from Halleck, who made no bones about being disgusted at the way Grant had let the war turn into a siege. Not that Halleck had anything against sieges. He believed in trenches with a kind of engineer's fundamentalism. No, what he despised was the way Grant had done it. Why go all the way south of the James and dig in there when, at a much lower cost in human life, Grant could have spaded his way from the Wilderness to Richmond, much as Halleck himself had burrowed the Army of the Tennessee from Shiloh to Corinth? Grant's obsession with wide envelopments, converging columns, and holding attacks seemed stupid to Halleck when there was a spade within reach.[15]

Grant remained a portrait of equanimity. He did not believe for a moment that Early could take Washington. It was so well protected by rivers and forts that militia and rear-echelon troops could hold it long enough for him to send veteran units to defend it if that proved necessary. His veteran units did not belong in the rear but up front, which was where he deployed them.

Not only did Grant think Early couldn't take Washington, neither did Early or, for that matter, Lee. All Early thought he was capable of was to throw a scare into the city, which might be enough to force Grant to send troops north, relieving some of the pressure on Lee. He did not stand a chance in the world of marching his troops down Pennsylvania Avenue. What Grant was looking for wasn't a way of holding Early at bay and defending the District in some heroic stand on Capitol Hill but a commander who would get into Early's rear, cut him off from the Shenandoah and destroy him once and for all.[16]

Grant nonetheless was obliged to calm northern nerves by sending twenty-five thousand men from the Petersburg front up to the capital. In the meantime, Lew Wallace deployed a blocking force of militia and raw volunteers along the Monocacy River, mainly to stop any Confederate move toward Baltimore. Early had nothing to gain by attacking Wallace, but the temptation was too great to resist. The Confederates had a three-to-one advantage in manpower and here was the chance of winning a battle at little cost—or so he imagined. He won the engagement but suffered casualties too high for a small and overextended force like his.[17]

The battle of the Monocacy also cost Early a day when he was fighting, not moving, and that was all Grant's troops needed to reach the District by sea. Following his victory Early pressed on to probe the girdle of forts ringing the capital. On July 11 he deployed his twelve thousand men near Fort Stevens, the northernmost bastion of Washington's defenses. Over the next twenty-four hours Confederate sharpshooters harassed Union artillerists, picking some of them off at ranges of half a mile. Early saw for himself how weakly held were the Union lines, but was even more aware of how exhausted his own troops were and how suicidal it would be to make an infantry assault against so much artillery. Curiosity satisfied, and doubts confirmed, he pulled out the night of July 13 and returned to the Shenandoah.[18]

Even so, after receiving reinforcements, Early sortied from the valley again at the end of July, sending another scare through Washington. This time Grant went up to the capital for a day to confer with the President and personally assured him the District was safe.

Clearly, though, something decisive had to be done about the Shenandoah. It was not only Lee's highway north but also the biggest granary in the Confederacy, and harvest time wasn't far off. After Hunter took over from Sigel, Grant had told Halleck he wanted Hunter's army to "eat out Virginia clear and clean, so far as they go [until] crows flying over it will have to carry their provender with them."[19]

To control the valley and defend Washington, however, destroying the crops wasn't enough. Grant decided to make Sheridan commander of Hunter's Army of the Shenandoah.

"I want Sheridan put in command of all the troops in the field," he informed Halleck, "with instructions to put himself South of the enemy, and follow him to the death." Lincoln, who spent much of each day in the telegraph office at the War Department, sent Grant a cable: "This, I think, is exactly right [but] it will neither be done nor attempted unless you watch it every day, and hour, and force it." Lincoln had no illusions about the eagerness of Stanton or Halleck to support Grant's way of war.[20]

Sheridan caught up with Early near Winchester in mid-September. Grant went to see him with a plan of attack, listened to what Sheridan had to say, kept his plan in his pocket and simply told him, "Go in." On September 19 Sheridan attacked and inflicted four thousand casualties, but sustained five thousand in return. Early nevertheless retreated and Sheridan pursued. Three days later, he attacked Early again, this time winning a clear victory. Thrilled at the news, Grant ordered artillery batteries within range of enemy positions to fire a one-hundred-gun salute, with live ammunition, the next morning in celebration.[21]

Four weeks later, at Cedar Creek, a reinforced, replenished Early attacked and nearly routed Sheridan's army. Then Sheridan arrived, rushing back from conferring with Halleck in Washington, formed another line of battle, counterattacked, and in two hours turned virtual defeat into a hands-down victory. Early retreated again, this time taking his command west, up into the Blue Ridge Mountains.[22]

The Shenandoah Valley had been so devastated by now that it could barely feed the people who lived there or provide forage for their animals. Pursuing Early farther into the mountains would do little or nothing to speed the end of the war. Besides, Lee was now so hard-pressed to hold Petersburg and Richmond that he could not reinforce Early again. There would be no more threats against Washington.

★

Around midnight, most of the men were asleep, and the bustle around Grant's headquarters came to a halt as officers drifted away to their tents, bidding one another good night; card games concluded with a rapid settling of debts; the camp fell silent. Grant, who spent up to twelve hours a day writing reports, telegrams and orders, finally had a chance to write a letter to Julia. If there wasn't much news in his letters, he apologized, it was because the fight for Richmond and Petersburg had settled into a siege.

Much of the time, he wrote her about his plans for after the war— where would they live? what would they live on? what should they do about the children's education? Admirers in Chicago wanted to buy him a house there, but he discouraged them: as general-in-chief he would have to stay close to Washington. In which case Philadelphia appealed. Washington repelled him—all those obnoxious politicians, their egos insufferably inflated, the endless petty squabbles, the stench of corruption, the labyrinthine political intrigues. Having written to his wife, he went to bed, by which time his staff was asleep, and woke up five hours later, before most of them were stirring.[23]

He missed Julia and the children, missed them terribly, but he could hardly expect her to come and live with him at City Point. The setting was beautiful enough—a bluff seventy-five feet above the confluence of the Appomattox and James Rivers. A long wooden staircase was built against the face of the bluff by Army engineers and the steamboat landing at the bottom was renovated.

There were splendid views in nearly every direction from the large, comfortable house that occupied the top of the bluff. A garden full of roses and honeysuckle surrounded it on three sides, but Grant spurned all that. He allowed his onetime West Point roommate Brigadier General Rufus Ingalls to live in the house. Ingalls was the quartermaster general of the Army of the Potomac, and he and Meade's commissary general lived there with their staffs, while Grant lived in a small tent set up on the lawn in front of the house.[24]

He seemed at times to be going out of his way to rough it. The lieutenant general's equipment and baggage, including the hospital tent he used for a headquarters and the small tent he slept in at night, were carried by a single Army wagon. His effects were easier to shift than those of some lieutenants. The simplicity of his life in the field was, perversely, close to being a kind of excess. No senior general had to live like this, and he was the only one who chose to do so. The Hannah Effect? Probably.[25]

When late fall arrived, though, changes had to be made. Grant couldn't expect his staff to live in tents through the winter. More than a dozen crude wooden huts were built on the lawn by Army carpenters, and among the thousands of cabins the Army built during the Civil War only one—Grant's—survives, at City Point. It is T-shaped, twenty-five feet long and, at the back, twenty-seven feet wide. It seems spacious only when compared to the tent it displaced. The front section consists of a single room that served as office, dining room, reception room, war room, and inner sanctum. At the back are two small bedrooms. With a tin roof over his head, Grant was finally able to send for Julia to come to City Point.[26]

When little Jesse and his sister, Nellie, came to stay with their parents, the cabin was horribly cramped, besides being depressingly crude. Grant may have liked it all the better for that. Not that Julia made any complaints. "I am snugly nestled away in my husband's log cabin. Headquarters can be as private as a home," she wrote a friend. "I enjoy being here [and] have such long talks with my husband. . . . Am I not a happy woman?"[27]

For all her well-developed liking for comfortable surroundings, Julia would rather be with Grant in this sparse hut than be without him in a palace. Grant's staff officers often found them sitting in the room at the front, chatting quietly, finding something better than riches or luxury in the pleasure of sitting side by side and holding hands as they talked or while Grant read a book to her.[28]

Julia entertained visitors at City Point that any society hostess might envy—the President and Mrs. Lincoln, Secretary of War Edwin McMasters Stanton, Secretary of State William Seward—setting out plates on a deal table covered with a large piece of shelter tent for her tablecloth. Grant, as always, ate the plainest food, and in small quantities. He loved fruit and liked oysters. The only meat he ate was beef, and it had to be well cooked. A hint of pinkness killed his appetite. Cigars were his one indulgence, and he was cutting back even on that. At City Point he got down to four smokes a day.[29]

That fall a noted Norwegian artist, Ole Peter Hansen Balling, was commissioned by Lincoln to paint a huge canvas showing the most important combat commanders of the Union Army. Balling moved into one of the City Point huts and set up his easel, to paint Grant from life. All twenty-seven figures in the painting were mounted, with Grant in the center foreground leading the other twenty-six generals to victory. One day while painting Grant, Balling remarked that in the five weeks he had been at City Point, he hadn't seen a single bottle of liquor. Grant broke into laughter. "How could I permit a single drop around, with all the slander I've received?"[30]

Lincoln—"dressed all in black, looking very much like a boss undertaker," according to Horace Porter—came to visit Grant several times at City Point. He usually arrived at the landing at the foot of the bluffs aboard the presidential steamer, the *River Queen*. The rapport between general-in-chief and commander-in-chief was immediate and intense. They might as well have known each other since childhood. The bond was partly similar frontier backgrounds, but it was more than that. "Mediocrity knows nothing higher than itself," observed Arthur Conan Doyle, "but talent instantly recognizes genius." The spark of greatness in each flared in the presence of the other. Lincoln was nonetheless worried about Grant as a potential rival, even if an unwilling one.

Early's raids had thrown a scare into the North, and the appearance of stalemate at Petersburg only added to northern gloom. Volunteering for the Army had almost stopped and the hated draft had gone into effect that summer. The *New York Herald*—the most influential paper of its day—was promoting Grant for the presidency, and so were other newspapers. So, too, were various congressmen, and the Missouri delegation to the Republican convention was sworn to vote for Grant.

He had been writing to his admirers in Congress for nearly a year, telling them he had no interest in running for office while there was still a war to be won. Grant's friends and staff said the same thing. He told Rear Admiral Daniel Ammen, who had known him since childhood and once rescued him from drowning, "I have always thought that the most slavish life a man could lead was that of a politician." And to another old friend he made a joke about the attempts to get him into politics. "I am not a candidate for any office," he said, "but I would like to be mayor of Galena long enough to fix the sidewalks, especially the one reaching my house."[31]

When Grant's former "superintendent of contrabands," Colonel John Eaton, stopped by the White House on August 12, Lincoln asked him, "Do you know what General Grant thinks of the effort now being made to nominate him for the presidency?"

Eaton said he knew nothing about it, and Lincoln asked him to go to City Point and learn what Grant had to say about the upcoming election. Once he reached Grant's headquarters, Eaton put the question plainly. "The question isn't whether you wish to run," he told Grant, "but whether you could be compelled to run in answer to the demand of the people for a candidate who should save the Union."

Grant pounded the arm of the chair he was sitting in. "They can't do it! They can't compel me to do it." When Eaton told Lincoln how Grant had responded, "the President," in Eaton's words, "fairly glowed with satisfaction."[32]

Even without a potential challenge from Grant, however, Lincoln was filled with foreboding. At a cabinet meeting on August 23 he passed a sheet of paper around the table and asked each man to sign his name on the back. They did so, without seeing what was on the front, which read, "This morning, as for some days past, it seems exceedingly probable that this Administration will not be re-elected. Then it will be my duty to so co-operate with the President elect, as to save the Union between the election and the inauguration; as he will have secured his election on such ground that he cannot possibly save it afterwards. A. Lincoln." When all had signed, he put the paper in his pocket.[33]

Eleven days later, on September 2, Sherman had soldiers on the streets of Atlanta. Grant heard about it a few hours later, but he waited two days, until the news was confirmed, before ordering another hundred-gun salute. The fall of Atlanta transformed Lincoln's prospects and justified Grant's strategy. While Grant was pinning Lee at Petersburg, Sherman had advanced deep into Georgia, and this time Lee had not been able to send reinforcements to help save it. "Atlanta is ours," crowed Sherman, "and fairly won!" Shortly afterward came Sheridan's victories in the Shenandoah. By the end of October Lincoln's re-election was certain.[34]

Meanwhile, Grant insisted that soldiers be allowed to vote, even if that was likely to work to the advantage of the Democratic candidate, George B. McClellan, former commander of the Army of the Potomac. He scrupulously refrained from saying anything publicly that could be read as an endorsement of Lincoln, even though he considered his re-election essential to winning the war. He also refused to allow political speakers from either party into Army camps.[35]

On Election Day, November 8, McClellan won much of the soldier vote, but it made no difference. Lincoln won nationally by what is, for presidential elections, a sizable margin—55 percent to 45 percent. In the Electoral College, where presidents are chosen irrespective of the people's will, he won 212 votes to only 21 for McClellan.

As the result clattered in over the telegraph wire, Grant teased his staff by pretending the early returns showed Lincoln defeated. He often laughed at himself, told funny stories, exercised a dry wit and reveled in harmless practical jokes. It seems surprising that anyone fell for them, but at least one general went to bed that night anticipating the inauguration of President McClellan.[36]

On November 10, with Lincoln's re-election beyond doubt, he sent a pithy telegram to Stanton: "The election having passed off quietly . . . is a victory worth more to the country than a battle won." War-weary and jaded though it was, the North would see this thing through.[37]

★

Most of the time his self-control was impeccable. He never showed physical fear, his moral courage was impressive, his impassivity in the face of crisis was almost uncanny, yet Grant was a deeply emotional man, someone who craved drama and excitement, a man who loathed routine, a man with almost no capacity for sitting still. Sometimes the facade cracked and the emotional Grant stood revealed. It cracked the day he heard about McPherson.

The three officers Grant came to admire most during the Civil War were Sheridan, Sherman and James B. McPherson, who had risen spectacularly, advancing from captain to major general in only three years. McPherson was young, handsome, charming, graduating first in his class at West Point, becoming an engineer, but this time an engineer with a fighter's heart.

Sherman made him commander of the Army of the Tennessee at the start of the Atlanta campaign and on July 22, 1864, McPherson rode down a Georgia road that was reported to be free of Confederates. McPherson soon discovered it wasn't. Just as he tried to turn his horse around and get back to the Union lines, a Confederate soldier shot him out of the saddle.

Next day an army telegrapher took the message to Grant's tent, where the general was seated at a small table, writing, and silently handed it to him. Grant almost reeled as he read the slip of paper in his hand. McPherson . . . *dead?* He closed his eyes, wishing the news, the fact of death itself, away. His lips began to twitch spasmodically as he forced himself not to shout out in his anger and pain, then the tears began to flow, streaming down his sunburned cheeks and into his beard.[38]

Grant's reaction was reported in the newspapers and McPherson's grandmother wrote to him to say how touched she was. He replied, "A nation grieves. . . . It is a selfish grief," he wrote, "because the nation had more to expect from him than from almost any man living. I join in this selfish grief, and add the grief of personal love. . . . I knew him well; to know him was to love. . . . Your bereavement is great, but can not exceed mine."[39]

Once Sherman had taken Atlanta there was a month-long pause while Grant and Sherman considered the next move. Clearly, Sherman could not remain in Atlanta indefinitely. The question came down to whether he should pursue and destroy the forty-thousand-man army of John Bell Hood or whether he should move toward Grant and the Army of the Potomac. Grant wanted Sherman to destroy Hood before moving east and early October found Sherman moving north, against Hood, who was threatening to advance into Tennessee and possibly Kentucky. If Hood eluded Sherman, he could reclaim large areas that Grant had spent two years securing for the Union.

Yet to have Sherman move to the East Coast, cutting across Lee's links with the rest of the South while Grant continued applying pressure at Petersburg, was Grant's kind of strategy. But if this *was* to be the strategy, just where would Sherman head for? There was no well-established Union base on the Georgia or South Carolina coasts, where he could be resupplied for the winter after finishing the long trek from Atlanta.

Grant imagined Sherman finding himself stranded deep in enemy territory, far from any assistance he might be able to give and watching his army whittled down to nothing, harassed by guerrilla bands, fighting simply to survive. Lincoln could picture the same thing, too. "The President feels much solicitude in respect to Sherman's proposed movement . . . a misstep might be fatal to his army," Stanton informed Grant.[40]

Rawlins was sent to see Sherman and appraise the situation in Georgia. He returned to City Point convinced that Sherman should devote all of his efforts to destroying Hood's army. Grant, however, had arrived at exactly the opposite conclusion while Rawlins was gone. When Rawlins discovered he couldn't change Grant's mind, he went to Stanton and urged him to stop the march to the sea.[41]

There were no councils of war at Grant's headquarters. Instead, he encouraged his staff to debate ideas—and tell him how wrong he was—in lengthy sessions around the campfire each night. Everyone could speak freely, whatever his rank. It was a military town meeting set outdoors. There was a tacit bargain at work, an unspoken agreement that those who lost an argument would support whatever decision Grant finally made just as loyally as those on the winning side. Rawlins scorned all that and betrayed the trust of those who trusted him. Once he learned of Rawlins's treachery, Grant never forgave him. Among soldiers, disloyalty is the greatest crime of all.[42]

Sherman settled the issue of strategy by abandoning the pursuit of Hood, handing it over to George Thomas and the Army of the Cumberland. It was hard for Grant, who had long been thinking about a march across the South, to tell him not to do it. Besides, he had a lot of faith in Sherman's judgment. Grant allowed Sherman to move east, toward Georgia's Atlantic coast.

Hood's army was, meanwhile, advancing into Tennessee. Thomas's senior corps commander, John Schofield, dug in at Franklin, fifteen miles south of Nashville, to fight a delaying action while Thomas prepared Nashville's defenses. Grant became impatient, then infuriated. He urged Thomas to attack Hood, not wait for Hood to attack him. Thomas did not move. On November 15 Hood launched a massive frontal assault on Schofield's position and lost six thousand men, to Schofield's twenty-three hundred.

Hood continued his advance. Schofield fell back from Franklin to Nashville and sent a message to Grant: "Many officers here are of the opinion that General Thomas is certainly too slow in his movements." It was a lie, but some years before, when Schofield was a cadet at West Point, he had been court-martialed. He been acquitted, but two officers had voted for his conviction and one was George H. Thomas. Here was a gold-plated chance for revenge, for if Grant fired Thomas, Schofield was likely to succeed him.[43]

Unaware of Schofield's machinations, Thomas was waiting to get his cavalry—commanded by Grant's onetime protégé James Harrison Wilson—remounted. No sooner were they ready for action than an ice storm blew up, and Wilson refused to risk his cavalry with so much ice on the ground.

Lincoln, monitoring the telegraph traffic, told Stanton to send a message to Grant: "The President feels solicitous about the disposition of General Thomas to lay in fortifications for an indefinite period. . . . This looks like the McClellan and Rosecrans strategy of do nothing and let the rebels raid the country . . ."[44]

Grant had an order drafted ousting Thomas and installing Schofield, but then decided not to send it without giving Thomas one more chance. "Delay no longer for weather or reinforcements," he told Thomas. But still Thomas waited for the ice to melt. On December 14, Grant sent for Major General John A. Logan, one of Sherman's corps commanders, who happened to be at City Point more or less by chance. He ordered

Logan to go to Nashville immediately. If, when he arrived there, no battle had been fought, Logan was to relieve Thomas at once.[45]

That night, temperatures rose rapidly across middle Tennessee. The ice melted. Thomas attacked on December 15 and something happened for the first, and only, time on a Civil War battlefield—one army annihilated another. Wilson's cavalry pursued Hood's broken army to destruction. Thomas was vindicated.

Grant, though, never acknowledged that. "I was fond of him," he later insisted, "and it was a severe trial to me even to think of removing him. But Thomas was an inert man. We used to say laughingly, 'Thomas is too slow to move, and too brave to run away.' " After the war Congress tried to make amends to Thomas for Grant's injustice to him by offering him a third star. He turned it down. Honor delayed was honor denied.[46]

Sherman's march to the sea had meanwhile followed its relentless course. The railroads lines that served Atlanta, one of the most important railheads in North America, were wrecked for fifty miles around. The countryside was reduced to little more than a wasteland. With every mile Sherman advanced, the impotence of the Confederacy to stop him became manifest. His sixty-thousand-man army met nothing that could be called opposition.

In early December he reached Savannah, which was held by ten thousand Confederates. Sherman blundered in assuming they would fight. He failed to cut the roads leading north to Charleston, forty miles away. Just as Sherman prepared to launch his assault, the rebels pulled out, racing up the road to Charleston.[47]

The Confederacy now consisted of little more than the Carolinas and the southern third of Virginia, with Sherman waging war in one and Meade in the other. Grant now turned his attention to capturing the last port open to rebel blockade runners—Wilmington, North Carolina. The port itself wasn't the problem. The challenge at Wilmington was Fort Fisher, the massive earthwork crammed with guns that protected both land and sea approaches to the port.

This mission fell within Butler's Department of Virginia and North Carolina, and Grant made it clear to Butler that he expected one of Butler's corps commanders, Major General Godfrey Weitzel, to direct the operation. Butler soon turned his fertile mind to the challenge of taking Fort Fisher. Why not, he reasoned, flatten the fort by blowing up a ship loaded with gunpowder close to the walls? Grant privately ridiculed what he called Butler's "gunpowder plot," but let him go ahead with it.

Butler came to confer with Grant about the Fort Fisher operation several times. Disembarking from his steamer, Butler would make a waddling ascent of the hundred-plus steps leading up the face of the bluff. He liked to underline his combat credentials by wearing a huge cavalry saber. Grant, writing in his cabin, knew when Butler had arrived because the saber banged noisily against every step on the long, slow ascent. Exchanging knowing smiles with his chief enlisted clerk, Sergeant M. Harrison Strong, he then waited through a good five minutes of clanking before Butler finally appeared at the top of the bluff, panting and sweating, ready to talk war.[48]

On December 8 Butler showed up at City Point and casually remarked that he intended to go on to Fort Fisher. Grant was surprised, not to say dismayed, but he did not forbid Butler to go. A department commander was supreme within his own department, and however unwise his decision to command the operation in person, he had both the rank and the right to do so.[49]

The Navy was responsible for towing Butler's powder boat into position, and made a mess of it. The boat, filled with two hundred tons of gunpowder, was exploded half a mile from the fort, doing no damage at all. Butler got his troops ashore, the Navy bombarded the fort, and when the hour approached for the troops to make their assault, Butler's nerve cracked and he called the whole thing off, re-embarked his men instead of digging in, and sailed back to Fortress Monroe.[50]

Grant had had enough. He told Halleck he wanted Butler removed, and wrote to Lincoln saying the same thing. With the election of an overwhelmingly Republican House and Senate, Lincoln no longer needed to conciliate Butler. In January 1865 the Beast was unceremoniously dismissed from command.[51]

As Butler, grumbling and aggrieved, packed up his effects at Fortress Monroe, Grant sent another expedition to capture Fort Fisher. This time it fell after a brief naval bombardment, followed by a vigorous infantry assault.

★

At the end of January 1865, Grant's trenches ran in a semicircle for nearly thirty miles, from the eastern suburbs of Richmond to Dinwiddie

Court House, on the southwestern edge of Petersburg. Throughout the winter Grant applied pressure at both ends of his line, extending it steadily, stretching Lee's dwindling manpower close to the breaking point. Confederate commissioners tried to open negotiations with Grant for an armistice. As much as anyone, he wanted a swift end to the war, but it wasn't for him to talk terms.

Lincoln came down to City Point to deal with the Confederates in person. They did not offer to surrender, and he wasn't interested in anything less. The commissioners departed empty-handed, well aware that the South was defeated, yet the fighting went on.[52]

On March 2, the day before Lincoln's second inaugural, Lee used a flag-of-truce meeting over prisoner exchanges as an excuse to send Grant a letter suggesting they get together to talk about an armistice. Grant informed the War Department and got a swift reply from Lincoln: No talks with Lee on anything but a Confederate surrender.[53]

Several weeks later, Lincoln was down at City Point to talk to Grant, Sherman and Sheridan about strategy. The day Lincoln arrived, March 24, Grant issued orders to concentrate the bulk of Meade's army on the left flank, attack westward, and cut the Southside Railroad. Meanwhile, Sheridan was to advance from his position near Lynchburg and cut the Richmond–Danville railroad. Grant was moving against Lee's railroads from two directions at once. If Lee concentrated to block one force, the other would be able to keep moving. The wide envelopment again.

He expected Lee to react with the only offensive move open to him—an attempted breakout. Next morning, March 25, Lee did exactly that. The Confederates launched a frontal assault on Fort Stedman, at the right end of Grant's line. In the space of three hours the Confederate attack was shattered.

That afternoon Lincoln and Grant reviewed one of Meade's corps, on a stretch of ground only a mile from Fort Stedman. The bands played and flags flew while Lincoln rode through the blue ranks on Grant's powerful mount, Cincinnati, and Grant rode alongside on his favorite horse, a black pony called Jeff Davis. During the review more than a thousand Confederates taken prisoner at Fort Stedman shuffled past, being herded into captivity.[54]

Grant expected Lee would now abandon Richmond and Petersburg and make a desperate dash south, to North Carolina, where he might link up with Joe Johnston. Sheridan was leading his Army of the

Shenandoah south to get in front of Lee when Meade decided to intervene. In recent months Grant had usually ignored Meade. The two men hardly saw each other all winter.

Meade feared that with Sheridan so far south, Lee might suddenly move east and attack the Union rear. He ordered Sheridan to go east instead of south. When Grant heard of it he made a thirty-mile ride over muddy roads to see Meade and get the order changed. He told him gently but firmly that here was a chance to smash Lee's army in the open. Destroy Lee's army, and Richmond would fall without a fight. Secure the rear, and Lee would get away.[55]

On April 5 Lee's divisions, pulling out of Richmond and Petersburg, converged on Amelia Court House, on the Richmond–Danville railroad, hoping to find rations. What they found instead was Sheridan's cavalry, blocking the road south. Lee had no choice but to swing his army to the west, toward Farmville, where he recrossed the Appomattox River, giving up all hope of joining forces with Johnston. He kept moving west, toward Appomattox Court House.[56]

The evening of April 7 Grant reached Farmville and wrote a note to Lee: "The result of the last week must convince you of the hopelessness of further resistance . . . and regard it as my duty to shift from myself the responsibility of further effusion of blood, by asking of you the surrender [of] the Army of Northern Virginia." After dinner he stood on a hotel porch, smoking, chatting with his aides and leaning against a railing. Dozens of regiments marched through Farmville that night and it wasn't long before some of the marching men realized that the man standing at the railing, puffing on a cigar, was Grant. They broke into cheers, and the cheers rippled up and down the column, renewed with added vigor as the head of each regiment passed the hotel, shaking the little town. After a couple of hours of being spontaneously feted by his men, Grant threw his last cigar butt into the street, said, "I think I'll retire," and headed upstairs.[57]

At four A.M. he was awakened to read Lee's reply. In it, Lee said *he* didn't think the situation was hopeless but asked what kind of terms Grant was offering. Grant wrote back that he would meet Lee "at any point agreeable to you, for the purpose of arranging definitely the terms upon which the surrender of the Army of Northern Virginia will be received."

Lee's soldiers had deserted in droves during the past few days. His army now numbered about nine thousand men. Yet he could not face reality, and tried to hide in a fantasy world where he and Grant would together work out an armistice that would bring the Civil War to an end without a surrender, without an admission of defeat. "To be frank," he informed Grant, "I do not think the emergency has arisen to call for the surrender of this Army." More bluster. "I cannot therefore meet with you with view to surrender the Army of N. Va." But he added, as if doing Grant a favor, that if Grant was willing to talk about a cessation of hostilities, "I shall be pleased to meet you at 10 a.m. tomorrow on the old stage road to Richmond . . ."[58]

Next morning, Sunday, April 9, Grant sent Lee a note rejecting the absurd pretense that they might somehow negotiate an end to the war. Lee was meanwhile coming to his senses and after more prevarication finally sent a message that read, "I therefore request an interview at such time and place as you may designate to discuss the terms of the surrender of this army." He also sent Longstreet to see Meade, to tell him he intended to surrender.[59]

A few hours later Grant and Lee finally met, in the parlor of Wilmer McLean, who had moved to Appomattox seeking respite from the war after his previous home had become the site of the opening battle, First Bull Run. Lee was gorgeously arrayed, in a brand-new uniform, red sash, shining boots, magnificent sword in a golden scabbard. Grant arrived travel-stained from two days in the saddle, in muddy boots, his pants tucked into the tops, wearing a private's rough woolen blouse and a lieutenant general's stars.

This brief meeting was one of the great moments in the war, a quasi-mythical passage of national reconciliation. It was invested with a cathartic emotional charge straight out of Greek drama and boasted a metatext on the world beyond this modest parlor: The tall, handsome man who looked like the conqueror possessed the trappings of power as romance but was in fact impotent; the other man possessed the romance of the real, the authentic, with mud on his boots and the crushing might of superior organization.

Grant claimed his shabbiness had made him self-conscious, that he feared Lee might mistake it for a calculated insult. In truth, he probably savored the contrast, for in an industrializing democracy rough at the edges, with a ferrous puritanism still dark in the mold, his muddy work wear was the raiment of kings.[60]

They chatted awkwardly for a few minutes about Mexico, mutual Army friends, even the weather, until Lee raised the subject of surrender. A small table was brought over and Grant sat down, writing in pencil in a field-order book. The Confederates would have to hand over their arms and all other military equipment. Officers could retain their side arms and whatever horses they owned. All those surrendered would be pledged not to take up arms again.

Lee put on his glasses, read the document through, then pointed out that many private soldiers in the cavalry and artillery owned their own horses. Grant relented. The written agreement would not be changed, he said, but added, "I will instruct the officers [who] receive the paroles to let all the men who claim to own a horse or mule take the animals home with them to work their little farms." Once a copy had been made in ink, Lee signed it, then bowed and departed.[61]

Riding away from the McLean house, Horace Porter, one of Grant's aides, said maybe Washington ought to be informed that Lee had quit. Grant dismounted, sat on a boulder at the edge of a field, and scribbled a short telegram to Stanton: "Gen. Lee surrendered the Army of Northern Va this afternoon . . ."[62]

Back at his headquarters, staff members who hadn't witnessed the surrender welcomed him back, and he could see it in their eyes—something like worship. He had to deflate it, get them—and himself—back to Earth. In an offhand way, he remarked wryly, "More of Grant's luck." Every success he'd won in the past four years had been ridiculed by his detractors and Lee's admirers as luck. In this instant, he joined the scoffers and mockers, laughed at himself, at them, at glory itself. Then he sat down and started writing dispatches.[63]

CHAPTER 25

★ ★ ★ ★

"A NATIONAL DISGRACE"

Two days after the surrender, Grant returned to City Point and prepared to leave at once for Washington. Congressman Elihu B. Washburne, who had come down to City Point, was surprised. "It seems to me you are in a great hurry and are getting away pretty quick," said Washburne.

"With the capture of Lee's army," Grant replied, "all the armies of the rebels will in due time surrender." What mattered now was to stop wasting money on a war that was as good as won, and he was going to Washington to tell Lincoln and Stanton how to do it—the parsimonious product of parsimonious parents.[1]

When Grant went to the White House on April 13 he took his youngest boy, Jesse, along and had a long chat with Lincoln, while Jesse fidgeted and wandered morosely around the room. No one knows exactly what was said, but Grant probably told Lincoln the government should put an end to all military contracting, stop enrolling troops and end all borrowing intended to finance the war. With Lee's surrender, there would be no more big batttles, no more campaigns. The struggle had effectively ended. It was safe to start reducing the size of the Army, cut military expenditures, and stop wasting money.

Washington that night was ablaze with lights and the streets were crowded with revelers celebrating Lee's surrender. Grant joined Lincoln on a tour of the illuminations, and they were cheered from one street corner to the next. Next morning, a Friday, the cabinet held its normal weekly session and Lincoln asked Grant to attend. When the meeting broke up, Lincoln said he and Mrs. Lincoln were going to Ford's Theater that night, to see *Our American Cousin.* Would the general and Mrs. Grant care to join them? Grant declined the invitation. Julia had arranged to travel to Burlington, New Jersey, that evening, he said, where two of the children were in school. She did not want to disappoint them, he told Lincoln. Mary Lincoln had also informed Julia that she and the President expected the Grants to attend the performance with them. Julia sent her a brief, impersonal message saying she had already made other arrangements. In truth, Julia couldn't stand the hysterical and self-dramatizing Mary Lincoln. The First Lady was absurdly jealous, highly irritable and almost devoid of common sense.[2]

A few hours later Grant, Julia and young Jesse boarded a Philadelphia-bound train, on the way to Burlington. When the train reached Philadelphia at midnight, the Grants went to a hotel to wait for the connecting train. A messenger arrived and handed Grant a telegram. It read, "The President was assassinated at Ford's Theatre at 10 30 tonight & cannot live . . ." After escorting Julia and Jesse to Burlington and assuring himself they were safe, Grant returned to Washington.[3]

By the time he got back to the capital, Lincoln was dead and Andrew Johnson had been sworn in as President. The secretary of state, William Seward, had been in bed recovering from a carriage accident and was knifed by one of Booth's accomplices, who had forced his way into Seward's home and attacked him in his sickbed. An attempt had also been made to kill Stanton, but he escaped unscathed. Julia was forever convinced that she and Ulyss had been stalked by none other than John Wilkes Booth himself and that an attempt would have been made to kill Grant had he not left the city when he did.

Yet Grant always regretted leaving. He blamed himself for not going to Ford's Theater that night. Grant was certain that he would have heard Booth open the door to Lincoln's box and been able to get his body between Booth's derringer and the seated President. His admiration for Lincoln added to the sense of loss and kept alive that feeling of guilt.

Lincoln's funeral was held in the White House four days after he died. Grant, who ever after revered the dead President as "incontestably the greatest man I ever knew," stood at the head of the catafalque throughout the service. Once more a lifetime of practiced calm failed and the tears flowed freely.[4]

For a week or so, Washington was filled with paranoid fears, alarming rumors, barely checked anger. Grant oversaw the Army's part in the hunt for the assassins and strove to bring a sense of military order and discipline to an angry city seething with talk. While Grant and the nation grieved for Lincoln, the war was still not at an end.

Sherman had advanced on Raleigh, North Carolina, and demanded the surrender of Joe Johnston's army. Sherman's hand was overwhelming. He not only had his own army at his disposal, but the Army of the Potomac was ready to reinforce him. Johnston, though, was a master of delaying tactics and bluff, and proceeded to make a complete fool of Sherman. Instead of surrendering, Johnston got Sherman to talk about a truce, and talk about a truce led to talk about a peace settlement, and before he knew it Sherman was negotiating the terms on which the South would stop fighting, something for which he had no authority whatever. Sherman had long believed in a hard war and a soft peace. Just how soft, Joe Johnston soon discovered.[5]

At six-thirty the evening of April 21 Grant was at work in the War Department when he received a copy of the agreement Sherman had concluded with Johnston, and which even now was being transmitted to the Confederate government for its approval or disapproval! Grant read it in amazement and sent a copy by mounted courier to Stanton, who was at home having dinner.

A cabinet meeting was called for eight P.M. Grant read aloud the telegram that Sherman had sent him. His listeners were stunned. Stanton angrily ticked off on the fingers of each hand what was wrong with it, before running out of fingers. The pact Sherman agreed with Johnston guaranteed southern property rights, for example. That could be interpreted as preserving slavery. It recognized the legitimacy of the state governments of the Confederacy. By implication, even the Confederate government was considered a sovereign power. The existing state governments of the Confederacy would not have to disarm. They would come back into the Union without being reformed, but the breakaway state of West Virginia might be forced to go back to being part of Virginia. And so on.[6]

Grant got permission to go and see Sherman and personally break the news to him that the government had repudiated the agreement with

Johnston. While Grant was heading south, Stanton let loose a blast in the newspapers that came close to calling Sherman an insubordinate fool. Stanton, who looked the part of a wrathful Old Testament patriarch, excelled at outrage. Halleck, Sherman's longtime mentor, joined in the chorus of criticism. Even Mrs. Sherman thought her husband had been too obliging to the rebels.[7]

Grant reached Sherman's headquarters three days later. He told Sherman not to get upset at the outcry from Washington. Nerves in the capital were stretched to breaking point and feelings were still running high over Lincoln's assassination. Even so, the new President demanded nothing less than a swift and complete capitulation. Under Grant's gaze, Sherman wrote out a message to Johnston that called for his surrender "on the same terms as were given to General Lee at Appomattox," and Johnston was told there was no room for further talk: If he did not comply within forty-eight hours, hostilities would be resumed. Johnston caved in promptly. Shortly afterward, Grant's former protégé James H. Wilson captured Jefferson Davis in South Carolina.[8]

When Grant returned to the War Department he was besieged by reporters. They wanted to talk about how Sherman had blundered, but he brushed that aside. From inside a cloud of thick cigar smoke, he talked instead about the "despair, misery and almost starvation" of the South. Now that the fighting had ended, the southerners—"an unfortunate, desolated race"—had to be treated with kindness and helped to recover from what the war had done to them and what they had done to themselves.[9]

It took two days—May 23 and 24—for the victorious Union armies to parade past the grandstand erected in front of the White House. Grant sat next to the new President, a man with few social graces and a burning inferiority complex. Andrew Johnson had been an illiterate blacksmith in a village in eastern Tennessee until he got married and his wife taught him to read. He became a tailor and turned his little shop into a place for political discussions, and that in turn got him elected an alderman. He went on to become governor of Tennessee, and then a United States senator. The fact that he was a War Democrat from a crucial border state got him chosen as Lincoln's running mate in 1864. No one then or later detected any hint of greatness in Johnson.[10]

As the jubilant, long-striding blue columns passed the reviewing stand under a forest of sparkling bayonets that swayed rhythmically to a martial tread, soldiers passing the presidential stand noticed Grant and broke into spontaneous cheers. Shouts of "Grant! Grant! Goodbye, old man!" echoed down the broad thoroughfare. Grant tried to push his chair farther back, until he was almost sitting behind the President. But still more columns swung past, behind battle flags torn by the musket balls of Shiloh, the canister of Gettysburg, streamers embroidered ANTIETAM, VICKSBURG, and other already legendary names fluttered as they advanced, and still the cheers for Grant went up, hour after hour. Johnson, whose crabbed nature had long since etched a permanently bitter expression onto his face, scowled into the middle distance, wounded and upstaged.[11]

★

Grant's well-advertised protests that military life did not appeal to him ring hollow. Julia wasn't fooled for a moment. "He was happy in the fight and din of battle," she knew, "but restless in the barracks. He could no more resist the sound of a fife or drum or a chance to fire a gun that a woman can resist bonnets."[12]

There was also Grant's enduring attachment to West Point. He never ceased to love the place, even though it had hurt him deeply. The demerit system had discouraged him from displaying his intellectual abilities to the full. And the way he had been denied a commission in the cavalry for losing his temper with a horse was unjust. In his youth, and for years afterward, he was the best rider in the Army. Men with far less ability than he and without anything approaching his knowledge of horses had been given cavalry assignments. Even when the Civil War began, the height of his ambition had been to command a cavalry brigade in the Army of the Potomac.[13]

The injustices inherent in the West Point system angered him all his life, yet Grant could not help his deep attachment to "the best school in the world," a place that for all its faults provided an excellent academic education, a camaraderie among the cadets that led to lifelong friendships, a competitive system that allowed poor boys to compete on equal terms with the rich, and, above all, a place where Grant's deepest faith—patriotism—was taught as the highest virtue a young man could aspire to.

In June 1865 Grant returned to West Point, stopping off en route in New York City as guest of honor at a celebration the Republican party had organized to mark Andrew Johnson's accession to the presidency. Whenever Johnson's name was mentioned in a speech, people sat on their hands. If they raised them, it was to stifle their yawns. But every mention of Grant triggered rapturous applause. The enthusiasm for Grant in New York was less a straw in the wind than a sky nearly black with bales of the stuff.[14]

He traveled up the Hudson to West Point aboard a dispatch boat. Grant planned to review the Corps of Cadets and have lunch with Winfield Scott, who was living in a hotel on the Academy's grounds in a golden retirement, regaled by adoring cadets and a procession of attractive, attentive young women. During the previous fall, Scott had published his autobiography—*Memoirs of Lieut.-General Scott, LL.D., Written by Himself*—and had immediately sent Grant a copy inscribed "From the Oldest to the Greatest General."[15]

When Grant arrived at the hotel, Scott greeted him in the same effusive manner—"I thank God you have passed through so much peril and glory unharmed. Welcome to my bachelor home!" Grant could hardly fail to have been touched by such warmth from this giant, whom he had first glimpsed as a cadet twenty-five years before and later served under in Mexico. They walked into lunch together arm in arm, like old comrades.

After reviewing the cadets, Grant made his way west, heading for Chicago. Large and boisterous crowds greeted him along the way. The excitement he generated, even though he usually said nothing, or nothing much, was a beacon of the political moment, a beacon that flashed INTERREGNUM. The true successor to Lincoln wasn't the Tennessee Tailor but Grant. The hero who had won the war was the only man the people—not the politicians—trusted to win the peace.

For now, all they could do was adore him, which they did. His hands became swollen and sore from being shaken; his fingers curled from the autographs he signed. When he reached Chicago, an attempt was made to smuggle him into the Sanitary Fair early in the morning, before the crowds arrived, so he might look at the exhibits in peace, but rumor had done its work and there were thousands of people already waiting.

Grant begged off shaking more hands or signing more autographs. A young woman shouted out that it didn't matter—the ladies did not want his orthography, still less to grasp his hand. What they wanted was to kiss him. "Well," said Grant, "none of them have offered to do it yet."

Hundreds of women rushed forward, swirled around him like a crinoline vortex, kissing and hugging him for nearly an hour, while Grant blushed a deep red, grew breathless—and probably aroused—and thoroughly enjoyed himself. He could usually manage to keep his head, he once warned Julia, "except in the presence of ladies."[16]

The question of where he would live still wasn't completely settled. During the war he had become friendly with several businessmen from Philadelphia, including the newspaper publisher George W. Childs. Grant hinted, to them and to others, that he would rather live in Philadelphia any day than in Washington, and Julia had enrolled Jesse in a school only a few miles away, in Burlington, New Jersey. When the war ended, Grant's admirers in the City of Brotherly Love promptly bought him a large, comfortable house. It was presented to Grant complete with expensive furniture, fine linen, and a cellar full of anthracite to keep it warm in the winter. Julia loved the house. Grant tried commuting—weekdays in the War Department, weekends with Julia.[17]

Galena, too, got involved in the give-Grant-a-home movement, and when he returned there on a brief visit in the summer of 1865, he was presented with a large house, but it wasn't new, nor was it as grand as some of the other residences.

Galena, it seems, had no illusions about him spending much time there. Still, it welcomed Grant warmly, pretending it really did remember him, when the fact was that few Galenans had ever met him during the ten months he lived there before the war. Someone had recalled the joke he made before the 1864 election about running for mayor so he could fix the sidewalks, especially the one reaching his home. A large banner greeted him now, emblazoned GENERAL, HERE IS YOUR SIDEWALK, and sure enough a brand-new sidewalk connected the gift home with the street.[18]

Commanding the Army proved even in peacetime to be a seven-day-a-week job. Much as Grant had suspected, he had little choice but to live in Washington. In the fall of 1865 he concluded the commuting had to stop. Major General Daniel Butterfield, war hero and composer of one of the world's most evocative tunes, "Taps," organized a fund drive among New York's richest to provide Grant with a Washington house. Butterfield raised $105,000, which was more than enough to buy the home at 205 I Street. Set among two acres of well-tended grounds and offering a panoramic view toward the Potomac, this was one of the finest homes in Georgetown. Butterfield paid off the mortgage, which came to $34,437.50, put $55,000 into government bonds and let Grant have the balance in cash.[19]

★

Andrew Johnson nurtured a poor boy's hatred of the rich and powerful of his native South. He blamed them for the tragedy of the Civil War. A month after the conflict ended, he told Grant he intended to hang those who had served as general officers in the Confederacy, starting with Robert E. Lee. Grant said that was out of the question. Under the agreement made at Appomattox, those officers who had sworn an oath to the United States and been paroled were exempt from punishment. "When can these men be tried?" said Johnson, exasperated.

"Never," Grant told him bluntly, "so long as they do not violate their paroles."[20]

Johnson refused to accept that, thinking that because Grant was under his orders he was also under his thumb. At which point Grant threatened to resign. Johnson blinked. If Grant resigned there would be a political crisis, one that could sweep Johnson straight out of the White House. The President backed down, but this proved to be only the first of the numerous clashes that characterized the relationship between the commanding general and his commander-in-chief for the next three and a half years.

Johnson made several gestures to appease Grant, giving his son Fred an appointment to the military academy and making Jesse Root Grant postmaster of Covington, Kentucky. He also had Grant made the first "General of the Army," which brought an unprecedented fourth star.

These efforts were doomed to fail, though, because in the fight over Reconstruction, Grant found himself increasingly on the side of the radical Republicans, who were determined to force racial justice on the South, while the President's sympathies were increasingly with those white southerners who refused to accept emancipated slaves as their equals.

When Congress passed the Civil Rights Act of 1866, making it a Federal offense to violate the civil rights of anyone, of whatever color, Johnson vetoed it. For the first time in history, Congress overrode a presidential veto of a major piece of legislation. Even so, neither the President nor the Federal courts made any attempt to enforce the law.[21]

Similarly, Congress passed three Reconstruction Acts. All three were vetoed by Johnson, and all three became law over his veto. It was obvious, though, that the President would not enforce them. By default, Reconstruction was left in the hands of the Army, yet the military was already hard-pressed simply to maintain order in the former Confederacy. What made military reconstruction impossible, however, was that southern resistance increasingly took the form of terrorism, and on a scale even the Army could do little to prevent; at least, not while the President and the courts were more likely to take the terrorists' side than the soldiers'. "The subjugation of the states to Negro domination," Johnson solemnly informed Congress, "would be worse than the military despotism under which they are now suffering." He was, he added, opposed to "the Africanization of the half of our country." Given the rampant racial violence of the time, this utterance is probably as close as any President has come to encouraging a lynch mob.[22]

Johnson, his political base shrinking by the day, tried to portray Grant as being his firm supporter, hoping Grant's popularity might keep his enemies at bay. In the fall of 1865, when Senator Carl Schurz published a report on the growing campaign of terror in the South, Johnson had Grant make a ten-day tour and report back to him on what he found. Grant's report said, in so many words, that conditions weren't as bad as Schurz had made out. Given the superficiality of Grant's investigation, whatever conclusion it arrived at wasn't going to be worth much, except as propaganda.[23]

It wasn't until the summer of 1866 that Grant was prepared to acknowledge that Reconstruction was failing. On May 1, 1866, a meeting in Memphis of freedmen and their white sympathizers was attacked by a mob that included the city police and Confederate veterans in their old uniforms. Forty-six people were murdered and more than a hundred injured. Grant was incensed. "A year ago they [the people of the South] were willing to do anything," he told a reporter from the *New York Times*. "Now they regard themselves as masters of the situation."[24]

In June Congress passed the Fourteenth Amendment, which imposed Reconstruction on southern courts: The due process clause demanded equal treatment before the law. Johnson encouraged the ten states of the former Confederacy to reject the amendment, and every one did so. There was also an antiblack riot in New Orleans that July, even bloodier and more destructive than the affray in Memphis.[25]

With midterm congressional elections drawing near, Johnson sought to counter his rapidly growing unpopularity by creating "the National Union Movement," an amorphous body of pro-Johnsonian political activists. Pretending to be above party, Johnson set the NUM machinery rolling with a meeting at the White House, into which a deeply reluctant Grant was dragooned. Then the President set off on a two-week tour of the Midwest, a jaunt that became known as the Swing Around the Circle, dragging Grant along with him.

The shameless way Johnson went grubbing for votes, by appealing to the worst instincts of a country still traumatized by war, appalled Grant. Johnson's speeches, he told Julia, were "a national disgrace." He felt sullied just by being there, but could hardly say as much to other people. Even so, he dropped some heavy hints. "The President is my superior officer, and I am under his command," he pointedly told a crowd in Cincinnati. And when a former aide, William Hillyer, was quoted as saying Grant supported Johnson, Hillyer got a swift response: No one, Grant told him bluntly, "is authorized to speak for me in political matters."[26]

In the end, Johnson found his Swing Around the Circle accomplished nothing except to demonstrate the popular fervor for Grant. No one was interested in Johnson. The President's solution to that problem was to get Grant out of the country. Napoleon III's attempt to impose one of his dim-witted relatives on the people of Mexico had ended with a firing squad and the first in a long line of military defeats for the French Foreign Legion. Johnson was sending a mission to Mexico to establish relations with the new government of Benito Juárez. He decided to assign Grant to this mission, and while he was away Johnson intended to replace Stanton, who was a radical Republican, with Sherman as secretary of war.

When Johnson informed Grant at a cabinet meeting that he was being sent to Mexico, Grant refused to go. "No power on Earth can compel me to it." Johnson was astonished, and told him he had no choice. If it were a military assignment, Grant argued back, that would be true. But this was a diplomatic assignment, and he could not be forced to take part. Grant was probably on weak ground here, but he had made his point. Johnson dropped the subject, still hoping to replace Stanton with Sherman. That part of the plan also came to grief, because Sherman refused to oblige. Grant would have seen Sherman's elevation over his head as betrayal, and the friendship between Grant and Sherman was too close to allow that.[27]

When the war ended Grant had been against enfranchising the freedmen. They would have to be educated first, he argued, before they could vote. The violent reaction to Reconstruction, epitomized by the attacks on peaceful demonstrations to promote black rights, changed his mind. Black suffrage, Grant concluded two years after the war, "is the only solution to our difficulties" in the South. His aide Colonel Cyrus B. Comstock noted the change in his diary—"The General is getting more and more Radical."[28]

Johnson, meanwhile, was demanding that Grant remove several military commanders, starting with Phillp Sheridan. Grant had sent Sheridan to Louisiana, where Sheridan brought the same combative, aggressive style to Reconstruction that he had applied to Confederate armies. He ousted local politicians, judges, even the governor of the state, for impeding Reconstruction. He installed Army officers as voter registrars and held voter registration drives under military protection. Grant fought hard to save Sheridan, but Johnson's authority as commander-in-chief ultimately left Grant no choice but to comply.[29]

Despite the growing antipathy between them, Johnson had no intention of ousting Grant. The general might become a political force outside the Army, but he remained subject to orders as long as he remained on active service. Congress nonetheless decided to secure Grant's position. The 1867 Army Appropriations Act contained a clause that said the commanding general of the armies of the United States could not be removed or transferred without his permission.

Congress was equally determined to keep Stanton in the War Department. Stanton, with his belief in a hard war and a vigorously reconstructed South, was a hero to radical Republicans. The radicals in Congress pushed through the Tenure of Office Act, which blocked the President from removing anyone who had been appointed to a government post with the advice and consent of the Senate. Johnson loathed Stanton and was as determined to get rid of him as Congress was to retain him. Johnson waited until Congress was out of session and, in August 1867, ordered Stanton's suspension from office. He later claimed he was trying to get the legislation before the Supreme Court, to have it decide on the law's constitutionality, but this was specious. Johnson informed the cabinet he would not apply for a writ of *quo war-*

ranto, which was the only sure way of getting the Court involved. Besides, the Court was already in such deep political trouble for blocking Reconstruction that there were moves in Congress to abolish it. The justices, taking fright, left the Tenure of Office Act alone. Its constitutionality was never challenged.[30]

For now, Johnson needed an acting secretary of war. He thrust the position on Grant, who did not want it but did not want anyone else to have it, either. Grant had no greater enemy in the cabinet than the secretary of the Navy, Gideon Welles, who was one of Johnson's staunchest admirers. A pro-Johnson secretary of war operating in partnership with a pro-Johnson naval secretary would have made life almost intolerable. In August 1867 Grant crossed the street from his headquarters at 17th and F streets and moved, reluctantly, into Stanton's office. He would be in a better position here to protect the Army, and officers such as Sheridan, than if he remained on the other side of the street.[31]

When Congress returned at the end of the year, the issue of what it had intended when it passed the Tenure of Office Act could finally be clarified. Grant had always had his doubts about whether the President had the legal power to suspend Stanton, but "the law was binding on me, constitutional or not, until set aside by the proper tribunal."[32]

On Saturday, January 11, 1868, he was informed by some of his congressional admirers that the Senate Military Affairs Committee was going to demand Stanton's reinstatement. What was more worrying, though, was that on a close reading of the Tenure of Office Act, it looked as if he could be judged to have acted illegally in taking Stanton's place, even temporarily—in which case he risked a ten-thousand-dollar fine and five years in prison. Shocked, Grant immediately went over to the White House and told Johnson he was worried by the legal penalties in the legislation. The President told him there was nothing to worry about and urged Grant to remain as acting secretary of war. At the very least, he did not want Grant to stand down and hand the office back to Stanton. Grant said he thought Stanton intended to resign, not return.[33]

On Monday, the Senate formally disapproved Stanton's suspension. Next day, during a cabinet meeting, Johnson assured Grant once more that his anxieties about legal penalties were exaggerated. I will pay the fine, he said. If necessary, I'll offer to serve your time in prison. Grant was incredulous. After leaving the meeting Grant had the adjutant general of the Army, Lorenzo Thomas, take the keys to the secretary's office to Stanton. When Johnson learned of Grant's action, he was outraged. He claimed that in the course of their conversation on January 11 Grant had promised to return the office of secretary of war to him.[34]

Johnson's version of what Grant had promised him was supported by Grant's archenemy Gideon Welles. This version nevertheless does not sound altogether convincing. Except with people he knew, liked and trusted, Grant worked by hints, by indirection; mostly he kept his own counsel. The fact that Johnson (and Welles) claimed that Grant expressed himself openly and unambiguously on an issue that had him worried about going to prison raises an interesting question about their veracity. Grant's most hostile biographer, William McFeely, states forthrightly that Grant was lying, but there is no independent evidence of this. What is far more likely is that Grant was opaque and Johnson read what he wanted into that opacity. Grant had being doing that to people most of his life.[35]

Besides, there is good evidence that Grant was cautious in any conversation with Johnson. Grant took an old friend, Judge Amos Webster, to the White House one day when he had to meet Johnson. As they departed from the President's office, Grant asked, "Did you notice that screen? Did you hear any noise?"

"I did," said Webster.

"A reporter was there taking down all I said!" Grant responded, evidently infuriated. Under such circumstances it isn't likely that Grant would have committed himself unambiguously to any demand that came from Johnson in respect to something as controversial as the Tenure of Office Act.[36]

The Johnson-Welles-McFeely version also seeks to ignore the fact that the President cannot order a military officer to commit an illegal act, and with the Tenure of Office Act on the statute books upheld by Congress and the Supreme Court declining to consider it, Johnson was attempting to flout the law. Constitutional lawyers have since argued that the Tenure of Office Act could not apply to Stanton. Because he had been appointed by Lincoln, they argue, Johnson was free to suspend him or to dismiss him. This issue was never tested, however, and Johnson was trying to get around the law, not overturn it. He was resorting to expediency, not principle, and brazenly tried to use Grant—and Grant's popularity—as a shield against the wrath of the radicals.

Even now, Johnson did not give up. His reaction to Stanton's return was to tell Grant not to obey any order from Stanton. Grant replied that such an instruction would have to be put in writing. Johnson wrote an endorsement on Grant's letter, ordering him "not to obey any order from the War Department . . . unless such order is known . . . to have been authorized by the Executive."[37]

Johnson made one last attempt to get rid of Stanton, by ordering Lorenzo Thomas to take over the War Department. Stanton dealt with that challenge by frightening Thomas with threats of arrest and criminal prosecution into returning to his duties as adjutant general.

The renewed tussle over Stanton so infuriated the congressional radicals that impeachment proceedings were started against Johnson. Grant followed the action in Congress closely, with all the inflamed hopes of an angry—even vengeful—man to see an enemy publicly humiliated. Johnson's conviction and removal from office, Grant informed a friend, "will give peace to the country."[38]

When the Senate voted on Johnson's impeachment, in May 1868, the President escaped conviction by a single vote. Grant was bitterly disappointed. It hardly mattered, though, for revenge—pluperfect in being the fate Johnson feared most—was in sight.

———— ★ ★ ★ ★ ————

CHAPTER 26

"LET US HAVE PEACE"

N ight after night they came to 205 I Street, trying to discover
whether Ulysses the Silent had an itch for the White House, and
to weigh up whether to back him if he did. More than fifty years later
his youngest son, Jesse, remembered them, the steady stream of senators and representatives who came calling, many of them famous men
in their day, like Senator Charles Sumner of Massachusetts, dressed
unforgettably in tartan trews and brilliant white spats. Others were less
famous, like Benjamin F. Wade, president pro tem of the Senate, but
powerful all the same. And mixed among the elected politicians were
the peripheral but inevitable figures—the journalists and the political
fixers. They too pulled on the bell at the front door, handed their hats to
the maid, and waited in the front parlor under the blank gaze of a marble bust of Lincoln until summoned upstairs to Grant's library, where he
met most of his visitors.[1]

This large room, with walnut bookcases covering three walls, was a
general's den. There were trophies of war wherever one looked—flags
and shells, banners and swords, bullets and daggers. Under the bronze,
fixed gaze of a bugler and a drummer boy—two small statues placed on
the mantel—they joked with Grant while trying to fathom his laughter,
told him how worried they were about Johnson, the national debt, or

Reconstruction, and wondered what that veiled look in his eye meant, and whether a Grant sigh could be read as agreement. From time to time he reached over to fortify himself with another round from the cigar stand. Four icons hung on the walls—treasured engravings of Washington and Lincoln, Sherman and Sheridan—were constant reminders that he relied for guidance and inspiration on men greater than his importuning visitors, whoever they were.[2]

Grant had long since made the transformation in his own mind from being a Democrat to being a Republican. The war had dissolved his old political allegiance. The question now was, What kind of a Republican? But try as they might, they could not get Grant to talk about it. Ben Wade was baffled and irritated. "I've often tried to find out whether Grant is for Congress or Johnson or what the devil he is for," he complained to a journalist, "but I can never get anything out of him. As quick as I talk politics, Grant will talk horse, and he can talk horse by the hour."[3]

Despairing of ever getting Grant to say, yes, he was a Republican, and, yes, he was interested in being President, Wade traveled all the way to Covington, Kentucky, to see whether old Jesse Root Grant, who had a long record of blabbing about what his son thought, could offer enlightenment. To Wade's disappointment, Jesse wasn't there. But Grant's self-regarding brother-in-law Michael J. Cramer, a Methodist preacher who had married Grant's sister Mary, was present and he was happy to talk, provided Wade promised not to tell Grant about it.

Grant, Cramer told Wade, was a Republican, strong on the rights of liberated slaves and a staunch believer in Reconstruction. Wade was so excited he whipped his slouch hat off, threw it in the air and broke one of the pendants dangling from the crystal chandelier in Jesse Grant's parlor. "That settles the matter. We shall propose Grant as the candidate of the Republican Party!" said Wade.[4]

The abolitionist element in the Republican party, such as Horace Greeley, editor of the *New York Tribune,* was never convinced, though, that Grant was really one of them. As for Wade, he soon developed his own desire to make a run for the presidency. There was also Ben Butler, another important radical. He was still smarting at Grant's wartime report that described him as being "bottled up" at Bermuda Hundred. One way or another, the radical wing of the Republican party did not want Grant.

Even so, the 1866 election had seen many radical Republicans either defeated or left hanging onto their seats by a handful of votes. Republican voters had made it plain that with the war over and won, what they wanted was moderation. That was more than enough to frighten the radicals, because the increasingly bitter struggle between Congress and Andrew Johnson had left the party with few leaders who were not tainted to some degree by radicalism. By 1868 virtually every Republican realized Grant was the only potential standard-bearer who could lead them to victory in the fall. Because whatever kind of Republicanism Grant practiced, no one, Republican or Democrat, believed he was a radical.[5]

The strange thing was that, although he kept silent, almost anyone could watch him thinking. When the weather was too wet or too cold, Grant took the streetcar to work, which astonished Washingtonians. And when the weather was good, he astonished them even more—he walked the mile and a half between his house on I Street and Army headquarters. It became something of a routine spectacle to see Grant striding along the sidewalks at a terrific pace, trailed by aides and clerks trotting to keep up. He walked the way he rode, at top speed. Grant, burning up the sidewalk, seemed utterly self-absorbed, deep in thought, chomping on a cigar, automatically raising his hat to anyone who raised his to him, frowning and veering away if any importuning passerby attempted to engage him in conversation.

After he had lived in the District for a few months, he could walk through a crowd and people would fall back, creating a space around him, they having become as silent as he, but gazing at him, fascinated, thrilled at the thought of brushing shoulders—metaphorically, of course—with History. The more astute observers noticed, however, that there was something about him which made Grant seem always to be alone, no matter how large the crowd, as if he lived within some personal force field that kept other people and their concerns on the periphery while the real Grant was somewhere else, traveling less through the streets than through his own thoughts.[6]

In early 1868 his mind turned increasingly to the presidency, impelled partly by his fraught relationship with Andrew Johnson, partly by the siren song played by his nightly visitors. If he stayed out of politics, his future looked good. With his $21,000-a-year salary and the interest on his government bonds, he had an income of roughly $25,000 a year.

Grant could expect a comfortable existence for the rest of his life. If, however, he was elected President, he would have to resign his position as general-in-chief. The presidential salary was $25,000 a year, so his income would rise to around $30,000, but he would have to entertain on a lavish scale and would be forced to go into debt. After four years—eight at the most—he would find himself unemployed and debt-ridden. The price of glory could turn out to be a chance to "study the poverty question" all over again.[7]

Besides, he wasn't a party politician. If anything, he had a soldier's natural longing to be above party. He much preferred the presidency to come seeking him than to feel that he had gone in search of the presidency. The jubilant shouts of "Grant! Grant! Grant!" that greeted him on his travels seemed to promise just that, and he later justified his entry into politics by saying that he owed a debt to the Republican party that could not be denied. But behind his growing interest in the Republican nomination was a feeling that a Grant presidency was the only sure way of securing the results of the war. Grant became convinced that a Democratic presidency would mean an appeasement of the South that made a mockery of the Union's sacrifices in blood and treasure.

In February 1868 the New York State Republican Convention endorsed Grant by acclamation. The movement for his nomination was becoming irresistible even without any word from Grant. Not even Julia was sure which way his mind was moving. One evening in April, Julia asked him point-blank: "Ulys, do you want to be President?"

"No," he replied. "But I don't see that I have anything to say about it. The national convention is about to assemble and, from all I hear, will nominate me, and I suppose if I am nominated, I will be elected."[8]

When the convention met, at Crosby's Opera House in Chicago in May, it took only one ballot to push Grant's nomination through. Stanton was waiting in the War Department telegraph office until the news clicked over the wire, then bustled across the street and fairly ran into Grant's office carrying a telegram. Panting and excited, he announced, "General, I have come to tell you that you have been nominated by the Republican Party for President of the United States!"[9]

Back in Chicago, the 650 delegates, having unanimously nominated Grant, were turning their energies to providing him with a running mate. In those days, the presidential candidate had no say in the matter. On the fifth ballot, the convention chose Schuyler Colfax, the Speaker of the House of Representatives. Colfax was the candidate of the radicals, and he offered a way of creating a ticket that both moderates and ultras could support. Colfax was considered both competent and honest. He turned out to be merely competent.[10]

While Grant's political admirers were jubilant and assumed he shared their excitement, his old Army friends knew better. Sheridan wrote to say, "I will not congratulate you because I believe you are sacrificing personal interests and comforts to give the Country a civil victory . . ."[11]

At the end of May, a delegation from the Republican National Committee arrived at Grant's home and solemnly informed him he had been nominated. Grant read out a brief and yawn-inducing acceptance speech. Julia looked on, not entirely delighted. She was less impressed by the historic importance of the occasion than by the sight of the two hundred people who were gathered around the steps at the front of the house to hear Grant's short speech. They were overflowing onto the flower beds and trampling her flowers.[12]

Grant's formal acceptance was couched in a letter to the president of the Republican National Committee that same day. He congratulated the convention delegates on their "wisdom, moderation and patriotism," looked forward to the election of an administration that would reduce taxation and the national debt, and concluded with a rare rhetorical flourish: "Let us have peace."[13]

Grant traveled to Galena several weeks later, with no intention of returning to Washington until after the election. The one aspect of running for the White House that Grant probably approved of was that the candidate was not expected to do much. His Democratic rival, however, could not afford to sit still. The Democrats nominated the governor of New York, Horatio Seymour. With the odds heavily against him, Seymour, in the closing weeks of the campaign, went on a speaking tour to appeal for votes and nearly closed the gap.

The campaign was really fought out in the newspapers, however. Grant was portrayed by the Democratic press as a butcher of his own troops, a drunkard, a madman, and a military dictator in waiting. The Republican press, meanwhile, extolled him as the savior of his country, and even Greeley's *New York Tribune* fell into line, running a poem by Miles O'Reilly every morning for the two months preceding election day:

So boys! a final bumper
*   While we all in chorus chant—*
"For next President we nominate
*   Our own Ulysses Grant!"*

And if asked what state he hails from
*   This our sole reply shall be,*
"From near Appomattox Court House,
*   With its famous apple tree."*

For 'twas there to our Ulysses
*   That Lee gave up the fight*
Now boys, "To Grant for President
*   And God defend the right!"*

Shortly before the election, the telegraph company ran a line from its Galena office up the hill to Congressman Elihu B. Washburne's house. After casting his ballot on Election Day, Grant and a small group of friends sat in Washburne's library monitoring the returns as they clicked in staccato bursts onto the telegrapher's pad. By two A.M. next day, it was evident he had won, if narrowly. Grant was not going to reach the White House on a tidal wave of public acclaim. His share of the popular vote was only 52.7 percent, a smaller percentage than Lincoln had won in 1864. The white vote had been split almost evenly between Grant and Seymour. His margin of victory in the popular ballot was due to the black vote. In the Electoral College, however, Grant had won 214–80. Dawn was breaking as Grant walked home alone. Julia, eager to hear the result, was waiting for him at the front door. "I am afraid," he told her, "I am elected."[14]

★

The morning of March 4, 1869, the skies over Washington were leaden with rain clouds and the side streets, still unpaved, were awash with mud. Andrew Johnson was holding his last cabinet meeting while his successor was getting into in a black dress suit and yellow kid gloves. Grant left the I Street house for the last time and stepped into an open carriage. The previous day he had sold the house and its contents to Sherman for sixty-five thousand dollars.[15]

Grant's carriage took its place at the head of the inaugural parade. By custom, the outgoing President should be seated beside him, but

Johnson said he would not ride with Grant, and Grant had said he would not allow Johnson in his carriage. Rather than have an empty seat beside him, Grant told his chief of staff, John Rawlins, to take Johnson's place.[16]

Grant had written his inaugural address entirely on his own. It was, for him, fairly striking: "The responsibilities of the position I feel, but accept them without fear. . . . The office has come to me unsought; I commence its duties untrammeled. . . . I shall on all subjects have a policy to recommend, but none to enforce against the will of the people . . ."

The principal theme of his speech was not Reconstruction but the urgent need to reduce the national debt. Between the War of 1812 and the Civil War, the United States had been virtually debt-free. The Civil War had forced the Federal government to impose an income tax, but it was limited to those who made more than six hundred dollars a year. The government raised most of the money it needed—and it needed a lot—by borrowing more than two billion dollars and by issuing greenbacks, which were also in effect promises of payment. Grant committed the government to retire the greenbacks and to do something about reducing the heavy financial burden of a huge national debt. The "Let us have peace" phrase had been a great success once before, so he used it again to conclude his speech.[17]

Next day, Grant sent his list of cabinet appointments to the Senate. Speculation about the names on this list had been intense, but Grant was as sphinxlike as ever. He told one journalist that he had been waking up in the middle of the night and searching under his pillow for his waistcoat—the list was in a waistcoat pocket and he was afraid Julia might have found it.[18]

By custom and practice, a President-elect was expected to consult with the leaders of his party over cabinet appointments. Grant, however, ignored the Republican chieftains and made up his own list in his own way. He had a view of the Constitution that was overly idealistic and fundamentally flawed. "This is a republic where the will of the people is the law of the land," he had told Johnson during the argument between them over removing Sheridan from command in Louisiana. Similarly, in his letter accepting the Republican party nomination he had said a President was "a purely Administrative officer," elected "to execute the will of the people."[19]

Grant understood, as any educated person did, that the Anglo-American version of democracy was based on representation. Yet his approach to politics was essentially emotional, mediated through a romantic attachment to democracy in its purest form—the town meeting. He clung to a patriot's vision of a sturdy, simple America, an Arcadian city-state where the people practiced direct democracy. Even if he could accept the fact that at the Federal level the people's will was expressed by their elected representatives, he resisted the corollary fact that those same representatives were more than mere mouthpieces. They were expected to offer their own judgment on what was best for the country, even if that meant modifying—at times even ignoring—the views of those who had voted for them. Such an idea was anathema not only to Grant but to many others whose idea of American democracy was based on nostalgia for an America that never was.

As for the law of the land, that was not made by the people either, but by nine unelected judges. Besides, if the will of the people was clear on major issues, there would not have been a Civil War. The people were often divided over fundamental choices. Far from being based on the will of the people, American government was an exercise in compromise and pragmatism. Grant, at forty-six the youngest man elected to the presidency up to that time, had a lot to learn. The absolute master of military bureaucracy was a complete neophyte when he grasped the levers of government.

Grant's romantic interpretation was in part an act of denial of what had happened to the country and its government. Until the 1850s America recognizably resembled the Jeffersonian ideal of a nation of small towns and self-reliant farmers, hardworking, honest and rich mainly in the dreams they had for the country they were creating. Industrialization was rapidly changing all that. In the 1870s the United States was becoming a country of cities and factories, its people urbanized and dependent on wages, their dreams revolving increasingly around money and material possessions.

Until the Civil War there was no government-issued paper money. There were gold coins and gold certificates, but most of the population, which numbered sixty million people, handled only a small amount of real money in the course of a lifetime. There was only about $100 million in gold in the entire country, and of that, roughly $20 million was in circulation. The government held onto the other $80 million. Some states allowed their banks to issue money, but it only circulated locally and was unlikely to hold its value long. Banks went bust all the time, which was why people who got their hands on gold were likely to keep it under the mattress and not in the bank.

When the war came, however, not even its gold reserve was enough for the Federal government to pay the bills. Once the greenback machine got rolling, it churned out a total of $450 million. Paper money and bottled whiskey sluiced through the corridors of power between 1861 and 1865, intoxicating a nation and eroding the old morality.

After the war, business flourished as never before, thanks to the rise of the corporation. The Fourteenth Amendment had been intended to aid blacks, but the chief beneficiary of the "due process" clause turned out to be the corporation, which until then had been considered a kind of conspiracy against the public interest. With the rise of the corporation (memorably criticized by one late-nineteenth-century reformer as being beyond anyone's control because "It has no soul to be damned and no posterior to be kicked"), lobbying struck deep roots in American government. Before 1860 American government was mainly about ideas. By the 1870s it was mainly about money.

Grant, however, preferred to imagine he had been elevated to the presidency of a simpler, cleaner system of government and a nation of small farmers, a nation much as it was before the war. He also retained his suspicion—if not disdain—for party politics. When a group of Republicans from Pennsylvania went to see him shortly before his inauguration to urge him to put at least one Pennsylvania Republican in the cabinet, he told them sternly, "I am not the representative of a political party."[20]

His cabinet list, containing six names, went to the Senate the day following his inauguration. It shook Washington like an earthquake. There was nothing in it for the party leaders. They had grown accustomed to considering government a system for rewarding their friends and punishing their enemies, by means of thousands of government jobs, from cabinet posts to pension clerks, customs collectors to Indian agents. Few of the jobs paid very much, but they were nevertheless highly sought after, and those that did offer a chance of dishonest riches were, inevitably, the most desired of all.[21]

Grant's refusal to consult with the party leaders left him free to make his own selections, in his own way, and the result was widely ridiculed.

Yet on any dispassionate view it was much the same mixture of excellence, mediocrity and inexplicability as that of the cabinets of his immediate predecessor, Andrew Johnson, and most of his successors. In the twentieth century, two cabinet members would go to prison, and the administrations of Andrew Johnson, McKinley, Wilson, Harding, Coolidge, Franklin Roosevelt, Truman, Eisenhower, Kennedy, Lyndon Johnson, Nixon, Carter, Reagan, Bush and Clinton would all be tainted by financial scandals.

Grant's longtime political supporter Congressman Elihu B. Washburne wanted to be secretary of state, but Grant did not think he was up to it. So he appointed Washburne ambassador to France, but let him be secretary for one week, thinking this might flatter Washburne's vanity while adding *éclat* to Washburne's diplomatic credentials. It was an original if slightly bizarre notion.[22]

Who then would be the real secretary of state? There was an obvious candidate in Charles Sumner, the preeminent figure in the Senate and chairman of the Foreign Affairs Committee. It made tactical sense to offer him the post. He was well qualified to take it, and if he turned it down, he might feel flattered all the same to have been asked. Grant foolishly did not offer it to him, and Sumner felt aggrieved. That mistake would reverberate throughout Grant's first administration.[23]

Grant might have made amends to Sumner if he had offered the post to Sumner's protégé, John Lothrop Motley, a writer and sometime ambassador to Austria, who had campaigned for Grant in Massachusetts. Adam Badeau urged Grant to consider Motley and arranged a meeting between them. Grant was horrified. For one thing, he discovered, Motley wore a monocle. Very European. More shocking, though, was Motley's hair. "He parts his hair in the middle!" Grant expostulated to Badeau. On the grounds of a hairstyle and a monocle, Grant turned down a perfectly suitable candidate for the State Department and appointed Motley ambassador to Great Britain instead.[24]

The State Department finally went to Hamilton Fish, although it is possible that it was Julia, not Grant, who found Fish. A former senator and governor of New York, Fish had been living contentedly in retirement for a decade when Julia became friendly with Mrs. Fish—so friendly, in fact, that she tried to persuade the Fishes to move back to Washington. She was making little headway until she suggested to Ulyss that he offer the State Department to Hamilton Fish. The reply from Fish was a swift no, but Grant persisted. The statesmanlike Fish proved to be an inspired selection.[25]

For secretary of the Treasury Grant chose the creator of the modern department store, Alexander T. Stewart of New York, who was fabulously rich, with a fortune estimated at $40 million. His nomination was promptly ratified. Then someone, name unknown, reminded the Senate that a law dating from 1789 barred anyone engaged in trade from being secretary of the Treasury. Grant asked Congress to repeal the law. Stewart, Grant suggested, could put his financial assets into a blind trust. This proposal was brusquely rejected as a trick. Nor did the repeal movement get anywhere: Sumner used his power to block it. The law was eventually repealed, and blind trusts became commonplace not only for cabinet officers but for Presidents, too. That had to wait nearly a century, however. Backward-looking in his political philosophy, Grant could paradoxically be ahead of his time in the practicalities. After only two months in the Treasury Department, Stewart returned to private life. Grant complained bitterly that the government had just lost the services of a man who "could have saved it a million a year."[26]

Recognizing at last that he needed the aid of Republican party leaders if he was going to create a successful administration, Grant relied on them to help him find a replacement for Stewart. The leadership chose a former governor of Massachusetts, George S. Boutwell, a mediocrity much like themselves.

For attorney general, Grant chose Massachusetts congressman E. Rockwood Hoar, a distinguished lawyer and a figure of exemplary rectitude. Grant would have put him on the Supreme Court had it not been for Ben Butler's implacable hostility to Hoar, who had been fighting Butler for years within the Republican circles back in Massachusetts.

Grant's secretary of the interior was a youthful Civil War hero, Major General Jacob D. Cox. It was a popular choice, but Cox was likely to prove problematic. He had entered politics by being elected governor of Ohio on the Republican ticket. But he was a strange kind of Republican—one who was not simply opposed to radicalism but also opposed voting rights for blacks. Cox went even further than that, though: he also wanted legally enforced racial segregation—Jim Crow, with the power of the Federal government behind it.

In the waning months of the Johnson administration, Stanton had stepped down as secretary of war, to be replaced by Major General John

Schofield. Grant wanted to retain Schofield and told him so, but when Rawlins learned of it, he demanded the place for himself. Grant was planning to send Rawlins out to Arizona, where the desert air might give him some relief from the agonies of terminal tuberculosis. Even on death's doorstep, however, Rawlins craved fame and an office he could not hope to fulfill.[27]

Grant felt unable to deny a dying man his wish. It made little enough difference that Rawlins spent virtually the whole of his six months as secretary of war too weak to get out of bed. Grant was capable of running the War Department himself, in whatever time he had to spare. He was really his own secretary of war, much as Franklin Roosevelt was his own secretary of the Navy. It was a measure, though, of how little claim Rawlins had to Grant's friendship that in September 1869, as Rawlins lay dying, surrounded by friends and family, Grant stayed away.[28]

For his Navy secretary, Grant chose another Philadelphia businessman, Adolph E. Borie. Grant had met Borie several times during the Civil War, and after being given a house in Philadelphia, he had gotten to know Borie fairly well. Borie knew nothing about his appointment to the cabinet until he read about it in the newspapers. Deeply reluctant, he accepted the post, but after only three months in it, he quit. Grant replaced him with a capable young lawyer from New Jersey, George M. Robeson.[29]

While assembling a cabinet, Grant was determined to get rid of the Tenure of Office Act. It limited his freedom to surround himself with advisers he trusted and undermined any chance of controlling his administration. The fact that there were several thousand government jobs at his disposal gave him leverage, and he used it ruthlessly. Incoming administrations usually kept party leaders happy by firing most of the current postmasters, pension clerks, customs collectors and so on. These were the spoils of office and were considered to belong to the leaders of the President's party more or less as their due. No President, including the saintly Lincoln, had challenged the spoils system.

Grant was the first to do so. He was not going to create any vacancies, he told the Republican leadership in Congress, unless and until the Tenure of Office Act was revoked. The House promptly fell into line and passed a bill repealing the act. The Senate was the real beneficiary of the Tenure of Office Act and balked at giving him what he demanded.

The clamor for patronage, however, was a powerful weapon, and after months of dithering and sulking the Senate finally agreed to give Grant nearly everything he wanted. For the sake of senatorial pride, it drew the line at an outright repeal. Grant cared little about that, not after the substance of presidential power was at last in his hands.[30]

———— ★ ★ ★ ★ ————

CHAPTER 27

"I WOULD NOT
FIRE A GUN"

Between election and inauguration comes speculation, mainly about what the new administration will do that is different from what the outgoing President did. As far as most people were concerned, the biggest challenge facing the government right now was either the national debt, which had grown more than twentyfold because of the war, or Reconstruction, which was turning, in some parts of the South, into war by other means.

Grant knew as well as anyone that Reconstruction had already run out of steam, that radicalism had been rejected with his election. He certainly did not doubt that the best chance of forcing fundamental change on the South was in the immediate aftermath of the war. Johnson had wasted that opportunity and, as so often in politics, once the initial impetus has passed from an attempted reform, it is virtually impossible to regenerate it. Even so, he had a responsibility to enforce the law. He could not wash his hands of the South.

Reconstruction, however, was not going to be his principal concern. The reason he became President, he told his old boyhood friend Daniel Ammen, was to do something about the debt, which currently stood at $2.5 billion.[1]

He planned to reduce, and eventually abolish, the wartime income tax, to count on customs duties and excise taxes to rise as the country recovered from the war, to keep a firm grip on government spending, and to use budget surpluses to help reduce the debt.[2]

One thing he wouldn't do was make poorly paid Federal workers bear the brunt of government cuts. When Congress introduced an eight-hour day for government employees in June 1869, Grant reacted imme-diately with a proclamation that "no reduction shall be made in the wages paid by the Government by the day to laborers, workmen and mechanics."[3]

Besides having to redeem or refinance more than a billion dollars in bonds that would fall due during the 1870s, the government was trying to abolish greenbacks and return to specie payment. Many Americans wanted their country back the way it was—with a small government, a simpler way of life, the world's hardest currency—gold—and a national debt so small it was barely noticeable.

As long as a soft currency—the greenback—operated alongside gold, there would be irresistible opportunities for currency speculation. During the war, gold speculation had made it so hard to sell government bonds that Wall Street became known as "General Lee's left wing."[4]

Almost as soon as the war ended, the Johnson administration began abolishing greenbacks, retiring $50 million of the $450 million that was issued during the war. It wasn't possible, however, to cut the money supply without also shrinking the economy. When Grant was inaugu-rated the country was sliding into a recession. If phasing out greenbacks wasn't handled carefully, the economy would be pushed into a deeper recession, possibly something worse.

In the meantime, the gold speculators were becoming more ambi-tious than ever. Enter two semilegendary figures, Jim Fisk and Jay Gould. Fisk was a flamboyantly dressed, loud-mouthed, youthful Wall Street speculator with voracious appetites. He had a reputation for guz-zling champagne by the magnum and bedding women by the score. His sexual adventuring would end with his being shot dead by a cuckolded husband at the age of thirty-eight, but in 1869 he stood at the height of his daring and ambition.

Gould was Fisk's antithesis. He dressed like a funeral director, was boringly faithful to his wife, drank milk instead of champagne, and knew how to strip a railroad of its financial assets before its sharehold-ers woke up to the fact they'd been robbed by a heavily bearded man armed with nothing but a fully loaded pen. Gould, too, would die young, but succumbing to a virus, not a bullet.

Gould and Fisk calculated that with only $15 million in gold and gold certificates circulating in New York, where the gold price was fixed, they could buy up the entire amount, or close to it, and force up the price. The result would be an orgy of speculation that would end as all such orgies do—in a collapse that triggered an economic panic. But before that happened, Fisk and Gould planned to sell their holdings for an enormous profit. They would be left immensely rich, while countless others would be left immensely poor. There was only one catch: the new administration in Washington.

The Federal government's gold reserve amounted to approximately $80 million, and the government could always force the price down by releasing some of its holdings. In the spring of 1869 it was already doing that, to a limited degree, selling $2.5 million in gold each month to buy up greenbacks. The question was, Could Grant's secretary of the Treasury, George Boutwell, be persuaded to reduce, or even halt, government gold sales long enough for Fisk and Gould to move in, corner the New York gold market, then sell their holdings for some astronomical amount before the price collapsed?

Enter the third figure in the plot, Abel R. Corbin, an elderly New York financier and his new bride, Virginia, maiden name Grant. Known to everyone as Jenny, Grant's sister was a thirty-seven-year-old wallflower, an old maid planted firmly on the shelf in Covington, Kentucky, with nothing much to look forward to except spending the rest of her uninteresting life with Jesse and Hannah, and then Corbin showed up, at about the time her brother was nominated for the presidency. Following a brief courtship Corbin, who at a spry sixty-six was nearly as old as Jesse Root Grant, asked her to marry him. She accepted and before long was living in New York, where Abel was forever entertaining Fisk and Gould.[5]

Whether Corbin married Jenny before the gold conspiracy was launched or whether it was launched as an idea that came to him and his pals after he married Grant's sister is impossible to say and probably not all that important. The fact is, Corbin was an obvious gold digger, so it isn't surprising to find him at the heart of a gold scam almost as soon as his honeymoon ended.

Through Corbin, Fisk and Gould now had access to the President and they wasted little time moving in. When Grant traveled to Boston in June 1869 to open a festival devoted to peace, he spent a couple of nights at Corbin's New York home, where he met Gould. From New York, he traveled to Boston aboard a steamboat owned by Jim Fisk.

Over dinner aboard the boat, the conversation moved fitfully from subject to subject. Grant didn't have much to say, but then someone mentioned the state of the economy and the risk of a financial panic. Grant suddenly came alive. "There is a certain fictitiousness about the prosperity of the country," said Grant. "This bubble might as well be tapped in one way as another." Fisk and Gould were appalled. The President, they gloomily concluded, was "a contractionist."[6]

During the summer, however, Grant began to wonder whether the Treasury was selling too much gold. The crops were ripening and the price of internationally traded commodities, such as wheat and corn, was fixed in gold, but farmers were paid for their crops in greenbacks. A high price for gold helped the farmers. Conversely, a low price hurt them, and they were already suffering the effects of the recession. It was hardly surprising that Grant, who considered himself a farmer at heart and farmers as the backbone of the nation, wanted to help them if he could.

In early September John Rawlins died and Grant, passing through New York on the way to the funeral, which would be held in Connecticut, stayed once again at Corbin's home. When Gould came to call on Corbin and Grant, the subject of the nation's finances came up again, and Gould was thrilled to discover that the President wasn't a contractionist after all. In fact, several days later Grant sent a message to Boutwell suggesting it might help the farmers if the government reduced its gold sales.[7]

Fisk and Gould, meanwhile, were busy buying. By mid-September they owned most of the gold and gold certificates on the New York market, and there were hundreds of lesser speculators following in their wake, holding contracts for future purchases of gold that exceeded the entire national gold reserve.

Hoping to keep Grant on their side, Fisk and Gould tried to bribe his secretary, Horace Porter, by placing an order for $500,000 in gold in Porter's name. When Porter learned of it, he immediately repudiated the transaction. They also tried to put pressure on Grant directly by getting Corbin to write to him, urging him not to permit government gold sales until the harvest was in.

When Grant received Corbin's letter, he was incensed. This was the first he knew that his brother-in-law had been speculating in the gold market. He probably sensed, too, that Corbin, Fisk and Gould had been trying to manipulate him. Stalking into Julia's room carrying Corbin's letter, intending to tell her about it, he found his wife writing a letter to Jenny. Grant had her add a few comments from himself: Corbin was to stop speculating in gold. At once.[8]

There was an implied threat in this demand, and when Julia's letter reached Corbin's house on Thursday, September 23, he, Gould and Fisk all realized Grant was preparing to ruin them. "I must get out instantly—instantly!" wailed Corbin. Gold, which had been stuck at $130 since spring, had started moving in recent days and had just touched $140. The millions in gold that they held had been transmogrified in the space of a few minutes into a bundle of dynamite and Grant was about to reach for a match.[9]

While the plotters huddled in Corbin's house were arguing over what to do, Grant was sending for Boutwell. He told the secretary of the Treasury he was getting worried about the sudden increase in the price of gold. There was virtually no gold left for people who really needed it. Customs duties, for example, had to be paid in gold. Banks settled transactions between themselves in gold. Grant showed him a pile of telegrams from hard-pressed bankers and merchants. There was no gold left for them to buy. The speculators had it all. Boutwell recommended the government sell enough gold to break the market. How much did he have in mind? asked Grant. "Three million dollars," said Boutwell. Grant told him, "I think you had better make it five million."[10]

Next morning, Friday, September 24, Fisk and Gould started pulling out of the market, just as the price of gold shot up to $162. It hovered there, poised to go even higher, when the news flashed over the wires— Boutwell had ordered the immediate sale of $4 million in gold. By half past twelve, the price had fallen to $135 an ounce. Fisk and Gould— and most of the smaller speculators riding on their coattails—were wiped out.

Julia was afraid that Fisk and Gould would try to implicate Grant in the plot, but he reassured her. "I had nothing to do with it, and I have no papers which could be tortured into anything disreputable."[11]

That did not stop Fisk and Gould from seeking revenge on the man who had ruined them. When Congress investigated the gold panic, they did not try to claim outright that he had taken bribes. Instead, they exaggerated their influence with him, to make it appear that he had been involved, without actually saying so. Meanwhile, they began a whispering campaign against Julia. She, ran the story, had pocketed a $100,000 bribe from Fisk and Gould for getting Grant to reduce government gold sales. People who already despised Grant, such as Henry Adams, swallowed such stories whole, their animus making them gullible. Anti-administration newspapers also added to the chorus of disapproval, transforming what was merely the gift of a $200 watch from Corbin to Grant as being a bribe of $25,000. Apart from rumors and innuendo from Fisk and Gould, swindlers on a cosmic scale, not a scrap of evidence was ever produced against either Grant or his wife.[12]

The chairman of the congressional committee that investigated the gold panic was James A. Garfield—no admirer of Grant. Far from it. When the lieutenant-general bill had been presented to Congress to give Grant a third star, Garfield had led the opposition against it. In his report on the gold plot, Garfield exonerated Grant and his family, with the exception of the gullible and greedy Corbin.[13]

The larger questions—of how to reduce the national debt and how to phase out paper money without wrecking the economy—remained. Grant had just had an embarrassing introduction to how difficult the economic struggle would prove to be.

★

Being President in peacetime was not remotely as exciting as being a general in wartime. It did not take Grant long to find the White House, with its bureaucratic routines and formal occasions, fundamentally tedious. The issues that fully engaged his interests and abilities nearly always involved national security, beginning with his attempt to purchase San Domingo, better known these days as the Dominican Republic.

Grant had never forgotten the nightmarish ordeal of shepherding women, children and desperately sick soldiers across the Isthmus of Panama in 1852. Not surprisingly, then, in his very first message to Congress he called for the construction of a canal linking the Caribbean and the Pacific. "To Europeans the benefits of the proposed canal are great. To Americans they are incalculable." The canal would be built by American engineers and remain under American control. During his presidency Grant sent no fewer than seven surveying expeditions to Central America to look for the best route across.[14]

There was more to Grant's canal ambitions, though, than his traumatic experiences as a young lieutenant. He believed that the United States would continue to grow bigger and richer and that as it did so its presence in the Caribbean and Central America, small though it was now, would increase dramatically. The Navy would need a large natural harbor, preferably with an adjacent expanse of level, well-drained ground, big enough to accommodate barracks, warehouses and workshops. One way or another, the Caribbean was going to become an American lake. The question was not whether military and naval bases would be needed but how long the decision could be delayed.

The pressure was already building. In the first year of Grant's presidency the United States risked being drawn into a war with Spain over Cuba. The Spanish occupation was punctuated by periodic revolts, which Spain suppressed with a brutality that outraged American opinion. Cuban insurgents were treated as heroes in the United States and what money they had was raised in American cities. Grant's sympathies were entirely with the Cubans, but he could not convince Charles Sumner, who dominated the Senate Foreign Affairs Committee, to support a strong American line against Spain.

A product of the Bostonian upper class and a man who carried all through life a love of learning that reflected Harvard at its best, Sumner lacked the judgment that distills knowledge into wisdom. His reputation in the Senate, however, was unassailable. Sumner enjoyed the enviable prestige of the living, still-breathing-and-with-scars-to-prove-it martyr. One of the most eloquent abolitionists in Congress, in 1856 he had been clubbed senseless at his Senate desk by Preston Brooks, a young representative from South Carolina. This brutal, irrational act was a curtain-raiser on the national disaster to come.[15]

Sumner was a strange, tormented character, and being beaten on the head may have left him with traces of brain damage. As he aged, even his friends were sometimes inclined to doubt his sanity. Tall and solidly built, he possessed fleshy, uninteresting features and seemed determined to make up for the dull face and form nature had provided by dressing eccentrically. Exactly the kind of thing Grant would hold against someone.

His private life was ghastly. Awkward and pompous around women, he did not marry until he reached his fifties. His bride was a vivacious widow half his age. Sumner's powers turned out to be entirely political.

According to his wife, the senator was impotent. She left him after nine months of sexual frustration and humiliation for them both. Embittered and frustrated, she made sure the entire world knew that the great man had all the virility of a dishrag.[16]

There was no more radical Republican in the Senate than Sumner, which made him completely antipathetic to Grant. So too did the way Sumner forever appropriated the intellectual high ground, as if that remote and lightly populated summit were the only place for an honest man to live. When Boutwell asked Grant one day whether he had ever heard Sumner converse, Grant shot back, "No, but I have heard him lecture."[17]

Sumner treated politics not as the art of the possible but as the pursuit of perfection, and damn the cost. He was extravagantly admired and just as bitterly hated. His enemies liked to spread the word that Sumner was a freethinker, and shortly after Grant was elected and someone solemnly informed him that Senator Sumner had no faith in the Bible, Grant replied drolly, "Well, he didn't write it."[18]

It can hardly have surprised Grant, then, to find that almost from the start of his administration he could not get Sumner to help him with the Cuban problem. Fish, meanwhile, was arguing that the solution wasn't a war but to buy the island outright. The insurgency was suppressed, however, before serious negotiations could begin.[19]

The United States needed a Caribbean policy that amounted to more than bobbing into the future on the ebb and flow of popular emotion. During the Johnson administration secretary of state William H. Seward had tried to lay the foundations of an American military presence in the Caribbean. Seward was a visionary. It was he who persuaded a reluctant Russia to sell, and a deeply suspicious Congress to buy, the remote, empty spaces of Alaska. Shortly before Grant was inaugurated, Seward tried to buy the Danish West Indies, but nothing had come of this. Meanwhile, Seward was also trying to negotiate with the government of San Domingo for a long-term lease on Samaná Bay, one of the best anchorages in the Caribbean. This initiative, too, failed to produce a result.[20]

Seward's contacts on San Domingo included a pair of American adventurers—James W. Fabens and William Lewis Cazneau. They had been speculating in San Domingan properties since the early 1860s and were on good terms with the island's leader, President Buenaventura

Báez. It was the nature of government in San Domingo, an island occupied mainly by the descendants of slaves, to be perennially broke and politically unstable.

When Grant was inaugurated, Báez was attempting to float a huge loan, with the aid of Fabens and Cazneau, on the London money market. Half the proceeds from the loan would go to Fabens, Cazneau and Báez, as their commission. What was left over would go into the government's coffers—maybe. When the proposed loan failed to materialize, Báez had another idea: He would sell his country to the United States. He would get rich, his trusty advisers—Fabens and Cazneau— would also get rich, and the United States would be left, in its wisdom and wealth, to wrestle with San Domingo's enduring problems of race and poverty.

Fabens traveled to Washington, managed to arrange a meeting with Grant and put this proposition to him. Grant was intrigued, not to say excited. He asked a Philadelphia businessman, Benjamin Hunt, to go to San Domingo and report back to him on conditions there. Hunt fell ill before he could depart and Grant had one of his secretaries, Colonel Orville Babcock, travel to San Domingo in Hunt's place.

At a cabinet meeting in mid-August 1869 Babcock, freshly returned from his Caribbean mission, handed out ore samples from San Domingo. The island, he said, was teeming with mineral wealth. He had brought back something else, as well—a treaty of annexation, signed by President Báez. Fish pointedly remarked that the treaty was of no value, saying that Babcock had no authority from the State Department to negotiate on behalf of the United States.[21]

Grant sent Babcock back to San Domingo in November, this time with the required diplomatic authority. In his luggage were a banker's draft for one hundred thousand dollars, hundreds of rifles, and tens of thousands of rounds of ammunition, just in case President Báez had to cope with unruly elements who didn't want to see their country sold to the United States. Babcock returned shortly before Christmas with a new treaty, properly negotiated. He also brought an agreement for a long-term lease on Samaná Bay in case the treaty failed or wasn't considered acceptable.[22]

The evening of January 2, 1870, Grant walked out of the White House wrapped in a cloak and crossed Lafayette Square to call on Senator Sumner. This was unprecedented. Presidents did not pay calls, but

Grant was attempting to reach Sumner through his vanity. He found the senator sitting down to dinner with a pair of well-known political journalists. Grant told Sumner about Babcock's treaty and asked for his support. "I expect, Mr. President, to support the measures of your administration," said Sumner. This was hardly a commitment, but Grant always believed it was, and so did the two journalists.[23]

Anyway, Grant did not expect Sumner to oppose annexation. On the contrary, he assumed Sumner would support it, because Sumner was, Grant later told a friend, "a man who had advocated the annexation of islands extending nearly to Asia."[24]

Opposition to the treaty was fierce and Grant asked Sumner's staunchest ally on the Foreign Affairs Committee, Senator Carl Schurz of Missouri, to come and see him. "You are a member of the Senate committee that has the San Domingo treaty under consideration," said Grant. "I wish you would support that treaty. Won't you do that?"

The more Schurz learned of just how Babcock had managed to get hold of the treaty, the more disgusted he had become. The $100,000 draft and the small arsenal of weapons looked like the tools of bribery and coercion to him. There were rumors, too, that Babcock himself was going to get rich from the deal. But what really bothered him, as he explained his position to Grant, was race—San Domingo had a population that was almost entirely black. Its people were "indigestible, unassimilable," he said. "Those tropical islands would, owing to their climatic conditions, never be predominantly settled by people of Germanic blood [and] the populations inhabiting them could not be trusted with a share in governing our country." Grant soon lost interest in talking to Schurz. This supposed champion of southern blacks was, once you scratched the surface, just another racist after all.[25]

Even so, Schurz's objections were widely shared on Capitol Hill. James A. Garfield, for example, believed that the United States would need military bases to protect its interests in the Caribbean, that it would have to take over at least one island someday, but he was opposed to buying San Domingo. Why? Because the people of the West Indies were "strangely degenerated by their mixture with native races"—they were a combination, that is, of blacks, Hispanics and Indians. Such people had no place in American life.[26]

Grant told Garfield that far from adding to America's racial problems, the acquisition of San Domingo would act as a safety valve, providing a place that persecuted blacks in southern states could move to and get a new start. The soil of the island was rich. With American investment, it would flourish and its people would prosper. Strategically, it was ideal. A naval base at Samaná Bay would allow the United States to dominate the Gulf of Mexico and control the approaches to the canal that would surely be built one day across Central America. America would lose nothing by acquiring San Domingo but would gain in both power and wealth. Garfield, however, would not be persuaded.[27]

One evening that summer another congressman, Rutherford B. Hayes of Ohio, stopped by the White House to talk to Grant about San Domingo. Like Garfield, Hayes was not in favor of the treaty, but unlike Garfield, he found himself impressed by the strength of the case Grant made for ratification of the San Domingo treaty. Grant spoke eloquently and at length on the economic and strategic advantages of a peaceful annexation. He was angry, too, he told Hayes, at the opposition. Sumner, he fumed, had "very little practical sense." As for Schurz, the man was "an infidel and an atheist" and, not content with being disloyal to the government of his native Germany, had immigrated to the U.S. and become disloyal to this government, too.[28]

When the treaty was reported out from the Foreign Affairs Committee in March 1870, Sumner, Schurz and three other members of the committee announced that they opposed ratification. Only two members of the committee were in favor. The possibility of leasing Samaná Bay was not even considered.

Some aspects of the treaty negotiation could be criticized on ethical or procedural grounds, but the debate was fueled less by moral scruples than by Sumner's wounded pride at not being involved before Babcock brought back the treaty; by an understandable suspicion of adventurers such as Fabens and Cazneau; by distaste for such an obvious opportunist as Báez; and by racism yielding one of its predictable by-products—stupidity. Extending American citizenship to another two hundred thousand black people when the black population of the United States was already at least six million was hardly going to undermine the American way of life.

The treaty Grant submitted to the Senate called for a plebiscite to determine the wishes of the people of San Domingo. Their country would not have vanished without their consent. Grant had no doubt that they would vote overwhelmingly in favor of annexation by the United States, and he was probably right.

When the treaty was finally voted on by the Senate, it fell far short of the two-thirds majority needed for ratification. It was a bitter blow to Grant. Even little Jesse noticed the change in his father's mood. Grant was normally optimistic and easygoing, but these days his son found him irascible and difficult. He asked his father what was so important about San Domingo. "Because it should belong to us," said Grant. "There is not one sound argument against annexation, and one day we shall need it badly."[29]

After failing to push the treaty through in 1870, Grant tried again, in 1871, when there was a new Congress. An independent commission was sent to examine conditions in San Domingo. The commission reported back in favor of annexation. Meanwhile, Grant prevailed on the Republican leadership in the Senate to remove Sumner from the Foreign Affairs Committee, over strenuous protests from Schurz. Grant submitted the San Domingo treaty to the Senate again, and failed again.

In the course of his life Grant never hated anyone quite the way he hated Sumner. They were so temperamentally unalike that friction was probably inevitable, and Sumner's affected way of calling him "Grawnt" was bound to offend. What was infuriating, however, was that although Sumner was a Republican, he was disloyal, a man who had wounded a Republican administration more than any Democrat could. One day the President and Massachusetts senator George Frisbie Hoar were walking past Sumner's house in Lafayette Square when Grant stopped, raised his arm and shook his fist at Sumner's windows. "The man who lives up there has abused me in a way I have never suffered from any other man living!"[30]

His sole consolation was his conviction that History would prove him right over San Domingo, as it has done. Little more than a decade after Grant's death, the United States went to war with Spain. It seized the best naval anchorage in Cuba, at Guantánamo Bay. More than a century later, Guantánamo Bay is full of U.S. Navy ships and defended by thousands of U.S. Marines. The war with Spain also provided an opportunity to seize Puerto Rico, an American possession to this day. In 1917 Denmark was asked to sell the Danish West Indian islands. Behind the offer was a none too subtle hint that if Denmark refused, the U.S. would take them by force. That was how Danish territory became, for $25 million, the U.S. Virgin Islands. And throughout the twentieth century, American forces have been dispatched repeatedly to the Dominican

Republic, Haiti and other Caribbean islands to defend American interests in the region.

What the United States has secured since Grant's death only by war, threats of war, military intervention, and military occupation, Grant, during his presidency, tried to obtain peacefully. "I would not fire a gun to annex territory," said Grant. "I consider it too great a privilege to belong to the United States for us to go around gunning for new territories."[31]

★

Even if he did not like living in the White House, Julia loved it, once she had made some improvements. The executive mansion had been neglected for years. The carpets were worn, the paintwork dingy, the furniture broken down, scratched and shabby. To Johnson, Lincoln and Presidents before them the White House had always been a workplace, never a home.

Julia changed all that. She was hardly installed as First Lady before she had it cleaned up and repainted. The furniture, drapes and carpets were replaced. Male members of the staff, accustomed to lounging about in their old clothes, playing cards and smoking, were ordered to wear dress suits and white gloves, leave their cards at home and given a choice between smoking and dismissal. The gates had been open ever since the iron fence had gone up around the South Lawn thirty years earlier. People were free to wander into the grounds, and a lot of them did so, including the drunks, the mentally ill and the homeless. No one had thought of locking the gates and keeping the public out until Julia did it and turned the White House grounds into a place where Jesse and his sister Nellie could play in safety. It was Julia who turned 1600 Pennsylvania Avenue into a clean, orderly and comfortable place to live.[32]

She also transformed social life in the mansion. There were two receptions each week, one in the afternoon for invited guests to call on the First Lady, the other on Wednesday evenings so the people could call on the President. Julia held her afternoon reception at two P.M. on Tuesdays, the day the cabinet met. Instead of receiving her callers alone, she invited cabinet wives to join her for lunch and then to stand in the receiving line, like maids of honor at a European court. She and most cabinet wives became good friends, and her receptions were a great success, with the Marine band providing background music and lots of handsome young officers in dress uniforms circulating about the room, adding to the charm of the occasion for Julia's female callers.[33]

Julia turned out to be the most popular First Lady since Dolley Madison. She was gregarious, sensible and unaffected. She got rid of lazy or incompetent staff, including the White House cook, a former Army sergeant who knew how to provide robust soldier fare—either roast beef or a roast turkey—and nothing else. At a stroke she revolutionized the White House dining experience. The sergeant's successor was a professional chef.[34]

Julia's eighty-three-year-old father moved into the White House and set up court in the reception room by the front door. He sat there for much of each day, gossiping with his cronies, casting a sharp eye over the stream of visitors, and chatting with his son Colonel Frederick Tracy Dent. He loved to talk politics, reminisce about his imagined days as a rich planter and powerful political figure back in Missouri, and denounce his son-in-law as "a turncoat" for having switched allegiance from the Democratic party to the Republicans. He was an old bore, but Julia still doted on him, and Grant still ignored him.[35]

Old Jesse Grant also came to Washington. He had embarrassed his son by getting involved in the campaign to nominate him for the presidency and played an active role in the election campaign that followed. His excitement at his son's success was almost palpable, and when Ulysses was inaugurated, Jesse was there to witness it. Even so, the two families did not simply fail to get along. There was a lot of personal dislike. Old Jesse and Julia's father loathed each other and made no pretense about it. So when Jesse came to Washington, which he did several times a year after his son became President, he did not stay at the White House. He moved into a nearby hotel.[36]

Grant's mother stayed away. Hannah would not watch her son's inauguration and did not visit the White House once during his presidency. When a neighbor back in Covington, Kentucky, remarked, "I think you must be very proud to think of your son being made President," she mumbled something, and it seems a good bet that it wasn't "Yes, I am." Hannah would never admit to being proud of anything. Pride was a sin.[37]

While Julia was turning the White House into something resembling a home, Grant was making some changes of his own. Lincoln's assassination had brought the creation of the Secret Service. When Grant moved into the White House there were guards throughout the mansion. He got rid of them. He was as unprotected as Presidents had traditionally been. Grant often walked the streets of Washington alone, as he had done in his days as a soldier.[38]

Meanwhile, he modernized the way the President's business was conducted. He had three colonels as secretaries—Horace Porter, Orville Babcock and Frederick Dent—plus one civilian, Robert Douglas, son of Stephen A. Douglas. The three colonels brought a quasi-military air to the President's offices on the second floor. They did not wear uniforms, but even in civilian dress they had an unmistakably military bearing. Poor Douglas soon felt frozen out and left to become a U.S. Marshal.

Before Grant became President almost anyone who wanted to see the President could enter the White House and hang about, in the corridors or on the stairs, hoping for a word. Lobbyists, visitors and tourists intermingled with the White House staff and presidential family in scenes of confusion hard for a later generation to imagine. Frederick Dent was put in charge of the reception room. All visitors had to report there and convince Dent that their business warranted an appointment with Grant. Otherwise he directed them to see either Babcock or Porter, or simply turned them away.[39]

Most days, Grant woke at seven, read the newspapers before going to take Julia to breakfast at half past eight, took a walk around the neighborhood if the weather was good, and went to his office at ten, where he spent the next five hours dealing with correspondence and official appointments. In late afternoon he would either have a buggy hitched to a team of handsome thoroughbreds and go for a drive or else take a stroll. Youngsters played baseball on the open ground between the Washington Monument and the South Lawn, and Grant sometimes took a bat in hand and tested the pitching before walking on, smoking a cigar. On Sundays, if the weather was fair, he liked to take a six-mile walk around Georgetown.[40]

Grant's relationship with his four children remained close. His eldest son, Fred, was at West Point, and the second eldest, Ulysses, Jr., was a student at Harvard. The two youngest, Nellie and Jesse, grew up in the White House.

The mansion's staff had never seen such mutual devotion between a President and his wife. Grant loved Julia to the point of uxoriousness and at times appeared henpecked. Grant found it hard to refuse her anything. There were limits, though. Julia felt embarrassed at the nation having a cross-eyed First Lady and arranged to have an operation to straighten her eyes. When Grant heard of it he made her cancel the operation. He loved her just as she was, he told her, including the strabismus.[41]

They walked to and from every meal arm in arm. His working day did not begin until he and Julia had spent half an hour or so chatting alone in her room each morning. To both of them, a happy marriage was a romance, not a limited partnership.

While in public Grant appeared alone in a crowd, within the White House he was surrounded by people who loved him, beginning with his family. Porter and Babcock were treated more like sons than secretaries. His affection for them was obvious. On Sundays, Grant's childhood friend Daniel Ammen, now an admiral, had a standing invitation for lunch. Old Army friends like Sherman, whom he had made general-in-chief, stopped by regularly.[42]

When senators and representatives came to call in the evening, they were likely to find Grant on the portico at the back of the White House, looking at the Washington Monument. Julia would probably be there, along with her father, a few female friends, and the two youngest children, Jesse and Nellie. This was the scene that Rutherford B. Hayes found when he came calling one summer's night in 1870. There was no real conversation, just small talk—the recent weather, West Point, the rapid growth of American cities—until the women decided it was time to go inside and took the children with them. Then Grant sent for cigars and the talk turned serious. Politics was a subject too complex, too important, for the delicate ears of women.

Being President had been hard at first, said Grant. But now he'd grown used to it. As he sat there, puffing a cigar and savoring the breeze that came up from the Potomac and swept across this side of the mansion, he probably believed it.[43]

————— ★ ★ ★ ★ —————

CHAPTER 28

"A CONDITION
OF LAWLESSNESS"

Even before he was inaugurated Grant found himself wrestling with the unwelcome legacy of Raphael Semmes. There was no sailor, North or South, who quite compared with the tall, handsome and courtly Semmes, Winfield Scott's naval aide in the Mexican War. By the time of Grant's election Semmes had concluded his military career and become a professor of moral philosophy, but during the Civil War he commanded the most successful of the Confederacy's small force of commerce raiders and blockade runners, the C.S.S. *Alabama*.

This lightly armed nine-hundred-ton steam-driven vessel was built in a British yard near Liverpool. Britain had declared its neutrality in the war and, as a neutral, considered itself free to continue trading with both sides in the conflict, buying wheat from the North and cotton from the South and selling weapons to both. Semmes collected the *Alabama* in August 1862 and during the following two years circumnavigated the globe, seizing or sinking more than sixty Union ships. The *Alabama*'s course reached its conclusion when she was sunk off Cherbourg by the U.S.S. *Kearsarge* in July 1864.

As soon as the war ended the Johnson administration began pressing the British to make good the losses inflicted by the *Alabama* and other raiders. They were not in a good position to resist. The *Alabama* had not sailed the seas openly as a Confederate warship, as the British had expected, but cloaked herself in the flags of various nations, pretending to be a merchant vessel, before closing in on her prey. She did not, that is, operate as the warship of a belligerent seeking battle. Semmes was too much like an old-fashioned pirate for the British, who were in the forefront of the international effort to eradicate piracy.

Even before the Civil War ended the British government was hoping for a fresh start with Washington. For a time it seemed they had one. Between Grant's election and his inauguration the American ambassador in London, Reverdy Johnson, reached a provisional settlement with the British foreign secretary, Lord Clarendon, outlining the way an agreement might be reached.

The British accepted that the *Alabama*'s activities flouted maritime law and were prepared to pay for actual losses caused to American public property, which didn't amount to more than $20 million. Direct losses suffered by private individuals and companies had already been settled by the insurance companies. What the British would not accept was claims for indirect or consequential losses flowing from the fact that they had sold arms to the South.

Grant was disgusted with the Johnson-Clarendon Convention. He thought Andrew Johnson was so eager to conclude a deal that he had conceded too much to the British. More than that, he was convinced Britain's declaration of neutrality when the Civil War began was a ploy, a move intended to hurt the Union and aid the Confederacy, an act so unjust it could not be settled without an admission of guilt and payment for indirect losses. Besides, this was exactly the kind of international issue that interested him. Grant resented being sidelined by a lame-duck President, a man he despised.

Sumner was more than indignant. He was incensed. Johnson hadn't bothered to consult him, even though he chaired the Senate Foreign Affairs Committee. Under the new administration, things were going to be done differently. The evening that Grant's cabinet list was sent to the Senate, Henry Adams went to Sumner's Lafayette Square house to ask what his old friend thought of Grant's choices. Sumner imperiously said it didn't matter that he had not been named secretary of state—he was going to control American foreign policy anyway, through his committee. And one of the first things he intended to do was get the agreement negotiated in London annulled. The British would have to pay for aid-ing the South by selling them the *Alabama* and other weapons. They should start by ceding Canada to the U.S. If they refused, war was certain to follow. American forces would fight around the globe, taking the conflict to all parts of the British Empire. America would emerge from the struggle stronger, while the British would see their empire fade away.[1]

Grant did not have to reject the Johnson-Clarendon Convention—Sumner was going to do it for him. Sumner showed Grant the draft of the speech he had prepared denouncing the agreement. At this stage in their relationship, Grant still thought it might be possible to work with Sumner. Who, he asked Sumner, ought to be the new American ambassador to London, the man who would tackle the British face to face? Sumner suggested his protégé, John Lothrop Motley, he of the monocle and hair parted in the middle. Grant made the appointment and on April 12, 1869, the Senate confirmed it.[2]

Next day Sumner rose on the Senate floor and tore into the provisional settlement of the *Alabama* claims (an expression that by now covered damage done by all the blockade runners). He did not simply condemn the Johnson-Clarendon Convention but raised the stakes sky-high. Britain had declared neutrality in the war for the Union, yet it was longstanding British policy to eliminate slavery by impounding ships involved in the slave trade. Nevertheless, Britain had been so hypocritically eager to profit from the war that it had built and sold the *Alabama* and other blockade runners to the Confederacy. The result was not only the devastation of the American merchant fleet but the prolongation of the war. The losses to the merchant fleet amounted to $110 million. The real cost, though, was "leaving twenty-five hundred millions as a national debt to burden the people." The United States, Sumner said, should demand that Britain pay accordingly.[3]

The senators went wild, cheering, shouting, stamping their feet, aroused to a patriotic fervor not seen since the grand review of the victorious Union armies four years earlier. The Johnson-Clarendon Convention, which did little more than establish a framework for arbitration, was dead on arrival. British immigration to the United States was discouraged. There were demands for a complete ban on all Anglo-American trade. And Sumner's idea that Britain use Canada as a down payment on the *Alabama* claims was presented to Congress by Senator Zachariah Chandler.

Nearly twenty years before, young Lieutenant Grant had sued Chandler after slipping on the ice outside Chandler's Detroit home and Chandler had only had to pay him six cents in damages after convincing the jury that the lieutenant was probably drunk when he fell. Since then Chandler had gone into politics and become a senator, and now he claimed that sixty thousand Michigan volunteers would spring to arms and overrun Canada in a month. All they needed was the word.[4]

Ironically, the British would have been glad to get rid of Canada, but the Canadians did not want independence. Nor did they want to be swallowed up by the United States. Even so, the wishes of the Canadians never figured in the calculations of Sumner, Chandler or the outraged American press.

For all the talk of war, however, the United States was not in a good position to wage one. The Navy had been demobilized following the Civil War. It now consisted of a motley collection of wooden sailing vessels. The Navy, like much of the nation, was trying to move back to a simpler past. The British fleet, on the other hand, consisted mainly of steel-clad vessels driven by steam.

It was the financial markets, however, that were the biggest barrier to waging war on the British Empire, not military calculations. The first economic consequences of Sumner's speech were that the value of government bonds nosedived and American businessmen went into shock. The country's industrialization was largely financed by British money. Where would business borrow if London's banks stopped their loans? American banks had almost nothing left to lend. Come to that, where would the government borrow? Grant and Treasury secretary George Boutwell were already struggling to pay the interest on the national debt. They hoped they might refinance it, over a longer term and at a lower rate of interest, but they could only do that with the help of financing from European—mainly British—banks. A war with Britain would almost certainly bring a repudiation of America's debt, or the equivalent—a failure to pay the interest.[5]

The war that Sumner and Chandler were looking forward to was likely to be over quickly, and less likely to end in national rejoicing than national bankruptcy. Sumner, eloquent in Latin and Greek, was a dunce at economics. "Of all the crazy acts Sumner ever did, and they are many," Henry Adams eventually concluded, "I think his speech [on the *Alabama* claims] the maddest."[6]

In the meantime, Grant hoped the British would settle the issue by giving up Canada, almost to the point of expecting them to do so. Fish was more realistic—no British government was any more likely to cede territory because it was being threatened with war than an American government would be.[7]

Although Grant was no more inclined to fire a gun to obtain Canada than he was to fire one to gain San Domingo, he remained heart and soul with the angry, anti-British mood that Sumner's speech had unleashed. When Sumner asked whether Grant was discomfited by the reaction to the speech, Grant said, "Not in the least. Let it go on." He regarded Britain almost as an enemy.[8]

Not surprisingly, then, a year after Sumner's speech, there was still no progress on the *Alabama* claims and there was no chance of moving things forward. In the Johnson-Clarendon Convention the British had suggested arbitration of the dispute, but in rejecting the convention the U.S. had said no to arbitration. Nor would Grant declare war and invade Canada.

He could either leave this quarrel to fester and hand it on to his successor or he could make a fresh start. Grant opted for the fresh start, and began by sending a new ambassador, Robert C. Schenck, a former Union Army general and currently a lame-duck member of the House of Representatives, to London. Schenck was an acknowledged authority on poker, which might have added to his qualifications as an amateur diplomat.[9]

Sumner's friend John Lothrop Motley was recalled. This was interpreted by Sumner, and by an irate Motley, as a mean-spirited attempt by Grant to avenge himself for Sumner's opposition to the San Domingo annexation, and they were probably right. Motley's instructions had been so vague that it would have been easy for Grant to launch a new policy without installing a new ambassador.[10]

The British were still pushing the idea of arbitration and, for want of a realistic alternative, Grant finally and reluctantly agreed. Boutwell had found it impossible to find European banks that would refinance the American debt. As long as the *Alabama* claims remained unresolved, there was a risk of war, and there's not much that makes bankers more nervous.

Two years after Sumner had whipped his countrymen into a xenophobic frenzy, he was no longer chairman of the Foreign Affairs Committee. At last the Treaty of Washington, committing both sides to submit the issue to arbitration, was sent to the Senate. It passed by a vote of 50 to 12, something that would never have happened had Sumner's power not been broken; but now, chastened, Sumner himself voted in the treaty's favor. Ratifications were exchanged in Washington on June 17, 1871—the ninety-fifth anniversary of the battle of Bunker Hill.

An international arbitration panel was established in Geneva, consisting of one American—Charles Francis Adams, father of Henry— one Englishman, a Swiss jurist, a Brazilian diplomat and an Italian count. At which point Fish nearly wrecked everything. The British expected the arbitration would deal solely with the actual losses caused to the U.S. government by the *Alabama* and the other raiders. Instead, Grant allowed Fish to demand that the arbitrators rule on the indirect losses—the claims, that is, that Sumner had talked about as part of the national debt. By Fish's calculation these came to a billion dollars. The British weren't prepared to allow the arbitrators anywhere near the indirect claims, even after the U.S. said privately that it was not going to press for compensation. For Grant what mattered wasn't money but vindication.[11]

His approach to an issue like this was always going to be colored by his enveloping sense of patriotism. But besides that, he shared the anger that millions of Americans felt when they contemplated the fact that the British had made a profit out of neutrality. Americans considered that kind of behavior cynical and immoral and crying out for punishment. The puritanism that in Britain was fading fast still occupied the uplands of the American conscience. As Grant told W. H. Smith, the White House correspondent of the *Washington Star,* what he wanted from the British more than money was an apology, an admission that they were in the wrong.[12]

Grant was also being encouraged to apply more pressure by Adam Badeau, his former military secretary. Badeau had been assigned to the American legation in London, where he did all he could to exalt his own position and back-stab his superiors. He informed Grant that the British government was so desperate to settle it would do almost anything to prevent the talks ending in failure.[13]

The sudden demand that the arbitrators rule on the validity of the American claim for indirect losses nearly destroyed Grant's new beginning. If this claim was pressed, it could only revive talk of war. Contrary to Badeau's advice, that was something the British were prepared to risk rather than concede the issue of the indirect claims.

Grant was left facing a stark choice—stick to the actual losses or be stuck with the blame for destroying the best, possibly the only, chance to settle the issue peacefully. It was simply too humiliating for him to contemplate a public retreat from the indirect claims and the Treaty of Washington looked as good as dead.

With the politicans unable to agree, it fell to two diplomats, one American and one British, to bring it back to life. They agreed to ask the arbitrators to make a declaration on the indirect claims, not a decision. The arbitrators promptly declared that they had no power to consider indirect claims. The arbitration would be limited to direct losses.

Grant probably never saw how dangerous a path he had been treading. His determination—like Sumner's—to see international relations in simplistic moral terms was a formula for more conflict, not less. Had the claim for indirect losses been pursued, not only would the British have pulled out of the arbitration, but no country would ever again have been able to afford neutrality, because the economic price imposed on neutral countries could ultimately prove more expensive than taking sides at the outset. Grant's approach to the *Alabama* claims was short-sighted, short-term and semi-Sumnerian. Only when he abandoned it could the Geneva arbitration go ahead.[14]

The result was an award to the United States of $15.5 million and the establishment of what is still one of the most important precedents in international law. There was also a considerable clarification of the rights and obligations of neutral countries in time of war. This was the first major dispute between the world's great powers to be settled not by force but by an international panel of arbitrators. It remains a landmark in the development of international law. While it is humanity's loss that this precedent has not been followed more often, it is nonetheless to Grant's credit that it was established at all.[15]

Building on what had been achieved in Geneva, he was able to press for and get a quick resolution of all the other outstanding disputes with the British, which mainly involved fisheries and the American-Canadian boundary. "For the first time in the history of the United States as a nation," Grant informed Congress, there was no "question of disputed boundary between our territory and the possessions of Great Britain on this continent." He had achieved what Washington had only been able to dream about: The United States was finally free of foreign entangle-ments.[16]

★

Reconstruction was nearly four years old when Grant was sworn in as President. As general-in-chief he had tried to impose the will of Con-gress on the defeated and occupied South, insofar as Andrew Johnson allowed him to do so. Grant had no doubt that only the military could make a success of Reconstruction, but the tools he needed were being stripped from his hands by the rapid demobilization of the Union Army. When the war ended, there were a quarter of a million Union soldiers occupying the ten former states of the Confederacy. Four years later there were eleven thousand soldiers in those states, of which nearly half were in Texas, guarding the Mexican border.

Johnson, meanwhile, allowed seven of the rebel states back into the Union without having to do anything beyond pledge their allegiance to the Federal government. This was all wrong, thought Grant. The former states should be considered territories and, like other territories, told they had to achieve certain standards before they could join the Union. Military occupation should continue, to ensure protection for the freed-men, until the former rebel states were prepared to treat black people the same as whites. Meanwhile, former slaves should be given the rudi-ments of an education. Only after they had learned to read and write should they be allowed to vote, and only after these southern territories had met the requirements of the Reconstruction Acts would they be readmitted into the Union. This process might take ten years, but it would have a much better chance of success than Johnson's policy of appeasing the former slaveholders and leaving blacks to their fate.[17]

Not that radical Reconstruction held out much promise of a happier outcome. The South had been flooded with carpetbaggers eager to loot whatever the war had not destroyed. At the same time, power at the state level was often thrust into the hands of blacks. While a few were able and conscientious, most were inexperienced, poorly educated and re-viled by the white people they had to deal with. The chaotic proceed-ings of the all-black legislature imposed on South Carolina were taken as proof by white people across the South that giving political power to blacks was the North's revenge for Fort Sumter, that it had nothing to do with justice and everything to do with punishment.

Reconstruction, as Grant inherited it as President, had failed, but he hoped there was still a chance to make it work. The Fourteenth Amendment, passed over Johnson's veto, forced the courts to recognize that black people had rights, yet blacks still did not have the most important political right of all—the ballot. The Fifteenth Amendment, which was already making its way through Congress when he became President, would put ballot papers in their hands. Grant, who in 1865 thought it was a mistake to allow illiterates to vote—and there was hardly a slave who could read and write—had changed his mind. By 1869 he thought giving blacks the vote was the last chance of saving Reconstruction.

The evening of March 30, 1870, he signed the Fifteenth Amendment into law. The Army fired a one-hundred-gun salute, announcing the event to Washington and the world. Tens of thousands of people, black and white, paraded by torchlight down Pennsylvania Avenue. Grant came out and from the front steps of the White House told the crowd he had no doubt that the rights guaranteed by the Fifteenth Amendment would be used wisely. He had written a message to Congress a few hours earlier, calling the amendment "the most important event that has occurred since the nation came into life."[18]

All the same, the new legislation was fundamentally flawed. During its passage through Congress it had, in effect, been gutted of the kind of provisions that would make a real difference. It did not, for one thing, extend voting rights to everyone regardless of race, creed, gender or color. Nor did it ban literacy tests, property ownership, or educational requirements. Ironically, it was northern states rather than the Old South that refused to budge over suffrage qualifications. California, for example, would not let the Chinese vote. In Rhode Island, naturalized citizens had to own real estate before they could vote, and other New England states imposed tests of literacy. In Pennsylvania, you had to prove you paid state taxes. And so on. Here, then, was a way of flouting the intention of the Fifteenth Amendment for any state so inclined.[19]

Congress nonetheless threw its weight behind the new law by passing an enforcement act in May 1870, punishing any use of force, bribery, or intimidation to deprive people of their voting rights. Three more enforcement acts followed, in an ongoing attempt to provide Federal protection for people exercising their Fifteenth Amendment rights, in the South or the North, whether in rural areas or the cities.

The last of the enforcement acts, which Grant signed into law in April 1871, was aimed specifically at the Ku Klux Klan. For the first time the Federal government would punish criminal acts committed by individuals. Until now, these had been dealt with by state and local governments. This new legislation altered the relationship between the individual and the Federal government, making him directly accountable to Washington for his actions. A few years earlier such a step would have been considered impossible.

The change was due entirely to the rise of terrorism. A number of white-supremacy organizations flourished in the South. The Klan was not only the biggest and best organized, but it had a prestige that eclipsed the rest. Established in Pulaski, Tennessee, in 1866, it was not expected to be anything more than a social club where Confederate veterans could sit around and exaggerate their exploits in the war and mock the damn Yankees until it became almost possible to forget who had actually won.

The Klan's grand wizard was Nathan Bedford Forrest, onetime slave dealer and feared Confederate general. Forrest's treatment of black soldiers during the war was like many a modern Balkan atrocity. In 1867, as the reaction to Reconstruction ignited violence across the South, it was but a short, hurried step from being a social club to becoming an organization that made bedsheets into garments, crosses into burning brands, and murder into something respectable people committed after the sun went down. The object of the Klan was not to bring back slavery but to maintain white supremacy. As its members, brandishing rifles and shotguns and ropes, galloped up to the wretched hovels and shacks of impoverished blacks, they were pursuing most of the benefits of slavery, but without the trouble and expense.[20]

Grant's efforts to enforce the rights of blacks were being hampered not only by the flawed character of the Fifteenth Amendment but by the continuing reduction of the military's presence in the South. Congress kept cutting the Army's budget and Sherman, as general-in-chief, reduced the number of troops stationed in the former Confederacy to little more than three thousand men. Sherman did not believe in Reconstruction. On the contrary. He opposed nearly every Reconstruction measure and enforced Grant's policies reluctantly. In a speech in New Orleans in May 1871 he openly derided the anti-Klan legislation. Sherman's contempt for Grant the politician came close to wrecking the friendship they had forged in the war. By the time Grant's first administration ended they were barely on speaking terms and Sherman had moved his headquarters to St. Louis.[21]

Grant, meanwhile, was smashing the Klan. The ink was hardly dry on the anti-Klan law before the Department of Justice began indicting hundreds of people in North Carolina. Soldiers made the arrests and Federal courts heard the cases. In Mississippi, some seven hundred people were indicted for terrorist activities. Grant declared South Carolina was "in a condition of lawlessness," suspended habeus corpus and unleashed a roundup of hundreds of suspected terrorists. An estimated two thousand Klansmen packed up their robes and quit the state.[22]

Many of those charged with crimes of violence pleaded guilty rather than risk being tried by an all-black jury, something that did not happen often, but often enough to frighten even hardened lynchers. Most of those indicted were convicted and punished. By 1872 the Klan had been shattered. The twentieth-century version is a re-creation, with no direct links to the original Klan. Breaking the KKK was Grant's biggest contribution to Reconstruction but, as he realized, it wasn't enough.[23]

One evening, sitting in the White House library with Jesse and Julia, he was plunged in gloom. A telegram had arrived from the governor of Louisiana, who feared yet another outbreak of mob violence was brewing. After a while Grant shifted in his chair and groaned. "Oh, if the South could only see!"[24]

———— ★ ★ ★ ★ ————

CHAPTER 29

"THE SUBJECT OF ABUSE AND SLANDER"

G rant hadn't been in the White House six months before he realized he'd made a serious misjudgment. However much he liked to think he was President by the will of the people and therefore free to ignore the selfish, blinkered wishes of the Republican party leadership, the reality was that when he pulled on the levers of power what he seemed to get in return was the sound of wheels spinning and gears clashing somewhere in the direction of Capitol Hill. Turning wishes into policy and policy into action was beyond whatever power it was that the people's will provided. He needed political allies and support-ers as he had once needed able men to command his armies.[1]

The Republican party, however, was no longer a cohesive force with a clear vision of the kind of country it wanted. During the forty years following the Revolutionary War, politics had been driven by two big ideas: creating a new national identity and securing the new nation's borders against the British, French and Spanish, all of whom had major possessions in North America. During the next forty years the big ideas were the abolition of slavery and the promotion of Manifest Destiny.

When the Civil War ended, radical Republicans seemed so commit-ted to imposing Reconstruction that racial equality seemed likely to become the big post–Civil War idea. That soon petered out. By the time

Grant became President most of the onetime radicals had lost their enthusiasm for racial equality and before Grant left the White House some, such as Carl Schurz, were arguing against it.[2]

Grant had no grand vision of his own to guide the country. He was progressive on racial justice and on the settlement of international disputes, and he even thought that war, with its promotion of new technologies, was a progressive force, lifting society to new peaks of civilization. That, however, was not the same as having a legislative program to present to Congress or a vision for rallying the people. His program consisted mainly of keeping the Republican party in the White House as long as possible in order to keep the Democrats out: Republicans had saved the Union; Democrats had threatened its destruction.

The place where he needed allies most was in the Senate, which was increasingly falling under the control of what became known as the Stalwart Republicans. They came mainly from the Midwest and Northeast—men like Zachariah Chandler of Michigan, Oliver P. Morton of Indiana and Roscoe Conkling of New York. There were Stalwarts in the House, too, who became reliable supporters, including Benjamin F. Butler. However much they had clashed during the war, Grant and Butler became allies in peace, once Grant was President.[3]

The Stalwarts were the first-generation machine politicians. They depended heavily on the spoils system, with its wide array of government jobs, to keep their machines well greased. Politics to them was about exercising power, not debating ideas. The price of working with and through the Stalwart Republicans was that Grant had to resign himself to the cynical—often dubious—way that patronage was dispensed.[4]

Of all the Stalwarts, the one Grant was closest to was Conkling. A tall, strikingly handsome man a few years younger than Grant, Conkling had a booming voice and a brilliant speaking style. He may have been the best orator of his time. Behind his charismatic personality was an impressive intellect, combined with a fiercely emotional and combative nature. If Conkling befriended a man, they were brothers; slight him once, and you had an enemy for life. Conkling also had a private life that scandalized and fascinated Washington.[5]

Chief Justice Salmon P. Chase's daughter, Katherine, was a renowned society beauty, and in 1869 Kate Chase had married a young millionaire senator from Rhode Island, William Sprague. It was the kind of match that makes headlines and is gushed over as a fairy tale in modern dress.

But Kate soon learned there was a problem with the charming, hand-some Sprague: The family business was failing and he was drinking heavily. Under the influence, he was a mean drunk, the kind who goes home and beats up his wife. The heretofore happily married Conkling and Kate Chase Sprague fell into each other's arms, and then into bed, and nearly everyone in Washington knew it. Julia and Conkling's wife— also named Julia—were good friends, and the two couples continued socializing as if Conkling were not the most notorious adulterer in North America. Grant appeared oblivious of Conkling's affair. It is hardly believable that no one told him, or at least hinted at it, yet he would have had no trouble ignoring it as a malicious and totally unfounded rumor being spread by Conkling's enemies. After all, there had been plenty of false stories spread about *him.*

The Republican opponents of the Stalwarts comprised the liberal wing of the party, led by Sumner and Schurz, who saw themselves as the high-minded guardians of Republicanism, devoted to principles, not patronage; ideas, not interests. They loathed Conkling and everything he stood for. Nonetheless, the men who scorned the Stalwarts and railed against "Grantism"—by which they meant corruption—proved no more capable than Grant of producing an inspiring alternative vision to the pursuit of money that marked the Gilded Age, and even less capable than he of providing a legislative program that addressed the five most important political issues of the day—Reconstruction, the national debt, Indian policy, reform of the spoils system, and settlement of the *Alabama* claims.

By the time the Republican convention came around in June 1872, some of the liberals were flirting with the Democrats and the most influential of the liberal newspapers, Horace Greeley's *New York Tribune,* was assailing Grant regularly. For a long time Grant had admired Greeley as a man of integrity, however much they disagreed on politics. But during the past year he had come to despise him. "The truth about Greeley," Grant told a reporter that summer, "is that he has been surrounding himself with men of disreputable character and wanting to put them into important offices. I could not provide for all of them, and most of them I could not afford—the country could not afford—to trust with any decent place. . . . Mister Greeley would have filled the civil service with all the worthless men in the country if I had let him. That is the trouble." The famously high-minded Greeley had disappointed him by proving to be a party politician at heart and not, as his admirers called him, the Philosopher.[6]

The anti-Grant elements in the party eventually split away. Forming the Liberal Republican faction, they nominated Greeley as their presidential candidate. Behind the scenes, encouraging and advising the Liberal Republicans, was Greeley's assistant, Whitelaw Reid—the same Reid, that is, who had shot to fame for his memorable nineteen-thousand-word description of the battle of Shiloh. Reid had portrayed Grant then as a bungling fool and was still standing his ground. According to Reid's view of political trends, Grant was not even likely to be nominated. And if nominated, he stood little chance of being elected. Bolstered by advice like this, Greeley not only secured the nomination of the Liberal Republicans, but the Democrats, overjoyed to see the Republicans fighting among themselves, made him their candidate, too.[7]

Following his nomination by the Republican party, Grant received an invitation from Conkling to come visit him at his home in Utica, New York. He replied he would be glad to do so, but "it will be better if I should not attend any convention or political meeting during the Campaign. It has been done, so afar as I remember, by but two Pres. candidates heretofore and both of them were public speakers, and both were beaten. I am no speaker and don't want to be beaten."[8]

This time he awaited the results in Washington, not in provincial Galena, and one October morning shortly before the election Congressman James Garfield, who never liked, let alone admired, Grant, stopped by the White House. There was no friendship between them. Garfield thought Grant was "not fit to be nominated." As for Grant, he considered Garfield and his friends impractical "damned literary fellows."[9]

Even so, he invited Garfield upstairs, and when the conversation got around to the Liberal Republicans, Grant chuckled. They reminded him of the time he was serving on the Mexican border with Zachary Taylor's Army of Observation, he said. The night air was filled with the howling of prairie wolves. It was a spine-chilling experience. One night it sounded to him as if there were at least a hundred of them howling their heads off in the darkness. His curiosity aroused, he had crept out of the camp, moving silently toward the source of the ruckus. When he finally got close enough to spot them, he could see just how many wolves were making so much noise—a grand total of two.[10]

On Election Day, Grant achieved a significantly greater margin of victory in both the popular vote and the Electoral College vote than he had won in 1869. In March 1873 he was duly inaugurated, on a bitterly cold day that made for a small crowd and misery for the West Point cadets who, by tradition, led the inaugural parade. At the inaugural ball that evening, the President's guests danced in their overcoats.

Grant's second inaugural address was just as platitudinous as the first. The most interesting part was the way he used a solemn state occasion to lash out at his critics. "From my candidacy for my present office in 1868 to the close of the last Presidential campaign," he intoned, "I have been the subject of abuse and slander scarcely ever equaled in political history, which today I feel I can disregard in view of your verdict, which I gratefully accept as my vindication."[11]

Privately, however, he disliked being President more than ever. He later described it to a friend, in terms reminiscent of Samuel Johnson's famous description of the writer's lot—"toil, envy, want, the patron and the jail." Grant characterized the presidency as "the care, the responsibility, the abuse, the ingratitude attending the honor of office."[12]

★

Jay Cooke was a dapper figure—prematurely gray, able, quick-witted and patriotic. During the Civil War the Lincoln administration at first found it hard, when victory seemed doubtful, to persuade the major banking houses of New York to buy government bonds. Cooke, who operated a small private bank, seized the opportunity and by the time the war ended had established himself as the man who financed the war. He seemed able to find buyers for however many bonds the government offered for sale. No banker had ever enjoyed the esteem that Jay Cooke possessed when the war ended. He seemed to have it all—the admiration of his countrymen, the gratitude of his government and vast personal riches.[13]

With peace, Cooke moved into financing another huge enterprise, the Northern Pacific Railroad, which would be driven two thousand miles from the Mississippi, across the high plains, over the mountains and through Oregon until it reached the sea. Building the transcontinental lines demanded huge amounts of capital and without government help they could not have been built at all. The government awarded the railroads generous land grants and the land was then used to secure bond issues that paid for track and labor and rolling stock and telegraph lines. Cooke shamelessly bribed congressmen to get the bill that authorized the transfer of millions of acres of Federal land to the Northern Pacific and generously financed the Republican National Committee during Grant's 1872 re-election campaign.[14]

Grant himself had an account at Cooke's bank and was a guest from time to time at Cooke's home, a vast and ugly pile of stone with pretentions to grandeur, called Ogontz, outside Philadelphia. He was there the evening of September 17, 1873, after entrusting Jesse to the pedagogical care of a nearby private school. Grant stayed the night. Next morning, messengers came hurrying up the drive at Ogontz with telegrams for the master of the house. The Northern Pacific had run out of money and its bonds were dropping by the minute. Cooke's bank was the biggest shareholder in the railroad. He was already as good as bankrupt. Ever the charming, urbane host, however, he did not trouble Grant with his personal worries and shortly before noon suavely bid his guest a safe return to Washington.[15]

By the time he reached the capital Grant knew of the failure of Cooke's banking house, dragged into oblivion by the defunct Northern Pacific. He knew, too, that the result was sure to be a financial panic. Over the next few days Grant and his recently installed secretary of the Treasury, W. D. Richardson, came under intense pressure to intervene and pump money into the economy.[16]

Richardson had recently retired $44 million in greenbacks, reducing the total in circulation to $356 million. Although he possessed the authority to retire greenbacks, he needed congressional approval to increase the money supply. Even so, Richardson quickly reissued $26 million of the money he'd just retired.

Despite these efforts, thousands of businesses failed that fall and hundreds of thousands of people were thrown out of work as one bank after another went bust. While bankers were wallowing in self-pity and emitting howls of despair, Grant was thinking there was something to be said for the wave of business failures sweeping the country. Bankruptcies were killing off the overextended, the unwisely invested, the overvalued, and the badly managed. Individuals would suffer, he knew that, but the economy as a whole would become stronger and ultimately more productive. The President was, without being aware of it or intending it, a proto-monetarist.[17]

The Panic of 1873 revealed as nothing else could that Reconstruction had lost its primacy as the touchstone of party politics. American political life had been realigned. The political divide was no longer North versus South but East versus West, cities versus rural areas, and hard money—gold—versus soft money—greenbacks.

The recession raging through Wall Street like a firestorm created even greater turmoil in the West. Farmers were already hurting from the high prices the railroads were demanding to move their crops. While modern farm machinery transformed the productivity of American agriculture, the cost of this equipment was beyond the reach of most farmers. It was the bigger, richer farms that profited. The smaller farms were squeezed out. With their debts climbing and their hopes of solvency plummeting, millions of farmers saw only one solution—print more greenbacks; inflate the currency.

The clamor for inflation from the farm belt had a miraculous effect on the eastern bankers, who had been urging the same thing when the Panic first struck. They were appalled at the prospect of seeing the loans they had made to the farmers and the government bonds they had bought being repaid in a highly inflated currency. Bad money in exchange for good—a banker's waking nightmare. Yet that was exactly what Congress, under pressure from the Midwest, was preparing to do in the winter of 1873.[18]

The legislation making its way through Congress was popularly and accurately known as the Inflation Bill. It would legalize Richardson's reissue of $26 million in greenbacks and authorize him to reissue the remaining $18 million, bringing the total value of greenbacks in circulation back to $400 million. There was no question that Congress would pass this bill. The only question was whether Grant would veto it. As the hour of decision approached, not even he could answer the question.

Although Grant welcomed what he saw as the purging effects of the Panic, scouring out the rotten parts of the economy and promoting healthy fresh growth, he still pictured himself as a farmer. And as the lot of the farmers grew more agonizing that winter, he could feel the pain of millions of families, worried sick over their debts and sinking into despair. He owned the old Dent farm in St. Louis now, and it was a bottomless money pit, swallowing a large chunk of his salary year after year. He also knew, unlike his hard-money friends Conkling and Hoar, what it was like to be poor, to work with your hands for twelve hours a day, out in the open whatever the weather, and have to pawn your watch just to buy presents for the children at Christmas. A hard-money man in his mind, Grant had a soft-money man's heart.

The promoters of the Inflation Bill had been careful to give it a seductive face: it appeared to do no more than restore the currency situation to where it had been during Grant's first administration. Yet it was a potential trap. If Grant put back every dollar that Richardson had withdrawn, the whole policy of phasing out greenbacks and returning to a currency based on gold would be wrecked. He would not be able to revive it, nor, in all likelihood, would his successor. The government would be adopting a new economic policy by default: In case of economic panic, print more money. And if that doesn't work, print even more.

In April 1874, when Congress finally passed the Inflation Bill, Grant remained as torn as ever. The evening of April 21, after everyone else in the White House had gone to bed, he sat alone in his office, still trying to decide. He read the legislation carefully. Then he wrote out a message approving the bill. Decision at last. And yet . . . He thought a while longer, picked up the message he had just written, tore it into pieces, and took up his pen again.[19]

"It is a fair inference that if in practice this measure should fail to create the abundance of circulation expected of it," he wrote, "the friends of the measure, particularly those out of Congress, would clamor for [more] inflation . . ." What the country was being asked to accept was "a departure from the true principles of national finance, national interest, national obligations to creditors, Congressional promises, party pledges, and of personal views and promises made by me . . ."[20]

For the rest of his life Grant was convinced that vetoing the Inflation Bill was one of the greatest things he ever did for his country. The struggle between the hard-money East and the soft-money West nevertheless continued for another twenty-five years, and the recession triggered by the Panic of 1873 proved one of the longest in the nation's history.

Did he do right? According to the economic orthodoxy of our time, no. Deflation always makes a recession worse. In the modern world, however, the United States has only one currency, not two. There is also the Federal Reserve Board to serve as a barrier to inflation. With two currencies in circulation and no Federal Reserve to control interest rates, Grant made the right choice. Had he signed the Inflation Bill, he would have wrecked the credit of the American government, seen inflation shoot into double figures, turned a recession into a depression, and drastically curbed the post–Civil War industrialization of the United States. Even so, it had been a hard decision to make, not because of the pressure put on him by others, but because it tested his moral courage— he had done the right thing that was hard rather than the easy thing that was wrong.

★

During the Vicksburg campaign Grant had startled, even scandalized, some officers by appointing a full-blooded Seneca Indian, Ely Parker, to his wartime staff. Indians, including Parker, were not citizens. Besides, most white people considered them hopelessly backward, completely immoral and absolutely untrustworthy. The prejudice against Indians was widespread and deep and made even worse by undeniable guilt at the way the Indians had been dispossessed of the continent.

Grant eventually promoted Parker, who served as an aide and secretary, to a brevet brigadier general's star. Parker was a qualified civil engineer before he ever met Grant, so his remarkable success in the Union Army wasn't a complete surprise, but it was only possible because Grant did not share the common prejudices of his time.

Parker's life was far removed from that of virtually all the other three hundred thousand Indians living within the borders of the United States. He remained in uniform after the war, serving at Army headquarters in Washington. A bachelor into his forties, he proposed marriage to a pretty, blond eighteen-year-old, Minnie Orton Sackett, and she accepted. Their wedding day was scheduled for December 17, 1868. Grant was going to give the bride away at the Episcopal Church of the Epiphany and the night before the wedding loaned Parker a fancy silk sash so he would look military and magnificent at the altar.

Next day, Parker stood up his fiancée. Unnerved by the prospect of marriage to a white woman, he had disappeared; drunk, his friends discovered, in some cheap hotel room. After tracking him down, his brother officers got him sobered up and on December 24 Parker and Minnie Sackett were married and Grant gave her away as if nothing had happened.[21]

Three months later Grant became President and he appointed Parker commissioner of Indian affairs. It was an appointment intended to bring about a revolution in the government's Indian policy. Since the war the

Army had waged several major offensives against the Plains Indians, reducing many tribes to a bleak choice between starvation and reservation. Most Indians now lived in grinding poverty and depended on government handouts.

The supplies the government provided passed through the hands of crooked Indian agents, who stole shamelessly and looked on with indifference as Indian families went hungry. The agents cynically enriched themselves further by selling whiskey and guns to the Indians, knowing that at some point drunken braves were likely to attack white settlers.

Lacking both citizenship and real military power, the Indians had no way to assert themselves politically. Their relationship with the government was based on 370 treaties, most of which had been broken by the white man, the rest by the Indians. The Fourteenth Amendment made everyone born within the borders of the United States an American citizen, but this excluded Indians living on reservations.

For three years following the Civil War the Army had conducted a vigorous campaign, directed by Sheridan, to break the military power of the Plains Indians. Grant had not blamed the Indians, however, for their resistance to white rule. "Indian wars," he wrote Sheridan, "have grown out of the mismanagement of the [Indian] bureau." He also held white settlers responsible. "Our white people seem never to be satisfied without hostilities with them," he told Sherman in disgust.[22]

Besides putting Ely Parker in charge of Indian affairs, Grant also appointed a Board of Indian Commissioners to provide independent advice on Indian policy. The board was supposed to last for just one year, but proved so useful it survived until 1934. He and the board agreed that the Indians had to earn a place in American society if they were to survive. He wanted them to become farmers and mechanics and to accept the values of a Christian society and, eventually, be converted to Christianity. In his first inaugural address he said he would promote "any course toward [the Indians] which tends to their civilization and ultimate citizenship."[23]

He persuaded Congress to increase the appropriation for Parker's office from $5 million to $7 million; the extra money would go into education and training. And to put a stop to corruption among the Indian agents, Grant dismissed nearly all of those currently employed by the Indian office. In doing so, he antagonized scores of congressmen,

for these were patronage posts they had long controlled. He antagonized them even more by replacing their appointees with religious
activists. He sought Indian agents among the Quakers. More than a hundred Army officers were also appointed as Indian agents. The Army
those days had far more officers than it needed and they provided a
good source of honest men.

Congress fought back. In 1870 it barred Army officers from filling
civil offices, thereby preventing them from serving as Indian agents.
Grant, however, would not go back to the bad old days and crooked old
ways. He recruited Protestant ministers to run the reservations, and
when he ran out of Protestants, he recruited Catholic priests. He even
recruited a religious Jew to serve as a reservation superintendent.[24]

Grant's policy was to keep the reservation Indians under the control
of the agents and the "roving Indians"—those living outside the reservations—under the control of the Army. Parker had no objections to
that. As a soldier, he had no patience with Indians who did not obey the
law. Nor could they expect much mercy from Sherman, now general-in-
chief of the army. He believed the only way to protect white settlements
and clear the way for the railroads was to herd virtually every Indian
onto the reservations.[25]

The Board of Indian Commissioners urged Grant to abolish the
treaty system as a way of dealing with Indian tribes, and he did so. Indians henceforth were to be considered wards of the government. In other
words, the government now had responsibility for their welfare.[26]

After only eighteen months in office, Parker was accused of corruption. A congressional committee investigated the charges and cleared
him of dishonesty but cast so much doubt on his administrative ability
he had little option but to resign. His successor, Francis A. Walker,
demonstrated as much honesty as Parker and possibly more skill.

Grant's Indian "peace policy" was popular east of the Mississippi,
where there were few Indians, and just as deeply resented west of the
great river. White settlers in the West considered it naive and dangerous,
and some Indian tribes seemed determined to prove the settlers were
right. In January 1870 the Piegan tribe in Montana attacked several pio-
neer settlements. The Army retaliated by killing nearly two hundred
Piegans, including many women and children. In 1871–72 the Army
waged an arduous campaign in Arizona agains the Apaches. There were
clashes with the Modocs of Oregon that led, in April 1873, to the mur-

der of the department commander, Major General Edward S. Canby, during what was supposed to be a peace parley.[27]

The worst trouble of all, though, came in South Dakota. There had been flare-ups involving the Sioux for more than a decade. The Sioux had secured possession of the Black Hills under a treaty signed in 1868, when they agreed to move onto a reservation provided they retained this, their most sacred hunting ground. Then, in 1874 Lieutenant Colonel George Armstrong Custer was sent into the Black Hills by Phil Sheridan, commander of the Department of the Missouri.

Custer's mission, ostensibly, was to survey sites for a possible fort. Other reservations had Army forts on them, so in itself this didn't mean much. But Custer emerged from the Black Hills claiming there was so much gold there it was possible to pick up nuggets among the roots of the grass. This inevitably set off a stampede of white gold hunters. The Army tried to keep them out, but it lacked the manpower—and possibly the willpower—to do so.

The government offered the Sioux $6 million for the Black Hills. They declined to sell. Grant was then advised by the commission handling the negotiations that the government should assert its rights under eminent domain, take the hills, and pay the Indians compensation. The Sioux were invited to send a delegation to Washington, and Grant told the Sioux bluntly they were being unreasonable in preventing white men from digging for gold. The government could not keep the gold hunters out. But if the Indians persisted in trying to stop them, there was certain to be bloodshed, and once blood was spilled, the government would be forced by the anger of white people across the nation to remove the Sioux from the Black Hills. The Sioux were still not persuaded.[28]

Throughout the next year the gold hunters poured into the Black Hills, and angry Sioux streamed off their reservation. In the spring of 1876 Sheridan ordered the Indians to go back. When they refused to do so, Sherman declared they were now at war with the United States.

The Army prepared an offensive, consisting of three converging columns under Major General Alfred H. Terry, to trap the roving Sioux bands and destroy them. One of Terry's columns would be commanded by Custer. Shortly before this offensive was launched, however, Custer was called to Washington to testify before a congressional committee that was investigating corruption charges against former secretary of war William Belknap. Custer did little more than repeat the rumors common on Army posts in the West about Belknap. More than that, though, he had a lot to say about Grant's brother Orvil.[29]

If Jesse and Hannah Grant produced one bad seed, Orvil was it. Twenty years earlier he had struck some of the customers of the Galena leather store as a shifty, untrustworthy figure. After the Civil War, Orvil opened his own leather business in Chicago, only to lose it in the great fire of 1871. After that Orvil bounced from one swindle to another. It was inevitable, then, that he would be gossiped about, and that was all Custer had to offer—gossip. Grant had no illusions about Orvil, but he was outraged when he read how Custer had derided his brother before a congressional committee.[30]

He ordered Sherman not to allow Custer to take part in Terry's operation. Virtually everyone in the Army realized this was going to be the last big Indian fight and there was probably hardly a combat-arms officer who did not want to be in on it. The press, meanwhile, carried stories that said Sherman considered Custer the only man capable of dealing with the hostile Sioux. Sherman responded with a scornful blast: "The Army possesses hundreds of officers who are competent for such an expedition."[31]

Although Grant almost never argued with anyone, he could carry a grudge as well as the next man. He intended to humiliate Custer much as Custer had humiliated Orvil, but Custer outflanked him by pleading with Sheridan to let him share whatever dangers his regiment, the Seventh Cavalry, was about to face. Sheridan in turn asked Grant to relent and Grant, who thought Sheridan the greatest soldier in the world, did so, but as a concession to Sheridan, not to Custer.[32]

So Custer got his way, blundered, let his ego dictate his actions, and led nearly three hundred soldiers into a massacre at the battle of the Little Big Horn in June 1876. As he led the nation in mourning, Grant said this was a battle that was "wholly unnecessary."[33]

Following Custer's death the Army had a free hand to destroy all Sioux bands outside their reservation. The Sioux gained nothing from destroying Custer except to bolster the badly battered self-esteem of Indians everywhere. More than a century later, the Little Big Horn battlefield is a popular honeymoon destination for Indian newlyweds.[34]

For anyone surveying the stripped and mutilated bodies of Seventh Cavalry troopers strewn across the burnished hills of Montana in summer, Grant's peace policy looked a failure, but in truth it outlived even this disaster. It was never going to resolve the fundamental racial and cultural tensions between Indians and whites. Even so, it provided a basis for a measure of justice in Indian affairs. More than that, though, it offered the first chance ever for what Grant called "the original occupants of this land" to secure a place in American life. No President could have done more. None had done as much.[35]

CHAPTER 30

★ ★ ★ ★

"LIKE A BOY GETTING OUT OF SCHOOL"

The longer Julia lived in the White House, the more she liked it. It was, she thought, "a bright and beautiful dream. I wish it might continue forever."[1] Grant's feelings were exactly the opposite. He hadn't cared for it much during his first term, liked it even less during the second. It wasn't as if there was somewhere else that he thought of as home. Neither the Galena gift house nor the one in Philadelphia meant much to him. He had no intention of living permanently in either place.

Since leaving his parents' home to go to West Point, Grant had moved from one temporary accommodation to the next. Stone barracks that were drafty and cold, tents in the mud, commandeered plantations with white pillars at the front and slave hovels at the rear, cramped wartime hotel rooms smelling of tobacco and spittoons, rented houses in places he did not know, gift homes that he had no sense of possessing—all seemed much the same to him. The White House was merely the latest stop. Although Grant had bought a property overlooking the ocean at Long Branch, New Jersey, he spent only a few months there each year. It was a bolt-hole, an escape from the cares of the White House and Washington's oppressive, enervating summers.

The craving for movement, the underlying itch that made him dread boredom, gave Grant something of a drifter's soul. He never had a permanent home in the way that most people do and all other Presidents have had. Whatever ties marked the frontiers of his mortal existence were entirely emotional, never material. He had no interest in money or material possessions or a spot on the Earth to call his own. His hinterland was occupied by his family, his friends and his flag. It was these, not property ownership or being a general or being President or any deep sense of place, that were the springs of his happiness and shaped his idea of success.

In his rootlessness and restlessness, as in his attachment to people and ideals rather than places and things, Grant was closer to the quintessential artist or intellectual than he would ever be to the solid bourgeois paterfamilias that nineteenth-century Americans expected from their Presidents. It helps explain why he was a mystery to contemporaries such as Sherman and to others who have studied him since, whether as admiring as Bruce Catton or as disdainful as William McFeely. Unable to find what they were looking for—someone much like their conventional middle-class selves, that is—they filed accounts of a hole that events swirled around, and missed the man.

Toward the end of June 1873 Grant was informed that his father was not expected to live much longer. He boarded a special train and headed for Covington, Kentucky. Jesse had been dying of cancer for more than a year. He expired, at age seventy-nine, before his eldest son reached his bedside. Grant was shaken and depressed at the old man's demise. A female neighbor and family friend tried to console him, but he was so prostrated by grief he couldn't utter a word in reply. Hannah moved to New York, to live with her daughter Virginia.[2]

Six months later Julia's father died in the White House at the age of eighty-seven, and Grant traveled with Julia to St. Louis to bury him. Julia, by all accounts, seemed almost stoical when her father died. It was Grant, renowned for his self-control, who at times appears to have been the more likely of the two to burst into tears.

Although he never considered the White House a real home, the East Room made a magnificent setting for the wedding of the Grants' only daughter, Nellie, in May 1874. Grant was dismayed, not to say depressed, however, at Nellie's intended. She had fallen in love with a reedy, etiolated Englishman, Algernon Sartoris. He was a nephew of the famous actress Fanny Kemble, a connection that cloaked this dull young man with a spurious glamour. Nellie may well have thought she was marrying into the English aristocracy; certainly the American press believed it. Yet the Sartorises were neither rich enough nor grand enough to count for much in English society. They were roughly on a par with glove manufacturers or successful merchants.

Grant duly gave Nellie away, then, while the wedding guests and the rest of the family chattered and laughed downstairs, he retreated upstairs, went into Nellie's room, threw himself on her bed in despair at losing his pretty eighteen-year-old daughter, and burst into tears. Nellie planned to move to England and live there. It was as if she had abandoned him.[3]

His three sons, however, remained a source of comfort and delight. Grant had secured a West Point place for his eldest son, Fred, but less for the career than for the education. In the years following the Civil War the Army had little to do. Grant knew as well as anyone how stultifying peacetime service in the infantry could be, and Fred was going to graduate near the bottom of his class. There was no chance of his becoming an engineer. "I do not want Fred to stay in the Army longer than to report for duty and serve a week or two," Grant told Fred's brother Buck (Ulysses, Jr.), a student at Harvard.[4]

During the holidays, when Fred and Buck returned to the White House or to the "cottage" in Long Branch, Grant devoted his evenings to them. At times like these he refused to engage in official business or receive visitors. He seemed to think he owed his children as much of his time as he owed his country.[5]

Meanwhile his scapegrace brother, Orvil, was proving how bad a Grant could be. Orvil had moved to Chicago after the war and opened a leather business of his own. When Mrs. O'Leary's cow kicked over the lantern that ignited the great Chicago fire of 1871, it burned down half the city's businesses, including Orvil's.

Desperate for a new source of income, he recommended one James E. McLean for appointment as collector of the Port of Chicago. The arrangement with McLean was that he would share his salary with Orvil. Once McLean was on the Federal payroll, however, Orvil began demanding a bigger share than originally agreed. McLean protested to Grant, and when he realized his brother was sharing McLean's salary, he fired McLean. Unfortunately, he could not get rid of Orvil so easily.[6]

Orvil moved on to another swindle. Teaming up with a crooked lawyer, J. H. Smith of Albany, New York, he cheated a widow with two small daughters out of the five thousand dollars that her husband had left her. Orvil and Smith convinced her that she should let them manage her money. There was no risk, they said. After all, the President of the United States had pledged to act as guarantor for up to fifteen thousand dollars for any money entrusted to Orvil's careful stewardship. They showed her a letter with U. S. Grant's signature forged on the bottom to prove it. She confidently handed over the five thousand dollars. Some months later she wrote to Grant asking him to make good the money his brother had stolen.[7]

Throughout the emotional tribulations of these years, Julia remained the fixed point in his rootless life. They were as close as ever. One hot, sunny day in May 1875 she took a sheet of paper and wrote across the top of it,

"Dear Ulys,

"How many years ago today is it that we were engaged? Just such a day as this was it not? Julia."

She had a servant take it to him.

Grant read it, then scribbled at the bottom of the page, "Thirty-one years ago. I was so frightened however that I do not remember whether it was warm or snowing. Ulys."[8]

★

On various occasions American historians have been asked to rate the Presidents, from best to worst. Some, like Eisenhower, have risen in esteem, while others, such as John Kennedy, have lost a portion of their luster. Grant, however, has not budged from his traditional place. Were it not for the handsome, statesmanlike features of Warren G. Harding immediately below him, Grant's bearded chin would be scraping the ground at the bottom of the presidential totem pole. Just as surely as the one thing that Americans know about Grant the soldier is that he was a hopeless drunkard, the one thing they know about Grant the man is that he was a hopeless President. Virtually the worst ever, it seems.

It looks strange, though, to place him lower than Presidents who accomplished nothing significant, such as Franklin Pierce, Chester Arthur, Millard Fillmore and Benjamin Harrison; or someone like James Buchanan, whose time in office helped precipitate a national disaster; not to mention those who made a bad national situation worse, like Andrew Johnson; or a crook like Richard Nixon. There is something at work in Grant's case that is almost like a posthumous revenge. Could he really have been so bad?

The obvious black mark against Grant's presidency is the succession of scandals that marked its eight-year passage, beginning with the Gold Corner. Few people ever thought he was personally on the take. On the contrary, Grant is often portrayed as a gullible, naive man far out of his depth, taken advantage of by people a lot smarter and greedier than he was. Even so, that kind of perception does not get a former President far with historians. If anything, it shakes faith in the Republic. The fundamental flaw in the Grant presidency, however, was less the man than the fact that the executive branch is not trapped in amber. It is a reflection—sometimes an unwelcome one—of American society and politics at a particular time, and the spirit of the age when Grant was sworn in was about as amoral as it gets in a God-fearing country.

Government salaries before the Civil War were, by general acknowledgment, low. Wartime prices made them derisory and Lincoln did nothing to correct the problem. He had more urgent worries to deal with. So, it turned out, did Andrew Johnson, who was busy trying to block Reconstruction and fight off impeachment. The result was inevitable. Crookedness proliferated at every level of government. By 1869 parts of the Federal bureaucracy, much of Congress, and both national political parties, were sustained by corruption. What had begun simply as a means of keeping food on the table or a candidate in office or a party in power had started to resemble a way of life.

In the conquered South, it was also a form of punishment. Radical governments in most southern states provided both a means and an excuse for stealing from a region that had been impoverished by war. One reason Reconstruction was so hated and resented was the license it seemed to give to predatory northerners to loot the weak and prostrate South.

In his first couple of years as President, Grant had little choice about coming to terms with the spoils system. That was the price he had to pay for the support of his party's leadership. Like other nineteenth-century Presidents, he was swamped with applications from job seekers. Much of his time was spent on this. The principles he applied seemed clear enough: "Every man holding place should be reliable and equal to the duties he has to perform and should be a Republican."[9] Yet he was invariably sympathetic to wounded veterans, of whatever party, who sought Federal jobs. Sometimes their injuries seemed to count for more than their competence. Anyone, in fact, who had a good sob story was likely to get a sympathetic hearing.

With Grant, as with his predecessors and successors alike, many of the people he placed in important posts were old friends and acquaintances. And nearly a dozen Grant and Dent relatives were given minor appointments. Jesse, for example, had taken immense pleasure in being the postmaster of Covington. The small salary meant nothing to him. Jesse Grant was one of the richest men in Kentucky. But holding even a minor Federal post added to a man's standing in the community, and the rich, too, can crave the crumbs of distinction.

For all such appointments, however, Grant paid a price. Democrats and Liberal Republicans in Congress and the press accused him of turning the Federal payroll into a monument to nepotism and favoritism. Grant was stung, and expressed his exasperation to an old friend, Joseph R. Jones, whom he had appointed minister to Belgium and, later, collector of customs for Chicago: "Sumner, Schurz, Dana and all think it preposterous in me to give appointments to persons who I ever knew and particularly to those who feel any personal friendship for me."[10]

The parceling out of Federal jobs was complicated by bitter factional rivalries at state level within the Republican party. Grant found himself drawn straight into bitter political fights being waged in places as far apart as Missouri and Massachusetts. He could neither resolve these patronage squabbles nor provide enough Federal appointments to keep every political faction in his party happy.

Nor could he avoid allowing his closest political supporters to control most of the top slots. The post of customs collector for the Port of New York, for example, was the jewel in the crown of Federal posts. The collector was responsible for more than $500 million a year in customs duties. The chances for personal enrichment were obvious. Grant's choice was a horse-loving businessman named Thomas Murphy, who used to come and talk bloodstock with him at Long Branch.

Grant gave Murphy the New York appointment while Roscoe Conkling was engaged in a bitter fight for supremacy in the New York Republican party with the state's other senator, Reuben Fenton. After Conkling finally broke Fenton's power, he wanted to mark his supremacy by putting his own man in as collector of customs for New York, and Grant owed Conkling too much to refuse him. So Murphy departed in 1871, to the glee of the Democratic press, which insisted, falsely, that he had been stealing millions, and Conkling's good friend and attorney Chester A. Arthur was given the job.[11]

During his first term, Grant pressed Congress to reform the Federal civil service. He wanted applicants to submit to competitive examinations, with promotion based strictly on tests of competence and knowledge. This kind of root-and-branch reform would kill the spoils system.[12]

Congress unenthusiastically gave him authority to establish the first Civil Service Board, a body that would supervise the system he envisaged and make further recommendations. The board he appointed comprised distinguished and capable men, but his hopes for civil service reform were swiftly crushed, mainly by his friends.[13]

Roscoe Conkling and other party leaders simply refused to countenance any major reform. They depended on the spoils system so heavily they could not imagine politics without it. They preferred incompetence they could control to ability they couldn't.

Grant did not have to go any distance to find crookedness in government. He had only to look out his windows. Then as now, the District of Columbia was a byword for corruption. Much of the money Congress provided for paving the muddy side streets, for example, had vanished in bribes and payoffs. Some five thousand dollars had gone into the pockets of one of the most self-righteous members of Congress, James A. Garfield, a man regarded as a champion of reform. Garfield was chairman of the congressional committee responsible for supervising the District's affairs and he seemed to assume he was entitled to a share of whatever bribes were on offer.[14]

Virtually the entire Republican party leadership in the House, in fact, was open to bribery. During the 1872 election, the *New York Sun* revealed that large amounts of Union Pacific Railroad stock had been distributed among congressional leaders in 1868 or sold to them for sums well below the stock's actual worth. The company organized to oversee construction of the railroad, Crédit Mobilier, had been used to drain it instead. The Federal government had given millions of acres of government land to the Union Pacific, land that in turn secured huge mortgages, which were supposed to provide working capital and fund purchases of rolling stock and building equipment. By 1868 the railroad's assets had been systematically looted and the company's directors made a preemptive strike to ward off any congressional inquiry; they sold railroad stock at well below its current market value to the congressional leadership. Some politicians, such as Garfield, even got their stock free.[15]

One of the congressmen implicated in the Crédit Mobilier scandal had gone on to become Grant's first Vice President, Schuyler Colfax. Another was Colfax's successor as veep, Henry Wilson. This was a scandal dating from the Andrew Johnson years, but because it broke during Grant's presidency, it has invariably added to *his* account. Once the *Sun*'s story was published, the Republican-dominated House conducted an investigation. It exonerated all the Republicans who'd taken Crédit Mobilier bribes and excoriated the two Democrats who had shared in the loot.

Scandal reached even into the cabinet room. Grant's choice for John Rawlins's successor as secretary of war was a large, massively bearded former soldier, William W. Belknap. Shortly after Belknap took office, his wife died. And shortly after that, Belknap married his vivacious young sister-in-law. The second Mrs. Belknap dressed well and spent lavishly.

Sutlers at Army posts had what amounted to a monopoly on sales to soldiers and local Indians. A sutler at a big post, such as Fort Sill, Oklahoma, could make a very good living. One who used his monopoly position to squeeze every last cent out of the troops and the Indians could even get rich. The sutler at Fort Sill, a rogue called Caleb P. Marsh, had made a deal with the first Mrs. Belknap, possibly with the connivance of the secretary of war, that if given a free hand, he would share the proceeds with her. The second Mrs. Belknap not only slipped into her sister's marital bed but continued the relationship with Marsh, too. At least, that was the rumor circulating among members of the House Appropriations Committee looking into Army expenditures in early 1876.

The morning of March 2, the secretary of the Treasury, Benjamin Bristow, went over to the White House, and Grant, who had just finished breakfast, met him in the parlor. The President was in a hurry to keep an appointment to have his portrait painted at the studio of Henry Ulke, only a block away. Bristow quickly explained the trouble Belknap was in while Grant got into his coat and hat. As a White House servant opened the front door so they could walk out to the street, there in front of them were Belknap and Secretary of the Interior Zachariah Chandler, about to enter.[16]

Belknap started babbling incoherently about the trouble he was in. Grant wasn't interested in excuses or even explanations and bluntly told Belknap he had to resign. "Impossible!" Belknap spluttered. "Such an act might even ruin you politically, Mr. President!"

Grant ignored this bluster. "I demand and shall immediately accept your resignation." He took Belknap up to his office and dictated a letter for Belknap to write out: "Mr. President, I hereby tender my resignation as Secretary of War, and request its immediate acceptance. Thanking you for your constant and continued kindness." Belknap wrote this brief farewell to office in a firm and steady hand, then signed it.[17]

Over the next few months, as Congress investigated the case of the sutler and the secretary's wives, it unearthed enough evidence to justify impeachment proceedings. But then it discovered something else—it could not impeach a private citizen, which was what Belknap had been since the morning of March 2. By forcing his immediate resignation, Grant had saved Belknap's worthless neck and put an immediate stop to this scandal. But another one—much bigger and more damaging to his reputation—was already coming to a head.[18]

★

Although it held the White House from 1861 to 1885, the Republican party was never as strong as it looked. It was essentially a northern party. The Democratic party was more cohesive and had a much broader base. It had a preeminent position in the South and held on to a large, traditional block of loyal voters in most northern states. Not only was the Republican party clinging to a vulnerable electoral base, but it was torn by factional infighting between its Liberal and Stalwart wings.

These internal squabbles took an interesting turn in the Midwest and the border states, where they became inextricably linked with whiskey frauds. The Lincoln administration had imposed high taxes on whiskey to help pay for the war. Border-state Democrats had siphoned off some of this money to help pay for McClellan's 1864 campaign. Cheating the government out of tax revenues on whiskey had become so prevalent under the Johnson administration that in 1868 Congress created a new post, supervisor of internal revenue. The supervisors were expected to crack down on these frauds and, in so doing, help reduce the national debt.

The frauds may have been discouraged somewhat during the first Grant administration, but stamping them out completely was impossible. The Republican party in the Midwest and the border states had become as dependent on whiskey-fraud money as the Democrats had ever been.[19]

The biggest of the various whiskey rackets had taken root in St. Louis, although there were similar operations under way in Chicago, Milwaukee and other cities. The presiding genius of the St. Louis frauds was someone Grant knew, a former Union Army brigadier general by the name of James McDonald.

Sherman had raised McDonald to a general's star during the Atlanta campaign, and remained his friend and supporter after the war. So McDonald found himself appointed superintendent of internal revenue for St. Louis. He was perfectly placed to manage the fraud and to conceal it at the same time.[20]

Grant was warned shortly after McDonald's appointment that he was "a bad egg" by Charles W. Ford, the manager of Grant's farm near St. Louis. McDonald, said Ford, was "a man that Republican papers denounce as being without sense, without truth and common honesty." Nothing came of Ford's warning. McDonald held on to his post.[21]

The St. Louis whiskey ring might have continued until the end of Grant's presidency had not the secretary of the Treasury, W. D. Richardson, chosen to resign in May 1874. Grant made Richardson a Federal judge and offered the Treasury job to a Kentucky lawyer-politician, Benjamin Helm Bristow, who had served as solicitor general in 1870–72.

Grant had created the post of solicitor general as a way of improving Federal law enforcement. The solicitor general would oversee all Federal prosecutions, freeing the attorney general to concentrate on running the department. Bristow had shown himself to be an energetic and competent lawyer. Nevertheless, he was also a man with a murky past.

The Union general commanding western Kentucky in 1863–64 had made local farmers buy permits for shipping their hogs and tobacco by rail. Military traffic had priority on rail shipments in wartime and the railroads were under direct Army control. The commander in Kentucky was engaging in extortion and using the war as camouflage. The general's local agents, who issued the permits, took a slice of the loot. Bristow, at that time a government lawyer, acted as one of his agents. Grant, however, knew nothing of this when he made Bristow solicitor general. He was still ignorant of it when he appointed him secretary of the Treasury in June 1874.[22]

Bristow insisted on appointing his own assistants, and Grant gave him a free hand. Even so, there was one person in his department whom he wasn't sure how to control, and that was the supervising architect of the Treasury, A. B. Mullett. With the rapid expansion of the Federal government following the Civil War, there was a huge construction program under way and Mullett, from his office in the Treasury Department, brought an artistic brilliance rare in government to the challenge of creating buildings that were both functional and beautiful while projecting the necessary gravitas.

Colonel William Crook, who managed the White House staff through five administrations, saw cabinet members come and cabinet members go. He remembered Bristow as "big, beefy, overgrown . . . trying to bully everyone."[23] Bristow, one of the founders of the American Bar Association, was so infatuated with himself that he went to see a "phrenologist." Afterward, he carefully pasted into his scrapbook the charlatan's report on what the bumps on Bristow's head signified— "intellectual vigor . . . strong perceptive power . . . brim-full of good-natured wit . . ."[24]

Given his rampant egotism, it was probably inevitable that Bristow would see in Mullett nothing but an obstacle to be crushed, because it was clear from their first meeting that Mullett found him boorish and overbearing. Mullett offered to resign the day they met, but Bristow talked him out of it. Bristow saw a possibility here, something he could turn to advantage—if he could fire Mullett, there was a chance for favorable publicity. As supervising architect, Mullett had developed a working relationship with the political boss that Congress had installed to run the District, Alexander Shepherd. Over time Mullett and Shepherd became friends, but Shepherd was considered a crook, and probably was. Bristow found it convenient to believe that Mullett had to be a crook, too.[25]

Alas, poor Mullett! He turned out to be as honest as he was gifted. No matter how diligently Bristow's underlings raked through Mullett's files and interrogated members of the architect's staff, there was nothing he could pin on the supervising architect except artistic talent. Mullett had been born in England, but came to the U.S. as a child. As supervising architect he designed handsome Roman Revival buildings, such as the San Francisco Mint, that have been admired for more than a century. A qualified engineer as well as a trained architect, Mullett was a major innovator and floated the San Francisco Mint on a concrete slab. It was probably the first earthquake-proof building in the world.

He also sought to create a new architectural vernacular, one that expressed both the eclectic nature of American culture and the French Second Empire aesthetic of the Gilded Age. His greatest achievement was the State-War-Navy Building next to the White House, known in our day as the Old Executive Office Building. Like the San Francisco Mint, it is a masterpiece of nineteenth-century American art, and Mullett is considered by the American Architectural Association to be one of the greatest architects in the nation's history.[26]

A man of Mullett's highly developed sensitivities was helpless against a ruthless political operator like Bristow, who embodied all the hallmarks of the philistine—a coarse-grained mind, vulgarity in dress and speech, greedy and aggressive by habit and instinct. Mullett quit, but Bristow shamelessly claimed he had fired him and lyingly spread the word around that Mullett was corrupt. Mullett tried to return to government service after Bristow left office, but Bristow had sufficiently ruined his reputation to make that impossible. Brokenhearted and in failing health, Mullett committed suicide.

Destroying Mullett launched Bristow's campaign to establish himself as a reformer, the one truly honest man in the crooked Grant administration. He bore down on the whiskey frauds by proposing to shift all the internal revenue supervisors from their current posts to similar duties in other cities. McDonald, for example, was slated to be transferred to Philadelphia. Moving the supervisors around would have resulted in the exposure of whiskey rings in half a dozen cities. McDonald hurriedly dispatched an intermediary to Washington, urging Grant to cancel the transfers.

The Republican party in Missouri had split during the first Grant administration into two irreconcilable factions—the Liberal Republicans, led by Carl Schurz, and Republicans loyal to Grant. According to McDonald's emissary, McDonald was the biggest obstacle to the machinations of the Liberal Republicans. Move him to Philadelphia, and the Schurz faction would prevail. Grant unwisely ordered Bristow to cancel the transfer program.[27]

Bristow continued collecting evidence and on May 10, 1875, the Treasury Department seized distilleries in St. Louis, Chicago, Evansville and Milwaukee. Dozens of people were arrested and hundreds of documents seized. Among those implicated were McDonald, Grant's brother Orvil, and Grant's secretary Brevet Brigadier General Orville Babcock.

Flushed with triumph, Bristow sought to portray Grant as a pawn and a dupe of the fraudsters, and informed Hamilton Fish, the secretary of state, that the President had told him, "Well, Mr. Bristow, there is at least one honest man in St. Louis on whom we can rely—John McDonald." To which Bristow had forthrightly responded, "McDonald is the head and center of all the frauds!" There is no evidence to corroborate Bristow's story, yet assuming it to be true, what does it tell us about Bristow? That he was trying to undermine the President within his own cabinet by holding him up to ridicule.[28]

He need not have bothered. Grant was doing a good job of that without Bristow's help. When a distant relation of Julia's wrote to him from St. Louis in July 1875 telling him how extensive the frauds were, Grant scribbled in the margin, "Let no guilty man escape unless it can be avoided," and forwarded the letter to Bristow.[29]

The qualification "unless it can be avoided" alluded to the possibility of letting some of the small fry escape punishment if they testified against the bigger fish. But then he had second thoughts. "I don't see why nine thieves should go unpunished," said Grant to his staff, "in order to catch the tenth." He ordered Federal prosecutors not to offer immunity in exchange for testimony. This action, which was motivated mainly by his fear that immunity would only encourage perjury, made it impossible in most cases to secure convictions.[30]

Grant's greatest failing, though, was a willful refusal to accept that Babcock had been involved in the whiskey ring. The day Babcock's trial opened in St. Louis, Grant called a special cabinet meeting and said he was thinking of going there to testify on Babcock's behalf. What did the cabinet think? It thought this was a bad idea and advised him to send a deposition instead. So Grant made a deposition, with Bristow and Attorney General Edwards Pierrepont as his witnesses, and the Chief Justice of the United States, Morrison R. Waite, signed the deposition. A week later this document was read out at Babcock's trial. Grant's testimony on behalf of Babcock secured his acquittal. The jurors were so impressed that each one wrote a personal letter of congratulations to Babcock.[31]

Even so, there was no shortage of evidence against him—a sheaf of telegrams, signed "Sylphe," that a handwriting expert testified Babcock had written. However much Grant believed in his innocence, Babcock at the very least had guilty knowledge of McDonald's activities. The likeliest explanation is that here was a soldier completely out of his depth in the murky business of party finances and political infighting in Missouri. The fact that the whiskey ring was financing Grant's supporters was probably good enough for Babcock. He also seems to have blinded himself to the equally obvious fact that McDonald and his friends were getting rich from this racket. There is nothing to show that Babcock himself gained so much as a dollar from it, and although Grant felt it politic to get a new secretary, Babcock still needed a salary and ended up as chief inspector of lighthouses. It was work that eventually cost him his life. He drowned off the Florida coast.[32]

Grant's biographer William McFeely says unequivocally that Grant perjured himself to save Babcock. He offers no new evidence to substantiate this remarkable contention; it is merely his interpretation of Treasury documents controlled by Bristow and congressional testimony from Grant's enemies.[33]

Bristow himself never testified before Congress. He relied instead on his principal assistant, Bluford Wilson, to cast doubt on Grant's honesty. Bristow refused at first to testify, claiming that his conversations with the President were privileged. Grant immediately gave him written permission to repeat all of their conversations to the committee investigating the whiskey frauds. Even with this carte blanche permission, Bristow still refused, on the grounds that he was protecting the powers of the President, which was simply absurd. By refusing to appear before Congress, he avoided any close examination of his own motives and conduct.[34]

As for Bluford Wilson, he did not have much of a reputation except as Bristow's hatchet man. He was, moreover, the brother of Grant's implacable enemy James Harrison Wilson, a man who secretly devoted a considerable amount of his time and part of his fortune to blackening Grant's name after Grant rejected his demands to be appointed secretary of war. "The Wilsons have disappointed me more than any persons I ever reposed confidence in," Grant sorrowfully told his old friend Elihu B. Washburne.[35]

To believe, as McFeely does, that Grant perjured himself requires a belief in the integrity of Bluford Wilson, which is stretching credulity to the breaking point. It is far more plausible that Grant testified as he did for the most obvious reason of all: he believed in Babcock's innocence—"strongly but wrongly," in the words of John Y. Simon, editor of the Grant *Papers*.[36]

Grant was like most people in repressing painful memories, and he could filter out bad news the way the inhabitants of wet regions put up an umbrella at the first hint of rain. When virtually the whole of Washington was buzzing with talk of the affair between Roscoe Conkling and Kate Sprague Chase, for example, Grant remained oblivious of it. If he started to read a newspaper that he could see was going to upset him, he would say, "Why should I read it?" and throw it to the ground.[37]

Grant's reputation for honesty was almost as solid as his reputation for horsemanship. Among many of his wartime acquaintances he was considered "tediously truthful." Within the cabinet, Hamilton Fish, himself an example of absolute probity, described Grant as "the most scrupulously truthful man I ever met," and he told John Russell Young, "I do not think it would have been possible for Grant to have told a lie, even if he had composed it and written it down."[38]

What hurt Grant most was not the Babcock indictment but the discovery of betrayal by someone else whom he trusted implicitly. He could not have been surprised that his brother Orvil was indicted. He was also probably less than amazed to find that one of Julia's brothers and a brother-in-law were involved. But when he learned that the manager of his farm, his old friend Charles W. Ford, was implicated he ordered that all the livestock be sold immediately, even though prevailing market conditions meant he would take a large financial loss. With the stock out of the way, he put the farm up for sale, but he failed to find anyone who wanted to buy a money-losing proposition. He rented out the farm, absorbing the losses but distancing himself from St. Louis as he did so. He rarely visited the city again. Ford, unable to clear his name, took his own life.[39]

While Grant's reputation was falling into the gutter, Bristow's was rising like a rocket. The breakup of the whiskey rings brought ringing praise from the *New York Times,* the *Chicago Tribune* and other major newspapers. Bristow had won the esteem of many Liberal Republicans. At the end of 1875, with the Republican convention only six months away, he began to see himself in a dazzling new light: Bristow the nominee . . . Bristow the candidate . . . Bristow the President!

Grant was outraged. He became convinced that his Treasury secretary had been intriguing against him all along, conspiring with his enemies in the party, using a place in the cabinet to back-stab his chief and turn what had been intended as a reform movement that would help clean up the Grant administration into a personal campaign to ruin his reputation and install Bristow as his successor. The nearer the convention approached, Bristow found, his ambition was exceeded only by the President's determination to block him.[40]

★

He could hardly wait to leave. According to the surgeon general, William Barnes, Grant returned to the White House from Capitol Hill one day toward the end of his presidency and walked into Julia's parlor. "I wish this was over," he moaned. "I wish I had this Congress off my hands. I wish I was out of it altogether. After I leave this place, I never want to see it again."

Julia looked up at him. "Why, Ulyss, how you talk! I never want to leave it."[41]

He did not even want to remind people he was the President. Portraits of his cabinet members were being shipped to Philadelphia for the Exhibition of 1876. Grant's old friend John Eaton stopped by the White House and told him he ought to send a portrait of himself. Julia agreed. "You know, Ulyss, you and Lincoln and Washington stand together. You ought to let them have something!" Grant wouldn't relent.[42]

For all the furor over the scandals of his administration, Grant remained the most popular man in American politics. Republican party regulars were almost desperate for a third term. So was Julia. At first, Grant tried to duck the issue, saying he could hardly decline something that he hadn't been offered. On May 30, 1875, however, the Pennsylvania Republican delegation voted to back Grant at the national convention. Grant immediately convened a cabinet meeting, told the cabinet that he would not run again, then wrote to the chairman of the Pennsylvania Republican Committee, saying he did not want another term.[43]

Once the message was on its way, he went and told Julia what he'd done. She was appalled. "And why did you not read your letter to me?"

"I know you too well. It would never have gone if I had read it to you."

"Oh, Ulyss! Was that kind to me? Was it just to me?"

"I do not want to be here another four years," said Grant. "I don't think I could stand it."[44]

Bristow resigned three weeks before the Republican convention met in Cincinnati and appeared to have a good chance of winning the nomination. Grant was backing Roscoe Conkling, but Bristow's biggest challenger wasn't Conkling. It was James G. Blaine, from the state of Maine. Blaine was damaged goods, though, both physically and ethically. He had been involved in a railroad swindle, which worked to Bristow's advantage. Unlike Blaine, Bristow had done a magnificent job of stuffing his skeletons into closets and keeping them there. Besides which, before a single convention ballot was cast, Blaine suffered a stroke.

Grant and Conkling nevertheless managed to block Bristow's push for the nomination. As Blaine's hopes crumbled and Bristow's supporters began drifting away, the convention looked for a compromise candidate and soon found one in the three-term governor of Ohio, Rutherford B. Hayes. He looked presidential, he had risen to a general's shoulder straps in the Union Army and, as far as anyone could tell, had never taken a dishonest dollar in his life. He was a rich man who owned much of Ohio.

Hayes's election seemed uncertain, though. The Democratic party had a strong candidate, a genuine reformer, in Governor Samuel J. Tilden of New York. Tilden was the lawyer who had smashed the Tweed ring. He was also an effective campaigner, so much so that he actually won the 1876 election—but that did not mean he would move into the White House.

There was widespread ballot-rigging and voter intimidation across the South in the election of 1876. The frauds the Democrats perpetrated in the South were exceeded only by the frauds that a shrinking and desperate Republican minority managed to effect with the support of Federal officials. Grant consistently and strongly pressed for honest elections in the South, but he could not impose them on his own party.

On November 9, the day following the election, Tilden was reported to have won 184 electoral votes. One more vote and he would be President. Everything now hung on four disputed states—Oregon, South Carolina, Louisiana and Florida. A fifteen-man electoral committee, drawn equally from the House, the Senate and the Supreme Court, was assembled to decide who should get these electoral votes.

While the committee was still trying to decide whom to install as President, Grant invited Hayes to come to the White House, but he felt unable to leave Ohio with the election still unsettled. Hayes sent his political adviser, James M. Comly, to Washington instead. Comly knew just what was on Grant's mind and, like Hayes, knew that Hayes would never become President without Grant's support. Comly wasted no time telling Grant that if Hayes was elected, he would not give Bristow a place in the cabinet. "At this point," Comly reported back to Hayes, "he drew the friendly cigars from his pocket."[45]

Party membership on the electoral committee was evenly divided: seven Republicans, seven Democrats and one independent. The independent, however, was elected to the Senate by the legislature of his home state, Illinois, and replaced by another supposed independent, but he turned out to be a closet Republican. The committee's Republican members, who now had a majority of eight to seven, promptly awarded all four states, and their electoral votes, to Hayes.

Even so, Hayes recognized he had no mandate of any kind. Grant was always convinced that had the black population of the South been allowed to vote as the law provided, Hayes would have won easily. The fact was, however, that he had lost to Tilden in the popular vote. And if he could not carry northern states like Delaware, Indiana and Rhode Island, the chances that he had actually carried three southern states whose people were virtually in revolt against Reconstruction was absurd. Seeking to do the decent thing, Hayes pledged he would serve for only one term, and kept his word.

Federal election law required inaugurations to take place on March 4, but in 1877 that day fell on a Sunday. Hayes insisted that he would not be inaugurated on the Sabbath. Grant arranged to let him have the presidency a day early, a symbolic act that only seemed to emphasize his eagerness to depart. The evening of March 3, Grant had Hayes and the Chief Justice come for dinner, and before the first course was served the three of them, along with several witnesses, went into the Red Room. Hayes was secretly sworn in as President two days before his inauguration, which took place Monday, March 5.[46]

Once Hayes had repeated the presidential oath in public, Grant was finally free. He later told his friend John Russell Young, "I was never as happy in my life as the day I left the White House. I felt like a boy getting out of school."[47]

———— ★ ★ ★ ★ ————

CHAPTER 31

"NO DESIRE TO TARRY"

E ven in a new and restless country there was no shortage of stay-puts, but Grant seemed born to travel. As a child, he had journeyed all over Ohio. As a young officer, he had seen Panama, Mexico and California. During the war, he had ridden through half the country blazing the victory trail. During the irksome Andrew Johnson years he sometimes fantasized about escaping to Europe on a long vacation. He probably hoped that by the time he came back he would find Johnson was out of the White House. After moving into the executive mansion himself, the novelty of being President soon wore off and the idea of escape, of Europe, nagged at him all over again.[1]

Grant was so eager to be gone that he began planning in earnest more than a year before his second term ended, and in January 1876 he talked about it with a reporter, J. Monroe Royce. To another journalist, John Russell Young of the *New York Herald*, he wistfully remarked, "I have never been abroad." Evidently Mexico didn't count as abroad. Once he'd seen Europe, Grant expected to return to Washington, where he would live out the rest of his days.[2]

It came as something of a surprise that Grant was able to travel far. Land rich and cash poor, he owned a considerable amount of property—the farm near St. Louis as well as two large houses, in Galena and

Long Branch. The St. Louis farm, however, continued swallowing cash even after it was rented out. Property taxes exceeded any revenue it would ever generate. And with his keen interest in bloodlines, Grant couldn't resist stocking it with thoroughbred horses and the finest cattle. He wasn't going to get much of a return on them, either.³

His $25,000 salary as President during his first term was nothing compared to his expenses. Just keeping the White House in operation cost around $35,000 a year. The government bore some of the burden, but the President had to cover the rest. He also had to pay for entertainments such as formal receptions and state dinners. The bill for champagne for a single dinner could come to nearly $2,000, while meals costing more than thirty dollars a plate had to be provided for up to one hundred guests.⁴

When his first term ended, Grant found himself in debt. He was afraid that by the time he left the White House he would be forced to sell his property just to square his accounts. He was saved from that humiliation only because Congress raised its own salaries early in his second term from $2,500 to $5,000 a year, and doubled the President's income, too.⁵

Even so, a salary of $50,000 a year did no more than cover his current expenses and pay off his debts. Grant also persisted in making his financial problems worse by giving away large sums of money. During the war he got into the habit of paying hotel bills and buying railroad tickets for his staff. Treating them, that is, as if they were members of his family. He continued in the same way when he became President. Besides, anyone who asked him for a handout—or even a small pension—was almost certain to get it. Hamilton Fish was astonished—if not appalled—at Grant's generosity. "He gave to all who asked of him [giving] from five to ten times the amount that the applicants could have reasonably or probably expected."⁶

Grant spent almost nothing on himself. He didn't much care about clothes and he never had an interest in jewelry. His sole indulgence was horses, and at one time he had twelve of them chewing contentedly in the White House stables. On that scale, horses were a rich man's hobby, but he never saw them in that light.

He might have resolved his perennial cash crisis when his father died, but Grant renounced his share of the old man's $150,000 fortune. He had done nothing to create this wealth, he said, and that meant he wasn't entitled to any of it. Although large sums passed through his hands over the years, Grant never managed to save anything. It was Julia who tried to save, but with a husband like Grant, her thrift wasn't going to take them far. It was ironic, but while Jesse and Hannah had always disliked Julia because they thought she was another spendthrift Dent, it was really their eldest son they had to worry about. He had no conception of savings. Whatever money he had, he spent, lost or gave away.[7]

Between the end of the Civil War and the close of his presidency, Grant's income just about covered his expenses and gifts to other people. He had nothing to show for twelve years of effort. And then, with his days in the White House nearly over, money seemed to rush up from underground and jump into his pockets. Grant had invested some of the proceeds from the fund that his friends and admirers in New York had presented to him at the end of the war in the Consolidated Virginia Mining Company. The company was gouging deep holes in the stark, gray landscape around Virginia City, Nevada, looking for silver. In 1873 it struck what became known as the Comstock Lode and by 1876 Grant's twenty-five shares, which had not cost him much, were worth a thousand dollars each. By selling his mining stock he would have all he needed for a leisurely and comfortable tour of the Old World.[8]

★

It was as if he feared he might never return. Before setting sail, Grant went back to his roots in Georgetown, Ohio. As with countless returnees before him, he found that what his imagination had long presented to him as the physical center of his being was in truth a dull and backward place, occupied by uninteresting people. They were overjoyed to see him—the great man paying his respects to his humble origins was bound to be greeted like a hero—but as he listened to them recall the old days and looked into their eyes, his spirit sank. These people were satisfied to pursue lives empty of accomplishment. There was no burning curiosity there, no restless desire to embrace the world or to challenge it. "The change I saw in them was so great," he told Hamilton Fish, "that I had no desire to tarry." The truth, though, was a revolutionary change *had* occurred . . . in him.[9]

Before sailing from Philadelphia, Grant had a uniform made; his last, as it turned out. His weight was now 184 pounds; he was nearly fifty pounds heavier at the end of his presidency than he had been at the end of the war. "I don't want to have to appear at full dress occasions in knee breeches and slippers," he told the tailor who measured him for the uniform. "I think I'll be more comfortable in a uniform, although I always get out of wearing brass buttons whenever I can." He also bought a cheap, off-the-peg suit to travel in, costing all of sixteen dollars.[10]

When he sailed from Philadelphia on May 17, 1877, aboard the steamship *Indiana,* the banks of the Delaware were black with well-wishers, while thousands of small craft escorted Grant's ship downriver to the sea. Grant's party consisted of himself, Julia, young Jesse and a maid. There were several journalists aboard, too, including the one Grant knew best and trusted, John Russell Young. Grant was news, in office or not.

Young was roughly the same height as Grant, stoutly built, with reddish hair and a neatly cropped mustache. An Ulsterman by birth, he had come to America as a child, gone into journalism, and become a protégé of Horace Greeley, who made him managing editor of the *New York Tribune.* He left to found his own newspaper, which quickly went under, and became a star reporter on the *New York Herald,* the most popular and innovative journal of the day.[11]

When the *Indiana* sailed up the Mersey and into Liverpool on May 28, it was as if the Delaware continued on the other side of the Atlantic—a river swarming with small craft under a forest of flags, the docks and surrounding streets choked with cheering, handkerchief-waving crowds. Grant was astounded. He had expected to be treated like another American tourist. The Liverpudlians welcomed him like one of their own—maybe even better.

Among the throng waiting to greet him was Adam Badeau, whom Grant had made consul general in London. Badeau arrived with a huge medal that a jeweler had made. It was, in effect, an ersatz version of the garish and feudal chivalric orders that European monarchs still bestow (with sash to match) on leading members of the political class. Badeau was inviting Grant to award this bauble to himself, as if he needed a jewel-encrusted dazzler to hold his own at official functions. It showed just how little Badeau understood Grant, who was never going to wear something as risible as this. He hardly wore the uniform, either. Grant preferred the sixteen-dollar suit.[12]

From Liverpool the Grants journeyed to London, where they stayed for a month, met Queen Victoria and made a side trip to Southampton to see Nellie and Algernon. The lord mayor of London hosted a banquet in Grant's honor at the eight-hundred-year-old Guildhall and a copy of the lord mayor's speech was given in advance to the ambassador, Edwards Pierrepont, as a courtesy. Pierrepont tried to read it to Grant, thinking it might help him prepare a speech in reply.

Grant said abruptly, "Don't read it! I shall get to thinking about it and then I shall have to write down what I want to say, and then I shall have to commit it to memory, and when I get up to speak I shall find I have not remembered it and I'll cave in and have to give up. I must trust entirely to the spur of the moment or I can't go through with it." His spontaneous reply on the night of the banquet was a success. One thing Grant learned to do on his travels was make a short, gracious and sometimes witty extemporaneous speech.[13]

While he was in Britain he visited a grand country house, grand enough, in fact, to have its own golf course. Grant's host invited him to play a few rounds and a caddy handed him a club. Grant carefully took his first swing at the ball, and missed it by six inches. On his second attempt, he hit the ground instead of the ball. Undaunted, he made a few more swings, missing every time. Grant handed the club back to the caddy as if everything had gone the way it should, and turned to his host. "I have always understood the game of golf was good outdoor exercise and especially for the arms. I fail to see, however, what use there is for a ball in the game."[14]

Grant spent eighteen months crisscrossing Europe. There was no pattern to his wanderings apart from a determination to see it all. He visited England, Scotland and Northern Ireland; Belgium and Holland; Germany, Austria and Switzerland; Poland and Russia; Norway, Denmark and Sweden; Portugal and Spain; France, Italy ("Venice would be a fine city if only it were drained," said Grant) and Greece. Wherever he went he was treated more like a head of state than a private citizen and sometimes got a twenty-one-gun salute.

Europe was still in shock from the Franco-Prussian War of 1870–71, which had ended with the unification of Germany. Italy, too, had recently broken free from Austria and been united by force of arms. Given Europe's political convulsions, it wasn't surprising that a reporter asked Grant before he departed if he expected to observe a war during his travels. "No," said Grant. "I should keep as far away as possible from the theater of war. It is at all times a sad and cruel business. I hate war with all my heart."[15]

In Paris, he and Young one day found themselves outside Les Invalides, the former military hospital beneath whose gorgeous dome Napoleon lies buried in a red porphyry tomb. Young was eager to see it. Grant declined and walked away. He would not even look at military paintings if he could avoid them. He caught sight of some at Versailles and thought them "disgusting." Hannah would have been proud of him.[16]

The Germans and French both wanted to honor him with military reviews and were astonished to discover the great general shunned reviews, parades, or any display of military power. What Grant wanted from Europe's leaders wasn't pomp but stimulating conversation, such as he got at his meeting with Bismarck, who talked frankly in fluent English about European politics and questioned Grant closely on the Civil War, all the while cradling a meerschaum in one hand and stroking a reclining wolfhound with the other. Grant told him it was a good thing the Civil War had not ended quickly. A short war would have saved the Union but not ended slavery. "And slavery meant the germs of a new rebellion. There had to be an end to slavery . . . no treaty was possible— only destruction."[17]

He liked meeting up with old friends, too, like Grenville Dodge, who owned a house on the Boulevard Haussmann in Paris. Dodge had served ably under Grant in the Shiloh and Vicksburg campaigns and Grant had made him a general. With Dodge and Young, but sometimes alone, Grant spent hours watching the crowds on the Champs-Elysées. He was bored by the pampered and often banal lives of the powerful and rich but forever fascinated with how ordinary people managed to succeed in the struggle for existence.[18]

The American ambassador to Spain, James Russell Lowell, was slightly irritated that Grant so obviously found the meetings Lowell had arranged to be tedious and had almost nothing to say to the people he met. Like other Beacon Hill patricians before him—Charles Sumner, Henry Adams—he concluded that Grant could not be very bright. "What he likes best," noted Lowell from those rarefied purlieus where disdain operates much as oxygen does closer to the ground—it makes life possible—"is to wander about the streets. After being here two days I think he knew Madrid better than I."[19]

Although he had avoided Napoleon's tomb, Grant had no objection to visiting that of Ferdinand and Isabella, where the king and queen lay buried side by side. As he and Julia stood in front of it, Grant turned to her. "Julia," he said, "this is how we should lie in death."[20]

Although he covered most of Europe by road and rail, Grant also liked traveling by ship. He journeyed up the Rhine by boat and saw much of the Mediterranean the same way. Julia found all travel tiring and was susceptible to seasickness, but Grant throve on new sights and seemed immune to *mal de mer.* Afloat or ashore, he rarely went to bed before midnight. Most nights after dinner, he stayed up playing cards and reminiscing about the war.[21]

And what did the Old World teach him? Not much. He took almost no interest in its cultural treasures or intellectual life. This was the age of Impressionism, of Manet, Monet and Renoir. In music, it was the era of Wagner and Brahms and Verdi. Intellectual horizons were being rolled back by radical thinkers such as Karl Marx and John Stuart Mill. In literature, Tennyson and Flaubert were both at the height of their powers. None of which meant anything to Grant. He preferred people and things to high art and radical ideas. Grant spent an hour on his only visit to an art exhibition, but at the Paris Exposition in March 1878 he stayed for most of the day, looking at state-of-the-art machinery whirring and clanking and steaming.

"I have seen nothing," he decided, "that would make me want to live outside of the United States," he wrote one old friend. But if he had to choose, "my preference would be for England." He had been impressed, too, he told another friend, by the "sturdy, independent, self-reliant people" of Northern Ireland. Grant noticed that living standards were generally lower in Europe, and blamed it on wars past and wars still to come. The United States was different—"We are the only first class power that is not compelled to grind the laborers to the last degree to pay the interest on [national] debts and to support large armies and navies."[22]

From time to time he wrote to friends back home to say he was homesick, weary of travel, and longing to return. No one would imagine from these letters that he was absolute master of his own schedule. He could go home whenever he wanted. Instead, he thought of new places to visit, new scenes to absorb, new people to meet. Somewhere in Europe he did make one important discovery—Europe wasn't enough. He had to see the whole world.

★

In December 1877 Grant sailed into the Bay of Naples and was shocked to find that sunny Italy could be bitterly cold and dismally wet. He sailed on to a warmer, dryer place, Egypt. The khedive put a palace at his disposal and Grant spent a month visiting tombs, pyramids and the great temple at Karnak. "I have seen more to interest me in Egypt than in any of my other travels," he informed his son Fred.[23]

He fell in love, too, with the easygoing, let-tomorrow-take-care-of-itself attitude of most of the people he met. The antiquities, however, were what really held his interest. He spent hours staring into the time-worn, wind-striated face of the Sphinx. "It looks," he thought, "as if it has kept on thinking through all eternity without talking too much." His kind of monument.[24]

From Egypt he traveled to Palestine and was horrified when he entered Jerusalem to find himself being escorted into the ancient and holy city by a military band. He and Julia had expected to slip in more or less unobserved, like other pilgrims. From Palestine he moved north, to Syria, and then on to Constantinople.

The sultan of Turkey, Abdul Hamid II, had been in power for only two years. Grant judged him a personable and intelligent young man, but felt the sultan was out of his depth politically. Events would in time prove Grant right. As he grew older, Abdul Hamid turned into a paranoid, murderous tyrant who ruled by terror until, in 1908, he was finally overthrown. Grant eagerly accepted an invitation to visit Abdul Hamid's stables and was enthralled to be told that the bloodlines of some of the Arabian stallions he was shown went back three hundred years.

The sultan wanted to know which horses he considered the best. Grant picked out two—a gray called Djeytan and a black with a white star on his forehead, called Missirli. Abdul Hamid then told him these two horses were his and refused to listen to Grant's protests that he couldn't accept such valuable gifts. In fact, though, Grant was secretly thrilled. Put to stud, these horses would improve American breeds.[25]

When spring arrived, Grant returned to France and resumed his exploration of the Old Continent. But when winter approached again, his mind turned to Egypt once more and he began planning to go home. He would see India, China, Australia and Japan on the way.

Grant sailed through the Suez Canal in January 1879 and reached Bombay in February. From the coast, he made his way to Delhi. Along the way he was the guest of the fabulously rich maharajah of Jaipur. When the maharajah organized a tiger hunt in Grant's honor he discovered something surprising—Grant was a great soldier who never went hunting. In India, a warrior with an aversion to blood sports was a creature unknown, almost unimaginable.[26]

In Delhi he was the guest of the viceroy, Edward George Lytton, an English aristocrat. A strange and unhappy man who had grown up in a strange and unhappy home, Lord Lytton was a novelist, not a politician. He hated India, despised the Indians, loathed his work, and was feeling at the end of his tether at the time the Grants showed up. One of Lytton's principal diversions was to write long and fanciful letters to his friends in England. It did not matter whether there was a word of truth in what he wrote. What mattered was to be amusing, to forget how unhappy he was, and maintain an insouciant image.

In a letter recounting what happened when the Grants came for dinner, Lytton described Grant as getting drunk, groping a female guest, being overcome with lust, copulating with Julia in front of the assembled company, and vomiting on her while engaged in coitus. Scores of people were present at this dinner. Not one ever suggested it was anything but another dull semiofficial occasion. Lytton's fantasy may have begun as a scene he played out in his head that evening, a novelist's way of enduring the tedium.[27]

William McFeely presents some of Lytton's tale as being true, even though all of it is nonsense, and he accepts Lytton's description of six British sailors having to pull Grant off the unresisting, vomit-smeared Julia as a kind of compliment to Grant's physical strength.[28]

Lytton's biographer Aurelia Harlan doesn't waste time on this story, probably because it is so obviously another of his numerous fantasies. Love of make-believe and a poet's disregard for mere facts so shaped his imagination that when Lytton came to write his autobiography, *Glenaveril,* he cast it in the form of a poem running to nearly fifteen thousand lines. But although *Glenaveril* is an acknowledged fantasy, this is not its greatest drawback. Lytton's odd tribute to himself is poetasting drivel.[29]

From India, Grant sailed through the Straits of Malacca and stopped in Singapore, where he was guest of honor at a banquet at which one of the speakers referred to the likelihood that the United States would put a limit on Chinese immigration and deny American citizenship to those already here. Grant made a short extemporaneous speech in reply. He had been stationed in California, he said, when the first wave of Chinese immigration arrived. The problem was not the number or the character of the immigrants but the conditions in which they lived and worked, which amounted to a form of slavery. The Union had fought a long, costly and bitter war to end slavery and it was intolerable that something so evil should be allowed to reappear in a different guise. Once the Chinese were treated like other immigrants, they would pose no more of a threat to American life than anyone else in a nation of immigrants.[30]

From Singapore he sailed on to Siam, met the king, then proceeded to Hong Kong, Canton, Shanghai, Tientsin and Peking. The Chinese viceroy, Li Hung-chang, told him, "You and I are the greatest men in the world." Grant himself came to think of Li Hung-chang as a great man, but he had serious doubts about China. Big and ancient though it was, it lacked the essentially adaptive nature of any great country. China, thought Grant, was too resistant to political change to be truly successful.[31]

Li Hung-chang and the head of the Chinese government, Prince Kung, knew that Grant intended to stop in Japan. They asked him to help settle the ongoing Sino-Japanese dispute over ownership of the Ryukyu Islands. Grant readily agreed to try to bring the two sides closer together.[32]

He was entranced by Japan from the moment he set foot on Japanese soil. The country's calm, carefully crafted beauty charmed him into submission. Grant marveled at the absence of locks on Japanese doors and windows. Although far from rich, the Japanese were orderly, hardworking and honest. The country was so peaceful, he jokingly told his old friend Daniel Ammen, "Japanese babies don't cry."[33]

Unlike China, he thought, Japan was progressive. Its people, from the emperor down, seemed eager to adopt or adapt whatever the West had to offer. Grant left Japan having failed to see anything beyond the surface of life, even though this was the only country where he was unable to avoid witnessing a military review. It never occurred to him that Imperial Japan was a quasi-military dictatorship. The charming young emperor was a glove puppet in the hands of his generals, whose interest in the West was not the gaining of democracy but the acquisition of artillery. They craved industrialization not to build a better life but to build battleships. In 1895 Japan resolved the dispute over the Ryukyus in its own way. It attacked China—the opening round in fifty years of conquest.

★

Julia had had enough. She had spent more than two years traveling with Ulyss. She was glad to see him so happy and relaxed after so many years of responsibility and hard work, but they couldn't travel forever and she wanted to go home. So Grant gave up all hope of visiting Australia. There was no way of sailing there directly from Japan. To reach Australia would mean traveling through half a dozen countries first. Enough was enough. From Japan they sailed eastward, destination Golden Gate.[34]

During the slow voyage across the Pacific John Russell Young gave Grant a book to read—the longest novel written up to that time, Victor Hugo's *Les Misérables.* Hugo, the son of one of Napoleon's generals, had written a celebrated description of the battle of Waterloo. Young noticed that Grant read *Les Misérables* "very slowly, almost like a man who is studying rather than reading. For two or three days we did not see him, except at meals." When Grant eventually emerged from his cabin, the book finally finished, it was late at night.

The two men strolled the deck, puffing on cigars. Young wanted to know what he thought of the chapter on Waterloo. "It is a very fine account," replied Grant. Then he launched into a detailed analysis of the battle—tactics, deployments, weapons, leadership. It was, he thought, the best-planned battle in Napoleon's career. Napoleon had failed only because providence was against him. He had spent almost the entire day at Waterloo flat on his back, seriously ill; the heavy rains of the previous two days aided the British and Prussians; Marshal Soult had not reached the battlefield; and so on.

From Napoleon, Grant moved on to analyze the campaigns of Frederick the Great, and the more he talked, the farther back he went, concluding with the campaigns of Julius Caesar. It poured out of him, hour after hour, this battle, that general, the shifting nature of warfare, the evolution of tactics, the development of weapons. Grant's understanding of the art of war was at last explained, and he revealed it not to Sherman or Sheridan, not to a class of awestruck West Point cadets, but to a civilian, in the middle of the night, aboard a steamship bobbing far out at sea, like a man conveying a secret.[35]

Grant sailed into San Francisco Bay in September, to be greeted by huge crowds. He brought with him two unusual traveling companions: a huge St. Bernard he had bought in Switzerland, called Ponto, and a smiling, attentive young manservant named Yanada, whom he had hired in Japan.

The Grants made a trip to Oregon and traveled around northern California before heading east again. Along the way they spent three days visiting the Comstock mine. He and Julia donned battered felt hats and long dusters and descended into the mine, lanterns in hand, paying homage to the source of the money that had paid for their trip.

From Nevada they journeyed on, to their Galena home. They weren't there long before they headed for Chicago and the reunion of the Army of the Tennessee. Chicago gave him a tumultuous hello, with a welcoming parade of eighty thousand people. Meeting up again with Sherman and Sheridan meant a lot more to him than any parade, but he had to review the marchers.

The speakers invited to these festivities included Mark Twain, who had met Grant briefly in 1869, in his office in the White House. Grant had greeted him dressed in a short, well-worn linen duster well spattered with ink. Twain, a former Confederate soldier, wasn't sure what to say to the Union's greatest general and admitted as much. "Mr. President, I'm a little embarrassed. Are you?" Grant had smiled at him, shook his hand, and said nothing. Twain decided Grant was possibly even more embarrassed than he was, but he was reading too much into Grant's inveterate shyness.[36]

Since then Twain had become fascinated with the Grant legend, without knowing much about the man. So he was thrilled to be invited to sit on the reviewing stand jutting out from the second floor of the Palmer House during the monster parade. The mayor of Chicago, Carter Harrison, introduced him to Grant. "General, let me present Mr. Clemens, a man almost as great as yourself."

Grant extended his hand and said wryly, "Mr. Clemens, I am not embarrassed. Are you?" Twain roared with laughter, then attempted to step to the back of the reviewing stand.

"I don't want to interrupt your speech," said Twain.

"But I'm not going to make any," Grant replied. "Stay where you are." Twain watched the parade sitting next to Grant and chatting with him.[37]

That evening, at Haverly's Theater, Twain was astonished at Grant's reaction to adulation. More than a thousand veterans of the Army of the Tennessee, accompanied by their wives, shouted themselves hoarse when Grant arrived. Grant then mounted the stage and, without saying a word, slouched in a chair in front of the multitude for half an hour, right leg crossed over the left, his face impassive, as if untouched by the surging tide of adoration being driven relentlessly at him with the brassy aid of an exuberant band. Sherman finally walked over, put a hand on Grant's shoulder, bent down, and whispered into his ear that he had to do *something*. Grant stood up, bowed, and sat down again. Before he went to bed that night, Twain, scourge of all that was pompous or meretricious, wrote to a friend, telling him he had never seen such self-control, such an "iron man."[38]

The next evening the reunion banquet was held at the Palmer House. One unforgettable night in 1861 Twain had been chased across Ralls County, Missouri, by these people, when they had arms in their hands. His unit had been routed in a brief skirmish with the Federals, and shortly after that Twain gave up soldiering. Having long ceased to identify himself with his former comrades, he embraced the former foe. "Imagine what it was like," he wrote his friend and fellow writer William Dean Howells, "to see a bullet-shredded old battle flag reverently unfolded to the gaze of a thousand middle-aged soldiers who hadn't seen it since they saw it advancing over victorious fields when they were in their prime. And imagine what it was like when Grant, their commander, stepped into view while they were still going mad over the flag, and right then in the midst of it all [the band] struck up 'When we were marching through Georgia.' Well, you should have heard the thousand voices lift that chorus and seen the tears stream down. If I live to be a hundred I sha'n't ever forget these things, nor be able to talk about them."[39]

Sherman proposed the first toast of the evening. Grant responded to it with a short, amusing speech that had a serious—and suitably patriotic—theme. Grant said that what he had learned from his travels was that other countries at last acknowledged the rightful place of the United States in the world—as one of the great powers. A small fort on the table in front of him erupted in fireworks, and the band swung into "The Stars and Stripes Forever."

After fourteen other orators had had their say, Twain spoke last. It was two in the morning and his audience was drowsy. He proposed a toast "To the Babies." There were, he estimated, three or four million cradles being rocked in the United States, and some of them held the nation's future leaders, and among these was "the future illustrious commander-in-chief of the American armies." But at present that budding hero was able to devote all of his attention to the pressing business of getting his big toe into his mouth. "An achievement," said Twain in an offhand way, "which the illustrious guest of this evening also turned his attention to some fifty-six years ago." That woke them up. A sense of alarm played over the faces of the diners. Was Twain going to ridicule Grant in public? And in his presence, too?

Twain paused just long enough for doubt and fear to get a good grip on them, then he let them have it. "And if the child is but the father to the man, there are mighty few who will *doubt that he succeeded!*" Grant laughed so hard he nearly fell off his chair. He roared, he shook, he wept. Twain had seen an iron man the night before. A challenge. Tonight he had gotten through the carapace, the shyness, the legend, reached the iron man and, for a few minutes, set him free.[40]

From Chicago the Grants continued their journey east until, in December, they were back where they'd begun, in Philadelphia. The mayor declared a holiday. Schools, stores and factories closed. At noon on December 16 an enormous parade stepped off under Grant's impassive gaze. It was four and a half hours before the last marcher strutted past. An estimated 350,000 people crowded the sidewalks. Up to half the population of Philadelphia was there, parading or spectating. And that wasn't the end of it. At night the parade came back, this time under torchlight, passing beneath a huge arch thrown across Chestnut Street near the Continental Hotel. Another four and a half hours of marching, singing, band music, cheers, emotion, adulation.[41]

Fervor like this—and he'd been on the receiving end of it from coast to coast—could have only one result. It was something Grant had foreseen, and dreaded, long before he came home. His political friends would try to make him President again.

———— ★ ★ ★ ★ ————

CHAPTER 32

"TO BE; TO DO;

TO SUFFER"

Leaving the United States provided no escape from the third-term question. It traveled around the world with Grant, in the shape of John Russell Young. The *New York Herald* had been pushing Grant's name in front of Americans since 1863. The paper's founder and proprietor, James Gordon Bennett, had been trying to get Grant into the White House while Lincoln was still in residence. After Bennett died in 1868, his son, James Gordon Bennett, Jr., took over and nothing changed. When Grant left the White House, the *Herald* was too closely identified with Grant to let him drop out of sight, out of mind. So, too, were Roscoe Conkling and the Stalwart Republicans. They yearned for Grant to ignore Washington's precedent and run for a third term.

Even so, Grant would have gone around the world with no one for company but Julia. It wasn't Grant's idea to have Young along—it was Bennett's. Grant had no objections, not because he was Bennett's dupe, but because he already knew and liked Young, who was perceptive, knowledgeable, and a good talker, even if he was sometimes too frank in what he wrote. The news Bennett wanted most from Young proved impossible to come by, though, because Grant kept saying he wasn't interested in running again. Then, one night in Málaga, during the visit to Spain, Grant said it was just possible he might do it.

During the past year the United States had been wracked by political violence and bitter labor disputes that were broken up by force. "I would not accept but on one condition," said Grant. "Namely, social or public affairs at home would render it necessary for me to go back as a military leader. . . . But I was never as happy in my life as the day I left the White House."[1]

Grant regularly saw American newspapers while he was away. "Some of them speculate on my designs," he told a friend. "They may know them, but if they do, I do not." And when a group of Americans Grant met abroad tried to raise the subject, Young noticed "he answered in an impatient way that he knew what the Presidency was and had had all he wanted."[2]

There is absolutely nothing in Grant's conversations or letters that indicates he returned to the United States with any intention of seeking a third term. Nevertheless, the pressure on him by the time he reached Philadelphia was intense, and it did not come only from Conkling and the Stalwarts. It came from the people. "The general popular favorite is Grant," a disapproving President Hayes told his diary.[3]

After his triumphal cross-country journey, Grant returned to Galena —a place he did not much care for, but it would do for now. Each morning he walked into town with Yanada and stopped at the post office to pick up his mail. Then he would go to see his old friend and wartime aide William Rowley for a chat, before going back up the hill to have lunch with Julia. Late in the afternoon he went into town again, heading for the offices of the *Galena Gazette,* where he read the telegrams that had come in during the day over the AP wire.[4]

According to Adam Badeau, Grant wanted badly to be nominated for a third term and be President again. He ought to know—Badeau visited Grant briefly in Galena shortly before the Republican convention met and went back to see Grant after it was over. The trouble is, Badeau's claims, although accepted without question by McFeely, lack corroboration. There is not one letter, not one diary entry, not one interview, memo or official document in which Grant expressed even a hint of a desire to run again. Yet there are dozens of letters, diary entries and recorded conversations in which Grant explicitly said he didn't want to be President.[5]

Badeau himself failed to offer so much as a letter from himself to a friend—Henry Adams, say—with a date in 1880 or earlier in which he had said Grant was hoping and maneuvering to be President. He waited until Grant was safely dead before he said this, and by then Badeau had been fired as Grant's research assistant and scorned by him as petulant, greedy and mentally unstable. In portraying Grant as he does, Badeau presents him as a duplicitous figure. That is not enough, however. Badeau informed the world that Grant only got as far as he did because he was in the hands of smarter, more ruthless men. His account of Grant is an act of revenge.[6]

The people Grant trusted—Julia, Fred, Buck, John Russell Young— had no doubts about Grant and the third term: He did not want it. A week before the Republican convention met in Chicago, Young went to Galena. Grant gave him a letter to carry to Senator Don Cameron of Pennsylvania, one of the Stalwart leaders who were trying to secure the nomination for Grant. In his letter, Grant repeated what he had told Young in Málaga—he did not want to be President again; it should go to someone who did want it, someone younger, energetic and enthusiastic. Barring an emergency, his friends should not put his name in nomination.[7]

Julia was appalled. She longed to return to Washington, to preside again over White House receptions, to be a social leader and a figure in her own right. In trying to sabotage his potential nomination, Grant was, as he rarely did, ignoring what Julia wanted.[8]

Cameron and Conkling paid no attention to his letter. They would try to nominate him regardless, and even if they could not put him over, they could use Grant as a battering ram to destroy Conkling's most powerful enemy, James G. Blaine. On the fourth day of the convention, the roll call of the states was made and when New York's turn came, Conkling swaggered dramatically down the central aisle of the convention floor, the cynosure of every eye, and instead of mounting the stage he jumped up on the reporter's table in front of it. The delegates could see him better that way, and he knew he made a magnificent sight. Tall, fair, handsome and dominating, Conkling looked as if he'd walked into the wrong century, a Viking chieftain who had momentarily put aside his sword and buckler in favor of a well-cut suit. Conkling stood on the table, reporters scribbling furiously at his feet, threw back his splendid head, projected his tremendous wedge-shaped physique, and roared the opening stanza of a poem that every man in the hall knew virtually by heart:

"And when asked what state he hails from,
Our sole reply shall be,
He comes from Appomattox
And its famous apple tree!"

The convention floor erupted in volcanic applause that ran on for twenty minutes. It wasn't only the Grant delegates who yelled and stamped their feet. Conkling had grabbed hold of the patriotic impulse with both hands and pulled on it like a bell rope.[9]

Grant was following developments from Rowley's office. A private wire had been installed there so Grant could monitor the convention. When news of Conkling's sensational speech flashed over the wire, Grant was alarmed. He said he was going home, and Buck followed him out to the street. "I'm afraid I may be nominated," said Grant, sounding depressed.[10]

Once the tumult died down, Conkling made a powerful speech nominating Grant, but he went on too long. And when Conkling finished, Garfield, who dreaded the idea of Grant back in the White House, made a clever speech that diluted much of the enthusiasm Conkling had generated, and he managed to do it without attacking Grant.

On the first ballot, Grant led with 304 votes—seventy-five short of victory and only twenty ahead of Blaine. In third place came Sherman's brother, Senator John Sherman of Ohio. Day after day, the convention voted, and nothing really changed. After six days and thirty-five ballots, Grant's tally had risen to 313. Sherman's vote was crumbling, and some of his friends sent Grant a telegram saying he could have the Sherman vote—which was enough to secure the nomination—in exchange for a promise to make Sherman secretary of the Treasury. Grant's answer was No.[11]

With the convention completely deadlocked, Garfield's name was put forward; he would be the compromise candidate. On the next ballot, he was nominated with a sigh of relief. The Stalwarts got a consolation prize: Conkling's close friend Chester A. Arthur was nominated for the vice presidency.

Young returned to Galena. Grant, he thought, was "rather glad" he hadn't been nominated. All the same, Grant hated failure, loathed defeat even if what was lost was something he did not want. Cameron and Conkling should never have put his name forward, he complained to Buck, unless success was certain.[12]

In the fall, he campaigned for Garfield, partly because he had an obsession with party unity, partly because he loathed the Democratic nominee, Winfield Scott Hancock. In 1864 Hancock, then serving as a corps commander under Grant, had received one vote at the Democratic convention. Grant was appalled. A soldier had only one duty in time of war, and it wasn't to apply his boot to the commander-in-chief. Ever since he got that one vote, Grant told a reporter, Hancock had been "crazy to be President." Grant dismissed him as "ambitious, vain and weak."[13]

Grant was nevertheless worried by Hancock's candidacy, because Hancock and the Democratic party seemed eager to appease the South. Reconstruction had been dead long before Grant left the White House, and the Hayes administration had conducted the funeral. That had done nothing to revive the Republican party in the South. On the contrary, it was almost impossible by 1880 for a Republican to be elected to anything in the former Confederacy. Grant campaigned in every southern state for Garfield, but it probably made no difference at all.

In the North, however, Grant remained the most popular man there was. There wasn't even a close second. Huge crowds turned out to hear him speak. By this time, he was an effective impromptu speaker. He never spoke for more than ten minutes, and he invariably stressed unity—of nation, of party—instead of making an explicit pitch for Garfield's election.[14]

On Election Day, Garfield narrowly defeated Hancock, who proved a better soldier than a political campaigner. Four months after being sworn in, Garfield was assassinated by a disappointed office seeker.

★

Grant lived in Galena reluctantly. The town bored him. The only reason he was there, he said, was that he could afford it, and then only "in a moderate way." He really wanted to be in New York or Washington, not here. "I have never felt identified with Galena," he told Young in 1876. He would like to live in Washington—"I feel at home there." The trouble was, he and Julia would be expected to entertain people, and they couldn't afford much entertaining. As for New York, the city was simply too expensive. But even after seeing the world, he ended up back in dull little Galena.[15]

He still hoped to sell the eight hundred acres he owned near St. Louis. For years he told himself they simply had to rise in value as the city expanded. That was what had happened to property around Chicago, but St. Louis grew much more slowly. Grant convinced himself his property was worth $100,000, refusing to accept, like millions before and since, that property is worth exactly what someone else will pay you for it. No one wanted his land. Given its continuing losses, he might have had trouble giving it away.[16]

He was rescued once again by his rich friends. They subscribed to what might be considered a second Grant escape fund. He was able to leave Galena behind and buy a handsome brownstone on East 66th Street in New York, within sight of Central Park. The house was so crammed with war memorabilia—flags, swords, bullets, weapons, uniforms—it looked like a military museum. There was also an impressive library, stocked with five thousand books.[17]

He also became a president again, this time of the Mexican Southern Railroad. He had disliked Mexico intensely when he first saw it, but by the time he left it, following Scott's brilliant campaign, Grant had come to love the country and its people, apart from the priests and the ruling class. He was eager ever afterward to help Mexico develop, and the railroad held the promise of modernization. Grant put his name and his contacts at the service of the Mexican Southern, which was almost entirely American owned, with offices at 2 Wall Street. Grant usually made his way there at around eleven A.M., Monday to Friday, spent a couple of hours on company business, then went home to have lunch with Julia.[18]

Occasionally he took the ferry across the Hudson to see his sister Virginia and his mother, who lived with her. In May 1883 Hannah died and Grant took his mother's remains back to Ohio, to be buried alongside Jesse.[19]

On Christmas Eve that year he fell on the icy sidewalk outside his house, badly injuring his left leg, the one that had been crushed when a horse fell on it in New Orleans twenty years before. He was in agony for weeks after his Christmas Eve fall and hobbled about on crutches for the rest of his life. This time the injured leg refused to heal, but he could still indulge his one recreation, driving a handsome pair of trotters at jolting speed through Central Park.

The fact that Grant had an office on Wall Street and that over the years he had become friendly with various millionaires was taken by those who disliked him as proof that he was not the man his admirers claimed. Hugh McCulloch, a millionaire banker who had served as secretary of the Treasury under Lincoln, Andrew Johnson and Chester A. Arthur, claimed that after he failed to secure the Republican nomination in 1880, Grant's "ambition now was to be rich. . . . For rich men he had great respect; for poor men . . . he had but little regard." McCulloch somehow fails to cite a single instance of Grant ever expressing admiration for the rich as a class, or expressing disdain for the poor, to support this assertion.[20]

The rich people Grant was friendly with were people he liked as individuals; their net worth was irrelevant. As his correspondence shows, they were people who amused him, people who put up with his jokes, people whose wives got on well with Julia, and people who had been kind to him. At the same time, he retained his long-established sympathy with the poor, in fact with anyone who had a hard life. He never forgot what it was like. Once, when Julia kept a cab waiting so long it cost him five dollars, he reminded her, "Julia, five dollars would have kept our whole family for a week at Hardscrabble!"[21]

Few of those who were truly close to Grant were rich. His friends since childhood, Daniel Ammen and Absalom Markland, had spent their careers on the government payroll. Some old friends had become rich, such as Horace Porter, the president of the Pullman Car Company, but their friendship was forged in the ten years when Porter served as Grant's aide and secretary. After leaving the White House, Grant probably spent more time with John Russell Young than he did with any of his millionaire friends.

It is even more telling that the greatest political cartoonist of the day, Thomas Nast, like the greatest American poet of the age, Walt Whitman, and the greatest contemporary American novelist, Mark Twain, all admired Grant from a perspective that trod on the toes of idolatry. A Grant who yearned to amass wealth and rub shoulders with plutocrats could never win the love of Walt Whitman. In reading a man's character, who is the better judge, an immortal artist like Whitman or an obscure and banal banker-politician named McCulloch?[22]

Grant hadn't changed. American manufacturers asked him to use his contacts with the Mexican government to help them sell their products in Mexico. Grant was willing to help, but whatever he received as a commission he intended to give to the Mexican government. His aim was to help Mexico develop, not get rich from its sweat.[23]

The railroad provided no more than a modest salary, and New York was, as he had foreseen, an expensive place to live. Buck—the not overly bright Ulysses S. Grant, Jr.—seemed to have the answer: go into partnership with Ferdinand Ward, a Wall Street speculator hailed in the press as "the Young Napoleon of Finance." Following his graduation from Harvard, Buck had gone on to Columbia Law School, and from there gravitated to the Street and into partnership with Ward, a young man in a hurry to get seriously rich. Ward wasn't overly scrupulous about how he did it, either.

Grant sold his St. Louis properties at last and managed to scrape together $100,000 to invest in Grant and Ward. He would draw a salary of $3,000 a month and share in the profits. Grant did not know it, but the young Napoleon was running what amounted to a huge Ponzi scheme. Investors—in this case more aptly known as "the suckers"—were invited to loan the firm of Grant and Ward large sums of money. At the end of three or six months, they received a dividend. With dividends running as high as 40 percent a year, the money was flooding in.

Ward was aided and abetted by another swindler, James D. Fish, president of the Marine Bank. Money that was deposited with the Marine Bank made its way swiftly into accounts at Grant and Ward. The backing of the bank was taken as proof that Grant and Ward stood on solid foundations, not worm-eaten planks.[24]

Grant never doubted that the money the firm accepted was more than covered by the value of the investments Ward was making. It wasn't that Grant was putting his faith in Ward, whom he barely knew; he was putting it in Buck. The trouble was, Buck knew no more than his father about the often crooked workings of Wall Street. No Securities and Exchange Commission policed the Gilded Age. This was capitalism red in tooth and claw, and the Street was a place where sheep got fleeced. It was an environment tailor-made for a cunning predator like Ward. He not only fooled Grant; he conned dozens of people who fancied they knew their way around the markets, including the president of the Erie Railroad, who handed over $800,000 without a qualm.[25]

Like all Ponzi schemes, Ward's needed more and more cash coming in to keep the phony "profits" flowing out. And like all Ponzi schemes, the pool of suckers eventually started to run dry. By May 1884 the word on the Street was that Grant and Ward was in trouble. The elder Grant was surprised rather than alarmed, and Ward convinced him all they were facing was what nowadays would be known as a short-term cash flow problem.

Grant's many admirers among the higher plutocracy included William H. Vanderbilt. On Sunday May 4, Grant went to see Vanderbilt and to ask his help. He left the Vanderbilt mansion with a check for $150,000, made out in his name, to use as he saw fit. The money was instantly swallowed up without making an iota of difference. The morning of May 6 the Marine Bank failed, bringing Grant and Ward down two hours later. The firm's liabilities were at least $16 million. Its assets were $57,000. Ward got ten years in Sing Sing. Grant got ruin and humiliation.

The situation looked desperate. At one point Grant and Julia had only $180 in cash. Admirers sent him several thousand dollars, which allowed him to put food on the table and pay the servants until the Galena house was sold, which realized $65,000, but Grant's creditors had claims amounting to more than $500,000. Vanderbilt offered to waive repayment of the $150,000 and Grant was prepared to accept this generosity, but Julia was too proud to agree to it. So Vanderbilt bought up most of the memorabilia that made the brownstone resemble a military museum, gave the items of enduring historic interest to the government for safekeeping, let Grant have the rest back, and said he considered the debt repaid.[26]

Overnight, Grant's normally firm handwriting turned into a spidery scrawl. To the pain from his leg were added the torments of neuralgia. His system seemed to be breaking down. One day that summer he bit into a peach, and instead of a fragrant, ripe deliciousness enchanting his palate, he felt a sharp, stabbing pain in the esophagus. It was his death sentence, written in the smoke of ten thousand cigars.

Grant did not seek medical assistance immediately. For some months he stoically endured the pain, but in the late fall he suffered severe choking fits. He finally revealed how serious his illness was to his doctor, who referred him to a throat specialist, John H. Douglas, who took a tissue sample. "Is it cancer?" Grant asked. Douglas replied, "The disease is serious, epithelial in character and sometimes capable of being cured."

It was February 1885 before all the laboratory tests were completed. The lab report left no doubt that Grant's cancer was out of control. Whether anything could have been done to halt its progress had Grant sought help sooner is doubtful. What was certain now was that Grant had only a few months to live.[27]

★

Before Grant went broke, in the days when he appeared to be a successful investor, people visited him in his office at 2 Wall Street and would start chatting and Grant would ask them to stay for lunch. All he had to offer, besides talk and cigars, were beans, bacon and coffee brought on a tray from a nearby restaurant, but for Mark Twain, a lunch like that was more than enough. Just being with Grant for an hour or two made even crude eats worth a trip to the city.

The more Twain knew Grant, the greater the fascination. He found that the iron man, the unmoving, seemingly unmoved, figure he had watched on the stage at Haverly's Theater in Chicago, was in truth deeply emotional, which was why he needed such extraordinary self-control. Twain marveled at Grant's gentleness, his generosity of spirit, his complete lack of bitterness over Ferdinand Ward, his bedrock integrity. Twain had never known anyone quite like Grant. In the circles of the famous and powerful, such modesty and transparent honesty were rare. And Grant liked Twain because Twain made him laugh and because he didn't seem to want anything—apart, that is, from a request that Grant write his memoirs.

One evening back in 1881, when Grant was visiting Twain in Hartford, Connecticut, that epicenter of small arms makers, insurance companies and American humor, Twain told Grant he ought to start writing. Grant said no, there wasn't much point in that. Adam Badeau had brought out his first volume of *The Military History of Ulysses S. Grant* back in 1868, just after Grant was nominated for the presidency. The book had flopped. And look what had happened to John Russell Young. His book *Around the World with General Grant,* published in 1879, had sunk almost without trace.[28]

Grant's doubts seemed justified when, in 1881, Badeau finally brought out volumes two and three of his account of Grant during the war. These flopped as comprehensively as volume one. However popular Grant was with the public, it looked as if few people thought his story was worth the price of a book.

In the summer of 1884, everything changed. Grant was asked by the Century Publishing Company to write four articles for *Century* magazine. The editors would pay him five hundred dollars per article. Grant agreed. He needed the money, and he needed the intellectual distraction. As he worked on his articles, about Shiloh and Vicksburg, the Wilderness and Appomattox, he began thinking about writing a book, but he wasn't sure he could do it. He had written millions of words in his life—letters and memos, orders and reports—but writing a book was a mystery.

Meanwhile, the editors from Century Publishing were urging him to write his memoirs. A score of Civil War generals, including Sherman, had already written theirs or were scribbling now. Without coming to any agreement with Century, he started writing his book, and in October 1884 Badeau moved into Grant's East 66th Street house to provide research assistance. Badeau convinced himself that he was Grant's ghostwriter. But that wasn't what Grant wanted or needed. A week or so after Badeau moved in, Absalom Markland stopped by and asked Grant if he really would be doing the writing. After all, Grant was in a lot of pain. "Yes," said Grant. "I am going to do it myself. If I do not do it myself it will not be mine."[29]

A couple of weeks later Mark Twain, who was on a lecture tour of New England, overheard the conversation of two people walking in front of him one rainy evening. One of them, who was connected with Century, said Grant was writing his memoirs. Next morning Twain appeared at 3 East 66th Street and asked how much Century was offering. When Grant said he was getting five hundred dollars for each magazine piece, Twain was appalled and said in so many words that Grant was being robbed. And when Grant told him that Century was offering a 10 percent royalty for a book, Twain said that was ridiculous—an insult, more robbery. Ten percent was reasonable for other authors, other books, but Grant's would be in a class all its own.

Down the years, countless writers have resented their dependence on publishers. Twain, like George Bernard Shaw and James Clavell, was one of the few who actually did something about it. He set up Charles Webster, one of his wife's relatives, as a publisher for *The Adventures of Huckleberry Finn*. Published in 1884, it had huge sales and was recognized from the first as a masterpiece of world literature.

Twain said Webster would gladly publish Grant's book, and on far more generous terms than Century's. After thinking about Twain's offer for two months and dickering with other publishers, Grant finally decided to let Webster publish his book. He reached this conclusion not because Twain said he would make more money that way but because Twain had been the first person to urge him to write his memoirs.

Twain's offer was a 20 percent royalty on every copy sold, or 70 percent of the publisher's profits. Grant said he was afraid Twain was being too generous. Seeing that the standard royalty rate was 10 percent, doubling it could mean publishing the book at a loss. Twain might ruin himself. So Grant opted for 70 percent of the profits, because if the book failed, Twain wouldn't have to pay him anything.

Meanwhile, there was the problem of what would happen to Julia. Wouldn't the creditors get all the money? Grant's friend George W. Childs, publisher of the *Philadelphia Ledger,* asked his lawyer, J. G. Rosegarten, about it. An unpublished manuscript, said Rosegarten, has no market value. If Grant wanted to give the rights to the manuscript to Julia, the creditors couldn't stop him. She could then sell her rights in the manuscript to Charles L. Webster, which is what she did.[30]

That spring of 1885, ten thousand subscription agents, dressed in faded blue uniforms and commemorative medals from Shiloh or Vicksburg or the Wilderness or Gettysburg, knocked on doors in the shadow of budding trees and asked if there was a Union veteran in the house. And a graying middle-aged man would appear and they would talk, one old soldier to another. Grant's book was a cause, an act of communion. This was more than business. The general was writing his memoirs; the general was dying. The memories flowed, of campgrounds, battlefields, glory days, old comrades. Then out came the big black leather-bound subscription book, and the writing case with its steel-nib pen and a small ink bottle appeared almost magically from a coat pocket. Here's where you sign. A two-volume set, only $3.50 for both volumes. Pay $1 down, the balance on delivery, a memorial to pass on to your children and your children's children. His story is your story, too. And they remembered waking rigid in every joint on the cold, wet ground, the dead friends, the hardtack with weevils crawling out of it, the haunting bugle calls, the acrid smoke that stung the eyes, the indescribable exhilaration of knowing you've been shot at and missed. And they wrote down their names. Loyal, loyal.

As the orders flooded in, Badeau turned sulky. He had signed a contract with Grant: $5,000 from the first $20,000 the book earned, with a further $5,000 from the next $10,000. Badeau decided that wasn't enough. He told Grant he now wanted $1,000 a month, plus 10 percent of the profits. He put his demands in a bathetic letter that reeked of self-pity. The more successful Grant's book was, he moaned, the less interest there would be in his three-volume work. He said, indirectly, that Grant was going to die, leaving him to complete the book. The glory of the memoirs would go entirely to Grant, while Badeau would bear up under the inglorious drudgery of putting them into publishable shape. His advice and insights were invaluable, Badeau claimed. No professional writer had his knowledge of the war; no professional soldier had his literary skills. All he sought was justice.

Grant was disgusted but not surprised. He had already taken the measure of Badeau. "I do not think the work would ever be done by you in the case of my death while $1,000 per month was coming in. . . . I understand you better than you do yourself. You are petulant, your anger is easily aroused, and you are overbearing, even to me." As for Badeau's claim that his book would suffer from the success of Grant's, "This is all bosh . . . the work of a distempered mind . . . if my book affects yours in any way it will be to call attention to it." Badeau was more or less thrown out of Grant's house in March 1885. Some years later he got his $10,000, but he had to sue the family for it.[31]

Grant worked steadily on his book, writing most of it in pencil, with Fred as his research assistant. Will alone seemed to be holding death in check, but his strength was deserting to the enemy all the same. To speed the flow of words, he decided to try dictating parts of his book and found he could dictate almost as well as he could write. One day, to Twain's envy and astonishment, he dictated ten thousand words. But Twain was also pained to see how thin he'd grown, how much weaker he was.[32]

On April 3, Grant was so racked by fever and pain that Doctor Douglas didn't expect him to survive, but he pulled through and went on with the book. Willpower had always forged the metal of his self-control and now it held him together, forcing him through the cocaine-drugged days and the morphine-drugged nights, writing, dictating, thinking, remembering.

His death was going to be all of a piece with his life. Grant left New York in June 1885 to die in a place he did not know and in someone else's house: rootless to the end. The summer's heat in the city was oppressive, and he was offered the use of a summer cottage at Mount

McGregor, a few miles from Saratoga Springs, New York. He traveled to Saratoga Springs in the comfort of Vanderbilt's private railroad car, but there he had to change to a narrow-gauge train. The pint-size engine and the small cars rocked and bumped up the steep mountainside. The last part of the trip had to be made on foot. This trip to Mount McGregor was such an ordeal it seemed unlikely Grant would survive it, but he rallied again. He couldn't die yet. The memoirs weren't finished.

Any slow, agonizing death cuts to the core of character, and Grant's way of dealing with it was turning into a book itself. Part of the secret of his success as a general stood revealed as he bent to his final task, not only in the power of his will but in the clarity of his mind. Drugs did not seem to color his thinking, nor did physical exhaustion, lack of sleep, intense pain, or impending oblivion. He treated all of these as irrelevant or, at most, irritants, and focused tightly on the task at hand.

To that dominating will and powerful mind was yoked an extraordinary memory. Sherman had been awestruck by Grant's ability to soak up details and remember them and in his own memoirs would remark, "I think Grant knew every tin can in my army." Others had noticed, too, how Grant could look at a map for a few moments and remember every detail as he planned the battle ahead, while his staff officers had to keep consulting it to follow the moves he was planning.

The memoirs, as he wrote them out in pencil or dictated them to a secretary, seemed to flow almost effortlessly. The result was a work two hundred pages longer than Twain and he had agreed. The prose was limpid, the thinking clear, the effort of production well concealed.

Grant had always possessed a dry sense of humor and an ability to charm people, despite his shyness. Not even the agonizing pain in his throat blunted either the humor or the charm, both of which were rooted in a strong sense of life's absurdities and brevity. He told the story, for example, of a lieutenant named Slaughter who was assigned to his regiment in the 1840s. Slaughter "was very liable to seasickness. It almost made him sick to see the wave of a table-cloth when the servants were spreading it." Shortly after graduating from West Point, Slaughter was ordered to California and made the long, seven-month voyage around Cape Horn. He was violently sick the whole way. When he arrived in California, there were orders waiting for him, saying there had been an administrative mistake—he was supposed to be assigned to a fort in the Great Lakes region. Slaughter returned to the East Coast, this time by the much shorter Isthmus of Panama route, but seasick all over again.

Arriving back on the East Coast, he found his orders had been changed once more, and he really did have to go to California. "He was as sick as ever, and had been so for more than a month while lying at anchor in the [San Francisco] bay. I remember him well, seated with his elbows on the table in front of him, his chin between his hands, and looking the picture of despair. At last he broke out, 'I wish I had taken my father's advice. He wanted me to go into the Navy; if I had done so, I should not have had to go to sea so much.' Poor Slaughter! It was his last sea voyage. He was killed by Indians in Oregon."[33]

Grant also recalled how Braxton Bragg had been famous in the pre–Civil War Army for his irascibility. For a time, Bragg had served as a company commander and post quartermaster. There was an occasion when he felt it his duty to make a requisition on behalf of his company, only to feel it was just as much his duty as post quartermaster to reject the requisition. Bragg then forwarded the paperwork to the post commander to decide the issue. The post commander was astounded. "My God, Mr. Bragg, you have quarrelled with every officer in the Army, and now you are quarreling with yourself!"[34]

Modest though he surely was, Grant was proud of his career as a soldier. Most of the time that pride was half-hidden in what he wrote, but in one place it broke clear into the light of day: "I had been in all the engagements in Mexico that it was possible for one person to be in," he wrote, as if afraid this distinction might pass unnoticed.[35]

He paid virtually no attention to his eight years as president. He judged, rightly, that whatever he might have achieved as commander-in-chief was far overshadowed by his accomplishments as general-in-chief. He was worried, all the same, about the great unresolved issue of the Civil War and Reconstruction—the place of blacks in American life.

"It is possible that the question of a conflict between the races may come up in the future, as did that between freedom and slavery before." He was still angry at the rejection of his attempt to acquire San Domingo, which "was freely offered to us, not only by the administration, but by all the people, almost without price." San Domingo, he insisted, could provide a decent living for up to fifteen million people. "I took it that the colored people would go there in great numbers, so as to have an independent state governed by their own race" yet still part of the United States and under the protection of the Federal government. It was not to be. Grant's sigh almost rises from the page.[36]

While he worked on his manuscript, people came to see him, such as his West Point classmate Simon Bolivar Buckner, who had helped him out when he was broke in New York in 1854 and surrendered to him at Fort Donelson in 1862. Grant took the warmth of their meeting as symbolizing something he profoundly longed for, reconciliation between North and South.

Union Army veterans, thousands of them, came to Mount McGregor just to get a glimpse of the general sitting on the cottage porch, writing his memoirs. They solemnly filed past, sometimes in quasi-military formation. Grant acknowledged them with a nod of his head or a wave of the hand.[37]

On July 1, with his revisions of the page proofs finally finished, he wrote out the preface. Grant chose to begin his book with a quote from *Imitation of Christ,* by the fifteenth-century mystic Thomas à Kempis. " 'Man proposes and God disposes.' There are but few important events in the affairs of men brought about by their own choice." Here, then, was his reading of the metatext not just of his life but of all human existence.

The work itself was going to provide for Julia long after he had departed. Mark Twain came to Mount McGregor for a few days and told him as much. More than 150,000 copies had already been ordered, and there was still more than half the country to be covered by the subscription agents. Financial success was certain now. As for its critical success, that too seemed likely. While Grant probably recognized that his work would prove an important contribution to the literature of the Civil War, Twain knew it was more than that. The style revealed the man; the book revealed the mind.

Grant's memoirs have the directness and limpidity of the purest English prose, as it was crafted first by William Tyndale and then spread throughout the English-speaking world in the King James Version of the Bible, most of which is lifted from Tyndale's version written a century earlier. Grant reached deep into himself and into the whole history of the Anglo-American people to grasp the core of its culture, the English language, and trusted in that narrative style that achieves its effects by never straining for effect, assembled it into vivid pictures sufficently understated to allow an intelligent reader's imagination room to expand, and shaped a literary architecture with a born artist's eye.

Grant's recollections were inevitably partial and selective, one man's interpretation of events. As with all memoirs, Grant's was at its best as a revelation of the way he remembered the events of his adventurous life and how he felt about them at the end of his days. What he was busy making with stubs of pencil on small pieces of paper was a great memoir, not a great history. Its truth was not in the details of what he described but in the story he told, of himself, of the war, of justice triumphant at last over a great evil. Those hundreds of thousands of Union Army veterans who handed over three dollars and four bits would get their taste of immortality.[38]

★

A few days after reaching Mount McGregor, Grant wrote a letter to Julia. "There are some things about which I would like to talk [but] the subject would be too painful to you and the children. . . . I had an idea that I could live until fall. . . . I see now that the time is approaching more rapidly." He told her that he had no particular wish to be buried in New York; they were almost strangers in the city. "I should myself select West Point," but Julia would not be allowed to join him there when her time came. So it was for her to choose his burial ground. He urged her to keep the children "in the paths of rectitude," and wrote that he would rather hear they were dying than learn that they had done something wrong. There was a postscript: "This will be found in my coat after my demise."[39]

Meanwhile, Julia decided that Ulyss and the rest of the family needed the comfort of religion to see them through the death watch, and Ulyss had never been baptized. She sent for the pastor of the church they had attended in Washington, the Reverend John Newman, a Methodist minister who specialized in the spiritual needs of the rich. Newman urged Grant to be baptized; Grant refused. Newman waited until Grant had another of his fainting spells and baptized him anyway. With Grant finally in the fold, Newman began pestering him to take communion. Grant told him that was out of the question, and it was. He would have to be conscious to take communion.[40]

One day Grant scrawled a note that read, "I think I am a verb instead of a personal pronoun. A verb is anything that signifies to be; to do; to suffer. I signify all three." His own personal trinity.

On July 8, Grant summoned the strength to write another letter to Julia, his last. He gave her instructions about various bequests and urged her to become close friends with his sister. The end was very near, he told her. "I never will leave Mt. McGregor alive." If it weren't for the fact that the book still needed revisions, "I would welcome the arrival of the Messenger of Peace, the earlier the better."[41]

Sometime that same day, Grant contemplated his life, one of the most eventful of the nineteenth century, trying to find some purpose to it, or at least a pattern. He failed. "It seems that one man's destiny in this world is quite as much a mystery as it is likely to be in the next. I never thought of acquiring rank in the profession I was allocated for." Yet he had become the first four-star general in American history. "I certainly never had any taste for political life." But he became President despite that. And, "If anyone suggested the idea of my becoming an author, as they frequently did, I was not sure whether they were making sport of me. . . . I have now written a book." All that remained were some last-minute corrections to the text. Ten days later, these were completed. He could go now.[42]

The preparations had been in place for weeks. An entire nation had become accustomed to waking each morning to wonder whether Grant was still alive. Fire bells in every town and city were going to be rung when the news came. Church bells would toll every thirty seconds for exactly thirty-one minutes: sixty-three peals, sixty-three years.[43]

The pain was so great he needed to die, needed to drop into the absolving emptiness. The end came at 8:08 A.M. on July 23, with Julia, the four children, three doctors, and his black valet, Harrison Tyrrell, gathered around his bed. Grant seemed to be sleeping when he half opened his eyes for a moment. He gasped, but so faintly it was almost a sigh. His grip on Julia's hand went slack.

One Sunday afternoon when Grant was still President, Dan Ammen had come to the White House for lunch, and as they talked about growing up in Georgetown, Ammen reminded Grant of how he had once saved Grant from drowning. Ammen expected Grant to say how glad he was to have been rescued, how joyful and wonderful it was to be alive. Instead, Grant responded, "I would not be willing to live my life over again, were it a matter of volition."[44]

For all the success as a soldier, the fame and prestige of the presidency, the adulation of millions, and the unbeatable bliss of a happy marriage, none of it mattered in the end, none of it made a difference. Once was enough.

NOTES

Chapter 1: "I Won't Go"

1. Albert D. Richardson, *Personal History of Ulysses S. Grant* (Hartford, Conn.: 1868), 18; Hamline Elijah Robinson, *Genealogical Notes: Genealogy of the Grant Family* (n.p. 1885), 21–22; William McFeely, *Grant* (New York: 1981), 5.
2. See Thomas P. Slaughter, *The Whiskey Rebellion* (New York: 1968), 176 passim.
3. Richardson, 41–42.
4. Jesse Root Grant, in *New York Ledger,* March 7, 1868.
5. Lloyd Lewis, *Captain Sam Grant* (Boston: 1950), 3–12, 295, 333.
6. J.C.A. Stagg, *Mr. Madison's War* (Princeton, N.J., 1983), Chapter 2.
7. Jesse Root Grant, op. cit.
8. Lewis, 11–13.
9. Jesse Root Grant, op. cit.
10. William E. Woodward, *Meet General Grant* (New York: 1928), 12–13.
11. Richardson, 49–50; Hamlin Garland, *Ulysses S. Grant: His Life and Character* (New York: 1898), 6; Phineas Camp Headley, *The Life and Campaigns of Gen. U.S. Grant* (New York: 1868), 19.
12. Richardson, 51.
13. Richardson, 52; Ishbel Ross, *The General's Wife* (New York: 1956), 54.
14. Letter, Isaac Lynch to Philip B. Swing, September 26, 1865, Grant Family Papers, Southern Illinois University (SIU).
15. Garland Notebooks, Hamlin Garland Papers, USC.
16. Ibid.
17. Jesse R. Grant, *In the Days of My Father, General Grant* (New York: 1925), 96.
18. Garland, 13.
19. "Chicago Home Visitor," supplement to *Chicago Daily Tribune,* May 25, 1865.
20. *New York Times,* July 30, 1885.
21. Ulysses S. Grant, *Personal Memoirs of U.S. Grant* (New York: 1885), I, 26.

22. Lewis, 22.
23. Ibid., 32–33.
24. Garland, 6.
25. Lewis, 33.
26. Garland, 12–13.
27. Garland Notebooks, loc. cit.; Grant Association *Newsletter* (Jan. 1971).
28. Jesse Root Grant, in *New York Ledger,* March 14, 1868.
29. *New York Times,* Aug. 4, 1885.
30. Grant, *Personal Memoirs,* I, 32; John Russell Young, *Around the World with General Grant* (New York: 1879), II, 450.

Chapter 2: "I, Cadet U. S. Grant"

1. Stephen E. Ambrose, *Duty, Honor, Country* (Baltimore, Md.: 1966), 18–23.
2. Lloyd Lewis, *Letters from Lloyd Lewis* (Boston: 1960), 69.
3. Lloyd Lewis, *Captain Sam Grant* (Boston: 1950), 61.
4. Ishbel Ross, *The General's Wife* (New York: 1956), 17.
5. Lewis, *Captain Sam Grant,* 65.
6. Ulysses S. Grant, *Personal Memoirs* (New York: 1885), I, 24.
7. Jack Waugh, *The Class of 1846* (New York: 1994), 12.
8. Charles Elliott, *Winfield Scott* (Boston: 1939), 237, 256.
9. Grant, *Personal Memoirs,* I, 41.
10. John Y. Simon, ed., *The Papers of Ulysses S. Grant* (Carbondale, Ill.: 1968), I, 3. Hereafter referred to as Grant *Papers.*
11. Rufus Ingalls in *New York Herald,* April 7, 1885.
12. Garland Notebooks, Hamlin Garland Papers, USC.
13. John Russell Young, *Around the World with General Grant* (New York: 1879), II, 450–51.
14. Grant *Papers,* I, 5–7.
15. *New York Tribune,* Aug. 2, 1885.
16. Stephen W. Sears, *George B. McClellan* (New York: 1988), 73; Young, *Around the World,* I, 214–15.
17. Albert D. Richardson, *Personal History of Ulysses S. Grant* (Hartford, Conn.: 1868), 93–94.
18. Marcus Cunliffe, *Soldiers and Civilians* (New York: 1968), 160.
19. Richardson, 90.
20. "Interview with James Longstreet," Hamlin Garland Papers, USC.
21. Ambrose, 99–103; Waugh, 62–65.
22. Grant, *Personal Memoirs,* I, 39.
23. Edward C. Marshall, *The Ancestry of General Grant and their Contemporaries* (New York: 1869), 66–68.

24. William C. Church, *Ulysses S. Grant and the Period of National Preservation and Reconstruction* (New York: 1897), 20; William E. Woodward, *Meet General Grant* (New York: 1928), 13–14.
25. Jesse R. Grant, *In the Days of My Father, General Grant* (New York: 1925), 54–55.
26. Ross, 52–53.
27. Richardson, 91.
28. Lewis, *Captain Sam Grant,* 74.
29. Ingalls, op. cit.; Henry Coppée, *The Life and Services of U. S. Grant* (New York: 1868), 22.
30. Young, *Around the World with General Grant,* II, 450.
31. Grant, *Personal Memoirs,* I, 40.
32. Waugh, 59.
33. Lewis, *Captain Sam Grant,* 84.
34. Richardson, 90.
35. Ibid., 93.
36. Church, 19; Richardson, 91–92; Ross, 56–57.
37. The original, signed simply "U," is in the Ulysses S. Grant Collection at Southern Illinois University.
38. Church, 20.
39. *Register of Punishments,* May 1, 1842, USMA Archives.
40. Ibid., March 18, 1843; *Post Orders: Special Order No. 42,* March 24, 1843.
41. James B. Fry, "An Acquaintance with Grant," *New American Review* 141 (July–Dec. 1885).
42. Ross, 17.
43. Grant, *Personal Memoirs,* I, 51.
44. Cadet Account Book, 1839–1843, Ulysses S. Grant Papers, Huntington Library.
45. Grant *Papers,* I, 23.
46. George W. Childs, *Recollections of General Grant* (Philadelphia: 1890), 43.

Chapter 3: "Be Shure and Write"

1. M. T. Burke (Garland interview), Hamlin Garland Papers, USC.
2. Ulysses S. Grant, *Personal Memoirs* (New York: 1885), I, 43–44.
3. William E. Woodward, *Meet General Grant* (New York: 1928), 56.
4. Robert Ferrell, ed., *Monterrey Is Ours! The Mexican War Letters of Lieutenant Dana* (Chapel Hill, N.C.: 1992), 15.
5. Jesse R. Grant, *In the Days of My Father, General Grant* (New York: 1925), 142.

6. Albert D. Richardson, *Personal History of Ulysses S. Grant* (Hartford, Conn.: 1868), 95.

7. Hamlin Garland, *Ulysses S. Grant: His Life and Character* (New York: 1920), 59; William Taussig, "Personal Recollections of General Grant," *Proceedings of the Missouri Historical Society* (Oct. 1903), 5.

8. John Y. Simon, ed., *Personal Memoirs of Julia Dent Grant* (Carbondale, Ill.: 1975), 46.

9. Emma Dent Casey, "When Grant Went a-Courtin,'" Grant Association *Newsletter* (July–Oct. 1968).

10. Simon, 43.

11. Lloyd Lewis, *Captain Sam Grant* (Boston: 1950), 35.

12. Jesse R. Grant, 29.

13. "Interview with General Longstreet," Hamlin Garland Papers, USC.

14. Simon, 51.

15. Grant *Papers,* I, 38; John W. Emerson, "Grant's Life in the West," *Midland Monthly* (Nov. 1896).

16. Simon, 48–49.

17. Frank A. Burr, *A New and Authentic Record of the Life and Deeds of General U.S. Grant* (Boston: 1885), 91–92.

18. Ishbel Ross, *The General's Wife* (New York: 1956), 20–21.

19. Simon, 49.

20. Grant, *Personal Memoirs,* II, 47–49.

21. Simon, 49–50.

22. Foster Coates, "The Courtship of General Grant," *Ladies' Home Journal* (Oct. 1890).

23. J. Fair Hardin, "Fort Jesup, Fort Selden, Camp Sabine, Camp Salubrity," *Louisiana Historical Quarterly* (Jan. 1934).

24. Grant *Papers,* I, 28.

25. *New York Times,* July 24, 1885.

26. Henry Edward Chambers, *Mississippi Valley Beginnings* (New York: 1922), 358.

27. Grant *Papers,* I, 52.

28. Ibid., 35.

29. Ibid., 51.

30. Letter, Grant to Julia Dent, Aug. 31, 1844, Grant *Papers,* I, 33.

31. Ross, 27.

32. Chambers, 359–60.

33. Grant *Papers,* I, 59.

34. Ibid., 65.

35. *New York Times,* July 24, 1885.

36. James Grant Wilson, *General Grant* (New York: 1897), 69–71.

37. Emma Dent Casey memoir.
38. Woodward, 26; *New York Times,* July 24, 1885.
39. John L. Crane, "Grant as a Colonel," *McClure's Magazine* (June 1896).
40. "Interview with General Longstreet," Hamlin Garland Papers, USC.
41. William C. Church, *Ulysses S. Grant and the Period of National Preservation and Reconstruction* (New York: 1897), 28–29.
42. George Lockhart Rives, *The United States and Mexico, 1821–1848* (New York: 1913), II, 141–42.
43. Holman Hamilton, *Zachary Taylor* (Indianapolis: 1941), 176.

Chapter 4: "The Flag Is Paramount"

1. John Russell Young, *Around the World with General Grant* (New York: 1879), I, 447–48.
2. Ulysses S. Grant, *Personal Memoirs of U. S. Grant* (New York: 1885), I, 68.
3. Robert Selph Henry, *The Story of the Mexican War* (New York: 1950), 19–20; Seymour V. Connor and Odie B. Faulk, *North America Divided: The Mexican War, 1846–1848* (New York: 1971), 26–32.
4. K. Jack Bauer, *The Mexican War, 1846–1848* (New York: 1974), 32–41; Henry, 17; cf. Frederick Merk, with Lois B. Merk, *Slavery and the Annexation of Texas* (New York: 1973).
5. Charles Sellers, *James K. Polk* (Princeton: 1966), II, 397, 401–5; Paul H. Bergeron, *The Presidency of James K. Polk* (Lawrence, Kan.: 1987), 82–85.
6. Frederick Merk, *The Monroe Doctrine and American Expansionism* (New York: 1966), 139–43; Connor and Faulk, 29–30.
7. Antonio López de Santa Anna, *Mi Historia Militar y Politica* (Mexico City: 1974), 41.
8. John W. Emerson, "Grant's Life in the West," *Midland Monthly* (Jan. 1897). The quotation is from Byron's "Destruction of Sennacherib."
9. Grant, *Personal Memoirs,* I, 95.
10. Bauer, 57.
11. Grant *Papers,* I, 85; Grant, *Personal Memoirs,* I, 92.
12. Bauer, 59–60.
13. Grant, *Personal Memoirs,* I, 98; Emerson, op. cit.
14. Grant *Papers,* I, 95–96.
15. Robert Ferrell, ed., *Monterrey Is Ours! The Mexican War Letters of Lieutenant Dana* (Chapel Hill, N.C.: 1992), 105.
16. Grant *Papers,* I, 88, 97.
17. Emerson, op. cit.; Grant *Papers,* I, 106–7.

18. Lewis, 167–68.
19. Emerson, op. cit.
20. Some writers, such as Lewis, have mistakenly assumed that because Hamer commanded a brigade he was a brigadier general. In both Mexico and the Civil War, brigades were often commanded by majors and colonels, but it was military courtesy to call anyone who commanded a brigade a "brigadier," regardless of his actual rank.
21. Emerson, op. cit.
22. Justin H. Smith, *The War with Mexico* (New York: 1920), I, 232–41; Bauer, 89–93.
23. Grant, *Personal Memoirs,* I, 112. The root cause of the problem was an ambiguous order from Taylor to Garland: Bauer, 95. Grant, however, had convinced himself that Taylor *never* issued orders that could be misunderstood.
24. Hamlin Garland, *Ulysses S. Grant: His Life and Character* (New York: 1898), 78.
25. Grant, *Personal Memoirs,* I, 115–16; Richardson, 110–11; Garland, 79–80, 101; William C. Church, *Ulysses S. Grant and the Period of National Preservation and Reconstruction* (New York: 1897), 33.
26. Smith, 258–61; Bauer, 99–102.
27. "Interview with General Longstreet," Hamlin Garland Papers, USC.
28. Grant *Papers,* I, 119.
29. Emerson, *Midland Monthly* (Feb. 1897).
30. Emerson, *Midland Monthly* (Jan. 1897).
31. Grant, *Personal Memoirs,* I, 103.

Chapter 5: "The Last Chance I Shall Ever Have"

1. Grant *Papers,* I, 124.
2. Ibid., 122.
3. Letter, Grant to Julia Dent, Feb. 25, 1847, MD, LC. This letter, like half a dozen others written during the war, contains a number of crossed out— in some instances virtually obliterated—lines; the work, presumably, of one of Grant's descendants. Wherever possible, I have given the complete version as reconstructed by me. Hence the difference between the material presented here and the letters as reproduced in the Grant *Papers.*
4. For a fascinating and important work on this subject, see Victor Davis Hanson, *The Western Way of War: Infantry Battle in Classical Greece* (New York: 1989).
5. Diary, March 9, 1847, Henry P. Judah Papers, MD, LC; Robert Ferrell, ed., *Monterrey Is Ours! The Mexican War Letters of Lieutenant Dana* (Chapel Hill, N.C.: 1992), 191.

6. John W. Emerson, "Grant's Life in the West," *Midland Monthly* (March 1897).
7. Diary, March 29–April 5, 1847, Henry P. Judah Papers, MD, LC; J. J. Oswandel, *Notes of the Mexican War* (Philadelphia: 1885), 97–99.
8. Ferrell, 196–97; Robert W. Johannsen, *To the Halls of the Montezumas* (New York: 1985), 170.
9. Albert D. Richardson, *Personal History of Ulysses S. Grant* (Hartford, Conn.: 1868), 126; A. E. Watrous, 218–19; Hamlin Garland, *Ulysses S. Grant: His Life and Character* (New York: 1898), 92.
10. William C. Church, *Ulysses S. Grant and the Period of National Preservation and Reconstruction* (New York: 1897), 38; Garland, 100.
11. Grant *Papers,* I, 134.
12. Emerson, op. cit.
13. Garland, 85.
14. Grant, *Personal Memoirs,* I, 141–44.
15. K. Jack Bauer, *The Mexican War, 1846–1848* (New York: 1974), 308–10; Robert Selph Henry, *The Story of the Mexican War* (Indianapolis: 1950), 353–55.
16. Letter, Frederick T. Dent to the Secretary of War, Oct. 5, 1847, Frederick T. Dent Papers, Southern Illinois University.
17. Letter, James M. Robertson to Frederick D. Grant, March 2, 1885, Grant *Papers,* MD, LC; John Luther Ringwalt, *Anecdotes of General Ulysses S. Grant* (Philadelphia: 1886), 59; Richardson, 121–22. Robertson was awarded a commission and concluded his career as a brigadier general.
18. Henry Coppée, *The Life and Services of General U. S. Grant* (New York: 1868), 25.
19. Bauer, 319–20.
20. Grant, *Personal Memoirs,* I, 156–57.
21. Robertson letter, op. cit.
22. Garland, 102; Richardson, 123–24; Grant, *Personal Memoirs,* I, 159.
23. John W. Emerson, "Grant's Life in the West," *Midland Monthly* (April 1897).
24. Church, 48. Grant's brevet commissions for El Molino del Rey and Chapultepec are reproduced in William H. Allen, *The American Civil War and Grant Album* (Boston: 1894).
25. George A. Agassiz, ed., *Meade's Headquarters, 1863–1865: Letters of Colonel Theodore Lyman from the Wilderness to Appomattox* (Boston: 1922), 313.
26. Michael Fellman, *Citizen Sherman* (New York: 1995), 13.
27. See Grant Association *Newsletter,* Jan. 1967.
28. Grady MacWhinney, *Braxton Bragg and Confederate Defeat* (New York: 1969), 33–34.

29. Edward J. Nichols, *Zach Taylor's Little Army* (Garden City, N.Y.: 1973), 58–59.
30. Grant, *Personal Memoirs,* I, 139.
31. Ibid., 166.
32. Ethan Allen Hitchcock, *Fifty Years in Camp and Field* (New York: 1909), 310–11.
33. Stanhope Bayne-Jones, *The Evolution of Preventive Medicine in the United States, 1607–1939* (Washington, D.C.: 1968), 86.
34. Letter, Grant to Julia Dent, June 10, 1846, Grant Papers, MD, LC.
35. Letter, Grant to Julia Dent, May 17, 1847, Grant Papers, MD, LC.
36. Grant *Papers,* I, 97.
37. Ibid., 149.
38. Ibid., 162; John M. Taylor, "Lieutenant Grant and the Missing Money," *Army* (Feb. 1982).

Chapter 6: "I Was No Clerk"

1. Grant *Papers,* I, 128.
2. Ibid., 74–75.
3. Letter, Grant to Julia Dent, May 17, 1847, Grant *Papers,* MD, LC.
4. Grant *Papers,* I, 89.
5. Ibid., 90.
6. Ibid., 160.
7. John Y. Simon, ed., *Personal Memoirs of Julia Dent Grant* (Carbondale, Ill.: 1975), 52–53.
8. Letter, Grant to Julia Dent, May 7, 1848, Grant Papers, MD, LC. This was crossed out, probably by a Grant descendant, some years later and does not appear in the published version of the letter.
9. Simon, 34.
10. William Taussig, "Personal Recollections of General Grant," Proceedings of the *Missouri Historical Society* (Oct. 1903), 3; Lloyd Lewis, *Captain Sam Grant* (Boston: 1950), 296.
11. Albert D. Richardson, *Personal History of Ulysses S. Grant* (Hartford, Conn.: 1868), 112; Ishbel Ross, *The General's Wife* (New York: 1956), 46.
12. HQ Order Book, 4th Infantry Regiment, July 23, 1848, USAMHI.
13. Simon, 55.
14. Ibid.; Ross, 48–49.
15. William C. Church, *Ulysses S. Grant and the Period of National Preservation and Reconstruction* (New York: 1897), 47.
16. Simon, 80.

17. Simon, 58.
18. Grant *Papers,* I, 174–78; Simon, 59.
19. Eunice Tripler, *Some Notes and Personal Recollections* (New York: 1920), 103; Lewis, 290.
20. Grant, *Personal Memoirs,* II, 139–40.
21. Richardson, 132; Friend Palmer, *Early Days in Detroit: Papers Written by General Friend Palmer* (Detroit: 1906), 225–26.
22. Simon, 66–67; Ross, 64.
23. Grant *Papers,* I, 195.
24. Richardson, 135; Lewis, 289.
25. William E. Woodward, *Meet General Grant* (New York: 1928), 105.
26. Grant *Papers,* I, 214.
27. Ibid., 220.
28. See HQ Order Book, 4th Infantry Regiment, May 5, 1849; July 23, 1849, USAMHI, for just two of many examples. Drunkenness was the most common court-martial offense in the regiment.
29. Lewis, 293–94; Ross, 68.
30. Hamlin Garland, *Ulysses S. Grant: His Life and Character* (New York: 1898), 111.
31. See Donald W. Beattie, *Sons of Temperance: Pioneers in Total Abstinence and Constitutional Prohibition,* Ph.D. dissertation (Boston University, 1966).
32. Simon, 71; cf. Grant *Papers,* I, 238.
33. Grant *Papers,* I, 243.
34. Ibid., 247, 283.

Chapter 7: "How Forsaken I Feel Here!"

1. Washington Irving, *The Adventures of Captain Bonneville, U.S.A.* (Norman, Okla.: 1961); cf. Edith Harrison Lovell, *Benjamin Bonneville: Soldier of the American Frontier* (Bountiful, Utah: 1992), 55–88.
2. Letter, Henry C. Hodges to William C. Church, Jan. 7, 1897, Church Papers, MD, LC.
3. Grant *Papers,* I, 238.
4. Hamlin Garland, "Grant's Quiet Years at Northern Posts," *McClure's Magazine* (March 1, 1897).
5. *Dayton Daily Journal,* Jan. 27, 1880.
6. Louis A. Arthur, ed., *Eunice Tripler: Some Notes of Her Personal Recollections* (New York: 1910), 107–8.
7. R. Z. Kirkpatrick, "General Grant in Panama," *Military Engineer,* (April–May 1934).

8. Grant *Papers,* I, 249–50; Grant, *Personal Memoirs,* I, 196.
9. Interview with Sergeant James Elderkin, Hamlin Garland Papers, USC; William S. Lewis, "Reminiscences of Delia Sheffield," *Washington Historical Quarterly* 15 (1924).
10. Grant *Papers,* I, 261–62.
11. Grant, *Personal Memoirs,* I, 197.
12. Hamlin Garland, *Ulysses S. Grant* (New York: 1898), 119.
13. Garland, "Grant's Quiet Years at Northern Posts."
14. Grant *Papers,* I, 252–53.
15. William C. Church, *Ulysses S. Grant and the Period of National Preservation and Reconstruction* (New York: 1897), 50.
16. David McCullough, *The Path Between the Seas* (New York: 1977), 26–27.
17. David Goodman, *Gold Seeking* (Stanford, Calif.: 1994), 203–13.
18. Grant *Papers,* I, 257.
19. Charles G. Ellington, *The Trial of Ulysses Grant* (Glendale, Calif.: 1987), 85–94; John W. Emerson, "Grant's Life in the West," *Midland Monthly,* (April 1897).
20. Grant *Papers,* I, 265.
21. Ibid., 263.
22. Grant, *Personal Memoirs,* I, 210.
23. Grant *Papers,* I, 267.
24. Ellington, 157–58.
25. Grant *Papers,* I, 268.
26. Ibid., 275.
27. Ibid., 271–74.
28. Albert D. Richardson, *Personal History of Ulysses S. Grant* (Hartford, Conn.: 1868), 146.
29. Richardson, 145; Letter, Henry C. Hodges to William C. Church, Jan. 7, 1897, Church Papers, MD, LC.
30. McFeely interview, Hamlin Garland Papers, USC; cf. Richardson, 149.
31. Lloyd Lewis, *Captain Sam Grant* (Boston: 1950), 310; John W. Emerson, "Grant's Life in the West," *Midland Monthly* (July 1897).
32. Grant *Papers,* I, 296–97.
33. Grant, *Personal Memoirs,* I, 203; Ogden interview, Hamlin Garland Papers, USC; Lewis, 316–19; Ellington, 119.
34. Grant *Papers,* I, 307.
35. Ibid., 288.
36. Ibid., 311–12.
37. Delia B. Sheffield, "Reminiscences of Delia Sheffield," *Washington Historical Quarterly* (Jan. 1924).

38. D. L. Thornbury, *California's Redwood Wonderland* (San Francisco: 1923), 69–87; Clara McGeorge Shields, "General Grant at Fort Humboldt in the Early Days," *U. S. Grant Association Newsletter* (April 1971).

39. George Crook, *The Autobiography of George Crook* (Norman, Okla.: 1968), 10.

40. Grant *Papers,* I, 316.

41. Richardson, 147; Lewis, 325; Ellington, 147.

42. There is no documentary evidence or eyewitness account to support the widely circulated story that Grant was forced to resign because of drunkenness. There is, on the other hand, a great deal of testimony to the contrary from people who were at Fort Humboldt at this time. The most thorough evaluation of the sources, pro and con, is in Ellington, 165–80.

43. Grant *Papers,* I, 328–29.

Chapter 8: "I Was Happy"

1. Grant *Papers,* I, 330–31.

2. John Y. Simon, ed., *Personal Memoirs of Julia Dent Grant* (Carbondale, Ill.: 1968), 73; Grant *Papers,* I, 481.

3. Grant, *Personal Memoirs,* I, 209.

4. John W. Emerson, "Grant's Life in the West," *Midland Monthly* (Sept. 1897).

5. Grant *Papers,* I, 297.

6. Simon, 72–73; Grant *Papers,* I, 323.

7. Buckner interview, Hamlin Garland Papers, USC; Arndt M. Stickels, *Simon Bolivar Buckner* (Chapel Hill, N.C.: 1940), 33–36.

8. Lloyd Lewis, *Captain Sam Grant* (Boston: 1950), 334.

9. Lewis, 339; Charles G. Ellington, *The Trial of Ulysses Grant* (Glendale, Calif.: 1987), 201–2.

10. Marcus Cunliffe, *Soldiers and Civilians* (New York: 1968), 142–43.

11. John Russell Young, *Around the World with General Grant* (New York: 1879), II, 451.

12. Jesse R. Grant, *In the Days of My Father, General Grant* (Philadelphia: 1920), 9.

13. Emerson, *Midland Monthly* (Sept. 1897).

14. Lewis, 341; Albert D. Richardson, *Personal History of Ulysses S. Grant* (Hartford, Conn.: 1868), 155.

15. Interview notes, Hamlin Garland Papers, USC.

16. Jesse Grant Cramer, *Letters of Ulysses S. Grant to His Father and Youngest Sister, 1857–78* (New York: 1912), 11–12.

17. Grant *Papers,* I, 347.

18. Michael Fellman, *Citizen Sherman* (New York: 1995), 54–57; William C. Church, *Ulysses S. Grant and the Period of National Preservation and Reconstruction* (New York: 1897), 57.

19. Hamlin Garland, *Ulysses S. Grant: His Life and Character* (New York: 1898), 139–40; Henry Coppée, *Grant and His Campaigns* (New York: 1866), 26n.

20. "Interview with General Longstreet," Hamlin Garland Papers, USC.

21. Richardson, 162. For a good recent appraisal of the Franco-Austrian War and its importance to the evolution of warfare in the industrial age, see Robert Epstein, *Napoleon's Last Victory and the Emergence of Modern War* (Lawrence, Kans.: 1995).

22. Simon, 77–78.

23. William Taussig, "Personal Recollections of General Grant," *Proceedings of the Missouri Historical Society* (Oct. 1903), 5; Ishbel Ross, *The General's Wife* (New York: 1956), 99.

24. Grant *Papers,* I, 339.

25. Simon, 80.

26. Grant *Papers,* I, 346–47.

27. Richardson, 161.

28. Ibid., 157.

29. Emerson, *Midland Monthly* (Sept. 1897).

30. Grant *Papers,* I, 348–49.

31. Grant *Papers,* I, 350–51.

32. Taussig, 6–7.

33. Grant, *Personal Memoirs,* I, 212–13; Church, 61.

34. Richardson, 162.

35. Ibid., 170. Julia Grant claims this occurred the night he learned he had not gotten the job as superintendent of county roads (Simon, 82), but she is almost certainly wrong about this.

36. Grant *Papers,* I, 355–56; James Grant Wilson, *The Life and Public Services of Ulysses Simpson Grant* (New York: 1885), 18.

37. Lewis, 373.

Chapter 9: "The South Will Fight"

1. Hamlin Garland, *Ulysses S. Grant: His Life and Character* (New York: 1898), 148; Lloyd Lewis, *Captain Sam Grant* (Boston: 1950), 373–74.

2. Kenneth Owens, *Galena, Grant and the Fortunes of War* (DeKalb, Ill.: 1963), 1–21; Timothy R. Mahoney, *River Towns in the Great West: The Structure of Provincial Urbanization in the American Midwest, 1820–1870* (Cambridge, Mass.: 1990), 268–72.

3. John Y. Simon, ed., *The Personal Memoirs of Julia Dent Grant* (Carbondale, Ill.: 1975), 82–83.

4. Ibid., 84.

5. Michael J. Cramer, *Ulysses S. Grant: Conversations and Unpublished Letters* (New York: 1898), 35.

6. Albert D. Richardson, *Personal History of Ulysses S. Grant* (Hartford, Conn.: 1868), 173.

7. Garland, 149; Lewis, 377.

8. Grant *Papers,* I, 359.

9. Leigh Leslie, "Grant and Galena," *Midland Monthly* (Sept. 1895).

10. Jesse R. Grant, *In the Days of My Father, General Grant* (New York: 1920), 11; Simon, 86.

11. Lewis, 391; Cramer, 29, 43.

12. Garland, 151; Ishbel Ross, *The General's Wife* (New York: 1956), 104. In her memoirs, Julia vigorously rebutted suggestions that Grant did not read much. Cf. Grant *Papers,* I, 316, and letter, Julia Grant to H. Clay Neville, Nov. 6, 1894, Huntington Library.

13. Grant *Papers* I, 352; Grant, *Personal Memoirs,* I, 214–15; Richardson, 156, 174–75.

14. Don E. Fehrenbacher, *Slavery, Law, and Politics: The Dred Scott Case in Historical Perspective* (New York: 1981), 120 passim.

15. Stephen B. Oates, *To Purge This Land with Blood* (New York: 1974).

16. Lewis, 360.

17. John W. Emerson, "Grant's Life in the West," *Midland Monthly* (Oct. 1897); John Russell Young, *Around the World with General Grant* (New York: 1879), II, 446.

18. Owens, 33.

19. John C. Smith, "Personal Recollections of General Ulysses S. Grant," GAR pamphlet (Chicago: 1904); Grant, *Personal Memoirs,* I, 217.

20. Lewis, 386.

21. *St. Louis Globe–Democrat,* July 24, 1885.

22. Grant *Papers,* II, 7.

23. James H. Wilson, *The Life of John A. Rawlins* (New York: 1916), 49.

24. Augustus L. Chetlain, *Recollections of Seventy Years* (Galena, Ill.: 1899), 70–71.

25. Grant *Papers,* II, 3–4.

26. Ibid., 6.

27. Augustus L. Chetlain, "Reminiscences of General Grant," *The Magazine of History* (April 1907); Chetlain, *Recollections of Seventy Years,* 73; Garland, 160.

Chapter 10: "I Can't Wait Any Longer"

1. Augustus V. Kautz memoir, 113; Kautz Papers, USAMHI.
2. *Chicago Tribune,* March 20, 1886. This article was written by Yates's private secretary, John Moses. Cf. Augustus L. Chetlain, *Recollections of Seventy Years* (Galena, Ill.: 1899), 72–73.
3. Grant *Papers,* II, 21.
4. Lloyd Lewis, *Captain Sam Grant* (Boston: 1950), 413–27.
5. Hamlin Garland, *Ulysses S. Grant: His Life and Character* (New York: 1898), 165.
6. Chetlain, 78.
7. Grant *Papers,* II, 35.
8. Grant, *Personal Memoirs,* I, 241; Church, 70.
9. Garland, 168–69.
10. Richard Yates and Catherine Y. Pickering, *Richard Yates: Civil War Governor* (Danville, Ill.: 1966), 205; Chetlain, 78; Albert D. Richardson, *Personal History of Ulysses S. Grant* (Hartford, Conn.: 1868), 184–85; Garland, 170.
11. Lewis, 427.
12. Grant *Papers,* II, 81.
13. Grant, *Personal Memoirs,* I, 242.
14. Richardson, 185.
15. Lewis, 428.
16. James L. Crane, "Grant as a Colonel," *McClure's Magazine* (June 1896).
17. Grant *Papers,* II, 46.
18. Grant, *Personal Memoirs,* I, 253.
19. John Parker interview, Hamlin Garland Papers, USC.
20. Church, 72–73.
21. H. A. Hannah interview, Hamlin Garland Papers, USC.
22. Church, 75–76; Crane, loc. cit.
23. Grant *Papers,* II, 60, 70.
24. Grant, *Personal Memoirs,* I, 250.
25. Crane, op. cit.
26. Grant *Papers,* II, 95–96, 105; John W. Emerson, "Grant's Life in the West," *Midland Monthly* (March 1898).
27. Emerson, *Midland Monthly* (Feb. 1898).
28. Letter, Grant to Julia Dent Grant, Aug. 15, 1861, Grant *Papers,* II, 115–16.
29. Bruce Catton, *Grant Moves South* (Boston: 1960), 27–28.
30. Unpublished Jessie Benton Frémont memoir, 248–50, Bancroft Library, UC Berkeley; Alan Nevins, *Frémont: Pathmarker of the West* (Lincoln, Nebr.: 1992), 493–94.

31. Grant, *Personal Memoirs,* I, 258–60.
32. Charles Elliott, *Winfield Scott* (Boston: 1939), 718–23.
33. Hoyt Sherman, "Recollections of General Grant," *Midland Monthly* (March 1899).
34. Jay Monaghan, *Swamp Fox of the Confederacy: The Life and Military Services of M. Jeff Thompson* (Tuscaloosa, Ala.: 1956), 29–41.
35. Grant *Papers,* II, 193.
36. Richardson, 192.
37. Grant *Papers,* II, 194–95.
38. Grant, *Personal Memoirs,* I, 264.
39. Grant *Papers,* II, 214.

Chapter 11: "We Will Cut Our Way Out"

1. William M. Polk, *Leonidas Polk: Bishop and General* (New York: 1915), 2 vols.
2. John C. Frémont, "In Command in Missouri," in Robert Johnson and Clarence Buel, eds., *Battles and Leaders of the Civil War* (New York: 1888), I, 278–88; unpublished Jesse Benton Frémont memoir, 293–301, Bancroft Library, UC Berkeley.
3. Letter, Grant to McClernard, Nov. 5, 1861, Grant *Papers,* III, 113.
4. Hamlin Garland, *Ulysses S. Grant: His Life and Character* (New York: 1898), 182; Nathaniel C. Hughes, *Battle of Belmont* (Chapel Hill, N.C.: 1991), 49–50.
5. *Official Records of the War Against the Rebellion* (hereafter cited as O.R.), III, 269–70; Albert D. Richardson, *Personal History of Ulysses S. Grant* (Hartford, Conn.: 1868), 197; Adam Badeau, *Military History of Ulysses S. Grant* (New York: 1882), I, 21.
6. William McFeely, *Grant* (New York: 1981), 92.
7. Henry Walke, "The Gunboats at Belmont and Fort Henry," *Battles and Leaders of the Civil War,* I, 360–61.
8. Letter, Grant to Jesse Root Grant, Nov. 8, 1861, Grant *Papers,* III, 137.
9. Ibid., II, 22.
10. Hughes, 127–28.
11. John H. Brinton, *Personal Memoirs of John H. Brinton* (New York: 1914), 77.
12. Garland, 184.
13. Hughes, 147–48.
14. Richardson, viii; Grant, *Personal Memoirs,* I, 276.
15. Hughes, 155.
16. Grant, *Personal Memoirs,* I, 281.

17. Bruce Catton, *Grant Moves South* (Boston: 1960), 79.
18. I have relied on the careful compilation in Hughes, *Battle of Belmont,* 184–85, for casualties; these figures are slightly higher than those in Grant's report, published in O.R., III, 310.
19. Grant *Papers,* III, 133, 141.
20. O.R., I, 267–72.
21. Grant, *Personal Memoirs,* I, 271.

Chapter 12: "This Is Not War"

1. Letter, Sylvanus Cadwallader to James H. Wilson, Feb. 25, 1887, Wilson Papers, MD, LC.
2. Grant Association *Newsletter,* vol. X, no. 3, April 1973.
3. James H. Wilson, *The Life of John A. Rawlins* (New York: 1902), 66–67.
4. Albert D. Richardson, *A Personal History of Ulysses S. Grant* (Hartford, Conn.: 1868), 189–90.
5. John H. Brinton, *Personal Memoirs of John H. Brinton* (New York: 1914), 37–38.
6. Report, Grant to the Adjutant General, Nov. 17, 1861, Grant *Papers,* III, 148. Although dated 1861, this report was not actually submitted until 1865, when Grant was general-in-chief.
7. John Y. Simon, ed., *Personal Memoirs of Julia Dent Grant* (Carbondale, Ill.: 1975), 92.
8. Letter, Grant to P. Casey, Dec. 31, 1861, Philip D. and Elsie O. Sang Collection, copy in Bruce Catton/Doubleday Collection, MD, LC.
9. Simon, 95–96; *Chicago Sunday Tribune,* Dec. 14, 1902.
10. Allan Nevins, *Frémont: Pathmarker of the West* (Lincoln, Nebr.: 1992), 499–500.
11. Letters, Lincoln to Frémont, Sept. 2, 1861, and to Orville H. Browning, Sept. 22, 1861, in Roy P. Basler, ed., *Collected Works of Abraham Lincoln* (New Brunswick, N.J.: 1953), IV, 506, 532.
12. Unpublished Jesse Benton Frémont memoir, 270–71, Bancroft Library, UC Berkeley; Andrew Rolle, *John Charles Frémont* (Norman, Okla.: 1992), 202–3.
13. Letter, Grant to Jesse Root Grant, Nov. 27, 1861, Grant *Papers,* III, 227.
14. James L. Crane, "Grant as a Colonel," *McClure's Magazine* (June 1896).
15. O.R., V, 37.
16. O.R., VIII, 388–91.
17. O.R., VII, 532.
18. Ibid.
19. O.R., I, 537.

20. John W. Emerson, "Grant's Life in the West," *Midland Monthly* (May 1898).
21. Grant, *Personal Memoirs,* I, 285–86.
22. Emerson, op. cit.
23. Letter, Joseph Russell Jones to E. B. Washburne, January 17, 1862, Washburne Papers, MD, LC.
24. O.R., VII, 120, 561.
25. Emerson, op. cit.
26. Letter, Halleck to McClellan, Jan. 24, 1862, McClellan Papers, MD, LC.
27. Grant, *Personal Memoirs,* I, 287.
28. Grant *Papers,* IV, 99.
29. William T. Sherman, *Memoirs* (New York: 1875), I, 219–20.
30. Grant *Papers,* IV, 103–14.
31. O.R., VII, 930–31.
32. O.R., I, 121–22, 571–72.
33. Emerson, op. cit.
34. Cf. letters, Grant to Julia Dent Grant, Sept. 22 and 25, 1861, Grant *Papers,* II, 299–300, 311–12.

Chapter 13: "Unconditional and Immediate Surrender"

1. Letter, Grant to Halleck, Feb. 3, 1862, Grant *Papers,* IV, 145.
2. Grant *Papers,* IV, 147; Benjamin Franklin Cooling, *Forts Henry and Donelson* (Knoxville, Tenn.: 1987), 92.
3. Letter, Grant to Julia Dent Grant, Feb. 4, 1862, Grant *Papers,* IV, 149.
4. Cooling, 100.
5. Field Orders No. 1, Feb. 5, 1862, Grant *Papers,* IV, 150–51.
6. O.R., VII, 126–27; William F. Crummer, *With Grant at Fort Donelson, Shiloh and Vicksburg* (Oak Park, Ill.: 1915), 14–16.
7. Jesse Taylor, "The Defense of Fort Henry," in Robert Johnson and Clarence Buel, eds., *Battles and Leaders of the Civil War* (New York: 1888), I, 370–71.
8. Crummer, 19–20.
9. Report, Grant to John H. Kelton, Feb. 6, 1862, Grant *Papers,* IV, 155–58
10. O.R., VII, 124.
11. Cooling, 120.
12. O.R., VII, 595, 628.
13. O.R., VII, 612.
14. John H. Brinton, *Personal Memoirs* (New York: 1914), 115.
15. Cooling, 110.
16. Brinton, 116.

17. Charles B. Coffin, *Drum-Beat of the Nation* (New York: 1888), 143.
18. Letter, Halleck to George W. Cullum, Feb. 10, 1862, *Naval Official Records,* XXII, 578; James Mason Hoppin, *The Life of Andrew Hull Foote* (New York: 1874), 229.
19. Grant, *Personal Memoirs,* I, 302; Cooling, 153.
20. Henry Walke, "The Western Flotilla at Fort Donelson, Island Number Ten, Fort Pillow and Memphis," in *Battles and Leaders of the Civil War,* I, 431–36.
21. Letter, Grant to Julia Dent Grant, Feb. 14, 1862, Grant *Papers,* IV, 211.
22. Letter, Grant to George W. Cullum, Feb. 15, 1862, Grant *Papers,* IV, 212.
23. Grant, *Personal Memoirs,* I, 305.
24. Note, Grant to Andrew H. Foote, Feb. 15, 1862, Grant *Papers,* IV, 214.
25. Grant, *Personal Memoirs,* I, 308.
26. Bruce Catton, *Grant Moves South* (Boston: 1960), 166.
27. Lewis Wallace, "The Capture of Fort Donelson," in *Battles and Leaders of the Civil War,* I, 421–22.
28. Grant, *Personal Memoirs,* I, 307.
29. Brinton, 121.
30. John W. Emerson, "Grant's Life in the West," *Midland Monthly* (June 1898).
31. Grant, *Personal Memoirs,* I, 311.
32. Brinton, 129–30.
33. Arndt M. Stickles, *Simon Bolivar Buckner* (Chapel Hill, N.C.: 1940), 170–73; Catton, 177.
34. Brinton, 133–34.
35. Letter, Grant to Julia Dent Grant, Feb. 16, 1862, Grant *Papers,* IV, 229.

Chapter 14: "It Begins to Look Like Home"

1. David Donald, *Lincoln* (New York: 1996), 334–35.
2. Hamlin Garland, *Ulysses S. Grant* (New York: 1898), 198.
3. O.R., VII, 637.
4. Letter, C. C. Washburn to Elihu B. Washburne, March 8, 1862, Washburne Papers, MD, LC; Grant, *Personal Memoirs,* I, 317–18. See Herman Hattaway and Archer Jones, *How the North Won* (Urbana, Ill.: 1983), Chapter 3, for an interesting appraisal of whether or not Grant could have put his ideas into practice.
5. Letter, Thomas A. Scott to Edwin M. Stanton, Feb. 17, 1862, Stanton Papers, MD, LC; Bruce Catton, *Grant Moves South* (Boston: 1960), 187; Ethan Allen Hitchcock, *Fifty Years in Camp and Field* (New York: 1909), 434–36, 473–74; O.R., VII, 628; Grant *Papers,* IV, 196–97n.

6. O.R., VII, 637–38.

7. Ibid., 662.

8. Ibid., 679–80.

9. Benjamin Franklin Cooling, *Forts Henry and Donelson* (Knoxville, Tenn.: 1987), 250; Grant *Papers,* IV, 320n; Grant, *Personal Memoirs,* I, 325.

10. Letter, Grant to Julia Dent Grant, Feb. 26, 1862, Grant *Papers,* IV, 292.

11. O.R., VII, 666.

12. Ibid., 680.

13. Ibid.

14. Telegram, Halleck to Grant, March 4, 1862, Record Group 107, National Archives.

15. John Russell Young, *Around the World with General Grant* (New York: 1879), II, 452.

16. Letter, C. C. Washburn to Elihu Washburne, March 7, 1862, Washburne Papers, MD, LC.

17. O.R., X, Pt. 2, 15.

18. Ibid., 22.

19. Ibid., 21.

20. Ibid., 13, 21.

21. Ibid., 32.

22. Letter, Grant to Julia Dent Grant, March 15, 1862, Grant *Papers,* IV, 375.

Chapter 15: *"Lick 'Em Tomorrow"*

1. Charles Roland, *Albert Sidney Johnston: Soldier of Three Republics* (Austin, Tex.: 1964); William Preston Johnston, *The Life of Gen. Albert Sidney Johnston* (New York: 1878).

2. Bruce Catton, *Grant Moves South* (Boston: 1960), 212–13.

3. Lloyd Lewis, *Sherman: Fighting Prophet* (Boston: 1933), 213: Grant, *Personal Memoirs,* I, 308.

4. Ulysses S. Grant, "The Battle of Shiloh," in Robert Johnson and Clarence Buel, eds., *Battles and Leaders of the Civil War,* I, 466.

5. Letter, Grant to Julia Dent Grant, April 3, 1862, Grant *Papers,* V, 7.

6. O.R., X, Pt. 1, 89, 331.

7. Thomas Jordan, "Notes of a Confederate Staff Officer at Shiloh," in *Battles and Leaders of the Civil War,* I, 595n.

8. Johnston, 569–71; Alfred D. Roman, *The Military Operations of General Beauregard* (New York: 1883), I, 278–79.

9. Hamlin Garland, *Ulysses S. Grant: His Life and Character* (New York: 1898), 202; Catton, 223.

10. Letter, Grant to Buell, April 6, 1862, Grant *Papers,* V, 17.

11. Emmett Crozier, *Yankee Reporters, 1861–1865* (New York: 1956), 208–11.

12. O.R., X, Pt. 1, 286–88, 599; Kenneth P. Williams, *Lincoln Finds a General* (New York: 1952), III, 362.

13. W. W. Belknap, *History of the 15th Iowa Volunteer Infantry* (Keokuk, Iowa: 1887), 189; John D. Billings, *Hardtack and Coffee* (Boston: 1887), 405–6.

14. O.R., X, Pt. 2, 50; Catton, 228.

15. O.R., X, Pt. 1, 278.

16. Letter, Grant to Commanding Officer Advance Forces, April 6, 1862, Grant *Papers,* V, 18.

17. Lew Wallace, *An Autobiography* (New York: 1906), I, 463–64; *Battles and Leaders,* I, 607.

18. Grant, *Battles and Leaders,* I, 468. There is an unsigned, undated letter on House of Representatives stationery in Series 10, Box 22, of the Ulysses Grant Papers in the Library of Congress. This document provides a detailed account by an artillery officer in W.H.L. Wallace's division. This item refers to a meeting between Grant and W.H.L. Wallace on the morning of April 6, during which Grant talked about the counterattack that he was preparing to launch with Lew Wallace's division.

19. Grant Association *Newsletter* (Jan. 1964; Oct. 1972); O.R., X, Pt. 1, 179–80.

20. Louis M. Starr, *Bohemian Brigade* (Madison, Wis.: 1987), 101.

21. *Chicago Tribune,* Jan. 27, 1869.

22. For a good description, see Wiley Sword, *Shiloh—Bloody April* (New York: 1974), 175.

23. Johnston, 611–15.

24. Don Carlos Buell, "Shiloh Reviewed," *Battles and Leaders of the Civil War,* I, 492–94; Johnston, 611–15.

25. Adam Badeau, *Military History of General Grant* (New York: 1868), 82.

26. Grant *Papers,* V, 341–42.

27. *Chicago Tribune,* Nov. 21, 1880.

28. O.R., X, Pt. 1, 339; Catton, 239–40.

29. *Army and Navy Journal* (Dec. 30, 1893).

30. Letter, Grant to Julia Dent Grant, April 30, 1862, Grant *Papers,* V, 103; Garland, 209.

31. Grant, *Personal Memoirs,* I, 349.

32. O.R., X, Pt. 1, 384.

33. O.R., X, Pt. 1, 570.

34. Letter, W. R. Rowley to Elihu B. Washburne, April 17, 1862, Washburne Papers, MD, LC.

35. Thomas Livermore, *Numbers and Losses in the Civil War* (Bloomington, Ind.: 1957), 79–80.

Chapter 16: *"Notoriety Has No Charms"*

1. Franc Wilkie, *Pen and Powder* (Boston: 1888), 154.
2. James G. Smart, *A Radical View: The "Agate" Dispatches of Whitelaw Reid* (Memphis: 1989), I, 119–73.
3. J.F.C. Fuller, *The Generalship of Ulysses S. Grant* (London: 1929), 111–13.
4. Emmett Crozier, *Yankee Reporters* (Philadelphia: 1939), 210–17.
5. Letters, Benjamin H. Campbell to Elihu B. Washburne, Dec. 17, 1861; William Bross to Simon Cameron, Dec. 30, 1861, Washburne Papers, MD, LC.
6. Letters, Elihu B. Washburne to John A. Rawlins, Dec. 21, and Rawlins to Washburne, Dec. 30, 1861, Washburne Papers, MD, LC.
7. Grant *Papers,* V, 22–23, 53–54.
8. Letters, William J. Kountz to Edwin Stanton, Feb. 8 and 10, 1862, Stanton Papers, MD, LC.
9. Letter, Grant to Julia Dent Grant, Feb. 16, 1862, Grant *Papers,* V, 229.
10. Letter, Grant to William J. Kountz, Jan. 29, 1862, Grant *Papers,* V, 110.
11. Letter, Grant to Julia Dent Grant, April 15, 1862, Grant *Papers,* V, 47.
12. Letters, L. S. Felt to Elihu B. Washburne, April 12, 1862; N. G. Speer to Washburne, April 17, 1862; Charles L. Stephenson to Washburne, April 19, 1862; E. Hampstead to Washburne, April 12, 1861; Washburne Papers, MD, LC.
13. J. P. Riordan interview in Hamlin Garland Papers, USC.
14. James L. McDonough, *Shiloh: In Hell Before Night* (Knoxville, Tenn.: 1977), 222–23; Joseph A. Frank and George A. Reaves, *"Seeing the Elephant": Recruits in the Battle of Shiloh* (New York: 1989), 140–45.
15. Jacob Ammen diary, April 8, 1862, Jacob Ammen Papers, Illinois Historical Society.
16. Letters, Grant to Julia Dent Grant, April 25, 30, 1862, Grant *Papers,* V, 72, 102.
17. Letter, Grant to Mrs. C. F. Smith, April 26, 1862, Grant *Papers,* V, 83–84.
18. Letter, Grant to Jesse Root Grant, April 26, 1862, Grant *Papers,* V, 78. Cf. Adam Badeau, *Military History of Ulysses S. Grant* (New York: 1868), I, 96–98.
19. Bruce Catton, *Grant Moves South* (Boston: 1960), 257.
20. Letter, W. R. Rowley to Elihu B. Washburne, April 19, 1862, Washburne Papers, MD, LC.

21. Letter, Grant to Elihu B. Washburne, May 14, 1862, Washburne Papers, MD, LC.

22. O.R., X, Pt. 1, 98–99; A. K. McClure, *Lincoln and Men of War-Times* (Philadelphia: 1892), 91–93. Doubts have been raised about McClure's reliability by noted Grant scholar Brooks D. Simpson, because other elements in McClure's account—particularly those relating to Halleck's role—are demonstrably untrue. Even so, Simpson himself concedes, "Certainly Lincoln may have uttered those words." See Brooks D. Simpson, "Alexander McClure on Lincoln and Grant," *Lincoln Herald* (Fall 1993).

23. O.R., X, Pt. 2, 105–6; James Grant Wilson, "Types and Traditions of the Old Army, Part II: General Halleck—A Memoir," *Journal of the Military Service Institute* (May–June 1905).

24. O.R., X, Pt. 2, 144; Catton, 266–67.

25. O.R., X, Pt. 2, 182–88.

26. O.R., X, Pt. 2, 97 passim; letter, Grant to Don Carlos Buell, April 7, 1862, Grant *Papers*, V, 20–21.

27. Grant, *Personal Memoirs*, I, 381.

28. Badeau, 105.

29. Catton, 275.

30. Grant, *Personal Memoirs*, I, 381.

31. Ibid., 382.

32. William T. Sherman, *Memoirs of W. T. Sherman* (New York: 1891), I, 255.

33. Grant's letters to Julia make it clear that all he really had in mind was a thirty-day leave back on the banks of the Gravois. See letters, Grant to Julia Dent Grant, May 23 and June 9, 1862, Grant *Papers*, V, 129–30, 140–41.

34. Sherman, loc. cit.

35. Badeau, I, 108n.

36. Grant *Papers*, V, 152, note 7. Cf. Lew Wallace, *An Autobiography* (New York: 1906), 11, 588–90; Robert E. and Katherine M. Morsberger, *Lew Wallace: Militant Romantic* (New York: 1980), 109–12.

Chapter 17: "One More Fight"

1. Letter, Grant to Julia Dent Grant, April 15, 1862, Grant *Papers*, VI, 47. Cf. Grant to George P. Ihrie, April 25, 1862, Grant *Papers*, VI, 47.

2. Adam Badeau, *Military History of Ulysses S. Grant* (New York: 1868), I, 94–95.

3. John Y. Simon, ed., *The Personal Memoirs of Julia Dent Grant* (Carbondale, Ill.: 1975), 101.

4. Grant *Papers*, VI, 219–20.

5. Grant, *Personal Memoirs*, I, 398.

6. Letter, Grant to Jesse Root Grant, Aug. 3, 1862, Grant *Papers,* VI, 263.
7. O.R., XVII, Pt. 2, 143.
8. O.R., XVI, Pt. 2, 734–35, 741.
9. Ibid., 315–16.
10. Letter, Grant to Julia Dent Grant, August 18, 1862, Grant *Papers,* VI, 308.
11. Report on Shiloh, Sept–Oct. 1862, Grant *Papers,* V, 340.
12. O.R., XVI, Pt. 1, 907–8; James L. McDonough, *War in Kentucky* (Knoxville, Tenn.: 1994), 117–18.
13. Shelby Foote, *The Civil War* (New York: 1958), I, 714.
14. Charles A. Dana, *Recollections of the Civil War* (New York: 1899), 115; William M. Lamers, *The Edge of Glory: A Biography of General William S. Rosecrans, U.S.A.* (New York: 1961), 14.
15. Grant, *Personal Memoirs,* I, 408; Report of the Joint Committee on the Conduct of the War (Washington, D.C.: 1865), III, 18 (hereafter referred to as CCW).
16. Foote, 718.
17. Badeau, 112.
18. Lamers, 108.
19. Badeau, 113n.
20. Ibid., 114; CCW, III, 20.
21. O.R., XVII, Pt. 1, 64–68.
22. Ibid., 160, 166.
23. Ibid., 168–69.
24. Kenneth P. Williams, *Lincoln Finds a General* (New York: 1952), IV, 90.
25. Thomas Livermore, *Numbers and Losses in the Civil War* (Bloomington, Ind.: 1957), 94. For good general accounts of this battle as seen by its two principals, see Lamers, Chapter 6, and Robert G. Hartje, *Van Dorn* (Nashville, Tenn.: 1967), Chapter 10.
26. CCW, III, 22–23; Lamers, 160–61.
27. O.R., XVII, Pt. 1, 156.
28. Simon, 104.
29. O.R., XVII, Pt. 1, 157–61; Grant, *Personal Memoirs,* I, 418.
30. O.R., XVII, Pt. 2, 287.
31. Ibid., 290; Simon, 105; A. Noel Blakeman, *Personal Recollections of the War of the Rebellion* (New York: 1897), III, 357.

Chapter 18: "Unmanageable and Incompetant"

1. John Riordan interview, Hamlin Garland Papers, USC.
2. Letter, McClernand to Lincoln, Jan. 16, 1863, Robert Todd Lincoln Papers, MD, LC; Moses Harrel interview, Hamlin Garland Papers, USC. Riordan and Harrell had served as infantry colonels under McClernand.

3. Stephen Ambrose, *Halleck* (Baton Rouge: 1962), 110–12; Howard K. Beale, ed., *The Diary of Gideon Welles* (New York: 1960), I, 387.

4. O.R., XVII, Pt. 2, 282.

5. James H. Wilson, *The Life of John A. Rawlins* (New York: 1907), 103.

6. See Grant *Papers,* VII, 274–76.

7. Sylvanus Cadwallader, *Three Years with General Grant* (New York: 1955), 18.

8. Adam Badeau, *Military History of General Grant* (New York: 1868), 130–31.

9. Michael Ballard, *Pemberton* (Jackson, Miss.: 1991), 84–86, 115–18.

10. O.R., XVII, Pt. 1, 472.

11. O.R., XVII, Pt. 1, 495–96.

12. Letter, Grant to Mary Grant, Dec. 15, 1862, Grant *Papers,* VII, 44–45.

13. Cadwallader, 22–23.

14. *Chicago Times Herald,* July 7, 1899.

15. The relevant documents are reproduced in Grant *Papers,* XIX, 17–21.

16. O.R., XVII, Pt. 2, 424; Grant *Papers,* VII, 50–54n; XIX, 37.

17. John Y. Simon, ed., *The Personal Memoirs of Julia Dent Grant* (Carbondale, Ill.: 1975), 107.

18. O.R., XVII, Pt. 1, 496–99.

19. Cadwallader, 34; Hamlin Garland, *Ulysses S. Grant* (New York: 1898), 218.

20. O.R., XVII, Pt. 2, 439–40.

21. Simon, loc. cit.

22. O.R., XVII, Pt. 2, 444.

23. Robert George Hartje, *Van Dorn* (Nashville, Tenn.: 1967), 261–63.

24. Letter, Grant to Silas Hudson, Jan. 14, 1863, Grant *Papers,* VII, 224–25; O.R., XXVII, Pt. 1, 515.

25. O.R., XVII, Pt. 2, 415.

26. O.R., LII, Pt. 1, 314.

27. O.R., XVII, Pt. 1, 420, 425.

28. William T. Sherman, *Memoirs of General W. T. Sherman* (New York: 1875), I, 284–88.

29. O.R., XVII, Pt. 1, 601–53; O.R., XVII, Pt. 2, 534–35; John F. Marszalek, *Sherman: A Soldier's Passion for Order* (New York: 1992), 206–7.

30. Letter, Grant to McClernand, Jan. 11, 1863, Grant *Papers,* VII, 210–11. This letter was never sent.

31. Sherman, 299.

32. O.R., XVII, Pt. 2, 555.

33. For the draft of this unsent letter, see Grant *Papers,* VII, 209–10n.

Chapter 19: *"Fortifications Almost Impregnible"*

1. David Donald, *Lincoln* (New York: 1995), 362–64.
2. O.R., XVII, Pt. 2, 523, 590–91.
3. Letter, Sylvanus Cadwallader to Carrie Cadwallader, November 13, 1862, Cadwallader Papers, MD, LC.
4. Grant *Papers,* VI, 317n; VII, 186–87n.
5. John Eaton, *Grant, Lincoln and the Freedmen* (New York: 1907), 30–31.
6. Grant *Papers,* VI, 315–16n.
7. Grant *Papers,* VIII, 26.
8. O.R., XXIV, Pt. 1, 8–9.
9. O.R., XXIV, Pt. 3, 18–19; letter, McClernand to Lincoln, Feb. 2, 1863, Robert Todd Lincoln Papers, MD, LC.
10. Letter, Grant to Silas Hudson, Jan. 14, 1863, Grant *Papers,* VII, 224–25.
11. Letter, Albert D. Richardson to S. H. Gay, March 20, 1863, Gay Papers, Columbia University.
12. O.R., XXIV, Pt. 1, 19.
13. William T. Sherman, *Memoirs of General W. T. Sherman* (New York: 1891), I, 317.
14. Eaton, 64.
15. John Y. Simon, ed., *Personal Memoirs of Julia Dent Grant* (Carbondale, Ill.: 1975), 111; David Dixon Porter, *Incidents and Anecdotes of the Civil War* (New York: 1891), 180–82. Porter claims he talked Thomas out of relieving Grant, but this is almost certainly untrue.
16. Charles A. Dana, *Recollections of the Civil War* (New York: 1899), 20–22.
17. Sylvanus Cadwallader, *Three Years with General Grant* (New York: 1955), 61–62; James H. Wilson, *The Life of John A. Rawlins* (New York: 1916), 120–21.
18. Letter, Cadwallader Washburn to Elihu B. Washburne, April 11, 1863, Washburne Papers, MD, LC.
19. Letters, Grant to David Farragut, March 20, 1863, O.R., XV, 300–301; Grant to David D. Porter, March 29, 1863, O.R., XXIV, Pt. 3, 151–52. In the first letter he forecasts a bloody frontal assault; in the second he anticipates landing an invasion force south of Vicksburg.
20. John F. Marszalek, *Sherman* (New York: 1992), 217.
21. Wilson, 114–16; Sherman, I, 315–16.
22. Simon, 112.
23. O.R., XXIV, Pt. 1, 30; O.R., XXIV, Pt. 3, 207–8.
24. Grant *Papers,* VII, 397n.
25. Grant *Papers,* VIII, 9–10, 112–13.

26. D. Alexander Brown, *Grierson's Raid* (Urbana, Ill.: 1962), 6–10.

27. Kenneth P. Williams, *Lincoln Finds a General* (New York: 1956), IV, 338.

28. Letter, Grant to Julia Dent Grant, May 3, 1863, Grant *Papers,* VIII, 155; O.R., XXIV, Pt. 1, 32.

29. J. H. Robinson interview, Hamlin Garland Papers, USC.

30. Ballard, 138–40.

31. O.R., XXIV, Pt. 1, 34–35; Ulysses S. Grant, "The Vicksburg Campaign," in *Battles and Leaders of the Civil War* (New York: 1887), III, 500.

32. Letter, Grant to William S. Hillyer, May 5, 1863, Grant *Papers,* VIII, 162.

33. Grant, *Battles and Leaders,* III, 501.

34. Benjamin Thomas and Harold M. Hyman, *Stanton* (New York: 1962), 268; O.R., XXIV, Pt. 1, 84.

35. Edward Bearss, *Grant Strikes a Fatal Blow* (Dayton: 1960), 512–21.

36. See Grant *Papers,* VIII, 214n.

37. Grant *Papers,* VIII, 224.

38. Hamlin Garland, *Ulysses S. Grant: His Life and Character* (New York: 1898), 230n; Frederick Dent Grant, "With Grant at Vicksburg," *The Outlook* (July 2, 1898).

39. Thomas Livermore, *Numbers and Losses in the Civil War* (Bloomington, Ind.: 1957), 100.

40. Grant, *Personal Memoirs,* I, 519.

41. Sherman, I, 324.

42. Frederick Dent Grant, op. cit.; Sherman, I, 352.

43. John Y. Simon, "Frederick Dent Grant at Vicksburg," Grant Association Newsletter (Oct. 1969).

44. O.R., XXIV, Pt. 1, 44–59.

45. Letter, Charles A. Dana to Edwin M. Stanton, May 24, 1863, Stanton Papers, MD, LC.

46. Williams, 408–9.

47. O.R., XXIV, Pt. 1, 102, 159–61; Wilson, 133–35.

48. For a thorough discussion of this issue, complete with the relevant documents, see Grant *Papers,* VIII, 322–25.

49. Letters, Grant to Julia Dent Grant, June 9 and 15, 1863, Grant *Papers,* VIII, 332, 376.

50. O.R., XXXVIII, 458; letter, Grant to Julia Dent Grant, June 29, 1863, Grant *Papers,* VIII, 444–45.

51. O.R., XXIV, Pt. 1, 59–60.

52. Garland, 235; Ballard, 179.

53. Naval O.R., XXV, 102.

54. Fred Grant, op. cit.; O.R., XXIV, Pt. 1, 44, 285; Grant, *Personal Memoirs,* I, 565.

Chapter 20: *"The Specticle Was Grand"*

1. Roy P. Basler, ed., *Collected Works of Abraham Lincoln* (New Brunswick, N.J.: 1953), VI, 326.
2. O.R., XXIV, Pt. 1, 63.
3. Howard K. Beale, ed., *The Diary of Gideon Welles* (New York: 1960), I, 378–79.
4. O.R., XXIV, Pt. 3, 540–42; cf. letter, Grant to Lincoln, Aug. 23, 1863, Grant *Papers,* IX, 195–97.
5. See the long letter from Halleck to Grant, Jan. 8, 1864, in O.R., XXXII, Pt. 2, 40–42.
6. O.R., XXIV, Pt. 3, 552.
7. Beale, I, 370.
8. Letters, Grant to Charles A. Dana, Aug. 5, 1863, and Grant to Elihu B. Washburne, August 30, 1863, Grant *Papers,* IX, 145–47, 217–18.
9. Grant *Papers,* IX, 222n; letter, Thomas K. Smith to William E. Brooks, n.d. but evidently Oct.–Nov. 1842, in the Lewis-Catton Notes, U. S. Grant Association, SIU.
10. Grant, *Personal Memoirs,* II, 28; Bruce Catton, *Grant Takes Command* (Boston: 1968), 26. Also see Frank Parker interview, Hamlin Garland Papers, USC. Parker, another eyewitness, claims Grant's horse stepped into a large pothole in the road, but this seems unlikely.
11. O.R., XXX, Pt. 3, 732.
12. Herman Hathaway and Archer Jones, *How the North Won* (Urbana, Ill.: 1986), 378.
13. William M. Lamers, *The Edge of Glory* (New York: 1961), 292–309.
14. Shelby Foote, *The Civil War* (New York: 1963), II, 689–91.
15. Grant *Papers,* IX, 281n.
16. O.R., XXX, Pt. 4, 404.
17. Grant, *Personal Memoirs,* II, 17–18.
18. James H. Wilson, *The Life of John A. Rawlins* (New York: 1907), 163.
19. Grant's recollection that Stanton carried two sets of orders, one leaving Rosecrans in command and the other replacing him with Thomas, is incorrect. Grant, *Personal Memoirs,* 18–19; Grant *Papers,* IX, 297n.
20. O.R., XXX, Pt. 3, 945.
21. John Y. Simon, ed., *The Personal Memoirs of Julia Dent Grant* (Carbondale, Ill.: 1975), 125.
22. O.R., XXX, Pt. 1, 218; Lamers, 390–93; Allan Peskin, *Garfield* (Norwalk, Conn.: 1987), 214–17.
23. O.R., XXX, Pt. 4, 479.

24. James L. McDonough, *Chattanooga—A Death Grip on the Confederacy* (Knoxville, Tenn.: 1984), 50.

25. Oliver Otis Howard, "Grant at Chattanooga," *Personal Recollections of the War of the Rebellion* (New York: 1891), 245–46; *Autobiography of Oliver Otis Howard* (New York: 1907), 460–61.

26. McDonough, 53.

27. Grant *Papers,* IX, 317–18n.

28. James H. Wilson interview, Hamlin Garland Papers, USC.

29. Horace Porter, *Campaigning with Grant* (New York: 1897), 5; Charles A. Dana, *Recollections of the Civil War* (New York: 1902), 133–34.

30. Lamers, 400. See also William Farrar Smith, *From Chattanooga to Petersburg Under Generals Grant and Butler* (Cambridge, Mass.: 1893), 9–14.

31. Porter, 7.

32. O.R., XXXI, Pt. 1, 56.

33. William F. Smith, "An Historical Sketch of the Military Operations Around Chattanooga," *Papers of the Military Historical Society of Massachusetts* (Boston: 1910), 177–79.

34. Grant, *Personal Memoirs,* II, 89–91; Grant, "Chattanooga," in *Battles and Leaders of the Civil War* (New York: 1887), III, 689; Francis McKinney, *Education in Violence: The Life of George H. Thomas* (Detroit: 1961), 281–82.

35. Smith, *From Chattanooga to Petersburg,* 17.

36. O.R., XXXI, Pt. 3, 216.

37. Diary, Nov. 20, 1863, William W. Smith Papers, MD, LC.

38. John F. Marszalek, *Sherman: A Soldier's Passion for Order* (New York: 1993), 244.

39. O.R., XXXI, Pt. 2, 746–47; McDonough, 113–14, 125.

40. Diary, Nov. 24, 1863, William W. Smith Papers, MD, LC.

41. Henry Villard, *Memoirs of Henry Villard* (Boston: 1904), II, 261; John Russell Young, *Around the World with General Grant* (New York: 1879), II, 306.

42. O.R., XXXI, Pt. 2, 575; Lloyd Lewis, *Sherman: Fighting Prophet* (New York: 1932), 316–25.

43. O.R., XXXI, Pt. 2, 116.

44. Unpublished memoir, "The Battle of Chattanooga," in Montgomery C. Meigs Papers, MD, LC.

45. Bruce Catton, *Grant Takes Command* (Boston: 1968), 65–67.

46. James H. Wilson interview, Hamlin Garland Papers, USC.

47. Thomas J. Wood, "The Battle of Missionary Ridge," in *Sketches of War History, 1861–1865,* Military Order of the Loyal Legion of the United

States (Cincinnati: 1888), IV, 37. Wood commanded one of the Union divisions in this assault.

48. Diary, Nov. 25, 1863, William W. Smith Papers, MD, LC.
49. Shelby Foote, *The Civil War* (New York: 1963), 854–55. In the original draft of his report on the battle, Grant wrote that the men had advanced up the ridge "without orders from me," but later crossed this out. Grant *Papers,* IX, 562.
50. Meigs, op. cit.
51. Diary, William W. Smith Papers, loc. cit.
52. Letter, Grant to Elihu B. Washburne, Dec. 2, 1863, Grant *Papers,* IX, 490–91.

Chapter 21: "Get All the Sunshine I Can"

1. Letter, Grant to Elihu B. Washburne, Dec. 12, 1863, Grant *Papers,* IX, 522.
2. See letter, Halleck to Francis Lieber, Dec. 27, 1863, Lieber Papers, Huntington Library.
3. Letter, John A. Rawlins to Elihu B. Washburne, Jan. 20, 1864, Eldridge Collection, Huntington Library.
4. Philip H. Sheridan, *Personal Memoirs of General P. H. Sheridan* (New York: 1888), I, 312–18; Grant, *Personal Memoirs,* II, 81.
5. O.R., XXXI, Pt. 1, 20.
6. O.R., XXXI, Pt. 2, 25; Grant, *Personal Memoirs,* II, 84.
7. O.R., XXXI, Pt. 2, 72; Pt. 3, 349–50.
8. Diary, Jan. 18, 1864, Cyrus B. Comstock Papers, MD, LC; O.R., XXXIII, 394–95.
9. "Notes of a Conversation with Mrs. Grant," Hamlin Garland Papers, USC.
10. *Congressional Globe,* 38th Congress, 1st. Session, I, 428–31. Cf. Grant *Papers,* X, 141–42n.
11. John Russell Young, *Around the World with General Grant* (New York: 1879), II, 446.
12. William E. Woodward, *Meet General Grant* (New York: 1928), 256.
13. Letter, James H. Wilson to Sylvanus Cadwallader, Sept. 8, 1904, Cadwallader Papers, MD, LC. Cf. James H. Wilson, *The Life of John A. Rawlins* (New York: 1907), 39.
14. Harrison Strong interview, Hamlin Garland Papers, USC; Horace Porter, *Campaigning with Grant* (New York: 1897), 7; Young, I, 306.
15. Letter, Cadwallader to James H. Wilson, June 21, 1897, Sylvanus Wilson Papers, MD, LC.

16. Gene Smith, *American Gothic* (New York: 1992), 66–67, 77.
17. This overheated and ultimately sad correspondence, consisting of more than twenty letters from Badeau, is to be found in the James H. Wilson Papers in the Firestone Library at Princeton University.
18. "An Interview with General Harry Wilson," Hamlin Garland Papers, USC.
19. Benjamin H. Thomas, ed., *Three Years with Grant* (New York: 1955).
20. Undated memo headed "Staff List" in Cadwallader Papers, MD, LC; James H. Wilson, *The Life of John A. Rawlins* (New York: 1907), 208, 395. Some of Wilson's letters are addressed to "General S. Cadwallader."
21. Henry Coppée, *Grant and His Campaigns* (New York: 1866), 458; Grant *Papers,* X, 259–60.
22. Garland, loc. cit.
23. Letter, Richard Henry Dana to his wife, April 21, 1864, Dana Papers, Massachusetts Historical Society.
24. Ibid.
25. Porter, 22.
26. Letter, Julius Nichols to Helen Smith, March 16, 1864, John Colton Smith Papers, MD, LC; Grant Association *Newsletter* (Jan. 1970); Noah Brooks, *Washington in Lincoln's Time* (New York: 1958), 134–35.
27. Helen Nicolay, *Lincoln's Secretary: A Biography of John G. Nicolay* (New York: 1949), 194–95; Howard K. Beale, ed., *Diary of Gideon Welles* (New York: 1960), 538–39.
28. A. E. Watrous, "Grant as His Son Saw Him: An Interview with Colonel Frederick Dent Grant," *McClure's Magazine* (May 1894).
29. Brooks, loc. cit.
30. Roy P. Basler, ed., *Collected Works of Abraham Lincoln* (New Brunswick, N.J.: 1953), VII, 234; Grant *Papers,* X, 195; diary, March 9, 1864, Cyrus B. Comstock Papers, MD, LC.
31. William O. Stoddard, Jr., *William O. Stoddard, Lincoln's Third Secretary* (New York: 1955), 197–98.

Chapter 22: "If It Takes ~~Me~~ All Summer"

1. O.R., XXXVI, Pt. 1, 12–18.
2. O.R., XXXII, Pt. 3, 312.
3. O.R., XXXIII, Pt. 3, 198.
4. Richard B. Irwin, "The Red River Campaign," *Battles and Leaders of the Civil War,* IV, 345–74.
5. O.R., XXXIV, Pt. 3, 331–32.
6. Letter, Grant to Jesse Root Grant, March 1, 1864, Grant *Papers,* X, 183.

7. Letter, Halleck to Francis Lieber, March 7, 1864, Lieber Papers, Huntington Library.

8. Stephen Ambrose, *Halleck* (Baton Rouge: 1960), 162–64.

9. Horace Porter, *Campaigning with Grant* (New York: 1897), 29.

10. Bruce Catton, *Grant Takes Command* (Boston: 1966), 159–60; letter, D. B. Birney to George T. Gross, April 24, 1864, Birney Papers, USAMHI.

11. Philip H. Sheridan, *Personal Memoirs of General P. H. Sheridan* (New York, 1891), I, 192–94; Grant, *Personal Memoirs,* II, 133–34.

12. A. A. Humphreys, *The Campaign of '64 and '65* (New York: 1883), 9–12; O.R., XXXIII, 827–29.

13. Ibid., XXXIII, 955.

14. Diary, December 15, 1877, John Russell Young Papers, MD, LC; Humphreys, 421–23; O.R. XXXIII, 1053.

15. Gordon Rhea, *The Battle of the Wilderness* (Baton Rouge: 1994), 60–61.

16. O.R., XXXVI, Pt. 1, 1.

17. Adam Badeau, *Military History of Ulysses S. Grant* (New York: 1868), 108; Albert D. Richardson, *A Personal History of U. S. Grant* (Hartford, Conn.: 1868), 393; Porter, 41–42.

18. Shelby Foote, *The Civil War* (New York: 1974), III, 148.

19. Freeman Cleaves, *Meade of Gettysburg* (Norman, Okla.: 1960), 207–13.

20. O.R., XXXVI, Pt. 2, 380.

21. Emory Thomas, *Robert E. Lee* (New York: 1995), 336–37.

22. O.R., XXXVI, Pt. 2, 403.

23. Ibid.

24. Vincent Flanagan, *The Life of General Gouverneur Kemble Warren* (Ph.D. dissertation, CUNY, 1969); Cf. Pfanz, *Gettysburg: The Second Day* (Chapel Hill, N.C.: 1984).

25. George A. Agassiz, ed., *Meade's Headquarters, 1863–1865: The Letters of Colonel Theodore Lyman* (Boston: 1922), 91.

26. Rhea, 189 et seq; Porter, 72–73.

27. Diary, May 6, 1864, Marsena Patrick Papers, MD, LC; Harrison Strong interview, Hamlin Garland Papers, USC.

28. Porter, 52.

29. James I. Robertson, *General A. P. Hill* (New York: 1987), 258–60.

30. William H. Armstrong, *Warrior in Two Camps* (Norman, Okla.: 1975), 90–91.

31. Diary, May 6, 1863, Marsena Patrick Papers, MD, LC.

32. Edward Steere, *The Wilderness Campaign* (Harrisburg, Pa.: 1994), 443.

33. Porter, 70–71.

34. Thomas Livermore, *Numbers and Losses in America's Civil War* (Bloomington, Ind.: 1959), 110–11.

35. James H. Wilson, *Under the Old Flag* (1912), I, 390–91; Porter, 71. See Bruce Catton, *Grant Takes Command* (Boston: 1968), 508n.
36. Diary, May 6, 1864, Charles Francis Adams II Papers, Massachusetts Historical Society.
37. Henry Wing, *When Lincoln Kissed Me* (New York: 1914), 37–39.
38. O.R., XXXVI, Pt. 2, 481.
39. Porter, 78–79; James H. Wilson, *The Life of John A. Rawlins* (New York: 1916), 215.
40. Adam Badeau, *Military History of Ulysses S. Grant* (New York: 1868), II, 139; Grant, *Personal Memoirs,* II, 213.
41. Undated memo, "A Second Talk with General Longstreet," Hamlin Garland Papers, USC; Theodore Lyman, "Uselessness of the Maps Furnished to Staff of the Army of the Potomac Previous to the Campaign of 1864," *Papers of the Military Historical Society of Massachusetts,* Vol. 4, (Boston: 1905).
42. William D. Matter, *If It Takes All Summer* (Chapel Hill, N.C.: 1988), 50, 53.
43. Cleaves, *Meade of Gettysburg,* 252–54.
44. Sheridan, I, 368–69.
45. Porter, 83–84; O.R., XXXVI, Pt. 2, 553.
46. Porter, 90.
47. Matter, 130–32; Vincent Esposito, ed., *West Point Atlas of American Wars* (New York: 1960), 128.
48. Matter, 158–67; Grant, *Personal Memoirs,* II, 224–25.
49. Humphreys, 83.
50. Porter, 114–15; Meade, *Life and Letters,* II, 197; Humphreys, 83n; Grant, *Personal Memoirs,* II, 563–64; Arthur Vernon Grant, Jr., "Unity of Command: The Command Relationship Between Generals Grant and Meade in the Campaigns of 1864–1865," M.A. thesis (Rice University, 1974), 1271–30.
51. Letter, Grant to Halleck, May 11, 1864, Grant *Papers,* 10, 422–23; Armstrong, 98.
52. Matter, 308–11.

Chapter 23: "Willing to Run the Risk of Defeat"

1. Benjamin F. Butler, *Autobiography and Reminiscences: Butler's Book* (Boston: 1892), 57–58, 78–85, 94–110; Howard P. Nash, Jr., *Stormy Petrel: The Life and Times of General Benjamin F. Butler* (Rutherford, N.J.: 1969), 10–22.
2. Robert S. Holzman, *Stormy Ben Butler* (New York: 1954), 84–88; Nash, 161–65; Rod Gragg, *Confederate Goliath* (Baton Rouge: 1991), 39.

3. James H. Wilson, *The Life of John A. Rawlins* (New York: 1916), 423.

4. Diary, March 11, 1864, Cyrus B. Comstock Papers, MD, LC.

5. The most recent biography, William H. C. Smith's *Napoleon III* (Paris: 1982), is at pains to offer favorable judgments, but his subject remains repellent.

6. O.R., XXXIII, 795.

7. Bruce Catton, *Grant Takes Command* (Boston: 1968), 246–47.

8. O.R., XXXVI, Pt. 2, 518.

9. O.R., XXXVI, Pt. 1, 20.

10. William F. Smith, "Butler's Attack on Drewry's Bluff," in *Battles and Leaders of the Civil War,* IV, 206–11.

11. Herbert M. Schiller, ed., *The Autobiography of William F. Smith* (Dayton, Ohio: 1990), 87–88; O.R., XXVI, Pt. 2, 117, 122, 125–26, 135, 152; William G. Robertson, *Back Door to Richmond* (Newark, Del.: 1987), 189–93; Herbert M. Schiller, *The Bermuda Hundred Campaign* (Dayton, Ohio: 1988), 253–57.

12. O.R., XXXVI, Pt. 1, 20.

13. O.R., XXXVI, Pt. 2, 43–44.

14. Horace Porter, *Campaigning with Grant* (New York: 1897); William Marvel, *Burnside* (Chapel Hill, N.C.: 1991), 372.

15. Grant, *Personal Memoirs,* II, 428; Adam Badeau, *Military History of U.S. Grant* (New York: 1868), II, 232–36.

16. O.R., XXVI, Pt. 3, 207.

17. A. A. Humphreys, *The Campaign of '64 and '65* (New York: 1883), 171–76; Philip H. Sheridan, *Personal Memoirs of General P. H. Sheridan* (New York: 1891), I, 395–407.

18. O.R., XXXVI, Pt. 3, 478.

19. Porter, 175.

20. Schiller, 94.

21. O.R., XXXVI, Pt. 3, 525.

22. Ibid., 526.

23. Schiller, 94, 113.

24. W. W. Smith (Garland interview), Hamlin Garland Papers, USC; O.R., XXVI, Pt. 3, 524.

25. Porter, 179; Grant, *Personal Memoirs,* II, 276.

26. See Grady McWhinney and Perry Jameson, *Attack and Die!* (Tuscaloosa, Ala.: 1982), for an interesting analysis of Lee's addiction to frontal assaults.

27. *Chicago Tribune,* April 12, 1885.

28. O.R., XXXVI, Pt. 3, 600, 638–39; Emory Thomas, *Robert E. Lee* (New York: 1995), 334–35.

29. Letter, Grant to Elihu B. Washburne, June 9, 1864, Washburne Papers, MD, LC.

30. Thomas, 341–44.

31. For an excellent recent analysis, see Brian Holden Reid, "Another Look at Grant's Crossing of the James, 1864," *Civil War History,* XXXIX, No. 4 (1993).

32. Douglas Southall Freeman, *R. E. Lee* (New York: 1935), III, 398.

33. W. W. Smith (Garland interview), Garland Papers, USC.

34. *Chicago Tribune,* April 27, 1880.

35. John Russell Young, *Around the World with General Grant* (New York: 1879), II, 627.

36. Porter, 199–200.

37. Grant *Papers,* XI, 34–35, 47–49.

38. David M. Jordan, *Winfield Scott Hancock* (Bloomington, Ind.: 1990), 142–43.

39. T. Harry William, *Napoleon in Gray* (Baton Rouge: 1950), 221–23.

40. William F. Smith, *From Chattanooga to Petersburg* (Cambridge, Mass.: 1893), 33; "The Movement Against Petersburg, June 15, 1864," *Military History Society of Massachusetts,* V, 89.

41. Schiller, 102–3.

42. O.R., XXVI, Pt. 1, 25; Butler, 688.

43. O.R., XL, Pt. 2, 59.

44. O.R., XL, Pt. 1, 313–14; Jordan, 143–44.

45. Theodore Lyman, *Meade's Headquarters* (Boston: 1922), 164.

46. Clifford Dowdey, *Lee's Last Campaign* (New York: 1952), 542–44.

47. Grant, *Personal Memoirs,* II, 292.

Chapter 24: "Gen. Lee Surrendered"

1. O.R., L, Pt. 2, 985; O.R., XL, Pt. 1, 35–36; George Meade, *The Life and Letters of George Gordon Meade* (New York: 1913), II, 216–17; Arthur Vernon Grant, Jr., "Unity of Command: The Command Relationship Between Generals Grant and Meade," M.A. thesis (Rice University, 1974), 213–14; diary, Aug. 4, 1864, Cyrus B. Comstock Papers, MD, LC; Benjamin Thomas and Harold Hyman, *Stanton* (New York: 1962), 321.

2. Diary, July 17, 1864, Cyrus B. Comstock Papers, MD, LC; letter, John A. Rawlins to Emma Rawlins, July 19, 1864, James H. Wilson Papers, MD, LC; O.R., XL, Pt. 2, 558–59, 598; O.R., XL, Pt. 3, 334; Herbert M. Schiller, ed., *Autobiography of William F. Smith* (Dayton, Ohio: 1990), 57, 113n.

3. O.R., XL, Pt. 2, 619–20; O.R., XL, Pt. 3, 4–5.

4. David Marvel, *Burnside* (Chapel Hill, N.C.: 1991), 394–95.

5. Joint Committee on the Conduct of the War, *The Battle of Petersburg* (Washington, D.C.: 1865), I, 110.

6. Horace Porter, *Campaigning with Grant* (New York: 1897), 264–65.

7. O.R., XL, Pt. 1, 125–26.

8. Porter, 267.

9. E. P. Alexander, *Military Memoirs of a Confederate* (New York: 1907), 598–99; Emory Thomas, *Robert E. Lee* (New York: 1995), 342; Grant *Papers,* XII, 263, 320, 323–24, 330.

10. O.R., XL, Pt. 1, 17–18, 134; Grant *Papers,* XII, 363.

11. Ulysses S. Grant, "Preparing for the Campaigns of 1864," in *Battles and Leaders of the Civil War,* IV, 112.

12. Franz Sigel, "Sigel in the Shenandoah Valley," in *Battles and Leaders,* IV, 487–91; Stephen D. Engle, *Yankee Dutchman: The Life of Franz Sigel* (Fayetteville, Ark.: 1993), 184–91.

13. O.R., XXXVII, Pt. 2, 259.

14. Letter, Charles A. Dana to John A. Rawlins, July 14, 1864, Grant *Papers,* XII, 252n–53.

15. Diary, July 15, 1864, Cyrus B. Comstock Papers, MD, LC.

16. Jubal A. Early, *War Memoirs: Autobiographical Sketch and Narrative of the War Between the States* (Bloomington: 1960), 392–94; "Early's March on Washington in 1864," *Battles and Leaders of the Civil War,* IV, 305–9.

17. Lew Wallace, *An Autobiography* (New York: 1906), II, 783–810; Benjamin Franklin Cooling, *Symbol, Sword and Shield: Defending Washington During the Civil War* (Shippensburg, Pa.: 1991), 191–92.

18. O.R., XXXVII, Pt. 2, 222–23, 229–30; Early, 394; Cooling, 206–207.

19. O.R., XLIII, Pt. 1, 719.

20. O.R., XXXVII, Pt. 2, 582; Roy P. Basler, ed., *Collected Works of Abraham Lincoln* (New Brunswick, N.J.: 1953), VIII, 476.

21. Letter, Grant to P. H. Sheridan, Sept. 20, 1864, Grant *Papers,* XII, 177.

22. Philip H. Sheridan, *Personal Memoirs of General P. H. Sheridan* (New York: 1891), II, 62–82.

23. Grant *Papers,* XII, 90–91, 189, 226, 278, 308, 345, 371, 379.

24. M. R. Morgan, "From City Point to Appomattox with General Grant," *Journal of the Military Services Institution* (Sept.–Oct. 1907); Porter, 212.

25. Harrison Strong (Garland interview), Hamlin Garland Papers, USC.

26. Jesse R. Grant, *In the Days of My Father, General Grant* (New York: 1925), 22; Porter, 329–30.

27. Letter, Julia Dent Grant to Lillian Rogers, Feb. 7, 1865, Grant Papers, MD, LC.

28. Ibid., 215.

29. Edwin S. Wheeler, *History of the 21st Connecticut Volunteer Infantry Regiment* (n.p., n.d.), 327; Noah Brooks, "Lincoln, Chase and Grant," *Century* (Feb. 1895).

30. Ralph McCabe, "Rare Painting Brought to Light Here," *Washington Sunday Star,* Sept. 27, 1931. McCabe based his story on Balling's diary.

31. Letter, Grant to Benjamin Burns, Dec. 17, 1863, Grant *Papers,* X, 541; Daniel Ammen, *The Old Navy and the New* (Philadelphia: 1891), 531; Walter B. Stevens, *Grant in St. Louis* (St. Louis: 1916), 82.

32. John Eaton, *Grant, Lincoln and the Freedmen* (New York: 1907), 186–91.

33. David Donald, *Lincoln* (New York: 1995), 529–30.

34. Porter, 285; Adam Badeau, *Military History of U. S. Grant* (New York: 1868), II, 545–46.

35. O.R., XLII, Pt. 2, 1045–46.

36. Morgan, op. cit.

37. O.R., XLII, Pt. 3, 581.

38. Samuel H. Beckwith, "With Grant in the Wilderness," *New York Times,* May 31, 1914. Beckwith was the telegrapher who handed Grant the message.

39. Letter, Grant to Lydia Slocum, Aug. 10, 1864, Grant *Papers,* XI, 397.

40. O.R., XXXIX, Pt. 3, 222.

41. O.R., XXXIX, Pt. 1, 35, 39; Pt. 2, 478; Pt. 3, 63–64, 222; Porter, 314–15.

42. Grenville M. Dodge, *Personal Recollections* (Council Bluffs, Iowa: 1914), 76; Grant, *Personal Memoirs,* II, 376.

43. James H. Wilson, *Under the Old Flag* (New York: 1912), II, 92–93; Winston Groom, *Shrouds of Glory* (New York: 1995), 233–35.

44. O.R., XLV, Pt. 2, 15–16.

45. O.R., XLV, Pt. 2, 114–15; Grant, *Personal Memoirs,* II, 382–83.

46. John Russell Young, *Around the World with General Grant* (New York: 1879), II, 295.

47. Shelby Foote, *The Civil War* (New York: 1974), III, 711–12.

48. M. Harrison Strong, in *Christian Science Monitor,* May 2, 1929.

49. Joint Committee on the Conduct of the War, *Inquiry into the Fort Fisher Expedition* (Washington, D.C.: 1865), II, 73; Benjamin F. Butler, *Autobiography and Reminiscence: Butler's Book* (Boston: 1892), 850.

50. Rod Gragg, *Confederate Goliath: The Battle of Fort Fisher* (New York: 1991), 88–98; Grant, *Personal Memoirs,* II, 393–94; Porter, 362–63.

51. O.R., XLVI, Pt. 2, 29; Porter, 373.

52. Grant, *Personal Memoirs,* II, 421–23; Alexander H. Stephens, manuscript memoir, Stephens Papers, MD, LC; Roy P. Basler, ed., *Collected Works of Abraham Lincoln* (New Brunswick, N.J.: 1953), VIII, 274–75; Howard C. Westwood, "Lincoln at the Hampton Roads Peace Conference," *Lincoln Herald* (Winter, 1979); Porter, 382–85.

53. O.R., XLVI, Pt. 2, 802, 824–25; Basler, VIII, 330–31.
54. Bruce Catton, *Grant Takes Command* (Boston: 1967), 435.
55. Young, 302–3; Grant, *Personal Memoirs,* II, 469; Sheridan, *Memoirs,* II, 177–78; Meade, II, 242.
56. Douglas Southall Freeman, *Lee's Lieutenants* (New York: 1935), IV, 66–72.
57. John Gibbon, *Personal Recollections of the Civil War* (New York: 1928), 306–7; Amos Webster (Garland interview), Hamlin Garland Papers, USC; O.R., XLVI, Pt. 1, 47.
58. O.R., XXXIV, Pt. 1, 55.
59. O.R., XLVI, Pt. 3, 664–65.
60. *New York Herald,* July 6, 1878.
61. Young, 457–58; Manuscript memoir, "Lee's Surrender," Orville E. Babcock Papers, Chicago Historical Society; Charles Marshall, *An Aide-de-Camp of Lee* (Boston: 1927); "Ely S. Parker's Narrative," Grant Papers, MD, LC.
62. Porter, 486; letter, Adam Badeau to Editors of *Century* magazine, Sept. 2, 1885, in E. B. Long, Notes, MD, LC.
63. M. Harrison Strong (Garland interview), Hamlin Garland Papers, USC; O.R., XLVI, Pt. 3, 663.

Chapter 25: "A National Disgrace"

1. *Chicago Tribune,* June 13, 1865.
2. Grant, *Personal Memoirs,* II, 508; Jesse R. Grant, *In the Days of My Father, General Grant* (New York: 1927), 35–38; John Y. Simon, ed., *Personal Memoirs of Julia Dent Grant* (Carbondale, Ill.: 1975), 155.
3. O.R., XLVI, Pt. 3, 744–45.
4. John Russell Young, *Around the World with General Grant* (New York: 1879), II, 354; Noah Brooks, *Washington in Lincoln's Time* (New York: 1958), 233–34.
5. Joseph E. Johnston, *Narrative of Military Operations* (Bloomington, Ind.: 1959), 399–403; William T. Sherman, *Memoirs of General W. T. Sherman* (New York: 1891), II, 327; O.R., XLVII, Pt. 1, 31–323; Michael Fellman, *Citizen Sherman* (New York: 1995), 240–44.
6. O.R., XLVII, Pt. 3, 206–7, 221; Howard K. Beale, ed., *Diary of Gideon Welles* (New York: 1960), II, 293–95; Benjamin Thomas and Harold Hyman, *Stanton* (New York: 1962), 405–7.
7. *New York Times,* April 24, 1865; John F. Marszalek, *Sherman: A Soldier's Passion for Order* (New York: 1993), 348.
8. O.R., XLVII, Pt. 1, 34.

9. *New York Tribune,* May 3, 1865; cf. letter, Grant to Julia Dent Grant, April 29, 1865, Grant *Papers,* XIV, 436–37.

10. The best, in fact only worthwhile, account of Johnson's life is Hans L. Trefousse, *Andrew Johnson* (New York: 1989).

11. Jesse R. Grant, 43–44.

12. *Chicago Sunday Tribune,* Dec. 14, 1902.

13. Young, I, 217.

14. *New York Times,* June 8, 1865.

15. Charles Elliott, *Winfield Scott* (Boston: 1939), 757–59.

16. *Chicago Tribune,* June 13, 1865.

17. Simon, 158.

18. *Chicago Tribune,* Aug. 19, 1865.

19. *Washington Star,* March 17, 1934.

20. Adam Badeau, *Grant in Peace* (New York: 1887), 26; Young, II, 460–61.

21. Martin E. Mantell, *Johnson, Grant and the Politics of Reconstruction* (New York: 1973), 16.

22. James D. Richardson, *Messages and Papers of the Presidents* (Washington, D.C.: 1898), VIII, 3764.

23. Report, Grant to Andrew Johnson, Dec. 18, 1865, Grant *Papers,* XV, 434–37; Brooks D. Simpson, *Let Us Have Peace* (Chapel Hill, N.C.: 1991), 118–24.

24. *New York Times,* May 24, 1866.

25. George C. Rable, *But There Was No Peace* (Athens, Ga.: 1987), 53–55.

26. *New York Tribune,* Sept. 29, 1866; cf. Grant *Papers,* XVI, 310n.

27. Marszalek, 370–71.

28. Diary, March 1, 1867, Cyrus B. Comstock Papers, MD, LC.

29. Letters, Grant to P. H. Sheridan, April 5, April 21, May 26, Sept. 8, 1867; Grant to Andrew Johnson, Aug. 17, 1867, Grant *Papers* XVII, 95–96, 122–23, 168, 277–78, 316–17.

30. Patricia C. Acheson, *The Supreme Court* (New York: 1961), 138–40.

31. "Note from General Schofield on the Grant-Stanton Affair," Hamlin Garland Papers, USC.

32. Letter, Grant to Johnson, Jan. 28, 1868, Andrew Johnson Papers, MD, LC.

33. Letters, Grant to Johnson, Jan. 14, 1868, and William S. Hillyer to Johnson, Jan. 14, 1868, both in Andrew Johnson Papers, MD, LC; Sherman to Grant, January 19, 1868, William T. Sherman Papers, MD, LC; Beale, *Diary of Gideon Welles,* III, 255–57; William B. Hesseltine, *Ulysses S. Grant, Politician* (New York: 1957), 107–8n.

34. Letters, Grant to John A. Bingham, Feb. 12, 1868, Grant *Papers,* XVIII, 149n; Johnson to Grant, Jan. 31, 1868, and Grant to Johnson, Feb. 3,

1868, both in Andrew Johnson Papers, MD, LC; Grant to Johnson, Badeau, 125; Thomas and Hyman, 566–69; Trefousse, 306–9.

35. William McFeely, *Grant* (New York: 1981), 270.
36. Amos Webster interview, Hamlin Garland Papers, USC.
37. Letter, with endorsement, Grant to Johnson, Jan. 24, 1868, Huntington Library; Badeau, 126.
38. Letter, Grant to Charles W. Ford, March 18, 1868, Grant *Papers,* XVIII, 205.

Chapter 26: "Let Us Have Peace"

1. Jesse R. Grant, *In the Days of My Father, General Grant* (New York: 1925), 49, 105–6.
2. *Washington Star,* March 17, 1934.
3. *New York Tribune,* July 26, 1885.
4. Michael J. Cramer, *Ulysses S. Grant: Conversations and Unpublished Letters* (New York: 1897), 67–68.
5. William B. Hesseltine, *Ulysses S. Grant, Politician* (New York: 1957), 90; *New York Sun,* May 9, 1872.
6. Frank Harrison, *Anecdotes and Reminiscences of General Ulysses S. Grant* (New York: 1885), 25.
7. Jesse R. Grant, interview, Hamlin Garland Papers, USC. John Russell Young, *Around the World with General Grant* (New York: 1879), II, 452; Adam Badeau, *Grant in Peace* (New York: 1887), 73–74.
8. John Y. Simon, ed., *The Personal Memoirs of Julia Dent Grant* (Carbondale, Ill.: 1975), 171.
9. Badeau, 144.
10. Willard H. Smith, *Schuyler Colfax* (Indianapolis: 1952), 270–81; Charles H. Coleman, *The Election of 1868* (New York: 1933), 92–94.
11. Grant *Papers,* XVIII, 266n. Sherman, too, wrote a letter of consolation rather than congratulation: Sherman to Grant, June 7, 1868, William T. Sherman Papers, MD, LC.
12. *New York Times,* May 30, 1868; Simon, loc. cit.
13. Letter, Grant to Joseph R. Hawley, May 29, 1865; Grant *Papers,* XVIII, 263–64.
14. Coleman, 363–64; Ulysses S. Grant III, *Ulysses S. Grant: Warrior and Statesman* (New York: 1968), 293–94.
15. Letters, Grant to Ellen Sherman, Feb. 2, 1869; to Sayles J. Bowen, Feb. 3, 1869; to William T. Sherman, Feb. 12, 1869, Grant *Papers,* XIX, 122 passim.
16. Howard K. Beale, ed., *Diary of Gideon Welles* (New Brunswick, N.J.: 1960), III, 542.

17. Inaugural Address, March 4, 1869, Grant *Papers,* XIX, 139–42.
18. Henry Adams, *The Letters of Henry Adams* (Boston: 1921), 152.
19. Hesseltine, 93; letter, Grant to Joseph R. Hawley, loc. cit.
20. *New York Times,* Feb. 26, 1869.
21. Grant *Papers,* XIX, 145.
22. Badeau, 162.
23. Edward Chalfant, *Better in Darkness* (New York: 1994), 165.
24. Badeau, 153.
25. Grant *Papers,* XIX, 151–52; James Grant Wilson, *General Grant* (New York: 1897), 299.
26. Grant *Papers,* XIX, 147–48; *New York Herald,* March 9, 1869.
27. James H. Wilson, *The Life of John A. Rawlins* (New York: 1916), 351–54.
28. Letter, Sylvanus Cadwallader to James H. Wilson, Sept. 17, 1904, Wilson Papers, MD, LC.
29. Grant *Papers,* XIX, 200–202; Badeau, 166.
30. Hesseltine, 150–56.

Chapter 27: "I Would Not Fire a Gun"

1. William B. Hesseltine, *Ulysses S. Grant, Politician* (New York: 1957), 67.
2. President's Annual Message, Dec. 6, 1869, Grant *Papers,* XX, 18–44.
3. Proclamation, May 19, 1869, Grant *Papers,* XIX, 189.
4. Meade Minnigerode, *Certain Rich Men* (New York: 1927), 142.
5. See Grant *Papers,* XX, 234n.
6. Maury Klein, *The Life and Legend of Jim Gould* (Baltimore: 1986), 103.
7. Letter, Grant to Boutwell, Sept. 12, 1869, Grant *Papers,* XIX, 243–44.
8. John Y. Simon, ed., *Personal Memoirs of Julia Dent Grant* (Carbondale, Ill.: 1975), 182.
9. Kenneth Akerman, *The Gold Ring* (New York: 1988), 166–69.
10. George S. Boutwell, *Reminiscences of Sixty Years in Public Affairs* (New York: 1902), II, 175.
11. William W. Smith interview, Hamlin Garland Papers, USC.
12. Edward Chalfant, *Better in Darkness* (New York: 1994), 182–203; letter, Grant to Corbin, Dec. 28, 1873, Grant *Papers,* MD, LC.
13. The committee hearings were published as *Gold Panic Investigation,* 41st Congress, 2nd Session, House Report 31 (Washington, D.C.: 1870); Alan Peskin, *Garfield* (Kent, Ohio: 1979), 311.
14. Message to Congress, March 30, 1870, Grant *Papers,* XX, 130–31; David McCullough, *The Path Between the Seas* (New York: 1977), 26–27.
15. David Donald, *Charles Sumner and the Coming of the Civil War* (New York: 1960), 290–95.

16. David Donald, *Charles Sumner and the Rights of Man* (New York: 1970), 314–20.
17. Boutwell, II, 215.
18. Louis A. Coolidge, *Ulysses S. Grant* (Boston: 1922), 290.
19. E. L. Pierce, *Memoirs and Letters of Charles Sumner* (Boston: 1891), IV, 409; Allan Nevins, *Inside the Grant Administration: The Diaries of Hamilton Fish* (New York: 1956), I, 191–200, 231–48.
20. Glyndon G. Van Deusen, *William Henry Seward* (New York: 1967), 528–31; John M. Taylor, *William Henry Seward* (New York: 1991), 274–75.
21. William Javier Nelson, *Almost a Territory: America's Attempt to Annex the Dominican Republic* (Newark, Del.: 1991), 71–76; Jacob D. Cox, "How Judge Hoar Ceased to be Attorney General," *Atlantic Monthly* (Aug. 1895).
22. Diary, Dec. 21, 1869, Hamilton Fish Papers; Charles C. Tansill, *The United States and Santo Domingo, 1798–1873* (Baltimore: 1938), 371–82; William B. Hesseltine, *Ulysses S. Grant, Politician* (New York: 1957), 193–98.
23. The quote is from Treasury Secretary Boutwell, a friend of Sumner's, who came in toward the end of the meeting. Sumner's recollection was different—"I am an Administration man. Whatever you do you will always find in me the most careful and candid consideration." If anything, this is even more evasive, but however he phrased it, Grant, Boutwell, and the two journalists alike believed Sumner had pledged his support. Donald, *Charles Sumner and the Rights of Man,* 435–37. Cf. Grant *Papers,* XX, 163–64.
24. Letter, Grant to John Russell Young, Nov. 21, 1877, J. R. Young Papers, MD, LC.
25. Carl Schurz, *The Reminiscences of Carl Schurz* (New York: 1908), III, 207–8.
26. Peskin, 338.
27. *New York Tribune,* April 6, 1870. The arguments that Grant deployed in favor of annexation are cogently summarized in an undated draft memorandum from 1869 or 1870 in Grant *Papers,* XX, 74–76. Cf. the interview with Grant published in the *New York Herald,* March 30, 1870.
28. Diary, July 1, 1870, Rutherford B. Hayes Papers, MD, LC.
29. Jesse R. Grant, *In the Days of My Father, General Grant* (New York: 1925), 138.
30. George F. Hoar, *Autobiography of Seventy Years* (New York: 1903), I, 210–11.
31. John Russell Young, *Around the World with General Grant* (New York: 1879), II, 449.

32. Jesse R. Grant, 57.
33. Emily Edson Briggs, *The Olivia Letters* (New York: 1906), 179–80, 257–60, 394.
34. Jesse R. Grant, 67.
35. William H. Crook, *Through Five Administrations* (New York: 1910), 181.
36. William W. Smith, loc. cit; Hamlin Garland Notebooks, Garland Papers, USC.
37. Smith, loc. cit.
38. Jesse R. Grant, 57, 153.
39. Crook, 154–56.
40. Ben Perley Poore and O. H. Tiffany, *Life of Grant* (Philadelphia: 1885), 49–50; Jesse R. Grant, 76–77; Hamlin Garland Notebooks, Garland Papers, USC.
41. Crook, 179.
42. Daniel Ammen, *The Old Navy and the New* (Philadelphia: 1891), 503.
43. Diary, July 1, 1870, Rutherford B. Hayes Papers, MD, LC.

Chapter 28: "A Condition of Lawlessness"

1. Edward Chalfant, *Better in Darkness* (New York: 1994), 167–68.
2. David Donald, *Charles Sumner and the Rights of Man* (New York: 1970), 369–70.
3. Charles Sumner, *The Works of Charles Sumner* (Boston: 1880), XIII, 76–88; Donald, 374–76.
4. *Congressional Globe,* 41st Congress, Special Session, 730, April 19, 1869.
5. Adrian Cook, *The Alabama Claims* (Ithaca, N.Y.: 1973), 105–6.
6. Letter, Adams to Carl Schurz, May 16, 1871, Henry Adams Papers, Massachusetts Historical Society, Boston.
7. Diary, Nov. 9 and 26, 1869, Hamilton Fish Papers, MD, LC.
8. Donald, 403.
9. William B. Hesseltine, *Ulysses S. Grant, Politician* (New York: 1957), 231.
10. Hamilton Fish Papers, MD, LC, July 1, 1870, Jan. 2, 1871; Adam Badeau, *Grant in Peace* (New York: 1887), 216.
11. Cook, 207–18; letter, Fish to John C. Hamilton, April 22, 1869, Hamilton Fish Papers, MD, LC.
12. *Washington Sunday Star,* Jan. 25, 1931.
13. Letter, Badeau to Grant, May 11, 1871, Grant *Papers,* MD, LC.
14. Cook, 218–37; Allan Nevins, *Inside the Grant Administration* (New York: 1956), 541–9.

15. L. Oppenheim, *International Law: A Treatise* (London: 1952), II, 34, 715–16.
16. James D. Richardson, *Messages and Papers of the Presidents* (Washington, D.C.: 1898), IX, 184–205.
17. John Russell Young, *Around the World with General Grant* (New York: 1879), II, 361–62.
18. Message to Congress, March 30, 1870, Grant *Papers,* XX, 130–31.
19. Eric Foner, *A Short History of Reconstruction 1863–1877* (New York: 1971), 192–93.
20. Jack Hurst, *Nathan Bedford Forrest* (New York: 1993), 284–87.
21. John F. Marszalek, *Sherman: A Soldier's Passion for Order* (New York: 1993), 423–27; Michael Fellman, *Citizen Sherman* (New York: 1995), 292–93.
22. Foner, 196–97; letter, Orville Babcock to Amos T. Ackerman, June 15, 1871, Grant Letter Book, Grant *Papers,* MD, LC.
23. Cf. Richard N. Current, "President Grant and the Continuing Civil War," in John Y. Simon and David L. Wilson, *Ulysses S. Grant: Essays and Documents* (Carbondale, Ill.: 1981).
24. Jesse R. Grant, *In the Days of My Father, General Grant* (New York: 1928), 194.

Chapter 29: "The Subject of Abuse and Slander"

1. *Philadelphia Press,* July 27, 1885.
2. Hans L. Trefousse, *Carl Schurz* (Knoxville, Tenn.: 1982) 188–89, 222–23.
3. William D. Mallam, "The Grant-Butler Relationship," *Mississippi Valley Historical Review* XLI, No. 2 (Sept. 1954); George F. Hoar, *Autobiography of Seventy Years* (New York: 1903), 361–62; William B. Hesseltine, *Ulysses S. Grant, Politician* (New York: 1957), 116–17.
4. See Richard E. Welch, Jr., *George Frisbie Hoar and the Half-Breed Republicans* (Cambridge, Mass.: 1971), and David Jay Rothman, *Power and Politics: The United States Senate, 1869–1901* (Cambridge, Mass.: 1966).
5. David Jordan, *Roscoe Conkling of New York* (Ithaca, N.Y.: 1971); John Russell Young, *Men and Memories* (New York: 1901), 214–23.
6. Letter, Grant to John Russell Young, Nov. 15, 1870, Young Papers, MD, LC; *New York Herald,* July 18, 1872.
7. Bingham Duncan, *Whitelaw Reid* (Athens, Ga.: 1975), 40–41; Royal Cortissoz, *The Life of Whitelaw Reid* (New York: 1921), I, 202–5.
8. Letter, Grant to Roscoe Conkling, July 15, 1872, Conkling Papers, MD, LC.

9. Alan Peskin, *Garfield* (Kent, Ohio: 1982), 309, 344.
10. Diary, October 19, 1872, James A. Garfield Papers, MD, LC.
11. Edward C. Richardson, *Messages and Papers of the Presidents* (Washington, D.C.: 1898), VII, 223.
12. *Chicago Tribune,* Sept. 1, 1885.
13. Ellis P. Oberholzer, *Jay Cooke, Financier of the Civil War* (Philadelphia: 1907).
14. Henrietta Melia Larson, *Jay Cooke, Private Banker* (New York: 1968), 291–95.
15. *New York Times,* Sept. 19, 1873.
16. Telegram, O. P. Morton to Grant, Sept. 19, 1873, and letter, Morton to Grant, March 22, 1874, both in Grant *Papers,* MD, LC.
17. Grant to Cowdrey, October 6, 1873, Grant Letter Book, MD, LC; diary, Nov. 18, 1873, James A. Garfield Papers, MD, LC.
18. Hesseltine, 333.
19. This was how Grant described it to an old Army friend, Jesse Seligman; *Philadelphia Press,* July 27, 1885.
20. Richardson, VII, 268–69; Hesseltine, 335–36.
21. William H. Armstrong, *Warrior in Two Camps* (Norman, Okla.: 1978), 132–33.
22. Letters, Grant to P. H. Sheridan, Dec. 24, 1868, Grant *Papers,* XIX, 99–100; Grant to W. T. Sherman, May 19, 1868, Grant *Papers,* XVIII, 257–58.
23. Inaugural Address, March 4, 1869, Grant *Papers,* XX, 140–42.
24. F. H. Smith (Garland interview), Hamlin Garland Papers, USC; Henry E. Fritz, *The Movement for Indian Assimilation, 1860–1890* (Philadelphia: 1963), 76–79; Armstrong, 150.
25. John F. Marszalek, *Sherman: A Soldier's Passion for Order* (New York: 1993), 393.
26. Francis Paul Prucha, *The Great Father* (Lincoln, Nebr.: 1984), 164–65; Fritz, 84–85.
27. Robert Wooster, *The Military and United States Indian Policy, 1865–1903* (New Haven, Conn.: 1982), 149.
28. *New York Daily Graphic,* June 5, 1875; *New York Times,* June 5, 1875.
29. Robert Utley, *Cavalier in Buckskin* (Norman, Okla.: 1988), 158–60.
30. *New York World,* May 1, 1876.
31. Letters, W. T. Sherman to P. H. Sheridan, April 28 and May 2, 1876, Philip Sheridan Papers, MD, LC; Sherman to Orville Babcock, May 4, 1876, Grant *Papers,* MD, LC.
32. Paul Andrew Hutton, *Phil Sheridan and His Army* (Lincoln, Nebr.: 1985), 311; Utley, 162–63.

33. *New York Times,* July 7, 1876.
34. See Evan O'Connell, *Son of the Morning Star* (San Francisco: 1984), 347–54, on the instant creation of the Custer myth.
35. Grant *Papers,* XX, 142; letter, John D. Lang to Grant, March 27, 1877, Grant *Papers,* MD, LC.

Chapter 30: "Like a Boy Getting out of School"

1. *Chicago Sunday Tribune,* Dec. 14, 1902.
2. *Cincinnati Commercial,* June 30, 1873; Eliza M. Shaw interview, Hamlin Garland Papers, USC; letters, O. H. Tiffany to Grant, June 30, 1873, and Aaron F. Perry, July 5, 1873, Grant *Papers,* MD, LC; Jesse R. Grant, *In the Days of My Father, General Grant* (New York: 1925), 95; William E. Woodward, *Meet General Grant* (New York: 1928), 14.
3. *New York Herald,* May 22, 1874; William H. Crook, *Through Five Administrations* (New York: 1910), 187.
4. Letter, Grant to Ulysses Grant, Jr., Dec. 8, 1870, Grant *Papers,* MD, LC.
5. William W. Smith interview, Hamlin Garland Papers, USC.
6. Letter, Grant to James E. McLean, Feb. 4, 1872, Grant *Papers,* MD, LC.
7. Letter, M. J. Crapser to Grant, July 29, 1874, Grant *Papers,* MD, LC.
8. Memo, May 22, 1875, Grant *Papers,* MD, LC.
9. Letter, Grant to James F. Casey, March 27, 1871, Grant *Papers,* MD, LC.
10. Letter, Grant to J. R. Jones, Nov. 7, 1871, Grant *Papers,* MD, LC.
11. David A. Jordan, *Roscoe Conkling of New York* (Ithaca, N.Y.: 1971), 172.
12. James D. Richardson, *Messages of the Presidents* VII, 156–59.
13. Letter, D. B. Eaton to Grant, Nov. 20, 1873, Grant *Papers,* MD, LC; William B. Hesseltine, *Ulysses S. Grant, Politician* (New York: 1955), 261–64, 359.
14. Alan Peskin, *Garfield* (Kent, Ohio: 1973), 377–79.
15. Ibid., 362.
16. Ross A. Webb, *Benjamin Helm Bristow* (Lexington, Ky.: 1963), 223.
17. Harry James Brown and Frederick D. Williams, eds., *The Diary of James A. Garfield* (East Lansing: 1957), III, 243–44; William H. Crook, *Through Five Administrations* (New York: 1910), 212–14; Jesse R. Grant, *In the Days of My Father, General Grant* (New York: 1925), 122; letter, Belknap to Grant, March 2, 1876, Grant *Papers,* MD, LC.
18. Richard E. Welch, Jr., *George Frisbie Hoar and the Half-Breed Republicans* (Cambridge, Mass.: 1966), 51–53.
19. *Chicago Tribune,* Dec. 21, 1868; letter, Carl Schurz to Grant, May 25, 1868, Grant *Papers,* XVIII, 267–68n; letter, Orvil L. Grant to Ulysses S. Grant, in *New York Tribune,* Jan. 5, 1870; James McDonald interview,

Hamlin Garland Papers, USC. The twenty-five-page transcript of the interview with McDonald has a handwritten note at the beginning that reads "Probably not by Garland." Yet it is evident that the typewriter that produced this transcript was the same machine used to transcribe the rest of Garland's notes for his biography of Grant, and the comments on McDonald's answers are typical of Garland's engaged yet skeptical approach to what those he interviewed told him. Even the questions posed are worded almost identically with those that appear in other transcripts. Short of any proof to the contrary, the only reasonable assumption is that Garland interviewed McDonald. Garland's conclusion, as this transcript makes clear, is that while McDonald sincerely believed Grant knew about the Whiskey Ring, McDonald was deluding himself.

20. James McDonald, *Secrets of the Great Whiskey Ring* (St. Louis: 1880), 121–25; Walter B. Stevens, *Grant in St. Louis* (St. Louis: 1916), 120–21.

21. Letter, Ford to Grant, May 30, 1870, Grant *Papers,* XX, 149–50.

22. Letter, T. W. Campbell to A. H. Burbridge, Dec. 27, 1876, Grant *Papers*, MD, LC. Campbell gives details of Bristow's involvement and includes sworn statements from people who claimed they were forced to bribe Bristow to move their hogs and tobacco during the war; Ross A. Webb, *Benjamin Helm Bristow* (Lexington, Ky.: 1963), 42–43.

23. Crook, 196–97.

24. Webb, 176–77.

25. Letters, A. B. Mullett to Grant, June 29 and 30, 1875, Grant *Papers,* MD, LC; D. Mullett Smith, *A. B. Mullett* (Washington, D.C.: 1990), 7–8.

26. See Elsa Santoyo, *Creating an American Masterpiece* (Washington, D.C.: 1988); *The Old Executive Office Building* (Washington, D.C.: 1984); *National Cyclopedia of American Biography* (New York: 1939), XXVII, 452.

27. U.S. Congress, 44th Cong., 1st Sess., House Miscellaneous Document 186, "Whisky Frauds," 366.

28. Diary, May 22, 1875, Hamilton Fish Papers, MD, LC.

29. Letter, William D. Barnard to Grant, July 19, 1875, Huntington Library.

30. Crook, 199.

31. Diary, Feb. 9, 1876, Hamilton Fish Papers, MD, LC.; Amos D. Webster interview, Hamlin Garland Papers, USC. Webster was the executor of Babcock's estate.

32. James McDonald interview, Hamlin Garland Papers, USC. McDonald gives considerable detail on Babcock's involvement, but says explicitly that Babcock did not profit personally from it.

33. William McFeely, *Grant* (New York: 1981), 415.

34. Letters, Grant to Bristow, July 12, 1876, and Bristow to Grant, July 13, 1876, Benjamin H. Bristow Papers, MD, LC.

35. Letter, Charles A. Gray to Reilly O'Beirne, Aug. 14, 1876; Grant to Edwards Pierrepont, July 29, 1876, and Pierrepont to Grant, Aug. 22, 1876, Grant *Papers,* MD, LC. Paul Pehrson, *James Harrison Wilson,* Ph.D. dissertation (University of Wisconsin, 1993), 253–73; letter, Grant to Washburne, Oct. 7, 1878, copy in Long-Catton Notes, MD, LC.
36. McFeely, 415; author interview with John Y. Simon.
37. John Russell Young, *Men and Memories* (New York: 1901), 475.
38. Horace Porter, *Campaigning with Grant* (New York: 1897), 340–41; *The Independent,* July 30, 1885; Young, 369.
39. Letters, Grant to E. F. Beale, Sept. 18, 1875, Grant *Papers,* MD, LC; Grant to Frederick T. Dent, Nov. 10, 1875, Frederick T. Dent Papers, SIU; Walter B. Stevens, *Grant in St. Louis* (St. Louis: 1916), x–xii.
40. Diary, Feb. 6 and 9, 1876, and memo dated March 6, 1876, Hamilton Fish Papers, MD, LC; letter, H. E. Monroe to Grant, Aug. 14, 1876, Grant *Papers*, MD, LC.
41. Amos D. Webster interview, Hamlin Garland Papers, USC.
42. John Eaton, *Grant, Lincoln and the Freedmen* (New York: 1907), 307.
43. Hamlin Garland, *Ulysses S. Grant* (New York: 1898), 431–32.
44. Ulysses S. Grant, Jr., interview, Hamlin Garland Papers, USC; John Y. Simon, *The Personal Memoirs of Julia Dent Grant* (Carbondale, Ill.: 1975).
45. Ari Hoogenboom, *Rutherford B. Hayes* (Lawrence, Kan.: 1995), 284.
46. Adam Badeau, *Grant in Peace* (New York: 1887), 252.
47. *Chicago Tribune*, Sept. 1, 1885.

Chapter 31: "No Desire to Tarry"

1. Letter, Grant to W. T. Sherman, Jan. 13, 1867, Grant *Papers,* XVII, 13–14.
2. J. Monroe Royce, "A Morning with General Grant," *New York Star,* Jan. 13, 1876; *Chicago Times,* Sept. 15, 1876.
3. Letters, Grant to Roscoe Conkling, Aug. 12, 1875, Conkling Papers, MD, LC; Grant to Nat Carlin, Oct. 27, 1873, Aug. 24, 1875, Eldridge Collection, Huntington Library. Cf. George R. Jones, *Joseph Russell Jones* (Chicago: 1964), 68.
4. Alan Peskin, *Garfield* (Norwalk, Conn.: 1987), 547; William Crook, *Through Five Administrations* (New York: 1921), 188.
5. Harry James Brown and Frederick D. Williams, eds., *Diary of James Garfield* (East Lansing: 1967), II, 165.
6. Hamilton Fish, in *The Independent,* July 30, 1885.
7. Ulysses S. Grant, Jr., interview, Hamlin Garland Papers, USC.
8. Letter, Grant to Charles H. Rogers, Dec. 6, 1875, Grant *Papers,* MD, LC; John Russell Young, *Around the World with General Grant* (New York:

1879), I, 202; Daniel Ammen, *The Old Navy and the New* (Philadelphia: 1891), 542; *Cincinnati Gazette,* Aug. 16, 1885; Jesse R. Grant, *In the Days of My Father, General Grant* (New York: 1925), 253; Allan Nevins, *Hamilton Fish* (New York: 1956), II, 893. Cf. Ulysses S. Grant, Jr., interview, loc. cit.

9. The *Independent,* July 30, 1885.

10. Pamphlet by John Bach MacMaster, "The Life, Memoirs and Death of General Grant," (n.p. 1885).

11. Joseph I. C. Clarke, *My Life and Memoirs* (New York: 1926); James L. Crouthamel, *Bennett's New York Herald and the Rise of the Popular Press* (Syracuse: 1989).

12. *New York Herald,* March 21, 1895.

13. Frank Harrison, *Memories and Anecdotes of General Grant* (New York: 1885); *The Independent,* July 30, 1885. Harrison says it was Badeau who tried to read the speech to him, but Pierrepont seems a more likely candidate.

14. Grant Association *Newsletter* (Oct. 1963).

15. J. Monroe Royce, op. cit.

16. John Russell Young, *Men and Memories* (New York: 1901), 477; *Around the World with General Grant,* I, 443.

17. Young, *Around the World,* 417; Young, *Men and Memories,* 274–76.

18. Grenville M. Dodge, *Personal Recollections of Abraham Lincoln, Ulysses S. Grant and William T. Sherman* (Council Bluffs, Iowa: 1911), 107.

19. Young, *Men and Memories,* 284–88; Charles Eliot Norton, *The Letters of James Russell Lowell* (New York: 1894), II, 232.

20. Unidentified newspaper clipping in Lewis-Catton Notes, SIU.

21. Diary, Feb. 1, 18, 20, 1878, John Russell Young Papers, MD, LC.

22. Letters, Grant to E. F. Beale, Nov. 4, 1877, Decatur House Papers, MD, LC; Grant to George W. Childs, Jan. 14, 1879, Grant *Papers,* SIU; Grant to Charles Rogers, Dec. 6, 1878, Grant *Papers,* MD, LC.

23. Letter, Grant to Fred Grant, Jan. 25, 1878, Grant *Papers,* MD, LC.

24. "Grant in Egypt," *New York Tribune,* Sept. 6, 1885.

25. Jesse R. Grant, 293; clipping from *Evening Star,* May 12, 1879, Grant Family Papers, SIU. The American consul in Constantinople at the time, Lloyd C. Griscom, claimed in his memoir, *Diplomatically Speaking,* that Grant refused to take the two horses because they were black and no American President had ever been drawn by black horses. He settled, says Griscom, for a pair of grays. The fact that one of the horses Grant finally accepted was black suggests Griscom's memory was faulty.

26. Young, *Men and Memories,* 482.

27. Mary Lutyens, *The Lyttons in India* (London: 1979), 150.

28. William McFeely, *Grant* (New York: 1981), 473.
29. Aurelia Brooks Harlan, *Owen Meredith* (New York: 1946), 233.
30. *Straits Times,* April 5, 1879.
31. Young, *Around the World,* II, 372; Young, *Men and Memories,* 303, 319; Cramer, 167–68.
32. Young, *Men and Memories,* II, 294–95, 300–302.
33. Ammen, 522.
34. Jesse R. Grant, 319; Adam Badeau, *Grant in Peace* (Hartford, Conn.: 1887), 518.
35. *Chicago Tribune,* Sept. 1, 1885.
36. Samuel L. Clemens, *Autobiography of Mark Twain* (New York: 1959), 241–42.
37. Albert Bigelow Paine, *Mark Twain* (New York: 1936), II, 653.
38. Charles H. Gold, "Grant and Twain in Chicago: The 1879 Reunion of the Army of the Tennessee," *Chicago History* (Sept. 1969); Justin Kaplan, *Mr. Clemens and Mark Twain* (New York: 1966), 225.
39. Henry Nash Smith and William M. Gibson, eds., *The Mark Twain–William Dean Howells Letters* (Cambridge, Mass.: 1967), II, 139.
40. Paul Fatout, ed., *Mark Twain Speaking* (Iowa City: 1976), 131–33; Paine, II, 655–57.
41. *Philadelphia Public Ledger,* Dec. 17, 1879; Ammen, 522.

Chapter 32: *"To Be; to Do; to Suffer"*

1. *Chicago Tribune,* Sept. 1, 1885.
2. Letter, Grant to John F. Long, Feb. 22, 1878, Huntington Library; diary, June 30, 1878, John Russell Young Papers, MD, LC.
3. Diary, Dec. 18, 1879, Rutherford B. Hayes Papers, MD, LC.
4. Florence Gratiot Bale, "Historic Galena" (Galena, Ill.: 1945), in Lewis-Catton Notes, SIU; letter, A. W. Glessner to U. S. Grant III, Nov. 17, 1933, Grant Family Papers, SIU.
5. William McFeely, *Grant* (New York: 1981), 478–83.
6. Adam Badeau, *Grant in Peace* (New York: 1887), 320–22.
7. Ulysses S. Grant interview and Julia Dent Grant interview, Hamlin Garland Papers, USC; *Chicago Tribune,* Sept. 1, 1885. This contains an interview with Young that had originally appeared in the *New York Herald.*
8. John Y. Simon, ed., *Personal Memoirs of Julia Dent Grant* (Carbondale, Ill.: 1975), 320–22.
9. *The Inter Ocean,* Number 6,026, in Grant Family Papers, SIU; Alan Peskin, *Garfield* (Norwalk, Conn.: 1978), 467; David A. Jordan, *Roscoe Conkling of New York* (Ithaca, N.Y.: 1979), 334.

10. Ulysses S. Grant, Jr., interview, Hamlin Garland Papers, USC.

11. Jesse R. Grant, *In the Days of My Father, General Grant* (New York: 1925), 329.

12. Ulysses S. Grant, Jr., interview, Hamlin Garland Papers, USC.

13. David A. Jordan, *Winfield Scott Hancock* (Bloomington, Ind.: 1988), 213–14, 289.

14. Peskin, 500–501; Albert B. Paine, *Mark Twain* (New York: 1912), II, 691–94.

15. *Chicago Tribune,* Sept. 15, 1876; letter, Grant to Mary King, Jan. 27, 1881, Grant *Papers,* MD, LC.

16. Letters, Grant to Fred Grant, Jan. 25, 1881, Grant *Papers,* SIU; to John F. Long, Sept. 24, 1881, Huntington Library; to Mary King, Jan. 27, 1881, Grant *Papers,* MD, LC.

17. *New York Herald Tribune,* April 24, 1927.

18. *Missouri Republican,* April 11, 1881; letter, Grant to R. Evans Peterson, June 8, 1882, Grant *Papers,* SIU.

19. *Cincinnati Times-Star,* April 27, 1927.

20. Hugh McCulloch, *Men and Measures of Half a Century* (New York: 1889), 360.

21. Jesse R. Grant interview, Hamlin Garland Papers, USC.

22. On Whitman and Grant, see Grant Association *Newsletter* (April 1964). McFeely takes the McCulloch view.

23. Letters, Grant to John F. Long, Dec. 23, 1883, Grant *Papers,* SIU; J. R. Young to Grant, Jan. 26, 1884, Grant *Papers,* MD, LC.

24. Franklin Spencer Edmonds, *Ulysses S. Grant* (Philadelphia: 1915), 321–29; Thomas Pitkin, *The Captain Departs* (Carbondale, Ill.: 1973), 2–8.

25. Paine, 804.

26. Letters, Julia Dent Grant to Clarence Seward and William H. Vanderbilt, Jan. 11, 1885, Grant Family Papers, SIU.

27. For examples of the change in his handwriting, see Grant to Childs, May 10, 1864, Grant *Papers,* MD, LC, and Grant to Cavender and Rouse, May 21, 1884, SIU. The diagnosis of throat cancer is in a letter from G. R. Elliott to John H. Douglas, Feb. 19, 1885, Grant *Papers,* MD, LC.

28. Samuel L. Clemens, *The Autobiography of Mark Twain* (New York: 1912), I, 26.

29. Letter, Absalom H. Markland to Julia Dent Grant, March 19, 1888, Grant Family Papers, SIU.

30. Letter, J. G. Rosegarten to George W. Childs, Nov. 5, 1884, Grant *Papers,* MD, LC.

31. *New York Herald,* March 18, 1887.

32. Dictations, Mark Twain Papers, Bancroft Library, UC Berkeley.

33. Grant, *Personal Memoirs,* I, 198–99.

34. Ibid., I, 86–87.

35. Ibid., I, 248.

36. Ibid., II, 550.

37. Pitkin, 65.

38. The total subscription produced $1,106,586.67. After printing costs, payments to the subscription agents, and incidental expenses, the gross profit came to a little less than $700,000. Julia's 70 percent produced a total of $474,873.59; account sheet for 1887 in Grant *Papers,* MD, LC.

39. Letter, Grant to Julia Dent Grant, June 29, 1885, Grant *Papers,* MD, LC.

40. Diary, John H. Newman Papers, Special Collections, West Point; letter, Jesse R. Grant to Hamlin Garland, Dec. 1, 1896, Hamlin Garland Papers, USC.

41. Letter, Grant to Julia Dent Grant, July 8, 1885, Grant *Papers,* MD, LC.

42. Memo, July 8, 1885, Grant *Papers,* MD, LC.

43. Clemens, 68.

44. Daniel Ammen, *Old Navy and the New* (Philadelphia: 1891), appendix, 34.

INDEX

GEOFFREY PERRET was born into an Anglo-American theatrical family and reared as a transatlantic commuter. He served in the U.S. Army from 1958 to 1961, and attended the University of Southern California, where he was elected Phi Beta Kappa; Harvard; and the University of California at Berkeley. His first book was an award-winning account of the American World War II home front, *Days of Sadness, Years of Triumph*. Perret is also the author of *A Country Made by War,* a military history of the United States; *There's a War to Be Won,* a chronicle of the United States Army in World War II; *Winged Victory,* a history of the Army Air Forces in World War II; and *Old Soldiers Never Die,* a biography of General Douglas MacArthur.

ABOUT THE TYPE

This book was set in Times Roman, designed by Stanley Morrison specifically for *The Times* of London. The typeface was introduced in the newspaper in 1932. Times Roman had its greatest success in the United States as a book and commercial typeface, rather than one used in newspapers.